SOFT COMPUTING

Neural Networks, Fuzzy Logic, Genetic Algorithm and Probabilistic Reasoning

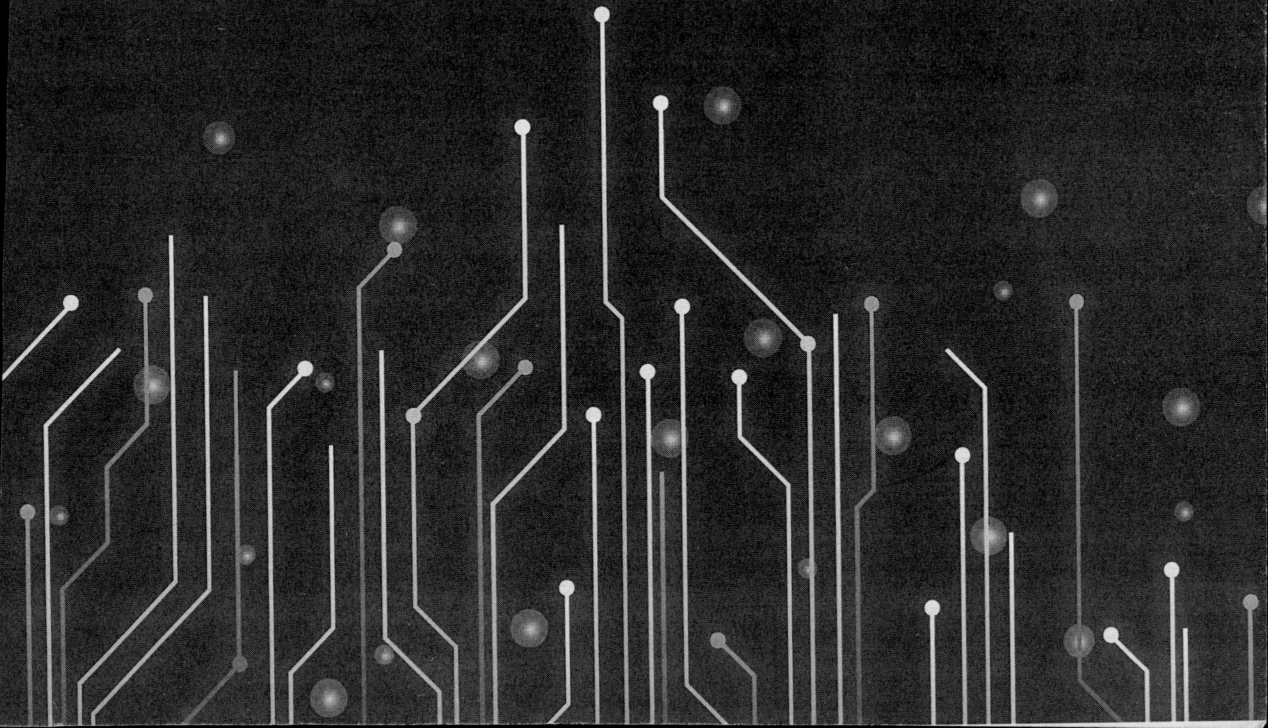

SOFT COMPUTING

Neural Networks, Fuzzy Logic, Genetic Algorithm and Probabilistic Reasoning

FOR

(All Indian Universities, Engineering and Technical Colleges and Institutions, IIT's and IT Organizations)

IKVINDERPAL SINGH

KHANNA BOOK PUBLISHING CO. (P) LTD.

Publisher of Engineering and Computer Books

4C/4344, Ansari Road, Darya Ganj, New Delhi-110002

Phone : 011-23244447-48 **Mobile:** +91-9910909320

E-mail : contact@khannabooks.com

Website : www.khannabooks.com

Dear Readers,

To prevent the piracy, this book is secured with HIGH SECURITY HOLOGRAM on the front title cover. In case you don't find the hologram on the front cover title, please write us to at contact@khannabooks.com or whatsapp us at +91-99109 09320 and avail special gift voucher for yourself.

Specimen of Hologram on front Cover title:

Moreover, there is a SPECIAL DISCOUNT COUPON for you with EVERY HOLOGRAM.

How to avail this SPECIAL DISCOUNT:

Step 1: Scratch the hologram
Step 2: Under the scratch area, your "coupon code" is available
Step 3: Logon to www.khannabooks.com
Step 4: Use your "coupon code" in the shopping cart and get your copy at a special discount
Step 5: Enjoy your reading!

Thanks,
Khanna Publishing House

ISBN: 978-93-80016-97-9

Soft Computing
by Ikvinderpal Singh

First Edition: 2010
Reprint: 2025, 2026

To view complete list of books, please scan the QR Code:

Published by:
Khanna Book Publishing Co. (P) Ltd.
CIN: U22110DL1998PTC095547

Visit us at: www.khannabooks.com
Write us at: contact@khannabooks.com

Printed in Bharat.

Dedicated to God
And
Our Parents

Preface

Soft computing refers to a collection of computational techniques in computer science, artificial intelligence, machine learning and some engineering disciplines which attempt to study, model and analyze very complex phenomena - those for which more conventional methods have not yielded low cost, analytic and complete solutions. Earlier computational approaches could model and precisely analyze only relatively simple systems. More complex systems arising in biology, medicine, humanities, management sciences and similar fields often remained intractable to conventional mathematical and analytical methods.

Soft computing differs from conventional (hard) computing in that, unlike hard computing, it is tolerant of imprecision, uncertainty, partial truth and approximation. In effect, the role model for soft computing is the human mind. The guiding principle of soft computing is: Exploit the tolerance for imprecision, uncertainty, partial truth and approximation to achieve tractability, robustness and low solution cost. The basic ideas underlying soft computing in its current incarnation have links to many earlier influences. Zadeh's 1965 paper of fuzzy sets; the 1973 paper on the analysis of complex systems and decision processes; and the 1979 report (1981 paper) on possibility theory and soft data analysis are just a few to name. The inclusion of neural computing and genetic computing in soft computing came at a later point.

This book on soft computing is designed to focus on the major components:

1. Neural Networks
2. Fuzzy Logic
3. Genetic Algorithm
4. Probabilistic Reasoning

We can also divide the book into three parts: Neural Networks, Fuzzy Logic and Genetic Algorithm, Probabilistic Reasoning

To conclude, we hope that the reader will find this book a helpful guide and a valuable source of information about soft computing concepts.

Part One provides a comprehensive discussion of the Artificial Neural Networks.

This part is intended for beginners, intermediate level, and all those who want to learn or expand their knowledge in Neural Networks. Since this is a part on the design of neural networks, our choice of topics was guided by two principles. First, we wanted to present the most useful and practical neural network architectures, learning rules and training techniques. Second, we wanted the book to be complete in it and to flow easily from one chapter to the next.

Indeed, we are strongly believed that Neural Networks are field of both intellectual interest and practical value to all such students and young professionals. Artificial neural networks not only provide an understanding into an important computational architecture and methodology, but they also provide an understanding of the mechanism of the biological neural network.

This book presents a wide variety of standard neural networks, with diagrams of the architecture, detailed statements of the training algorithm, and several examples of the application for each net. Derivations, theorems and proofs are included when they serve to illustrate the important features of a particular neural network.

The use of an interactive programming style is emphasized throughout the text. The chapters are mainly organized in increasing degree of complexity.

Chapter 1 describes the evolution of neural network, Biological neural network and Artificial neural network, advantages and disadvantages of ANN, various applications of neural networks. It covers the important concept of various network architectures of ANN.

Chapter 2 it covers the concept of Perceptron, its algorithm and architecture. It also deals with various types of Perceptrons. It also covers the important concept of Linear Separability and XOR problem.

Chapter 3 Covers the Backpropagation network, its algorithm and architecture. It also covers the use of Backpropagation.

Chapter 4 deals with Adaline and Madaline Networks. It covers concept of Adaptive Linear Combiner and its architectures with the help of algorithmic approach.

Chapter 5 describes the Supervised and Unsupervised learning, Networks like Competitive learning, Kohonen Self Organizing Map(SOM), Learning Vector Quantization. It also presents detailed analysis of Hebbian Learning.

Chapter 6 explains one of the complex concepts, Counter Propagation Network. It covers all concepts of CPN building blocks and CPN data processing.

Chapter 7 covers Adaptive Resonance Theory, Architecture and algorithm of ART1 and ART2 has been given in detail.

Chapter 8 covers all the description of Neocognitron, its algorithm and architecture. It also covers the data processing of Neocognitron in detail.

Chapter 9 explains the special concept of Bidirectional Associative Memory, its algorithm and architecture is given with the help of example.

Chapter 10 presents the Case studies, Speech Recognition and Stock Market Prediction. At the end detailed description of Neural Networks in Medicine is given using suitable examples.

Part Two discusses detail description of Fuzzy Logic and Genetic Algorithm.

This part is meant for a wide range of readers who wish to learn the basic concepts of Fuzzy logic. It can also be helpful for programmers, researchers and management experts who use Fuzzy logic techniques. Fuzzy logic techniques have been clearly dealt with suitable examples. Genetic algorithm operators and the various classifications have been discussed in lucid manner, so that a beginner can understand the concepts with minimal effort.

Chapter 11 covers the introduction to Fuzzy systems, uncertainty, classical logical theory, two valued logic, Multi- valued logic, fuzzy logic theory, advantages and disadvantages of fuzzy logic and the vocabulary of fuzzy logic. It also covers relationship between fuzzy logic and approximate reasoning, Propositional fuzzy logic, Predicate fuzzy logic, higher order fuzzy logic.

Chapter 12 deals with fuzzy logic, objectives of fuzzy logic, linguistic variables, fuzzy reasoning, applications areas of fuzzy logic, fuzzy logic for control, fuzzy sets, design membership function, basic operations in fuzzy sets, possibility theory, fuzzy rules.

Chapter 13 discusses the definition, properties, and operations of classical and fuzzy sets. It contains solved sample problems related to the classical and fuzzy sets. It also covers the concept of fuzzy quantifiers, fuzzy numbers, cardinality of fuzzy set, height of a fuzzy set, types of membership functions and possibility theory.

Chapter 14 deals with Cartesian product of the relation along with the cardinality, operations, properties, and composition of classical and fuzzy relations. It also covers the concept of Fuzzy tolerance and equivalence relation, Fuzzy Graphs and Fuzzy Arithmetic.

Chapter 15 discusses the Fuzzy if then rules, types of fuzzy rules, formation of rules, composition of rules, and aggregation of fuzzy rules. It also covers the properties of fuzzy rules, fuzzy rule based models, defuzzification, fuzzy inference system, sugeno and mamdani method.

Chapter 16 describes various application of fuzzy logic, Fuzzy logic in industrial automation, Fuzzy logic supervisory control for coal power plant, Optimization of a water treatment system, Fuzzy logic in chemical industry, Truck speed limiter control by fuzzy logic, Fuzzy logic and neuro-fuzzy in appliances, Fuzzy logic in adaptive heating system control, Fuzzy logic in data analysis of environmental data for traffic control, Fuzzy technology in sonar system and Fuzzy logic in automotive engineering.

Chapter 17 presents Neuro-Fuzzy Systems, Neural Networks, Network Architectures of ANN, Cooperative fuzzy neural network, hybrid fuzzy neural network, properties of neuro-fuzzy system, Architectures of neuro-fuzzy systems, ANFIS architecture and Examples of neuro-fuzzy modeling.

Chapter 18 is devoted to the most important concept of Genetic Algorithm, Methodology of genetic algorithms, Genetic Operators, Basic steps of the genetic algorithm, Working of Genetic Algorithm, Binary GA implementation and Design issues in GA.

Part Three discusses detail description of Probabilistic Reasoning.

This part is meant for a wide range of readers who wish to learn the basic concepts of Probabilistic Reasoning.

Chapter 19 covers the introduction to Probability Theory, it also includes various types of probability, classical probability, statistical probability, permutation and combination, conditional probability, Baye's Theorem and Solved problems.

Chapter 20 deals with random variable and mathematical expectation; it also includes the Solved problems to clear the concept.

Chapter 21 describes the concept of theoretical distributions, Binomial Distribution, Poisson Distribution, Normal Distribution. All the distributions are explained with the help of examples.

Chapter 22 deals with Fuzzy logic and Probability theory. It covers the concept of vagueness, imprecision, axiomatic structure of probability and fuzzy logic. It also includes concepts like Properties about probability of fuzzy events, Conditional probability of fuzzy events, Independence fuzzy events, Baye's theorem for fuzzy events and fuzzy measures.

This book can be used by a wide reader audience, ranging from beginners to practicing professionals. It is well suited for advanced or beginning college level students as a complete book for an introductory Soft Computing cause, as a supplementary text, or as an effective independent study guide.

Each and Every chapter contains clear statements of definitions and principles together with illustrative and other descriptive material.

Suggestions for improvement of the book will be gratefully accepted for future editions.

Ikvinderpal Singh

ips_sikand@yahoo.com

Acknowledgements

First we would like to thanks almighty for giving us courage to bring up this book. We duly acknowledge the contribution of our colleagues Prof. Harbhajan Singh, Prof. Sukhwinder Kaur, Prof. Kawaljit Kaur, Prof. Mani Arora, Mr. Baljinder Singh, Mr. Jagbir Singh, Mr. Sukhwant Singh, Mr. Avtar Singh Sandhu, Mr. Lovedeep Singh, Mr. Kanwarpal Singh, Mr. Navjeet Singh, Mr. Manpreet Singh, Mrs. Mandeep Kaur, Mrs. Jyoti Maini and Mr. Kawaljeet Singh for their valuable co-operation and guidance. We are grateful to Mr. Puneet Khanna M/s Khanna Book Publishing Co. Ltd. for his encouragement and motivation during this project.

Ikvinderpal Singh

Contents

Part - III: Probabilistic Reasoning

Introduction to Soft Computing

Soft Computing (SC) an innovative approach to constructing computationally intelligent systems, has just come into the limelight. It is now realized that complex real-world problems require intelligent systems that combine knowledge, techniques, and methodologies from various sources. These intelligent systems are supposed to possess humanlike expertise within a specific domain, adapt themselves and learn to do better in changing environment, and explain how they make decisions or take actions. In confronting real-world computing problems, it is frequently advantageous to use several computing techniques synergistically rather than exclusively, resulting in construction of complementary hybrid intelligent systems. The quintessence of designing intelligent systems. The quintessence of designing intelligent systems of this king is neuro-fuzzy computing: neural networks that recognize patterns and adapt themselves to cope with changing environments; fuzzy inference systems that incorporate human knowledge and perform interference and decision making. The integration of these two complementary approaches, together with certain derivative-free optimization techniques, results in a novel discipline called neuro-fuzzy and soft computing.

As a prelude, we shall provide a bird's-eye view of relevant intelligent system approaches, along with bits of their history, and discuss the features of neuro-fuzzy and soft computing.

WHAT IS SOFT COMPUTING?

Soft computing differs from conventional (hard) computing in that, unlike hard computing, it is tolerant of imprecision, uncertainty, partial truth, and approximation. In effect, the role model for soft computing is the human mind. The guiding principle of soft computing is: Exploit the tolerance for imprecision, uncertainty, partial truth, and approximation to achieve tractability, robustness and low solution cost. The basic ideas underlying soft computing in its current incarnation have links to many earlier influences, among them Zadeh's 1965 paper on fuzzy sets; the 1973 paper on the analysis of complex systems and decision processes; and the 1979 report (1981 paper) on possibility theory and soft data analysis. The inclusion of neural computing and genetic computing in soft computing came at a later point.

At this juncture, the principal constituents of Soft Computing (SC) are Fuzzy Logic (FL), Neural Computing (NC), Evolutionary Computation (EC) Machine Learning (ML) and Probabilistic Reasoning (PR), with the latter subsuming belief networks, chaos theory and parts of learning theory. What is important to note is that soft computing is not a melange. Rather, it is a partnership in which each of the partners contributes a distinct methodology for addressing problems in its domain. In this perspective, the principal constituent methodologies in SC are complementary rather than competitive. Furthermore, soft computing may be viewed as a foundation component for the emerging field of conceptual intelligence.

- Neural Networks
- Fuzzy Systems
- Evolutionary Computation
- Machine Learning
- Probabilistic Reasoning

IMPORTANCE OF SOFT COMPUTING

The complementarily of FL, NC, GC, and PR has an important consequence: in many cases a problem can be solved most effectively by using FL, NC, GC and PR in combination rather than exclusively. A striking example of a particularly effective combination is what has come to be known as "neurofuzzy systems." Such systems are becoming increasingly visible as consumer products ranging from air conditioners and washing machines to photocopiers and camcorders. Less visible but perhaps even more important are neurofuzzy systems in industrial applications. What is particularly significant is that in both consumer products and industrial systems, the employment of soft computing techniques leads to systems which have high MIQ (Machine Intelligence Quotient). In large measure, it is the high MIQ of SC-based systems that accounts for the rapid growth in the number and variety of applications of soft computing.

The conceptual structure of soft computing suggests that students should be trained not just in fuzzy logic, neurocomputing, genetic programming, or probabilistic reasoning but in all of the associated methodologies, though not necessarily to the same degree.

SOFT COMPUTING CONSTITUENTS AND CONVENTIONAL ARTIFICIAL INTELLIGENCE

Soft computing is an emerging approach to computing which parallels the remarkable ability of the human mind to reason and learn in an environment of uncertainly and imprecision. (Lotfi A. Zadeh, 1992)

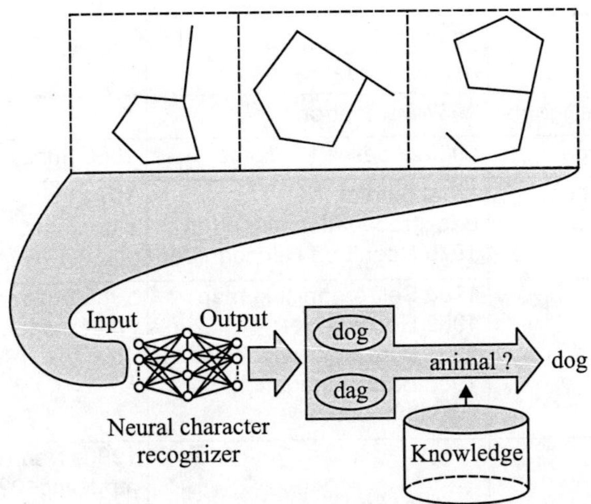

Figure 1: A neural character recognizer and a knowledge base cooperate in responding to three hand-written characters that form a word "dog".

Table 1 Soft computing constituents (the first three items) and conventional artificial intelligence.

Methodology	Strength
Neural network	Learning and adaptation
Fuzzy set theory	Knowledge representation via fuzzy if-then rules
Genetic algorithm and simulated annealing	Systematic random search
Conventional AI	Symbolic manipulation

Soft computing consists of several computing paradigms, including neural networks, fuzzy set theory, approximate reasoning, and derivative-free optimization methods such as genetic algorithms and simulated annealing. Each of these constituent methodologies has its own strength, as summarized in Table 1. The seamless integration of these methodologies forms the core of soft computing; the synergism allows soft computing to incorporate human knowledge effectively, deal with imprecision an uncertainty, and learn to adapt to unknown or changing environment for better performance. For learning and adaptation, soft computing requires extensive computation. In this sense, soft computing shares the same characteristics as computational intelligence.

In general, soft computing does not perform much symbolic manipulation, so we can view it as a new discipline that complements conventional artificial intelligence (AI) approaches, and vice versa. For instance, Figure 1 illustrates a situation in which a neural character recognizer and a knowledge base are used together to determine the meaning of a hand-written word. The neural character could be either an "o" or "a". If the knowledge base provides an extra piece of information that the given word is related to animals, then the answer "dog" is picked up correctly.

Figure 2 is a list of conventional AI approaches and each of the soft computing constituents in chronological order.

1940s	1947 Cybemetics	1943 McCulloch-Pitts neuron model		
1950s	1956 Artificial Intelligence	1957 Perceptron		
1960s	1960 Lisp language	1960s Adaline Madaline	1965 Fuzzy Sets	
1970s	Mid-1970s Knowledge Engineering (expert systems)	1974 Birth of Backpropagation algorithm 1975 Cognitron Neocognitron	1974 Fuzzy controller algorithm	1970s Genetic
1980s		1980 Self-organizing map 1982 Hopfield Net 1983 Boltzmann machine 1986 Backpropagation algorithm boom	1985 Fuzzy modeling (TSK model)	mid- 1980's Artificial life Immune modeling
1990s			1990s Neuro-fuzzy modeling1991 ANFIS 1994 CANFIS	1990 Genetic programming

Figure 2: A historical sketch of soft computing constituents and conventional AI approaches.

FROM CONVENTIONAL AI TO COMPUTATIONAL INTELLIGENCE

Humans usually employ natural languages in reasoning and drawing conclusions. Conventional AI research focuses on an attempt to mimic human intelligent behaviour by expressing it in language forms or symbolic rules. Conventional AI basically manipulates symbols on the assumption that such behavior can be stored in symbolically structured knowledge bases. This is the so-called physical symbol system hypothesis. Symbolic systems provide a good basis for modeling human experts in some narrow problem areas if explicit knowledge is available. Perhaps the most successful conventional AI product is the knowledge is available. Perhaps the most successful conventional AI product is the knowledge-based system or expert system (ES); it is represented in a schematic form in Figure 3.

Conventional AI literature reflects earlier work on intelligent systems. Many AI precursors defined AI in light of their own philosophy; some representative AI definitions are listed next along with a couple of ES definitions.

- "AI is the study of agents that exist in an environment and perceive and act." (S. Russell and P. Norvig)
- "AI is the art of making computers do smart things." (Waldrop)
- "AI is the activity of providing such machines as computers with the ability to display behavior that would be regarded as intelligent if it were observed in humans". (R. McLeod)
- "ES is a computer program using expert knowledge to attain high levels of performance in a narrow problem area." (D. A. Waterman).
- "ES is a caricature of the human expert, in the sense that it knows almost everything about almost nothing."

These definitions provide a conspicuous AI framework although they may be somewhat ephemeral because the conceptual framework is metamorphosing rapidly. The reader may well wonder, "Has AI become obsolete already?"

Calling soft computing constituents "parts of modern AI" inevitably depends on personal judgment. It is true that today many books on modern AI describe neural networks and perhaps other soft computing components.

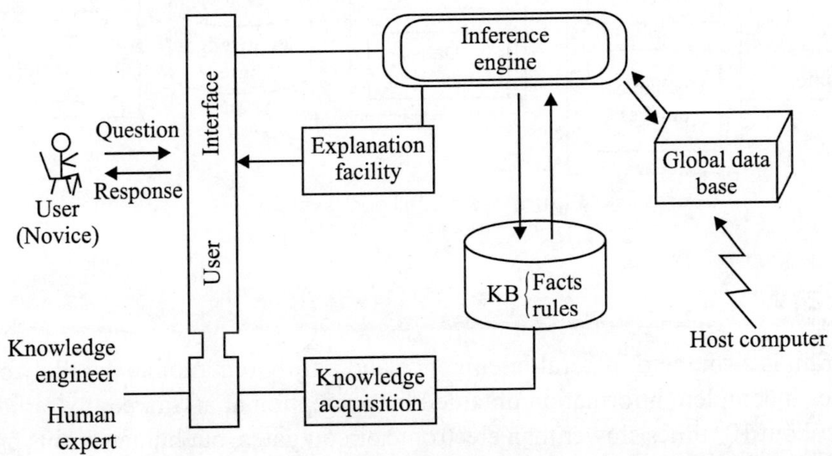

Figure 3: An expert system: one of the most successful (conventional) AI products

This means that the AI field is steadily expanding; the boundary between AI and soft computing is becoming indistinct and, obviously, successive generations of AI methodologies will be growing more sophisticated. Further discussion of these philosophical AI territories is beyond the scope of this book.

In practice, the symbolic manipulations limit the situations to which the conventional AI theories can be applied because knowledge acquisition and representation are by no means easy, but are arduous takes. More attention has been directed toward biologically inspired methodologies such as brain modeling, evolutionary algorithms, and immune modeling; they simulate biological mechanisms responsible for generating natural intelligence. These methodologies are somewhat orthogonal to conventional AI approaches and generally compensate for the shortcomings of symbolicism.

The long-term goal of AI research is the creation and understanding of machine intelligence. From this perspective, soft computing shares the same ultimate goal with AI. Figure 4 is a schematic representation of an intelligent system that can sense its environment (perceive) and act on its perception (react). An easy extension of ES may also result in the same ideal computationally intelligent system sought by soft computing researchers. Soft computing is apparently evolving under AI influences that sprang from cybernetics (the study of information and control in humans and machines).

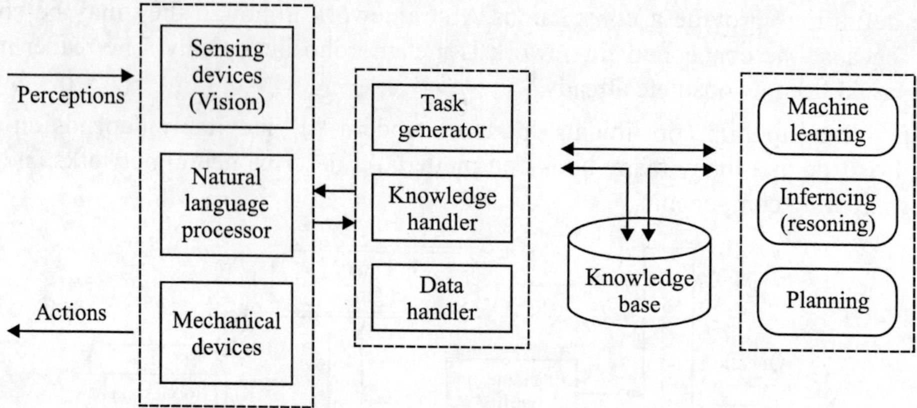

Figure 4: An intelligent system

NEURAL NETWORKS

The human brain is a source of natural intelligence and a truly remarkable parallel computer. The brain processes incomplete information obtained by perception at an incredibly rapid rate. Nerve cells function about 10^6 times slower than electronic circuit gates, but human brains process visual and auditory information much faster than modern computers.

Inspired by biological nervous systems, many researchers, especially brain modelers, have been exploring artificial neural networks, a novel nonalgorithmic approach to information processing. They model the brain as a continuous-time nonlinear dynamic system in connectionist architectures that are expected to mimic brain mechanisms to simulate intelligent behavior. Such connectionism replaces symbolically structured representations with distributed representations in the form of weight between a massive set of interconnected neurons (or processing units). It does not need critical decision flows in its algorithms.

A variety of connectionist approaches have been studied; some representative methodologies and their computational capacities are discussed in subsequent chapters.

FUZZY SET THEORY

The human brain interprets imprecise and incomplete sensory information provided by perceptive organs. Fuzzy set theory provides a systematic calculus to deal with such information linguistically, and it performs numerical computation by using linguistic labels stipulated by membership functions. Moreover, a selection of fuzzy if-then rules forms the key component of a fuzzy inference system (FIS) that can effectively model human expertise I a specific application.

Although the fuzzy inference system has a structured knowledge representation in the form of fuzzy if-then rules, it lacks the adaptability to deal with changing external environments. Thus, we incorporate neural network learning concepts in fuzzy inference systems, resulting in neuro-modeling, a pivotal technique in soft computing.

We discuss fuzzy sets, fuzzy rules, neuro-fuzzy modeling, genetic algorithms and fuzzy inference systems in PART 2.

EVOLUTIONARY COMPUTATION

Natural intelligence is the product of millions of years of biological evolution. Simulating complex biological evolutionary process may lead us to discover how evolution propels living systems toward higher-level intelligence. Greater attention is thus being paid to evolutionary computing techniques such genetic algorithms (GAs), which are based on the evolutionary principle of natural selection. Immune modeling and Artificial Life are similar disciplines and are based on the assumption that chemical and physical laws may be able to explain living intelligence. in particular, Artificial Life, and inclusive paradigm, attempts to realize lifelike behavior by imitating the processes that occur in the development or mechanics of life.

Heuristically informed search techniques are employed in many AI applications. When a search space is too large for an exhaustive (blind, brute-force) search and it is difficult to identify knowledge that can be applied to reduce the search space, we have no choice but to use other, more efficient search techniques to find less-than-optimum solutions., the GA is a candidate technique for this purposes; it offers the capacity for population-based systematic random searches. Simulated annealing and random search are other candidates that explore the search space in a stochastic manner.

MACHINE LEARNING

Machine learning is a scientific discipline that is concerned with the design and development of algorithms that allow computers to evolve behaviors based on empirical data, such as from sensor data or databases. A major focus of machine learning research is to automatically learn to recognize complex patterns and make intelligent decisions based on data; the difficulty lies in the fact that the set of all possible behaviors given all possible inputs is too complex to describe generally in programming languages, so that in effect programs must automatically describe programs. Artificial intelligence is a closely related field, as also probability theory and statistics, data mining, pattern recognition, adaptive control, and theoretical computer science.

Algorithm Types

Machine learning algorithms are organized into taxonomy, based on the desired outcome of the algorithm.

- **Supervised learning** generates a function that maps inputs to desired outputs. For example, in a classification problem, the learner approximates a function mapping a vector into classes by looking at input-output examples of the function.
- **Unsupervised learning** models a set of inputs, like clustering.

- **Semi-supervised learning** combines both labeled and unlabeled examples to generate an appropriate function or classifier.
- **Reinforcement learning** learns how to act given an observation of the world. Every action has some impact in the environment, and the environment provides feedback in the form of rewards that guides the learning algorithm.
- **Transduction** tries to predict new outputs based on training inputs, training outputs, and test inputs.
- **Learning to learn** learns its own inductive bias based on previous experience.

PROBABILISTIC REASONING

The aim of a **probabilistic logic** (or **probability logic**) is to combine the capacity of probability theory to handle uncertainty with the capacity of deductive logic to exploit structure. The result is a richer and more expressive formalism with a broad range of possible application areas. Probabilistic logic is a natural extension of traditional logic truth tables: the results they define are derived through probabilistic expressions instead. The difficulty with probabilistic logics is that they tend to multiply the computational complexities of their probabilistic and logical components.

CHARACTERISTICS OF SOFT COMPUTING

With neuro-fuzzy modeling as a backbone, the characteristics of soft computing can be summarized as follow:

1. **Human expertise:** Soft computing utilizes human expertise in the form of fuzzy if-then rules, as well as in conventional knowledge representations, to solve practical problems.
2. **Biologically inspired computing models:** Inspired by biological neural networks, artificial neural networks are employed extensively in soft computing to deal with perception, pattern recognition, and nonlinear regression and classification problems.
3. **New optimization techniques:** Soft computing applies innovative optimization methods arising from various sources; they are genetic algorithms (inspired by the evolution and selection process), simulated annealing (motivated by thermodynamics), the random search method, and the downhill Simplex method. These optimization methods do not require the gradient vector of an objective function, so they are more flexible in dealing with complex optimization problems.
4. **Numerical computation:** Unlike symbolic AI, soft computing relies mainly on numerical computation. Incorporation of symbolic techniques in soft computing is an active research area within this field.
5. **New application domains:** Because of the numerical computation, soft computing has found a number of new application domains besides that of AI approaches. These application domains are mostly computation intensive and include adaptive signal processing, adaptive control, nonlinear system identification, nonlinear regression, and pattern recognition.

6. **Model-free learning:** Neural networks and adaptive fuzzy inference systems have the ability to construct models using only target system sample data. Detailed insight into the target system helps set up initial model structure, but it is not mandatory.
7. **Intensive computation:** Without assuming too much background knowledge of the problem being solved, neuro-fuzzy and soft computing rely heavily on high-speed number-crunching computation to find rules or regularity in data sets. This is a common feature of all areas of computational intelligence.
8. **Fault tolerance:** Both neural networks and fuzzy inference systems exhibit fault tolerance. The deletion of a neuron in a neural network, or a rule in a fuzzy inference system, does not necessarily destroy the system. Instead, the system continues performing because of its parallel and redundant architecture, although performance quality gradually deteriorates.
9. **Goal driven characteristics:** Neuro-fuzzy and soft computing are goal driven; the path leading from the current state to the solution does not really matter as long as we are moving toward the goal in the long run. This is particularly true when used with derivative-free optimization schemes, such as genetic algorithms, simulated annealing, and the random search method. Domain-specific knowledge helps reduces the amount of computation and search time, but it is not a requirement.
10. **Real-world applications:** Most real-world problems are large code scale and inevitably incorporate built-in uncertainties; this precludes using conventional approaches that require detailed description of the problem being solved. Soft computing is an integrated approach that can usually utilize specific techniques within subtasks to construct generally satisfactory solutions to real-world problems.

The field of soft computing is evolving rapidly; new techniques and applications are constantly being proposed. We can see that a firm foundation for soft computing is being built through the collective efforts of researchers in various disciplines all over the world. The underlying driving force is to construct highly automated, intelligent machines for a better life tomorrow, which is already just around the corner.

PART - I
Artificial Neural Networks

1. Fundamentals of Neural Networks
2. Perceptrons
3. Backpropagation
4. Adaline and Madaline
5. Supervised and Unsupervised Learning
6. Counter Propagation Network
7. Adaptive Resonance Theory
8. Neocognitron
9. Bidirectional Associative Memory
10. Case Studies

CHAPTER 1

Fundamentals of Neural Networks

1.1 INTRODUCTION

For many decades, it has been a goal of science and engineering to develop intelligent machines with a large number of simple elements. References to this subject can be found in the scientific literature of the 19th century. During the 1940s, researchers desiring to duplicate the function of the human brain, have developed simple hardware (and later software) models of biological neurons and their interaction systems. McCulloch and Pitts published the first systematic study of the artificial neural network. Four years later, the same authors explored network paradigms for pattern recognition using a single layer perceptron. In the 1950s and 1960s, a group of researchers combined these biological and psychological insights to produce the first artificial neural network (ANN).Initially implemented as electronic circuits, they were later converted into a more flexible medium of computer simulation. However, researchers such as Minsky and Papert later challenged these works. They strongly believed that intelligence systems are essentially symbol processing of the kind readily modeled on the Von Neumann computer. For a variety of reasons, the symbolic–processing approach became the dominant method. Moreover, the perceptron as proposed by Rosenblatt turned out to be more limited than first expected. Although further investigations in ANN continued during the 1970s by several pioneer researchers such as Grossberg, Kohonen, Widrow, and others, their works received relatively less attention. The primary factors for the recent resurgence of interest in the area of neural networks are the extension of Rosenblatt, Widrow and Hoff' s works dealing with learning in a complex, multi-layer network, Hopfield mathematical foundation for understanding the dynamics of an important class of networks, as well as much faster computers than those of 50s and 60s.

The interest in neural networks comes from the networks' ability to mimic human brain as well as its ability to learn and respond. As a result, neural networks have been used in a large number of applications and have proven to be effective in performing complex functions in a variety of fields. These include pattern recognition, classification, vision, control systems, and prediction . Adaptation or learning is a major focus of neural net research that provides a degree of robustness to the NN model. In predictive modeling, the goal is to map a set of input patterns onto a set of output patterns.

NN accomplishes this task by learning from a series of input/output data sets presented to the network. The trained network is then used to apply what it has learned to approximate or predict the corresponding output.

1.2 HISTORICAL BACKGROUND OF NEURAL NETWORKS

Neural network simulations appear to be a recent development. However, this field was established before the advent of computers, and has survived at least one major setback and several eras.Many importand advances have been boosted by the use of inexpensive computer emulations. Following an initial period of enthusiasm, the field survived a period of frustration and disrepute. During this period when funding and professional support was minimal, important advances were made by relatively few reserchers. These pioneers were able to develop convincing technology which surpassed the limitations identified by Minsky and Papert. Minsky and Papert, published a book (in 1969) in which they summed up a general feeling of frustration (against neural networks) among researchers, and was thus accepted by most without further analysis. Currently, the neural network field enjoys a resurgence of interest and a corresponding increase in funding.

The history of neural networks that was described above can be divided into several periods:

1. **First Attempts:** There were some initial simulations using formal logic. McCulloch and Pitts (1943) developed models of neural networks based on their understanding of neurology. These models made several assumptions about how neurons worked. Their networks were based on simple neurons which were considered to be binary devices with fixed thresholds. The results of their model were simple logic functions such as "a or b" and "a and b". Another attempt was by using computer simulations. Two groups (Farley and Clark, 1954; Rochester, Holland, Haibit and Duda, 1956). The first group (IBM reserchers) maintained closed contact with neuroscientists at McGill University. So whenever their models did not work, they consulted the neuroscientists. This interaction established a multidiscilinary trend which continues to the present day.

2. **Promising & Emerging Technology:** Not only was neroscience influential in the development of neural networks, but psychologists and engineers also contributed to the progress of neural network simulations. Rosenblatt (1958) stirred considerable interest and activity in the field when he designed and developed the Perceptron. The Perceptron had three layers with the middle layer known as the association layer.This system could learn to connect or associate a given input to a random output unit.

   Another system was the ADALINE (ADAptive LInear Element) which was developed in 1960 by Widrow and Hoff (of Stanford University). The ADALINE was an analogue electronic device made from simple components. The method used for learning was different to that of the Perceptron, it employed the Least-Mean-Squares (LMS) learning rule.

3. **Period of Frustration & Disrepute:** In 1969 Minsky and Papert wrote a book in which they generalised the limitations of single layer Perceptrons to multilayered systems. In the book they said: "...our intuitive judgment that the extension (to multilayer systems) is sterile". The significant result of their book was to eliminate funding for research with neural network

simulations. The conclusions supported the disenhantment of reserchers in the field. As a result, considerable prejudice against this field was activated.

4. **Innovation:** Although public interest and available funding were minimal, several researchers continued working to develop neuromorphically based computaional methods for problems such as pattern recognition.

   During this period several paradigms were generated which modern work continues to enhance.Grossberg's (Steve Grossberg and Gail Carpenter in 1988) influence founded a school of thought which explores resonating algorithms. They developed the ART (Adaptive Resonance Theory) networks based on biologically plausible models. Anderson and Kohonen developed associative techniques independent of each other. Klopf (A. Henry Klopf) in 1972, developed a basis for learning in artificial neurons based on a biological principle for neuronal learning called heterostasis.

   Werbos (Paul Werbos 1974) developed and used the back-propagation learning method, however several years passed before this approach was popularized. Back-propagation nets are probably the most well known and widely applied of the neural networks today. In essence, the back-propagation net. is a Perceptron with multiple layers, a different thershold function in the artificial neuron, and a more robust and capable learning rule.

   Amari (A. Shun-Ichi 1967) was involved with theoretical developments: he published a paper which established a mathematical theory for a learning basis (error-correction method) dealing with adaptive patern classification. While Fukushima (F. Kunihiko) developed a step wise trained multilayered neural network for interpretation of handwritten characters. The original network was published in 1975 and was called the Cognitron.

5. **Re-emergence:** Progress during the late 1970s and early 1980s was important to the re-emergence on interest in the neural network field. Several factors influenced this movement. For example, comprehensive books and conferences provided a forum for people in diverse fields with specialized technical languages, and the response to conferences and publications was quite positive. The news media picked up on the increased activity and tutorials helped disseminate the technology. Academic programs appeared and courses were inroduced at most major Universities (in US and Europe). Attention is now focused on funding levels throughout Europe, Japan and the US and as this funding becomes available, several new commercial with applications in industry and finacial institutions are emerging.

6. **Today:** Significant progress has been made in the field of neural networks-enough to attract a great deal of attention and fund further research. Advancement beyond current commercial applications appears to be possible, and research is advancing the field on many fronts. Neurally based chips are emerging and applications to complex problems developing. Clearly, today is a period of transition for neural network technology.

1.3 WHAT IS NEURAL NETWORK?

Work on artificial neural networks, commonly referred to as "neural networks" has been motivated right from its inception by the recognition that the human brain computes in an entirely different way from the conventional digital computer. The brain is a highly complex, nonlinear and parallel computer (information-processing system). It has the capability to organize its structural constituents known as neurons so as to perform certain computations (e.g., pattern recognition, perception, and motor control) many times faster than the fastest digital computer in existence today. Consider for example, human vision, which is an information-processing (Marr. 1982: Levine, 1985: Churchland and Sejnowski, 1992). It is the function of the visual system to provide a representation of the environment around us and, more important to supply the information we need to interact with the environment. To be specific the brain routinely accomplishes perceptual recognition tasks (e.g. recognizing a familiar face embedded in an unfamiliar scene) in approximately 100-200 ms, whereas tasks of mush lesser complexity may take days on a conventional computer.

For another example, consider the sonar of a bat. Sonar is an active echo-location system. In addition to providing information about how far away a target e.g. a flying insect) is, a bat sonar conveys information about the relative velocity of the target, the size of the target, the size of various features of the target, and the azimum and evaluation of the target (Suga, 1990a, b). The complex neural computations needed to extract all this information from the target echo occur within a brain the size of a plum. Indeed, an echo-locating bat can pursue and capture its target with a facility and success rate that would be the envy of a radar or sonar engineer.

How, then does a human brain or the brain of a bat do it? At birth a brain has great structure and the ability to build up its own rules through what we usually refer to as "experience." Indeed, experience is built up over time, with the most dramatic development (i.e., hard-wiring) of the human brain taking place during the first two years from birth; but the development continues well beyond that stage.

A "developing" neuron is synonymous with a plastic brain: Plasticity permits the developing nervous system to adapt to its surrounding environment. Just as plasticity appears to be essential to the functioning of neurons as information-processing units in the human brain, so it is with neural networks made up of artificial neurons. In its most general form, a neural network is a machine that is designed to model the way in which the brain performs a particular task or function of interest; the network is usually implemented by using electronic components or is simulated in software on a digital computer. Our interest in this book is confined largely to an important class of neural networks that perform useful computations through a process of learning. To achieve good performance, neural networks employ a massive interconnection of simple computing cells referred to as "neurons" or "processing units." We may thus offer the following definition of a neural network viewed as an adaptive machine:

A neural network is a massively parallel distributed processor made up of simple processing units, which has a natural propensity for storing experiential knowledge and making it available for use. It resembles the brain in two respects:

1. *Knowledge is acquired by the network from its environment through a learning process.*
2. *Interneuron connection strengths, known as synaptic weights, are used to store the acquired knowledge.*

The procedure used to perform the learning process is called a learning algorithm, the function of which is to modify the synaptic weights of the network in an orderly fashion to attain a desired design objective. The modification of synaptic weights provides the traditional method for the design of neural networks. Such an approach is the closest to linear adaptive filter theory, which is already well established and successfully applied in many diverse fields (Widrow and Stearns, 1985; Hykin, 1996). However, it is also possible for a neural network to modify its own topology, its own topology, which is motivated by the fact that neurons in the human brain can die and that new synaptic connections can grow.

Neural networks are also referred to in literature as neurocomputers, connectionist networks, parallel distributed processors, etc. Throughout the book we use the term "neural networks"; occasionally the term "neurocomputer" or "connectionist network" is used.

1.4 BENEFITS OF NEURAL NETWORKS

It is apparent that a neural network derives its computing power through, first, its massively parallel distributed structure and, second, its ability to learn and therefore generalize. Generalization refers to the neural network producing reasonable outputs for inputs not encountered during training (learning). These two information-processing capabilities make it possible for neural networks to solve complex (large-scale) problems that are currently intractable. In practice, however, neural networks cannot provide the solution by working individually. Rather, they need to be integrated into a consistent system engineering approach. Specifically, complex problem of interest is decomposed into a number of relatively simple tasks, and neural networks are assigned a subset of te tasks that match their inherent capabilities. It is important to recognize, however, that we have a long way to go (if ever) before we can build a computer architecture that mimics a human brain.

The use of neural networks offers the following useful properties and capabilities:

1. **Nonlinearity:** An artificial neuron can be linear or nonlinear. A neural network, made up of an interconnection of nonlinear neurons, is itself nonlinear. Moreover, the nonlinearity is of a special kind in the sense that it is distributed throughout the network. Nonlinearity responsible for generation of the input signal (e.g., speech signal) is inherently nonlinear.
2. **Input-Output Mapping:** A popular paradigm of learning called learning with a teacher or supervised learning involves modification of the synaptic weights of a neural network by applying a set of labeled training samples or task examples. Each example consists of a unique input signal and a corresponding desired response. The network is presented with an example picked at random from the set, and the synaptic weights (free parameters) of the network are modified to minimize the difference between the desired response and the actual response of the network produced by the input signal in accordance with an appropriate statistical criterion. The training of the network is repeated for many examples in the set until the network reaches a steady state where the are no further significant changes in the synaptic weights. The previously applied training examples may be replied during the training session but in a different order. Thus the network learns from the examples by constructing an input-output mapping for the problem at hand. Such an approach brings to mind the

study of nonparametric statistical inference, which is a branch of statistics dealing with model-free estimation, or, from a biological viewpoint, tabula rasa learning (Geman et. al., 1992): the term "nonparametric" is used here to signify the fact that no prior assumptions are made on a statistical model for the input data. Consider, for example, a pattern classification task, where the requirement is to assign an input signal representing a physical object or event to one of several prespecified categories (classes). In a nonparametric approach to this problem, the requirement is to "estimate" arbitrary decision boundaries in the input signal space for the pattern-classification task using a set of example, and to do so without invoking a probabilistic distribution model. A similar point of view is implicit in the supervised learning paradigm, which suggest a close analogy between the input-output mapping performed by a neural network and nonparametric statistical interface.

3. **Adaptivity:** Neural networks have a built-in capability to adapt their synaptic weights to change sin the surrounding environment. In particular a neural network trained to operate in a specific environment can be easily retained to deal with minor changes in the operating environment conditions. Moreover, when it is operating in a nonstationary environment (i.e., one where statistics change with time), a neural network can be designed to change sits synaptic weights in real time. The natural architecture oa a neural network for pattern classification, adaptive capability of the network, make it a useful tool in adaptive pattern classification, adaptive signal processing, and adaptive control. As a general rule, it may be said that the more adaptive we make a system, all the time ensuring that the system is required to operate in a nonstationary environment. It should be emphasized, however, that adaptivity does not always lead to robustness: indeed, it may do the very opposite. For example, an adaptive short time constants may change reapidly and therefore tend to respond to spurious disturbances, causing a drastic degradation in system performance. To realize the full benefits of adaptivity, the principal time constants of the system should be long enough for the system to ignore spurious disturbances and yet short enough to respond to meaningful changes in the environment: the problem described here is referred to as the stability-plasticity dilemma (Grossberg, 1988b).

4. **Evidential Response:** In the context of pattern classification, a neural network can be designed to provide information not only about which particular pattern to select, but also about the confidence in the decision made. This latter information may e used to reject ambiguous patterns, should they arise, and thereby improve the classification performance of the network.

5. **Contextual Information:** Knowledge is represented by the very structure an activation state of the neural network. Every neuron in the network is potentially affected by the global activity of all other neurons in the network. Consequently, contextual information is dealt with naturally by a neural network.

6. **Fault Tolerance:** A neural network, implemented in hardware from, has the potential to be inherently fault tolerant, of capable of robust computation, in the sense that its performance degrades gracefully under adverse operating conditions. For example, if a neuron or its connecting links are damaged, recall of a stored pattern is impaired in quality. However, due

to the distributed nature of information stored in the network, the damage has to be extensive before the overall response of the network is degraded seriously. Thus, in principle, a neural network exhibit exhibits a graceful degradation in performance rather than catastrophic failure. There is some empirical evidence for robust computation, but usually it is uncontrolled. In order to be assured that the neural network is in fact fault tolerant, it may be necessary to take corrective measres in designing the algorithm uses to train the network (Kerlirzin and Vallet, 1993).

7. **VLSI Implementability:** The massively parallel nature of a neural network makes it potentially fast for the computation of certain tasks. This same feature makes a neural network well suited for implementation using very-large-scale-integrated (VLSI) technology. One particular beneficial virtue of VLSI is that it provides a means of capturing truly complex behavior in a highly hierarchical fashion (Mead, 1989).

8. **Uniformity of Analysis and Design:** Basically, neural networks enjoy universality as information processors. We say this in the sense that the same notation is used in all domains involving the application of neural networks. This feature manifests itself in different ways:
   - Neurons, in one form or another, represent an ingredient common to all neural networks.
   - This commonality makes it possible to share theories and learning algorithms in different applications of neural networks.
   - Modular networks can be built through a seamless integration of modules.

9. **Neurobiological Analogy:**The decision of a neural network is motivated by analogy with the brain, which is a living proof that fault tolerant parallel processing is not only physically possible but also fast and powerful. Neurobiologists look to (artificial) neural networks as a research tool for the interpretation of neurobiological phenomena. On the other hand, engineers look to neurobiology for new ideas to solve problems more complex that those based on conventional hard-wired design techniques. These two viewpoints are illustrated by the following respective examples:
   - In Anastasio (1993), linear system models of the vestibulo-ocular reflex are compared to neural network models based on recurrent networks that are described in Section 1.6 and discusses in detail in Chapter 15. The vestibulo-ocular reflex (VOR) is part of the oculomotor system. The function of VOR is to maintain visual (i.e., retinal) image stability by making eye rotations that are opposite to head rotations. The VOR is mediated by premotor neurons in the vestibular nuclei that process head rotation signals from vestibular sensory neurons and send the results to the eye muscle motor neurons. The VOR is well suited for modeling because its input (head rotation) and its output (eye rotation) can be precisely specified. It is also a relatively simple reflex and the neuro-physiological properties of its constituent neurons have been well described. Among the three neural types, the premotor neurons (reflex interneurons) in the vestibular nuclei are the most complex and therefore most interesting. The VOR has previously been modeled using lumped, linear system descriptors and control theory. These models were useful in explaining some of the overall properties of the VOR,

but gave little insight into the properties of its constituent neurons. This situation has been greatly improved through neural network modeling. Recurrent network models of VOR (programmed using an algorithm called real-time recurrent learning that is described in Chapter 15) can reproduce and help explain many of the static, dynamic, nonlinear, and distributed aspects of signal processing by the neurons that mediate the VOR, especially the vestibular nuclei neurons (Anastasio, 1993).

- The retina, more than any other part of the brain is where we begin to put together the relationships between the outside worked represented by a visual sense, its physical image projected onto an array of receptors, and the first neural images. The retina is a thin sheet of neural tissue that lines the posterior hemihphere of the eyeball. The retina's task is to convert an optical image into a neural image for transmission down the optic nerve to a multitude of centers for further analysis. This is a complex task, as evidenced by the synaptic organization of the retina. In all vertebrate retinas the transformation from optical to neural image involves three stages (Sterling, 1990):
  - (i) Photo transduation by a layer of receptor neurons.
  - (ii) Transmission of the resulting signals (produced in response to light) by chemical synapses to a layer of bipolar cells
  - (iii) Transmission of these signals, also by chemical synapses, to output neurons that are called ganglion cells.

At both synaptic stages (i.e., from receptor to bipolar cells, and from bipolar to ganglion cells) there are specialized laterally connected neurons called horizontal cells and amacrine cells, respectively. The task of these neurons is to modify the transmission across the synaptic layers. There are also centrifugal elements called inter-plexiform cells; their task is to convey signal from the inner synaptic layer back to the outer one. A few researchers have built electronics chips that mimic the structure of the retina (maahowald and Mead, 1989: Boahen and Ardreou, 1992; Boahen, 1996). These electronic chips are called neromorphic integrated circuits,a term coined by Mead (1989). A neuromophic imaging sensor consist of an arrya of photoreceptors combined with analog circuitry at each picture element (pixel). It emulates the retina in that it can adapt locally to changes in brightness, detect edges, and detect motion. The neurobiological integrated circuits is useful in another important way: It provide a hope and belief, and to a certain extent an existence of proof, that physical understanding of neurobiological structures could have a productive influence on the art of electronics and VLSI technology.

With inspiration from neurobiology in mind, it seems appropriate that we take a brief look at the human brain and its structural levels of organization.

1.5 HUMAN BRAIN

The human nervous system may be viewed as a three-stage system, as depicted in the block diagram of Fig. 1.1. Central to the system is the brain, represented by the neural (nerve) net, which continually receives information, perceives it, and makes appropriate decisions. Two sets of arrows are shown in the figure. Those pointing from left to right indicate the forward transmission of information-bearing signals through the system. The arrows pointing from right to left signify the presence of feed-back in the system. The receptors convert stimuli from the human body or the external environment into electrical impulses that convey information to the neural net (brain). The effectors convert electrical impulses generated by the neural net into discernible responses as system outputs.

The struggle to understand the brain has been made easier because of the pioneering work of Random y Cajal (1911), who introduced the idea of neurons as structural constituents of the brain. Typically, neuron are five to six orders of magnitude slower than silicon logic gates; events in a silicon chip happen in the nanosecond (10^{-3}s) range. However, the brain makes up for the relatively slow rate of operation of a neuron by having a truly staggering number of neurons (nerve cells) with massive interconnections between them. It is estimated that there are approximately 10 billion neurons in the human cortex, and 60 trillion synapses or connections (Shepherd and Koch, 1990). The net result is that the brain is an enormously efficient structure. Specifically, the energetic efficiency of the brain is approximately 10^{-16} joules (J) per operation per second, whereas the corresponding value for the best computers in use today is about 10^{-6} joules per operation per second (Faggin, 1991).

Synapses are elementary structural and function units that mediate the interactionsbetween neurons. The most common kind of synapse is a chemical synapse, which operates as follows. A presynaptic process liberates a transmitter substance that diffuses across the synaptic junction between neurons and then acts on a postsnaptic process. Thus a synapse converts a presynaptic electrical signal into a chemical signal and thenback into a postsynaptic electrical signal (Spherd and Koch 1990). In electrical terminology, such an element is said to be a nonreciprocal two-part device. In traditional descriptions of neural organization, it is assumed that a synapse is a simple connection that can impose excitation or inhibition, but not both on the receptive neuron.

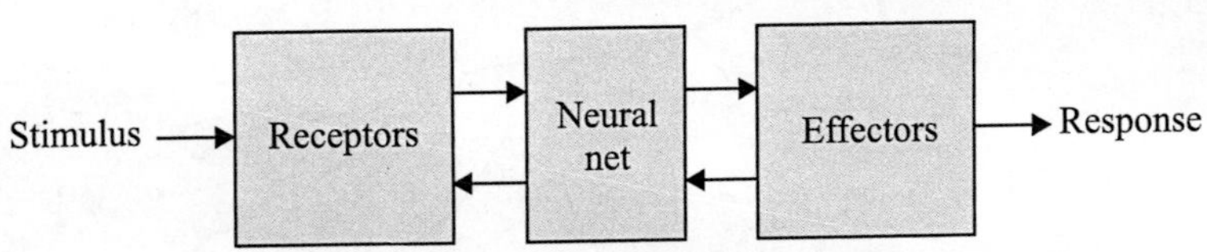

Figure 1.1: Block diagram representation of nervous system.

Earlier we mentioned that plasticity permits the developing nervous system to adapt to its surrounding environment (Eggermont, 1990; Churchland and Sejnowski, 1992). In an adult brain, plasticity may be accounted fro by two mechanism: the creation of new synaptic connections between neurons, and the modification of existing synapses. Axons, the transmission lines, and dendrites, the receptive zones, constitute two types of cell filaments that are distinguished on morphological grounds: an axon has a smoother surface, fewer branches, and greater length, whereas a dendrite (so called because of its resemblance to a tree) has an irregular surface and more branches (Freeman, 1975). Neurons come in a wide variety of shapes and sizes in different parts of the brain. Figure 1.2 illustrates the shape of a pyramidal cell, which is one of the most common types of cortical neurons. Like many other types of neurons, it receives most of its inputs through denritic spines; see the segment of dendrite in the insert in Figure 1.2 for detail. The pyramidal cell can receive 10,000 or more synaptic contacts and it can project onto thousands of target cells.

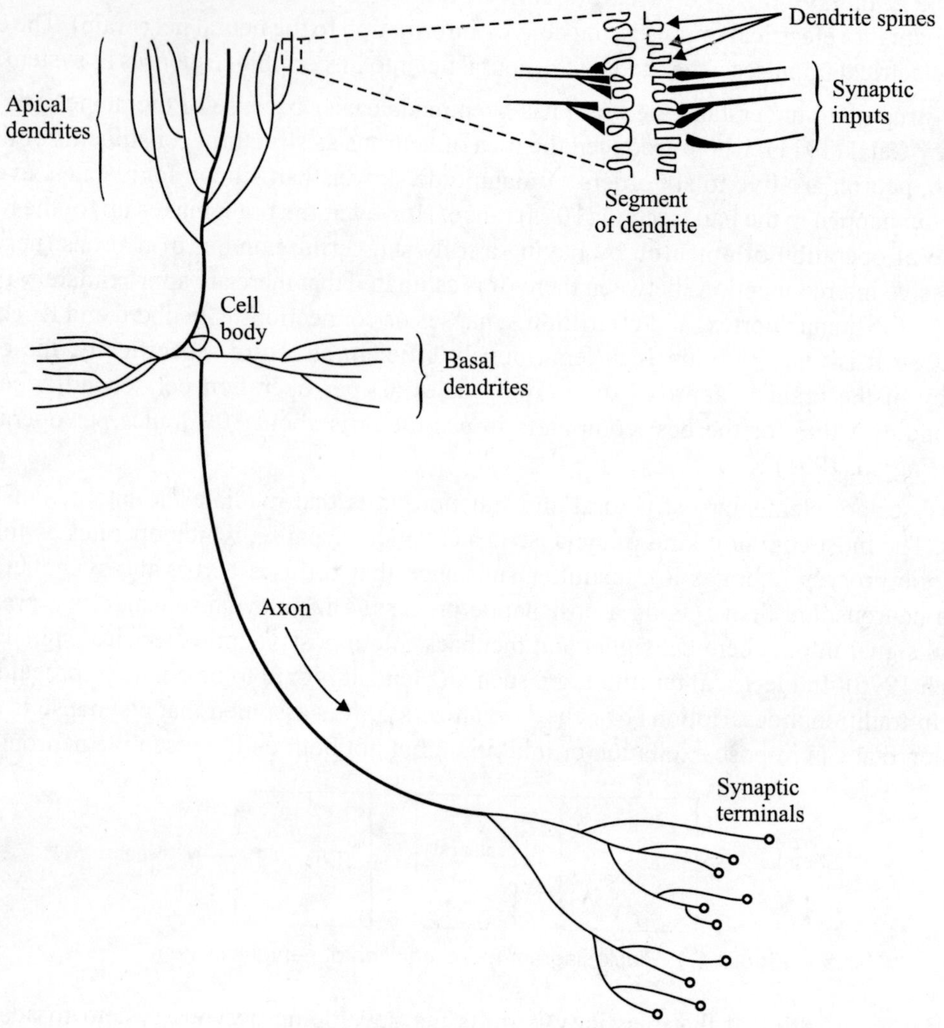

Figure 1.2: The pyramidal cell.

The majority of neurons encode their outputs as a series of brief voltage pulses. These pulses, commonly known as action potentials or spikes, originate are or close to the cell body of neurons and then propagate across the individual neurons at constant velocity and amplitude. The reasons for the use of action potentials for communication among neurons are based on the physics of axons. The axon of a neuron is very long and thin and is characterized by high electrical resistance and very large capacitance. Both of these elements are distributed across the axon. The axon may therefore be modeled as an RC transmission line, hence the common use of "cable equation" as the terminology for describing signal propagation along an axon. Analysis of this propagation mechanism reveals that when a voltage is applied at one end of the axon it decays exponentially with distance, dropping to an insignificant level by the time it reaches the other end. The action potentials provide a way to circumvent this transmission problem (Anderson, 1995).

In the brain there are both small-scale and large-scale anatomical organizations, and different functions take place at lower and higher levels. Figure 1.3 shows a hierarchy of interwoven levels of organization that has emerged from the extensive work done on the analysis of local regions in the brain (Shepherd and Koch, 1990; Churchland and Sejnowski, 1992). The synapses represent the most fundamental level, depending on molecules and ions for their action. At the next levels we have neural microcircits, dendritic trees, and then neurons. A neural microcircuit refers to an assembly of synapses organized into patters of connectivity to produce a functional operation of interest.

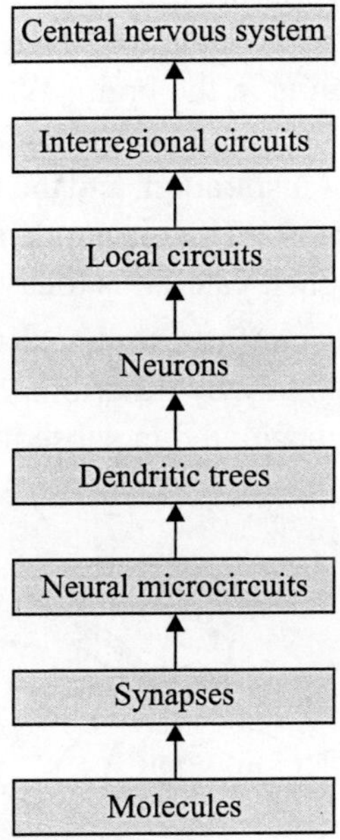

Figure 1.3: Structural organization of levels in the brain.

A neural microcircuit may be likened to a silicon chip made up of an assembly of transistors. The smallest size of microcircuits is measured in milliseconds. The neural micrometers (μm), and their fastest speed of operation is measured in milliseconds. The neural microcircuits are grouped to form dendritic subunits within the dendritic trees of individual neurons. The whole neuron, about 100 mm in size, contains several dendritic subunits. At the next level of complexity we have local circuits (about 1 mm in size) made up of neurons with similar or different properties; these neural assemblies performoperations characteristic of a localized region in the brain. This is followed by interregional circuits made up of pathways, columns, and topographic maps, which involve multiple region located in different parts of the brain.

Topographic maps are organized to respond to incoming sensory information. These maps are often arranged in sheets, as in the superior colliculus, where the visual,audiotory, and somatosensory maps are stacked in adjacent layers in such a way that stimuli from corresponding points in space lie above or below each other. Figure 1.4 presents a çytoarchitectural map of the cerebral cortex as worked out by Brodmann (Brodal, 1981). This figure shows clearly that different sensory inputs (motor, somatosensory, visual, auditory, etc.) are mapped onto corresponding areas of the cerebral cortex in an orderly fashion. At the final level of complexity, the topographic maps and other interregional circuits mediate specific types of behavior in the central nervous system.

It is important to recognize that the structural levels of organization described herein are a unique characteristic of the brain. They are nowhere to be found in a digital compute, and we are nowhere close to re-creating them with artificial neural networks. Nevertheless, we are inching our way toward a hierarchy of computational levels similar to that described in Fig. 1.3. The artificial neurons we use to build our neural networks are truly primitive in comparison to those found in the brain. The neural networks we are presently able to design are just as primitive compared to the local circuits and the interregional circuits in the brain. What is really satisfying, however, is the remarkable progress that we have made on so many fronts during the past two decades. With neurobiological analogy as the source of inspiration, and the wealth of theoretical and technological tools that we are bringing together, it is certain that in another decade our understanding of artificial neural networks will be much more sophisticated it is today.

Our primary interest in this book is confined to the study of official neural networks from an engineering perpective.[2] We begin the study by describing the models of (artificial) neurons that form the basis of the neural networks considered in subsequent chapters of the book.

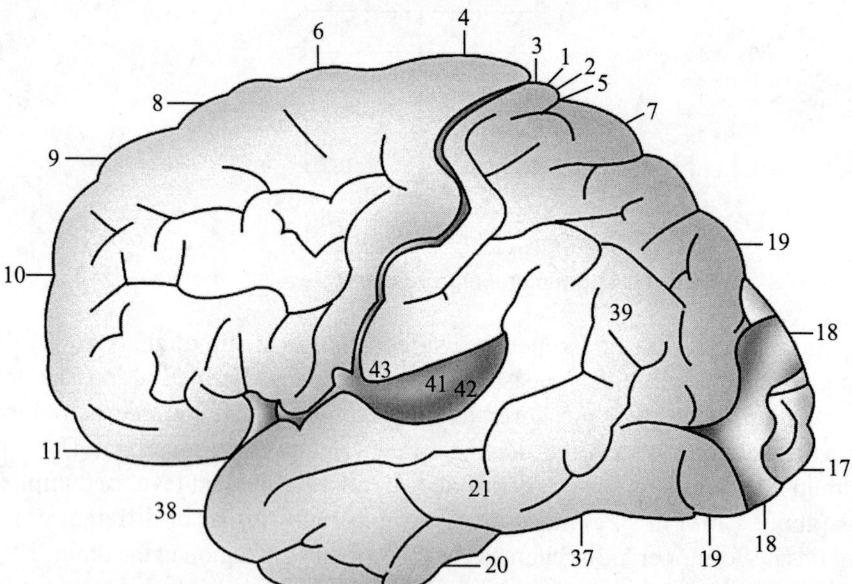

Figure 1.4: Cytoarchitectural map of the cerebral cortex. The different areas are identified by the thickness of their layers and types of cells within them. Some of the most important specific areas are as follows. Motor cortex: motor strip, area 4; premotor area, area 6; frontal eye fields, area 8. Somatosensory cortex: areas 3, 1, 2. Visual cortex: areas 17, 18, 19. Audiotory cortex: area 41 and 2.

1.6 BASIC STRUCTURE OF A NEURON

1.6.1 Model of Biological Neurons

In general, the human nervous system is a very complex neural network. The brain is the central element of the human nervous system, consisting of near 10^{10} biological neurons that are connected to each other through sub-networks. Each neuron in the brain is composed of a body, one axon and multitude of dendrites. The neuron model shown in Figure 1.5 serves as the basis for the artificial neuron. The dendrites receive signals from other neurons. The axon can be considered as a long tube, which divides into branches terminating in little endbulbs. The small gap between an endbulb and a dendrite is called a synapse. The axon of a single neuron forms synaptic connections with many other neurons. Depending upon the type of neuron, the number of synapses connections from other neurons may range from a few hundreds to 104.

The cell body of a neuron sums the incoming signals from dendrites as well as the signals from numerous synapses on its surface. A particular neuron will send an impulse to its axon if sufficient input signals are received to stimulate the neuron to its threshold level. However, if the inputs do not reach the required threshold, the input will quickly decay and will not generate any action. The biological neuron model is the foundation of an artificial neuron as will be described in detail in the next section.

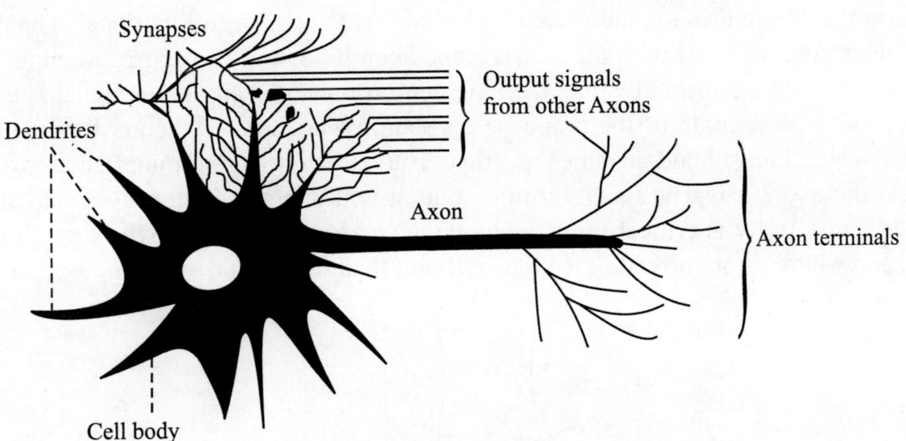

Figure 1.5: A biological neuron.

1.6.2 The Biological Neuron

The brain is a collection of about 10 billion interconnected neurons. Each neuron is a cell [right] that uses biochemical reactions to receive, process and transmit information.

A neuron's dendritic tree is connected to a thousand neighbouring neurons. When one of those neurons fire, a positive or negative charge is received by one of the dendrites. The strengths of all the received charges are added together through the processes of spatial and temporal summation. Spatial summation occurs when several weak signals are converted into a single large one, while

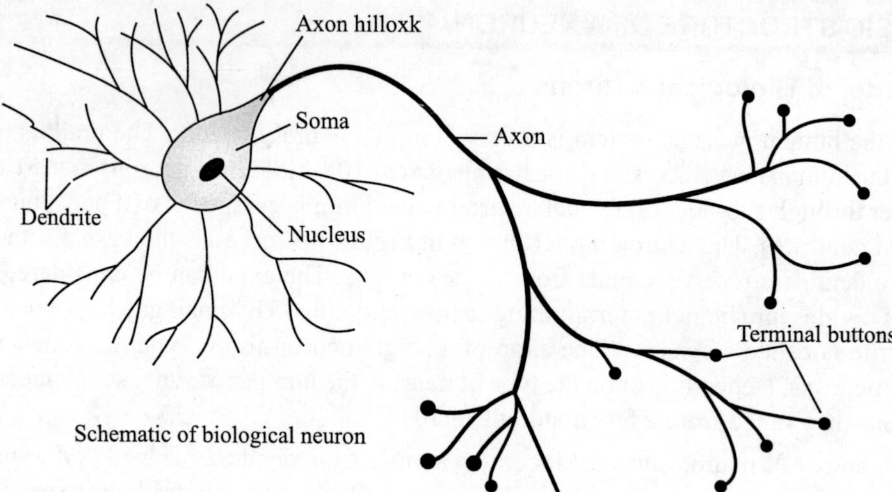

Figure 1.6: Biological Neuron

temporal summation converts a rapid series of weak pulses from one source into one large signal. The aggregate input is then passed to the soma (cell body). The soma and the enclosed nucleus don't play a significant role in the processing of incoming and outgoing data. Their primary function is to perform the continuous maintenance required to keep the neuron functional. The part of the soma that does concern itself with the signal is the axon hillock. If the aggregate input is greater than the axon hillock's threshold value, then the neuron fires, and an output signal is transmitted down the axon. The strength of the output is constant, regardless of whether the input was just above the threshold, or a hundred times as great. The output strength is unaffected by the many divisions in the axon; it reaches each terminal button with the same intensity it had at the axon hillock. This uniformity is critical in an analogue device such as a brain where small errors can snowball, and where error correction is more difficult than in a digital system.

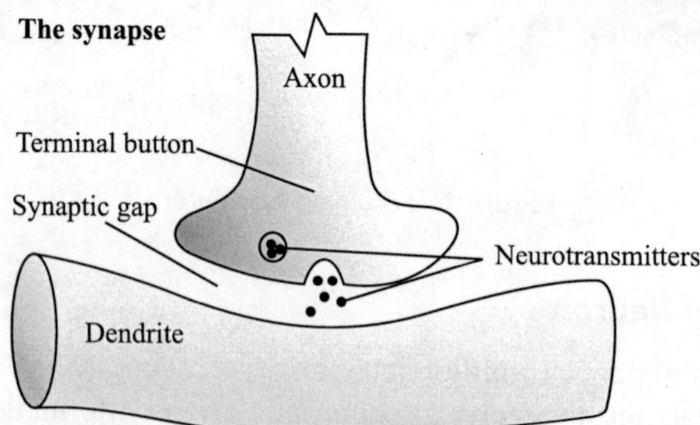

Figure 1.7: Components of biological neuron

Each terminal button is connected to other neurons across a small gap called a synapse [left]. The physical and neurochemical characteristics of each synapse determines the strength and polarity of the new input signal. This is where the brain is the most flexible, and the most vulnerable. Changing the constitution of various neuro- transmitter chemicals can increase or decrease the amount of stimulation that the firing axon imparts on the neighbouring dendrite. Altering the neurotransmitters can also change whether the stimulation is excitatory or inhibitory. Many drugs such as alcohol and LSD have dramatic effects on the production or destruction of these critical chemicals. The infamous nerve gas sarin can kill because it neutralizes a chemical (acetylcholinesterase) that is normally responsible for the destruction of a neurotransmitter (acetylcholine). This means that once a neuron fires, it keeps on triggering all the neurons in the vicinity. One no longer has control over muscles, and suffocation ensues.

1.7 WHAT IS AN ARTIFICIAL NEURAL NETWORK?

An artificial neural network is a system based on the operation of biological neural networks, in other words, is an emulation of biological neural system. Why would be necessary the implementation of artificial neural networks? Although computing these days is truly advanced, there are certain tasks that a program made for a common microprocessor is unable to perform; even so a software implementation of a neural network can be made with their advantages and disadvantages.

1.7.1 Advantages

1. A neural network can perform tasks that a linear program can not.
2. When an element of the neural network fails, it can continue without any problem by their parallel nature.
3. A neural network learns and does not need to be reprogrammed.
4. It can be implemented in any application.
5. It can be implemented without any problem.

1.7.2 Disadvantages

1. The neural network needs training to operate.
2. The architecture of a neural network is different from the architecture of microprocessors therefore needs to be emulated.
3. Requires high processing time for large neural networks.
4. Another aspect of the artificial neural networks is that there are different architectures, which consequently requires different types of algorithms, but despite to be an apparently complex system, a neural network is relatively simple.

Artificial neural networks (ANN) are among the newest signal-processing technologies in the engineer's toolbox. The field is highly interdisciplinary, but our approach will restrict the view to the engineering perspective. In engineering, neural networks serve two important functions: as pattern classifiers and as nonlinear adaptive filters. We will provide a brief overview of the theory, learning rules, and applications of the most important neural network models. Definitions and

Style of Computation An Artificial Neural Network is an adaptive, most often nonlinear system that learns to perform a function (an input/output map) from data. Adaptive means that the system parameters are changed during operation, normally called the training phase . After the training phase the Artificial Neural Network parameters are fixed and the system is deployed to solve the problem at hand (the testing phase).

The Artificial Neural Network is built with a systematic step-by-step procedure to optimize a performance criterion or to follow some implicit internal constraint, which is commonly referred to as the learning rule . The input/output training data are fundamental in neural network technology, because they convey the necessary information to "discover" the optimal operating point. The nonlinear nature of the neural network processing elements (PEs) provides the system with lots of flexibility to achieve practically any desired input/output map, i.e., some Artificial Neural Networks are universal mappers . There is a style in neural computation that is worth describing.

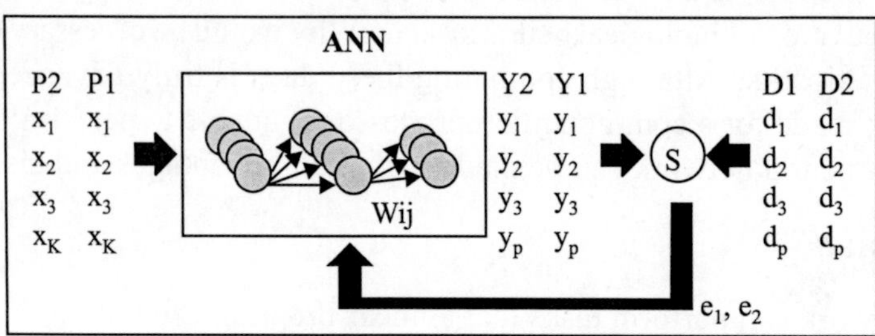

Figure 1.8: Working of artificial neuron

An input is presented to the neural network and a corresponding desired or target response set at the output (when this is the case the training is called supervised). An error is composed from the difference between the desired response and the system output. This error information is fed back to the system and adjusts the system parameters in a systematic fashion (the learning rule). The process is repeated until the performance is acceptable. It is clear from this description that the performance hinges heavily on the data. If one does not have data that cover a significant portion of the operating conditions or if they are noisy, then neural network technology is probably not the right solution. On the other hand, if there is plenty of data and the problem is poorly understood to derive an approximate model, then neural network technology is a good choice. This operating procedure should be contrasted with the traditional engineering design, made of exhaustive subsystem specifications and intercommunication protocols. In artificial neural networks, the designer chooses the network topology, the performance function, the learning rule, and the criterion to stop the training phase, but the system automatically adjusts the parameters. So, it is difficult to bring a priori information into the design, and when the system does not work properly it is also hard to incrementally refine the solution. But ANN-based solutions are extremely efficient in terms of development time and resources, and in many difficult problems artificial neural networks provide performance that is difficult to match with other technologies. Denker 10 years ago said that "artificial neural networks are the second best way to implement a solution" motivated by the simplicity of their design and because of their universality, only shadowed by the traditional design obtained by studying the physics of the problem. At present, artificial neural networks are emerging as the technology of choice for many applications, such as pattern recognition, prediction, system identification, and control.

1.7.3 Some other Definitions of A Neural Network Include

... a neural network is a system composed of many simple processing elements operating in parallel whose function is determined by network structure, connection strengths, and the processing performed at computing elements or nodes.

A neural network is a massively parallel distributed processor that has a natural propensity for storing experiential knowledge and making it available for use. It resembles the brain in two respects:

1. Knowledge is acquired by the network through a learning process.
2. Interneuron connection strengths known as synaptic weights are used to store the knowledge.

ANNs have been applied to an increasing number of real-world problems of considerable complexity. Their most important advantage is in solving problems that are too complex for conventional technologies — problems that do not have an algorithmic solution or for which an algorithmic solution is too complex to be found. In general, because of their abstraction from the biological brain, ANNs are well suited to problems that people are good at solving, but for which computers are not. These problems includes pattern recognition and forecasting (which requires the recognition of trends in data).

1.8 WHO IS DEVELOPING NEURAL NETWORKS?

It presents a very brief summary of the history of neural networks, in terms of the development of architectures and algorithms that are widely used today. Neural network simulations appear to be a recent development. However, this field was established before the advent of computers, and has survived at least one major setback and several eras. The history of neural networks shows the interplay among biological experimentation, modeling, and computer simulation/hardware implementation. Thus, the field is strongly interdisciplinary.

Many important advances have been boosted by the use of inexpensive computer emulations. Following an initial period of enthusiasm, the field survived a period of frustration and disrepute. During this period when funding and professional support was minimal, important advances were made by relatively few researchers. These pioneers were able to develop convincing technology which surpassed the limitations identified by Minsky and Papert. Minsky and Papert, published a book (in 1969) in which they summed up a general feeling of frustration (against neural networks) among researchers, and was thus accepted by most without further analysis. Currently, the neural network field enjoys a resurgence of interest and a corresponding increase in funding.

1.8.1 The Beginning of Neural Nets: The 1940s

(i) McCulloch-Pitts neurons

Warren McCulloch and Walter Pitts designed what are generally regarded as the first neural networks

[McCulloch & Pitts, 1943]. These researchers recognized that combining many simple neurons into neural systems was the source of increased computational power. The weights on a McCulloch-Pitts neuron are set so that the neuron performs a particular simple logic function, with different neurons performing different functions. The neurons can be arranged into a net to produce any output that can be represented as a combination of logic functions. The flow of information through the net assumes a unit time step for a signal to travel from one neuron to the next. This time delay allows the net to model some physiological processes, such as the perception of hot and cold.

The idea of a threshold such that if the net input to a neuron is greater than the threshold then the unit fires is one feature of a McCulloch-Pitts neuron that is used in many artificial neurons today. However, McCulloch-Pitts neurons are used most widely as logic circuits [Anderson & Rosenfeld, 1988].

McCulloch and Pitts subsequent work [Pitts & McCulloch, 1947] addressed issues that are still important areas today, such as translation and rotation invariant pattern recognition.

(ii) Hebb learning

Donald Hebb, a psychologist at McGill University, designed the first learning law for artificial neural networks [Hebb, 1949]. Hebb's principle can be described as a method of determining how to alter the weights between model neurons. The weight between two neurons increases if the two neurons activate simultaneously—and reduces if they activate separately. Nodes that tend to be either both positive or both negative at the same time have strong positive weights, while those that tend to be opposite have strong negative weights. Refinements were subsequently made to this rather general statement to allow computer simulations [Rochester, Holland, Haibt & Duda, 1956].

The idea is closely related to the correlation matrix learning developed by Kohonen (1972) and Anderson (1972) among others. An expanded form of Hebb learning [McClelland & Rumelhard, 1988] in which units that are simultaneously off also reinforce the weight on the connection between them will be presented in next chapters

1.8.2 The Golden Age of Neural Networks: The 1950s and 1960s

Although today neural networks are often viewed as an alternative to(or complement of) traditional computing, it is interesting to note that John von Neumann, the "father of modern computing," was keenly interested in modeling the brain [von Neumann, 1958]. Johnson and Brown (1988) and Anderson and Rosenfeld (1988) discuss the interaction between von Neumann and early neural network researchers such as Warren McCulloch, and present further indication of von Neumann's views of the directions in which computers would develop.

(i) Perceptrons

Together with several other researchers [Block, 1962; Minsky & Papert, 1988 (originally published 1969)], Frank Rosenblatt (1958, 1959, 1962) introduced and developed a large class of artificial neural networks called perceptrons. The most basic perceptron is composed of an input layer and output layer of nodes, each of which are fully connected to the other. Assigned to each connection is a weight which can be adjusted so that, given a set of inputs to the network, the associated connections will produce a desired output. The adjusting of weights to produce a particular output is called the "training" of the network which is the mechanism that allows the network to learn. Perceptrons are among the earliest and most basic models of artificial neural networks, yet they are at work in many of today is complex neural net applications.

The perceptron learning rule uses an interactive weight adjustment that is more powerful than the Hebb rule. Perceptron learning can be proved to converge to the correct weights if there are weights that will solve the problem at hand (i.e., allow the net to reproduce correctly all of the training input and target output pairs). Rosenblatt's 1962 work describes many types of perceptrons. Like the neurons developed by McCulloch and Pitts and by Hebb, perceptrons use a threshold output function.

The early successes with perceptrons led to enthusiastic claims. However, the mathematical proof of the convergence of iterative learning under suitable assumptions was followed by a demonstration of the limitations regarding what the perceptron type of net can learn [Minsky & Papert, 1969].

(ii) Adaline

Bernard Widrow and his student, Marcian (Ted) Hoff [Widrow & Hoff, 1960], developed a learning rule (which usually either bears their names, or is designated the least mean squares or delta rule) that is closely related to the perceptron learning rule. The perceptron rule adjusts the connection weights to a unit whenever the response of the unit is incorrect. (The response indicates a classification of the input pattern). The delta rule adjusts the weights to reduce the difference between the net input to the output unit and the desired output. This results in the smallest mean squared error. The similarity of models developed in psychology by Rosenblatt to those developed in electrical engineering by Widrow and Hoff is evidence of the interdisciplinary nature of neural networks. The difference in learning rules, although slight, leads to an improved ability of the net to generalize (i.e., respond to input that is similar, but not identical, to that on which it was trained). The Widrow-Hoff learning rule for a single-layer network is a precursor of the backpropagation rule for multilayer nets.

Work by Widrow and his students is sometimes reported as neural network, research, sometimes as adaptive linear systems. **ADALINE** (**Adaptive Linear Neuron** or later **Adaptive Linear Element**) is a single layer neural network. Adaline is a single layer neural network with multiple nodes where each node accepts multiple inputs and generates one output. It consists of a weight, a bias and a summation function. The difference between Adaline and the standard (McCulloch-Pitts) perceptron is that in the learning phase the weights are adjusted according to the weighted sum of the inputs (the net). In the standard perceptron, the net is passed to the activation (transfer) function and the function's output is used for adjusting the weights.

There have been many interesting applications of ADALINES, from neural networks for adaptive antenna systems [Widrow, Mantey, Griffinths, & Goode, 1967] to rotation-invariant pattern recognition to a variety of control problems, such as broom balancing and backing up a truck [Widrow, 1987l Tolat & Widrow, 1988; Nguyen & Widrow, 1989]. MADALINES are multilayer extensions of ADALINES [Widrow & Hoff, 1960; Widrow & Lehr. 1990]. **Madaline** (Multiple Adaline) is a two layer neural network with a set of ADALINEs in parallel as its input layer and a single PE (processing element) in its output layer. For problems with multiple input variables and one output, each input is applied to one Adaline. For similar problems with multiple outputs, madalines in parallel can be used. The madaline network is useful for problems which involve prediction based on multiple inputs, such as weather forecasting (Input variables: barometric pressure, difference in pressure. Output variables: rain, cloudy, sunny).

A MADALINE (many Adaline) network is created by combining a number of Adalines. The network of ADALINES can span many layers. The use of Multiple Adalines help counter the problem of non linear separability.

1.8.3 The Quiet years: The 1970s

In spite of Minsky and Papert's demonstration of the limitations of perceptrons (i.e., single-layer nets), research on neural networks continued. Many of the current leaders in the field began to publish their work during the 1970s. (Widrow, of course, had started somewhat earlier and is still active.)

(i) Kohonen

The early work of Teuvo Kohonen (1972), of Helsinki University of Technology, dealt with associative memory neural nets. His more recent work [Kohonen, 1982] has been the development of self-organizing feature maps that use a topological structure for the cluster units.

The Kohonen network (Kohonen, 1982, 1984) can be seen as an extension to the competitive learning network, although this is chronologically incorrect. Also, the Kohonen network has a different set of applications. In the Kohonen network, the output units in S are ordered in some fashion, often in a twodimensional grid or array, although this is application-dependent. The ordering, which is chosen by the user1, determines which output neurons are neighbours.

These nets have been applied to speech recognition (for Finnish and Japanese words) [Kohonen, Torkkola, Shozakai, Kangas, & Venta, 1987; Kohonen, 1988], the solution of the "Traveling Saleman Problem" [Angeniol, Vaubois, & Le Texier, 1988], and musical composition [Kohonen, 1989b].

(ii) Anderson

James Anderson, of Brown University, also started his research is neural networks with associative memory nets [Anderson 1968, 1972]. He developed these ideas into his "Brain-State-in-a-Box" [Anderson, Silverstein, Ritz, & Jones, 1977], which truncates the linear output of earlier models to prevent the output from becoming too large as the net iterates to find a stable solution (or memory). Among the areas of application for these nets are medical diagnosis and learning multiplication tables. Anderson and Rosenfeld (1988) and Anderson, Pellionisz, and Rosenfeld (1990) are collections of fundamental papers on neural network research. The introductions to each are especially useful.

(iii) Grossberg

Stephen Grossberg, together with his many colleagues and coauthors, has had an extremely prolific and productive career. Because of his interest in how brains give rise to minds, Grossberg's work focuses upon the design principles and mechanisms that enable the behavior of individuals, or machines, to adapt autonomously in real time to unexpected environmental challenges. His research has included fields as vision and image processing; object and event learning and pattern recognition; audition, speech and language; cognitive information processing; reinforcement learning and cognitive-emotional interactions; autonomous navigation; adaptive sensory-motor control and robotics; self-organizing neurodynamics; mental disorders; and neural network technology. Grossberg has published 15 books, over 450 research articles, and has 7 patents. Klimasaukas (1989) lists 146 publications by Grossberg from 1967 to 1988. His work which is very mathematical and very biological, is widely known [Grossberg, 1976, 1980, 1982, 1987, 1988]. Grossberg is director of the Center for Adaptive Systems at Boston University.

(iv) Carpenter

Together with Stephen Grossberg, Gail Carpenter has developed a theory of self-organizing neural networks called adaptive resonance theory [Carpenter & Grossberg, 1985, 1987a, 1987b, 1990]. Adaptive resonance theory nets for binary input patterns (ART1) and for continuously valued inputs (ART2) will be examined in Chapter 7.

1.8.4 Renewed Enthusiasm: The 1980s

(i) Backpropagation

Two of the reasons for the "quiet years" of the 1970s were the failure of a single-layer network has severe restrictions: the class of tasks that can be accomplished is very limited. In this chapter we will focus on feed-forward networks with layers of processing units. Minsky and Papert (Minsky & Papert, 1969) showed in 1969 that a two layer feed-forward network can overcome many restrictions, but did not present a solution to the problem of how to adjust the weights from input to hidden units. An answer to this question was presented by Rumelhart, Hinton and Williams in 1986 (Rumelhart, Hinton, & Williams, 1986), and similar solutions appeared to have been published earlier (Werbos, 1974; Parker, 1985; Cun, 1985). The central idea behind this solution is that the errors for the units of the hidden layer are determined by back-propagating the errors of the units of the output layer. For this reason the method is often called the back-propagation learning rule. Back-propagation can also be considered as a generalisation of the delta rule for non-linear activation functions1 and multilayer networks.

This method was also discovered independently by David Parker (1985) and by LeCun (1986) before it became widely known. It is very similar to yet an earlier algorithm in optimal control theory [Bryson & Ho, 1969]. Parker's work came to the attention of the Parallel distributed Processing Group led by psychologists David Rumelhart, of the University of California at San Diego, and James McClelland, of Carnegie-Mellon University, who refined and publicized it [Rumelhart, Hinton, & Williams, 1986a, 1986b; McClelland & Rumelhart, 1988].

(ii) Hopfield nets

A **Hopfield net** is a form of recurrent artificial neural network invented by John Hopfield. Hopfield nets serve as content-addressable memory systems with binary threshold units. They are guaranteed to converge to a local minimum, but convergence to one of the stored patterns is not guaranteed. Together with David Tank, a researcher at AT&T, Hopfield has developed a number of neural networks based on fixed weights and adaptive activations [Hopfield, 1982, 1984; Hopfield & Tank, 1985, 1986; Tank & Hopfield, 1987]. These nets can serve as associative memory nets and can be used to solve constraint satisfaction problems such as the "Traveling Salesman Problem." An article in Scientific American [Tank & Hopfield, 1987] helped to draw popular attention to neural nets, as did the message of a Nobel prize – winning physicist that, in order to make machines that can do what humans do, we need to study human cognition.

(iii) Neocognitron

Kunihiko Fukushima and his colleagues at NHK Laboratories in Tokyo have developed a series of specialized neural nets for character recognition. One example of such a net, called a neocognitron, is described in Chapter 8. The neocognitron design evolved from an earlier model called the cognitron, and there are several versions of the neocognitron itself. This deficiency was corrected in the neocognitron [Fukushima, 1988; Fukushima, Miyake, & Ito, 1983].

(iv) Boltzmann machine

A Boltzmann machine is the name given to a type of stochastic recurrent neural network by Geoffrey Hinton and Terry Sejnowski. Boltzmann machines can be seen as the stochastic, generative counterpart of Hopfield nets. They were one of the first examples of a neural network capable of learning internal representations, and are able to represent and (given sufficient time) solve difficult combinatoric problems. However, due to a number of issues discussed below, Boltzmann machines with unconstrained connectivity have not proven useful for practical problems in machine learning or inference. They are still theoretically intriguing, however, due to the locality and Hebbian nature of their training algorithm, as well as their parallelism and the resemblance of their dynamics to simple physical processes. If the connectivity is constrained, the learning can be made efficient enough to be useful for practical problems. A number of researchers have been involved in the development of nondeterministic neural nets, that is, nets in which weights or activations are changed on the basis of a probability density function [Kirkpatric, Gelatt, & Vecchi, 1983; Geman & Geman, 1984; Ackley, Hinton & Sejnowski, 1985; Szu & Hartly, 1987]. These nets incorporate such classical ideas as simulated annealing and Bayesian decision theory.

(v) Hardware implementation

Another reason for renewed interest in neural networks (in addition to solving the problem of how to train a multilayer net) is improved computational capabilities. Optical neural nets [Farhat, Psaltis, Prata, & Paek, 1985] and VLSI implementations [Sivilatti, Mahowald, & Neadm 1987] are being developed. An **optical neural network** is a physical implementation of an artificial neural network with optical components. Some artificial neural networks that have been implemented as optical neural networks include the Hopfield neural network and the Kohonen self-organizing map with liquid crystals.

Carver Mead, of California Institute of Technology, who also studies motion detection, is the coinventor of software to design microchips. He is also cofounder of Synaptics, Inc., a leader in the study of neural circuitry.

Nobel laureate Leon Cooper, of Brown University, introduced one of the first multilayer nets, the reduced coulomb energy network. Cooper is chairman of Nestor, the first public neural network company [Johnson & Brown, 1988], and the holder of several patents for information-processing systems [Klimasauskas, 1989].

Robert Hecht-Nielsen and Todd Gutschow developed several digital neurocomputer at TRW, Inc., during 1983-85. Funding was provided by the Defense Advanced Research Projects Agency (DARPA) [Hecth-Nielsen, 1990]. DARPA (1988) is a valuable summary of the state of the art in artificial neural networks (especially with regard to successful applications). To quite from the preface to his book, Neurocomputing, Hecth-Nielsen is "and industrialist, an adjunct academic, and a philanthropist without financial portfolio" [Hecht-Nielsen 1990]. The founder of HNC, Inc., he is also a professor at the University of California, San Diego, and the developer of the counter propagation network.

1.9 VARIOUS TYPES OF ARTIFICIAL NEURAL NETWORKS

Network	Application	Description
ADALINE Adaline Network	**Pattern Recognition** Classification of Digits 0-9	The Adaline is essentially asingle-layer backpropagation network. It is trained on a pattern recognition task, where the aim is to classify a bitmap representation of the digits 0-9 into the corresponding classes. Due to the limited capabilities of the Adaline, the network only recognizes the exact training patterns. When the application is ported into the multi-layer backpropagation network, a remarkable degree of fault-tolerance can be achieved.
BPN Backpropagation Network	**Time-Series Forecasting** Prediction of the Annual Number of Sunspots	This program implements the now classic multilayer backpropagation network with bias terms and momentum. It is used to detect structure in time-series, which is presented to the network using a simple tapped delay-line memory. The program learns to predict future sunspot activity from historical data collected over the past three centuries. To avoid overfitting, the termination of the learning procedure is controlled by the so-called stopped training method.

Network	Application	Description
HOPFIELD Hopfield Model	**Autoassociative Memory** Associative Recall of Images	The Hopfield model is used as an autoassociative memory to store and recall a set of bitmap images. Images are stored by calculating a corresponding weight matrix. Thereafter, starting from an arbitrary configuration, the memory will settle on exactly that stored image, which is nearest to the starting configuration in terms of Hamming distance. Thus given an incomplete or corrupted version of a stored image, the network is able to recall the corresponding original image.
BAM Bidirectional Associative Memory	**Heteroassociative Memory** Association of Names and Phone Numbers	The bidirectional associative memory can be viewed as a generalization of the Hopfield model, to allow for a heteroassociative memory to be implemented. In this case, the association is between names and corresponding phone numbers. After coding the set of exemplars, the network, when presented with a name, is able to recall the corresponding phone number and vice versa. The memory even shows a limited degree of fault-tolerance in case of corrupted input patterns.
BOLTZMAN Boltzmann Machine	**Optimization** Traveling Salesman Problem	The Boltzmann machine is a stochastic version of the Hopfield model, whose network dynamics incorporate a random component in correspondence with a given finite temperature. Starting with a high temperature and gradually cooling down, allowing the network to reach equilibrium at any step, chances are good, that the network will settle in a global minimum of the corresponding energy function. This process is called simulated annealing. The network is then used to solve a well-known optimization problem: The weight matrix is chosen such that the global minimum of the energy function corresponds to a solution of a particular instance of the traveling salesman problem.
CPN Counterpropagation Network	**Vision** Determination of the Angle of Rotation	The counterpropagation network is a competitive network, designed to function as a self-programming lookup table with the additional ability to interpolate between entries. The application is to determine the angular rotation of a rocket-shaped object, images of which are presented to the network as a bitmap pattern. The performance of the network is a little limited due to the low resolution of the bitmap.

Network	Application	Description
SOM Self-Organizing Map	**Control** Pole Balancing Problem	The self-organizing map is a competitive network with the ability to form topology-preserving mappings between its input and output spaces. In this program the network learns to balance a pole by applying forces at the base of the pole. The behavior of the pole is simulated by numerically integrating the differential equations for its law of motion using Euler's method. The task of the network is to establish a mapping between the state variables of the pole and the optimal force to keep it balanced. This is done using a reinforcement learning approach: For any given state of the pole, the network tries a slight variation of the mapped force. If the new force results in better control, the map is modified, using the pole's current state variables and the new force as a training vector.
ART1 Adaptive Resonance Theory	**Brain Modeling** Stability-Plasticity Demonstration	This program is mainly a demonstration of the basic features of the adaptive resonance theory network, namely the ability to plastically adapt when presented with new input patterns while remaining stable at previously seen input patterns.

1.10 WHY USE A NEURAL NETWORK?

Neural networks, with their remarkable ability to derive meaning from complicated or imprecise data, can be used to extract patterns and detect trends that are too complex to be noticed by either humans or other computer techniques. A trained neural network can be thought of as an "expert" in the category of information it has been given to analyze. This expert can then be used to provide projections given new situations of interest and answer "what if" questions.

1. **Adaptive learning:** An ability to learn how to do tasks based on the data given for training or initial experience.
2. **Self-Organisation:** An ANN can create its own organisation or representation of the information it receives during learning time.
3. **Real Time Operation:** ANN computations may be carried out in parallel, and special hardware devices are being designed and manifactured which take advantage of this capability.
4. **Fault Tolerance via Redundant Information Coding:** Partial destruction of a network leads to the corresponding degradation of performance. However, some network capabilites may be retained even with major network damage.

1.11 HOW NEURAL NETWORKS DIFFER FROM TRADITIONAL COMPUTING

Neural networks offer a different way to analyze data, and to recognize patterns within that data, than traditional computing methods. However, they are not a solution for all computing problems. Traditional computing methods work well for problems that can be well characterized. Balancing checkbooks, keeping ledgers, and keeping tabs of inventory are well defined and do not require the special characteristics of neural networks. Table 1.1 identifies the basic differences between the two computing approaches. Traditional computers are ideal for many applications. They can process data, track inventories, network results, and protect equipment. These applications do not need the special characteristics of neural networks. Expert systems are an extension of traditional computing and are sometimes called the fifth generation of computing. (First generation computing used switches and wires. The second generation occurred because of the development of the transistor. The third generation involved solid-state technology, the use of integrated circuits, and higher level languages like COBOL, Fortran, and "C". End user tools, "code generators," are known as the fourth generation.) The fifth generation involves artificial intelligence.

Table 1.1: Comparison of computing approaches

Characteristics (Including Expert Systems)	**Traditional Computing Neuralnetworks**	**Artificial**
Processing style Functions	SequentialLogically (left brained) via Rules Concepts Calculations	Parallel Gestault (right brained) via Images Pictures Controls
Learning Method Applications	by rules (didactically) Accountingword processing math inventory digital communications	by example (Socratically) Sensor processing speech recognition, pattern recognition text recognition

Typically, an expert system consists of two parts, an inference engine and a knowledge base. The inference engine is generic. It handles the user interface, external files, program access, and scheduling. The knowledge base contains the information that is specific to a particular problem. This knowledge base allows an expert to define the rules which govern a process. This expert does not have to understand traditional programming. That person simply has to understand both what he wants a computer to do and how the mechanism of the expert system shell works. It is this shell, part of the inference engine, that actually tells the computer how to implement the expert's desires. This implementation occurs by the expert system generating the computer's programming itself, it does that through "programming" of its own. This programming is needed to establish the rules for a particular application. This method of establishing rules is also complex and does require a detail oriented person. Efforts to make expert systems general have run into a number of problems. As the complexity of the system increases, the system simply demands too much computing resources and becomes too slow. Expert systems have been found to be feasible only when narrowly confined. Artificial neural networks offer a completely different approach to problem solving and they are sometimes called the sixth generation of computing. They try to provide a tool that both programs itself and learns on its own. Neural networks are structured to provide the capability to solve problems without the benefits of an expert and without the need of programming. They can seek patterns in data that no one knows are there. A comparison of artificial intelligence's expert systems and neural networks is contained in Table 1.2.

Table 1.2: Comparisons of expert systems and neural networks

Characteristics Used for Expert Systems	Von Neumann Architecture	Artificial NeuralNetworks
Processors	VLSI(traditional processors)	Artificial NeuralNetworks; variety of technologies;hardware developmentis on going
Processing Approach	Separate	The same
Processing Approach	Processes problem rule at a one time; sequential	Multiple,simultaneously
Connections	Externally programmable	Dynamically selfprogramming
Self learning	Only algorithmic parameters modified	Continuously adaptable
Fault tolerance	None without special processors	Significant in thevery nature of the interconnected neurons
Neurobiology in design	None	Moderate
Programming	Through a rule based complicated	Self-programming;but network must beset up properly
Ability to be fast	Requires big processors	Requires multiple custom-built chips

Expert systems have enjoyed significant successes. However, artificial intelligence has encountered problems in areas such as vision, continuous speech recognition and synthesis, and machine learning. Artificial intelligence also is hostage to the speed of the processor that it runs on. Ultimately, it is restricted to the theoretical limit of a single processor. Artificial intelligence is also burdened by the fact that experts don't always speak in rules. Yet, despite the advantages of neural networks over both expert systems and more traditional computing in these specific areas, neural nets are not complete solutions. They offer a capability that is not ironclad, such as a debugged accounting system. They learn, and as such, they do continue to make "mistakes." Furthermore, even when a network has been developed, there is no way to ensure that the network is the optimal network. Neural systems do exact their own demands. They do require their implementor to meet a number of conditions. These conditions include:

- a data set which includes the information which can characterize the problem.
- an adequately sized data set to both train and test the network.
- an understanding of the basic nature of the problem to be solved so that basic first-cut decision on creating the network can be made. These decisions include the activization and transfer functions, and the learning methods.
- an understanding of the development tools.

- adequate processing power (some applications demand real-time processing that exceeds what is available in the standard, sequential processing hardware. The development of hardware is the key to the future of neural networks).

Once these conditions are met, neural networks offer the opportunity of solving problems in an arena where traditional processors lack both the processing power and a step-by-step methodology. A number of very complicated problems cannot be solved in the traditional computing environments. For example, speech is something that all people can easily parse and understand. A person can understand a southern drawl, a Bronx accent, and the slurred words of a baby. Without the massively paralleled processing power of a neural network, this process is virtually impossible for a computer. Image recognition is another task that a human can easily do but which stymies even the biggest of computers. A person can recognize a plane as it turns, flies overhead, and disappears into a dot. A traditional computer might try to compare the changing images to a number of very different stored patterns.

This new way of computing requires skills beyond traditional computing. It is a natural evolution. Initially, computing was only hardware and engineers made it work. Then, there were software specialists - programmers, systems engineers, data base specialists, and designers. Now, there are also neural architects. This new professional needs to be skilled different than his predecessors of the past. For instance, he will need to know statistics in order to choose and evaluate training and testing situations. This skill of making neural networks work is one that will stress the logical thinking of current software engineers.

In summary, neural networks offer a unique way to solve some problems while making their own demands. The biggest demand is that the process is not simply logic. It involves an empirical skill, an intuitive feel as to how a network might be created.

1.12 NEURAL NETWORKS IN PRACTICE

Given this description of neural networks and how they work, what real world applications are they suited for? Neural networks have broad applicability to real world business problems. In fact, they have already been successfully applied in many industries.

Since neural networks are best at identifying patterns or trends in data, they are well suited for prediction or forecasting needs including:

1. Sales forecasting
2. Industrial process control
3. Customer research
4. Data validation
5. Risk management
6. Target marketing

But to give you some more specific examples; ANN are also used in the following specific paradigms: recognition of speakers in communications; diagnosis of hepatitis; recovery of telecommunications from faulty software; interpretation of multimeaning Chinese words; undersea mine detection; texture analysis; three-dimensional object recognition; handwritten word recognition; and facial recognition.

1.13 APPLICATIONS OF NEURAL NETWORKS

The *1988 DARPA Neural Network Study* [DARP88] lists various neural network applications, beginning in about 1984 with the adaptive channel equalizer. This device, which is an outstanding commercial success, is a single- neuron network used in long-distance telephone systems to stabilize voice signals. The DARPA report goes on to list other commercial applications, including a small word recognizer, a process monitor, a sonar classifier, and a risk analysis system.

Neural networks have been applied in many other fields since the DARPA report was written, as described in the next table.

Aerospace	High-performance aircraft autopilot, flight path simulation, aircraft control systems, autopilot enhancements, aircraft component simulation, and aircraft component fault detection
Automotive	Automobile automatic guidance system, and warranty activity analysis
Banking	Check and other document reading and credit application evaluation
Industry	Business Applications
Defense	Weapon steering, target tracking, object discrimination, facial recognition, new kinds of sensors, sonar, radar and image signal processing including data compression, feature extraction and noise suppression, and signal/image identification
Electronics	Code sequence prediction, integrated circuit chip layout, process control, chip failure analysis, machine vision, voice synthesis, and nonlinear modeling
Entertainment	Animation, special effects, and market forecasting
Financial	Real estate appraisal, loan advising, mortgage screening, corporate bond rating, credit-line use analysis, credit card activity tracking, portfolio trading program, corporate financial analysis, and currency price prediction
Industrial	Prediction of industrial processes, such as the output gases of furnaces, replacing complex and costly equipment used for this purpose in the past
Insurance	Policy application evaluation and product optimization
Manufacturing	Manufacturing process control, product design and analysis, process and machine diagnosis, real-time particle identification, visual quality inspection systems, beer testing, welding quality analysis, paper quality prediction, computer-chip quality analysis, analysis of grinding operations, chemical product design analysis, machine maintenance analysis, project bidding, planning and management, and dynamic modeling of chemical process system
Industry	Business Applications

Industry	Business Applications
Medical	Breast cancer cell analysis, EEG and ECG analysis, prosthesis design, optimization of transplant times, hospital expense reduction, hospital quality improvement, andemergency-room test advisement
Oil and gas	Exploration
Robotics	Trajectory control, forklift robot, manipulator controllers, and vision systems
Speech	Speech recognition, speech compression, vowel classification, and text-to-speech synthesis
Securities	Market analysis, automatic bond rating, and stock trading advisory systems
Telecommunications	Image and data compression, automated information services, real-time translation of spoken language, and customer payment processing systems
Transportation	Truck brake diagnosis systems, vehicle scheduling, and routing systems

1.13.1 Pattern Recognition

The act of recognition can be divided into two broad categories: recognizing concrete items and recognizing abstract items. The recognition of concrete items involves the recognition of spatial and temporal items. Examples of spatial items are fingerprints, weather maps, pictures and physical objects. Examples of temporal items are waveforms and signatures. Recognition of abstract items involves the recognition of a solution to a problem, an old conversation or argument, etc. In other words, recognizing items that do not exist physically.

In this article, I am concerned with recognition of concrete items. Applications include finger print identification, voice recognition, face recognition, character recognition, signature recognition and classification of objects in scientific/research areas such as astronomy, engineering, statistics, medical, machine learning and neural networks. Recognition of an item involves three levels of processing: input filtering, feature extraction and classification

- **Filtering** is removing unwanted information or data from input. Depending on the application, the filter algorithm or method will change. For example, consider finger print identification. Each time we scan our fingerprints through a (non-ink) fingerprint device, the scanned output may be different. The difference may be due to a change in contrast or brightness or in the background of the image. There could be some distortion. In order to process the input, we may need only lines in the fingerprints and we may not need the other parts or background of the fingerprint. In order to filter out the unwanted portion of the image and replace it with a white background, we need a filter mechanism. Once the image is filtered through the filter mechanism, we will get standard clean finger prints only with lines, which in turn helps with the process of feature extraction.
- **Feature extraction** is a process of studying and deriving useful information from the filtered input patterns. The derived information may be general features, which are evaluated to ease further processing. For example, in image recognition, the extracted features will contain information about gray shade, texture, shape or context of the image. This is the main

information used in image processing. The methods of feature extraction and the extracted features are application dependent.

- **Classification** is the final stage of the pattern recognition. This is the stage where an automated system declares that the inputted object belongs to a particular category. There are many classification methods in the field. Classification method designs are based on the following concepts.

1.13.2 More Useful Applications

- **Member-roster concept:** Under this template-matching concept, a set of patterns belonging to a same pattern is stored in a classification system. When an unknown pattern is given as input, it is compared with existing patterns and placed under the matching pattern class.
- **Common property concept:** In this concept, the common properties of patterns are stored in a classification system. When an unknown pattern comes inside, the system checks its extracted common property against the common properties of existing classes and places the pattern/object under a class, which has similar, common properties.
- **Clustering concept:** Here, the patterns of the targeted classes are represented in vectors whose components are real numbers. So, using its clustering properties, we can easily classify the unknown pattern. If the target vectors are far apart in geometrical arrangement, it is easy to classify the unknown patterns. If they are nearby or if there is any overlap in the cluster arrangement, we need more complex algorithms to classify the unknown patterns. One simple algorithm based on the clustering concept is Minimum Distance Classification. This method computes the distance between the unknown pattern and the desired set of known patterns and determines which known pattern is closest to the unknown and, finally, the unknown pattern is placed under the known pattern to which it has minimum distance. This algorithm works well when the target patterns are far apart.
- **Detection of medical phenomena:** A variety of health-related indices (e.g., a combination of heart rate, levels of various substances in the blood, respiration rate) can be monitored. The onset of a particular medical condition could be associated with a very complex (e.g., nonlinear and interactive) combination of changes on a subset of the variables being monitored. Neural networks have been used to recognize this predictive pattern so that the appropriate treatment can be prescribed.
- **Stock market prediction:** Fluctuations of stock prices and stock indices are another example of a complex, multidimensional, but in some circumstances at least partially-deterministic phenomenon. Neural networks are being used by many technical analysts to make predictions about stock prices based upon a large number of factors such as past performance of other stocks and various economic indicators.
- **Credit assignment:** A variety of pieces of information are usually known about an applicant for a loan. For instance, the applicant's age, education, occupation, and many other facts

may be available. After training a neural network on historical data, neural network analysis can identify the most relevant characteristics and use those to classify applicants as good or bad credit risks.

- **Monitoring the condition of machinery:** Neural networks can be instrumental in cutting costs by bringing additional expertise to scheduling the preventive maintenance of machines. A neural network can be trained to distinguish between the sounds a machine makes when it is running normally ("false alarms") versus when it is on the verge of a problem. After this training period, the expertise of the network can be used to warn a technician of an upcoming breakdown, before it occurs and causes costly unforeseen "downtime."
- **Engine management:** Neural networks have been used to analyze the input of sensors from an engine. The neural network controls the various parameters within which the engine functions, in order to achieve a particular goal, such as minimizing fuel consumption.
- **Character Recognition:** The idea of character recognition has become very important as handheld devices like the Palm Pilot are becoming increasingly popular. Neural networks can be used to recognize handwritten characters.
- **Image Compression:** Neural networks can receive and process vast amounts of information at once, making them useful in image compression. With the Internet explosion and more sites using more images on their sites, using neural networks for image compression is worth a look.
- **Traveling Saleman's Problem:** Interestingly enough, neural networks can solve the traveling salesman problem, but only to a certain degree of approximation.
- **Neural Networks in Medicine:** Neural networks are being used increasingly in the field of medicine. They are particularly well suited to problems with a high degree of complexity for which there is no algorithmic solution or the solution is too complex for traditional techniques to determine. Medical areas that have seen the successful implementation of this technology include drug development, patient diagnosis, and image analysis. Two major cornerstones are the detection of coronary artery disease and the processing of EEG signals.
- **NeuroXL Predictor and Classifier:** Neuro XL Predictor and Classifier are both add-ins to Microsoft Excel that harness the power of artificial intelligence for forecasting and classification tasks. They both have easy-to-use interfaces that hide the underlying complexity of the networks, so the time between installing the product and performing useful classifications and predictions is short.
- **Advanced Technology for Forecasting and Classification:** Neural networks are a well-established technology for solving prediction and classification problems, using training and testing data to build a model. The data involves historical data sets containing input variables, or data fields, which correspond to an output. The network uses the training data to "learn" the solution to the problem by example. Since the network learns in this way, no complex models need to be created. Also, it is not necessary for your data to be complete or show a clear trend - neural networks can still converge to a solution under these conditions. Because they are modeled after the human brain, these networks are well suited to problems

that people are good at solving but computers are not. These problems include pattern recognition and forecasting (which requires the recognition of trends in data). However, unlike humans, these networks are not affected by factors such as fatigue, emotional state, and working conditions.

1.14 THE FIRST ARTIFICIAL NEURON

Much of this section is taken from (Fausett, 1994). As mentioned in the research history McCulloch and Pitts (1943) produced the first neural network, which was based on their artificial neuron. Although this work was developed in the early forties, many of the principles can still be seen in the neural networks of today.

We can make the following statements about a McCulloch-Pitts network

- The activation of a neuron is binary. That is, the neuron either fires (activation of one) or does not fire (activation of zero).

For the network shown below the activation function for unit Y is

$$f(y\_in) = 1, \text{ if } y\_in >= t \text{ else } 0$$

where y_in is the total input signal received t is the threshold for Y.

- Neurons is a McCulloch-Pitts network are connected by directed, weighted paths.
- If the weight on a path is positive the path is excitatory, otherwise it is inhibitory.
- All excitatory connections into a particular neuron have the same weight, although different weighted connections can be input to different neurons.
- Each neuron has a fixed threshold. If the net input into the neuron is greater than the threshold, the neuron fires.
- The threshold is set such that any non-zero inhibitory input will prevent the neuron from firing.
- It takes one time step for a signal to pass over one connection.

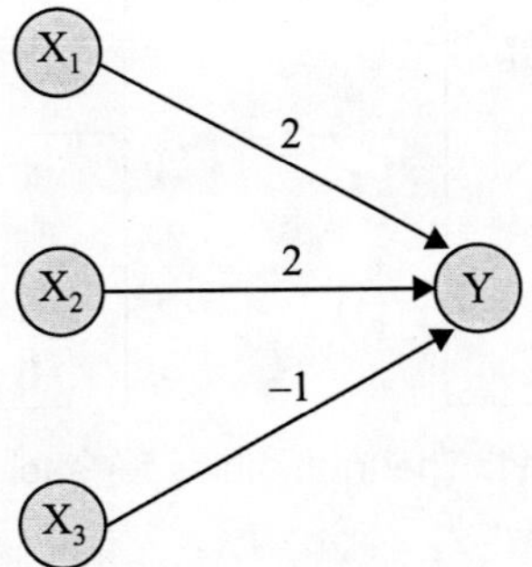

Figure 1.9: Mcculloch and pitts model

A sample McCulloch-Pitts network is shown above and some of the statements can be observed.

In particular, note that the threshold for Y has equal 4 as this is the only value that allows it to fire, taking into account that a neuron cannot fire if it receives a nonzero inhibitory input. Using the Mc Culloch-Pitts model we can model logic functions. Below we show and describe the architecture for four logic functions (the truth tables for each function is also shown)

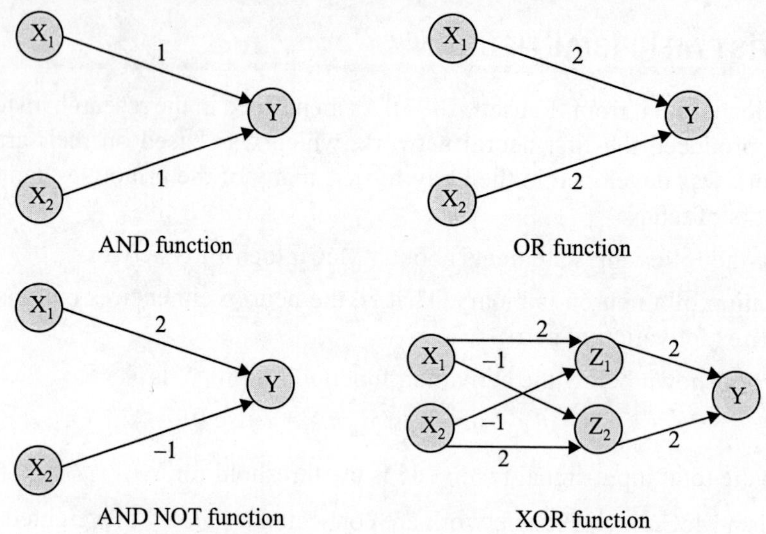

Figure 1.10: Architecture for four logic functions

AND		
X_1	X_2	Y
1	1	1
1	0	0
0	1	0
0	0	0

AND NOT		
X_1	X_2	Y
1	1	0
1	0	1
0	1	0
0	0	0

OR		
X_1	X_2	Y
1	1	1
1	0	1
0	1	1
0	0	0

XOR		
X_1	X_2	Y
1	1	0
1	0	1
0	1	1
0	0	0

Figure 1.11: The truth tables for each function

1.14.1 AND Function

As both inputs (X_1 and X_2) are connected to the same neuron the connections must be the same, in this case 1. To model the AND function the threshold on Y is set to 2.

1.14.2 OR Function

This is almost identical to the AND function except the connections are set to 2 and the threshold on Y is also set to 2.

1.14.3 AND NOT Function

Although the truth table for the AND NOT function is shown above it deserves just a small explanation as it is not often seen in the textbooks. The function is not symmetric in that an input of 1,0 is treated differently to an input of 0,1. As you can see from the truth table the only time true (value of one) is returned is when the first input is true and the second input is false. Again, the threshold on Y is set to 2 and if you apply each of the inputs to the AND NOT network you will find that we have modeled X_1 AND NOT X_2.

1.14.4 XOR Function

XOR can be modeled using AND NOT and OR;

$$X_1 \text{ XOR } X_2 = (X_1 \text{ AND NOT } X_2) \text{ OR } (X_2 \text{ AND NOT } X_1)$$

(To prove it draw the truth table)

This explains the network shown above. The first layer performs the two AND NOT's and the second layer performs the OR. Both Z neurons and the Y neuron have a threshold of 2.As a final example of a McCulloch-Pitts network we will consider how to model the phenomenon that if you touch something very cold you initially perceive heat. Only after you have left your hand on the cold source for a while do you perceive cold. This example (from Fausett, 1994) is an elaboration of one originally presented by (McCulloch and Pitts, 1943).

To model this we will assume that time is discrete. If cold is applied for one time step then heat will be perceived. If a cold stimulus is applied for two time steps then cold will be perceived. If heat is applied then we should perceive heat.

Take a look at this figure. Each neuron has a threshold of 2. This, as we shall see, allows us to model this phenomenon.

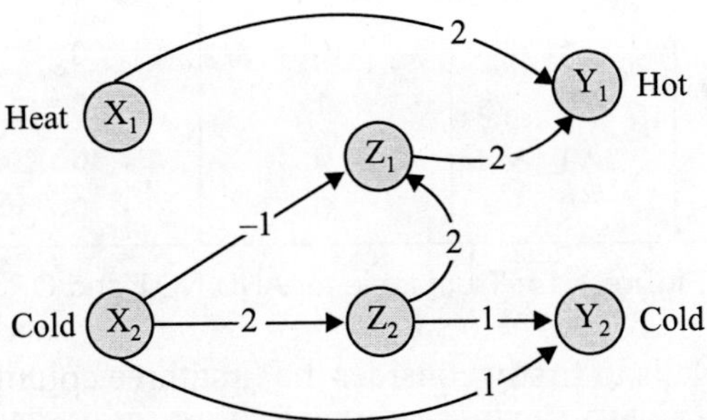

Figure 1.12: Neuron model having weights

First though, remember that time is discrete, so it takes time for the stimulus (applied at X_1 and X_2) to make its way to Y_1 and Y_2 where we perceive either heat or cold.

Therefore, at t(0), we apply a stimulus to X_1 and X_2.

At t(1) we can update Z_1, Z_2 and Y_1.

At t(2) we can perceive a stimulus at Y_2.

At t(2+n) the network is fully functional.

Before we see if the network performs as we hope let's consider what we are trying to do. Input to the system will be (1,0) or (0,1), which represents hot and cold respectively. We want the system to perceive cold if a cold stimulus is ap plied for two time steps. That is

$$Y_2(t) = X_2(t-2) \textbf{ AND } X_2(t-1) \qquad \text{(formula 1)}$$

This truth table (i.e. the truth table for AND) shows that this model is correct

$X_2(t-2)$	$X_2(t-1)$	$Y_2(t)$
1	1	1
1	0	0
0	1	0
0	0	0

Figure 1.13: Truth table for AND

We want the system to perceive heat if either a hot stimulus is applied or a cold stimulus is applied (for one time step) and then removed. We can express this as follows

$$Y_1(t) = [\, X_1(t-1) \,] \textbf{ OR } [\, X_2(t-3) \textbf{ AND NOT } X_2(t-2) \,] \qquad \text{(formula 2)}$$

This truth table shows that it gives us the required result

X2(t–3)	X2(t–2)	AND NOT	X1(t–1)	OR
1	1	0	1	1
1	0	1	1	1
0	1	0	1	1
0	0	0	1	1
1	1	0	0	0
1	0	1	0	1
0	1	0	0	0
0	0	0	0	0

Figure 1.14: Truth table for AND NOT and OR

The way to read this table is to firstly consider the first three columns. This gives the result (in the AND NOT column) of the AND NOT expression in the formula. This result is then OR'ed with the $X_1(t-1)$ to give the final column in the table, which is the result of the entire expression. You can see that if we apply heat (i.e. $X_1(t-1)$) then we always perceive heat as the output. If we apply cold for one time step (i.e. the row in red) we also perceive heat as the output.

So, if we are convinced that we have the correct logical statements to represent the hot/cold problem, we now need to convince ourselves that the network above represents the logical statements.

The figure of the network shows that

$$Y_1(t) = X_1(t-1) \textbf{ OR } Z_1(t-1) \quad \text{(formula 3)}$$

(compare this to the OR network we developed earlier).

Now consider the Z_1 neuron. This is how it is formed

$$Z_1(t-1) = Z_2(t-2) \textbf{ AND NOT } X_2(t-2) \quad \text{(formula 4)}$$

(again, compare this to the AND NOT network above).

Now Z_2, this is simply

$$Z_2(t-2) = X_2(t-3) \quad \text{(formula 5)}$$

If we take formula 3, and substitute in formula 4 and 5 we end up with

$$Y_1(t) = [\, X_1(t-1) \,] \textbf{ OR } [\, X_2(t-3) \textbf{ AND NOT } X_2(t-2) \,] \quad \text{(formula 6)}$$

which is the same as formula 2, showing that our network (Y_1 anyway) works correctly (as we have proved formula 2 works using a full analysis by using the truth table).We can perform a similar analysis for Y_2, and show that Y_2 in the network acts in the way we developed above (formula 1). You should do this to convince yourself that this is correct.

1.14.5 Modelling A Neuron

To model the brain we need to model a neuron. Each neuron performs a simple computation. It receives signals from its input links and it uses these values to compute the activation level (or output) for the neuron. This value is passed to other neurons via its output links. The input value received of a neuron is calculated by summing the weighted input values from its input links. That is

$$in_i = \Sigma_j W_{j,i} a_j$$

An activation function takes the neuron input value and produces a value which becomes the output value of the neuron. This value is passed to other neurons in the network.

This is summarised in this diagram and the notes below.

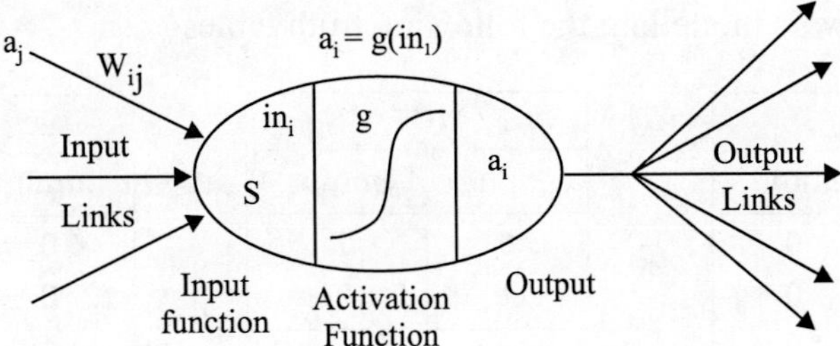

Figure 1.15: Labelled diagram of artificial neural network

a_j : Activation value of unit j
$w_{j,i}$: Weight on the link from unit j to unit i
in_i : Weighted sum of inputs to unit i
a_i : Activation value of unit i (also known as the output value)
g : Activation function

A neuron is connected to other neurons via its input and output links. Each incoming neuron has an activation value and each connection has a weight associated with it. The neuron sums the incoming weighted values and this value is input to an activation function. The output of the activation function is the output from the neuron. Some common activation functions are shown below.

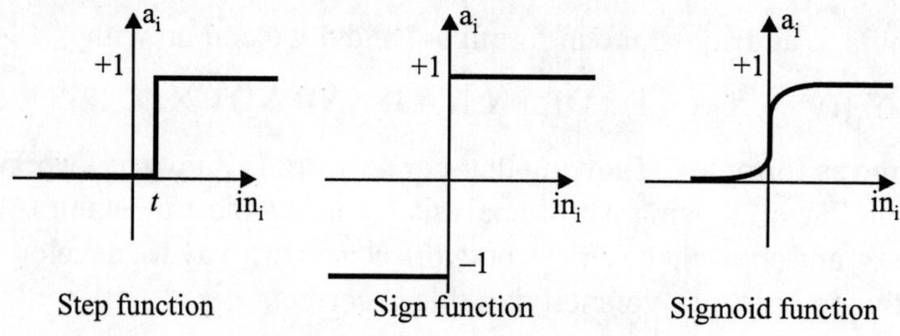

Figure 1.16: Activation functions

These functions can be defined as follows.

$$Step_t(x) = 1 \text{ if } x >= t, \text{ else } 0$$
$$Sign(x) = +1 \text{ if } x >= 0, \text{ else } -1$$
$$Sigmoid(x) = 1/(1+e^{-x})$$

On occasions an identify function is also used (i.e. where the input to the neuron becomes the output). This function is normally used in the input layer where the inputs to the neural network are passed into the network unchanged.

1.14.6 Some Simple Networks

We can use what we have learnt above to demonstrate a simple neural network which acts as a logic gate. The diagram below is modelling the following truth tables

AND		
$Input_1$	$Input_2$	Output
0	0	0
0	1	0
1	0	0
1	1	1

NOT	
Input	Output
0	1
1	0

OR		
$Input_1$	$Input_2$	Output
0	0	0
0	1	1
1	0	1
1	1	1

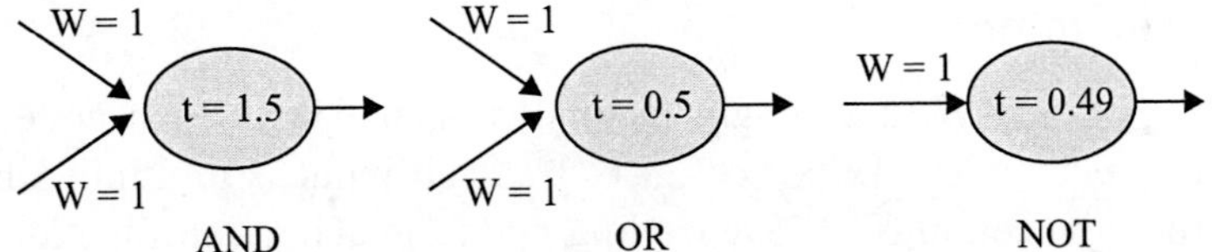

Figure 1.17: Simple networks with truth tables

In these networks we are using the step activation function.

You should convince yourself that these networks produce the correct output for all the allowed inputs. You will notice that each neuron has a different threshold. From a computational viewpoint it would be easier if all the neurons had the same threshold value and the actual threshold was somehow modelled by the weights.

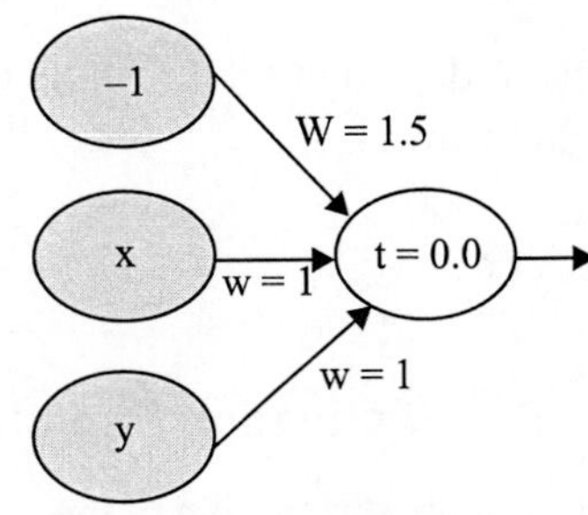

Figure 1.18: AND Network

In fact, it is possible to do exactly this. Consider this network

It is the same as the AND network in the diagram above except that there is an extra input neuron whose activation is always set to –1. The threshold of the neuron is represented by the weight that links this extra neuron to the output neuron.This means the threshold of the neuron can be set to zero. You might like to work through this network using the four possible combinations of x and y and convince yourself that the network operates correctly.This advantage of this method is that we can always set the threshold for every neuron to zero and from a computational point of view, when "training" the network, we only have to update weights and not both thresholds and weights.

1.15 ELEMENTS OF ARTIFICIAL NEURAL NETWORKS

An artificial neuron as shown in Figure 1.19, is the basic element of a neural network.It consists of three basic components that include weights, thresholds, and a single activation function .

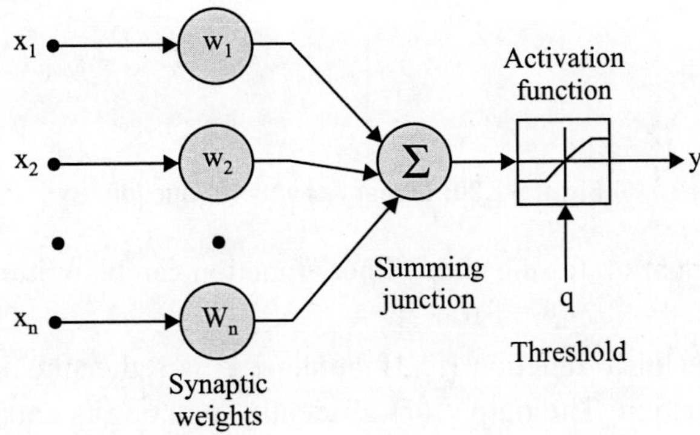

Figure 1.19: Basic Elements of an Artificial Neuron

1.15.1 Weighting Factors

The values $W_1, W_2, W_3, \ldots\ldots, W_n$ are weight factors associated with each node to determine the strength of input row vector $X = [x_1\ x_2\ x_3\ \ldots\ldots,\ x_n]^T$. Each input is multiplied by the associated weight of the neuron connection X^TW. Depending upon the activation function, if the weight is positive, X^TW commonly excites the node output; whereas, for negative weights, X^TW tends to inhibit the node output.

1.15.2 Threshold

The node's internal threshold θ is the magnitude offset that affects the activation of the node output y as follows:

$$y = \underset{i\ 1}{\overset{n}{}} (X_i W_i) \qquad (1.1)$$

1.15.3 Activation Function

In this subsection, five of the most common activation functions are presented. An activation function performs a mathematical operation on the signal output. More sophisticated activation functions can also be utilized depending upon the type of problem to be solved by the network.

1.15.3.1 Linear function

As is known, a linear function satisfies the superposition concept. The function is shown in Figure 1.20.

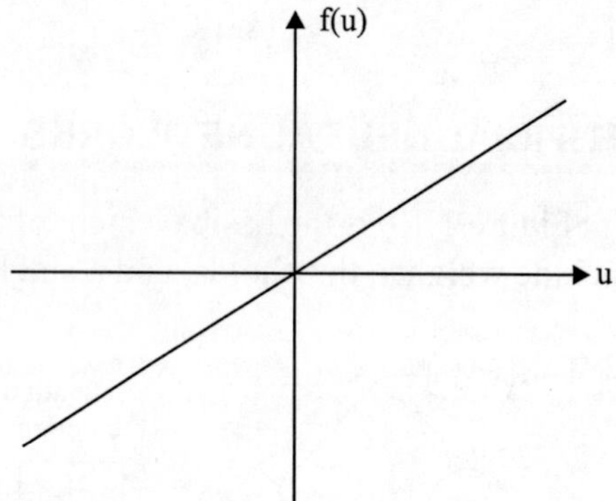

Figure 1.20: Linear Activation Function

The mathematical equation for the above linear function can be written as

$$y = f(u) = a \cdot u \qquad (1.2)$$

where a is the slope of the linear function 1.2. If the slope α is 1, then the linear activation function is called the identity function. The output (y) of identity function is equal to input function (u). Although this function might appear to be a trivial case, nevertheless it is very useful in some cases such as the last stage of a multilayer neural network.

1.15.3.2 Threshold function

A threshold (hard-limiter) activation function is either a *binary* type or a *bipolar* type as shown in Figures 1.21 and 1.22, respectively. The output of a *binary* threshold function can be written as:

$$y = f(u) =$$

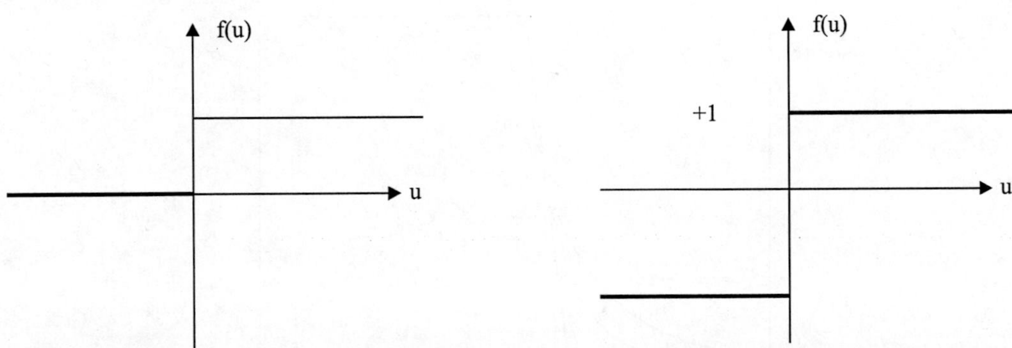

Figure 1.21: Binary threshold activation function

Figure 1.22: Bipolar threshold activation function.

The neuron with the hard limiter activation function is referred to as the McCulloch-Pitts model.

$$\begin{array}{l} 0 \text{ if } u < 0 \\ 1 \text{ if } u \quad 0 \end{array}$$

1.15.3.3 Piecewise linear function

This type of activation function is also referred to as saturating linear function and can have either a binary or bipolar range for the saturation limits of the output. The mathematical model for a symmetric saturation function (Figure 1.23) is described as follows:

$$y = f(u) = \begin{array}{l} -1 \text{ if } u \quad -1 \\ u \text{ if } -1 \quad u \quad 1 \\ 1 \text{ if } u \quad 1 \end{array}$$

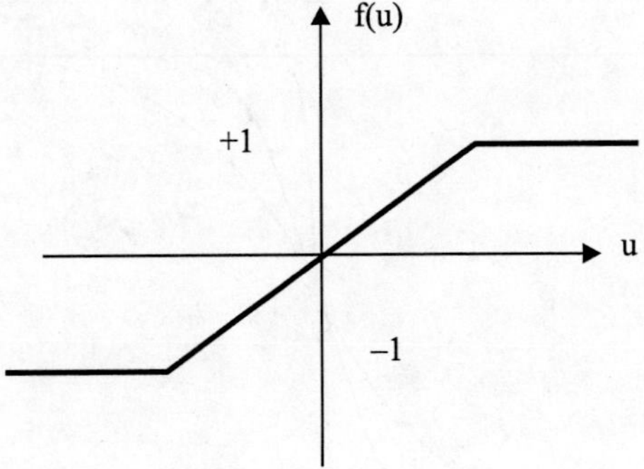

Figure 1.23: Piecewise linear activation function.

1.15.3.4 SIGMOIDAL (S SHAPED) FUNCTION

This nonlinear function is the most common type of the activation used to construct the neural networks. It is mathematically well behaved, differentiable and strictly increasing function. A sigmoidal transfer function can be written in the following form:

$$f(x) = \frac{1}{1+e^{-ax}}, \quad 0 \quad f(x) \quad 1$$

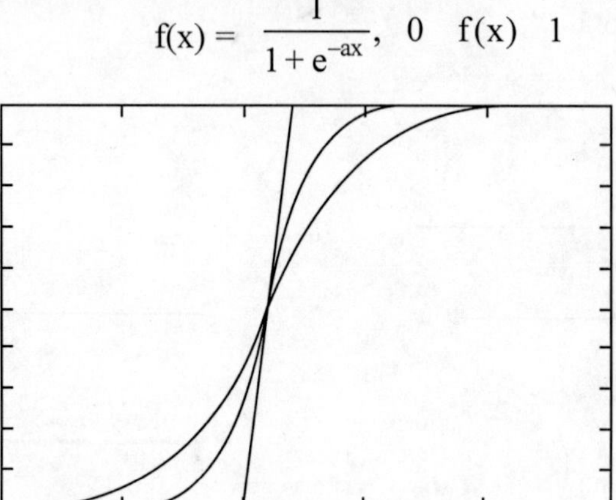

Figure 1.24: A sigmoid activation function.

where a is the shape parameter of the sigmoid function. By varying this parameter, different shapes of the function can be obtained as illustrated in Figure 1.24. This function is continuous and differentiable.

1.15.3.5 *Tangent hyperbolic function*

This transfer function is described bteby the following mathematical form:

$$f(x) = \frac{e^{x} \quad e^{-x}}{e^{x} \quad e^{-x}} -1 \quad f(x) \quad 1$$

It is interesting to note that the derivatives of Equations 2.5 and 2.6 can be expressed in terms of the individual function itself (please see problems appendix). This is important for the learning development rules to train the networks as shown in the next chapter.

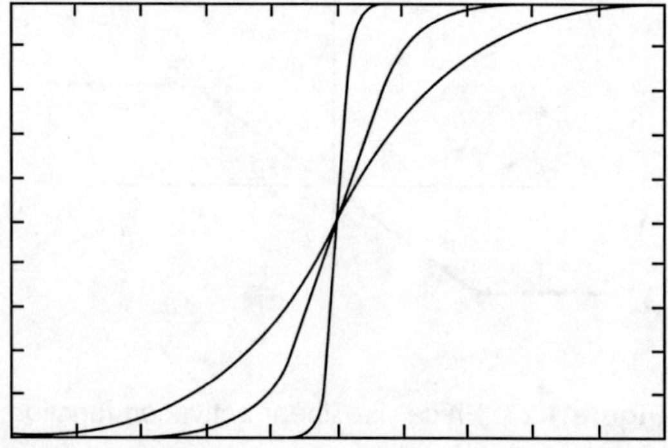

Figure 1.25: A tangent hyperbolic activation function.

Example 1.1: Consider the following network consists of four inputs with the weights as shown

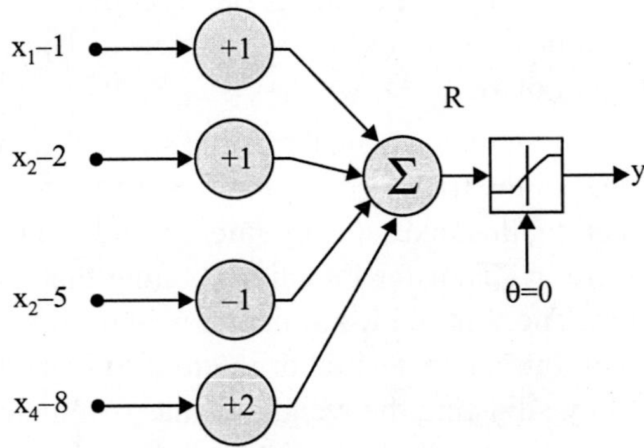

Figure 1.26: Neuron structure

The output R of the network, prior to the activation function stage, is calculated as follows:

$$R = W^T \cdot X \quad [1 \;\; 1 \;\; -1 \;\; 2] \cdot \begin{matrix} 1 \\ 2 \\ 5 \\ 8 \end{matrix} \quad 14$$

With a binary activation function, and a sigmoid function, the outputs of the neuron are respectively as follow:

$$y\ (\text{Threshold}) = 1;$$
$$y\ (\text{Sigmoid}) = 1.5*2^{-8}$$

1.16 ARCHITECTURE OF ARTIFICIAL NEURAL NETWORK

1.16.1 Simple Neuron

A neuron with a single scalar input and no bias appears on the left below.

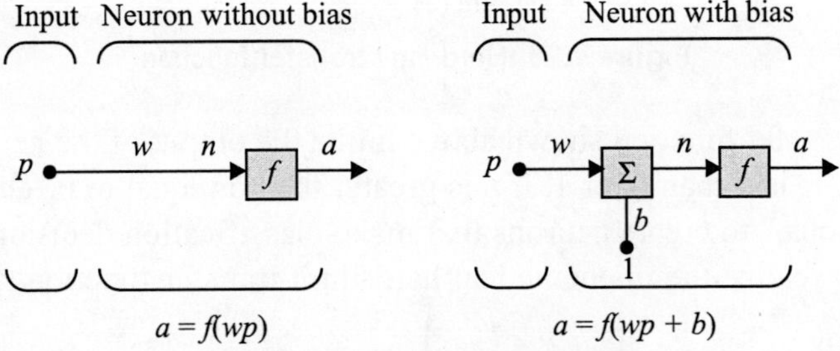

Figure 1.27: Simple Neuron

The scalar input p is transmitted through a connection that multiplies its strength by the scalar weight w to form the product wp, again a scalar. Here the weighted input wp is the only argument of the transfer function f, which produces the scalar output a. The neuron on the right has a scalar bias, b. You can view the bias as simply being added to the product wp as shown by the summing junction or as shifting the function f to the left by an amount b. The bias is much like a weight, except that it has a constant input of 1.

The transfer function net input n, again a scalar, is the sum of the weighted input wp and the bias b. This sum is the argument of the transfer function f. Here f is a transfer function, typically a step function or a sigmoid function, that takes the argument n and produces the output a. Examples of various transfer functions are in "Transfer Functions". Note that w and b are both adjustable scalar parameters of the neuron. The central idea of neural networks is that such parameters can be adjusted so that the network exhibits some desired or interesting behavior. Thus, you can train the network to do a particular job by adjusting the weight or bias parameters, or perhaps the network itself will adjust these parameters to achieve some desired end.

All the neurons in the Neural Network ToolboxTM software have provision for a bias, and a bias is used in many of the examples and is assumed in most of this toolbox. However, you can omit a bias in a neuron if you want. As previously noted, the bias b is an adjustable (scalar) parameter of the neuron. It is not an input. However, the constant 1 that drives the bias is an input and must be treated as such when you consider the linear dependence of input vectors in Chapter 4, "Linear Filters."

1.16.2 Transfer Functions

Many transfer functions are included the Neural Network Toolbox software. A complete list of them can be found in the reference pages. Three of the most commonly used functions are shown below.

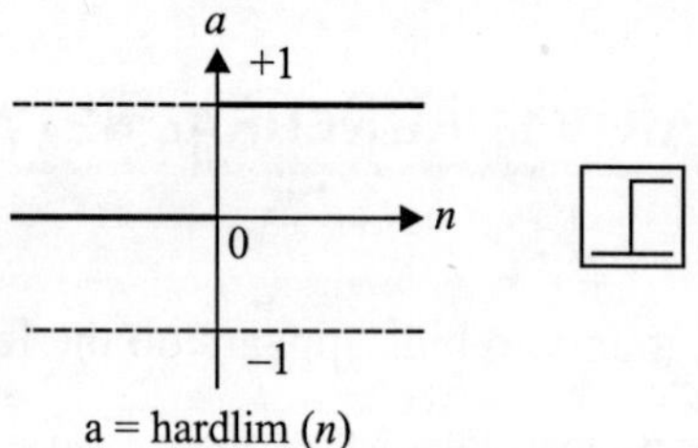

Figure 1.28: Hard-limit transfer function

The hard-limit transfer function shown above limits the output of the neuron to either 0, if the net input argument n is less than 0, or 1, if n is greater than or equal to 0. This function is used in Chapter 2, "Perceptrons," to create neurons that make classification decisions. The toolbox has a function, hardlim, to realize the mathematical hard-limit transfer function shown above. Try the following code:

```
n = –5:0.1:5; plot (n, hardlim (n),'c + :');
```

It produces a plot of the function hardlim over the range –5 to +5.

All the mathematical transfer functions in the toolbox can be realized with a function having the same name.

The following figure illustrates the linear transfer function.

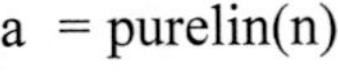

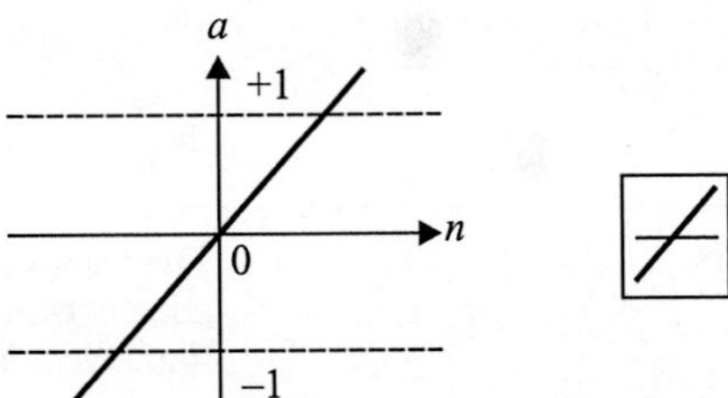

Figure 1.29: Linear transfer function

Neurons of this type are used as linear approximators in Chapter 4, "Linear Filters."

The sigmoid transfer function shown below takes the input, which can have any value between plus and minus infinity, and squashes the output into the range 0 to 1.

a = logsig(n)

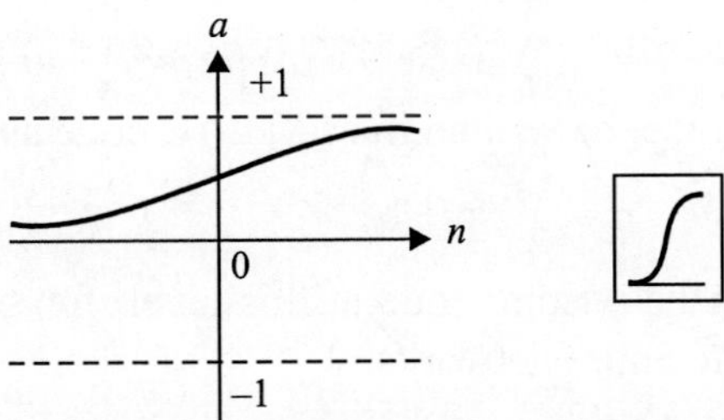

Figure 1.30: Log-sigmoid transfer function

This transfer function is commonly used in backpropagation networks, in part because it is differentiable.The symbol in the square to the right of each transfer function graph shown above represents the associated transfer function. These icons replace the general *f* in the boxes of network diagrams to show the particular transfer function being used.

For a complete listing of transfer functions and their icons, see the reference pages. You can also specify your own transfer functions.

You can experiment with a simple neuron and various transfer functions by running the demonstration program.

1.16.3 Neuron with Vector Input

A neuron with a single R-element input vector is shown below. Here the individual element inputs

$$P_1, P_2 \ldots. P_R$$

are multiplied by weights

$$w_{1,1}, w_{1,2} \ldots.. w_{1,R}$$

and the weighted values are fed to the summing junction. Their sum is simply **Wp**, the dot product of the (single row) matrix **W** and the vector **p**.

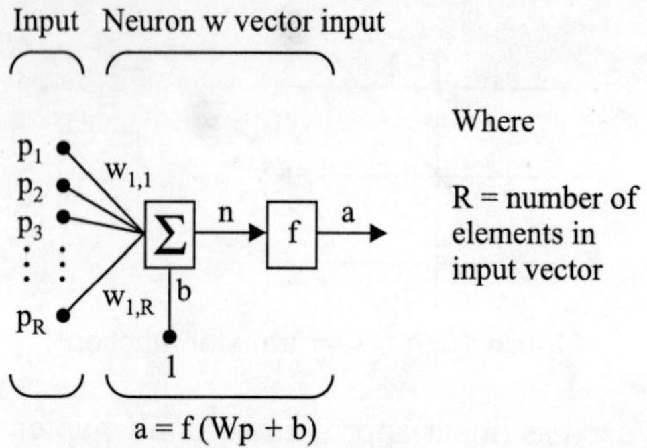

Figure 1.31: Neuron with vector input

The neuron has a bias b, which is summed with the weighted inputs to form the net input n. This sum, n, is the argument of the transfer function f.

$$n = w_{1,1}, P_1 + w_{1,2}, P_2 ..... w_{1,R}, P_R + b$$

This expression can, of course, be written in MATLAB code as

$$n = W*p + b$$

However, you will seldom be writing code at this level, for such code is already built into functions to define and simulate entire networks.

1.16.4 Abbreviated Notation

The figure of a single neuron shown above contains a lot of detail. When you consider networks with many neurons, and perhaps layers of many neurons, there is so much detail that the main thoughts tend to be lost. Thus, the authors have devised an abbreviated notation for an individual neuron. This notation, which is used later in circuits of multiple neurons, is shown.

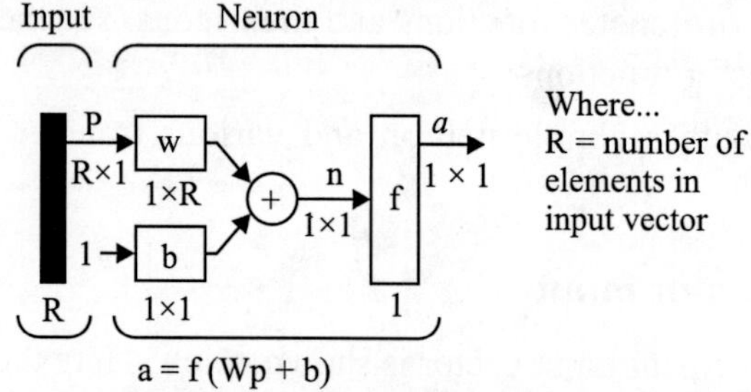

Figure 1.32: Abbreviated notation of neural network

Here the input vector **p** is represented by the solid dark vertical bar at the left. The dimensions of **p** are shown below the symbol **p** in the figure as R×1. (Note that a capital letter, such as R in the previous sentence, is used when referring to the size of a vector.) Thus, **p** is a vector of R input elements. These inputs postmultiply the single-row, R-column matrix **W**. As before, a constant 1 enters the neuron as an input and is multiplied by a scalar bias b. The net input to the transfer function f is n, the sum of the bias b and the product **Wp**. This sum is passed to the transfer function f to get the neuron's output a, which in this case is a scalar. Note that if there were more than one neuron, the network output would be a vector.

A layer of a network is defined in the previous figure. A layer includes the combination of the weights, the multiplication and summing operation (here realized as a vector product **Wp**), the bias b, and the transfer function f. The array of inputs, vector **p**, is not included in or called a layer.

Each time this abbreviated network notation is used, the sizes of the matrices are shown just below their matrix variable names. This notation will allow you to understand the architectures and follow the matrix mathematics associated with them.

As discussed in "Transfer Functions", when a specific transfer function is to be used in a figure, the symbol for that transfer function replaces the f shown above. Here are some examples.

Figure 1.33: Transfer functions

You can experiment with a two-element neuron by running the demonstration program.

1.17 NETWORK ARCHITECTURES

Two or more of the neurons shown earlier can be combined in a layer, and a particular network could contain one or more such layers. First consider a single layer of neurons.

1.17.1 A Layer of Neurons

A one-layer network with *R* input elements and *S* neurons follows. Inputs Layer of Neurons

In this network, each element of the input vector **p** is connected to each neuron input through the weight matrix **W**. The ith neuron has a summer that gathers its weighted inputs and bias to form its own scalar output n(i). The various n(i) taken together form an S-element net input vector **n**. Finally, the neuron layer outputs form a column vector a. The expression for a is shown at the bottom of the figure.

Note that it is common for the number of inputs to a layer to be different from the number of neurons (i.e., R is not necessarily equal to S). A layer is not constrained to have the number of its inputs equal to the number of its neurons.

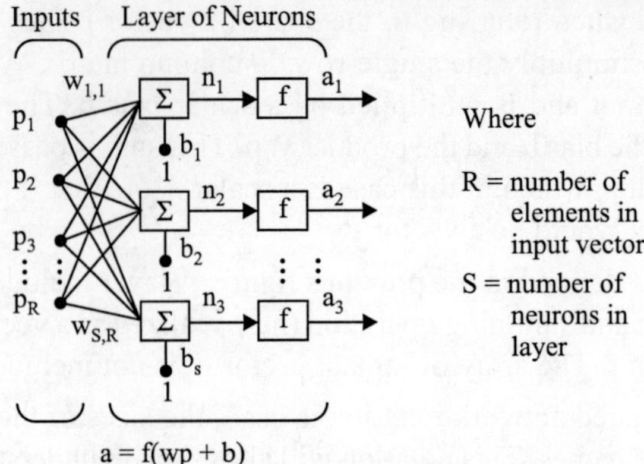

Figure 1.34: Input-Layer Neural Network

You can create a single (composite) layer of neurons having different transfer functions simply by putting two of the networks shown earlier in parallel. Both networks would have the same inputs, and each network would create some of the outputs.

The input vector elements enter the network through the weight matrix W.

$$w = \begin{matrix} w_{1,1} & w_{1,2} & \cdots & w_{1,R} \\ w_{2,1} & w_{2,2} & \cdots & w_{2,R} \\ \\ w_{S,1} & w_{S,2} & \cdots & w_{S,R} \end{matrix}$$

Note that the row indices on the elements of matrix **W** indicate the destination neuron of the weight, and the column indices indicate which source is the input for that weight. Thus, the indices in $w_{1,2}$ say that the strength of the signal *from* the second input element *to* the first (and only) neuron is $w_{1,2}$.

The *S* neuron R input one-layer network also can be drawn in abbreviated notation.

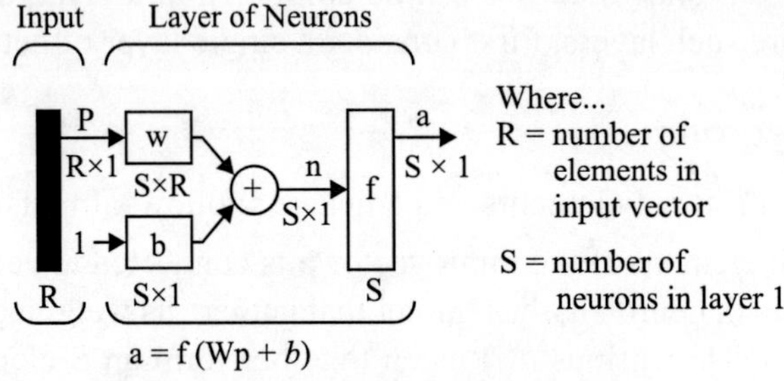

Figure 1.35: Abbreviated notation

Here **p** is an R length input vector, **W** is an S × R matrix, and a and b are S length vectors. As defined previously, the neuron layer includes the weight matrix, the multiplication operations, the bias vector **b**, the summer, and the transfer function boxes.

1.17.2 Inputs and Layers

To describe networks having multiple layers, the notation must be extended. Specifically, it needs to make a distinction between weight matrices that are connected to inputs and weight matrices that are connected between layers. It also needs to identify the source and destination for the weight matrices.

We will call weight matrices connected to inputs *input weights;* we will call weight matrices coming from layer outputs *layer weights.* Further, superscripts are used to identify the source (second index) and the destination (first index) for the various weights and other elements of the network. To illustrate, the one-layer multiple input network shown earlier is redrawn in abbreviated form below.

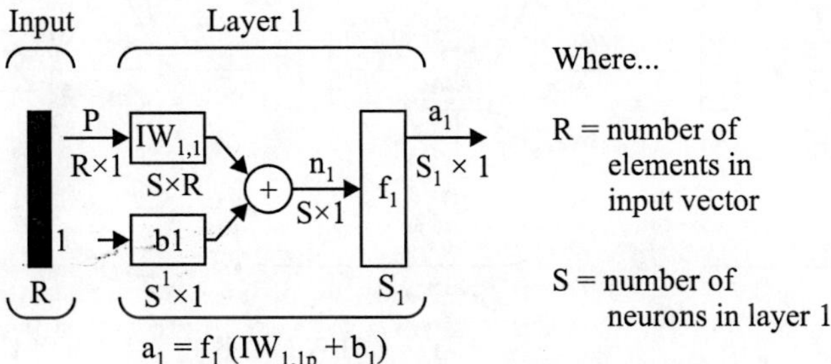

Figure 1.36: Inputs and layers

As you can see, the weight matrix connected to the input vector **p** is labeled as an input weight matrix ($\mathbf{IW}^{1,1}$) having a source 1 (second index) and a destination 1 (first index). Elements of layer 1, such as its bias, net input, and output have a superscript 1 to say that they are associated with the first layer. "Multiple Layers of Neurons" uses layer weight (**LW**) matrices as well as input weight (**IW**) matrices.

1.17.3 Multiple Layer of Neurons

A network can have several layers. Each layer has a weight matrix **W**, a bias vector **b**, and an output vector **a**. To distinguish between the weight matrices, output vectors, etc., for each of these layers in the figures, the number of the layer is appended as a superscript to the variable of interest. You can see the use of this layer notation in the three-layer network shown below, and in the equations at the bottom of the figure.

The network shown above has R^1 inputs, S^1 neurons in the first layer, S2 neurons in the second layer, etc. It is common for different layers to have different numbers of neurons. A constant input 1 is fed to the bias for each neuron. Note that the outputs of each intermediate layer are the inputs to the following layer. Thus layer 2 can be analyzed as a one-layer network with S^1 inputs, S^2 neurons, and an $S^2 \times S^1$ weight matrix W^2. The input to layer 2 is $\mathbf{a}^1$; the output is $\mathbf{a}^2$. Now that all the vectors and matrices of layer 2 have been identified, it can be treated as a single-layer network on its own. This approach can be taken with any layer of the network.

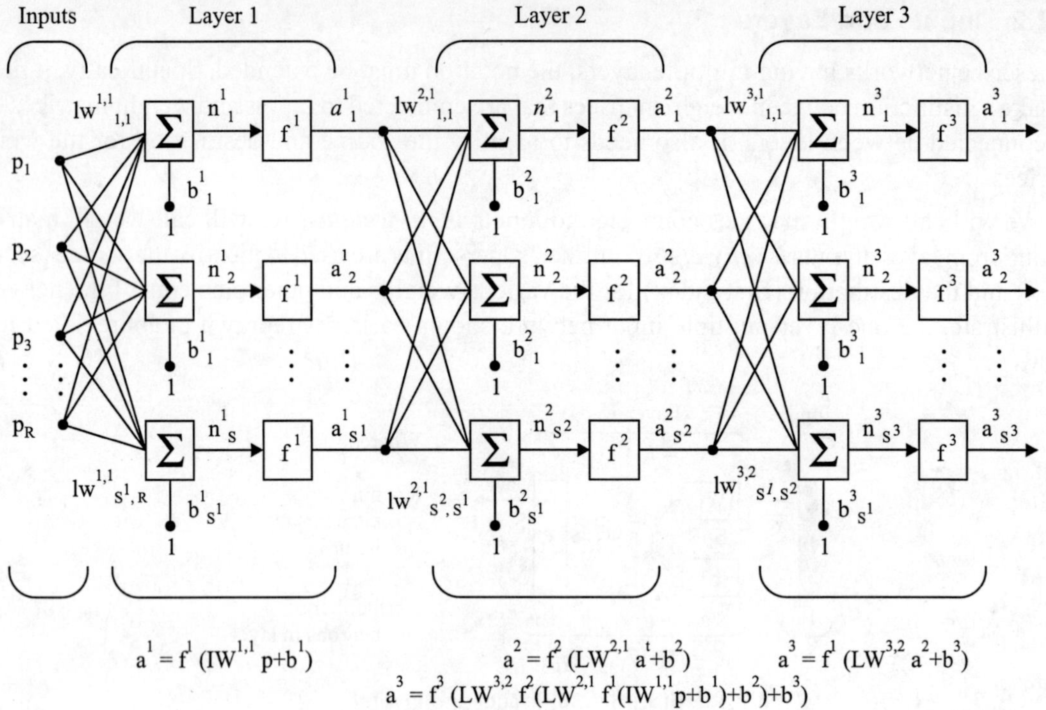

Figure 1.37: Multiple layers of neurons

The layers of a multilayer network play different roles. A layer that produces the network output is called an *output layer*. All other layers are called *hidden layers*. The three-layer network shown earlier has one output layer (layer 3) and two hidden layers (layer 1 and layer 2). Some authors refer to the inputs as a fourth layer. This toolbox does not use that designation.

The same three-layer network can also be drawn using abbreviated notation.

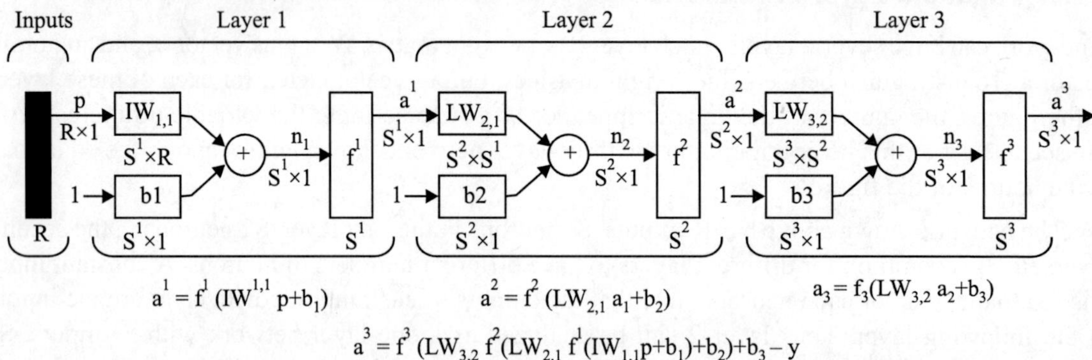

Figure 1.38: Abbreviated notation of multiple layers neural network

Multiple-layer networks are quite powerful. For instance, a network of two layers, where the first layer is sigmoid and the second layer is linear, can be trained to approximate any function (with a finite number of discontinuities) arbitrarily well. This kind of two-layer network is used extensively in Chapter 3, "Backpropagation."

Here it is assumed that the output of the third layer, $\mathbf{a}^3$, is the network output of interest, and this output is labeled as $\mathbf{y}$. This notation is used to specify the output of multilayer networks.

1.17.4 Input and Output Processing Functions

Network inputs might have associated processing functions. Processing functions transform user input data to a form that is easier or more efficient for a network.For instance, map min max transforms input data so that all values fall into the interval [–1, 1]. This can speed up learning for many networks. Remove constant rows removes the values for input elements that always have the same value because these input elements are not providing any useful information to the network. The third common processing function is fix unknowns, which recodes unknown data (represented in the user's data with Null values) into a numerical form for the network. fix unknowns preserves information about which values are known and which are unknown. Similarly, network outputs can also have associated processing functions. Output processing functions are used to transform user-provided target vectors for network use. Then, network outputs are reverse-processed using the same functions to produce output data with the same characteristics as the original user-provided targets.

EXERCISES

1. What do you mean by Neural network?
2. Discuss historical background of the neural network?
3. What are the various benefits of neural network?
4. Explain the working of human brain with the block diagram?
5. What is biological neural network? Explain all the components of pyramidal cells?
6. Explain various structural levels in the brain with the help of cerebral cortex diagram?
7. Explain basics structure of a biological neuron with the help of labeled diagram?
8. What are the various components of biological neuron? Explain with the help of the diagram?
9. What is artificial neural network? What are the advantages and disadvantages of artificial neural network?
10. Explain the working of artificial neuron?
11. What are the various types of artificial neural networks?
12. Why we use a neural network?
13. How neural networks differ from traditional computing?
14. Give comparison of computing approaches?

15. Give comparison of expert system and neural network?
16. What are the practical application of artificial neural network?
17. What are the various application of neural network? Explain all in detail?
18. What is pattern recognition? Explain the processing levels of pattern recognition?
19. Explain the McCulloch and pitts model?
20. Explain the architecture of AND, OR, AND NOT, XOR functions with the help of truth tables?
21. Explain the modeling of a neuron with the help of labeled diagram of artificial neural network?
22. Explain various simple networks with the diagrams?
23. What are the various elements of neural networks?
24. Explain the various types of activation functions?
25. Explain the architecture of single neuron and explain various transfers functions?
26. Explain the concept of neuron with vector input using diagrammatic approach?
27. Explain the abbreviated notation of artificial neuron network with the help of labeled diagram?
28. What are the various networks architecture of neural network?
29. Explain the working of input layer neural network with the help of diagram?
30. Explain the abbreviated notations input layer of neurons?
31. Explain the working of multiple layer of neurons with the help of diagram?
32. Explain the abbreviated notations of multiple layer of neurons?

CHAPTER 2

Perceptrons

2.1 INTRODUCTION

This chapter has a number of objectives. First, it introduces you to learning rules, methods of deriving the next changes that might be made in a network, and training, a procedure whereby a network is actually adjusted to do a particular job. Along the way, this chapter describes a toolbox function to create a simple perceptron network and functions to initialize and simulate such networks. The perceptron is used as a vehicle for tying these concepts together. Rosenblatt [Rose61] created many variations of the perceptron.

One of the simplest was a single-layer network whose weights and biases could be trained to produce a correct target vector when presented with the corresponding input vector. The training technique used is called the perceptron learning rule. The perceptron generated great interest due to its ability to generalize from its training vectors and learn from initially randomly distributed connections. Perceptrons are especially suited for simple problems in pattern classification. They are fast and reliable networks for the problems they can solve. In addition, an understanding of the operations of the perceptron provides a good basis for understanding more complex networks.This chapter defines what is meant by a learning rule, explains the perceptron network and its learning rule, and tells you how to initialize and simulate perceptron networks.

2.2 NEURON MODEL

A perceptron neuron, which uses the hard-limit transfer function hardlim, is shown in Figure 2.1.

Each external input is weighted with an appropriate weight $w1j$, and the sum of the weighted inputs is sent to the hard-limit transfer function, which also has an input of 1 transmitted to it through the bias. The hard-limit transfer function, which returns a 0 or a 1, is shown in Figure 2.2.

The perceptron neuron produces a 1 if the net input into the transfer function is equal to or greater than 0; otherwise it produces a 0.

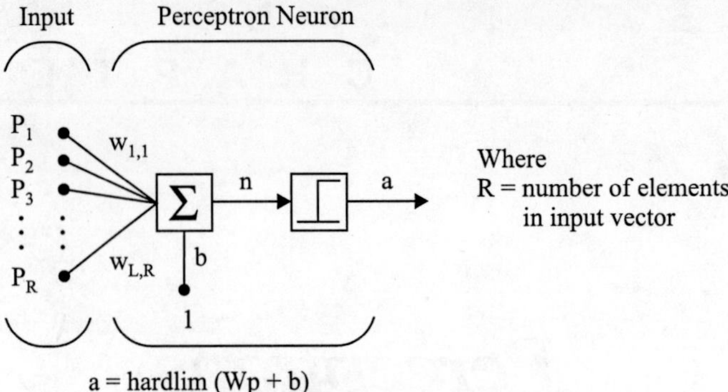

Figure 2.1: Perceptron neuron model

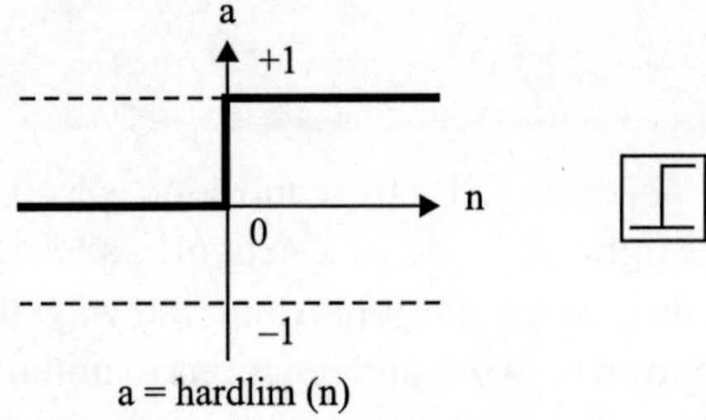

Figure 2.2: Transfer function

The hard-limit transfer function gives a perceptron the ability to classify input vectors by dividing the input space into two regions. Specifically, outputs will be 0 if the net input *n* is less than 0, or 1 if the net input *n* is 0 or greater. The following figure show the input space of a two-input hard limit neuron with the weights $w_{1,1} = -1$, $w_{1,2} = 1$ and a bias $b = 1$.

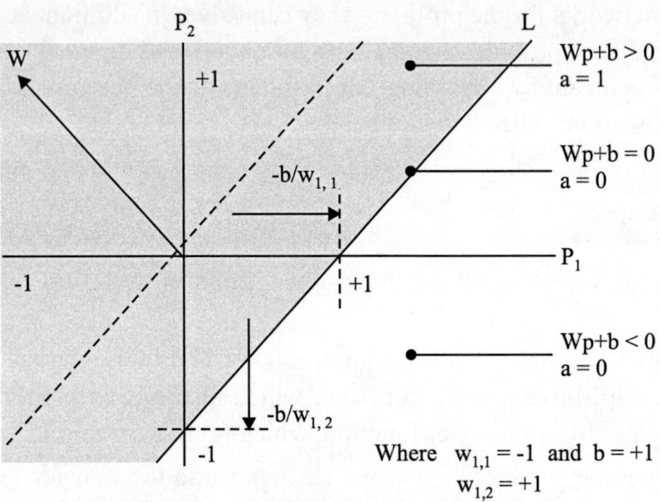

Figure 2.3: Decision boundaries

Two classification regions are formed by the *decision boundary* line L at **Wp** + b = 0. This line is perpendicular to the weight matrix **W** and shifted according to the bias b. Input vectors above and to the left of the line L will result in a net input greater than 0 and, therefore, cause the hard-limit neuron to output a 1. Input vectors below and to the right of the line L cause the neuron to output 0. You can pick weight and bias values to orient and move the dividing line so as to classify the input space as desired. Hard-limit neurons without a bias will always have a classification line going through the origin. Adding a bias allows the neuron to solve problems where the two sets of input vectors are not located on different sides of the origin. The bias allows the decision boundary to be shifted away from the origin, as shown in the plot above.

2.3 PERCEPTRON ARCHITECTURE

The perceptron network consists of a single layer of S perceptron neurons connected to *R* inputs through a set of weights $w_{i,j}$, as shown below in two forms. As before, the network indices *i* and *j* indicate that $w_{i,j}$ is the strength of the connection from the *j*th input to the *i*th neuron.

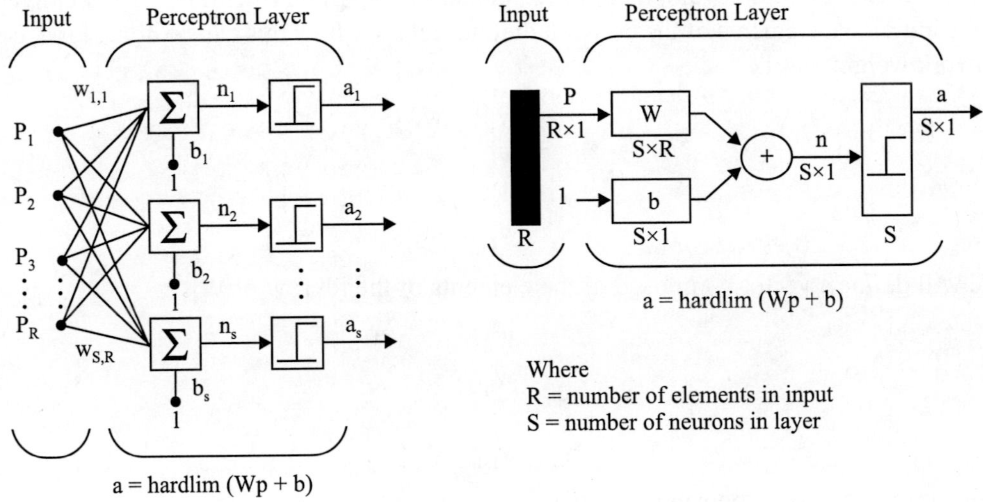

Figure 2.4: Perceptron Architecture

The perceptron learning rule described shortly is capable of training only a single layer. Thus only one-layer networks are considered here. This restriction places limitations on the computation a perceptron can perform. The types of problems that perceptrons are capable of solving are discussed in "Limitations and Cautions".

Before we present the perceptron learning rule, let's explain and out investigation of the perceptron network, which we began in 2.3. The general perceptron network is shown in Figure 2.5.

The output of the network is given by

$$a = \text{hardlim}\,(Wp + b) \tag{2.1}$$

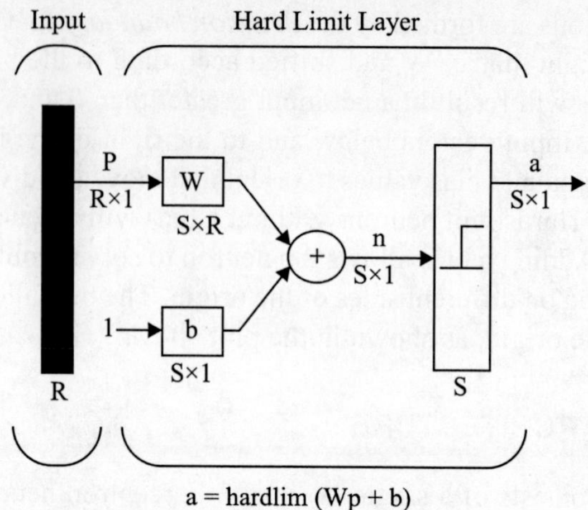

Figure 2.5: Perceptron network

It will be useful in out development of the perceptron learning rule to be able to conveniently reference individual elements of the network output. Let's see how this can be done. First, consider the network weight matrix:

$$W = \begin{matrix} w_{1,1} & w_{1,2} & \cdots\cdots & w_{1,R} \\ w_{2,1} & w_{2,2} & \cdots\cdots & w_{2,R} \\ \vdots & \vdots & \vdots & \vdots \\ w_{S,1} & w_{S,2} & \cdots\cdots & w_{S,R} \end{matrix} \tag{2.2}$$

We will define a vector composed of the elements of the ith row of W:

$$w = \begin{matrix} w_{i,1} \\ w_{i,1} \\ \vdots \\ w_{i,R} \end{matrix} \tag{2.3}$$

Now we can partition the weight matrix:

$$W = \begin{matrix} {}_1w^T \\ {}_2w^T \\ \vdots \\ {}_Sw^f \end{matrix} \tag{2.4}$$

This allows us to write the ith element of the network output vactor as

$$a_i = \text{hardlim}\ (n_i) = \text{hardlim}\ ({}_iw^T\ p + b). \tag{2.5}$$

Recall that the hardlim transfer function (shown at left) is defined as:

$$a = \text{hardlim}\ (n) = \begin{matrix} 1 \text{ if } n \quad 0 \\ 0 \text{ otherwise} \end{matrix} \tag{2.6}$$

Therefore, if the inner product of the ith row of the weight matrix with the input vector is greater than or equal to $-b_i$, the output will be 1, otherwise the output will be 0. Thus each neuron divides the input space into two regions. It is useful to investigate the boundaries between these regions. We will begin with the simple case of a single-neuron perceptron with two inputs.

2.3.1 Algorithm

The algorithm given here is suitable for either binary or bipolar input vectors (n-tuples), with a bipolar target, fixed q, and adjustable bias. The threshold q does not play the same role as in the step function; thus, both a bias and a threshold are needed. The role of the threshold is discussed following the presentation of the algorithm the algorithm is not particularly sensitive to the initial values of the weights or the value of the learning rate.

Step 1: Initialize weights and bias.

(For simplicity, set weights and bias to zero.)

Set learning rate α $(0 < \alpha \leq 1)$.

(For simplicity, α can be set to 1.)

Step 2: While stopping condition is false, do Steps 3 – 7.

Step 3: For each training pair s:t, do Steps 3–5.

Step 4: Set activations fo input units:

$$x_i = s_i$$

Step 5: Compute response of output unit:

$$y \text{ in} = b \qquad \underset{i}{} x_i w_i \, ;$$

$$y = \begin{matrix} 1 & \text{if } y\_in > \\ 0 & \text{if } - \quad y\_in \\ -1 & \text{if } y\_in < - \end{matrix}$$

Step 6: Update weights and bias if an error occurred for this pattern.

If $y \neq t$,

$w_i(\text{new}) = w_i(\text{old}) + \alpha t x_i$,

$b(\text{new}) = b(\text{old}) + \alpha t$.

else

$w_i(\text{new}) = w_i(\text{old})$,

$b(\text{new}) = b(\text{old})$.

Step 7: Test stopping condition:

If no weights changed in step2, stop; else, continue.

2.4 SINGLE-NEURON PERCEPTRON

Let's consider a two-input perceptron with one neuron, as shown in Figure 2.6. The output of this network is determined by

$$a = \text{hardlim}(n) = \text{hardlim}(Wp + b)$$
$$= \text{hardlim}({}_1w^T p + b) = \text{hardlim}(w_{1,1}p_1 + w_{2,2}p_2 + b) \quad (2.7)$$

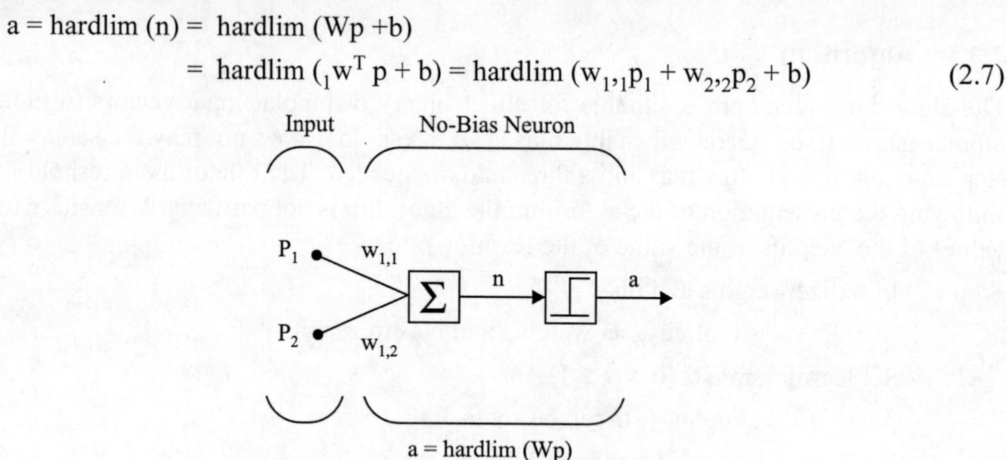

Figure 2.6: Two-input/output perceptron

The decision boundary is determined by the input vectors for which the net input n is zero:

$$n = {}_1w^T p + b = \text{hardlim } w_{1,1}p_1 + w_{2,2}p_2 + b = 0 \quad (2.8)$$

To make the example more concrete, let's assign the following values for the weights and bias:

$$w_{1,1} = 1, w_{1,2} = 1, b = -1. \quad (2.9)$$

The decision boundary is then

$$n = {}_1w^T p + b = \text{hardlim } w_{1,1}p_1 + w_{2,2}p_2 + b = p_1 + p_2 - 1 = 0. \quad (2.10)$$

This defines a line in the input space. On one side of the line the network output will be 0; on the line and on the other side of the line the output will be 1. To draw the line, we can find the points where it intersects the p_1 and p_2 axes. To find the p_2 intercept set $p_1 = 0$:

$$P_2 = -\frac{b}{w_{1,2}} = \frac{-1}{1} = 1 \text{ if } p_1 = 0 \quad (2.11)$$

To find the p_1 intercept, set $p_2 = 0$:

$$P_2 = \frac{b}{w_{1,1}} = \frac{-1}{1} = 1 \text{ if } p_1 = 0 \quad (2.12)$$

The resulting decision boundary is illustrated in Figure 4.3.

To find out which side of the boundary corresponds to an output of 1, we just need to test one point. For the input p $[2\ 0]^T$, the network output will be

$$a = \text{hardlim}({}_1w^T p + b) = \text{hardlim } [1\ 1] \begin{matrix}2\\0\end{matrix} - 1 = 1 \quad (2.13)$$

Therefore, the network output will be 1 for the region above and to the right of the decision boundary. This region is indicated by the shared area in Figure 2.7.

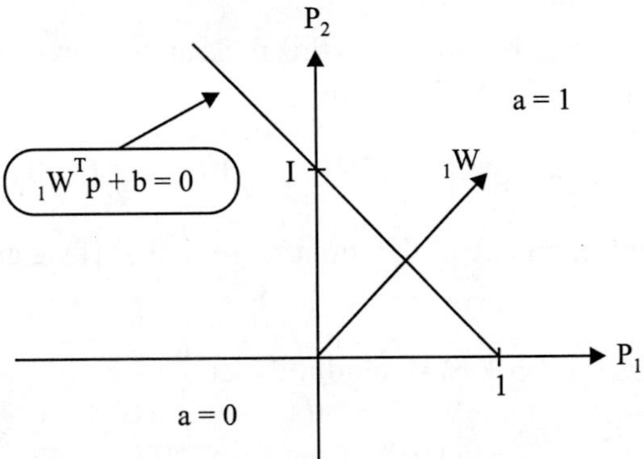

Figure 2.7: Decision boundary for two-input perceptron

We can also find the decision boundary graphically. The first step is to note that the boundary is always orthogonal to ${}_1w$, as illustrated in the adjacent figure. The boundary is defined by

$$ {}_1w^T p + b = 0 \tag{2.14}$$

For all points on the boundary, the inner product of the input vector with the weight vector is the same. This implies that these input vectors will all have the same projection onto the weight vector, so they must lie on a line orthogonal to the weight vector. In addition, any vector in the shaded region of Figure 2.7 will have an inner product greater that –b, and vectors in the unshared region will have inner products less than –b. Therefore the weight vector ${}_1w$ will always point toward the region where the neuron output is 1.

After we have selected a weight vector with the correct angular orientation, the bias value can be computed by selecting a point on the boundary and satisfying Eq. (2.14).

Let's apply some of these concepts to the design of a perception network to implement a simple logic function: the AND gate. The input/target pairs for the AND gate are

$$P_1 = \begin{matrix}0\\0\end{matrix}, t_1 = 0 \quad P_2 = \begin{matrix}0\\1\end{matrix}, t_2 = 0 \quad P_3 = \begin{matrix}1\\0\end{matrix}, t_3 = 0 \quad P_4 = \begin{matrix}1\\1\end{matrix}, t_4 = 1$$

The first step of the design is to select a decision boundary. We want to have a lime that separates the dark circles and the light circles. There are an infinite number of solution to this problem. It seems reasonable to choose the line that falls "halfway" between the categories of inputs, as shown in the adjacent figure.

Next we want to choose a weight vector that is orthogonal to the decision boundary. The weight vector can be any length, so there are infinite possibilities. One choice is

$$ {}_1w = \begin{matrix} 2 \\ 2 \end{matrix} \tag{2.15} $$

as displayed in the figure to the left.

Finally, we need to find the bias b. We can do this picking a point on the decision boundary and satisfying Eq. (2.14). If we use p = [1.5 0] we find

$$ {}_1w^T p + b = [2\ 2] \begin{matrix} 1.5 \\ 0 \end{matrix} + b = 3 + b = 0 \quad b = -3, \tag{2.16} $$

We can now test the network on one of the input/target pairs. If we apply p_2 to the network, the output will be

$$ a = \text{hardlim}\ ({}_1w^T p + b) = \text{hardlim}[2\ 2] \begin{matrix} 0 \\ 1 \end{matrix} - 3 \tag{2.17} $$

$$ a = \text{hardlim}\ (-1) = 0 $$

which is equal to the target output t_2. Verify for your that all inputs are correctly classified.

To experiment with decision boundaries, use the Neural Network Design Demonstration Decision Boundaries.

2.5 MULTIPLE-NEURON PERCEPTRON

Note that for perceptron with multiple neurons, as in figure 2.5 , there will be one decision boundary for each neuron. The decision boundary for neuron i will be defined by

$$ {}_iw^T p + b_i = 0 \tag{2.18} $$

A single-neuron perception can classify input vectors into two categories, since its output can be either 0 or 1. A multiple-neuron perceptron can classify inputs into may categories. Each category is represented by a different output vector. Since each element of the output vector can be either 0 or 1, there are a total of 2^S possible categories, where S is the number of neurons. Explaination is given in 2.14, 2.15.

2.6 LEARNING RULES

A *learning rule* is defined as a procedure for modifying the weights and biases of a network. (This procedure can also be referred to as a training algorithm.) The learning rule is applied to train the network to perform some particular task. Learning rules in this toolbox fall into two broad categories: supervised learning, and unsupervised learning.

In *supervised learning*, the learning rule is provided with a set of examples (the *training set*) of proper network behavior

$$ \{p_1, t_1\}, \{p_2, t_2\}, \ldots. \{p_Q, t_Q\} $$

Where P_q is an input to the network, and T_q is the corresponding correct (*target*) output. As the inputs are applied to the network, the network outputs are compared to the targets. The learning rule is then used to adjust the weights and biases of the network in order to move the network outputs closer to the targets. The perceptron learning rule falls in this supervised learning category.

In *unsupervised learning*, the weights and biases are modified in response to network inputs only. There are no target outputs available. Most of these algorithms perform clustering operations. They categorize the input patterns into a finite number of classes. This is especially useful in such applications as vector quantization.

2.6.1 Perceptron Learning Rule

Now that we have examined the performance of perceptron networks, we are in a position to introduce the perceptron learning rule. This learning rule is an example of supervised training, in which the learning rule is provided with a set of examples of proper network behavior:

$$\{p_1, t_1,\}, \{p_2, t_2\} \ldots\ldots \{p_q, t_q\} \tag{2.19}$$

where p_q is an input to the network and t_q is the corresponding target output. As each input is applied to the network, the network output is compared to the target. The learning rule then adjusts the weights and biases of the network in order to move the network output closer to the target.

2.6.2 Test Problem

In our presentation of the perceptron learning rule we will begin with a simple test problem and will experiment with possible rules to develop some intuition about how the rule should work. The input/target pairs for our test problem are

$$P_1 = \begin{matrix} 1 \\ 2 \end{matrix}, t_1 = 1 \quad P_2 = \begin{matrix} -1 \\ 2 \end{matrix}, t_2 = 0 \quad P_3 = \begin{matrix} 0 \\ -1 \end{matrix}, t_3 = 0$$

The problem is displayed graphically in the adjacent figure, where the two input vectors whose target is 0 are represented with a light circle O, and the vector whose target is 1 is represented with a dark circle •. This is a very simple problem, and we could almost obtain a solution by inspection. This simplicity will help us gain some intuitive understanding of the basic concepts of the perceptron learning rule.

The network for this problem should have two-inputs and one output. To simplify out development of the learning rule, we will begin with a network without a bias. The network will then have just two parameters, $w_{1,1}$ and $w_{1,2}$ as shown in Figure 2.8

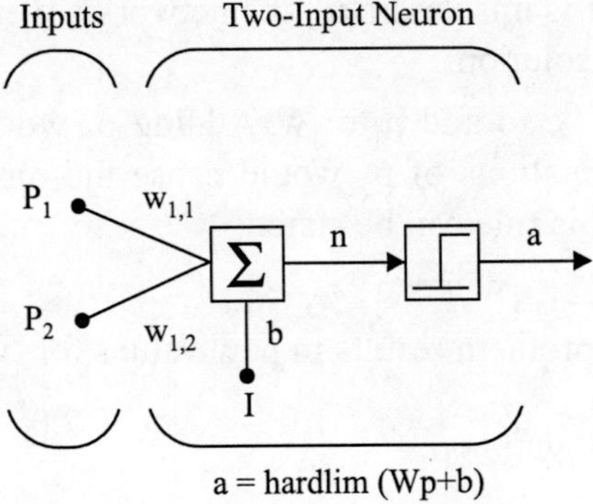

Figure 2.8: Test Problem Network

By removing the bias we are left with a network whose decision boundary must pass through the origin. We need to be sure that this network is still able to solve the test problem. There must be an allowable decision boundary that can separate the vectors p_2 and p_3 from the vector p_1. The figure to the left illustrates that there are indeed an infinite number of such boundaries.

The adjacent figure shown the weight vectors that correspond to the allowable decision boundaries. (Recall that the weight vector is orthogonal to the decision boundary.) We would like a learning rule that will find a weight vector that points in one of these directions. Remember that the length of the weight vector does not matter; only its direction is important.

2.6.3 Constructing Learning Rules

Training begins by assigning some initial values for the network parameters. In this case we are training a two-input/single-output network without a bias, so we only have to initialize its two weights. Here we set the elements of the weight vector, ${}_1w$, to the following randomly generated values:

$$ {}_1w^T = [1.0 - 0.8] \tag{2.20}$$

We will now begin presenting the input vectors to the network. We begin with p_1:

$$a = \text{hardlim}\,({}_1w^T p_1) = \text{hardlim}\ [1.0\ -0.8]\ \begin{matrix}1\\2\end{matrix}$$

$$a = \text{hardlim}\,(-0.6) = 0 \tag{2.21}$$

The network has not returned the correct value. The network output is 0, while the target response, t_i is 1.

One approach would be to set ${}_1w$ equal to p_1. The initial weight vector results in a decision boundary that incorrectly classifies the vector p_1. We need to alter the weight vector so that it points more toward p_1 so that in the future it has a better chance of classifying it correctly.

One approach would be to set ${}_1w$ equal to p_1. This is simple and would ensure that p_1 was classified properly in the future. Unfortunately, it is easy to construct a problem for which this rule cannot find a solution. The diagram to the lower left shown a problem that cannot be solved with the weight vector pointing directly at either of the two class 1 vectors. If we apply the rule ${}_1w = p$ every time one of these vectors is misclassified, the network's weights will simply oscillate back and forth and will never find a solution.

Another possibility would be to add $p_1$to ${}_1w$. Adding p_1 would make ${}_1w$ point more in the direction of p_1. repeated presentations of p_1 would cause the direction of ${}_1w$ to asymptotically approach the direction of p_1. This rule can be stated:

If t = 1 and a = o, then ${}_1w^{new} = {}_1w^{old} + p$ (2.22)

Applying this rule our test problem results in new values for ${}_1w$:

$$ {}_1w^{new} = {}_1w^{old} + p_1 = \begin{matrix}1.0\\-0.8\end{matrix} + \begin{matrix}1\\2\end{matrix}\ \ \begin{matrix}2.0\\1.2\end{matrix} \tag{2.23}$$

This operation is illustrated in the adjacent figure.

We now move on to the next input vector and will continue making changes to the weights and cycling through the inputs until they are all classified correctly.

The next input vector is p_2. When it is presented to the network we find:

$$a = \text{hardlim}\,({}_1w^T p_2) = \text{hardlim} = \begin{bmatrix}2.0 & -1.2\end{bmatrix}\begin{bmatrix}-1\\2\end{bmatrix}$$

$$a = \text{hardlim}\,(0.4) = 1 \tag{2.24}$$

The target t_2 associated with p_2 is 0 and the output a is 1. A class 0 vector was misclassified as a 1.Since we would now like to move the weight vector ${}_1w$ away from the input, we can simply change the addition in Eq. (2.22) to subtraction:

If $t = 0$ and $a = 1$, then $\quad {}_1w^{new} = {}_1w^{old} - p.$ (2.25)

If we apply this to the test problem we find

$${}_1w^{new} = {}_1w^{old} - p_2 = \begin{bmatrix}2.0\\1.2\end{bmatrix} + \begin{bmatrix}-1\\2\end{bmatrix} \begin{bmatrix}3.0\\-0.8\end{bmatrix} \tag{2.26}$$

Which is illustrated in the adjacent figure.

Now we present the third vector p_3:

$$a = \text{hardlim}\,({}_1w^T p_3) = \text{hardlim} = \begin{bmatrix}3.0 & -0.8\end{bmatrix}\begin{bmatrix}0\\-1\end{bmatrix}$$

$$a = \text{hardlim}\,(0.8) = 1 \tag{2.27}$$

The current ${}_1w$ results in a decision boundary that misclassifies p_3. This is a situation for which we already have a rule, so ${}_1w$ will be updated again, according to Eq. (2.25):

$${}_1w^{new} = {}_1w^{old} + p_3 = \begin{bmatrix}3.0\\-0.8\end{bmatrix} + \begin{bmatrix}0\\-1\end{bmatrix} \begin{bmatrix}3.0\\0.2\end{bmatrix} \tag{2.28}$$

The diagram to the left shows that the perceptron has finally learned to classify the three vectors properly. If we present any of the input vectors to the neuron, it will output te correct class for that input vector.

This bring us to our third and final rule: if it works, don't fix it.

if $\quad t = a$, then $\quad {}_1w^{new} = {}_1w^{old}$ (2.29)

Here are the three rules, which cover all possible combinations of output and target values:

If $\quad t = 1$ and $a = 0$ then $\quad {}_1w^{new} = {}_1w^{old} + p.$

If $\quad t = 0$ and $a = 1$, then $\quad {}_1w^{new} = {}_1w^{old} - p.$ (2.30)

If $\quad t = a$, then $\quad {}_1w^{new} = {}_1w^{old}$

2.7 PERCEPTRON LEARNING RULE (LEARNP)

Perceptrons are trained on examples of desired behavior. The desired behavior can be summarized by a set of input, output pairs

$$p_1t_1, p_2t_2, \ldots, p_qt_q$$

where **p** is an input to the network and **t** is the corresponding correct (target) output. The objective is to reduce the error **e**, which is the difference **t** - **a** between the neuron response **a** and the target vector **t**. The perceptron learning rule learnp calculates desired changes to the perceptron's weights and biases, given an input vector **p** and the associated error **e**. The target vector **t** must contain values of either 0 or 1, because perceptrons (with hardlim transfer functions) can only output these values.

Each time learnp is executed, the perceptron has a better chance of producing the correct outputs. The perceptron rule is proven to converge on a solution in a finite number of iterations if a solution exists.If a bias is not used, learnp works to find a solution by altering only the weight vector **w** to point toward input vectors to be classified as 1 and away from vectors to be classified as 0. This results in a decision boundary that is perpendicular to **w** and that properly classifies the input vectors.

There are three conditions that can occur for a single neuron once an input vector **p** is presented and the network's response **a** is calculated:

Case 1: If an input vector is presented and the output of the neuron is correct (**a** = **t** and **e** = **t** – **a** = 0), then the weight vector **w** is not altered.

Case 2: If the neuron output is 0 and should have been 1 (**a** = 0 and **t** = 1, and **e** = **t** – **a** = 1), the input vector **p** is added to the weight vector **w**. This makes the weight vector point closer to the input vector, increasing the chance that the input vector will be classified as a 1 in the future.

Case 3: If the neuron output is 1 and should have been 0 (**a** = 1 and **t** = 0, and **e** = **t** – **a** = –1), the input vector **p** is subtracted from the weight vector **w**. This makes the weight vector point farther away from the input vector, increasing the chance that the input vector will be classified as a 0 in the future.

2.8 EXAMPLE FOR LEARNING RULE

The perceptron learning rule can be written more succinctly in terms of the error **e** = **t** – **a** and the change to be made to the weight vector Δw:

Case 1: If **e** = 0, then make a change Δw equal to 0.

Case 2: If **e** = 1, then make a change Δw equal to $\mathbf{p}^T$.

Case 3: If **e** = –1, then make a change Δw equal to $-\mathbf{p}^T$.

All three cases can then be written with a single expression:

$$\Delta w = (t - \alpha)p^T = ep^T$$

You can get the expression for changes in a neuron's bias by noting that the bias is simply a weight that always has an input of 1:

$$\Delta b = (t - \alpha)\,(1) = e$$

For the case of a layer of neurons you have

$$\Delta W = (t - \alpha)(p)^T = e(p)^T$$

and

$$\Delta b = (t - \alpha) = e$$

The perceptron learning rule can be summarized as follows:

$$W^{new} = W^{old} + ep^T$$

and

$$b^{new} = b^{old} + e$$

where

$$\mathbf{e = t - a}$$

Now try a simple example. Start with a single neuron having an input vector with just two elements. Here are input vectors with the values –2 and 2, and outputs with values 0 and 1.

net = newp([–2 2;–2 2], [0 1]);

To simplify matters, set the bias equal to 0 and the weights to 1 and – 0.8:

net.b{1} = [0];
w = [1 –0.8];
net.IW{1,1} = w;

The input target pair is given by

p = [1; 2]; t = [1];

You can compute the output and error with

a = sim(net,p)

a = 0

e = t – a

e = 1

and use the function learnp to find the change in the weights.

dw = learnp(w,p,[],[],[],[],e,[],[],[])

dw = 1.2

The new weights, then, are obtained as

w = w + dw

w = 2.0000 + 1.2000

The process of finding new weights (and biases) can be repeated until there are no errors. Recall that the perceptron learning rule is guaranteed to converge in a finite number of steps for all problems that can be solved by a perceptron. These include all classification problems that are linearly separable. The objects to be classified in such cases can be separated by a single line.

2.8.1 Training (Train)

If sim and learnp are used repeatedly to present inputs to a perceptron, and to change the perceptron weights and biases according to the error, the perceptron will eventually find weight and bias values that solve the problem, given that the perceptron *can* solve it. Each traversal through all the training input and target vectors is called a *pass*. The function train carries out such a loop of calculation. In each pass the function train proceeds through the specified sequence of inputs, calculating the output, error, and network adjustment for each input vector in the sequence as the inputs are presented.

Note that train does not guarantee that the resulting network does its job. You must check the new values of **W** and **b** by computing the network output for each input vector to see if all targets are reached. If a network does not perform successfully you can train it further by calling train again with the new weights and biases for more training passes, or you can analyze the problem to see if it is a suitable problem for the perceptron. Problems that cannot be solved by the perceptron network are discussed in Limitations and Cautions.

To illustrate the training procedure, work through a simple problem. Consider a one-neuron perceptron with a single vector input having two elements. This network, and the problem you are about to consider, are simple enough that you can follow through what is done with hand calculations if you want. Suppose you have the following classification problem and would like to solve it with a single vector input, two-element perceptron network.

$$P_1 = \begin{matrix}2\\2\end{matrix}, t_1 = 0 \quad P_2 = \begin{matrix}1\\-2\end{matrix}, t_2 = 1 \quad P_3 = \begin{matrix}-2\\2\end{matrix}, t_3 = 0 \quad P_4 = \begin{matrix}-1\\1\end{matrix}, t_4 = 1$$

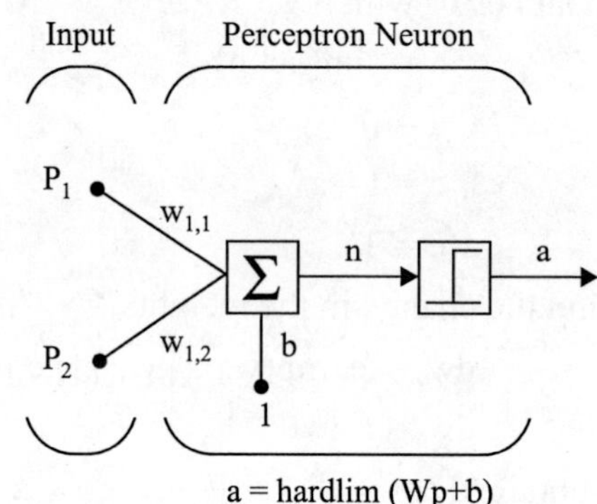

Figure 2.9: Perceptron Training

Use the initial weights and bias. Denote the variables at each step of this calculation by using a number in parentheses after the variable. Thus, above, the initial values are **W**(0) and *b*(0).

$$w(0) \quad [0 \ 0] \quad b(0) \quad 0$$

Start by calculating the perceptron's output *a* for the first input vector $\mathbf{p}_1$, using the initial weights and bias.

$$a = \text{hardlim}\,(W(0)p_1 + b(0))$$

$$= \text{hardlim}\quad 0\ 0 \quad \begin{matrix}2\\2\end{matrix} \quad 0 \quad \text{hardlim}\,(0) \quad 1$$

The output a does not equal the target value t_1, so use the perceptron rule to find the incremental changes to the weights and biases based on the error.

$$e = t_1 - a = 0 - 1 = -1$$

$$\Delta W = ep^T \quad (\ 1)[2\ 2] \quad [\ 2\ \ 2]$$

$$\Delta b = e = (-1) = -1$$

You can calculate the new weights and bias using the perceptron update rules.

$$W^{new} = w^{old} \quad ep^T \quad [0\ 0] \quad [\ 2\ \ 2] \quad [\ 2\ \ 2] \quad W(1)$$

$$b^{new} = b^{old} + e = 0 + (-1) = -1 = b(1)$$

Now present the next input vector, $\mathbf{p}_2$. The output is calculated below.

$$a = \text{hardlim}\,(W(1)p_2 + b(1))$$

$$= \text{hardlim} \quad 2\ \ 2 \quad \begin{matrix}2\\2\end{matrix} \quad 1 \quad \text{hardlim}\,(1) \quad 1$$

On this occasion, the target is 1, so the error is zero. Thus there are no changes in weights or bias, so

$$W(2) = W(1) = [-2\ -2] \text{ and } p(2) = p(1) = -1.$$

You can continue in this fashion, presenting $\mathbf{p}_3$ next, calculating an output and the error, and making changes in the weights and bias, etc. After making one pass through all of the four inputs, you get the values W (4) = [–3 –1] b (4) = 0 and. To determine whether a satisfactory solution is obtained, make one pass through all input vectors to see if they all produce the desired target values. This is not true for the fourth input, but the algorithm does converge on the sixth presentation of an input. The final values are

$$W(6) = [-2\ -3] \text{ and } b(6) = 1$$

This concludes the hand calculation. Now, how can you do this using the train function?

The following code defines a perceptron like that shown in the previous figure, with initial weights and bias values of 0.

```
net = newp([–2 2; –2 2],[0 1]);
```

Consider the application of a single input.

```
p = [2; 2];
```

having the target

```
t = [0];
```

Set epochs to 1, so that train goes through the input vectors (only one here) just one time.

```
net.trainParam.epochs = 1;
net = train(net,p,t);
```

The new weights and bias are

```
w = net.iw{1,1}, b = net.b{1}
w = –2 –2
b = –1
```

Thus, the initial weights and bias are 0, and after training on only the first vector, they have the values [–2 –2] and –1, just as you hand calculated.

Now apply the second input vector P_2. The output is 1, as it will be until the weights and bias are changed, but now the target is 1, the error will be 0, and the change will be zero. You could proceed in this way, starting from the previous result and applying a new input vector time after time. But you can do this job automatically with train.

Apply train for one epoch, a single pass through the sequence of all four input vectors. Start with the network definition.

```
net = newp([-2 2;-2 2],[0 1]);
net.trainParam.epochs = 1;
```

The input vectors and targets are

```
p = [[2; 2] [1; –2] [–2; 2] [–1; 1]]
t = [0 1 0 1]
```

Now train the network with

```
net = train(net, p, t);
```

The new weights and bias are

```
w = net.iw{1, 1}, b = net.b{1}
w = –3  –1
b = 0
```

This is the same result as you got previously by hand.

Finally, simulate the trained network for each of the inputs.

```
a = sim(net, p)
a = 0  0  1  1
```

The outputs do not yet equal the targets, so you need to train the network for more than one pass. Try more epochs. This run gives a mean absolute error performance of 0 after two epochs:

```
net.trainParam.epochs = 1000;
net = train(net,p,t);
```

Thus, the network was trained by the time the inputs were presented on the third epoch. (As you know from hand calculation, the network converges on the presentation of the sixth input vector. This occurs in the middle of the second epoch, but it takes the third epoch to detect the network convergence.) The final weights and bias are

w = w = net.iw{1,1}, b = net.b{1}

w = –2 –3

b = 1

The simulated output and errors for the various inputs are

a = sim(net, p)

a = 0 1 0 1

error = a – t

error = 0 0 0 0

You confirm that the training procedure is successful. The network converges and produces the correct target outputs for the four input vectors.The default training function for networks created with newp is trainc. (You can find this by executing net.trainFcn.)

This training function applies the perceptron learning rule in its pure form, in that individual input vectors are applied individually, in sequence, and corrections to the weights and bias are made after each presentation of an input vector. Thus, perceptron training with train will converge in a finite number of steps unless the problem presented cannot be solved with a simple perceptron.The function train can be used in various ways by other networks as well. Type help train to read more about this basic function.

You might want to try various demonstration programs. For instance, demop1 illustrates classification and training of a simple perceptron.

2.9 LIMITATIONS AND CAUTIONS

Perceptron networks should be trained with adapt, which presents the input vectors to the network one at a time and makes corrections to the network based on the results of each presentation. Use of adapt in this way guarantees that any linearly separable problem is solved in a finite number of training presentations.

As noted in the previous pages, perceptrons can also be trained with the function train, which is discussed in detail in the next chapter. Commonly when train is used for perceptrons, it presents the inputs to the network in batches, and makes corrections to the network based on the sum of all the individual corrections. Unfortunately, there is no proof that such a training algorithm converges for perceptrons. On that account the use of train for perceptrons is not recommended.

Perceptron networks have several limitations. First, the output values of a perceptron can take on only one of two values (0 or 1) because of the hard-limit transfer function. Second, perceptrons can only classify linearly separable sets of vectors. If a straight line or a plane can be drawn to separate the input vectors into their correct categories, the input vectors are linearly separable. If the vectors are not linearly separable, learning will never reach a point where all vectors are classified properly. However, it has been proven that if the vectors are linearly separable, perceptrons trained adaptively will always find a solution in finite time. You might want to try demop6. It shows the difficulty of trying to classify input vectors that are not linearly separable.

It is only fair, however, to point out that networks with more than one perceptron can be used to solve more difficult problems. For instance, suppose that you have a set of four vectors that you would like to classify into distinct groups, and that two lines can be drawn to separate them. A two-neuron network can be found such that its two decision boundaries classify the inputs into four categories. For additional discussion about perceptrons and to examine more complex perceptron problems.

2.10 OUTLIERS AND THE NORMALIZED PERCEPTRON RULE

Long training times can be caused by the presence of an *outlier* input vector whose length is much larger or smaller than the other input vectors. Applying the perceptron learning rule involves adding and subtracting input vectors from the current weights and biases in response to error. Thus, an input vector with large elements can lead to changes in the weights and biases that take a long time for a much smaller input vector to overcome. You might want to try demop4 to see how an outlier affects the training.

By changing the perceptron learning rule slightly, you can make training times insensitive to extremely large or small outlier input vectors.Here is the original rule for updating weights:

$$\Delta w = (t - a)\, p^T = ep^T$$

As shown above, the larger an input vector **p**, the larger its effect on the weight vector **w**. Thus, if an input vector is much larger than other input vectors, the smaller input vectors must be presented many times to have an effect. The solution is to normalize the rule so that the effect of each input vector on the weights is of the same magnitude:

$$\Delta w = (t \quad a)\frac{p^T}{|p|} \quad e\frac{p^T}{|p|}$$

The normalized perceptron rule is implemented with the function learnpn, which is called exactly like learnp. The normalized perceptron rule function learnpn takes slightly more time to execute, but reduces the number of epochs considerably if there are outlier input vectors. You might try demop5 to see how this normalized training rule works.

2.11 PERCEPTRON LEARNING RULE CONVERGENCE THEOREM

Perceptron Convergence Theorem

Says that there if there is a weight vector **w*** such that f(**w*****p**(q)) = t(q) for all q, then for any starting vector **w**, the perceptron learning rule will converge to a weight vector (not necessarily unique and not necessarily **w***) that gives the correct response for all training patterns, and it will do so in a finite number of steps.

Idea of the proof

The idea is to find upper and lower bounds on the length of the weight vector. If the length is finite, then the perceptron has converged, which also implies that the weights have changed a finite number of times.

Proof

1. Assume that the inputs to the perceptron originate from two linearly separable classes. **That is, the classes can be distinguished by a perceptron**. Let X_1 be the subset of training vectors belonging to C1. That is, **p**(1), **p**(2),... . Let X_2 be the set of training vectors belonging to C2. That is, **p**(1), **p**(2),... . Then we can say that $X_1 \cup X_2$ is the complete training set X.
2. Given the set of vectors X_1 and X_2 to train this perceptron to train this perceptron, the training process (as we have seen) involves the adjustment of the weight vector **w** such that C1 and C2 are linearly separable. That is, there exists some **w** such that
$$\mathbf{w}^T\mathbf{p} > 0 \text{ for every input vector } \mathbf{p}\ \varepsilon\ C1 \quad (1)$$
$$\mathbf{w}^T\mathbf{p} < 0 \text{ for every input vector } \mathbf{p}\ \varepsilon\ C2$$
3. What need to do is find some **w** such that the above is satisfied, which is the purpose of the perceptron algorithm.

   One algorithm for adapting the weight vector for the perceptron algorithm can be formulated as follows (there are others):

   a. If the kth member of the training set **p**(k) is correctly classified at the kth iteration no correction is made to **w**. This is done according to the following rule:
$$\mathbf{w}(k+1) = \mathbf{w}(k) \text{ if } \mathbf{w}^T\mathbf{p}(k) > 0 \text{ and } \mathbf{p}(k) \in C1$$
$$\mathbf{w}(k+1) = \mathbf{w}(k) \text{ if } \mathbf{w}^T\mathbf{p}(k) < 0 \text{ and } \mathbf{p}(k) \in C2 \quad (2)$$

   b. Otherwise, the weight vector of the perceptron is updated according to the following rule:
$$\mathbf{w}(k+1) = \mathbf{w}(k) + \mathbf{p}(k) \text{ if } \mathbf{w}^T\mathbf{p}(k) < 0 \text{ and } \mathbf{p}(k) \in C1$$
$$\mathbf{w}(k+1) = \mathbf{w}(k) - \mathbf{p}(k) \text{ if } \mathbf{w}^T\mathbf{p}(k) > 0 \text{ and } \mathbf{p}(k) \in C2 \quad (3)$$
4. The proof begins assuming that **w**(1) = **0** (i.e., the zero vector). Suppose that $\mathbf{w}^T(k)\mathbf{p}(k) < 0$ for k = 1, 2, ..., and all the input vectors $\mathbf{p}(k) \in X1$ (or C1).

   Here, the perceptron **incorrectly** classifies the vectors **p**(1), **p**(2), ... since the second condition in Equation (1) is violated (i.e., $\mathbf{w}^T(k)\mathbf{p}(k)$ should be greater than 0). Now we can use Equation (3) to write the adjustments to the weight matrix according to the perceptron learning rule
$$\mathbf{w}(k+1) = \mathbf{w}(k) + \mathbf{p}(k) \text{ for } \mathbf{p}(k) \in C1 \quad (4)$$
   Recall, what we are doing is modifying the weight vector so that it points in the right direction.
5. Given the initial condition **w**(1) = **0**, we can iteratively solve for **w**(k+1) obtaining:
$$\mathbf{w}(k+1) = \mathbf{p}(1) + \mathbf{p}(2) + \ldots + \mathbf{p}(k) \quad (5)$$

Exercise: Show $\mathbf{w}(k+1) = \mathbf{p}(1) + \mathbf{p}(2) + ... + \mathbf{p}(k)$

Answer:

$\mathbf{w}(1) = \mathbf{0}$

$\mathbf{w}(2) = \mathbf{w}(1) + \mathbf{p}(1) = \mathbf{p}(1)$

$\mathbf{w}(3) = \mathbf{w}(2) + \mathbf{p}(2) = \mathbf{w}(1) + \mathbf{p}(1) + \mathbf{p}(2) = \mathbf{p}(1) + \mathbf{p}(2)$

$\mathbf{w}(4) = \mathbf{w}(3) + \mathbf{p}(3) = \mathbf{w}(2) + \mathbf{p}(2) + \mathbf{p}(3) = \mathbf{w}(1) + \mathbf{p}(1) + \mathbf{p}(2) + \mathbf{p}(3)$
$= \mathbf{p}(1) + \mathbf{p}(2) + \mathbf{p}(3)$

So, in general:

$\mathbf{w}(k+1) = \mathbf{p}(1) + \mathbf{p}(2) + ... + \mathbf{p}(k)$

Since C1 and C2 are assumed to be linearly separable, then there exists a wo that can correctly classify all input vectors belonging to C1 and C2.

In this proof, we have assumed the existence of **wo** for which

$$\mathbf{w}_o^T \mathbf{p}(k) > 0 \text{ if } \mathbf{p}(k) \in C1$$

and

$$\mathbf{w}_o^T \mathbf{p}(k) < 0 \text{ if } \mathbf{p}(k) \in C2$$

This is equivalent to the existence of a weight vector **wo** for which

$$\mathbf{w}_o^T \mathbf{p}(k) > 0 \text{ if } \mathbf{p}(k) \in C1 \cup C2 \text{ or } X$$

The reason is that the training set can be considered to consist of two parts:

$$C1 = \{\mathbf{p} \text{ such that the target value is } 1\}$$

and

$$C2 = \{\mathbf{p} \text{ such that the target value is } 0\}$$

So we can think of the training set X as

$$X = C1 \cup C2$$

Where

$$C2 = \{-\mathbf{p} \text{ such that } \mathbf{p} \in C2\}$$

Now, if the response for the network is incorrect, then this allows the weights to be updated according to:

$$\mathbf{w}(k+1) = \mathbf{w}(k) + \mathbf{p}(k)$$

since $-\mathbf{w}_o^T \mathbf{p}(k) < 0 = \mathbf{w}_o^T \mathbf{p}(k) > 0$ if $\mathbf{p}(k)\ \varepsilon$ C2. Now in this case the perceptron is updated by $\mathbf{w}(k+1) = \mathbf{w}(k) - (-\mathbf{p}(k)) = \mathbf{w}(k+1) = \mathbf{w}(k) + \mathbf{p}(k)$ since $\mathbf{w}^T\mathbf{p}(k) > 0$ and $\mathbf{p}(k)\ \varepsilon$ C2.

For the solution **wo**, we can define some $\alpha > 0$ as

$$\alpha = \min_{p(x)\ \varepsilon X} w_o^T p(k) \qquad (6)$$

which is just the minimum (scalar) value of all $W_o^T\, p(k)$ for all p ε X.

By multiplying each side of Equation (5) by woT, we get

$$w_o^T\, \mathbf{w}\, (k+1) = \mathbf{w}_o^T\, \mathbf{p}(1) + \mathbf{w}_o^T\, \mathbf{p}(2) + ... + \mathbf{w}_o^T\, \mathbf{p}(k)$$

6. And, by applying Equation (6), we get

$$w_o^T\, w(k+1) \geq k\alpha \tag{7}$$

since has to be greater than or equal to k X min $W_o^T\, p(k)$

$$p(x)\ \varepsilon X$$

7. Next, use the Cauchy-Swartz inequality for $\mathbf{w}_o^T$ and $\mathbf{w}_o^T$ (k+1), which states for any two vectors **x** and **y**:

$$[x \cdot y]^2 \leq ||x||^2\, ||y||^2$$

or $\quad ||x||^2\, [x \cdot y]^2$

where $\quad ||\mathbf{x}||$ is the Euclidian norm.

Example. Suppose x = [–1 0 4].

Then, $\quad ||x|| = \sqrt{(-1) + 0^2 + 4^2} = \sqrt{17}$

Thus, we can say:

$$||\, w_o^T\, ||^2\, ||w(k+1)||^2 \geq [\, w_o^T\, w\, (k+1)]^2 \tag{8}$$

8. From Equation (7), we know by applying Cauchy-Swartz that

$$w_o{}^T w\, (k+1) \geq k\alpha \Rightarrow$$

$$||w_o{}^T||^2 ||w(k+1)||^2 \geq [k\alpha] \Rightarrow$$

$$||w_o{}^T||^2\, ||w(k+1)||^2 \geq [k^2\alpha^2]$$

and we get:

$$||w(k+1)||^2 \geq \frac{k^2\ \ 2}{||w_0||^2} \tag{9}$$

which shows that the squared length of the weight vector ($||\mathbf{w}(k+1)||^2$) grows by a factor of k^2, where k is the number of time the weights have changed.

9. So, what we have established from Equation (9) is a **lower-bound** in the terms of the squared Euclidian norm of the weight vector **w** at iteration k + 1.

But there is another aspect we must consider. In order to show that the weights cannot continue to grow indefinitely, we must establish an **upper- bound** for the weight vector **w**.

10. To find an **upper-bound**, we now do the following. Write Equation (4) as the following (where q is the number of patterns in X):

$$\mathbf{w}(k+1) = \mathbf{w}(k) + \mathbf{p}(k) \text{ for } k = 1, ..., q\ \mathbf{p}(k)EX$$

11. After taking the square of the Euclidian norm, we get

$$||\mathbf{w}(k+1)||^2 = ||\mathbf{w}(k)||^2 + 2\mathbf{w}^T(k)\ \mathbf{p}(k) + ||\mathbf{p}(k)||^2 \qquad (10)$$

12. But assuming that the perceptron incorrectly classifies an input vector belonging to X (i.e., we have to make the adjustment $\mathbf{w}(k+1) = \mathbf{w}(k) + \mathbf{p}(k)$) since $\mathbf{w}^T(k)\ \mathbf{p}(k) < 0$, then from Equation (10), it follows that:

$$||\mathbf{w}(k+1)||^2 \leq ||\mathbf{w}(k)||^2 + ||\mathbf{p}(k)||^2$$

Exercise: Why can we make this claim?

Answer: Because since the input vector **p**(k) was incorrectly classified, this implies that $\mathbf{w}^T(k)\ \mathbf{p}(k) < 0$. Thus, given that $||\mathbf{w}(k+1)||^2 = ||\mathbf{w}(k)||^2 + 2\mathbf{w}^T(k)\ \mathbf{p}(k) + ||\mathbf{p}(k)||^2$, then clearly $2\mathbf{w}^T(k)\ \mathbf{p}(k)$ must be < 0 also. Thus, we can claim that:

$$||\mathbf{w}(k+1)||^2 \leq ||\mathbf{w}(k)||^2 + ||\mathbf{p}(k)||^2.$$

We can rewrite the above as:

$$||\mathbf{w}(k+1\ )||^2 - ||\mathbf{w}(k)||^2\ ||\mathbf{p}(k)||^2 \qquad (11)$$

13. Adding these quantities for k = 1, ..., q (where q is the number of patterns in C1) and using the initial condition that **w**(1) = **0**, it can be shown (**this will be for homework**) that:

$$||w(K+1)||^2 \leq \sum_{i\ 1}^{k} ||P(n)||^2 \quad k \qquad (12)$$

where $\beta > 0$ and is defined by the following:

$$\beta = \max_{p(k)\ \varepsilon X} ||p(k)||^2 \qquad (13)$$

14. Equation (13) says that the Euclidian norm of the weight vector **w**(k+1), grows at most linearly with the number of iterations, k, given the input patterns. In other words,

$$||w(k+1)||^2 \leq k\beta. \qquad (14)$$

15. Thus, we have established both upper and lower bounds for a perceptron to classify correctly the input patterns **p**(k) for k = 1 ,...,q for two class C1 and C2 given they are lineary separable.
16. Observe that ||w(k+1)||² £ kb conflicts with the earlier result of

$$||w(k+1)||^2 \geq \frac{k^2\ \ ^2}{||w_0||^2}.$$

namely, it can be shown that they don't agree for ||**w**(k+1)|| for large values of k.

So we can state that k cannot be larger than some k max for which Equations (9) and (14) are **both** satisfied; and they must be equal to determine the maximum number of iterations for the two linearly separable classes to converge. To determine this, set Equations (9) and (14) equal to each other and substitute and solve for k max. Thus we get

$$\frac{k_{max}^2 \quad ^2}{||w_0||^2} = k_{max}\, b,$$

$$k_{max} = \frac{||w_0||^2}{2}$$

which means that changing the weights of the perceptron must terminate after at most kmax iterations, which means that the machine has solved the (linearly separable) problem correctly.

2.12 THE MULTILAYER PERCEPTRON NEURAL NETWORK MODEL

The following diagram illustrates a perceptron network with three layers:

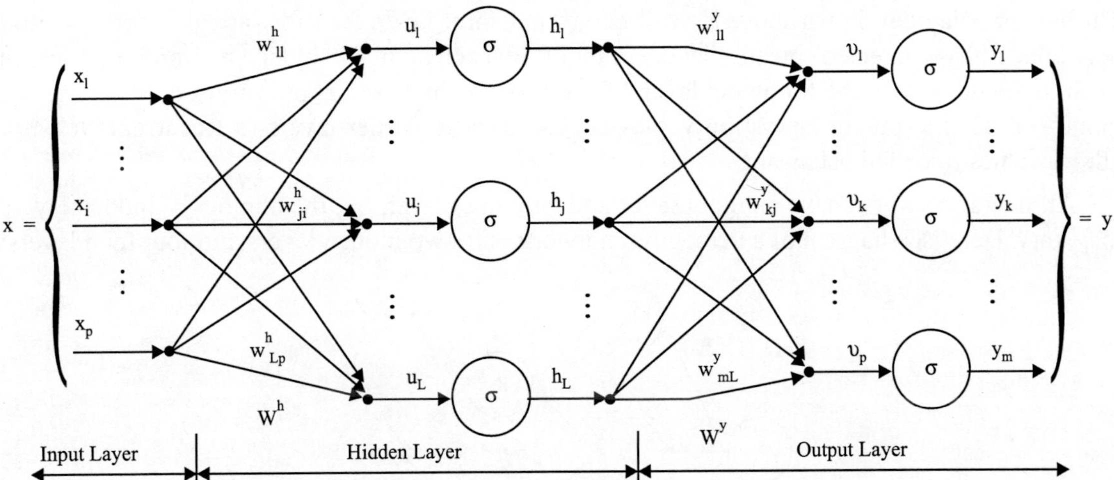

Figure 2.10: The multilayer perceptron neural network model

This network has an **input layer** (on the left) with three neurons, one **hidden layer** (in the middle) with three neurons and an **output layer** (on the right) with three neurons. There is one neuron in the input layer for each predictor variable. In the case of categorical variables, N–1 neurons are used to represent the N categories of the variable.

1. **Input Layer:** A vector of predictor variable values (x_1 ... x_p) is presented to the input layer. The input layer (or processing before the input layer) standardizes these values so that the range of each variable is –1 to 1. The input layer distributes the values to each of the neurons in the hidden layer. In addition to the predictor variables, there is a constant input of 1.0, called the bias that is fed to each of the hidden layers; the bias is multiplied by a weight and added to the sum going into the neuron.
2. **Hidden Layer:** Arriving at a neuron in the hidden layer, the value from each input neuron is multiplied by a weight (w_{ji}), and the resulting weighted values are added together producing

a combined value u_j. The weighted sum (u_j) is fed into a transfer function, σ, which outputs a value h_j. The outputs from the hidden layer are distributed to the output layer.

3. **Output Layer**: Arriving at a neuron in the output layer, the value from each hidden layer neuron is multiplied by a weight (w_{kj}), and the resulting weighted values are added together producing a combined value v_j. The weighted sum (v_j) is fed into a transfer function, ό, which outputs a value y_k. The y values are the outputs of the network.

If a regression analysis is being performed with a continuous target variable, then there is a single neuron in the output layer, and it generates a single y value. For classification problems with categorical target variables, there are N neurons in the output layer producing N values, one for each of the N categories of the target variable.

2.12.1 Multilayer Perceptron Architecture

The network diagram shown above is a full-connected, three layer, feed-forward, perceptron neural network. "Fully connected" means that the output from each input and hidden neuron is distributed to all of the neurons in the following layer. "Feed forward" means that the values only move from input to hidden to output layers; no values are fed back to earlier layers (a Recurrent Network allows values to be fed backward).

All neural networks have an input layer and an output layer, but the number of hidden layers may vary. Here is a diagram of a perceptron network with two hidden layers and four total layers:

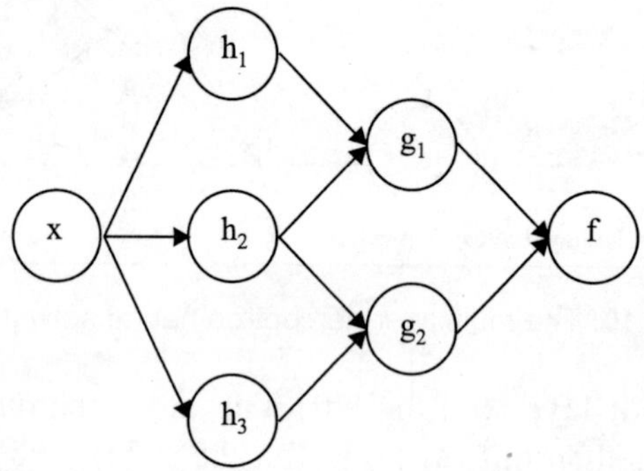

Figure 2.11: Multilayer Perceptron Architecture

When there is more than one hidden layer, the output from one hidden layer is fed into the next hidden layer and separate weights are applied to the sum going into each layer.

2.12.2 Training Multilayer Perceptron Networks

The goal of the training process is to find the set of weight values that will cause the output from the neural network to match the actual target values as closely as possible. There are several issues involved in designing and training a multilayer perceptron network:

- Selecting how many hidden layers to use in the network.

- Deciding how many neurons to use in each hidden layer.
- Finding a globally optimal solution that avoids local minima.
- Converging to an optimal solution in a reasonable period of time.
- Validating the neural network to test for overfitting.

2.12.3 Selecting The Number of Hidden Layers

For nearly all problems, one hidden layer is sufficient. Two hidden layers are required for modeling data with discontinuities such as a saw tooth wave pattern. Using two hidden layers rarely improves the model, and it may introduce a greater risk of converging to a local minima. There is no theoretical reason for using more than two hidden layers. DTREG can build models with one or two hidden layers. Three layer models with one hidden layer are recommended.

2.12.4 Deciding How Many Neurons to Use in the Hidden Layers

One of the most important characteristics of a perceptron network is the number of neurons in the hidden layer(s). If an inadequate number of neurons are used, the network will be unable to model complex data, and the resulting fit will be poor. If too many neurons are used, the training time may become excessively long, and, worse, the network may *over fit* the data. When overfitting occurs, the network will begin to model random noise in the data. The result is that the model fits the training data extremely well, but it generalizes poorly to new, unseen data. Validation must be used to test for this.

DTREG includes an automated feature to find the optimal number of neurons in the hidden layer. You specify the minimum and maximum number of neurons you want it to test, and it will build models using varying numbers of neurons and measure the quality using either cross validation or hold-out data not used for training. This is a highly effective method for finding the optimal number of neurons, but it is computationally expensive, because many models must be built, and each model has to be validated. If you have a multiprocessor computer, you can configure DTREG to use multiple CPU's during the process.

The automated search for the optimal number of neurons only searches the first hidden layer. If you select a model with two hidden layers, you must manually specify the number of neurons in the second hidden layer.

2.12.5 Finding A Globally Optimal Solution

A typical neural network might have a couple of hundred weighs whose values must be found to produce an optimal solution. If neural networks were linear models like linear regression, it would be a breeze to find the optimal set of weights. But the output of a neural network as a function of the inputs is often highly nonlinear; this makes the optimization process complex.

If you plotted the error as a function of the weights, you would likely see a rough surface with many local minima such as this:

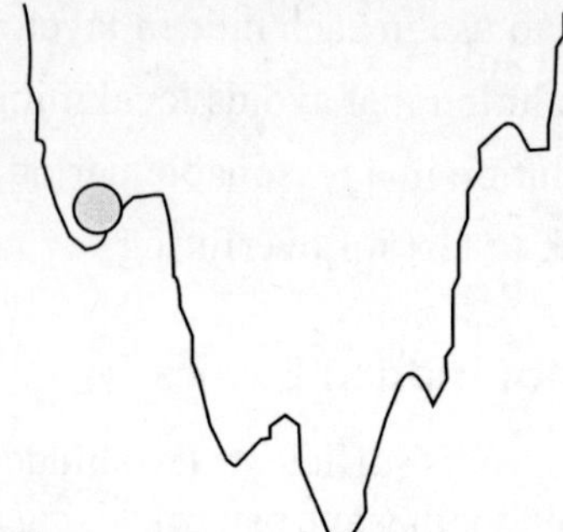

Figure 2.12: Optimal Solution

This picture is highly simplified because it represents only a single weight value (on the horizontal axis). With a typical neural network, you would have a 200-dimension, rough surface with many local valleys.

Optimization methods such as steepest descent and conjugate gradient are highly susceptible to finding local minima if they begin the search in a valley near a local minimum. They have no ability to see the big picture and find the global minimum.

Several methods have been tried to avoid local minima. The simplest is just to try a number of random starting points and use the one with the best value. A more sophisticated technique called *simulated annealing* improves on this by trying widely separated random values and then gradually reducing ("cooling") the random jumps in the hope that the location is getting closer to the global minimum.

DTREG uses the Nguyen-Widrow algorithm to select the initial range of starting weight values. It then uses the conjugate gradient algorithm to optimize the weights. Conjugate gradient usually finds the optimum weights quickly, but there is no guarantee that the weight values it finds are globally optimal. So it is useful to allow DTREG to try the optimization multiple times with different sets of initial random weight values. The number of tries allowed is specified on the Multilayer Perceptron property page.

2.13 LINEAR SEPARABILITY

When two sets of points in a two-dimensional graph can be completely separated by a single line, they are said to be **linearly separable**. In general, two groups are linearly separable in n-dimensional space if they can be separated by an (n – 1)-dimensional hyperplane. For 2-dimensional inputs, if there exists a line (whose equation us $w_0 + w_1w_1 + w_2w_2 = 0$) that separates all samples of one class from the other class, then an appropriate perceptron (with weights w_0, w_1, w_2 for the connections from inputs 1, x_1, x_2, respectively) can be derived from the equation of the separating line. Such classification problems are said to be "linearly separable," i.e., separable by a linear combination of inputs.

The close correspondence between perceptron weights and the coefficients of terms in the equations of lines can be used to arrive at the converse result as well. If there is a simple perceptron (with weight ω_0, ω_1, ω_2 for the connections from inputs 1, ω_1, ω_2, respectively) that can separate samples of two classes, then we can obtain the equation $(\omega_0 + \omega_1 x_1 + \omega_0, \omega_2 x_2 = 0)$ of a line that separates samples of the two classes.

Therefore, if the samples are NOT linearly separable, i.e., no straight line can possibly separate samples belonging to two classes, then there CANNOT be any simple perceptron that achieves the classification task. This is the fundamental limitation of simple perceptron, considered here for 2-dimensional input samples. Example of linearly nonseparable classes are illustrated in Figure 2.13. Most real-life classification problem are linearly nonseparable, and hence cannot be solved using perceptrons.

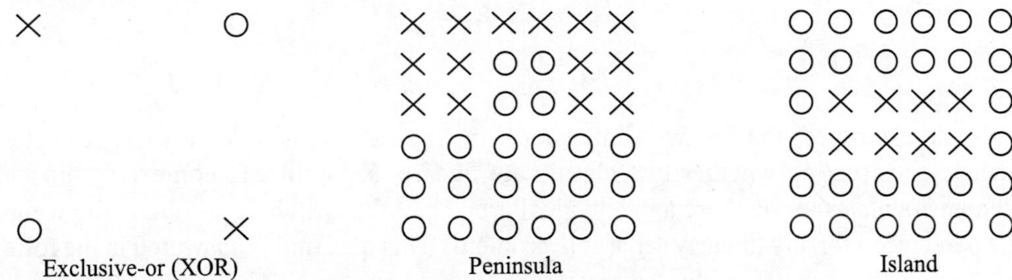

Figure 2.13: Examples of linearly nonseparable classes: crosses indicate samples of one class, and circles indicate samples of another class.

So far, we have examined with two input dimensions (say x_1, x_2). If there is only one input dimension (say x), then the 2-class problem can be solved using a perceptron if and only if there is some value x_0 of x such that all samples of one class occur for $x > x_0$, and all samples of the other class occur for $x < x_0$. (See Figure 2.14)

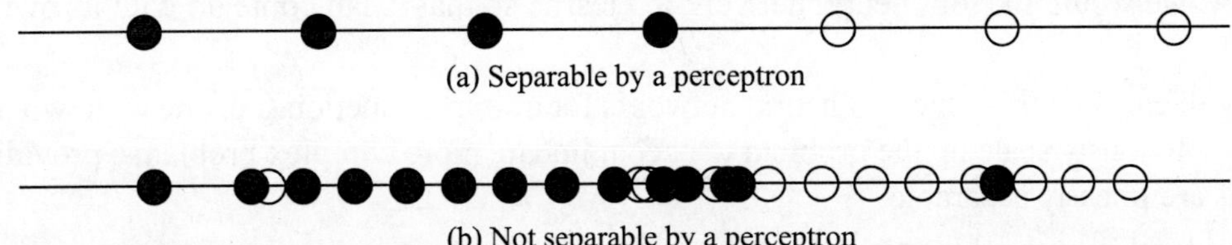

Figure 2.14: Classification Problems in One-dimensional Input Space.

If there are 3 input dimensions, a 2-class problem can be solved using a perceptron if and only if there is a plane that separates samples of different classed. As in the 2-dimensional case, coefficients of terms in the equation of the plane correspond to the weights of the perceptron. For spaces having a higher number of input dimensions, out geometric intuitions need to be suitably extended, imagining "hyperplanes" that can separate samples of different classes. Each hyperplane in n dimensions is defined by the equation

$$\omega_0, \omega_1 x_1 + \omega_2 x_2 + \ldots + \omega_n x_n = 0$$

dividing the n-dimensional space into two regions, in which $\omega_0 + \omega_1 x_1 + \omega_2 x_2 \ldots + \omega_n \omega_n > 0$ and $\omega_0 + \omega_1 x_1 + \omega_2 x_2 \ldots + \omega_n x_n < 0$, respectively. This again corresponds exactly with the decision made by the perception whose weights are $\omega_1 + \omega_2, \ldots, \omega_n$ and threshold is w_0, as shown in Figure 2.15.

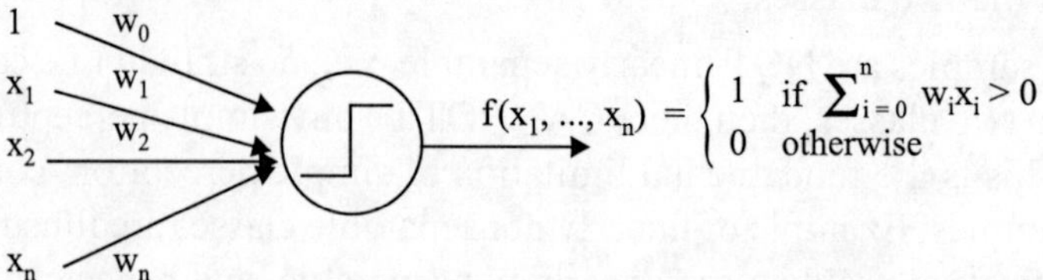

Figure 2.15: Generic perceptron for n-dimensional input space, implementing the hyperplane

$$\sum_{i=0}^{n} W_i X_i = 0.$$

For simple examples, and for two-dimensional input spaces, it is relatively easy to determine by geometric construction whether two classes are linearly separable. Become very difficult for higher-dimensional spaces. Is there a mechanical procedure that will help us obtain the weights of a suitable perceptron for any linearly separable problem? This question is answered in the following section.

2.14 LEARNING LINERALY SEPARABLE FUNCTIONS

With a function such as AND (with only two inputs) we can easily decide what weights to use to give us the required output from the neuron. But with more complex functions (i.e. those with more than two inputs it may not be so easy to decide on the correct weights). Therefore, we would like our neural network to “learn” so that it can come up with its own set of weights.

We will consider this aspect of neural networks for a simple function (i.e. one with two inputs). We could obviously scale up the problem to accommodate more complex problems, providing the problems are linearly separable.

Consider this truth table (AND) and the neuron that we **hope** will represent it.

AND		
$Input_1$	$Input_2$	Output
0	0	0
0	1	0
1	0	0
1	1	1

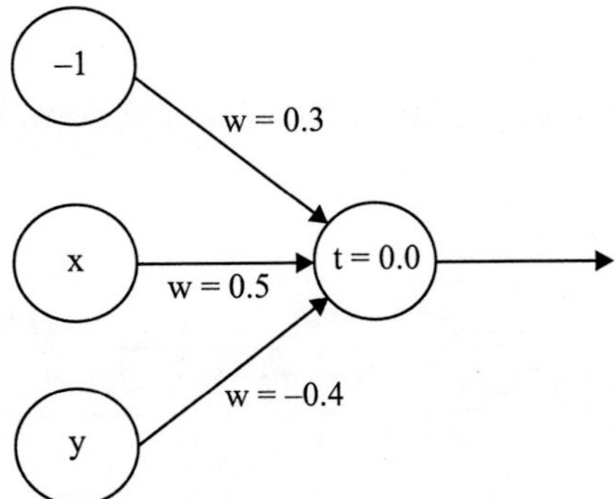

Figure 2.16: AND Map

In fact, all we have done is set the weights to random values between –0.5 and 0.5

By applying the activation function for each of the four possible inputs to this neuron (try it) it actually gives us the following truth table

???		
$Input_1$	$Input_2$	Output
0	0	0
0	1	0
1	0	1
1	1	0

Which can be graphically represented as follows

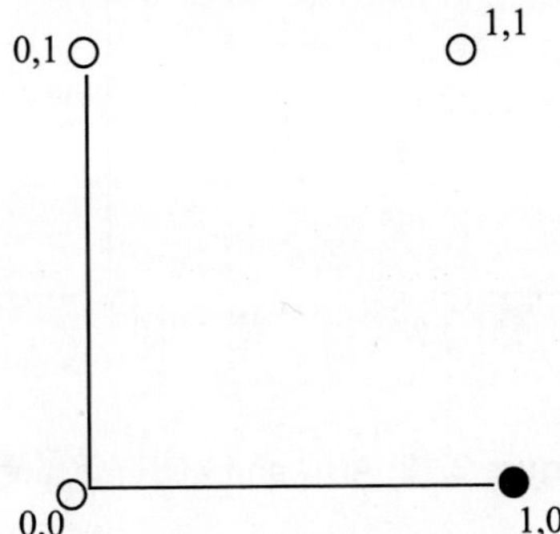

Figure 2.17: Graphic Function

The network, obviously, does not represent the AND function so we need to adjust the weights so that it "learns" the function correctly.

2.14.1 Example of Linearly Separable

We have already seen that perceptrons can represent the AND, OR and NOT logic functions. But does it follow that a perceptron (a single-layer, feed-forward network) can represent any boolean function?

Unfortunately, this is not the case.

XOR		
$Input_1$	$Input_2$	Output
0	0	0
0	1	1
1	0	1
1	1	0

To see why, consider these two truth tables

AND		
$Input_1$	$Input_2$	Output
0	0	0
0	1	0
1	0	0
1	1	1

We can represent these two truth tables graphically. Like this

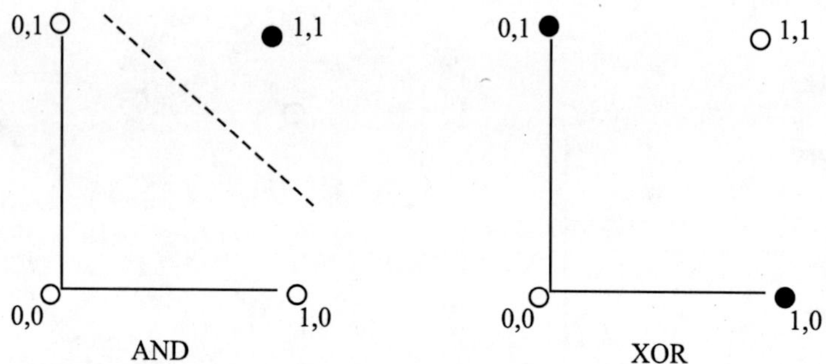

Figure 2.18: AND and XOR function

(where a filled circle represents an output of one and a hollow circle represents an output of zero).

If you look at the AND graph you will see that we can divide the one's from the zero's with a line. This is not possible with XOR.Functions such as AND are called linearly separable.It was the proof by Minsky & Papert in 1969 that perceptrons could only learn linearly separable functions that led to decline in neural network research until the mid 1980's when it was proved that other network architectures could learn these type of functions.Although, only being able to learn linearly separable functions is a major disadvantage of the perceptron it is still worth studying as it is relatively simple and can help provide a framework for other architectures.It should however, be realised that perceptrons are not only limited to two inputs (e.g. the AND function). We can have n inputs which gives us an n-dimension problem.When n = 3 we can still visualise the linear separability of the problem (see diagram below).

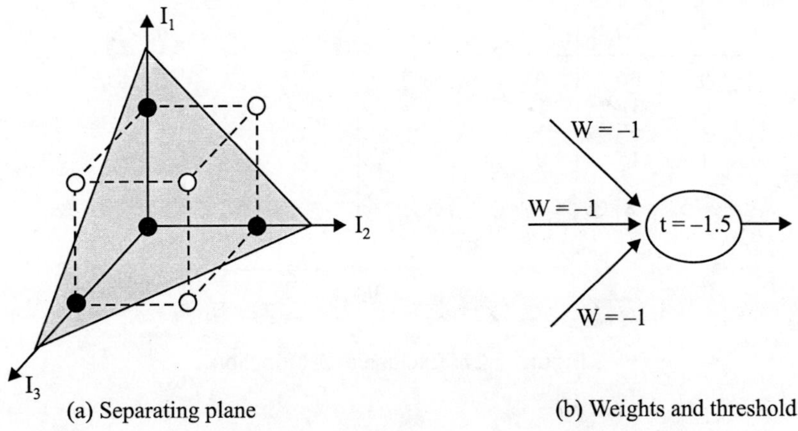

Figure 2.19: Seperating Plane

But once n is greater than three we find it difficult to visualise the problem.

2.15 LINEAR SEPARABILITY AND THE XOR PROBLEM

Consider two-input patterns (X_1, X_2) being classified into two classes as shown in figure 2.20. Each point with either symbol of x or 0 represents a pattern with a set of values (X_1, X_2). Each pattern is classified into one of two classes. Notice that these classes can be separated with a single line L. They are known as linearly separable patterns. Linear separability refers to the fact that classes of patterns with n-dimensional vector $x = (x_1, x_2, \ldots, x_n)$ can be separated with a single decision surface. In the case above, the line represents the decision surface.

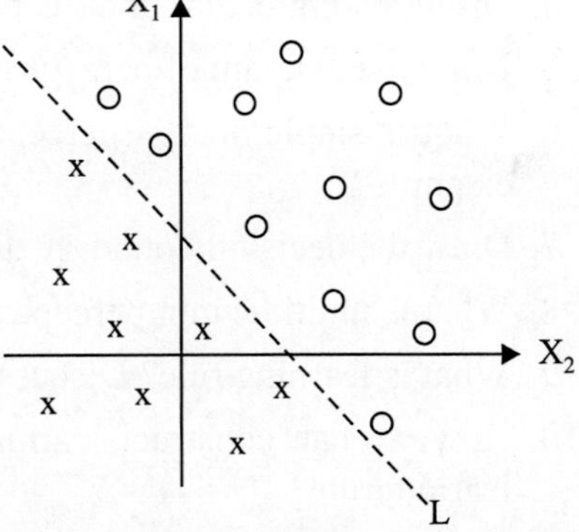

Figure 2.20: Linearly Separable Pattern

The processing unit of a single-layer perceptron network is able to categorize a set of patterns into two classes as the linear threshold function defines their linear separability. Conversely, the two classes *must* be linearly separable in order for the perceptron network to function correctly. Indeed, this is the main limitation of a single-layer perceptron network.

The most classic example of linearly inseparable pattern is a logical exclusive-OR (XOR) function. Shown in figure 2.21 is the illustration of XOR function that two classes, 0 for black dot and 1 for white dot, cannot be separated with a single line. The solution seems that patterns of (X_1, X_2) can be logically classified with two lines L_1 andL_2 .

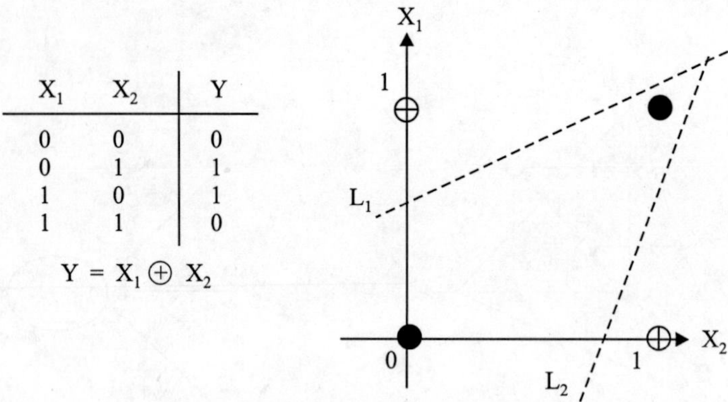

X_1	X_2	Y
0	0	0
0	1	1
1	0	1
1	1	0

$Y = X_1 \oplus X_2$

Figure 2.21: Exclusive-OR function

EXERCISES

1. What is perceptron?
2. Explain the concept of perceptron neuron model with the help of diagram?
3. What is decision boundary? Explain with the help of example?
4. Discuss architecture of perceptron with the help of diagram?
5. Draw the diagram of perceptron net4work and explain its working?
6. What is single neuron perceptron? Explain with the help of two input/output perceptron example?
7. Draw the decision boundary diagram for two input perceptron and also explain it?
8. What is multi neuron perceptron?
9. What is learning rule? Discuss the perceptron learning rule with the help of test problem?
10. How we can construct learning rules for perceptron network? Explain one example of learningrule?
11. How we can train a network? Explain the perceptron training with the help of example?
12. What are the limitations of perceptron network?
13. Explain the convergence theorem of perceptron learning rule?

14. Explain the model of multi layer perceptron neural network with the help of the labeled diagram?
15. Explain the architecture level of multi layer perceptron?
16. Write various steps used for training multi layer perceptron network?
17. What is linear separability? Explain the linearly separable classes with the help of examples?
18. How we can say AND function is linear separable?
19. What is separating plane? Explain with the help of the example?
20. Explain the XOR problem with the help of linear separability?

CHAPTER 3

Backpropagation

3.1 INTRODUCTION

There are many potential computer applications that are difficult to implement because there are many problems unsuited to solution by sequential process. Applications that must perform some complex data translation, yet have no predefined mapping function to describe the translation process, or those that must provide a "best guess" as output when presented with noisy input data are but two examples of problems of this type. An ANS that we have found to be useful in addressing problems requiring recognition of complex patterns and performing nontrivial mapping functions is the backpropagation network (BPN), formalized first by Werbos , and later by Parker and by Rummelhart and McClelland. This network, illustrated generically in Figure 3.1, is designed to operate as a multilayer, feedforward network, using the supervised mode of learning. The chapter begins with a discussion of an example of a problem mapping character image to ASCII, which appears simple, but can quickly overwhelm traditional approaches. Then, we look at how the backpropagation network operates to solve such a problem. Following that discussion is a detailed derivation of the equations that govern the learning process in the backpropagation network.

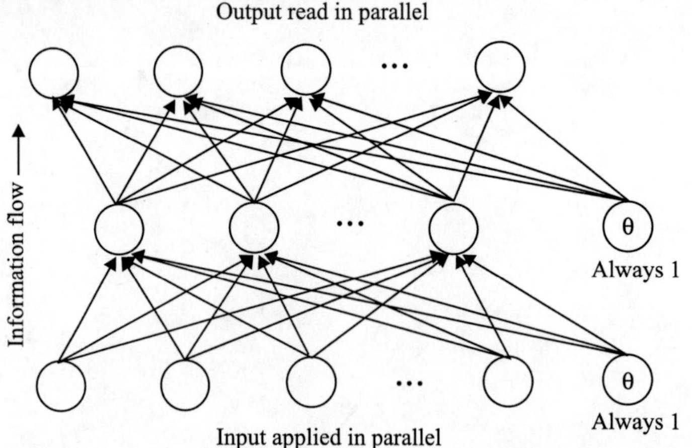

Figure 3.1: The general backpropagation network architecture is shown.

3.2 THE BACKPROPAGATION NETWORK

To illustrate some problems that often arise when we are attempting to automate complex pattern-recognition applications, let us consider the design of a computer program that must translate a 5 × 7 matrix of binary numbers representing the bit-mapped pixel image of an alphanumeric character to its equivalent eight-bit ASCII code. This basic problem, pictured in Figure 3.2, appears to be relatively trivial at first glance. Since there is no obvious mathematical function that will perform the desired translation, and because it would undoubtedly take too much time (both human and computer time) to perform a pixel-by-pixel correlation, the best algorithmic solution would be to use a lookup table.

The lookup table needed to solve this problem would be a one-dimensional linear array of ordered pairs, each taking the form:

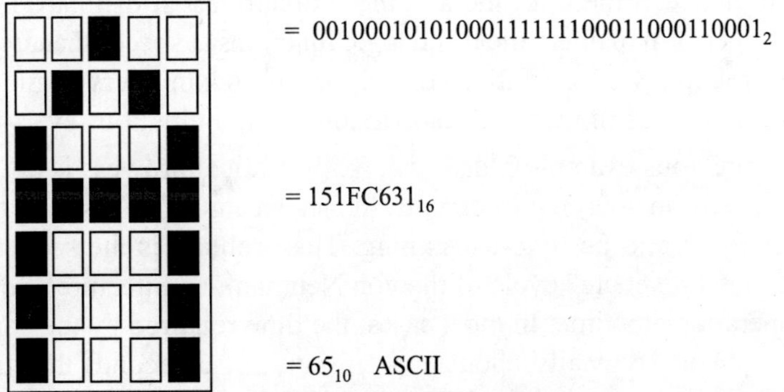

Figure 3.2: Each character image is mapped to its corresponding ASCII code.

The first is the numeric equivalent of the bit-pattern code, which we generate by moving the system rows of the matrix to a single row and considering the result to be a 35-bit binary number. The second is the ASCII code associated with the character. The array would contain exactly the same number of ordered-pairs as there were characters to convert. The algorithm needed to perform the conversion process would take the following form.

Although the lookup-table approach is reasonability fast and easy to maintain, there are many situations that occur in real systems that cannot be handled by this method. For example, consider the dame pixel-image-to-ASCII conversion process in a more realistic environment. Let's suppose that our character image scanner alters a random pixel in the input image matrix due to noise when the image was read. This single pixel error would cause the lookup algorithm to return either a null or the wrong ASCII code, since the match between the input pattern and the target pattern must be exact.

Now consider the amount of additional software (and, hence, CPU time) that must be added to the lookup-table algorithm to improve the ability of the computer to "guess" at which character the noisy image should have been. Single-bit errors are fairly easy to find and correct. Multibit errors become increasingly difficult as the number of bit errors grows. To complicate matters even further, how could our software compensate for noise on the image if that noise happened to make an "O" look like a "Q", or an "E" look like an "F"? If our character-conversion system had to produce an accurate output all the time, an inordinate amount of CPU time would be spent eliminating noise form the from the input pattern prior to attempting to translate it to ASCII.

One solution to this dilemma is to take advantage of parallel nature of neural networks to reduce the time required by a sequential processor to perform the mapping. In addition, system-development time can be reduced because the network can learn the proper algorithm without having someone deduce that algorithm in advance.

3.3 THE BACKPROPAGATION APPROACH

Problem such as the noisy image-to-ASCII example are difficult to solve by computer due to the basic incompatibility between the machine and the problem. Most of today's computer systems have been designed to perform mathematical and logic functions at speeds that are incomprehensible to humans. Even the relatively unsophisticated desktop microcomputers commonplace today can perform hundreds of thousands of numeric comparisons or combinations every second.

However, as our previous example illustrated, mathematical prowess is not what is needed to recognize complex patterns in noisy environments. In fact, an algorithmic search of even a relatively small input space can prove to be time-consuming. The problem is the sequential nature of the computer itself; the "fetch-execute" cycle of the von Neumann architecture allows the machine to perform only one operation at a time. In most cases, the time required by the computer to perform each instruction is so short (typically about one-millionth of a second) that the aggregate time required for even a large program is insignificant to the human users. However, for applications that must search through a large input space, or attempt to correlate all possible permutations of a complex pattern, the time required by even a very fast machine can quickly become intolerable.

What we need is a new processing system that can examine all the pixels in the image in parallel. Ideally, such a system would not have to be programmed explicitly; rather, it would adapt itself to "learn" the relationship between a set of example patterns, and would be able to apply the same relationship to new input patterns. This system would be able to focus on the features of an arbitrary input that resemble other patterns seen previously, such as those pixels in the noisy image that "look" like a known character, and to ignore the noise. Fortunately, such a system exists: we call this system the backpropagation network (BPN).

3.3.1 BPN Operation

We will cover the details of the mechanics of backpropagation. A summary description of the network operation is appropriate here, to begin with, the network learns a predefined se of input-output example pairs by using a two-phase propagate-adapt cycle. After an input pattern has been applied as a stimulus to the first later of network units, it is propagated through each upper layer until an output is generated. This output pattern is then compared to the desired output, and an error signal is computed for each output unit.

The error signals are then transmitted backward from the output layer to each node in the intermediate layer that contributes directly to the output. However, each unit in the intermediate layer receives only a portion of the total error signal, based roughly on the relative contribution the unit made to the original output. This process repeats, layer by layer, until each node in the network has received an error signal that describes its relative contribution to the total error. Based on the error signal received, connection weights are then updated by each unit ti cause the network to converge toward a state that allows all the training patterns to be encoded.

The significance of this process is that, as the network trains, the nodes in the intermediate layers organize themselves such that different nodes learn to recognize different features of the total input space. After training, when presented with an arbitrary input pattern that is noisy or incomplete, the units in the hidden layers of the network will respond with an active output if the new input contains a pattern that resembles the feature the individual units learned to recognize during training. Conversely, hidden-layer units have a tendency to inhibit their outputs if the input pattern does not contain the feature that they were trained to recognize.

As the signals propagate through the different layers in the network, the activity pattern present at each upper layer can be thought of as a pattern with features that can be recognized by units in the subsequent layer. The output pattern generated can be thought of as a feature map that presence of many different feature combinations at the input. The total effect of this behavior is that the BPN provides an effective means of allowing a computer system examine data patterns that may be incomplete or noisy, and to recognize subtle patterns from the partial input.

Several researchers have shown that during training, BPNs tend to develop internal relationships between nodes so as to organize the training data into classes of patterns. This tendency can be extrapolated to the hypothesis that all hidden-layer units BPN are somehow associated with specific features of the input pattern as a result of training. Exactly what the association is may or may not be evident to the human observer. What is important is that the network has found an internal representation that enables it to generate the desired outputs when given the training inputs. This same internal representation can be applied to inputs that were not used during training. The BPN will classify these previously unseen inputs according to the features they share with the training examples.

3.4 ARCHITECTURE OF BACKPROPAGATION

A multilayer neural network with one layer of hidden units (the Z units) is shown in figure 6.1. The output units (the Y units) and the hidden units also may have biases (as shown). The bias on a typical output unit Y_k is denoted by z_{ok}; the bias on a typical hidden unit Z_j is denoted v_{0j}. These bias terms act like weights on connections from units whose output is always 1. (These units are shown in figure 6.1 but are usually not displayed explicitly.) Only the direction of information flow for the feedforward phase of operation is shown. During the backpropagation phase of learning, signals are sent in the reverse direction.

The algorithm in Section 3.4.1 is presented for one hidden layer, which is adequate for a large number of applications.

3.4.1 Algorithm

As mentioned earlier, training a network by backpropagation involves three stages: the feeedforward of the input training pattern, the backpropagaiton of the associated error, and the adjustment of the weights.

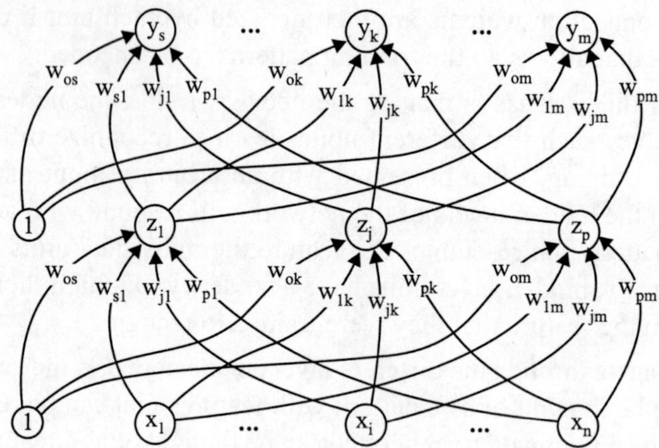

Figure 3.3: Backpropagation neural network with one hidden layer.

During feedforward, each input unit (X_i) receives an input signal and broadcasts this signal to the each of the hidden units Z_1,.....Z_p. Each hidden unit then computes its activation and sends its signal (z_j) to each output unit. Each output unit (Y_k) computes its activation (y_k) to form the response of the net for the given input pattern.

During training, each output unit compares its computed activation y_k with its target value t_k to determine the associated error for that pattern with that unit. Based on this error, the factor $á_k$ (k = 1,..., m) is computed. A_k is used to distribute the error at output unit Y_k back to all units in the previous layer (the hidden units that are connected to Y_k). It is also used (later) to update the weights between the output and the hidden layer. In a similar manner, the factor á, (j = 1, ... ,p) is computed for each hidden unit Z_j. It is not necessary to propagate the error back to the input layer, but $á_j$ is used to update the weights between the hidden layer and the input layer.

After all of the á factors have been determined, the weights for all layers are adjusted simultaneously. The adjustment to the weight w_{jk} (from hidden unit Z_j to output unit Y_k) is based on the factor $á_k$ and the activation z_j of the hidden unit Z_j. The adjustment to the weight v_{ij} (from input unit x_i to hidden unit Z_j) is based on the factor á, and the activation x_i of the input unit.

Nomenclature

The nomenclature we use in the training algorithm for the backpropagation net is as follows:

x Input training vector:

$x = (x_1, \ldots, x_i, \ldots, x_n)$

t Output target vector:

$t = (t_1, \ldots, t_k, \ldots, t_m)$.

σ_k Portion of error correction weight adjustment for w_{jk} that is due to an error at output unit Y_k; also, the information about the error at unit Y_k that is propagated back to the hidden units that feed into unit Y_k.

σ_j Portion of error correction weight adjustment for v_{ij} that is due to the backpropagation of error information from the output layer to hidden unit Z_j.

α Learning rate.

X_i Input unit i;

For an input unit, the input signal and output signal are the same, namely, x_i.

v_{oj} Bias on hidden unit j.

Z_j Hidden unit j:

The net input to Z_j is denoted z_in_j:

$$z\_in_j = V_{oj} \quad \underset{i}{} X_i V_{ij} .$$

The output signal (activation) of Z_j is denoted z_j:

$z_j = f(z\_in)$.

w_{ok} Bias on output unit k.

Y_k Output unit k:

The net input to Y_k is denoted y_in_k:

$$y\_in_k = w_{ok} \quad \underset{i}{} z_j w_{jk} ..$$

The output signal (activation) of Y_k is denoted y_k:

$y_k = f(y\_in_k)$.

Activation Function

An activation function for a backpropagation net should have several important characteristics: It should be continuous, differentiable, and monotonically nondecreasing. Furthermore, for computational efficiency, it is desirable that its deriavative be easy to compute. For the most commonly used activation functions, the value of the derivative (at a particular value of the independent variable) can be expressed in terms of the value of the function (at that value of the independent variable). Usually, the function is expected to saturate, i.e., approach finite maximum and minimum values asymptotically.

One of the most typical activation functions is the binary sigmoid function, which has range of (0, 1) and is defined as

$$f_1(x) = \frac{1}{1 \quad \exp(\quad x)}$$

with

$$f_1(x) = f_1(x) = f_1(x)[1 - d_1(x)].$$

This function is illustrated in Figure 3.4.

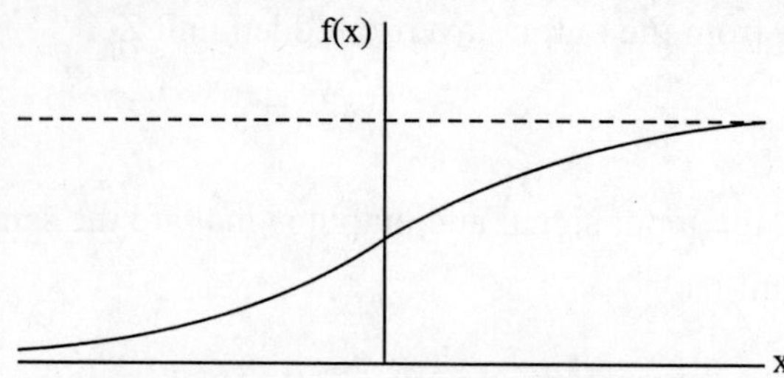

Figure 3.4: Binary sigmoid range (0, 1).

Another common activation function is bipolar sigmoid, which has range of (-1, 1) and is defined as

$$f_2(x) = \frac{2}{1 \quad \exp(\ x)}$$

with

$$f_2(x) = \frac{1}{2}[1 + f_2(x)][1 - f_2(x)].$$

This function is illustrated in Figure 6.3 Note that the bipolar sigmoid function a closely related to the function

$$\tanh(x) \ v_{oj} + \sum_{i \ 1}^{b} x_i v_{ij}$$

Figure 3.5: Bipolar sigmoid, range (–1, 1).

Training Algorithm

Either of the activation functions defined in the previous section can be used in the standard backpropagation algorithm given here. The form of the date 9especially the target values) is an important factor is choosing the appropriate function. The relevant considerations are discussed further in the next section. Other suitable activation functions are given in chapter 1 . Note that because of the simple relationship between the value of the function and its derivative, no additional evaluations of the exponential are required to compute the derivatives needed during the backpropagation phase of the algorithm.

The algorithm is as follows:

Step 1: Initialize Weights.

(Set to small random values).

Step 2: While stopping condition is false, do Steps 3-10.

Step 3: For each training pair, do Steps 4-9.

Feedforward:

Step 4: Each unit (X_i, i = 1,..., n) receives input signal x_i and broadcasts this signal to all units in the layer above (the hidden units).

Step 5: Each hidden unit (Z_j, j = 1,..., p) sums its weighted input signals.

$$z\_in_j = v_{oj} + \sum_{i=1}^{b} x_i v_{ij}$$

applies its activation function to compute its output signal.

$$z_j = f(z\_in_j).$$

and sends this signal to all units in the layer above (output units).

Step 6: Each output unit (Y, k = 1,..., m) sums its weighted input signals.

$$y\_in_k = w_{ok} + \sum_{j=1}^{p} z_i w_{ij}$$

and applies its activation function to compute its output signal.

$$y_k = f(y\_in_k).$$

Backpropagation of error:

Step 7: each output unit (Y_k, k = 1,..., m) receives a target pattern corresponding to the input training pattern, computes its error information term.

$$\delta_k = (t_k - y_k)\, f'(y\_in_k),$$

calculate its weight correction term (used to update w_{jk} later).

$$\Delta w_{jk} = \alpha \ddot{a}_k z_j.$$

calculates its bias correction term (used to update w_{ok} later).

$$\Delta w_{ok} = \alpha \delta_k,$$

and sends δ_k to units in the layer below.

Step 8: Each hidden unit (Z_j, j = 1,.../ p) sums its delta inputs (from units in the layer above).

$$\delta\_in_j = \sum_{i=1}^{m} {}_k w_{jk}$$

multiplies by the derivative of its activation function to calculate its error information term.

$$\Delta_j = \delta\_in_j\, f'(z\_in_j),$$

calculates its weight correction term (used to update v_{ij} later),

$$\Delta v_{ij} = \alpha\delta_k x_i,$$

and calculates its bias correction term (used to update v_{oj} = later),

$$\Delta v_{oj} = \text{áä}_{j.}$$

Update weights and biases:

Step 9: Each output unit (Y_k, k = 1,…, m) updates its bias and weights (j = 0, …, p):

$$w_{jk}(\text{new}) = w_{jk}(\text{old}) + \Delta w_{jk},$$

Each hidden unit (Z_j, j = 1,…., p) updates its bias and weights (i = 0,…, n):

$$v_{ij(\text{new})} = v_{ij}(\text{old}) + \Delta v_{ij}.$$

Step 10: Test stopping condition.

3.5 USING BAKPROPAGATION

The perception learning rule of Frank Rosenblatt and the LMS algorithm of Bernard Windrow and Marcian Hoff were to train single-layer perceptron-like networks. As we have discussed in previous chapters, these single-layer networks suffer from the disadvantage that they are only able to solve linearly separable classification problems. Both Rosenblatt and Widrow were aware of these limitations and proposed multilayer networks that could overcome them, but they were not able to generalize their algorithms to train these more powerful networks.

Apparently the first description of an algorithm to train multilayer networks was contained in the thesis of Paul Verbose in 1974. This thesis presented the algorithm in the context of general networks, with neural networks as a special case, and was not disseminated in the neural network community, It was not until the mid 1980s that the back propagation algorithm was rediscovered and widely publicized. It was rediscovered independently by David Rumelhart, Geoffrey Hinton and Ronald Williams, David Parker, and Yawn Le Cun . The algorithm was popularized by its inclusion in the book parallet Distributed Processing, which described the work of the Parallel Distributed processing Group led by psychologists David Rumelhart and James McClelland. The publication of this book soured a torrent of research in neural networks. The multilayer perception, trained by the back propagation algorithm, is currently the most widely used neural network.

In this chapter we will first investigate the capabilities of multilayer networks and then present the back propagation algorithm.

3.6 MULTILAYER PERCEPTRONS

We first introduced the notation for multilayer networks in Chapter 2. For ease of reference we have reproduced the diagram of the three-layer perception in Figure 3.6. Note that we have simply cascaded three perception networks, The output of the first network is the input to the second network, and the output of the second network is the input to the third network Each layer may have a different number of neurons, and even a different transfer function .Recall from Chapter 2 that we are using Superscripts to identify the layer number, Thus, the weight matrix for the first layer is written as W^1 and the weight matrix for the second layer is written W^2. To identify the structure of a multilayer network, we will sometimes use the following shorthand notation, where the number of input is followed by the number of neurons in each layer:

$$R - S^1 - S^2 - S^3 \tag{3.1}$$

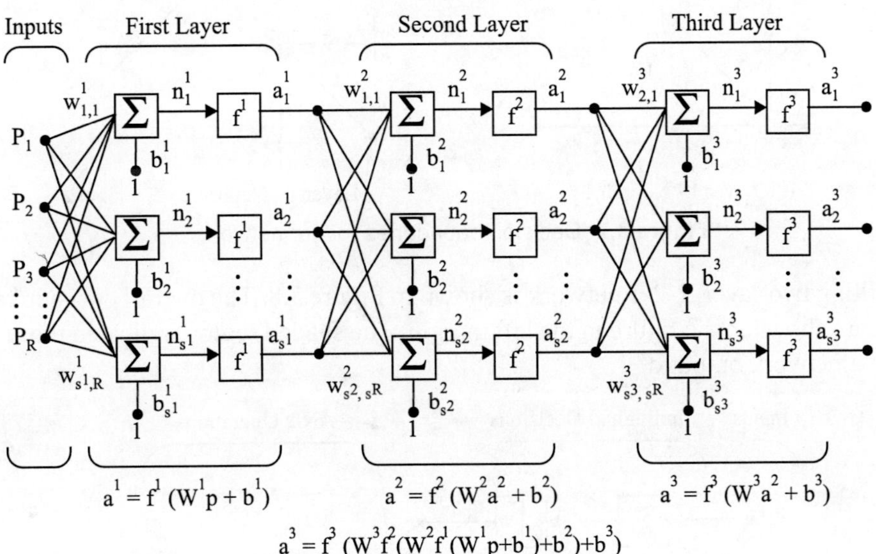

Figure 3.6: Three-layer network

Let's now investigate the capabilities of these multilayer perception networks. First we will look at the use of multilayer networks for pattern classification, and then we will discuss their application to function approximation.

3.6.1 Pattern Classification

To illustrate the capabilities of the multilayer perceptron for pattern classification, consider the classic exclusive-or (XOR) problem. The input/target pairs for the XOR gate are

$$P_1 = \begin{matrix} 0 \\ 0 \end{matrix}, t_1 = 0 \quad P_2 = \begin{matrix} 0 \\ 1 \end{matrix}, t_2 = 1 \quad P_3 = \begin{matrix} 1 \\ 0 \end{matrix}, t_3 = 0 \quad P_4 = \begin{matrix} 1 \\ 1 \end{matrix}, t_4 = 0$$

This problem, which is illustrated graphically in the figure to the left, was used by Minsky and Papert in 1969 to demonstrate the limitations of the single-layer perceptron. Because the two categories are not linearly separable, a single-layer perceptron cannot perform the classification. A two-layer network can solve the XOR problem. In fact, there are many different multilayer solutions. One solution is to use two neurons in the first layer to create two p decision boundaries. The first boundary separates p_1 from the other patterns, and the second boundary separates p_4. Then the second layer is used to combine the two boundaries together using an AND operation. The decision boundaries for each first-layer neuron are shown in Figure 3.7.

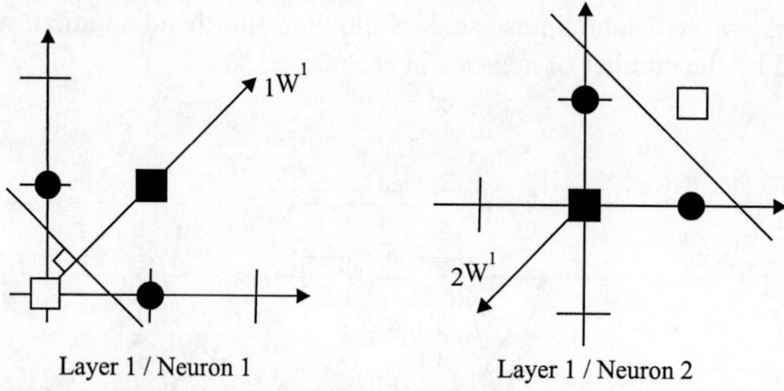

Figure 3.7: Decision boundaries for xor network

The resulting two-layer, 2-2-1 network is shown in Figure 3.8. The overall decision regions for this network are shown in the figure in the left margin. The shaded region indicated those input that will produce a network output of 1.

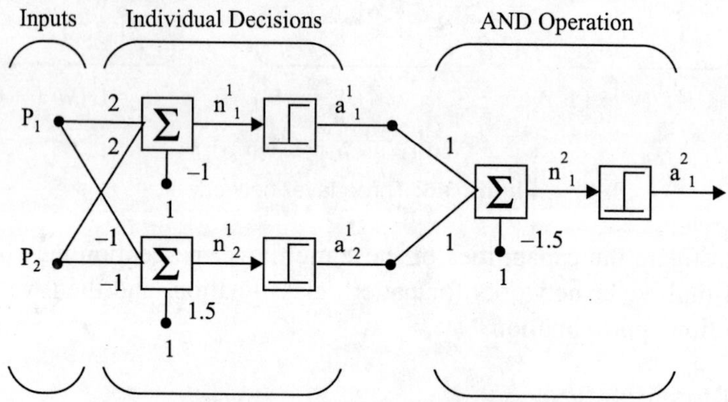

Figure 3.8: Two-layer XOR network

3.6.2 Function Approximation

Up to this point in text we have viewed neural networks mainly in the in the context of pattern classification. It is also instructive to view networks as function approximates. In control systems, for example, the objective is to find an appropriate feedback function that maps from measured outputs to control inputs. In adaptive filtering (Chapter 4) the objective is to find a function that maps from delayed values of an input single to an appropriate output single. The following example will illustrate the flexibility of the multilayer perceptron for implementing functions.Consider the two-layer, 1-2-1 network shown in figure 3.9. For this example the transfer function for the first layer is log-sigmoid and the transfer function for the second layer is linear. In other words.

$$f^1(n) = \frac{1}{1 \quad e^{-n}} \text{ and } f^2(n) = n. \quad (3.2)$$

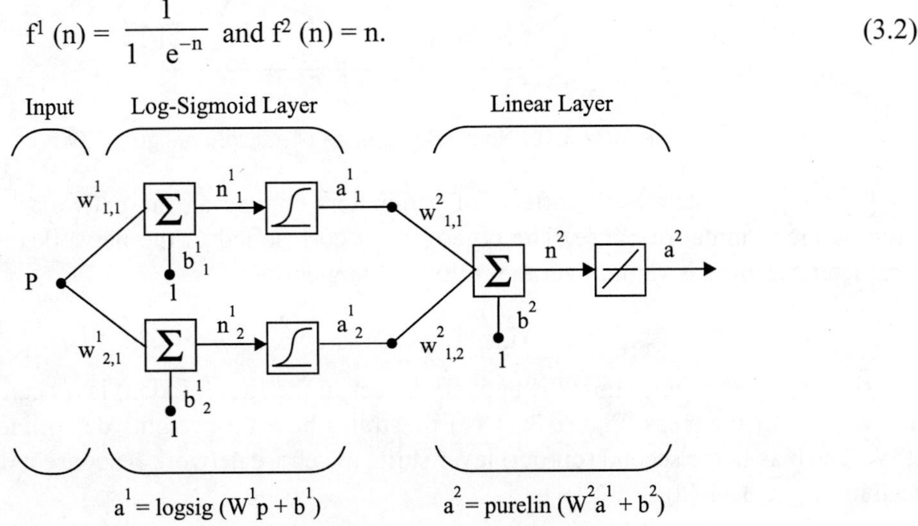

Figure 3.9: Example function approximation network

Suppose that the nominal values of the weight and biases for this network are

$$w^1_{1.1} = 10, w^1_{2.1} = 10, b^1_1 = -10, b^1_2 = 10,$$

$$w^2_{1,1} = 1, w^2_{1.2} = 2, b^2 = 0$$

The network response for these parameters is shown in Figure 3.10, which plots the network output a as the input p is varied over the range [–2, 2]. Notice that the response consists of two steps, one for each of the log-sigmoid neurons in the first layer. By adjusting the network parameters we can change the shape and location of each step, as we will see in the following discussion.

The centers of the steps occur where the net input to a neuron in the first layer is zero:

$$n^1_1 = w^1_{1,1}\,p + b^1_1 = 0 \quad p = -\frac{b^1_1}{w^1_{1,1}} = \frac{-10}{10} = 1, \quad (3.3)$$

$$n^1_2 = w^1_{1,2}\,p + b^1_2 = 0 \quad p = -\frac{b^1_2}{w^1_{1,2}} = \frac{-10}{10} = 1, \quad (3.4)$$

The steepness of each step can be adjusted by changing the network weight.

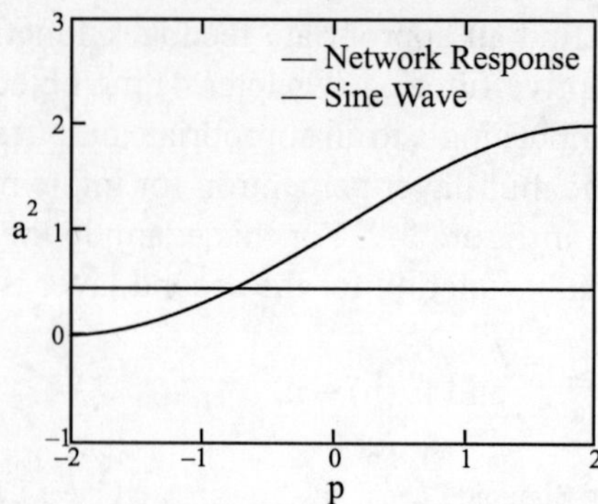

Figure 3.10: Nominal response of network of figure 3.6

Figure 3.10 illustrates the effects of parameters change on the network response. The blue curve is the nominal response. The other curves correspond to the network response when one parameter at a time is varied over the following ranges:

$$-1 \quad w_{1,1}^2 \quad 1, -1 \quad w_{1,2}^2 \quad b_2^1 \quad 20, -1 \quad b^2 \quad 1. \tag{3.5}$$

Figure 3.11 (a) shows how the network biases in the first (hidden) layer can be used to locate the position of the steps. Figure 3.11 (b) illustrates how the weights determine the slope of the steps. The bias in the second (output) layer shifts the entire network response u or down, as can be seen in Figure 3.11 (d).

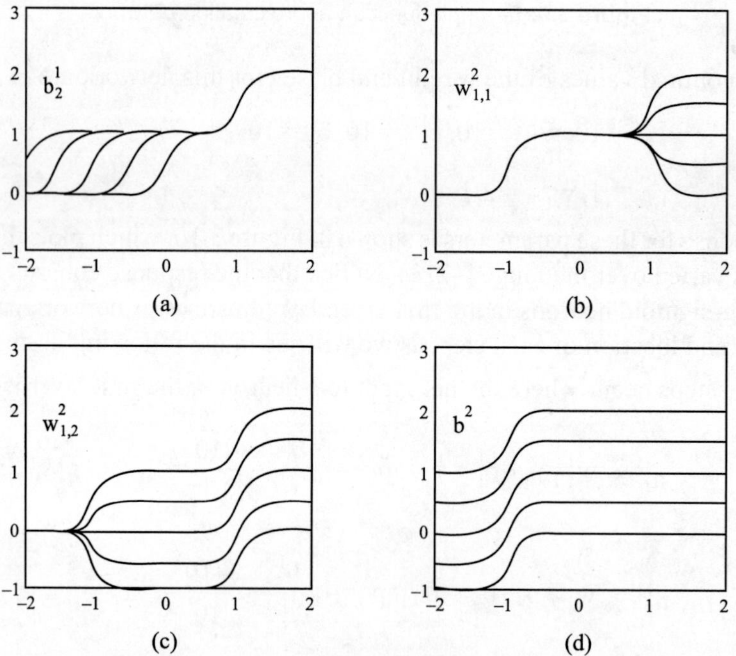

Figure 3.11: Effect of parameter changes on network response

From this example we can see how flexible the multilayer network is. It would appear that we could use such networks to approximate almost any function, if we had a sufficient number of neurons in the hidden layer. In fact, it has been shown that two-layer networks, with sigmoid transfer functions in the hidden layer and linear transfer functions in the output layer, can approximate virtually any function of interest to any degree of accuracy, provided sufficiently many hidden units are available .

Now that we have some idea of the power of multilayer perceptron networks for pattern recognition and function approximation, then next step is to develop an algorithm to train such networks.

3.7 THE BACKPROPAGATION ALGORITHM

It will simplify our development of the backpropagation algorithm if we use the abbreviated notation for the multilayer network, which we introduced in Chapter 2. The three-layer network in abbreviated notation is shown in Figure 3.12.

As we discussed earlier, for multilayer networks the output of one layer becomes the input to the following layer. The equations that describe this operation are

$$a^{m+1} = f^{m+1}(W^{m+1} a^m + b^{m+1}) \text{ for } m = 0, 1, \ldots, M-1 \tag{3.6}$$

where M is the number of layers in the network. The neurons in the first layer revive external inputs:

$$a^0 = p, \tag{3.7}$$

which provides the starting point for Eq. (3.6). The outputs of the neurons in the last layer are considered the network outputs:

$$a = a^M \tag{3.8}$$

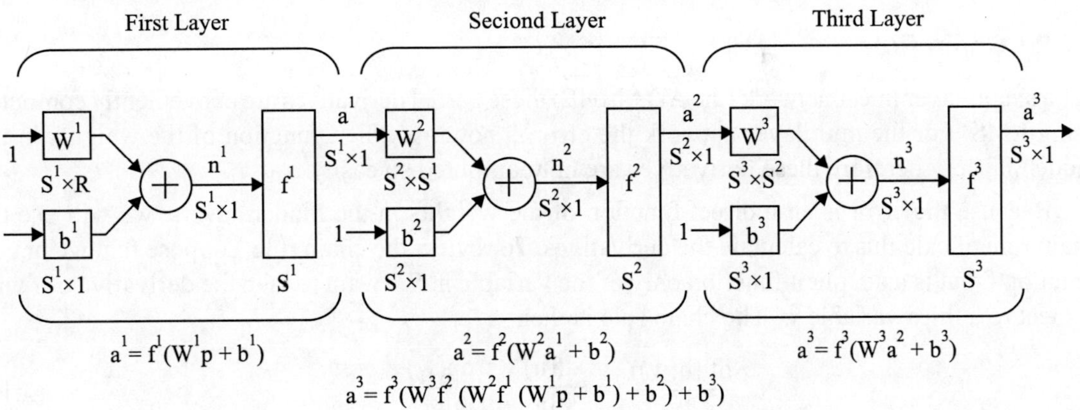

Figure 3.12: Three-layer network abbreviated notation

3.7.1 Performance Index

The backporpagation algorithm for multilayer networks is a generalization of the LMS algorithm of Chapter 4, and both algorithms use the same performance index: mean square error. The algorithm is provided with a set of examples of proper network behavior:

$$\{p_1, t_1\}, \{p_2, t_2\}, \ldots\ldots, \{p_Q, t_Q\}, \tag{3.9}$$

where p_q is an input to the network, and t_q is the corresponding target output. As each input is applied to the network, the network output is compared to the target. The algorithm should adjust the network parameters in order to minimize the mean square error:

$$F(x) = E[e^2] = E[(t - a)^2] \tag{3.10}$$

Where x is the vector of network weights and biases (as in Chapter 4). If the network has multiple outputs this generalizes to

$$F(x) = E[e^T e] = E[(t - a)^T (t - a)] \tag{3.11}$$

As with the LMS algorithm, we will approximate the mean square error by

$$F(x) = (t(k) - a(k))^T (t(k) - a(k)) = e^T(k)\, e(k), \tag{3.12}$$

where the expectation of the squared error has replaced by the squared error at iteration k.

The steepest descent algorithm for the approximate mean square error is

$$w^m_{i,j}(k+1) = w^m_{i,j}(k) - \frac{F}{w^m_{i,j}}, \tag{3.13}$$

$$b^m_i(k+1) = b^m_i(k) - \frac{F}{b^m_i}, \tag{3.14}$$

where α is the learning rate.

So far, this development is identical to that for the LMS algorithm. Now we come to the difficult part – the computation of the partial derivatives.

3.7.2 Chain Rule

For a single-layer linear network (the ADALINE) these partial derivatives are conveniently computed using LMS. For the multilayer network the error is not an explicit function of the weights in the hidden layers, therefore these derivatives are not computed so easily.

Because the error is an indirect function of the weights in the hidden layers, we will use the chain rule of calculus to calculate the derivatives. To review the chain rule, suppose that we have a function f that is an explicit function only of the variable n. We want to take the derivative of f with respect to a third variable w. The chain rule is then:

$$\frac{df(n(w))}{dw} = \frac{df(n)}{dw} \quad \frac{dn(w)}{dw} \tag{3.15}$$

For example, if

$f(n) = e^n$ and $n = 2w$, so that $f(n(w)) = e^2$ (3.16)

then

$$\frac{df\,(n(w))}{dw} = \frac{df(n)}{dw} \quad \frac{dn(w)}{dw}(e^n)(2) \qquad (3.17)$$

We will use this concept to find the derivatives in Eq. (3.13) and Eq. (3.14):

$$\frac{F}{w^m_{i,j}} = \frac{F}{n^m_i} \quad \frac{{}^{m}_{i}}{w^m_{i,j}} \qquad (3.18)$$

$$\frac{F}{b^m_i} = \frac{F}{n^m_i} \quad \frac{{}^{m}_{i}}{b^m_i} \qquad (3.19)$$

The second term in each of these equations can be easily computed, since the net input to layer m is an explicit function of the weights and bias in that layer:

$$n^m_i = \mathop{\quad}_{j\;1}^{S^{m\;1}} w^m_i \, a^{m\;1}_j \quad b^m_i \qquad (3.20)$$

Therefore

$$\frac{n^m_i}{w^m_{i,j}} = a^{m-1}_j, \frac{n^m_i}{b^m_i} = 1 \qquad (3.21)$$

If we now define

$$s^m_i \equiv \frac{F}{n^m_i} \qquad (3.22)$$

(the sensitivity of F to changes in the ith element of the net input at layer m), then Eq. (3.18) and Eq. (3.19) can be simplified to

$$\frac{F}{w^m_{ij}} = s_i^{m-1} a_j^{m-1}, \qquad (3.23)$$

$$\frac{F}{b^m_i} = s_i^m \qquad (3.24)$$

We can now express the approximate steepest descent algorithm as

$$w^m_{i,j}(k+1) = w^m_{i,j}(k) - \quad s^m_i \, a^{m-1}_j \qquad (3.25)$$

$$b^m_i(k+1) = b^m_i(k) - a\,s^m_i, \qquad (3.26)$$

In matrix form this becomes:

$$W^m(k+1) = W^m(k) - \alpha s^m (a^{m-1}) \qquad (3.27)$$

$$b^m(k+1) = b^m(k) - \alpha s^m, \qquad (3.28)$$

where

$$s^m \equiv \partial F = \begin{bmatrix} \frac{F}{n_1^m} \\ \frac{F}{n_2^m} \\ \vdots \\ \frac{F}{n_1^m S^m} \end{bmatrix}$$

SUMMARY

Let's summarize the backpropagation algorithm. The first step is to propagate the input forward through the network:

$$a^0 = p, \tag{3.30}$$

$$a^{m+1} = f^{m+1} (W^{m+1}a^m + b^{m+1}) \text{ for } m = 0, 1,\ldots, M-1, \tag{3.31}$$

$$a = a^M, \tag{3.32}$$

The next step is to propagate the sensitivities backward through the network:

$$s^M = -2F^M (n^M) (t - a), \tag{3.33}$$

$$s^m = F^m (n^m) (W^{m+1})^T s^{m+1}, \text{ for } m = M-1,\ldots, 2, 1. \tag{3.34}$$

Finally, the weights and biases are updated using the approximate steepest descent rule:

$$W^m (k+1) = W^m (k) - \alpha s^m (a^{m-1})^{T,} \tag{3.35}$$

$$b^m (k+1) = b^m (k) - \alpha s^m \tag{3.36}$$

Example: To illustrate the backporpagatin algorithm, let's choose a network and apply it to a particular problem. To begin, we will use the 1-2-1 network that we discussed earlier in this chapter. For convenience we have reproduced the network in Figure 3.13.

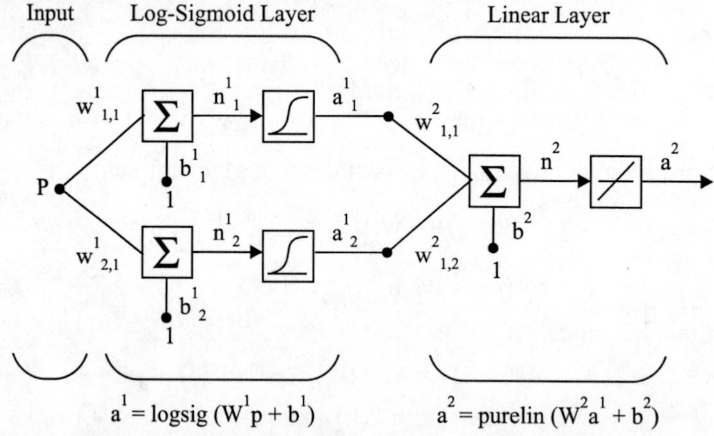

Figure 3.13: Example Function Approximation Network

Next we want to define a problem for the network to solve. Suppose that we want to use the network to approximate the function

$$g(p) = 1 + \sin \frac{}{4} p \quad \text{for } -2 \leq p \leq 2. \tag{3.37}$$

To obtain our training set we willevaluate this function at several values of p.

Before we begin the backpropagation algorithm we need to choose some initial values for the network weights and biases. Generally these are chosen to be small random values. In the next chapter we will discuss some reasons for this. For now let's choose the values.

$$w^1(0) \begin{matrix} -0.27 \\ -0.41 \end{matrix}, b^1(0) = \begin{matrix} -0.48 \\ -0.13 \end{matrix}, W^2(0) = [0.09 - 0.17], b^2(0) = [0.48].$$

The response of the network for these initial values is illustrated in Figure 3.14, along with the sine function we wish to approximate.

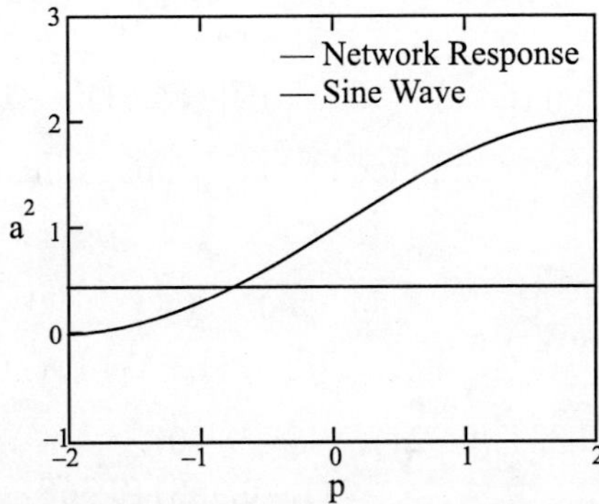

Figure 3.14: Initial Network Response

Now we are ready to start the algorithm. For our initial input we will choose p = 1:

$$a^0 = p = 1$$

The output of the first layer is then

$$a^1 = f^1(W^1a^0 + b^1) = \log\text{sig} \begin{matrix} -0.27 \\ -0.41[1] \end{matrix} + \begin{matrix} -0.48 \\ -0.13 \end{matrix} = \text{logsig} \begin{matrix} -0.75 \\ 0.54 \end{matrix}.$$

$$\begin{matrix} \dfrac{1}{1 \quad e^{0.75}} \\ \dfrac{1}{1 \quad e^{0.54}} \end{matrix} = \begin{matrix} 0321 \\ 0.368 \end{matrix}$$

The second layer output is

$$a^2 = f^2(W^2a^1 + b^2) = \text{purelin}([0.09 - 0.17] = \begin{matrix} 0.321 \\ 0.368 \end{matrix} \quad [0.48] \quad [0.446]$$

The error would then be

$$e = t - a = \{1 + \sin\frac{p}{4}\} - a^2 = \{1 + \sin\frac{1}{4}\} - 0.446 = 1.261.$$

The next stage of the algorithm is to backporpagate the sensitivities. Before we begin the backpropagation, recall that we will need the derivatives of the transfer functions, f^1 (n) and f^2 (n). For the first layer

$$f^1(n) = \frac{d}{dn}\ \frac{1}{1+e^{-n}}\ \frac{e^{-n}}{(1\ \ e^{-n})^2} = 1 - \frac{1}{1+e^{-n}}\ \frac{1}{1+e^{-n}} = (1-a^1)\,(a^1)$$

For the second layer we have

$$f^2(n) = \frac{d(n)}{dn} = 1$$

We can now perform the backpropagation. The starting point is found at the second layer, using Eq. (3.33):

$$s^2 = -2F^2\,(n^2)\,(t - a) = -2\,[f^2(n^2)]\,(1.261) = -2\,[1]\,(1.261) = -2.522.$$

The first layer sensitivity is then computed by backpropagating the sensitivity from the second layer, using Eq. (3.34):

$$s^1 = F^1(n^1)\,(W^2)^T s^2 = \begin{matrix} (1-a_1^1) & (a_1^1) & 0 \\ 0 & (1-a_2^1) & (a_2^1) \end{matrix}\ \begin{matrix} 0.09 & \\ 0.17 & -2.522 \end{matrix}$$

$$= \begin{matrix} (1-0.321)(0.321) & 0 \\ 0 & (1-0.368)\,(0.368) \end{matrix}\ \begin{matrix} 0.09 \\ 0.17 \end{matrix}\ [2.522]$$

$$\begin{matrix} 0.218 & 0 \\ 0 & 0.233 \end{matrix}\ \begin{matrix} 0.227 \\ 0.429 \end{matrix}$$

$$= \begin{matrix} -0.0495 \\ 0.0997 \end{matrix}$$

The final stage of the algorithm is to update the weights. For simplicity, we will use a learning rate $\alpha = 0.1$. (In Chapter 12 the choice of learning rate will be discussed in more detail.) From Eq. (3.35) and Eq. (3.36) we have

$$W^2(1)\ W^2(0) - \alpha s^2(a^1)^T = [0.09 - 0.17]\ -0.1\ [-2.522]\ [0.321\ 0.368]$$
$$= [0.171\ -0.0772],$$

$$b^2(1) = b^2(0) - \alpha s^2 = [0.48]\ -0.1\ [-2.522] = [0.732],$$

$$W^1(1) = W^1(0) - \alpha s^1(a^0)^T = \begin{matrix} -0.27 \\ -0.41 \end{matrix} - 0.1\ \begin{matrix} 0\ .0495\,[1] \\ 0.0997 \end{matrix} = \begin{matrix} -0.265 \\ -0.420 \end{matrix}$$

$$b^1(1) = b^1(0) - \alpha s^1 = \begin{matrix} -0.48 \\ -0.13 \end{matrix}\ 0.1\ \begin{matrix} -0.0495 \\ 0.0997 \end{matrix} = \begin{matrix} -0.475 \\ -0.140 \end{matrix}$$

This completes the first iteration of the backpropagation algorithm. we next proceed to choose another input p and perform another iteration of the algorithm. we continue to iterate unitl the difference between the network response and the target function reaches some acceptable level.

3.8 PRINCIPLES OF TRAINING MULTI-LAYER NEURAL NETWORK USING BACKPROPAGATION

The project describes teaching process of multi-layer neural network employing *backpropagation* algorithm. To illustrate this process the three layer neural network with two inputs and one output,which is shown in the picture below, is used:

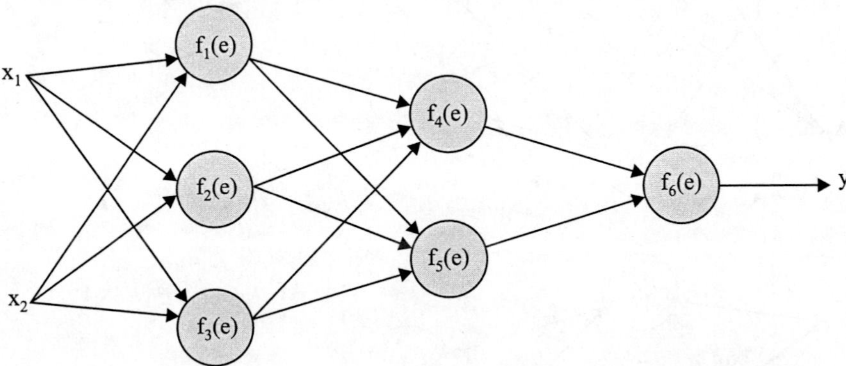

Each neuron is composed of two units. First unit adds products of weights coefficients and input signals. The second unit realise nonlinear function, called neuron activation function. Signal e is adder output signal, and y = f(e) is output signal of nonlinear element. Signal y is also output signal of neuron.

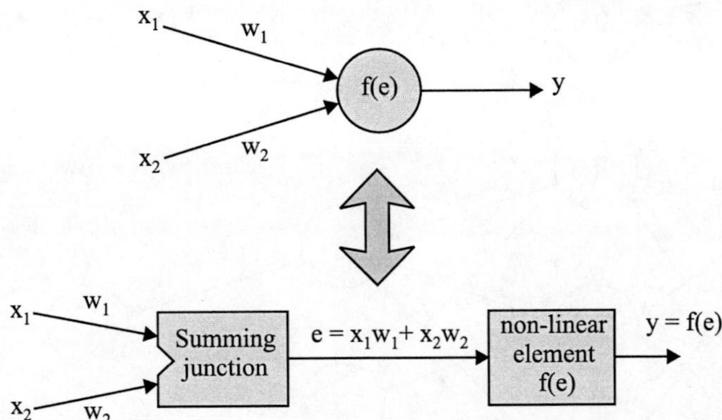

To teach the neural network we need training data set. The training data set consists of input signals (x_1 and x_2) assigned with corresponding target (desired output) z. The network training is an iterative process. In each iteration weights coefficients of nodes are modified using new data from training data set. Modification is calculated using algorithm described below: Each teaching step starts with forcing both input signals from training set. After this stage we can determine output signals values for each neuron in each network layer. Pictures below illustrate how signal is propagating through the network, Symbols $w_{(xm)n}$ represent weights of connections between network input x_m and neuron n in input layer. Symbols y_n represents output signal of neuron n.

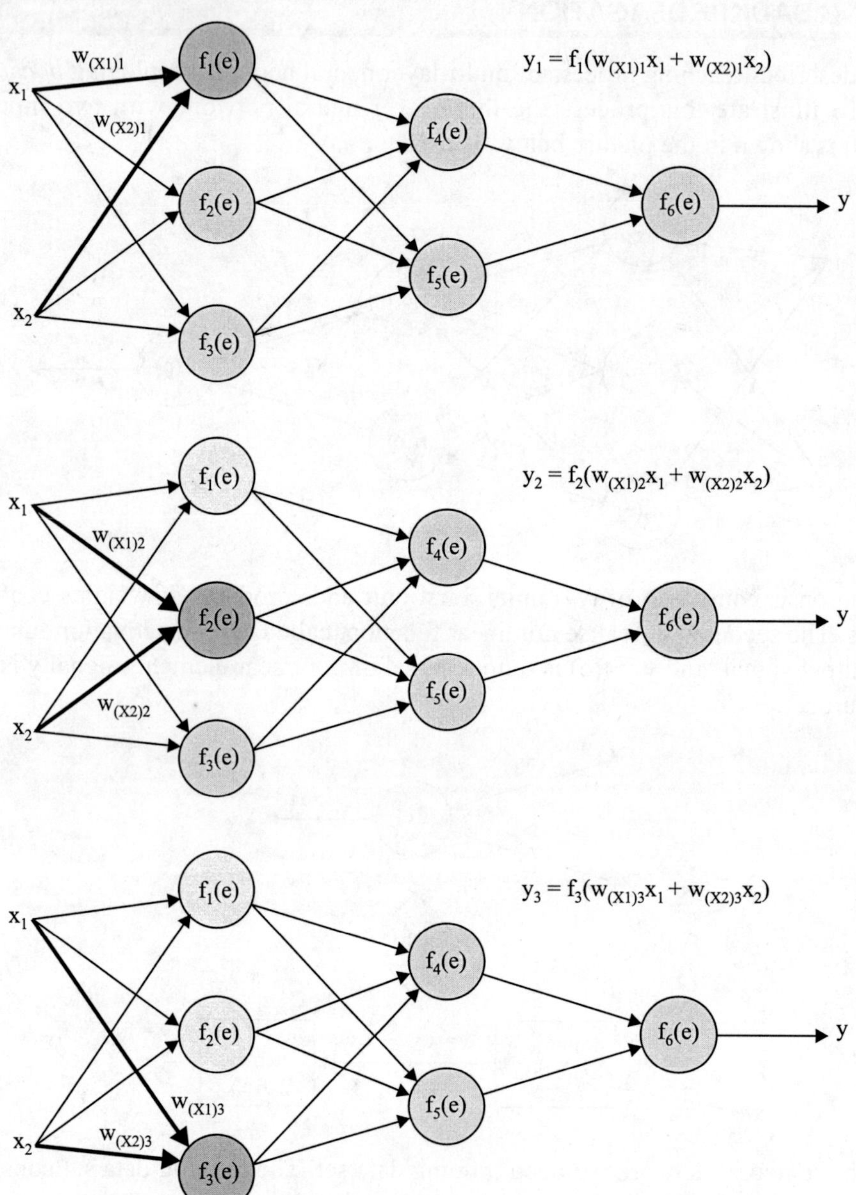

Propagation of signals through the hidden layer. Symbols w_{mn} represent weights of connections between output of neuron m and input of neuron n in the next layer.

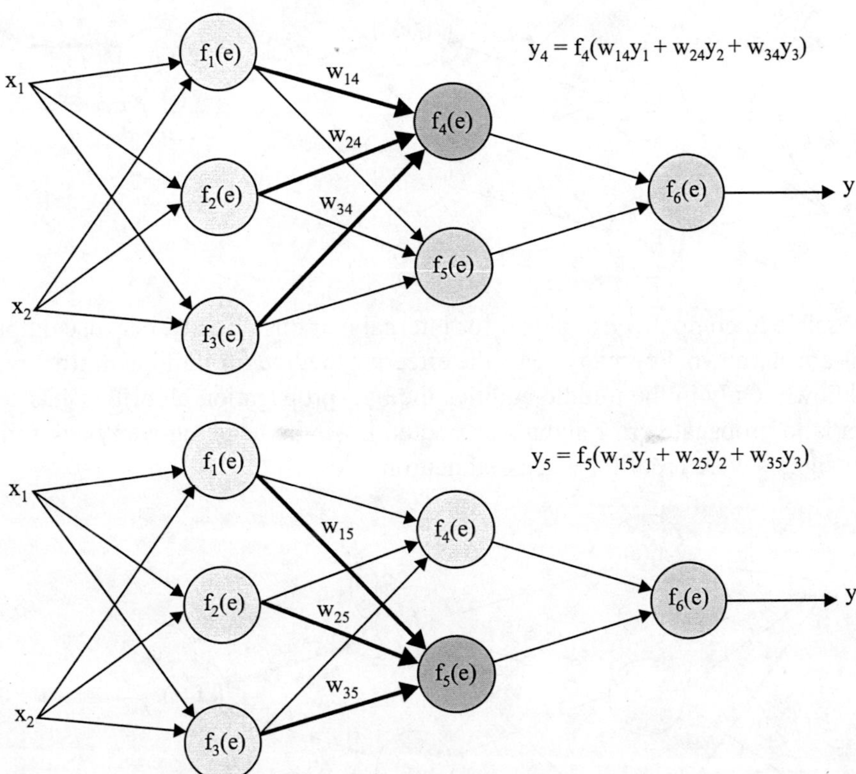

Propagation of signals through the output layer.

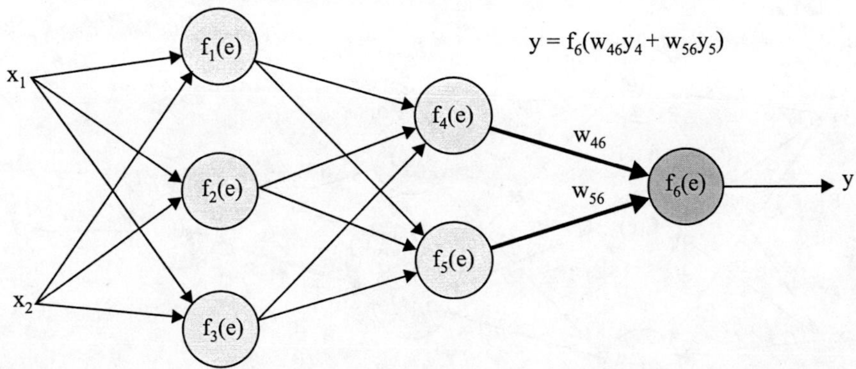

In the next algorithm step the output signal of the network y is compared with the desired output value (the target), which is found in training data set. The difference is called error signal of output layer neuron.

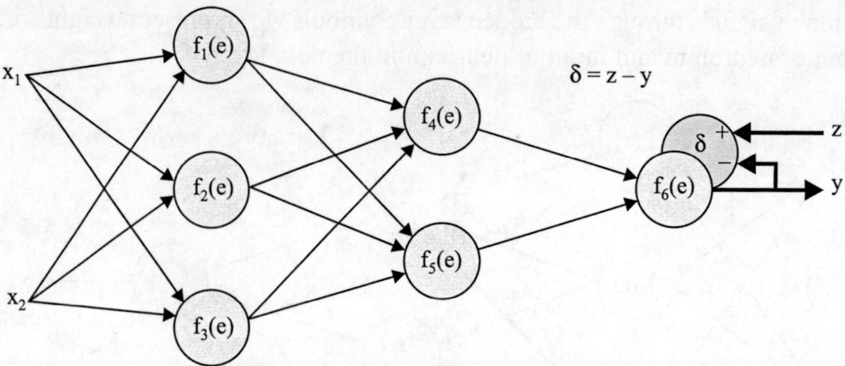

It is impossible to compute error signal for internal neurons directly, because output values of these neurons are unknown. For many years the effective method for training multiplayer networks has been unknown. Only in the middle eighties the backpropagation algorithm has been worked out. The idea is to propagate error signal (computed in single teaching step back to all neurons, which output signals were input for discussed neuron.

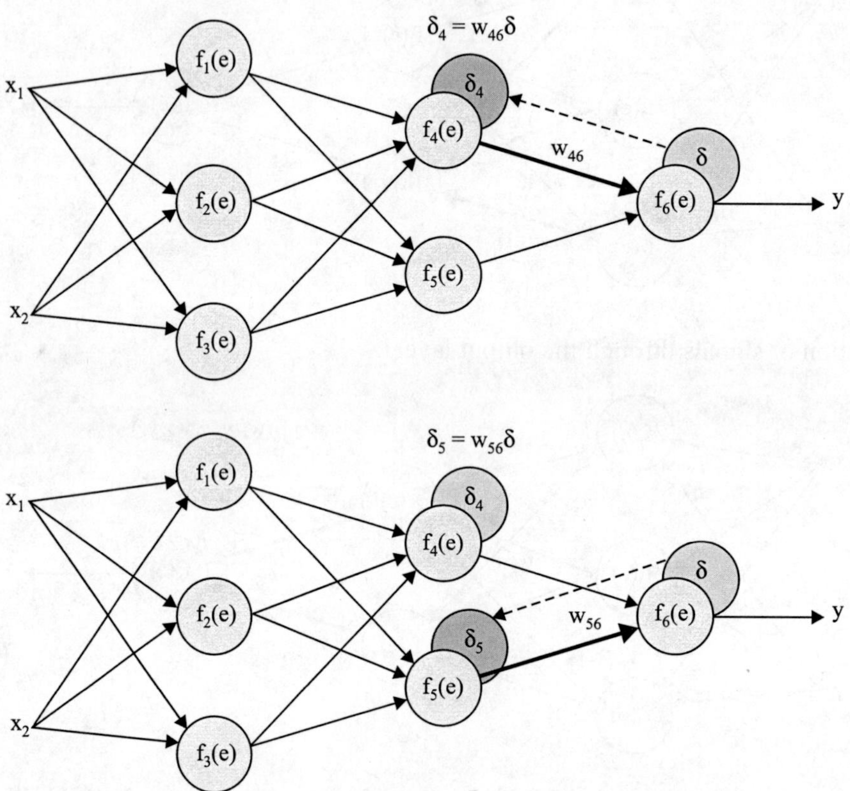

The weights' coefficients w_{mn} used to propagate errors back are equal to this used during computing output value. Only the direction of data flow is changed (signals are propagated from output to inputs one after the other). This technique is used for all network layers. If propagated errors came from few neurons they are added. The illustration is below:

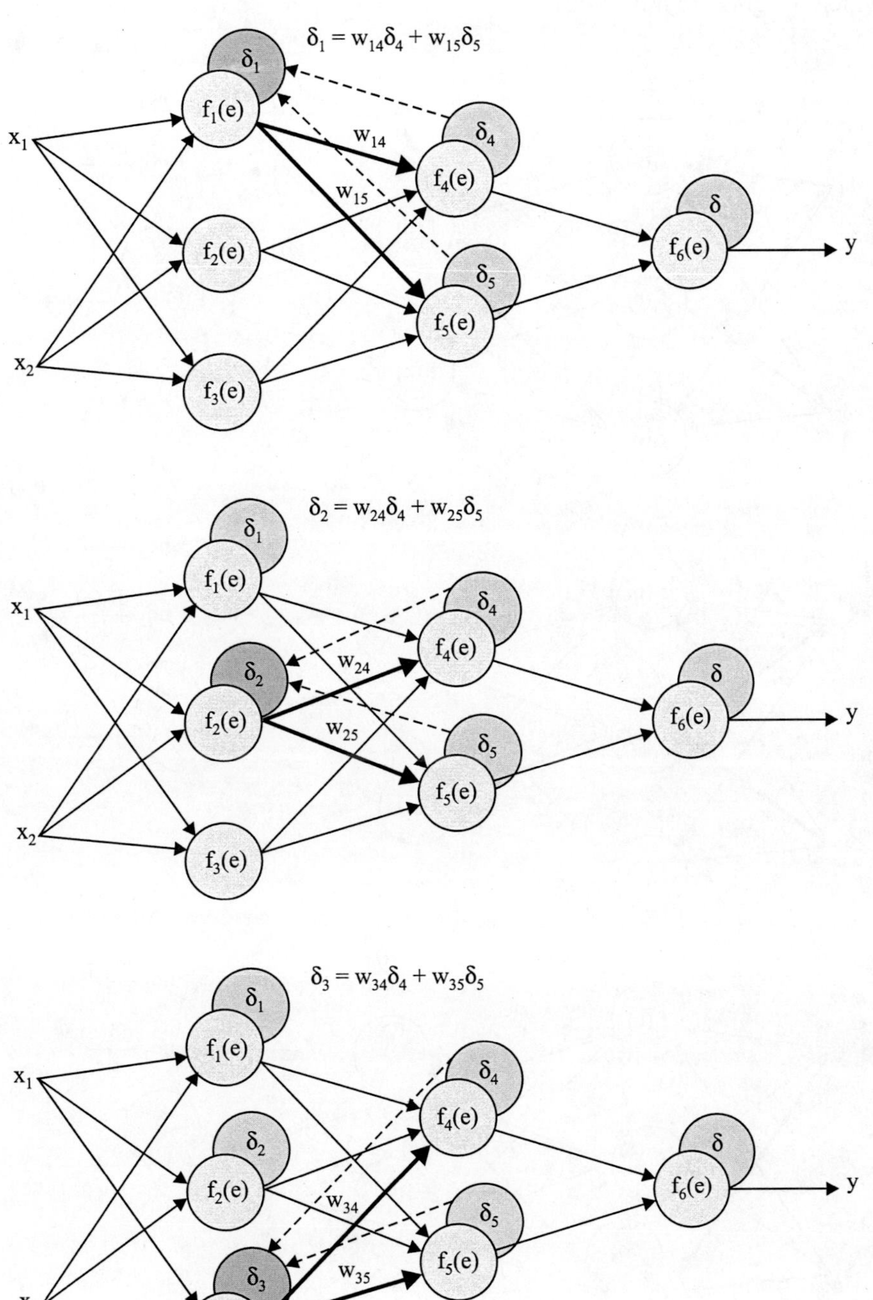

When the error signal for each neuron is computed, the weights coefficients of each neuron input node may be modified. In formulas below df(e)/de represents derivative of neuron activation function (which weights are modified).

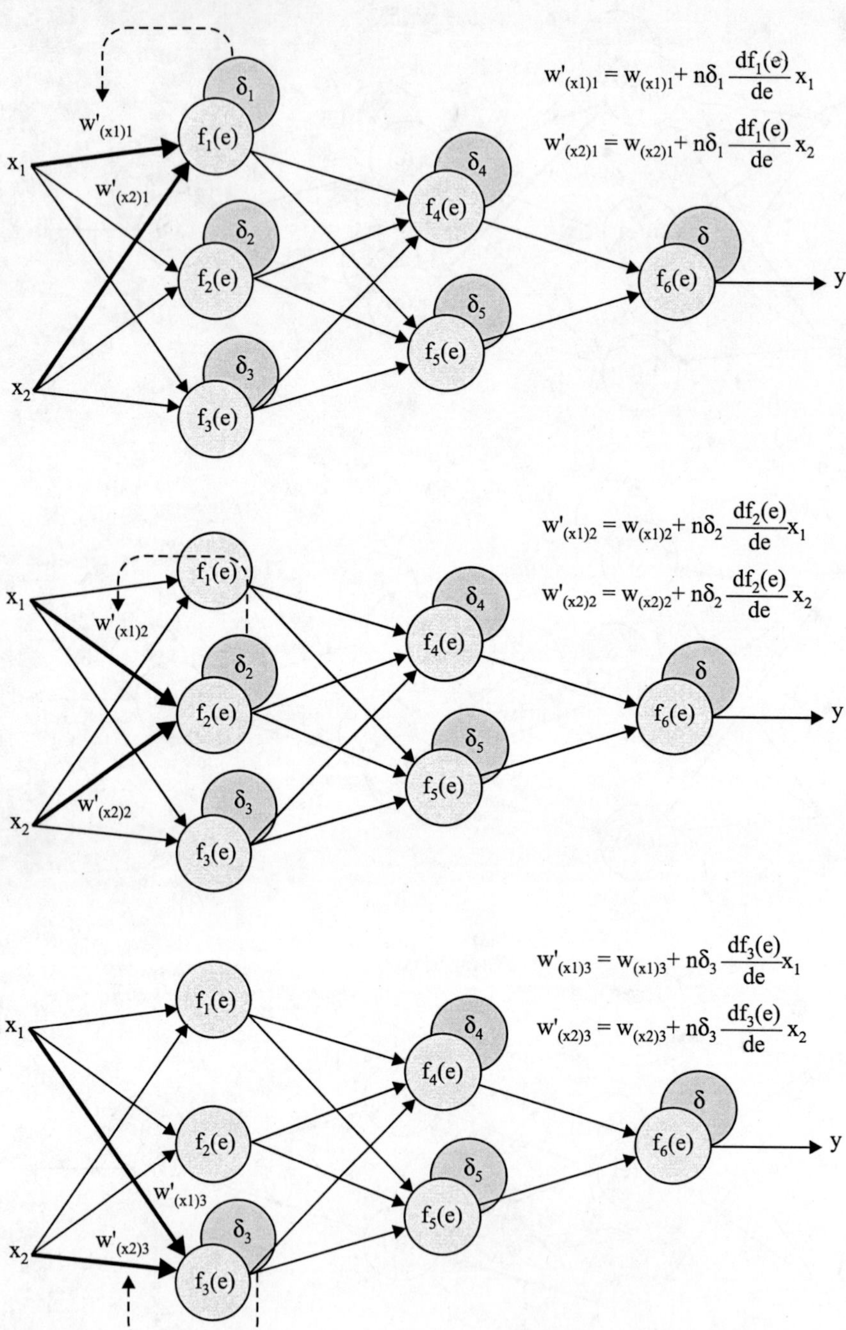

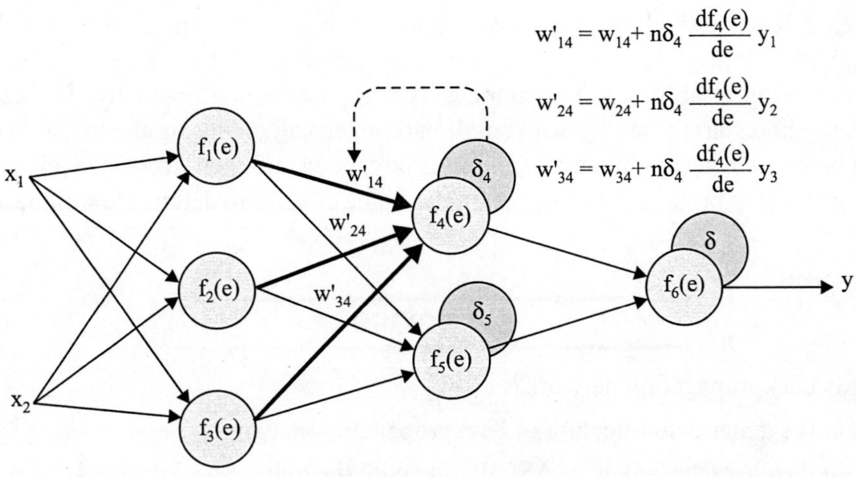
$w'_{14} = w_{14} + n\delta_4 \frac{df_4(e)}{de} y_1$
$w'_{24} = w_{24} + n\delta_4 \frac{df_4(e)}{de} y_2$
$w'_{34} = w_{34} + n\delta_4 \frac{df_4(e)}{de} y_3$
x1
x2
f1(e)
f2(e)
f3(e)
f4(e)
f5(e)
f6(e)
δ4
δ5
δ
w'14
w'24
w'34
y

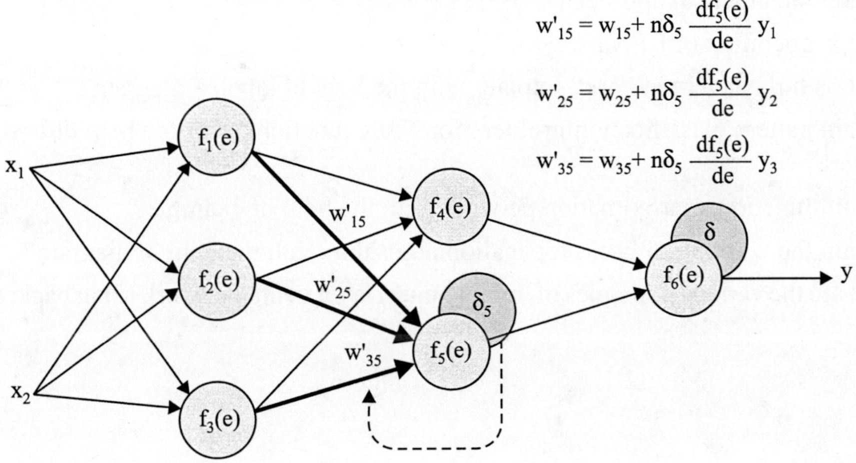
$w'_{15} = w_{15} + n\delta_5 \frac{df_5(e)}{de} y_1$
$w'_{25} = w_{25} + n\delta_5 \frac{df_5(e)}{de} y_2$
$w'_{35} = w_{35} + n\delta_5 \frac{df_5(e)}{de} y_3$
x1
x2
f1(e)
f2(e)
f3(e)
f4(e)
f5(e)
f6(e)
δ5
δ
w'15
w'25
w'35
y

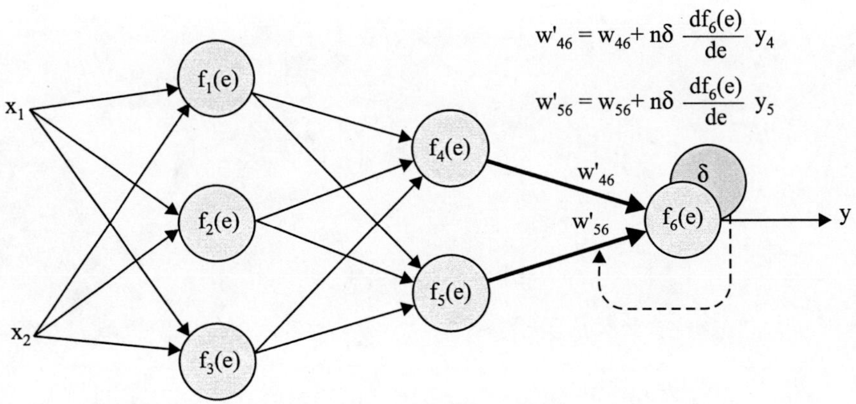
$w'_{46} = w_{46} + n\delta \frac{df_6(e)}{de} y_4$
$w'_{56} = w_{56} + n\delta \frac{df_6(e)}{de} y_5$
x1
x2
f1(e)
f2(e)
f3(e)
f4(e)
f5(e)
f6(e)
δ
w'46
w'56
y

Coefficient affects network teaching speed. There are a few techniques to select this parameter. The first method is to start teaching process with large value of the parameter. While weights coefficients are being established the parameter is being decreased gradually. The second, more complicated, method starts teaching with small parameter value. During the teaching process the parameter is being increased when the teaching is advanced and then decreased again in the final stage. Starting teaching process with low parameter value enables to determine weights coefficients signs.

EXERCISES

1. What is backpropagation network?
2. Explain the general architecture of backpropagation network?
3. Explain the character image of ASCII code with the help of backpropagation network?
4. Explain the practical approach of BPN network?
5. What is operation of BPN network?
6. What is three layer network? Explain with the help of labeled diagram?
7. Explain pattern classification problem for XOR functions with the help of two layer XOR network?
8. Explain function approximation network with the help of example?
9. Explain the working of backpropagation algorithm with the help of diagram?
10. What are the various principles of training multi layer neural network using backpropagation?

CHAPTER 4

Adaline and Madaline

4.1 INTRODUCTION

The ADALINE (adaptive linear neuron) networks discussed in this chapter are similar to the perceptron, but their transfer function is linear rather than hard-limiting. This allows their outputs to take on any value, whereas the perceptron output is limited to either 0 or 1. Both the ADALINE and the perceptron can only solve linearly separable problems. However, here the LMS (least mean squares) learning rule, which is much more powerful than the perceptron learning rule, is used. The LMS, or Widrow-Hoff, learning rule minimizes the mean square error and thus moves the decision boundaries as far as it can from the training patterns.

In this chapter, you design an adaptive linear system that responds to changes in its environment as it is operating. Linear networks that are adjusted at each time step based on new input and target vectors can find weights and biases that minimize the network's sum-squared error for recent input and target vectors. Networks of this sort are often used in error cancellation, signal processing, and control systems. The pioneering work in this field was done by Widrow and Hoff, who gave the name ADALINE to adaptive linear elements.

Signal processing developed as an engineering discipline with the advent of electronic communication. Initially, analog filters using resistor-inductor-capacitor (RLC) circuits were designed to remove noise from the communication signals. Today, signal processing has evolved into a many-faceted technology, with the emphasis having shifted from turned circuit implementation to digital signal processors (DSPs) that can perform the same types of filtering applications by executing convolution filters implemented in software. The basis for the industry remains the design and implementation of filters to perform noise removal from information-bearing signals.

4.2 REVIEW OF SIGNAL PROCESSING

We begin our discussion of the Adaline and Madaline networks with a review of basic signal-processing theory. An understanding of this material is essential if we are to appreciate the operation and applications of these network. However, this material is also typically covered as part of an undergraduate curriculum in information coding and data communication. Therefore, readers already comfortable with signal-processing concepts may skip this first section without fear of missing material relevant to the Adaline and Madaline topics. For those readers who are not familiar with the techniques commonly used to implement electronic communications and signal processing, we shall begin by describing briefly the data-encoding and modulation schemes used in an amplitude-modulation (AM) radio transmission. As part of this-discussion, we shall illustrate the need for filters in the communications industry. We will then review the concepts of the frequency domain, the four basic filter types, and Fourier analysis. This preliminary section concludes with a brief overview of digital signal processing, because many of the concepts realized in digital fitters are directly applicable to the Adaline and Madaline (and many other) neural networks.

4.2.1 Signal Processing and Filters

Signal processing is an engineering discipline that deals primarily with the implementation of filters to remove or reduce unwanted frequency components from an information-bearing signal. Let's consider, for example, an AM radio broadcast. Electronic communication techniques, whether for audio signals or other data, consist of signal encoding and modulation. Information to be transmitted-in this case, audiblc sounds, such as voice or music-can be encoded electronically by an analog signal that exactly reproduces the frequencies and amplitudes of the original sounds. Since the sounds being encoded represent a continuum from silence through voice to music, the instantaneous frequency of the encoded signal will vary with time, ranging from 0 to approximately 10,000 hertz (Hz).

Rather than attempt to transmit this encoded signal directly, we transform the signal into a form more suitable for radio transmission. We accomplish this transformation by modulating the amplitude of a high-frequency carrier signal with the analog information signal. This process is illustrated in Figure 4.1. Here, the carrier is nothing more than a sine wave with a frequency mush greater than the information signal. For AM radio, the carrier frequency will be in the range of 550 to 1600 kilohertz (KHz). Since the frequency of the carrier is significantly greater than is the maximum frequency of the information signal, little information is lost by this modulation. The modulated signal can then be transmitted to a receiving station (or broadcast to anyone with a radio receiver), where the signal is demodulated and is reproduced as sound.

The most obvious reason for a filter in AM radio is that different people have different preferences in music and entertainment. Therefore, the government and the communication industry have allowed many different radio stations to operate in the same geographical area, so that everyone's tastes in entertainment can be accommodated. With so many different radio stations all broadcasting in close proximity, how is it that we can listen to only one station at a time? The answer is to allow each receiver to be tuned by the user to a selectable frequency. In tuning the radio, we are essentially changing the frequency-response characteristics of a bandpass filter inside the radio. This filter allows only the signals from the station is which we are interested to pass, while eliminating all the other signals being broadcast within the spectrum of the AM radio.

To illustrate how the bandpass filter operates, we will change out reference from the time domain to the frequency domain. We begin by constructing a two-axis graph, where the x axis represents increasing frequencies and the y axis represents decreasing attenuation in a unit called the decibel (dB). Such a graph us illustrated in Figure 4.2(a). For the AM radio example, let us imagine that there are seven AM radio stations, labeled. A through G, operating in the area where we are listening. The frequencies at which these stations transmit are graphed as vertical lines located on the frequency axis at the point corresponding to their transmitting, or carrier, frequency. The amplitude of the lines, as illustrated in Figure 4.2(a), is almost 0 dB, indicating that each station is transmitting at full power, and each can be received equally well.

Now we will tune bandpass filter to select one of the seven stations. The frequency response of a typical bandpass filter is illustrated in Figure 4.2(b). Notice that the frequency-response curve is such that all frequencies that fall outside the inverted notch are attenuated to very little attenuation-hence the name "bandpass filter."

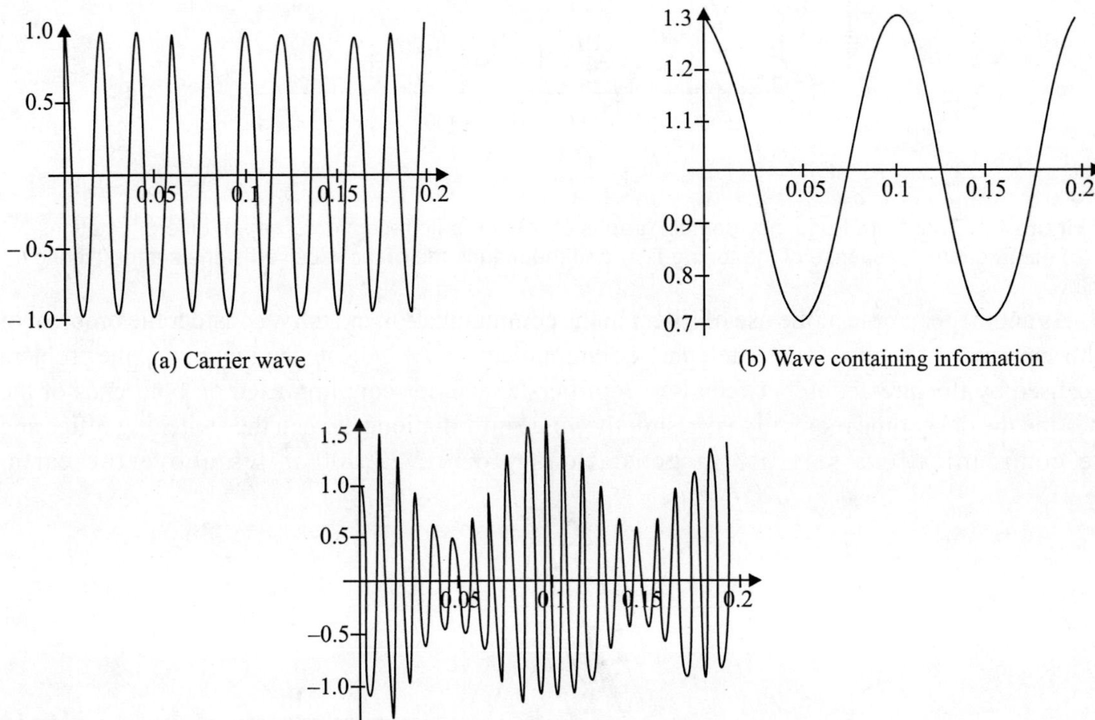

Figure 4.1: Information-encoding and amplitude-modulation techniques for electronic communication are shown. (a) The carrier wave has a frequency much higher than that of (b) The information-bearing signal (c) The carrier wave is modulated by the information-bearing signal.

To tune our radio receiver to any one of the seven broadcasting stations, we simply adjust the frequency response of the filter such that the carrier frequency of the desired station is within the passband.

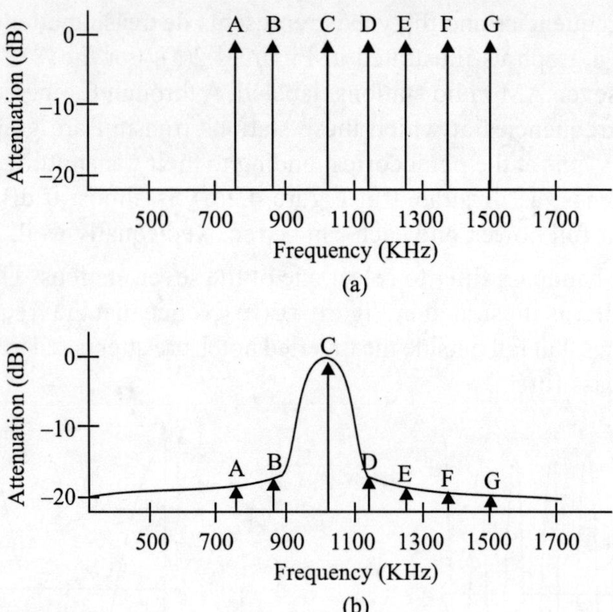

Figure 4.2: These are frequency domain graphs of (a) AM radio reception of seven different stations, (b) the frequency response of the tuning filter and the magnitude of the received signals after filtering.

As another example of the use of filters in the communication industry, consider the problem of echo suppression in long-distance telephone communication. As indicated in Figure 4.3, the problem is caused by the interaction between the amplifiers and series coupling used on both ends of the line, and the delay time required to transmit the voice information between the switching office and the communications satellite in geostationary orbit, 23,000 miles above the earth.

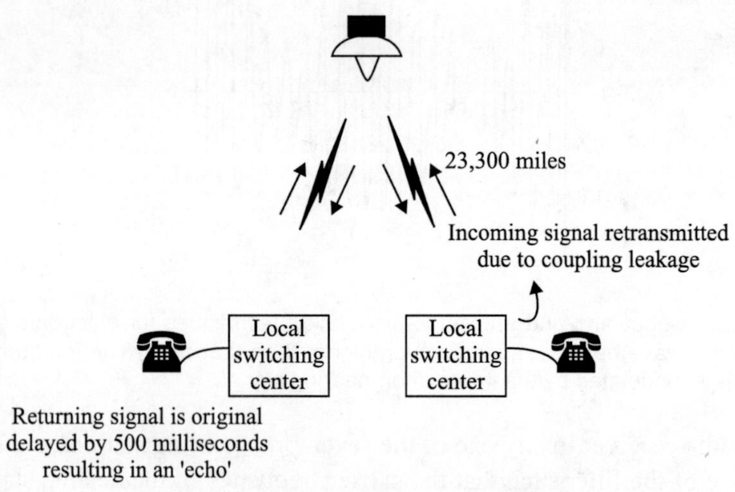

Figure 4.3: Echo can occur in long-distance telecommunications.

Specifically, you hear an echo of your own voice in the telephone when you speak. The signal carrying your voice arrives at the receiving telephone approximately 270 milliseconds after you speak. This delay is the amount of time required by the microwave signal to travel the 46,000 miles between the transmitting station, the satellite, and the receiving station on the ground. Once received and routed to the destination telephone, the signal is again amplified and reproduced as sound on the receiving handset.

Unfortunately, it is also often picked u by the transmitter at the receiving end, due to imperfections in the devices used to decouple the incoming signals. It can then be reamplified and fed back to you approximately 1/2 second after you spoke. The result is echo. Obviously, a simple bandpass filter cannot be used to remove the echo, because there is no way to distinguish the echoed signal from valid signals.

To solve problem such as these, the communications industry has developed many different types of filters. These filters not only are used in electronic communications, but also have an application base that includes radar and sonar imaging, electronic warfare, and medical technology. However, all the application-specific filter implementations can be grouped into four general filter types: lowpass, highpass, bandpass, and bandstop. The characteristic frequency response of these filters is depicted in Figure 4.4. The adaptive filter, which is the subject of the remainder of the chapter, has characteristics unique to the application it serves. It can reproduce the characteristics of any of the four basic filter types, alone or in combination.

As we shall show later, the adaptive filter is ideally suited to the telephone-echo problem just discussed.

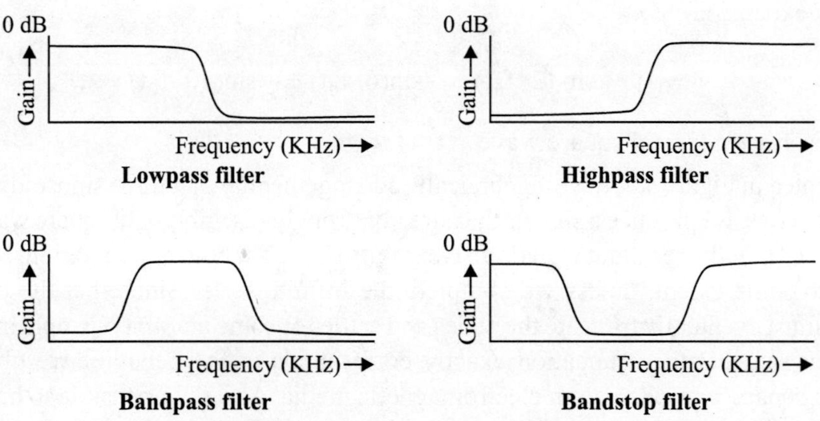

Figure 4.4: Frequency-response characteristics of the four basic filter types are shown.

4.2.2 Fourier Analysis and The Frequency Domain

To analyze a signal-processing problem that requires a filter. we must leave the time domain and find a tool for translating our filter models into the frequency domain. Because most of the signals we will analyze cannot be completely understood in the time domain.

For example, most signals consist not only of a fundamental frequency, but also harmonics that must be considered, or they consist of many discrete frequency components that must be accounted for by the filters we design. There are many tools that we can use to help understand the frequency-domain nature of signals. One of the most commonly used is the Fourier series. It has been shown that any periodic signal can be modeled as an infinite series of sines and cosines. The Fourier series, which describes the frequency-domain nature of periodic signals, is given by the equation.

$$x(t) = \underset{n\ \ 0}{a_n \cos(2\ \ f_0 t)} \qquad \underset{n\ \ 0}{b_n \sin(2\ \ bf_0 t)}$$

Where f_0 is the fundamental frequency of the signals in the time domain, and the coefficients, a_n and $b_{n,}$ are needed to modulate the amplitude of the individual terms of the series.

This series is useful for describing the discrete frequency components that comprise a nontrivial periodic signal. As an illustration, a square wave can be decomposed into a summation of frequency, as is illustrated in Figure 4.5.

Since a square wave is useful for representing binary information in data transmission , it is important that we understand the frequency-domain nature of such a signals. From Inspection the domain, we can observe that the square wave is ideally suited to binary data representation because there are two distinct states (a 1 and a 0) , and the transition time between states is negligible.

It is difficult, however, to obtain a perfect square wave in any practical electronic circuit, due in part to the effects to the transmitting media on the signals. To illustrate why this is so, consider the Fourier series expansion.

$$x(t) = \sin(2\ \ f_0 t) + \frac{1}{3}\sin(6\ \ f_0 t) + \frac{1}{5}\sin(10\ \ f_0 t) + ...$$

Which describes a typical square wave.

As illustrated in Figure 4.5, if we algebraically add together the first three sinusoidal components of this Fourier series, we produce a signals that already strongly resembles the square wave. However, we should notice that the resultant signals also exhibits ripple sin both active regions. These ripples will remain to some extent, unless we complete the infinite series.Since that the obviously not practical, we must eventually truncate the series and settle for some amount of ripple in the resulting signals.It turns out that this truncation exactly corresponds to the behavior we observed when transmitting a square wave across an electromagnetic media. As it is impossible to have a medium of infinite bandwidth, it follows that it is impossible to transmit all the frequency components of a square wave.

Thus when we transmit a periodic square wave, we can observe the frequency-domain effects in the time-domain signals as overshoot, undershoot, and ripple.

This example shows that the Fourier series can be a powerful tool in helping us to understand the frequency domain nature of any periodic signals, and to predict ahead of time what transmission effects we must consider as we design filters for our signals-processing applications.

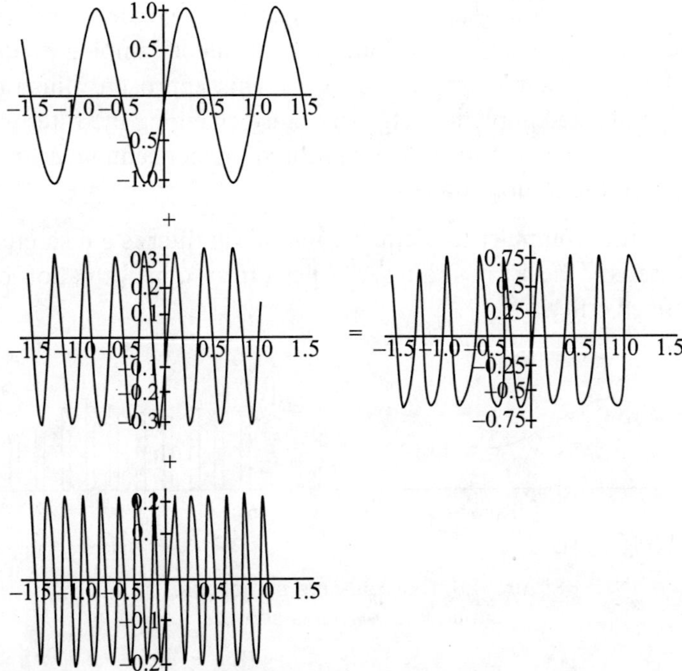

Figure 4.5: The first three frequency-domain components of a square wave are shown. Notice that the sine waves each have different magnitudes, as indicated by the coordinates on the y axis, even though they are graphed to the same height.

We can also apply Fourier analysis to a periodic signals, by evaluating the Fourier integral, which is given by

$$X(f) = \quad x(t)e^{-j2\ \ ft}dt.$$

We will not, however belabor this point. Our purpose here is merely to understand the frequency-domain nature of signals. Readers interested in investigating Fourier analysis further are referred to Kaplan.

4.2.3 Filter Implementation and Digital Signal Processing

Early implementations of the four basic filters were predominantly tuned RLS circuits. This approach had a basic limitation, however, in that the filters had only a very small range of adjustability. Aside from our being able to change the resonant frequency of the filter by adjusting a variable capacitor or inductor, the filter were pretty much fixed once implemented, leaving little room for change as applications become more sophisticated.

The next step in the evolution of filter design came about with the event of digital computer system, and, just recently, with the availability of microcomputer chips with architectures customtailored for signal-processing applications. The basic concept underlying digital filter implementation is the idea that a continuous analog signal can be sampled periodically, quantized, and processed by a fairly standard computer system. This approach, illustrated in Figure 4.6, overcome the limitation of fixed implementation, because changing the filter was simply a matter of rewriting the software for the computer. We will therefore concentrate on what goes on within the software simulation of the analog filter.

We assume that the computer implementation of the filter is a discrete time, linear, time-invariant system that satisfy these constraints can perform a transformation on an input signal, based on some predefined criteria

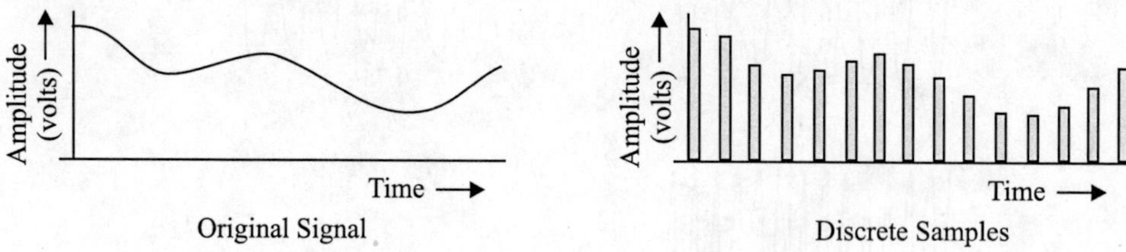

Figure 4.6: Discrete-time sampling of a continuous signal is shown.

to produce an output that corresponds to the input as though it had passed through an analog filter. Thus, a computer, executing a program that applies a given transformation operation, R, to discrete, digitized approximations of a continuous input signal, x(n), can produce an output value y(n) for each input sample, where n is the discrete timestep variable. In its role in performing this transformation, the computer can be thought of as a digital filter. Moreover, any filter can be completely characterized by its response, h(n), to the unit impulse function, represented as b(n) .More precisely.

$$h(n) = R\,[\partial(n)]$$

The benefit of this formulation is that, once the system response to the unit impulse is known, the system output for any input is given by

$$Y(n)\ R[x(n)] = \qquad h(i)\ x(n-i)$$

where x(n) is the system input

This equation is meaningful to us in that it describes a convolution some between the input signal and the unit inpluse response of the system. The process can be pictured as a window slidingpast a scene of interest. As illustrated in Figure 4.7, for each time step, the system output is produced by transposing and sifting h(n) one position to the right. The summation is then performed over all nonzero values of x(n) for the finite length of the filter.

In this manner, we can realize the filter by repetitively performing floating-point multiplications and additions, coupled with sample time delays and shift operations. Repetitive mathematical operations are what computer to best; therefore, the convolution sum provides us with a mechanism for building the digital signal processing are referred to Oppenheim and Schafer or Hamming.

It is sufficient for our purposes to note that the convolution sum is a sum-of–products operation similar to the type of operation an ANS PE performs when computing its input activation signal. Specifically, the Adaline uses exactly this sum-of-products calculation, without the sample time delays and shift operations., to determine how much input stimulation it receives from an instantaneous input signal. As we shall see in the next section, the Adaline extends the basis filter operation one step further, in that it has implemented within itself a means of adapting the weighting coefficients to allow it to increase or decrease the stimulation it receives the next time it is presented with the same signal.

The ability of the Adaline to adapt us weighting coefficients is extremely useful. When writing a digital filter program on a computer, the programmer must know exactly how to specify the filtering algorithm and what the details of the signal characteristics are.

If modification are desired, or if the signal characteristics change, reprogramming is requires, When the programmer uses an Adaline, the problem shifts to one of being able to specify the desired output signal. given a particular input signal. The Adaline takes the input and the desired output, and adjusts itself so that it can perform the desired transformation. Further-more, if the signal characteristics, the Adaline can adapt automatically we shall now expend these ideas, and begin our investigation of the adaline

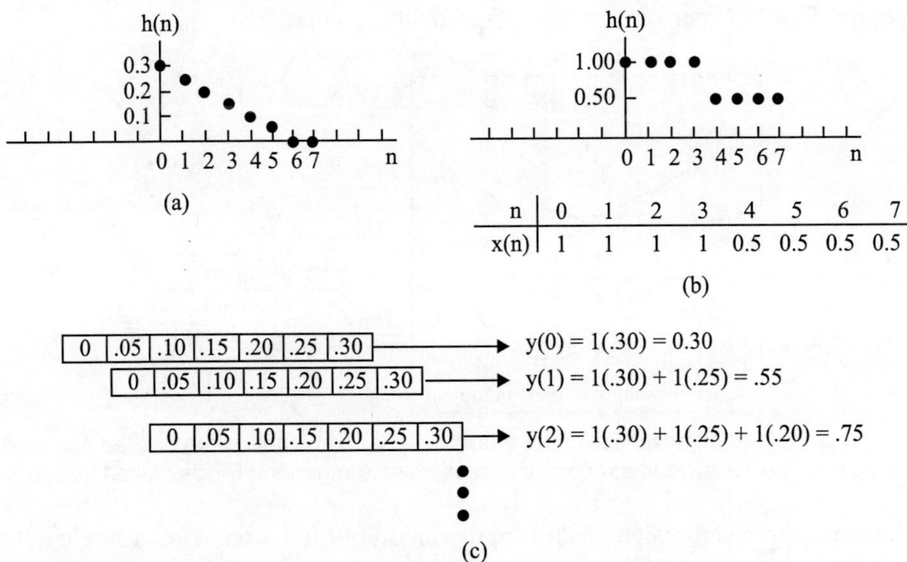

Figure 4.7: Convolution sum calculation is shown (a) The process begins by determining the desired response of the filter to the unit impulse function at eight discrete timesteps. (b) The input signal is sampled and quantized eight times. (c) The output of the filter is produced for each timestep by multiplication of each term in (a) with the corresponding value of (b) for all valid timesteps.

4.3 ADALINE AND THE ADAPTIVE LINEAR COMBINER

The Adaline is a device consisting of a single processing element; as such , it is not technically a neural network. Nevertheless, it is a very important structure that deserve close study. Moreover, we will show how it can form the basis of a network in a later section.

The term Adaline is an acronym: however, its meanings has changed some-what over the years. Initially called the ADAptive LINear Element, when neural networks fell out of favor in the late 1960s. It is almost identical in structure to the general PE described in Chapter 1. Figure 4.8 shows the Adaline structure. There are two basic modifications required to make the general PE structure into an Adaline. The first modification is the addition of a connection with weight,w_0, which we refer to as the bias term. This term is a weight on a connection that has its input value always equal to 1. The inclusion of such a term is largely a matter of experience. We show it here for completeness, but it will not appear in the discussion of the next sections. We shall resurrect the idea of a bias term in Chapter 3, on the backpropagation network.

The second modification is the addition of a bipolar condition on the output. The dashed box in Figure 4.8 encloses a part of the Adaline called the adaptive linear combiner (ALC). (If the output of the ALC is positive, the Adaline output is +1. If the ALC output is negative, the Adaline output is -1. Because much of the interesting processing takes place in the ALC portion of the Adaline, we shall concentrate on the ALC. Later, we shall add back the binary output condition.

The processing done by the ALC is that of the typical processing element described in the previous chapter. The ALC performs a sum-of-products calculation

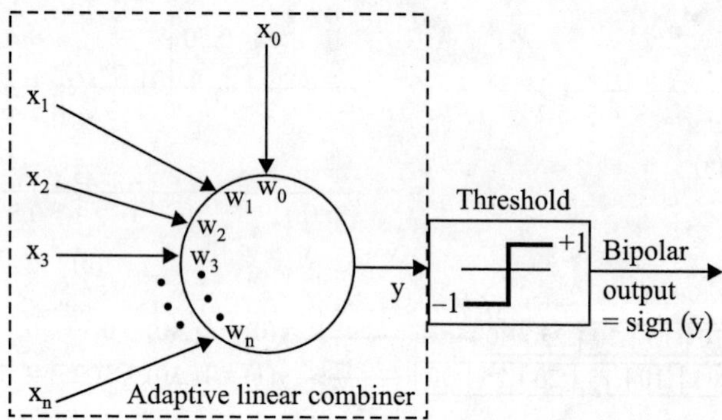

Figure 4.8: The complete Adaline consist of the adaptive linear combiner, in the dashed box, and a bipolar output function. The adaptive linear combiner resembles the general PE described in Chapter 1.

using the input and weight vectors, and applies an output function to get a single output value. Using the notation in Figure 4.8.

$$y = u_0 \quad \overset{n}{\underset{j\;1}{}} \; w_j x_j$$

Where w_0 is the bias weight. If we make the identification, $x_0 = 1$, we can rewrite the preceding equation as

$$y = \quad {}^{n}_{j\ 1} \quad w_j x_j$$

or, in vector notation,

$$y = w^t x \tag{4.1}$$

The output function in this case is the identity function, as is the activation function. The use of the identity function as both output and activation function means that the output is the same as the activation, which is the same as the net input to the unit.

The Adaline (or the ALC) is is ADAptive in the sense that there exists a well-defined procedure for the given input. What output value is correct depends on the particular processing function being performed by the device. The Adaline (or the ALC) is Linear because the output is a simple linear function of the input values. It is a NEuron only in the very limited sense of the PEs described in the previous chapter. The Adaline could also be said to be a LINear Element, avoiding the NEuron issue altogether. In the next section, look at a method to train the Adaline to perform a given processing function.

4.3.1 Algorithm

A training algorithm for an ADALINE is as follows:

Step 1: Initialize weights.
(Small random values are usually used.)
Set learning rate á.
(See comments following algorithm.)

Step 2: While stopping condition is false, do Steps 3-7.

Step 3: For each bipolar training pair s:t, do Steps 4-6.

Step 4: Set activations of input units, i = 1 …, n:

$$x_i = s_i.$$

Step 5: Compute net input to output unit:

$$y\_in = b + \quad {}_{i} \quad x_i w_i.$$

Step 6: Update bias and weights, i = 1, …, n:

$$b(new) = b(old) + á(t - y\_in).$$

$$w_i(new) = w_i(old) + á(t - y\_in)x_i.$$

Step 7: Test for stopping condition.

If the largest weight change that occurred in Step 3 is smaller that a specified tolerance, then stop; otherwise continue.

4.3.2 The LMS Learning Rule

Given an input vector, x, it is straightforward to determine a set of weights, w, which will result in a particular output value, y. Suppose we have a set of input vectors {$x_1, x_2, \ldots, x_L$}, each having its own, perhaps unique, correct or desired output value d_k, k = 1, L. The problem of finding a single weight vector that can successfully associate each input vector with its desired output value is no longer simple. In this section, we develop a method called the least-mean-square (LMS) learning rule, which is one method of finding the desired weight vector. We refer to this process of finding the weight vector as training the ALC. The learning rule can be embedded in the device itself, which can then self-adapt as inputs and desired outputs are presented to it. Small adjustments are made at the weight values as each input-output combination is processed until the ALC gives correct outputs. In a sense, this procedure is a true training procedure, because we do not need to calculate the value of the weight vector explicitly. Before describing the training process detail, let's perform the calculation manually.

Calculation of w*. To begin, let's state the problem a little differently: Given examples, (x_1, d_1), (x_2, d_2),..., (x_L, d_L), of some processing function that associates input vectors, x_k, with (or maps to) the desired output values, d_k, what is the best weight vector, w*, for an ALC that performs this mapping?

To answer this question, we must first define what is is that constitutes th... once the best weight vector is found, we would like the application of each inpu... the precise, corresponding output value. Thus, we want to eliminate, or at leas... difference between the desired output and the actual output for each input vector. the approach we select her is to minimize the mean squared error for the set of input vectors.

If the actual output value is y_k for the input vector, then the corresponding error te... $- y_k$. The mean squared error, or expectation value of the error, is defined by

$$(\ ^2_k) = \frac{1}{L} \ ^{L}_{k\ 1} \ ^2_k \tag{4.2}$$

where L is the number of input vectors in the training set.[1]

Using Eq. (4.1), we can expand the mean squared error as follows:

$$(\ ^2_k) = \{(d_k - w^t x_k)^2 \tag{4.3}$$

$$= \{d_k^2) + w^t (x_k x_k^t\} \, w - 2\{d_k x_k^t)w \tag{4.4}$$

In going from Eq. (4.3) to Eq. (4.4), we have made the assumption that the training set is statistically stationary, meaning that any expectation values vary slowly with respect to time. This assumption allows us to factor out the weight vectors from the expectation value terms in Eq. (4.4)

4.4 IMPORTANT ADAPTIVE FUNCTIONS

This chapter introduces the function adapt, which changes the weights and biases of a network incrementally during training. You can type help linnet to see a list of linear and adaptive network functions, demonstrations, and applications.

4.4.1 Linear Neuron Model

A linear neuron with *R* inputs is shown below.

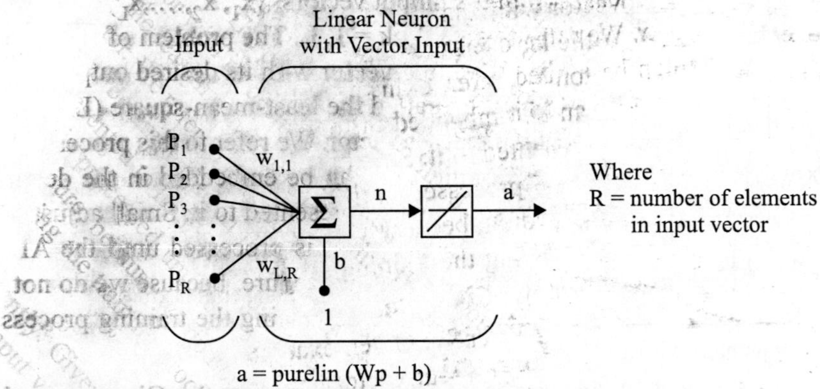

Figure 4.9: Linear neuron model

This network has the same basic structure as the perceptron. The only difference is that the linear neuron uses a linear transfer function, named purelin.

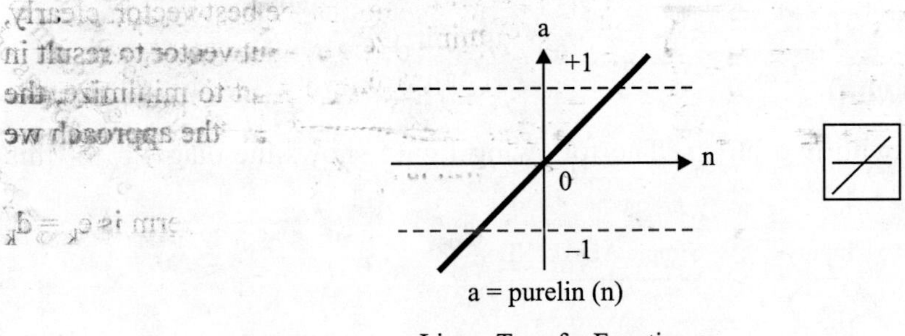

Linear Transfer Function

The linear transfer function calculates the neuron's output by simply returning the value passed to it.

$$a = \text{purelin}(n) = \text{purelin}(Wp + b) = Wp + b$$

This neuron can be trained to learn an affine function of its inputs, or to find a linear approximation to a nonlinear function. A linear network cannot, of course, be made to perform a nonlinear computation.

4.5 ADAPTIVE LINEAR NETWORK ARCHITECTURE

The ADALINE network shown below has one layer of S neurons connected to R inputs through a matrix of weights **W**.

This network is sometimes called a MADALINE for Many ADALINEs.

Note that the figure on the right defines an S-length output vector **a**.

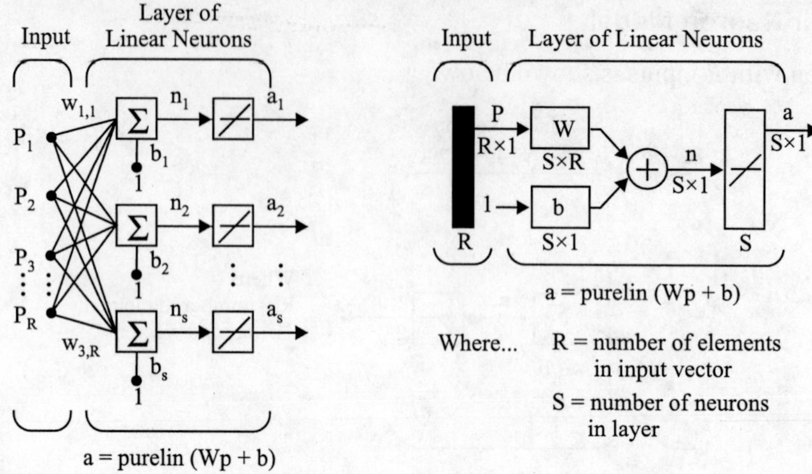

Figure 4.10: Adaptive linear network architecture

The Widrow-Hoff rule can only train single-layer linear networks. This is not much of a disadvantage, however, as single-layer linear networks are just as capable as multilayer linear networks. For every multilayer linear network, there is an equivalent single-layer linear network.

4.5.1 Single Adaline (Newlin)

Consider a single ADALINE with two inputs. The following figure shows the diagram for this network.

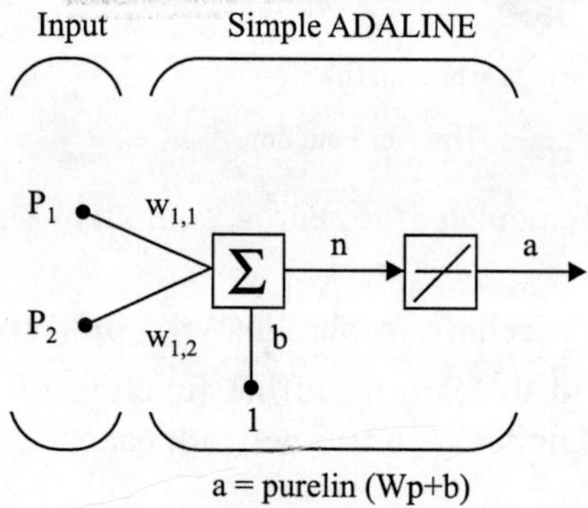

Figure 4.11: Single adaline

The weight matrix **W** in this case has only one row. The network output is

$$a = \text{purelin}(n) = \text{purelin}(wp + b) = wp + b$$

or

$$a = w_{1,1}p_1 + w_{1,2}p_2 + b$$

Like the perceptron, the ADALINE has a *decision boundary* that is determined by the input vectors for which the net input n is zero. For n = 0 the equation Wp + b = 0 specifies such a decision boundary, as shown below.

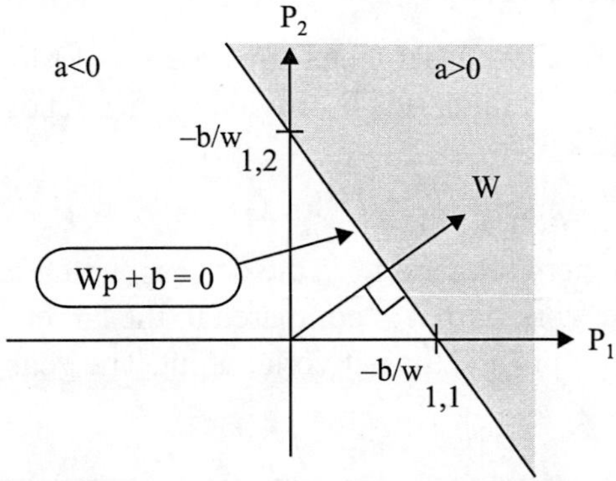

Input vectors in the upper right gray area lead to an output greater than 0. Input vectors in the lower left white area lead to an output less than 0. Thus, the ADALINE can be used to classify objects into two categories.

However, ADALINE can classify objects in this way only when the objects are linearly separable. Thus, ADALINE has the same limitation as the perceptron. We can create a network similar to the one shown using this command:

```
net = newlin ([–1 1; –1 1], 1);
```

The first matrix of arguments specifies typical two-element input vectors, and the last argument 1 indicates that the network has a single output. The network weights and biases are set to zero, by default. You can see the current values using the commands:

```
W = net.IW{1,1}
W = 0 0
```

and

```
b = net.b{1}
b = 0
```

You can also assign arbitrary values to the weights and bias, such as 2 and 3 for the weights and –4 for the bias:

```
net.IW{1,1} = [2 3];
net.b{1} = –4;
```

You can simulate the ADAPLINE for a particular input vector.

```
p = [5; 6];
a = sim(net, p)
a = 24
```

To summarize, you can create an ADALINE network with newlin, adjust its elements as you want, and simulate it with sim. You can find more about newlin by typing help newlin.

4.5.2 Least Mean Square Error

Like the perceptron learning rule, the least mean square error (LMS) algorithm is an example of supervised training, in which the learning rule is provided with a set of examples of desired network behavior.

$$mse = \{P_1, t_1\}, \{P_2, t_2\} \ldots \{P_Q, t_Q\}$$

Here $\mathbf{p}_Q$ is an input to the network, and $\mathbf{t}_Q$ is the corresponding target output. As each input is applied to the network, the network output is compared to the target. The error is calculated as the difference between the target output and the network output. The goal is to minimize the average of the sum of these errors.

$$mse = \frac{1}{Q}\sum_{k=1}^{Q} e(k)^2 = \frac{1}{Q}\sum_{k=1}^{Q} (t(k) - a(k)^2)$$

The LMS algorithm adjusts the weights and biases of the ADALINE so as to minimize this mean square error. Fortunately, the mean square error performance index for the ADALINE network is a quadratic function. Thus, the performance index will either have one global minimum, a weak minimum, or no minimum, depending on the characteristics of the input vectors. Specifically, the characteristics of the input vectors determine whether or not a unique solution exists.

4.5.3 LMS Algorithm (Learnwh)

Adaptive networks will use the LMS algorithm or Widrow-Hoff learning algorithm based on an approximate steepest descent procedure. Here again, adaptive linear networks are trained on examples of correct behavior.

The LMS algorithm, shown above.

$$w(k+1) = w(k) + 2\ e(k)p^T(k)$$

$$b(k+1) = b(k) + 2\alpha e(k)$$

4.5.4 Adaptive Filtering (Adapt)

The ADALINE network, much like the perceptron, can only solve linearly separable problems. It is, however, one of the most widely used neural networks found in practical applications. Adaptive filtering is one of its major application areas.

4.5.5 Tapped Delay Line

You need a new component, the tapped delay line, to make full use of the ADALINE network. Such a delay line is shown in the next figure. The input signal enters from the left and passes through *N*-1 delays. The output of the tapped delay line (TDL) is an *N*-dimensional vector, made up of the input signal at the current time, the previous input signal, etc.

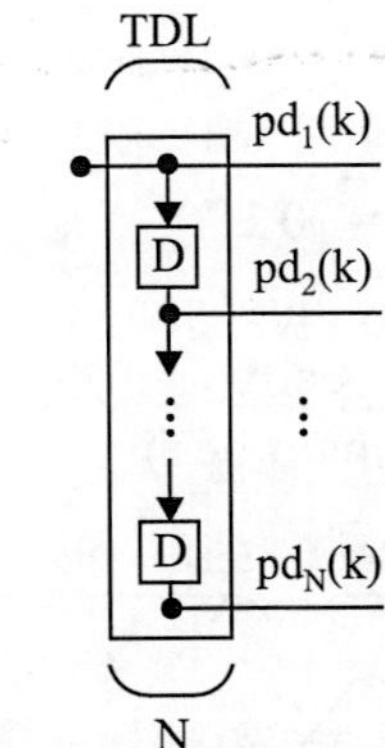

Figure 4.12: Tapped delay line

4.5.6 Adaptive Filter

You can combine a tapped delay line with an ADALINE network to create the *adaptive filter* shown in the next figure.

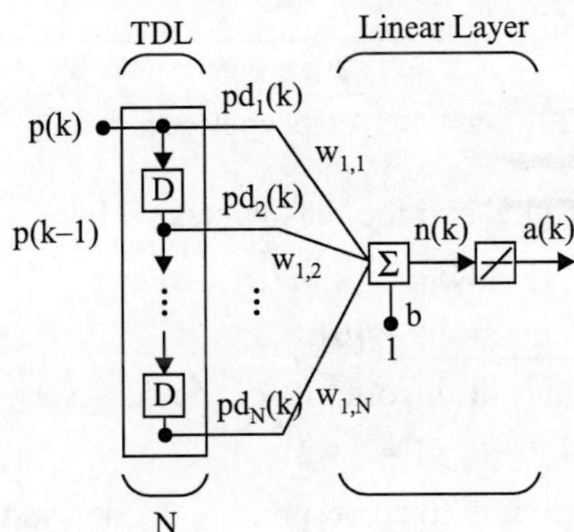

Figure 4.13: Adaptive filter

The output of the filter is given by

$$a(k) = \text{purelin}(wp + b) = \sum_{i=1}^{R} w_{1,i}\, a(k - i + 1) + b$$

In digital signal processing, this network is referred to as a *finite impulse response (FIR)* filter. Take a look at the code used to generate and simulate such an adaptive network.

4.5.7 Adaptive Filter Example

First define a new linear network using newlin.

Assume that the input values have a range from 0 to 10. You can now define the single output network.

net = newlin([0,10],1);

Specify the delays in the tapped delay line with

net.inputWeights{1,1}.delays = [0 1 2];

This definition indicates that the delay line connects to the network weight matrix through delays of 0, 1, and 2 time units. (You can specify as many delays as you want, and can omit some values if you like. They must be in ascending order.)

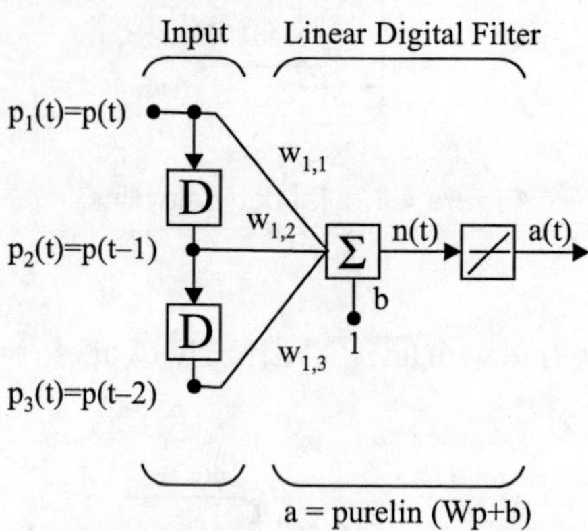

Figure 4.14: Adaptive filter example

You can give the various weights and the bias values with

net.IW{1,1} = [7 8 9];

net.b{1} = [0];

Finally, define the initial values of the outputs of the delays as

pi = {1 2};

These are ordered from left to right to correspond to the delays taken from top to bottom in the figure. This concludes the setup of the network. To set up the input, assume that the input scalars arrive in a sequence:

First the value 3, then the value 4, next the value 5, and finally the value 6. You can indicate this sequence by defining the values as elements of a cell array in curly braces.

p = {3, 4, 5, 6};

Now, you have a network and a sequence of inputs. Simulate the network to see what its output is as a function of time.

[a,pf] = sim(net,p,pi)

This simulation yields an output sequence

a = [46] [70] [94] [118]

and final values for the delay outputs of

pf = [5] [6]

The example is sufficiently simple that you can check it without a calculator to make sure that you understand the inputs, initial values of the delays, etc. The network just defined can be trained with the function adapt to produce a particular output sequence. Suppose, for instance, you want the network to produce the sequence of values 10, 20, 30, 40.

t = {10 20 30 40};

You can train the defined network to do this, starting from the initial delay conditions used above. Specify 10 passes through the input sequence with

net.adaptParam.passes = 10;

Then launch the training with

[net,y,E,pf,af] = adapt(net,p,t,pi);

This code returns the final weights, bias, and output sequence shown here.

wts = net.IW{1,1}

wts = 0.5059 3.1053 5.7046

bias = net.b{1}

bias = –1.5993

y = [11.8558] [20.7735] [29.6679] [39.0036]

Presumably, if you ran additional passes the output sequence would have been even closer to the desired values of 10, 20, 30, and 40. Thus, adaptive networks can be specified, simulated, and finally trained with adapt. However, the outstanding value of adaptive networks lies in their use to perform a particular function, such as prediction or noise cancellation.

4.6 PREDICTION EXAMPLE

Suppose that you want to use an adaptive filter to predict the next value of a stationary random process, p(t). You can use the network shown in the following figure to do this prediction.

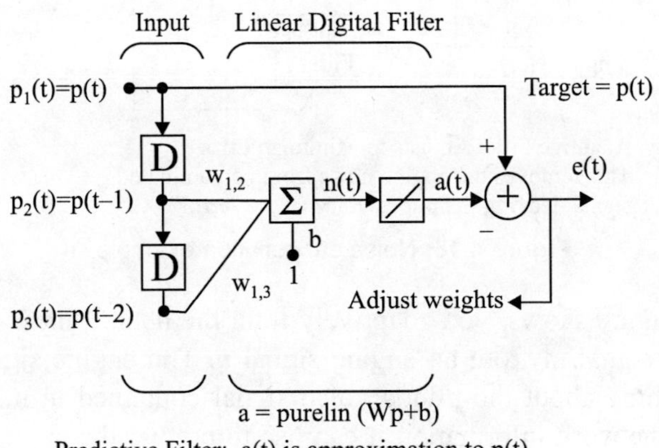

Figure 4.15: Prediction Example

The signal to be predicted, p(t), enters from the left into a tapped delay line. The previous two values of p(t) are available as outputs from the tapped delay line. The network uses adapt to change the weights on each time step so as to minimize the error e(t) on the far right. If this error is 0, the network output a(t) is exactly equal to p(t), and the network has done its prediction properly.

Given the autocorrelation function of the stationary random process p(t), you can calculate the error surface, the maximum learning rate, and the optimum values of the weights. Commonly, of course, you do not have detailed information about the random process, so these calculations cannot be performed. This lack does not matter to the network. After it is initialized and operating, the network adapts at each time step to minimize the error and in a relatively short time is able to predict the input p(t).

4.7 NOISE CANCELLATION EXAMPLE

Consider a pilot in an airplane. When the pilot speaks into a microphone, the engine noise in the cockpit combines with the voice signal. This additional noise makes the resultant signal heard by passengers of low quality. The goal is to obtain a signal that contains the pilot's voice, but not the engine noise. You can cancel the noise with an adaptive filter if you obtain a sample of the engine noise and apply it as the input to the adaptive filter.

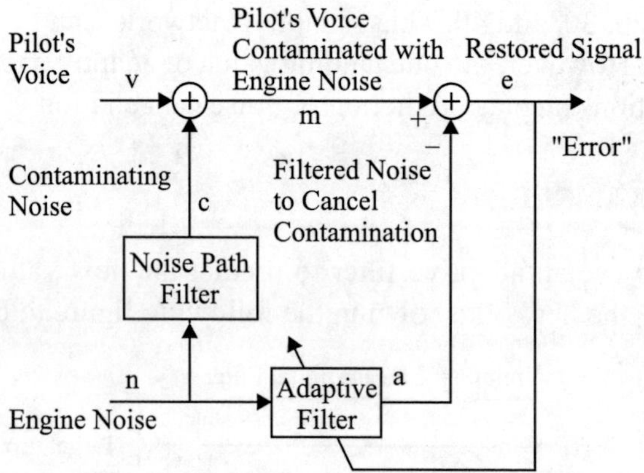

Figure 4.16: Noise cancellation example

As the preceding figure shows, you adaptively train the neural linear network to predict the combined pilot/engine signal m from an engine signal n. The engine signal n does not tell the adaptive network anything about the pilot's voice signal contained in m. However, the engine signal n does give the network information it can use to predict the engine's contribution to the pilot/engine signal m.

The network does its best to output m adaptively. In this case, the network can only predict the engine interference noise in the pilot/engine signal m. The network error e is equal to m, the pilot/ engine signal, minus the predicted contaminating engine noise signal. Thus, e contains only the pilot's voice. The linear adaptive network adaptively learns to cancel the engine noise. Such adaptive noise canceling generally does a better job than a classical filter, because it sibtracts from the signal rather than filtering it out the noise of the signal m.

4.8 MULTIPLE NEURON ADAPTIVE FILTERS

You might want to use more than one neuron in an adaptive system, so you need some additional notation. You can use a tapped delay line with *S* linear neurons, as shown in the next figure.

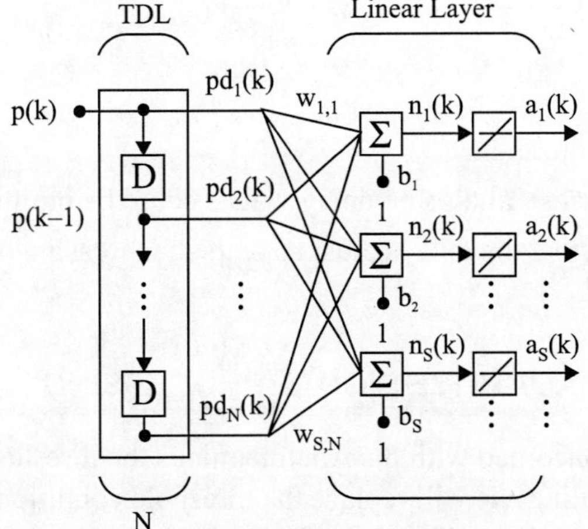

Figure 4.17: Multiple adaptive filters

Alternatively, you can represent this same network in abbreviatedform

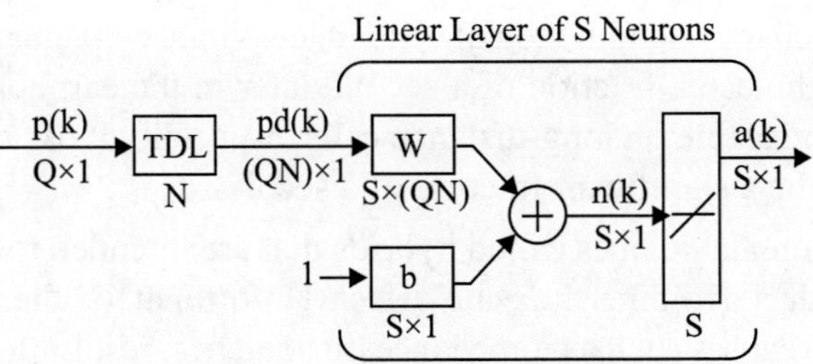

Figure 4.18: Abbreviated notation

If you want to show more of the detail of the tapped delay line—and there are not too many delays—you can use the following notation:

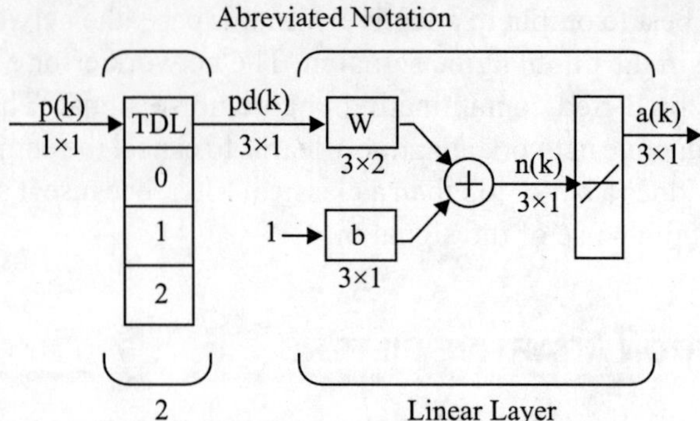

Figure 4.19: Abbreviated nmotation with TDL

Here, a tapped delay line sends to the weight matrix:

- The current signal
- The previous signal
- The signal delayed before that

You could have a longer list, and some delay values could be omitted if desired.

The only requirement is that the delays must appears in increasing order as they go from top to bottom.

4.9 APPLICATION OF ADAPTIVE SIGNAL PROCESSING

Up to now, we have been concerned with the Adaline minus the threshold condition on the output. In Section 4.11, on the Madaline, we will replace the threshold condition and examine networks. In this section, we will look at a few examples of adaptive signal processing using only the ALC portion of the Adaline.

4.9.1 ECHO Cancellation in Telephone Circuits

You may have experienced the phenomenon of echo in telephone conversations: you hear the words you speak into the mouthpiece a fraction of a second later in the earphone of the telephone. The echo tends to be most noticeable on long-distance calls, especially those over satellite links where transmission delays can be a significant fraction of a second.

Telephone circuits contain devices called hybrids that are intended to isolate incoming signals from outgoing signals, thus avoiding the echo effect. Unfortunately, these circuits do not always perform perfectly, due to causes such as impedance mismatches, resulting in some echo back to the speaker. Even when the echo signal has been attenuated by a substantial amount, it still may be audible, and hence an annoyance to the speaker.

Certain echo-suppression devices rely on relays that open and close circuits in the outgoing lines so that incoming voice signals are not sent back to the speaker. When transmission delays are long, as with satellite communications, these echo suppressors can result in a loss of parts of words.

This choppy-speech effect is perhaps more familiar that the echo effect. An adaptive filter can be used to remove the echo effect without the choppiness of the relays used in other echo suppression circuits.

Figure 4.20 is a block diagram of a telephone circuit with an adaptive filter used as an echo-suppression device. The echo is caused by a leakage of the incoming voice signal to the output line through the hybrid circuit. This leakage adds to the output signal coming from the microphone. The output of the adaptive filter, y, is subtracted from the outgoing signal, $s + n^l$, where s is the outgoing pure voice signal and n^l is the noise, or echo caused by leakage of the incoming voice signal through the hybrid circuit. The success of the leakage through the hybrid circuit.

Notice that the input to the filter is a copy of the incoming signal, n, and that the error is a copy of the outgoing signal,

$$\varepsilon = s + n^l - y \tag{4.5}$$

We assume that y is correlated with the noise. n^l, but not with the pure voice signal, s. If the quantity, $n^l - y$, is some echo still remains in the outgoing signal. Squaring and taking expectation values of both sides of Eq. (4.5) gives

$$(\varepsilon^2 = (s^2) + ((n^l - y)^2) + 2\,(s(n^l - y)) \tag{4.6}$$

$$= (s^2) + ((n^l - y)^2) \tag{4.7}$$

Equation (4.7) follows, since is s is not correlated with either y or n^l, resulting in the last term in Eq. (4.6) being equal to zero.

The signal power, (s^2), is determined by the source of the voice signal-say, some amplifier at the telephone switching station local to the sender. Thus, (s^2) is no directly affected by changes in (ε^2).

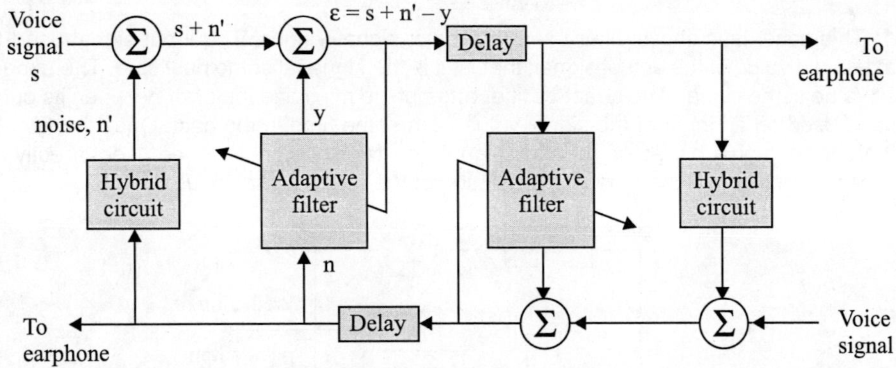

Figure 4.20: This figure is a schematic of a telephone circuit using an adaptive filter to cancel echo. The adaptive filter is depicted as a box; the slanted arrow represents the adjustable weights.

The adaptive filter attempts to minimize (ε^2), and in doing so, minimizes $((n^l - y)^2)$, the power of the uncanceled noise on the outgoing line. Since there is only one input to the adaptive filter, the device would be configured as a transverse filter. Widrow and Stearns suggest sampling the incoming signal at a rate of 8 KHz and using 128 weight values.

4.9.2 Other Applications

Rather than go into the details of the many applications that can be addressed by these adaptive filters, we refer you once again to the excellent text by Widrow and Stearns. In this section, we shall simply suggest a few broad areas where adaptive filters can be used in addition to the echo-cancellation application we have discussed.

Figure 4.21 shows an adaptive filter that is used to predict the future value of a signal based on its present value. A second example is shown in Figure 4.22. In this example, the adaptive filter learns to reproduce the output from some plant based on inputs to the system. This configuration has many uses as an adaptive control system. The plant could represent many things, including a human operator. In that case, the adaptive filter could learn how to respond to changing conditions by watching the human operator. Eventually, such a device might result in an automated control system, leaving the human free for more important tasks.[2]

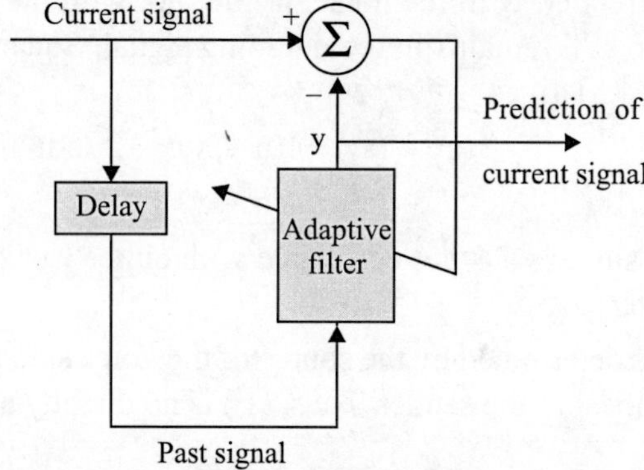

Figure 4.21: This schematic shows filter used to predict signal values. The input signal used to train the network is a delayed value of the actual signal; that is, it is the signal at some past time. The expected output is the current value of the signal. The adaptive filter attempts to minimize the error between its output and the current signal, based on an input of the signal value from some time in the past. Once the filter is correctly predicting the current signal based on the past signal, the current signal can be used directly as an input without the delay. The filter will then make a prediction of the future signal value.

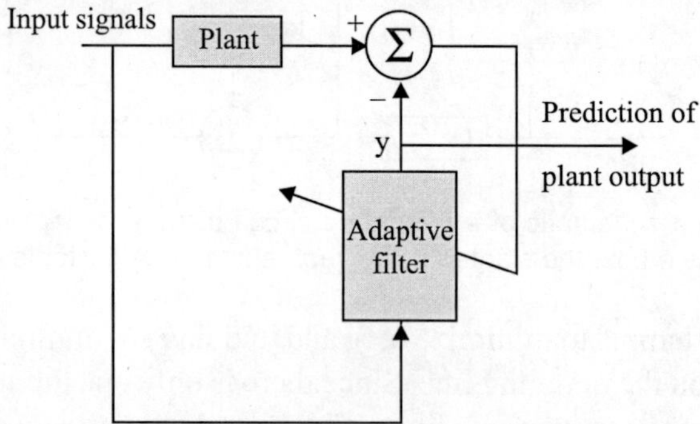

Figure 4.22: This example shows an adaptive filter used to model the output from a system, called the plant. Inputs to the filter are the same as those to the plant. The filter adjusts its weights based on the difference between its output and the output of the plant.

Another useful application of these devices is in adaptive beam-forming antenna arrays. Although the term antenna is usually associated with electromagnetic relation, we broaden the definition here to include any spatial array of sensors. The basic task her is to learn to steer the array. At any given time, a signal may be arriving from any given direction, but antennae usually are directional in their reception characteristics. They respond to signals in some directions, but not in others. The antenna array with adaptive filters learns to adjust its directional characteristics in order to respond to the incoming signal no matter what the direction is, while reducing its response to unwanted noise signals coming in from other directions.

Of course, we have only touched on the number of applications for these devices. Unlike many other neural-network architectures, this is a relatively mature device with a long history of success. In the next section, we replace the binary output condition on the ALC circuit so that the latter becomes, once again, the complete Adaline.

4.10 THE MADALINE

It also has some of the same limitations as the perceptron. For example, a two-input Adaline cannot compute the XOR function. Combining Adalines in a layered structure can overcome this difficulty, as we did in Chapter 2 with the perceptron. Such a structure is illustrated in Figure 4.23.

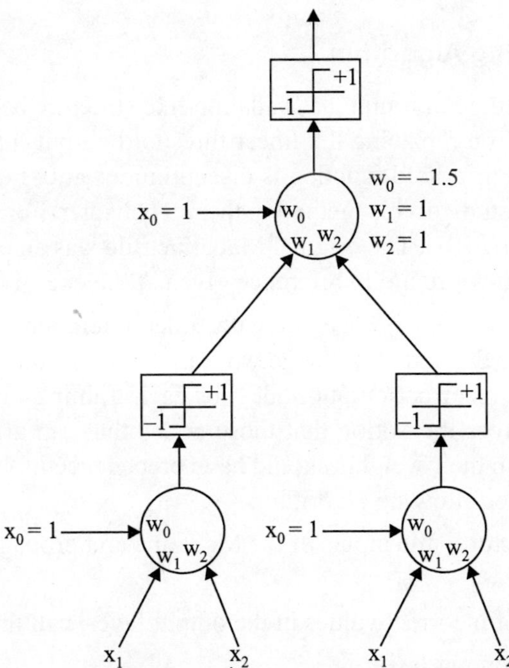

Figure 4.23: Many Adalines (the Madaline) can compute the XOR function of two inputs. Note the addition of the bias terms to each Adaline. A positive analog output from an ALC results in a+1 output from the associated Adaline; a negative analog output results in a -1. Likewise, any inputs to the device that are binary in nature must use ± rather than 1 and 0.

4.10.1 Madaline Architecture

Madaline is the acronym for Many Adalines. Arranged in a multilayered architecture as illustrated in Figure 4.24, the Madaline resembles the general neural-network structure shown in Chapter 1. In this configuration, the Madaline could be presented with a large-dimensional input vector-say, the pixel values from a raster scan. With suitable training, the network could be taught to respond with a binary +1 on one of several output nodes, each of which corresponds to a different category of input image.

Examples of such categorization are {cat, dog, armadillo, javelina} and {Flogger, Tom Cat, Eagle, Fulcrum}. In such a network, each of four nodes in the output layer corresponds to a single class. For a given input pattern, a node would have a +1 output if the input pattern corresponded to the class represented by that particular node. The other three nodes would have a –1 output. If the input pattern were not a member of any known class, the results from the network could be ambiguous.

To train such a network, we might be tempted to begin with the LMS algorithm at the output layer. Since the network is presumably trained with previously identified input patterns, the desired output vector is known. What we do not know is the desired output for a given node on one of the hidden layers. Furthermore, the LMS algorithm would operate on the analog outputs of the ALC, not on the bipolar output values of the Adaline. For these reasons, a different training strategy has developed for the Madaline.

4.10.2 The MRII Training Algorithm

It is possible to devise a method of training a Madaline-like structure based on the LMS algorithm; however, the method relies on replacing the linear threshold output function with a continuously differentiable function (the threshold function is discontinuous at 0; hence, it is not differentiable there). We will take up the study of this method in the next chapter. For now we consider a method known as Madaline rule II (MRII). The original Madaline rule was an earlier method that we shall not discuss here. Details can be found in reference given at the end of this chapter.

MRII resembles a trial-and-error procedure with added intelligence in the form of a minimum disturbance principle. Since the output of the network is a series of bipolar units, training amounts to reducing the number of incorrect output nodes for each training input pattern. The minimum disturbance principle enforces the notion that those nodes that can affect the output error while incurring the least change in their weights should have precedence in the learning procedure. This principle is embodied in the following algorithm:

1. Apply a training vector to the inputs of the Madaline and propagate it through to the output units.
2. Count the number of incorrect values in the output layer; call this number the error.
3. For all units on the output layer.
   (a) Select the first previously unselected node whose analog output is closest to zero. (This node is the node that can reverse its bipolar output with the change in its weights – hence the term minimum disturbance.

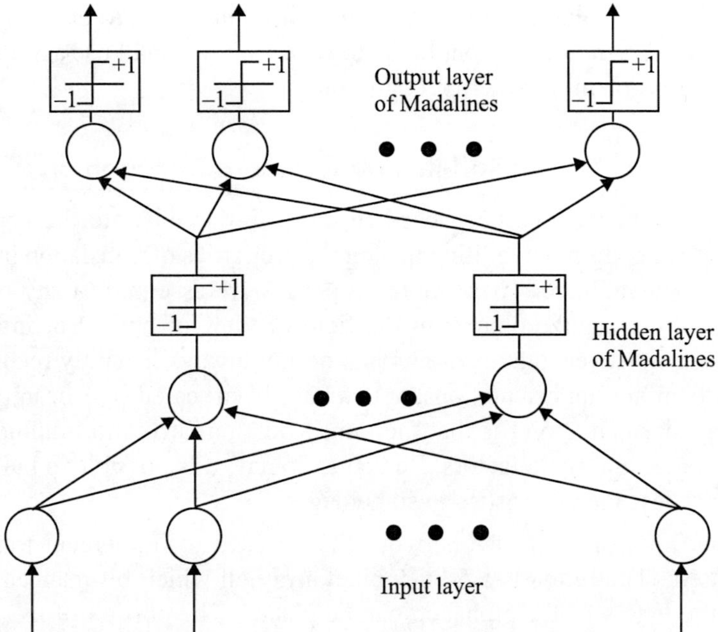

Figure 4.24: Many Adalines can be joined in a layered neural network such as this one.

(b) Change the weights on the selected unit such that the bipolar output of the unit changes.

(c) Propagate the input vector forward from the inputs to the outputs once again.

(d) If the weight change results in a reduction in the number of errors, accept the weight change; otherwise, restore the original weights.

4. Repeat step 3 for all layers except the input layer.
5. For all units on the output layer.

   (a) Select the previously unselected pair of units whose analog outputs are closest to zero.

   (b) Apply a weight correction to both units, in order to change the bipolar output of each.

   (c) Propagate the input vector forward from the inputs to the outputs.

   (d) If the weight change results in a reduction in the number of errors, accept the weight change; otherwise, restore the original weights.

6. Repeat step 5 for all layers except the input layer.

If necessary, the sequence in steps 5 and 6 can be repeated with triplets of units, or even larger combinations, until satisfactory results are obtained. Preliminary indications are that pairs are adequate for modest-sized networks with up to 25 units per layer.

At the time of this writing, the MRII was still undergoing experimentation to determine its convergence characteristics and other properties. Moreover, a new learning algorithm, MRIII, has been developed. MRIII is similar to MRII, but the individual units have a continuous output function, rather than the bipolar threshold function. In the next section, we shall use a Madaline architecture to examine a specific problem in pattern recognition.

4.10.3 A Madaline for Translation-invariant Pattern Recognition

Various Madaline structures have been used recently to demonstrate the applicability of this architecture to adaptive pattern recognition having the properties of translation invariance, rotation invariance, and scale invariance. These three properties are essential to any robust system that would be called on to recognize objects in the field of view of optical or infrared sensors, for example. Remember, however, that even humans do not always instantly recognize objects that have been rotated to unfamiliar orientations, or that have been scaled significantly smaller or larger than their everyday size. The point is that there may be alternatives to training in instantaneous recognition at all angles and scale factors. Be that as it may, it is possible to build neural-network devices that exhibit these characteristics to some degree.

Figure 4.25 shows a portion of a network that is used to implement translation-invariant recognition of pattern. The retina is a 5-by-5-pixel array on which bit-mapped representation of patterns, such as the letters of the alphabet, can be placed. The portion of the network shown is called a slab. Unlike a layer, a slab does not communicate with other slabs in the network, as will be seen shortly. Each Adaline in the slab receives the identical 25 inputs from the retina, and computes a bipolar output in the usual fashion; however, the weights on the 25 Adalines share a unique relationship.

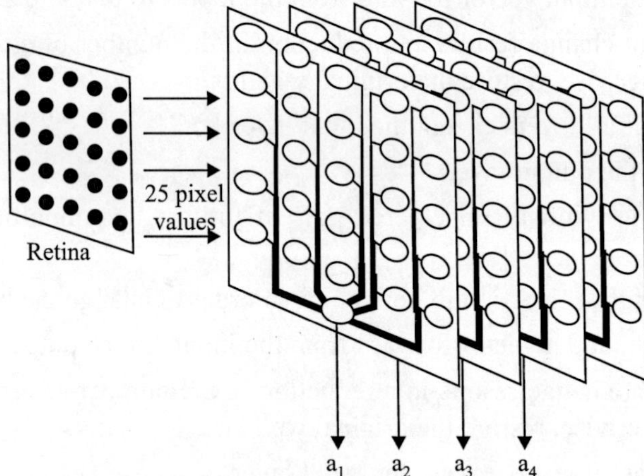

Figure 4.25: This single slab of Adalines will give the same output (either +1 ro -1) for a particular pattern on the retina, regardless of the horizontal or vertical alignment of that pattern on the retina. All 25 individual Adalines are connected to a single Adaline that computes the majority functions; If most of the inputs are +1, the majority element responds with a +1 output. The network derives its translation-invariance properties from the particular configuration of the weights. See the text for details.

Consider the weights on the top-left Adaline as being arranged in a square matrix duplicating the pixel array on the retina. The Adaline to the immediate right to the top-left pixel has the identical set of weight values, nut translated one pixel to the right: The rightmost column of weights on the first unit wraps around to the left to become the leftmost column on the second unit. Similarly, the unit below the top-left unit also the identical weights, but translated one pixel down. The bottom row of weights on the first unit becomes the top row of the unit under it. This translation continues across each row and down each column in a similar manner. Figure 4.26 illustrates some of these weight matrices. Because of this relationship among the weight matrices, a single pattern on the retina will elicit identical responses from the slab, independent of the pattern's translational position on the retina. We encourage you to reflect on this result for a moment (perhaps several moments), to convince yourself of its validity.

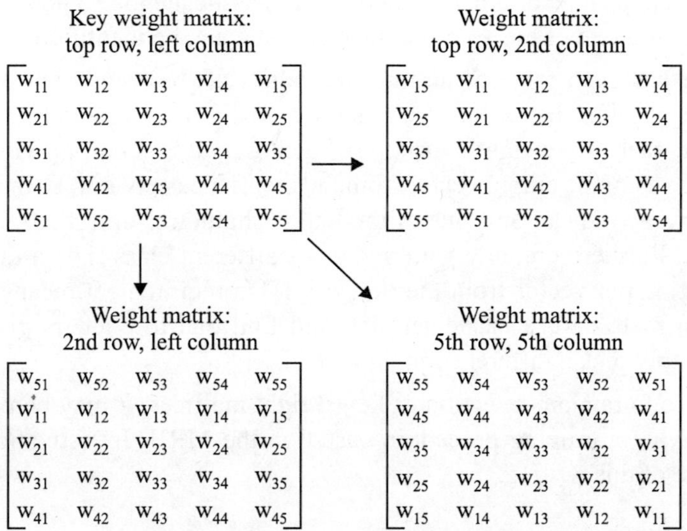

Figure 4.26: The weight matrix in the upper left is the key weight matrix. All other weight matrices on the slab are derived from this matrix. The matrix to the right of the key weight matrix represents the matrix on the Adaline directly to the right of the one with the key weight matrix has wrapped around to become the first column, with the other columns shifting one space to the right. The matrix below the key weight matrix is the one on the Adaline directly below the Adaline with the key weight matrix. The matrix diagonal to the key weight matrix represents the matrix on the Adaline at the lower right of the slab.

The majority node is a single Adaline that computes a binary output based on the outputs of the majority of the Adalines connecting to it. Because of the translational relationship among the weight vectors, the placement of a particular pattern at any location on the retina will result in the identical output from the majority element (we impose the restriction that patterns that extend beyond the retina boundaries will wrap around to the opposite side, just as the various weight matrices are derived from the key weight matrix). Of course, a pattern different from the first may elicit a different response from the majority element. Because only two responses are possible, the slab can differentiate two classes on input patterns. In terms of hyperspace, a slab is capable of dividing hyperspace into two regions.

To overcome the limitation of only two possible classes, the retina can be connected to multiple slabs, each having different key weight matrices (Widrow and Winter's term for the weight matrix on the top-left element of each slab). Given the binary nature of the output of each slab, a system of n slabs could differentiate 2^n different pattern classes. Figure 4.27 shows four such slabs producing a four-dimensional output capable of distinguishing 16 different input-pattern classes with translational invariance.

Let's review the basic operation of the translation invariance network in terms of a specific example. Consider the 16 letters A ® P, as the input patterns we would like to identify regardless of their up-down or left-right translation on the 5-by-5 pixel retina. These translated retina patterns are the inputs to the slab of the network. Each retina pattern results in an output pattern from the invariance network that maps to one of the 16 input classes (in this case, each class represents a letter). By using a lookup table, or other method, we can associate the 16 possible outputs from the invariance network with one of the 16 possible letters that can be identified by the network.

So far, nothing has been said concerning the values of the weights on the Adalines of the various slabs in the system. That is because it is not actually necessary to train those nodes in the usual sense. In fact, each key weight matrix can be chosen at random, provided that each input-pattern class result in a unique output vector from the invariance network. Using the example of the previous paragraph, any translation f one of the letters should result in the same output from the invariance network. Furthermore, any pattern from a different class (i.e., a different letter) must result in a different output vector from the network. This requirement means that, if you pick a random key weight matrix for a particular slab and find that tow letters give the same output pattern, you can simply pick a different weight matrix.

As an alternative to random selection of key weight matrices, it may be possible to optimize selection by employing a training procedure based on the MRII. Investigations in this area are outgoing at the time of this writing.

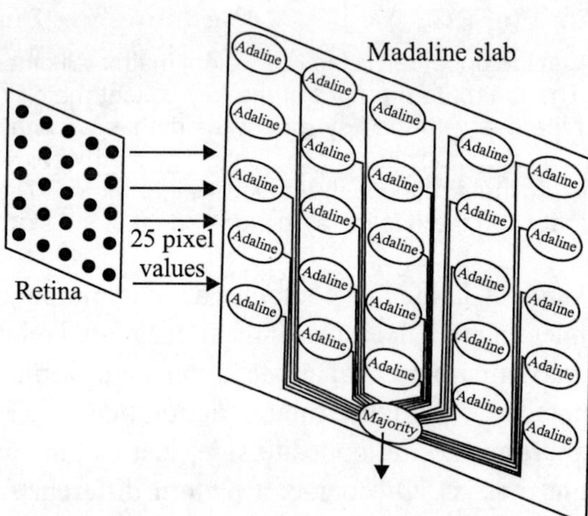

Figure 4.27: Each of the four slabs in the system depicted here will procedure a + 1 or a – 1 output value for every pattern that appears on the retina. The output vector is a four-digit binary number, so the system can potentially differentiate up to 16 different classes of input patterns.

EXERCISES

1. What is Adaline?
2. How adaline is useful for signal processing?
3. What do you signal processing and filters?
4. How we can remove the problem of Echo from long distance communication?
5. What is Fourier analysis and frequency domain?
6. What do you mean digital signal processing?
7. What is adaline? Explain the adaptive linear combiner with the help of diagram?
8. Explain the LMS learning rule?
9. Explain the various adaptive functions?
10. Explain the architecture of adaptive linear network with the help of labeled diagram?
11. Draw the diagram of decision boundary of adaline?
12. What is tapped delay line?
13. Explain the working of adaptive filter with the of example?
14. What is predictive filter? Explain with the help of example?
15. Explain the techniques of noise cancellation with the help of proper diagram?
16. What do you mean by multiple neuron adaptive filter?
17. Draw the abbreviated notation of multiple adaptive filter?
18. Explain the technique of echo cancellation in telephone circuits?
19. What are the various application of adaptive filters explain any one of them?
20. What is madaline? Explain the architecture of madaline?
21. Discuss training algorithm of madaline rule II?
22. Explain the translation invariant pattern recognition?

CHAPTER 5

Supervised and Unsupervised Learning

5.1 INTRODUCTION

Supervised learning is a machine learning technique for learning a function from training data. The training data consist of pairs of input objects (typically vectors), and desired outputs. The output of the function can be a continuous value (called regression), or can predict a class label of the input object (called classification). The task of the supervised learner is to predict the value of the function for any valid input object after having seen a number of training examples (i.e. pairs of input and target output). To achieve this, the learner has to generalize from the presented data to unseen situations in a "reasonable" way (see inductive bias). (Compare with unsupervised learning.) The parallel task in human and animal psychology is often referred to as concept learning. The network is supplied with a sequence of both input data and desired (target) output data network is thus told precisely by a "teacher" what should be emitted as output. The teacher can during the learning phase "tell" the network how well it performs ("reinforcement learning") or what the correct behavior would have been ("fully supervised learning"). In supervised learning we have perceptron , Backpropagation network and adaline network described in recent chapters.

Unsupervised learning is a class of problems in which one seeks to determine how the data are organized. It is distinguished from supervised learning (and reinforcement learning) in that the learner is given only unlabeled examples.Unsupervised learning is closely related to the problem of density estimation in statistics. However unsupervised learning also encompasses many other techniques that seek to summarize and explain key features of the data.One form of unsupervised learning is clustering. Another example is blind source separation based on Independent Component Analysis (ICA).

Among neural network models, the Self-Organizing Map (SOM) and Adaptive resonance theory (ART) are commonly used unsupervised learning algorithms. The SOM is a topographic organization in which nearby locations in the map represent inputs with similar properties. The ART model allows the number of clusters to vary with problem size and lets the user control the degree of similarity between members of the same clusters by means of a user-defined constant called the vigilance parameter. ART networks are also used for many pattern recognition tasks, such as automatic target recognition and seismic signal processing. The first version of ART was "ART1", developed by Carpenter and Grossberg(1988).

Self-organizing in networks is one of the most fascinating topics in the neural network field. Such networks can learn to detect regularities and correlations in their input and adapt their future responses to that input accordingly. The neurons of competitive networks learn to recognize groups of similar input vectors. Self-organizing maps learn to recognize groups of similar input vectors in such a way that neurons physically near each other in the neuron layer respond to similar input vectors.

Learning vector quantization (LVQ) is a method for training competitive layers in a supervised manner. A competitive layer automatically learns to classify input vectors. However, the classes that the competitive layer finds are dependent only on the distance between input vectors. If two input vectors are very similar, the competitive layer probably will put them in the same class. There is no mechanism in a strictly competitive layer design to say whether or not any two input vectors are in the same class or different classes.LVQ networks, on the other hand, learn to classify input vectors into target classes chosen by the user.

5.2 COMPETITIVE LEARNING

The prototypic competitive learning ("self-organizing") model is the Kohonen network (named after the Finnish researcher who pioneered the research). A Kohonen network is a two-layered network, much like the Perceptron. But the output layer for a two-neurode input layer can be represented as a two-dimensional grid, also known as the "competitive layer". The input values are continuous, typically normalized to any value between –1 and +1. Training of the Kohonen network does not involve comparing the actual output with a desired output. Instead, the input vector is compared with the weight vectors leading to the competitive layer. The neurode with a weight vector most closely matching the input vector is called the **winning neurode**.

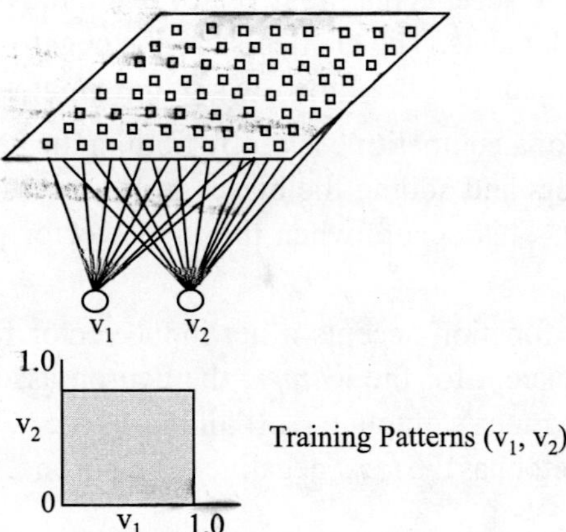

Figure 5.1: Network with training patterns

For example, if the input vector is (0.35, 0.8), the winning neurode might have weight vector (0.4, 0.78). The learning rule would adjust the weight vector to make it even closer to the input vector. Only the winning neurode produces output, and only the winning neurode gets its weights adjusted. In more sophisticated models, only the weights of the winning neurode and its immediate neighbors are updated.

After training, a limited number of input vectors will map to activation of distinct output neurodes. Because the weights are modified in response to the inputs, rather than in response to desired outputs, competitive learning is called **unsupervised** learning, to distinguish it from the **supervised** learning of Perceptrons, Adalines and Backpropagation. In supervised learning, comparison is made between actual outputs and desired outputs supplied by an external supervisor. There is no external supervisor in competitive learning. The neurons in a competitive layer distribute themselves to recognize frequently presented input vectors.

5.2.1 Architecture

The architecture for a competitive network is shown below.

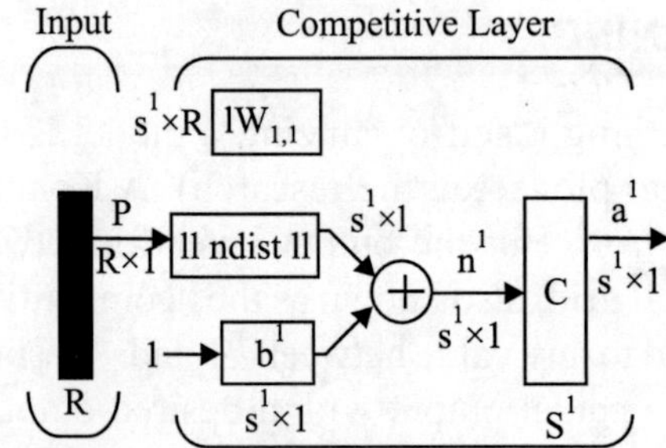

Figure 5.2: Architecture for a competitive network

The ||dist|| box in this figure accepts the input vector **p** and the input weight matrix $\mathbf{IW}^{1,1}$, and produces a vector having S_1 elements. The elements are the negative of the distances between the input vector and vectors ${}_i\mathbf{IW}^{1,1}$ formed from the rows of the input weight matrix.

Compute the net input $\mathbf{n}^1$ of a competitive layer by finding the negative distance between input vector **p** and the weight vectors and adding the biases **b**. If all biases are zero, the maximum net input a neuron can have is 0. This occurs when the input vector **p** equals that neuron's weight vector.

The competitive transfer function accepts a net input vector for a layer and returns neuron outputs of 0 for all neurons except for the *winner*, the neuron associated with the most positive element of net input $\mathbf{n}^1$. The winner's output is 1. If all biases are 0, then the neuron whose weight vector is closest to the input vector has the *least* negative net input and, therefore, wins the competition to output a 1.

5.2.2 Creating a Competitive Neural Network (NEWC)

You can create a competitive neural network with the function newc. A simple example shows how this works.

Suppose you want to divide the following four two-element vectors into two classes.

```
p = [.1 .8 .1 .9; .2 .9 .1 .8]
p = 0.1000   0.8000   0.1000   0.9000
    0.2000   0.9000   0.1000   0.8000
```

There are two vectors near the origin and two vectors near (1,1).

First, create a two-neuron layer with two input elements ranging from 0 to 1. The first argument gives the ranges of the two input vectors, and the second argument says that there are to be two neurons.

```
net = newc([0 1; 0 1],2);
```

The weights are initialized to the centers of the input ranges with the function midpoint. You can check to see these initial values as follows:

```
wts = net.IW{1,1}
wts = 0.5000   0.5000
      0.5000   0.5000
```

These weights are indeed the values at the midpoint of the range (0 to 1) of the inputs, as you would expect when using midpoint for initialization.

The biases are computed by initcon, which gives

```
biases = net.b{1}
biases = 5.4366
         5.4366
```

Now you have a network, but you need to train it to do the classification job.

Recall that each neuron competes to respond to an input vector **p**. If the biases are all 0, the neuron whose weight vector is closest to **p** gets the highest net input and, therefore, wins the competition and outputs 1. All other neurons output 0. You want to adjust the winning neuron so as to move it closer to the input.

5.3 KOHONEN'S SELF-ORGANIZING MAP (SOM)

The basic Self-Organizing Map (SOM) can be visualized as a sheet-like neural-network array, the cells (or nodes) of which become specifically tuned to various input signal patterns or classes of patterns in an orderly fashion. The learning process is competitive and unsupervised, meaning that no teacher is needed to define the correct output (or actually the cell into which the input is mapped) for an input. In the basic version, only one map node (winner) at a time is activated corresponding to each input. The locations of the responses in the array tend to become ordered in the learning process as if some meaningful nonlinear coordinate system for the different input features were being created over the network.

During the training phase, a SOM builds a representation of training samples. The trained network can be used to map any input vector onto two-dimensional space.

The objective of SOM training is to ensure that different parts of the network respond similarly to similar input vectors. So, the training mainly involves analyzing the behaviour of the network for a training sample and adjusting the weights of synapses to ensure that the network exhibits a similar behaviour for a similar input.

The training procedure involves following steps.

- Initialize the weights to small random values
- Choose a random training sample, assign the input vector to the input neurons and run the network.
- The output of a neuron in output layer represents the similarity between its weight vector (source synapse weights) and the input vector. The output neuron which has the highest output value is declared as the **winner neuron** for current input.
- Calculate the distance of each output neuron from the winner using a Neighborhood function
- Update the weights of synapses using following formulae. (This adjusts the weights corresponding to winner and its neighbors such that, a neuron close to the current winner wins for a similar input)

Similarity = Difference between source neurons output and the synapse weight

Weight Change = (Learning Rate) * (Neighborhood value of target neuron) * Similarity

- Similarly, train all samples in a random order. This completes one **training cycle** (or Training Epoch)
- Repeat the steps to complete the specified number of training epochs.

The trained SOM maps any input vector to a winner neuron, which can be interpreted as the position of vector in two-dimensional space.

Kohonon's SOMs are a type of unsupervised learning. The goal is to discover some underlying structure of the data. However, the kind of structure we are looking for is very different than, say, PCA or vector quantization. Kohonen's SOM is called a topology-preserving map because there is a topological structure imposed on the nodes in the network. A topological map is simply a mapping that preserves neighborhood relations.

In the nets we have studied so far, we have ignored the geometrical arrangements of output nodes. Each node in a given layer has been identical in that each is connected with all of the nodes in the upper and/or lower layer. We are now going to take into consideration that physical arrangement of these nodes. Nodes that are "close" together are going to interact differently than nodes that are "far" apart.

What do we mean by "close" and "far"? We can think of organizing the output nodes in a line or in a planar configuration. The goal is to train the net so that nearby outputs correspond to nearby inputs.

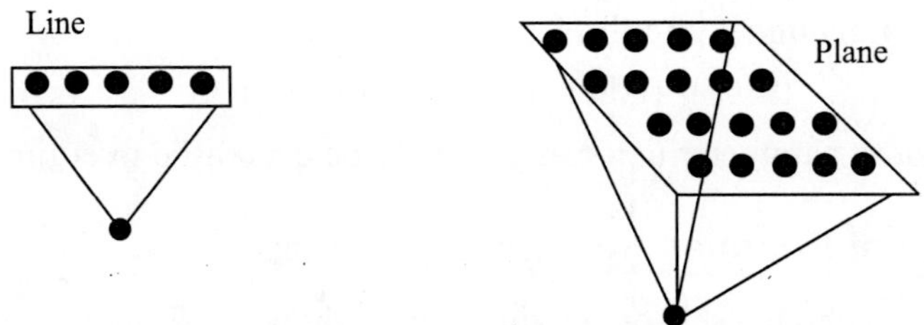

Figure 5.3: Kohonen's self-organizing map

The goal is to train the net so that nearby outputs correspond to nearby inputs.

E.g. if x_1 and x_2 are two input vectors and t_1 and t_2 are the locations of the corresponding winning output nodes, then t_1 and t_2 should be close if x_1 and x_2 are similar. A network that performs this kind of mapping is called a feature map.In the brain, neurons tend to cluster in groups. The connections within the group are much greater than the connections with the neurons outside of the group. Kohonen's network tries to mimick this in a simple way.

5.3.1 Simple Algorithm for Kohonon's Self Organizing Map

- Assume output nodes are connected in an array (usually 1 or 2 dimensional)
- Assume that the network is fully connected - all nodes in input layer are connected to all nodes in output layer.
- Use the competitive learning algorithm as follows:
- Randomly choose an input vector x
- Determine the "winning" output node i, where w_i is the weight vector connecting the inputs to output node i.

Note: the above equation is equivalent to $w_i\ x >= w_k\ x$ only if the weights are normalized. \

$$|\omega_i - x| \leq |\omega_k - x| \quad k$$

- Given the winning node i, the weight update is

$$w_k\ (new) = w_k\ (old) + \mu\ \chi\ (i, k)\ (x - w_k)$$

where χ (i, k) is called the neighborhood function that has value 1 when i = k and falls off with the distance $|r_k - r_i|$ between units i and k in the output array. Thus, units close to the winner as well as the winner itself, have their weights updated appreciably. Weights associated with far away output nodes do not change significantly. It is here that the toplogical information is supplied. Nearby units receive similar updates and thus end up responding to nearby input patterns.

The above rule drags the weight vector wi and the weights of nearby units towards the input x.

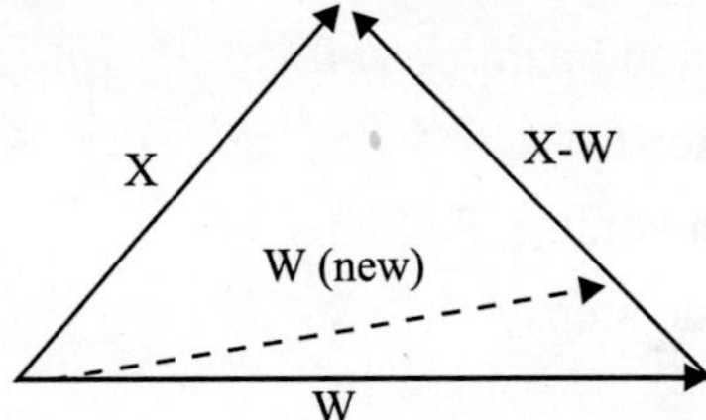

Example of the Neighborhood Function is:

$$\chi\,(i, k) = e\,(-|r_k - r_i|^2)/(2s^2)$$

where σ^2 is the width parameter that can gradually be decreased over time.

5.3.2 Architecture of Kohonen Self-organizing Map

The architecture of the Kohonen self-organizing map is shown in Figure 5.4.

Neighborhoods of the unit designated by # of radii R = 2, 1 and 0 in a one-dimensional topology (with 10 cluster units) are shown in Figure 5.5.

The neighborhoods of radii R = 2, 1 and 0 are shown in Figure 5.6 for a rectangular grid and in Figure 5.7 for a hexagonal grid 9each with 49 units). In each illustration, the winning unit is indicated by the symbol "#" and the other units are denoted by "*".

Note that each unit has eight nearest neighbors in the rectangular grid, but only six in the hexagonal grid. Winning units that are close to the edge of the grid will have some neighborhoods that have fewer units than that shown in the respective figure. (Neighborhoods do not "wrap around" from one side of the grid to the other; "missing" units are simply ignored.)

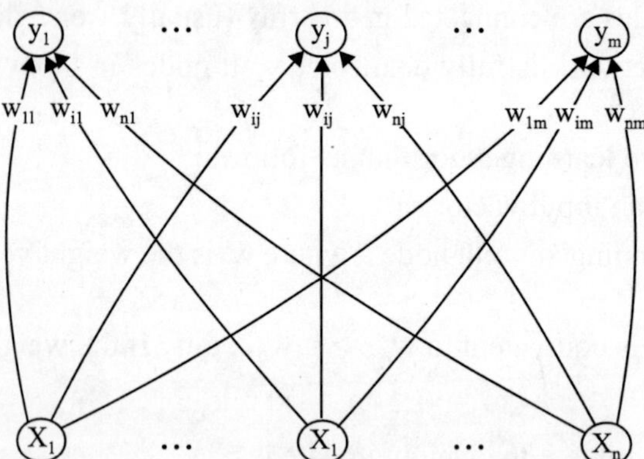

Figure 5.4: Kohonen self-organizing map.

  *   *   *   {*   (*   [#]   *)   *}   *   *

{}R = 2   ()R = 1   {}R = 0

Figure 5.5: Linear array of cluster units.

5.3.3 Algorithm

Step 1: Initialize weights w_{ij}. (Possible choices are discussed below.)

Set topological neighborhood parameters.

Set learning rate parameters.

Step 2: While stopping condition is false, do Steps 3-9.

Step 3: For each input vector x, do steps 4-6.

Step 4: For each j, compute:

$$D(j) = \sum_{i} (w_{ij} - x_i)^2$$

Step 5: Find index J such that D(J) is a minimum.

Step 6: For all units j within a specified neighborhood of J, and for all i:

$$w_{ij}(\text{new}) = w_{ij}(\text{old}) + \alpha[x_i - w_{ij}(\text{old})].$$

Step 7: Update learning rate.

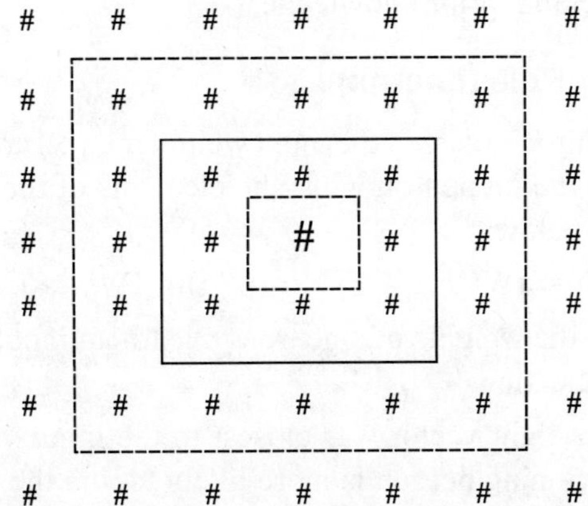

Figure 5.6: Neighborhoods for rectangular grid.

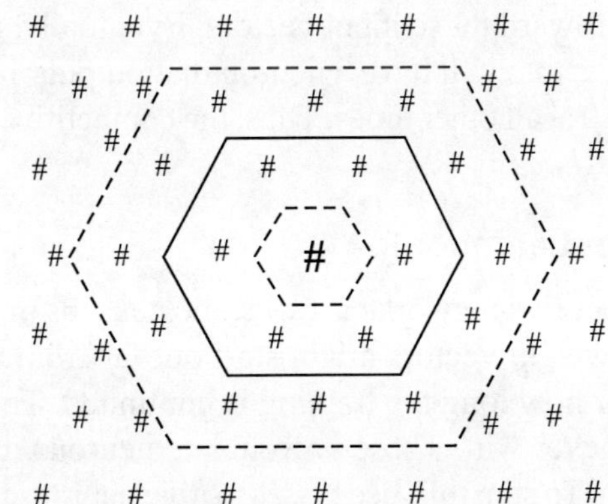

Figure 5.7: Neighborhoods for hexagonal grid.

Step 8: Reduce radius of topological neighborhood at specified times.

Step 9: Test stopping condition.

Alternative structures are possible for reducing R and α.

The learning rate α is a slowly decreasing function of time (or training epochs). Kohonen indicates that a linearly decreasing function is satisfactory for practical computations; a geometric decrease would produce similar results.

The radius of the neighborhood around a cluster unit also decreases as the clustering process progresses.

The formation of a map occurs in two phases: the initial formation of the correct order and the final convergence. The second phase takes much longer than the first and requires a small value for the learning rate. Many iterations through the training set may be necessary, at least in some applications [Kohonen, 1989a].

Random values may be assigned for the initial weights. If some information is available concerning the distribution of clusters that might be appropriate for a particular problem, the initial weights can be taken to reflect that prior knowledge.

5.3.4 Kohonen Learning Rule (Learnk)

The weights of the winning neuron (a row of the input weight matrix) are adjusted with the *Kohonen learning* rule. Supposing that the ith neuron wins, the elements of the ith row of the input weight matrix are adjusted as shown below.

$$_{i}IW^{1,1}(q) = {}_{i}IW^{1,1}(q-1) + \alpha\,(p(q) - {}_{i}IW^{1,1}(q-1))$$

The Kohonen rule allows the weights of a neuron to learn an input vector, and because of this it is useful in recognition applications.

Thus, the neuron whose weight vector was closest to the input vector is updated to be even closer. The result is that the winning neuron is more likely to win the competition the next time a similar vector is presented, and less likely to win when a very different input vector is presented. As more and more inputs are presented, each neuron in the layer closest to a group of input vectors soon adjusts its weight vector toward those input vectors. Eventually, if there are enough neurons, every cluster of similar input vectors will have a neuron that outputs 1 when a vector in the cluster is presented, while outputting a 0 at all other times. Thus, the competitive network learns to categorize the input vectors it sees.

5.3.5 Bias Learning Rule (Learncon)

One of the limitations of competitive networks is that some neurons might not always be allocated. In other words, some neuron weight vectors might start out far from any input vectors and never win the competition, no matter how long the training is continued. The result is that their weights do not get to learn and they never win. These unfortunate neurons, referred to as dead neurons, never perform a useful function. To stop this, use biases to give neurons that only win the competition rarely (if ever) an advantage over neurons that win often. A positive bias, added to the negative distance, makes a distant neuron more likely to win. To do this job a running average of neuron outputs is kept. It is equivalent to the percentages of times each output is 1. This average is used to update the biases with the learning function learncon so that the biases of frequently active neurons become smaller, and biases of infrequently active neurons become larger.

As the biases of infrequently active neurons increase, the input space to which those neurons respond increases. As that input space increases, the infrequently active neuron responds and moves toward more input vectors. Eventually, the neuron responds to the same number of vectors as other neurons.

This has two good effects. First, if a neuron never wins a competition because its weights are far from any of the input vectors, its bias eventually becomes large enough so that it can win. When this happens, it moves toward some group of input vectors. Once the neuron's weights have moved into a group of input vectors and the neuron is winning consistently, its bias will decrease to 0. Thus, the problem of dead neurons is resolved.

The second advantage of biases is that they force each neuron to classify roughly the same percentage of input vectors. Thus, if a region of the input space is associated with a larger number of input vectors than another region, the more densely filled region will attract more neurons and be classified into smaller subsections.

5.3.6 Training

Now train the network for 500 epochs. You can use either train or adapt.

```
net.trainParam.epochs = 500;
net = train(net, p);
```

Note that train for competitive networks uses the training function trainr. You can verify this by executing the following code after creating the network.

```
net.trainFcn
```

This code produces

```
ans = trainr
```

For each epoch, all training vectors (or sequences) are each presented once in a different random order with the network and weight and bias values updated after each individual presentation.

Next, supply the original vectors as input to the network, simulate the network, and finally convert its output vectors to class indices.

```
a = sim(net,p)
ac = vec2ind(a)
```

This yields

```
ac = 1 2 1 2
```

You see that the network is trained to classify the input vectors into two groups, those near the origin, class 1, and those near (1, 1), class 2.

It might be interesting to look at the final weights and biases. They are

```
wts = 0.1000 0.1467
      0.8474 0.8525
biases = 5.4961
         5.3783
```

(You might get different answers when you run this problem, because a random seed is used to pick the order of the vectors presented to the network for training.) Note that the first vector (formed from the first row of the weight matrix) is near the input vectors close to the origin, while the vector formed from the second row of the weight matrix is close to the input vectors near (1, 1). Thus, the network has been trained—just by exposing it to the inputs—to classify them.

During training each neuron in the layer closest to a group of input vectors adjusts its weight vector toward those input vectors. Eventually, if there are enough neurons, every cluster of similar input vectors has a neuron that outputs 1 when a vector in the cluster is presented, while outputting a 0 at all other times. Thus, the competitive network learns to categorize the input.

5.4 SELF-ORGANIZING FEATURE MAPS

Self-organizing feature maps (SOFM) learn to classify input vectors according to how they are grouped in the input space. They differ from competitive layers in that neighboring neurons in the self-organizing map learn to recognize neighboring sections of the input space. Thus, self-organizing maps learn both the distribution (as do competitive layers) and topology of the input vectors they are trained on.

The neurons in the layer of an SOFM are arranged originally in physical positions according to a topology function. The function gridtop, hextop, or randtop can arrange the neurons in a grid, hexagonal, or random topology. Distances between neurons are calculated from their positions with a distance function. There are four distance functions, dist, boxdist, linkdist, and mandist. Link distance is the most common.

Here a self-organizing feature map network identifies a winning neuron i^* using the same procedure as employed by a competitive layer. However, instead of updating only the winning neuron, all neurons within a certain neighborhood $N_{i*}(d)$ of the winning neuron are updated, using the Kohonen rule. Specifically, all such neurons i $N_{i*}(d)$ are adjusted as follows:

- ${}_iw(q) = {}_iw(q-1) + \alpha(p(q) - {}_iw(q-1))$

or

- ${}_iw(q) = (1-\alpha)_i w(q-1) + \alpha p(q)$

Here the *neighborhood* $N_{i*}(d)$ contains the indices for all of the neurons that lie within a radius d of the winning neuron i^*.

$$N_i(d) = \{j, d_{ij} \le d\}$$

Thus, when a vector **p** is presented, the weights of the winning neuron *and* its close neighbors move toward **p**. Consequently, after many presentations, neighboring neurons have learned vectors similar to each other.

Another version of SOFM training, called the *batch algorithm*, presents the whole data set to the network before any weights are updated. The algorithm then determines a winning neuron for each input vector. Each weight vector then moves to the average position of all of the input vectors for which it is a winner, or for which it is in the neighborhood of a winner.

To illustrate the concept of neighborhoods, consider the figure below. The left diagram shows a two-dimensional neighborhood of radius d = 1 around neuron 13. The right diagram shows a neighborhood of radius d = 2. These neighborhoods could be written as

$$N_{13}(1) = \{8, 12, 13, 14, 18\}$$

and

$$N_{13}(1) = \{3, 7, 8, 9, 11, 12, 13, 14, 15, 17, 18, 19, 23\}$$

$N_{13}(1)$ $N_{13}(2)$

The neurons in an SOFM do not have to be arranged in a two-dimensional pattern. You can use a one-dimensional arrangement, or three or more dimensions. For a one-dimensional SOFM, a neuron has only two neighbors within a radius of 1 (or a single neighbor if the neuron is at the end of the line). You can also define distance in different ways, for instance, by using rectangular and hexagonal arrangements of neurons and neighborhoods. The performance of the network is not sensitive to the exact shape of the neighborhoods.

5.4.1 Architecture

The architecture for this SOFM is shown below.

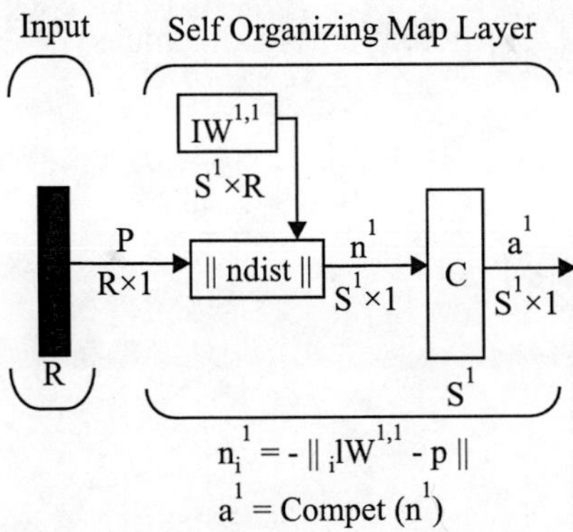

Figure 5.8: Architecture for this SOFM

This architecture is like that of a competitive network, except no bias is used here. The competitive transfer function produces a 1 for output element $\mathbf{a}^1_i$ corresponding to i^*, the winning neuron. All other output elements in $\mathbf{a}^1$ are 0. Now, however, as described above, neurons close to the winning neuron are updated along with the winning neuron. You can choose from various topologies of neurons. Similarly, you can choose from various distance expressions to calculate neurons that are close to the winning neuron.

5.4.2 Creating a Self-organizing Map Neural Network (NEWSOM)

You can create a new SOM network with the function newsom. This function defines variables used in two phases of learning:

Ordering-phase learning rate

Ordering-phase steps

Tuning-phase learning rate

Tuning-phase neighborhood distance

These values are used for training and adapting.

Consider the following example.

Suppose that you want to create a network having input vectors with two elements that fall in the ranges 0 to 2 and 0 to 1, respectively. Further suppose that you want to have six neurons in a hexagonal 2-by-3 network. The code to obtain this network is

```
net = newsom([0 2; 0 1],[2 3]);
```

Suppose also that the vectors to train on are

```
P = [.1 .3 1.2 1.1 1.8 1.7 .1 .3 1.2 1.1 1.8 1.7;...
0.2 0.1 0.3 0.1 0.3 0.2 1.8 1.8 1.9 1.9 1.7 1.8]
```

You can plot all of this with

```
plot(P(1,:), P(2,:),'.g',' markersize',20)
hold on
plotsom(net.iw{1,1},net.layers{1}.distances)
hold off
```

to give

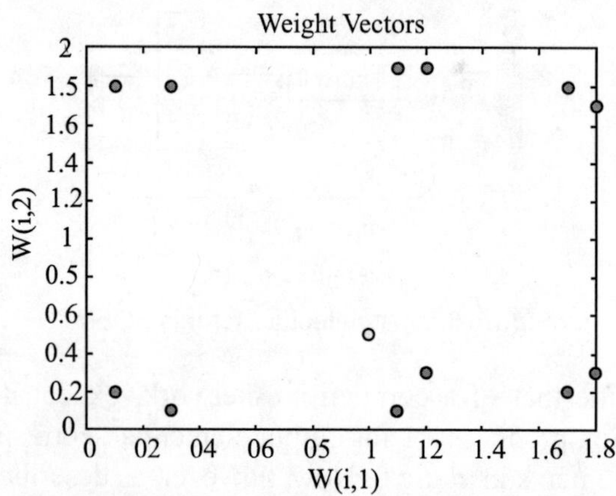

Figure 5.9: Neurons in a hexagonal 2-by-3 network

The various training vectors are seen as fuzzy gray spots around the perimeter of this figure. The initialization for newsom is midpoint. Thus, the initial network neurons are all concentrated at the black spot at (1, 0.5). When simulating a network, the negative distances between each neuron's weight vector and the input vector are calculated (negdist) to get the weighted inputs. The weighted inputs are also the net inputs (netsum). The net inputs compete (compete) so that only the neuron with the most positive net input will output a 1.

5.4.3 Training (LEARNSOMB)

The default learning in a self-organizing feature map occurs in the batch mode (trainbuwb). The weight learning function for the self-organizing map is learnsomb.

First, the network identifies the winning neuron for each input vector. Each weight vector then moves to the average position of all of the input vectors for which it is a winner or for which it is in the neighborhood of a winner. The distance that defines the size of the neighborhood is altered during training through two phases.

5.4.4 Ordering Phase

This phase lasts for the given number of steps. The neighborhood distance starts at a given initial distance, and decreases to the tuning neighborhood distance (1.0). As the neighborhood distance decreases over this phase, the neurons of the network typically order themselves in the input space with the same topology in which they are ordered physically.

5.4.5 Examples

Two examples are described briefly below. You might try the demonstrations demosm1 and demosm2 to see similar examples.

5.4.5.1 One-dimensional Self-organizing Map

Consider 100 two-element unit input vectors spread evenly between 0° and 90°.

```
angles = 0:0.5*pi/99:0.5*pi;
```

Here is a plot of the data.

```
P = [sin(angles); cos(angles)];
```

A a self-organizing map is defined as a one-dimensional layer of 10 neurons. This map is to be trained on these input vectors shown above. Originally these neurons are at the center of the figure.

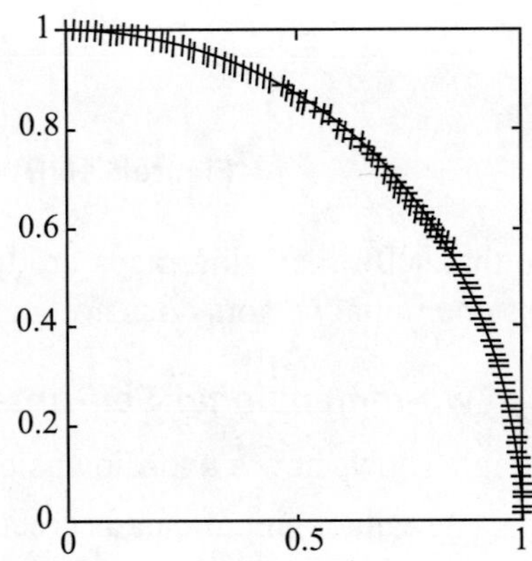

Figure 5.10: One-dimensional self-organizing map

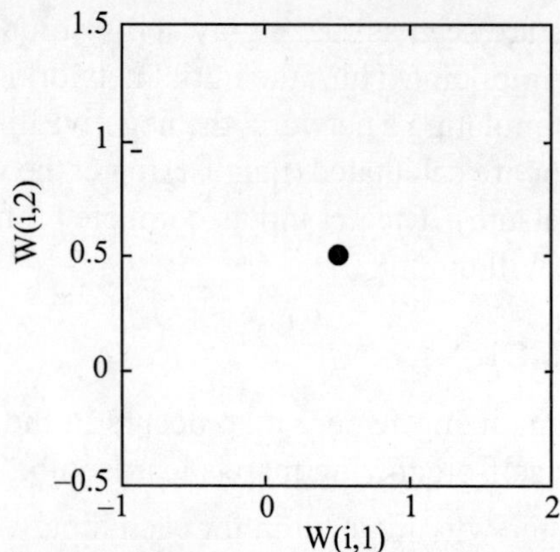

Figure 5.10(A): Neurons are at the center

Of course, because all the weight vectors start in the middle of the input vector space, all you see now is a single circle. As training starts the weight vectors move together toward the input vectors. They also become ordered as the neighborhood size decreases. Finally the layer adjusts its weights so that each neuron responds strongly to a region of the input space occupied by input vectors. The placement of neighboring neuron weight vectors also reflects the topology of the input vectors.

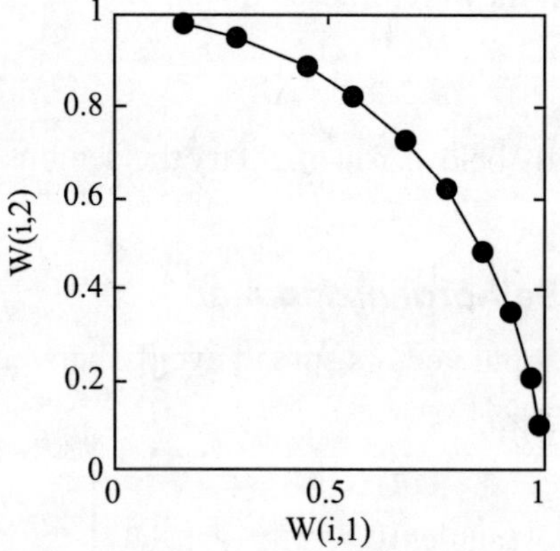

Figure 5.10(B): Input vectors in a random order

Note that self-organizing maps are trained with input vectors in a random order, so starting with the same initial vectors does not guarantee identical training results.

5.4.5.2 Two-dimensional Self-organizing Map

This example shows how a two-dimensional self-organizing map can be trained.

First some random input data is created with the following code:

```
P = rands(2,1000);
```

Here is a plot of these 1000 input vectors.

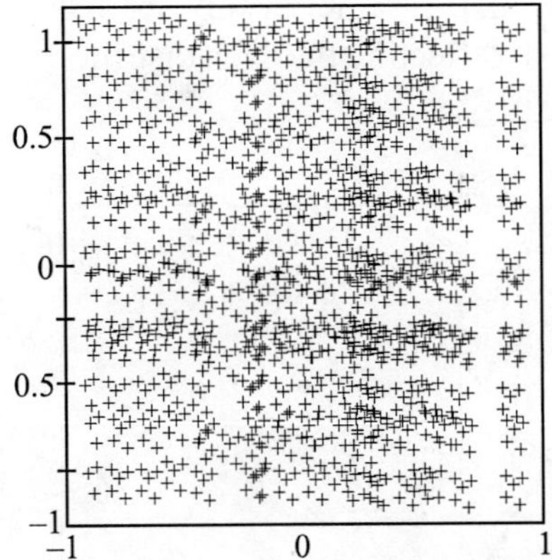

Figure 5.11: Two-dimensional self-organizing map can be trained using 1000 input vectors

A 5-by-6 two-dimensional map of 30 neurons is used to classify these input vectors. The two-dimensional map is five neurons by six neurons, with distances calculated according to the Manhattan distance neighborhood function mandist. The map is then trained for 5000 presentation cycles, with displays every 20 cycles. Here is what the self-organizing map looks like after 40 cycles.

The weight vectors, shown with circles, are almost randomly placed. However, even afteronly 40 presentation cycles, neighboring neurons, connected by lines, have weight vectors close together.

Here is the map after 120 cycles.

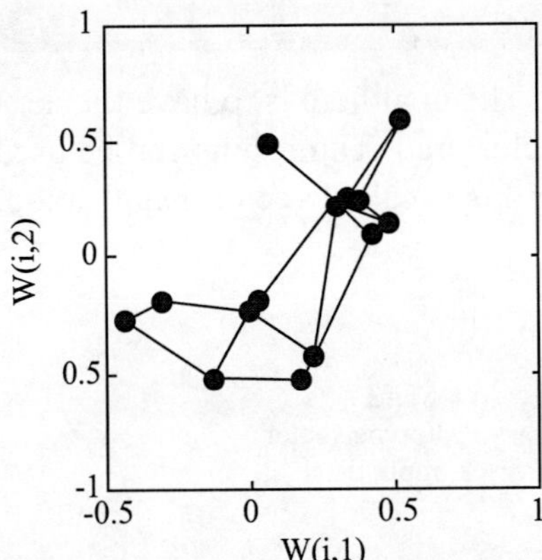

Figure 5.11(A): Self-organizing map looks like after 40 cycles

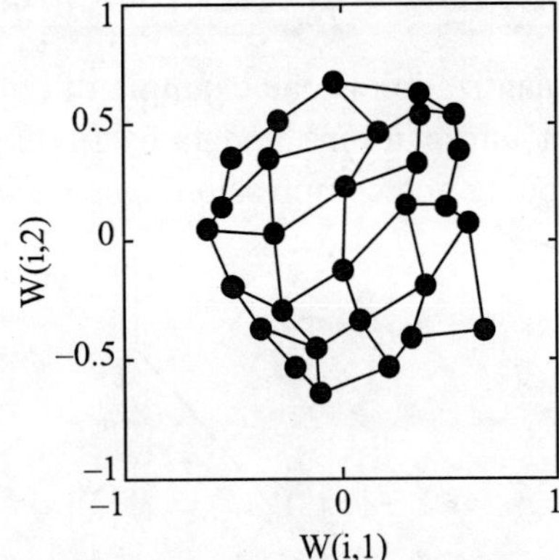

Figure 5.11(B): Self-organizing map looks like after 120 cycles

After 120 cycles, the map has begun to organize itself according to the topology of the input space, which constrains input vectors.

The following plot, after 500 cycles, shows the map more evenly distributed across the input space.

Finally, after 5000 cycles, the map is rather evenly spread across the input space. In addition, the neurons are very evenly spaced, reflecting the even distribution of input vectors in this problem.

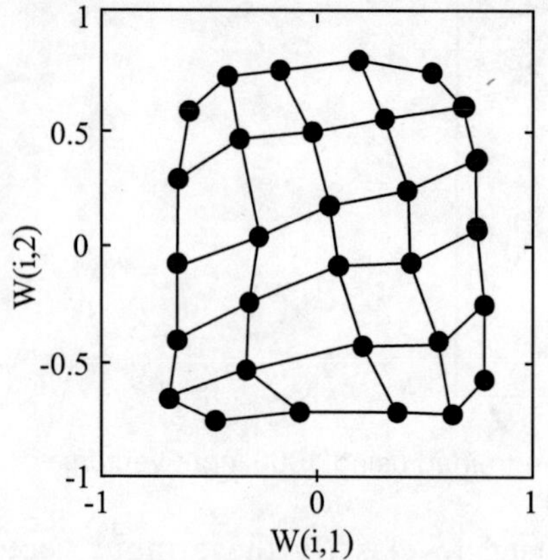

Figure 5.11(C): Self-organizing map looks like after 500 cycles

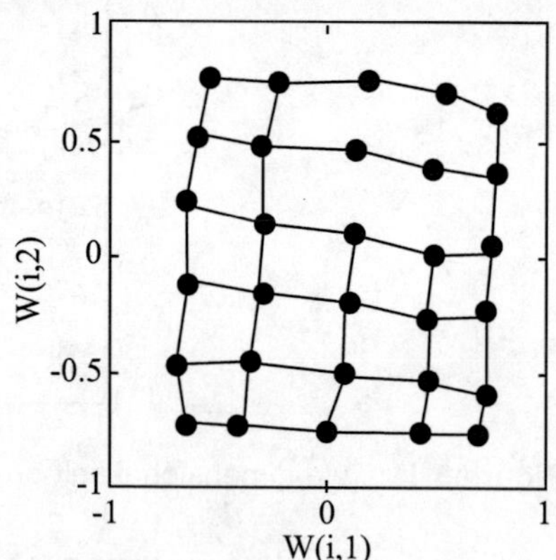

Figure 5.11(D): Self-organizing map looks like after 5000 cycles

Thus a two-dimensional self-organizing map has learned the topology of its inputs' space.It is important to note that while a self-organizing map does not take long to organize itself so that neighboring neurons recognize similar inputs, it can take a long time for the map to finally arrange itself according to the distribution of input vectors.

5.5 VECTOR QUANTIZATION (VQ)

Vector quantization is one example of competitive learning. The goal here is to have the network "discover" structure in the data by finding how the data is clustered. The results can be used for data encoding and compression. One such method for doing this is called vector quantization.

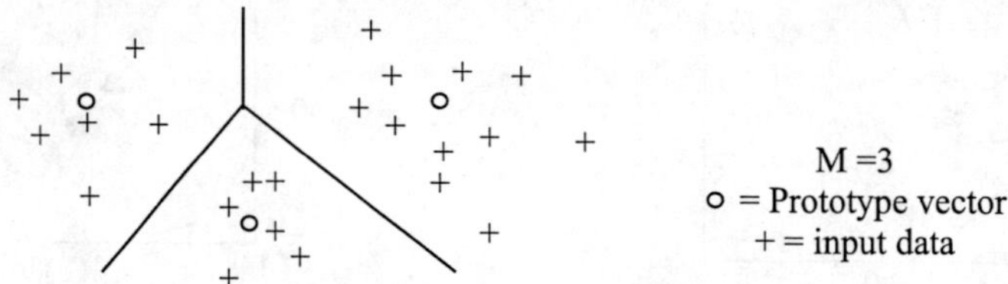

Figure 5.12: Vector quantization

In vector quantization, we assume there is a codebook which is defined by a set of M prototype vectors. (M is chosen by the user and the initial prototype vectors are chosen arbitrarily).

An input belongs to cluster i if i is the index of the closest prototype (closest in the sense of the normal euclidean distance). This has the effect of dividing up the input space into a Voronoi tesselation

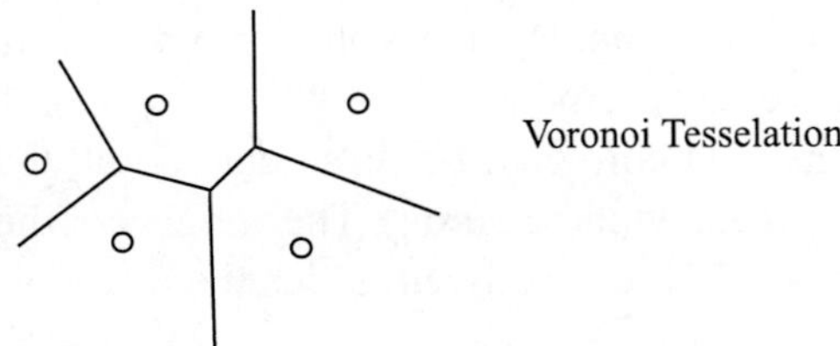

Figure 5.13: Normal euclidean distance

5.5.1 Implementing Vector Quantization With A Network

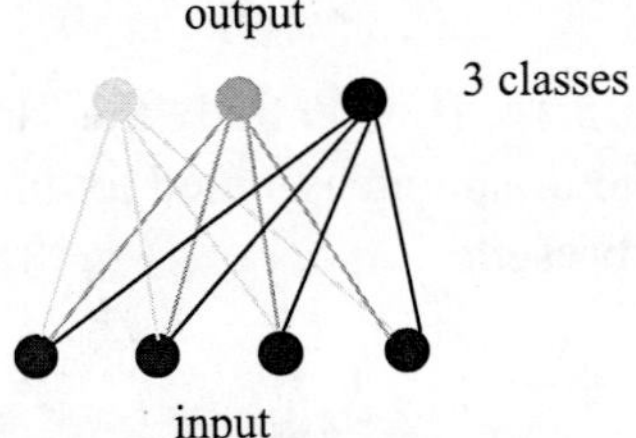

The prototypes are ripresented by the weight vectors connecting to each output node

Here there are 3 prototypes

w_1 = the weights connecting to output 1

w_2 = the weights connecting to output 2

w_3 = the weights connecting to output 3

Algorithm

- Choose the number of clusters M
- Initialize the prototypes $w_{*1}, \ldots w_{*m}$ (one simple method for doing this is to randomly choose M vectors from the input data)
- Repeat until stopping criterion is satisfied:
- Randomly pick an input x
- Determine the "winning" node k by finding the prototype vector that satisfies

$$| w_{*k} - x | <= | w_{*i} - x | \text{ (for all i)}$$

Note: if the prototypes are normalized, this is equivalent to maximizing $w_{*i}\, x$

- Update only the winning prototype weights according to

$$w_{*k}(\text{new}) = w_{*k}(\text{old}) + \alpha(x - w_{*k}(\text{old}))$$

This is called the standard competitive learning rule.

5.5.2 Learning Vector Quantization Networks

Learning Vector Quantization (LVQ), is a prototype-based unsupervised classification algorithm. LVQ is the unsupervised counterpart of vector quantization systems.

LVQ can be understood as a special case of an artificial neural network, more precisely, it applies a winner-take-all Hebbian learning-based approach. It is a precursor to Self-organizing maps (SOM) and related to neural gas, and to the k-Nearest Neighbor algorithm (k-NN). LVQ was invented by Teuvo Kohonen.

The network has three layers: an input layer, a Kohonen classification layer, and a competitive output layer. The network is given by prototypes W = (w(i), ..., w(n)). It changes the weights of the network in order to classify the data correctly. For each data point, the prototype (neuron) that is closest to it is determined (called the winner neuron). The weights of the connections to this neuron are then adapted, i.e. made closer if it correctly classifies the data point or made less similar if it incorrectly classifies it.

An advantage of LVQ is that it creates prototypes that are easy to interpret for experts in the field.

LVQ can be a source of great help in classifying text documents.

5.5.2.1 Representation of LVQ

The architecture of an LVQ neural net, shown in Figure 5.14, is essentially the same as that of a Kohonen self-organizing map (without a topological structure being assumed for the output units). In addition, each output unit has a known class that it represents.

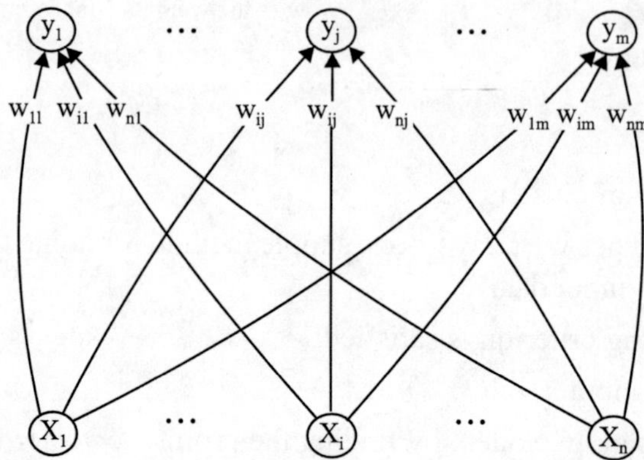

Figure 5.14: Learning vector quantization neural net.

Algorithm

The motivation for the algorithm for the LVQ net is to find the output unit that is closest to the input vector. Toward that end, if x and w_c belong to the same class, then we move the weights toward the new input vector; if x and w_c belong to different classes, then we move the weights away from this input vector.

The nomenclature we use is as follows:

x	training vector $(x_1, \ldots, x_i, \ldots, x_n)$.
T	correct category or class for the training vector.
w	weight vector for jth output unit $(w_{ij}, \ldots, w_{ij}, \ldots w_{nj})$.
C	category or class represented by jth output unit.
$\|\|x - w_j\|\|$	Education distance between input vector and (weight vector for) jth output unit.

Step 1: Initialize reference vectors (several strategies are discussed shortly);

Initialize learning rate, $\alpha(0)$.

Step 2: While stopping condition is false, do Steps 3-7.

Step 3: For each training input vector x, do Steps 4-5.

Step 4: Find J so that $||x - w_j||$ is a minimum.

Step 5: Update w_j as follows:

if $T = C_j$, then

$$w_j(new) = w_j(old) + \alpha[x - w_j(old)];$$

if $T \neq C_j$,

then

$$w_j(new) = w_j(old) - \alpha[x - w_j old)].$$

Step 6: Reduce learning rate.

Step 7: Test stopping condition:

The condition may specify a fixed number of iterations (i.e., executions of Step 1) or the learning rate reaching a sufficient small value.

5.5.2.2 Architecture of LVQ

The LVQ network architecture is shown below.

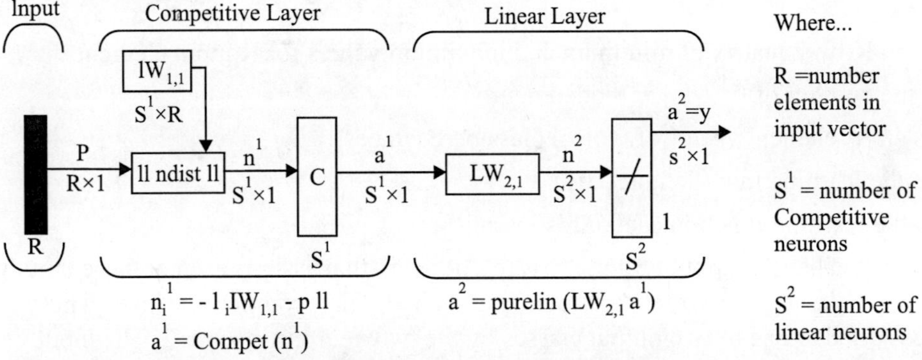

Figure 5.15: LVQ network architecture

An LVQ network has a first competitive layer and a second linear layer. The competitive layer learns to classify input vectors in much the same way as the competitive layers of Self-Organizing and Learning Vector Quantization Nets described in this chapter. The linear layer transforms the competitive layer's classes into target classifications defined by the user. The classes learned by the competitive layer are referred to as *subclasses* and the classes of the linear layer as *target classes*.

Both the competitive and linear layers have one neuron per (sub or target) class. Thus, the competitive layer can learn up to S^1 subclasses. These, in turn, are combined by the linear layer to form S^2 target classes. (S^1 is always larger than S^2.)

For example, suppose neurons 1, 2, and 3 in the competitive layer all learn subclasses of the input space that belongs to the linear layer target class 2. Then competitive neurons 1, 2, and 3 will have $\mathbf{LW}^{2,1}$ weights of 1.0 to neuron $\mathbf{n}^2$ in the linear layer, and weights of 0 to all other linear neurons. Thus, the linear neuron produces a 1 if any of the three competitive neurons (1, 2, or 3) wins the competition and outputs a 1. This is how the subclasses of the competitive layer are combined into target classes in the linear layer.

In short, a *1* in the ith row of $\mathbf{a}^1$ (the rest to the elements of $\mathbf{a}^1$ will be zero) effectively picks the ith column of $\mathbf{LW}^{2,1}$ as the network output. Each such column contains a single 1, corresponding to a specific class. Thus, subclass 1's from layer 1 are put into various classes by the $\mathbf{LW}^{2,1}\mathbf{a}^1$ multiplication in layer 2.

You know ahead of time what fraction of the layer 1 neurons should be classified into the various class outputs of layer 2, so you can specify the elements of $\mathbf{LW}^{2,1}$ at the start. However, you have to go through a training procedure to get the first layer to produce the correct subclass output for each vector of the training set. This training is discussed in Training. First, consider how to create the original network.

5.5.2.3 *Creating An LVQ Network (NewLVQ)*

You can create an LVQ network with the function newlvq,

net = newlvq(PR, S1, PC, LR, LF)

where

PR is an R-by-2 matrix of minimum and maximum values for R input elements.

S^1 is the number of first-layer hidden neurons.

PC is an S^2-element vector of typical class percentages.

LR is the learning rate (default 0.01).

LF is the learning function (default is learnlv1).

Suppose you have 10 input vectors. Create a network that assigns each of these input vectors to one of four subclasses. Thus, there are four neurons in the first competitive layer. These subclasses are then assigned to one of two output classes by the two neurons in layer 2. The input vectors and targets are specified by

P = [–3 –2 –2 0 0 0 0 2 2 3; 0 1 –1 2 1 –1 –2 1 –1 0];

and Tc = [1 1 1 2 2 2 2 1 1 1];

It might help to show the details of what you get from these two lines of code.

P = –3 –2 –2 0 0 0 0 2 2 3

0 1 –1 2 1 –1 –2 1 –1 0

Tc = 1 1 1 2 2 2 2 1 1 1

A plot of the input vectors follows.

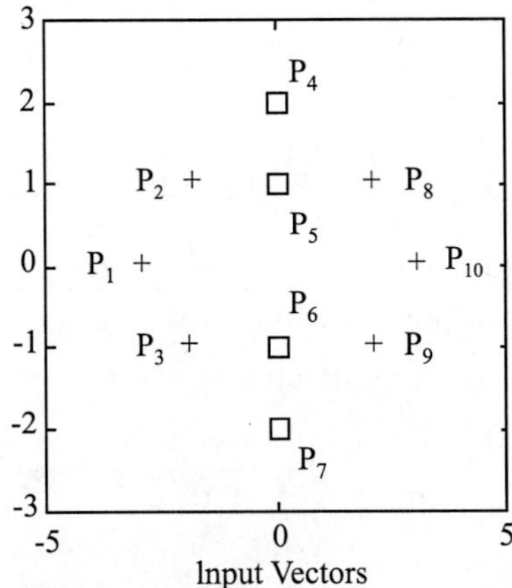

Figure 5.16: Creating an lvq network with 10 input vectors

As you can see, there are four subclasses of input vectors. You want a network that classifies $\mathbf{p}_1$, $\mathbf{p}_2$, $\mathbf{p}_3$, $\mathbf{p}_8$, $\mathbf{p}_9$, and $\mathbf{p}_{10}$ to produce an output of 1, and that classifies vectors $\mathbf{p}_4$, $\mathbf{p}_5$, $\mathbf{p}_6$, and $\mathbf{p}_7$ to produce an output of 2. Note that this problem is nonlinearly separable, and so cannot be solved by a perceptron, but an LVQ network has no difficulty.

Next convert the Tc matrix to target vectors.

T = ind2vec(Tc);

This gives a sparse matrix T that can be displayed in full with

targets = full(T)

which gives

```
targets = 1 1 1 0 0 0 0 1 1 1
          0 0 0 1 1 1 1 0 0 0
```

This looks right. It says, for instance, that if you have the first column of P as input, you should get the first column of targets as an output; and that output says the input falls in class 1, which is correct. Now you are ready to call newlvq.

Call newlvq with the proper arguments so that it creates a network with four neurons in the first layer and two neurons in the second layer. The first-layer weights are initialized to the centers of the input ranges with the function midpoint. The second-layer weights have 60% (6 of the 10 in Tc above) of its columns with a 1 in the first row, (corresponding to class 1), and 40% of its columns will have a 1 in the second row (corresponding to class 2).

net = newlvq(P,4,[.6 .4]);

Confirm the initial values of the first-layer weight matrix.

net.IW{1,1}

ans = 0 0

0 0

0 0

0 0

These zero weights are indeed the values at the midpoint of the ranges (-3 to +3) of the inputs, as you would expect when using midpoint for initialization.

You can look at the second-layer weights with

net.LW{2,1}

ans = 1 1 0 0

0 0 1 1

This makes sense too. It says that if the competitive layer produces a 1 as the first or second element, the input vector is classified as class 1; otherwise it is a class 2.

You might notice that the first two competitive neurons are connected to the first linear neuron (with weights of 1), while the second two competitive neurons are connected to the second linear neuron. All other weights between the competitive neurons and linear neurons have values of 0. Thus, each of the two target classes (the linear neurons) is, in fact, the union of two subclasses (the competitive neurons).You can simulate the network with sim. Use the original P matrix as input just to see what you get.

Y = sim(net,P);

Yc = vec2ind(Y)

Yc = 1 1 1 1 1 1 1 1 1 1

The network classifies all inputs into class 1. Because this is not what you want, you have to train the network (adjusting the weights of layer 1 only), before you can expect a good result. The next two sections discuss two LVQ learning rules and the training process.

5.5.3 LVQ1 Learning Rule (Learnlv1)

LVQ learning in the competitive layer is based on a set of input/target pairs.

$$\{p_1, t_1\}, \{p_2, t_2\}, \ldots, (p_Q, t_Q\}$$

Each target vector has a single 1. The rest of its elements are 0. The 1 tells the proper classification of the associated input. For instance, consider the following training pair.

$$p_1 \quad \begin{matrix} 2 \\ 1 \\ 0 \end{matrix}, \; t_1 \quad \begin{matrix} 0 \\ 0 \\ 1 \\ 0 \end{matrix}$$

Here there are input vectors of three elements, and each input vector is to be assigned to one of four classes. The network is to be trained so that it classifies the input vector shown above into the third of four classes.

To train the network, an input vector **p** is presented, and the distance from **p** to each row of the input weight matrix $\mathbf{IW}^{1,1}$ is computed with the function ndist. The hidden neurons of layer 1 compete. Suppose that the ith element of n^1 is most positive, and neuron i* wins the competition. Then the competitive transfer function produces a 1 as the *i**th element of $\mathbf{a}^1$. All other elements of $\mathbf{a}^1$ are 0.

When $\mathbf{a}^1$ is multiplied by the layer 2 weights $\mathbf{LW}^{2,1}$, the single 1 in $\mathbf{a}^1$ selects the class *k** associated with the input. Thus, the network has assigned the input vector **p** to class *k** and will be 1. Of course, this assignment can be a good one or a bad one, for t_{k*} can be 1 or 0, depending on whether the input belonged to class k* or not. Adjust the *i**th row of $\mathbf{IW}^{1,1}$ in such a way as to move this row closer to the input vector **p** if the assignment is correct, and to move the row away from **p** if the assignment is incorrect. If **p** is classified correctly,

$$(a^2_{k*} \quad t_{k*} \quad 1)$$

compute the new value of the *i**th row of $\mathbf{IW}^{1,1}$ as

$$_{i*}IW^{1,1}(q) = {}_{i*}IW^{1,1}(q-1) + \alpha(p(q) - {}_{i*}IW^{1,1}(q-1))$$

On the other hand, if **p** is classified incorrectly,

$$(a^2_{k*} \quad 1 \quad t_{k*} \quad 1)$$

compute the new value of the i*th row of $\mathbf{IW}^{1,1}$ as

$$_{i*}IW^{1,1}(q) = {}_{i*}IW^{1,1}(q-1) - \alpha(p(q) - {}_{i*}IW^{1,1}(q-1))$$

You can make these corrections to the i* th row of $\mathbf{IW}^{1,1}$ automatically, without affecting other rows of $\mathbf{IW}^{1,1}$, by back propagating the output errors to layer 1.

Such corrections move the hidden neuron toward vectors that fall into the class for which it forms a subclass, and away from vectors that fall into other classes.

The learning function that implements these changes in the layer 1 weights in LVQ networks is learnlv1. It can be applied during training.

5.5.4 Training

Next you need to train the network to obtain first-layer weights that lead to the correct classification of input vectors. You do this with train as with the following commands. First, set the training epochs to 150. Then, use train:

```
net.trainParam.epochs = 150;
net = train(net,P,T);
```

Now confirm the first-layer weights.

```
net.IW{1,1}
ans = 0.3283   0.0051
     –0.1366   0.0001
     –0.0263   0.2234
      0       –0.0685
```

The following plot shows that these weights have moved toward their respective classification groups.

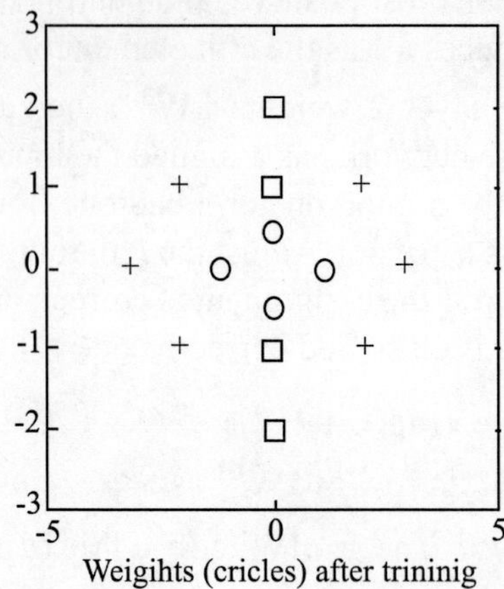

Figure 5.17: Weights after train network

To confirm that these weights do indeed lead to the correct classification, take the matrix P as input and simulate the network. Then see what classifications are produced by the network.

```
Y = sim(net,P);
Yc = vec2ind(Y)
```

This gives

```
Yc = 1 1 1 2 2 2 2 1 1 1
```

which is expected. As a last check, try an input close to a vector that was used in training.

```
pchk1 = [0; 0.5];
Y = sim(net,pchk1);
Yc1 = vec2ind(Y)
```

This gives

```
Yc1 = 2
```

This looks right, because pchk1 is close to other vectors classified as 2. Similarly,

```
pchk2 = [1; 0];
Y = sim(net,pchk2);
Yc2 = vec2ind(Y)
```

gives

```
Yc2 = 1
```

This looks right too, because pchk2 is close to other vectors classified as 1.

You might want to try the demonstration program demolvq1. It follows the discussion of training given above.

5.6 HEBBIAN LEARNING

In 1949, Donald Hebb wrote: "When the axon of cell A is near enough to excite a cell B and repeatedly or persistently takes part in firing it, some growth process or metabolic change takes place in one or both cells such that A's efficiency, as one of the cells firing B, is increased". As a result, a learning method evolved for artificial neural networks, called Hebbian learning, which is an instance of an unsupervised learning procedure. In Hebbian learning, weights between learning nodes are adjusted so that each weight better represents the relationship between the nodes. Nodes which tend to be positive or negative at the same time will have strong positive weights while those which tend to be opposite will have strong negative weights. Nodes that are uncorrelated will have weights near zero.

For example, if two nodes A and B are often simultaneously active, Hebbian learning will increase the connection strength between the two so that excitation of either one tends to cause excitation of the other. On the other hand, if nodes A and C were of opposite activations at all times, then Hebbian learning would gradually decrease the connection in between below zero so that an excited A or C would inhibit the other. Hebbian learning has four features interesting to the cognitive scientist: first it is unsupervised; second it is a local learning rule, meaning that it can be applied to a network in parallel; third it is simple and therefore requires very little computation; fourth it is biologically plausible.

Formally, Hebb's rule for the modification of a weight w_{ij} from neuron i to j with a learning rate h is defined as

$$\Delta w_{ij} = \eta ij.$$

This rule is not entirely unproblematic, because there exists no bound on the weight of the connection. A common solution to this problem is the introduction of a decay function for each connection. However, given the controlled usage of Hebbian learning in the neural optimal controller constructed here, this step is not necessary.

5.6.1 Hebb NET

The earliest and simplest learning rule for a neural net is generally known as the Hebb rule. Hebb proposed that learning occurs by modification of the synapse strengths (weights) in a manner such that if two interconnected neurons are both "on" at the same time, then the weight between those neurons should be increased. The original statement only talks about neurons firing at the same time (and does not say anything about reinforcing neurons that do not fire at the same time). However, a stronger form of learning occurs if we also increase the weights if both neurons are "off" at the same time. We use this extended Hebb rule [McClelland & Rumelhart, 1988] because of its improved computational power and shall refer to it as the Hebb rule.

We shall refer to a single-layer (feedforward) neural net trained using the (extended) Hebb rule as a Hebb net. The Hebb rule is also used for training other specific nets that are discussed later. Since we are considering a single-layer net, one of the interconnected neurons will be an input unit and one an output unit (since no input units are connected to each other, nor are any output units interconnected). If data are represented in bipolar form, it is easy to express the desired weight update as

$$w_i(\text{new}) = w_i(\text{old}) + x_i y.$$

If the data are binary, this formula does not distinguish between a training pair in which an input unit is "on" and the target value is "off" and a training pair in which both the input unit and the target value are "off".

5.6.2 Algorithm

Step 1: Initialize all weights:

$$w_i = 0 \ (i = 1 \text{ to } n).$$

Step 2: For each input training vector and target output pair, s : t, do steps 3 – 5.

Step 3: Set activations for input units:

$$x_i = s_i (i = 1 \text{ to } n).$$

Step 4: Set activation for output unit:

$$y = t.$$

Step 5: Adjust the weights for

$$w_i(\text{new}) = w_i(\text{old}) + x_i y (i = 1 \text{ to } n).$$

Adjust the bias:

$$b(\text{new}) = b(\text{old}) + y.$$

Note that the bias is adjusted exactly like a weight from a "unit" whose output signal is always 1.

The weight update can also be expressed in vector form as

$$w(\text{new}) = w(\text{old}) + xy.$$

This is often written in terms of the weight change, Δw, as

$$\Delta w = xy$$

and

$$w(\text{new}) = w(\text{old}) + \Delta w.$$

There are several methods of implementing the Hebb rule for learning.

EXERCISES

1. What is supervised and unsupervised learning?
2. Difference between supervised and unsupervised learning?
3. What do you mean competitive learning model?
4. Explain the architecture of competitive network?
5. How we can create a competitive neural network?

6. What is Kohonen's self organizing map?
7. Write the algorithm for Kohonen's self organizing map?
8. Explain the learning rule of Kohonen's self organizing map?
9. What is self organizing features map?
10. Explain the architecture of SOFM?
11. How can create a self organizing map neural network?
12. Explain the example of one dimensional and two dimensional self organizing map?
13. What is vector quantization?
14. How we can implement vector quantization with a network?
15. Explain the architecture of LVQ network?
16. How we can create LVQ network with ten input vectors?
17. Explain the learning rule of LVQ network?
18. How we can train LVQ network?
19. What is Hebbian learning?
20. Difference between Hebbian and competitive learning?

CHAPTER 6

Counter Propagation Network

6.1 INTRODUCTION

Robert Hecht-Nielsen developed the counter-propagation network as a means to combine an unsupervised Kohonen layer with a teachable output layer. This is yet another topology to synthesize complex classification problems, while trying to minimize the number of processing elements and training time. The operation for the counter-propagation network is similar to that of the Learning Vector Quantization network in that the middle Kohonen layer acts as an adaptive look-up table, finding the closest fit to an input stimulus and outputting its equivalent mapping.

The first counter-propagation network consisted of a bi-directional mapping between the input and output layers. In essence, while data is presented to the input layer to generate a classification pattern on the output layer, the output layer in turn would accept an additional input vector and generate an output classification on the network's input layer. The network got its name from this counter-posing flow of information through its structure. Most developers use a uni-flow variant of this formal representation of counter-propagation. In other words. there is only one feedforward path from input layer to output layer.

An example network is shown in Figure 6.1. The uni-directional counter-propagation network has three layers. If the inputs are not already normalized before they enter the network., a fourth layer is sometimes added. The main layers include an input buffer layer, a self-organizing Kohonen layer, and an output layer which uses the Delta Rule to modify its incoming connection weights. Sometimes this layer is called a Grossberg Outstar layer.

The size of the input layer depends upon how many separable parameters define the problem. With too few, the network may not generalize sufficiently. With too many, the processing time takes too long.

For the network to operate properly, the input vector must be normalized. This means that for every combination of input values, the total "length" of the input vector must add up to one. This can be done with a preprocessor, before the data is entered into the counter-propagation network. Or, a normalization layer can be added between the input and Kohonen layers. The normalization layer requires one processing element for each input, plus one more for a balancing element. This layer modifies the input set before going to the Kohonen layer to guarantee that all input sets combine to the same total.

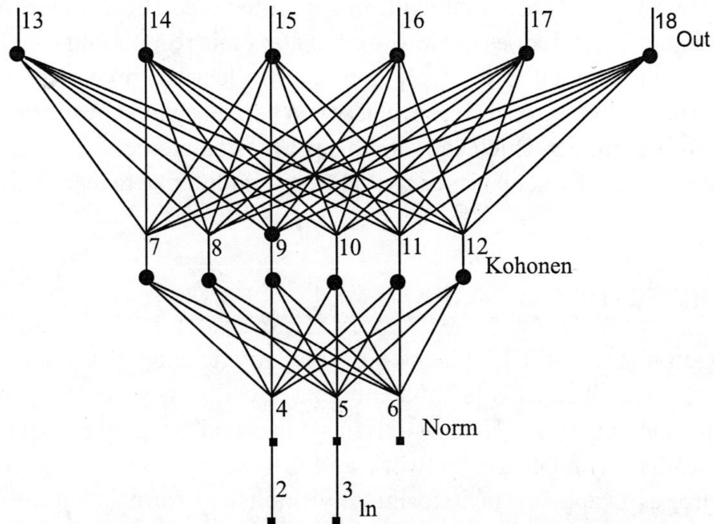

Figure 6.1: An example counter propagation network.

Normalization of the inputs is necessary to insure that the Kohonen layer finds the correct class for the problem. Without normalization, larger input vectors bias many of the Kohonen processing elements such that weaker value input sets cannot be properly classified. Because of the competitive nature of the Kohonen layer, the larger value input vectors overpower the smaller vectors.

Counter-propagation uses a standard Kohonen paradigm which self-organizes the input sets into classification zones. It follows the classical Kohonen learning law .This layer acts as a nearest neighbor classifier in that the processing elements in the competitive layer autonomously adjust their connection weights to divide up the input vector space in approximate correspondence to the frequency with which the inputs occur. There needs to be at least as many processing elements in the Kohonen layer as output classes. The Kohonen layer usually has many more elements than classes simply because additional processing elements provide a finer resolution between similar objects.

The output layer for counter-propagation is basically made up of processing elements which learn to produce an output when a particular input is applied. Since the Kohonen layer includes competition, only a single output is produced for a given input vector. This layer provides a way of decoding that input to a meaningful output class. It uses the Delta Rule to back-propagate the error between the desired output class and the actual output generated with the training set. The errors only adjust the connection weights coming into the output layer. The Kohonen layer is not effected.

Since only one output from the competitive Kohonen layer is active at a time and all other elements are zero, the only weight adjusted for the output processing elements are the ones connected to the winning element in the competitive layer. In this way the output layer learns to reproduce a certain pattern for each active processing element in the competitive layer. If several competitive elements belong to the same class, that output processing element will evolve weights in response to those competitive processing elements and zero for all others.

There is a problem which could arise with this architecture. The competitive Kohonen layer learns without any supervision. It does not know what class it is responding to. This means that it is possible for a processing element in the Kohonen layer to learn to take responsibility for two or more training inputs which belong to different classes. When this happens, the output of the network will be ambiguous for any inputs which activate this processing element. To alleviate this problem, the processing elements in the Kohonen layer could be pre-conditioned to learn only about a particular class.

6.2 CPN ARCHITECTURE

The counterpropagation network (CPN) is the most recently developed of the models that we have discussed so far in this text. The CPN is not so much a new discovery as it is a novel combination of previously existing network types. Hecht-Nielsen synthesized the architecture from a combination of a structure known as a competitive network and Grossberg's outstar structure. Although the network architecture, as it appears in its originally published form in Figure 6.2, seems rather formidable, we shall see that the operation of the network is quite straightforward.

Given a set of vector pairs, (x_1, y_1), (x_2, y_2) ..... (x_L, y_L), the CPN can learn to associate an x vector on the input layer with a y vector at the output layer. If the relationship between x and y can be described by a continuous function, Φ, such that $y = \Phi(x)$, the CPN will learn to approximate this mapping for any value of x in the range specified by the set of training vectors. Furthermore, if the inverse of Φ exists, such that x is a function of y, then the CPN will also learn the inverse mapping, $x = \Phi^{-1}(y)^1$. For a great many cases of practical interest, the inverse function does not exist. In these situations, we can simplify the discussion of the CPN by considering only the forward-mapping case, $y = \Phi(x)$.

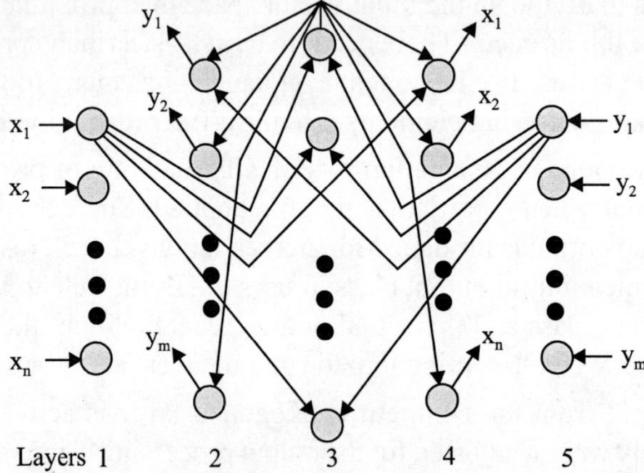

Figure 6.2: This spiderlike diagram of the CPN architecture has five layers: two input layers (1 and 5), one hidden layer (3), and two output layers (2 and 4). The CPN gets its name from the fact that the input vectors on layers 1 and 2 appear to propagate through the network in opposite directions.

In Figure 6.3 we have reorganized the CPN diagram and have restricted our consideration to the forward-mapping case. The network now appears as a three-layer architecture, similar to, but not exactly like, the backpropagation network discussed in Chapter 3. An input vector is applied to the units on layer 1. Each unit on layer 2 calculates its net-input value, and a competition is held to determine which unit has the largest net-input value. That unit is the only unit that sends a value to the units in the output layer. We shall postpone a detailed discussion of the processing until we have examined the various components of the network.

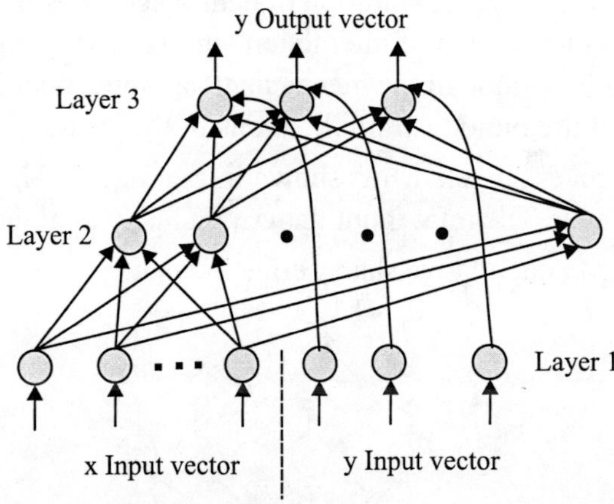

Figure 6.3: The forward-mapping CPN is shown. Vector pairs from the training set are applied to layer 1. After training is complete, applying the vectors (x, 0) to layer 1 will result in an approximation, y^1, to the corresponding y vector, at the output layer, layer 3.

CPNs are interesting for a number of reasons. By combining existing network types into a new architecture, the CPN hints at the possibility of forming other, useful networks from bits and pieces of existing structures. Moreover, instead of employing a single learning algorithm throughout the network, the CPN uses a different learning procedure on each layer. The learning algorithms allow the CPN to train quite rapidly with respect with respect to other networks that we have studied so far. The tradeoff is that the CPN may not always yield sufficient accuracy for some applications. Nevertheless, the CPN remains a good choice for some classes of problems, and it provides an excellent vehicle for rapid prototyping of other applications. In the next section, we shall examine the various building blocks from which the CPN is constructed.

6.3 CPN BUILDING BLOCKS

The PEs and network structures that we shall study in this section play an important role in many of the subsequent chapters in this text. For that reason, we present this introductory material in some detail. There are four major components: an input layer that performs some processing on the input data, a processing element called an instar, a layer of instars knows as a competitive network, and a structure known as an outstar. In section 6.4, we shall return to the discussion of the CPN.

6.3.1 The Input Layer

Discussions of neural networks often ignore the input-layer processing elements, or consider them simply as pass-through units, responsible only for distributing input data to other processing elements. Computer simulations of networks usually arrange for all input data to be scaled or normalized to accommodate calculations by the computer's CPU. For example, input-value magnitudes may have to be scaled to prevent overflow error during the sum-of-product calculations that dominate most network simulations. Biological systems do not have the benefits of such preprocessing: they must rely on internal mechanisms to prevent saturation of neural activities by large input signals. In this section, we shall examine a mechanism of interaction among processing elements that overcomes this noise-saturation dilemma. Although the mechanism has some neurophysiological plausibility, we shall not examine any of the biological implications of the model.

Examine the layer of processing elements shown in Figure 6.4. There is one input value, I_i for each of the n units on the layer. The total input pattern intensity is given by

$I = \Sigma_I I_i$. Corresponding to each I_i, we shall define a quantity

$$\theta_I = I_i (\Sigma I_i)^{-1} \tag{6.1}$$

Figure 6.4: This later of input units has n processing elements, $\{v_1, v_2, \ldots, v_n\}$ Each input value, I_i is connected with an excitatory connection (arrow with a plus sign) to its corresponding processing element, v_i. Each I_i is connected also to every other processing element, v_k, $k^1 i$, with an inhibitory connection (arrow with a minus sign). This arrangement is known as on-center, off-surround. The output of the layer is proportional to the normalized reflectance pattern.

The vector, $(\theta_1, \theta_2, \ldots, \theta_n)^t$, is called a reflectance pattern. Notice that this pattern is normalized in the sense that $\Sigma_I \theta_I = 1$.

The reflectance pattern is independent of the total intensity of the corresponding input pattern. For example, the reflectance pattern corresponding to the image of a person's face would be independent of whether the person were being viewed in bright sunlight or in shade. We can usually recognize a familiar person in a wide variety of lighting conditions, even if we have not seen her previously in the identical situation. This experience suggests that our memory stores and recalls reflectance patterns. The outputs of the processing elements in Figure 6.4 are governed by the set of differential equations,

$$x_i = -Ax_i + (B - x_i)I_i - x_i \underset{k \quad i}{I_k} \tag{6.2}$$

where $0 < x_i(0) < B$, and $A, B > 0$. Each processing element receives a net excitation (on-center) of $(B - x_i)I_i$ from its corresponding input value. I_i. The addition of inhibitory connections (off-surround), $-x_i I_k$, from other units is responsible for preventing the activities activity of the processing element from rising in proportion to the absolute pattern intensity, I_i. Once an input pattern is applied, the processing elements quickly reach an equilibrium state ($x_i = 0$) with

$$x_i^{eq} = {}_i\frac{BI}{A \quad 1} \tag{6.3}$$

where we have used the definition of θ_I in Eq. (6.1). The output pattern is normalized, since

$$x_i = \frac{BI}{A+I} = B\,\frac{A+1}{I}^{-1}$$

which is always less than B. Thus, the pattern of activity that develops across the input units is proportional to the reflectance pattern, rather than to the original input pattern.

After the input pattern is removed, the activities of the units do not remain at their equilibrium values, nor do they return immediately to zero. The activity patterns persists for some time while the term $-Ax_i$ reduces the activities gradually back to a value of zero. An input layer of the type discussed in this section is used for both the x-vector and y-vector portions of the CPN input layer shown in Figure 6.2. When performing a digital simulation of the CPN, we can simplify the program by normalizing the input vectors in software. Whether the input-pattern normalization is accomplished using Eq. (6.2), or by some preprocessing in software, depends n the particular implementation of the network.

6.3.2 The Instar

The hidden layer of the CPN comprises a set of processing elements known as instars. In this section, we shall discuss the instar individually. In the following section, we shall examine the set of instars that operate together to form the CPN hidden layer. The instar is a single processing element that shares its general structure and processing functions with many other processing elements described in this text. We distinguish it by specific way in which it is trained to respond to input data.

Let's begin with a general processing element, such as the one in Figure 6.5(a). If the arrow representing the output is ignored, the processing element can be redrawn in the starlike configuration of Figure 6.5(b). The inward-pointing arrows identify the instar structure, but we restrict the use of the term instar to those units whose processing and learning are governed by the equation in this section. The net-input value is calculated, as usual, by the dot product of the input and weight vectors, net = I. w. We shall assume that the input vector, I. and the weight vector, w, have been normalized to a length of 1.

The output of the instar is governed by the equation

$$y = -ay + b \text{ net} \tag{6.4}$$

where $a, b > 0$.

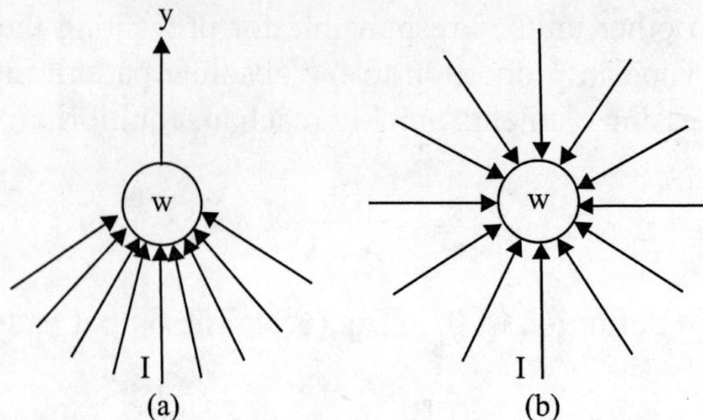

Figure 6.5: This figure shows (a) the general form of the processing element with input vector I, weight vector w, and output value y; and (b) the instar form of the processing element in (a).

6.3.3 Competitive Networks

In the previous section; we saw how an individual instar could learn to respond to a certain group of input vectors clustered together in a region of space. Suppose we have several instars grouped in a layer, as shown in Figure 6.6, each of which responds maximally to a group of input vectors in a different region of space. We can say that this layer of instars classifies any input vector, because the instar with the strongest response for any input vector, because the instar with the strongest response for any given input identifies the region f space in which the input vector lies.

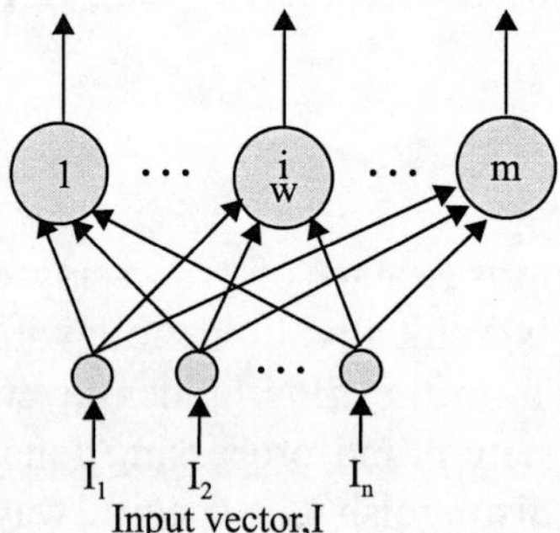

Figure 6.6: A layer of instars arrange in a competitive network. Each unit receives the input vector $I = (I_1, I_2 \ldots I_n)^t$ and the ith unit has associated with it the weight vector, $w_i = (w_{i1}, w_{i2} \ldots, w_{in})^t$. Net-input values are calculated in the usual way: $net_i = I. w_i$. The winner of the competition is the unit with the largest net input.

Rather than our examining the response of each instar to determine which is the largest, our task would be simpler if the instar with the largest response were the only unit to have a nonzero output. This effect can be accomplished if the instars compete with one another for the privilege of turning on. Since there is no external judge to decide which instar has the largest net input, the units must decide among themselves who is the winner. This decision process requires communication among all the units on the layer; it is also complicates the analysis, since there are more inputs to each unit than just the input from the previous layer. In the following discussion, we shall be focusing on unit activities, rather that on unit output values.

Figure 6.7 illustrates the interconnections that implement competition among the instars. The unit activations are determined by differential equations. There is a variety of forms that these differential equations can take; one of the simplest is

$$x_i = -Ax_i + (B - x_i)\,[f(x_i) + net_i] - x_i \sum_{k\ i} f(E_k) + \sum_{k\ i} net_k \qquad (6.5)$$

where A, B > 0 and $f(x_i)$ is an function that we shall specify shortly. This equation should be compared to Eq. (6.2).We can convert Eq. (6.2) to

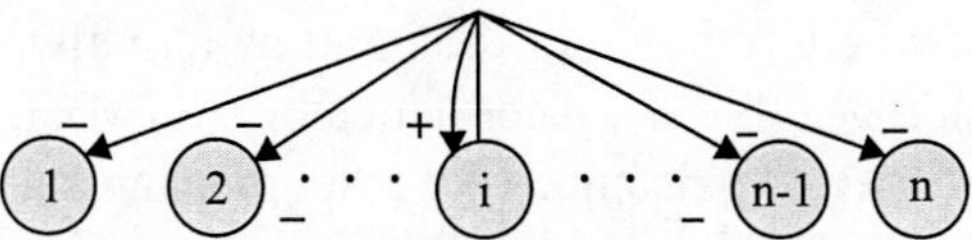

Figure 6.7: An on-center off-surround system for implementing competition among a group of instars. Each unit receives a positive feedback signal to itself and sends an inhibitory signal to all other units on the layer. The unit whose weight vector most closely matches the input vector sends the strongest inhibitory signals to the other units and receives the largest positive feedback from itself.

Eq. (6.5) by replacing every occurrence of I_j in Eq. (6.2) with $f(x_j) + net_j$, for all j. The relationship between the constants A and B, and the form of the function, $f(x_j)$, determine how the solutions to Eq.(6.5) evolve in time. We shall now look at specific cases.

Equation (6.5) is somewhat easier to analyze if we convert it to a pair of equations: one that describes the reflectance variables, $X_i = x_i / \Sigma_k x_k$, and one that describes the total pattern intensity, $x = \Sigma_k x_k$. First, rearrange Eq. (6.5) as follows:

$$x_i = -Ax_i + B[f(x_i) + net_i] - x_i\,[\Sigma f(x_k) + \Sigma net_k]$$

Next sum over i to get

$$x = -Ax + (B - x) \sum_k f(xX_k) + \sum_k net_k \qquad (6.6)$$

Now, substitute xX_i into Eq. (6.5) and use Eq. (6.6) to simplify the result. If we make the definition $g(w) = w^{-1} f(w)$, then we get

$$xX_i = BxX_i - \sum_k X_k[g(xX_i) - g(xX_k)]\ \ B(1 - X_i)net_i - BX_i \sum_{k\ 1} net_k \qquad (6.7)$$

We can now evaluate the asymptotic behavior of Eqs. (6.6) nd (6.7). Let's begin with the simple, linear case of f(w) = w. Since $g(w)\ w^{-1} f(w)$, g(w) = 1 and the first term on the right of Eq. (6.7) is zero. The reflectance variables stabilize at

$$X_i = \frac{net_i}{\sum_k net_k}$$

so the activities become

$$x_i = \frac{X^{eq} net_i}{\sum_k net_k}$$

where x^{eq} comes from setting Eq. (6.6) equal to zero. This equation shows that the units will accurately register any pattern presented as an input. Now let's look at what happens after the input pattern is removed.

Let $net_i = 0$ for all i. Then, X_i is identically zero for all time and the reflectance variables remain constant. The unit activations now depend only on x, since $x_i = xX_i$. Equation (6.6) reduces to

$$x = (B - A - x)x$$

If $B \leq A$, then $x < 0$ and $x \to 0$. However, if $B > A$, then $x \to B - A$ and the activity pattern becomes stored permanently on the units. This behavior is unlike the behavior of the input units described by Eq. (6.2), where removal of the input pattern always resulted in a decay of the activities. We shall call this storage effect short-term memory (STM). Even though the effect appears to be permanent, we can assume the existence of a reset mechanism that will remove the current pattern so that another can be stored. Figure 6.8 illustrates a simple example for the linear output function.

For our second example, we assume a faster-than-linear output function, $f(w) = w^2$. In this case $g(w) = w$. Notice that the first term on the right of Eq. (6.7) contains the factor $[g(xX_i) - g(xX_k)]$. For the quadratic output function, this expression reduces to $x[X_i - X_k]$. If $X_i < X_k$ for all values of $k \neq i$, then the first term in Eq. (6.6) is an excitatory term. If $X_i < X_k$ for $k \neq i$, then the first term in Eq. (6.6) becomes an inhibitory term. Thus, this network tends to enhance the activity of the unit with the largest value of X_i. This effect is illustrated in Figure 6.9. After the input pattern is removed, X_i will be greater than zero for only the unit with the largest value of X_i.

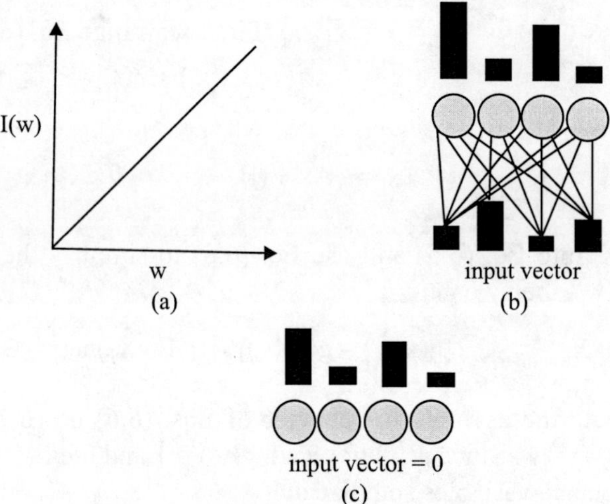

Figure 6.8: This series of figure shows the result of applying a certain input vector to units having a linear output function. (a) The graph of output function, f(w)=w. (b) This figure shows the result of the sustained application of the input vector. The units reach equilibrium activities as shown. (c) After removal of the input vector, the units reach equilibrium such that the pattern is stored in STM.

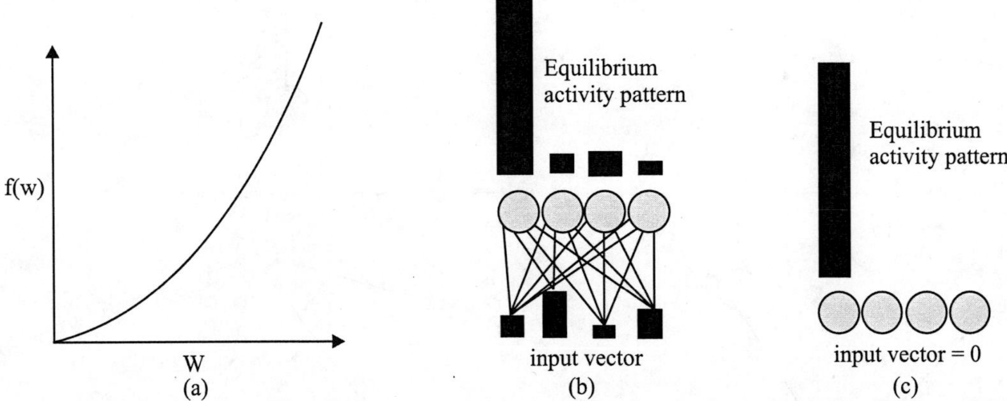

Figure 6.9: This series of figures is analogous to those in fig 6.9. but with units having a quadratic output function. (a) The graph of quadratic output function. (b) While the input vector is present, the network tends to enhance the activity of the unit with the largest activity. For the given input pattern, the unit activities reach the equilibrium values shown. (c) After the input pattern is removed, all activities but the largest decay to zero.

6.3.4 The Outstar

The final leg of our journey through CPN components brings us to Grossberg's outstar structure. As Figure 6.10 shows, an outstar is composed of all of the units in the CPN outer layer and a single hidden-layer unit. Thus, the outer-layer units participate in several different outstar: one for each unit in the middle layer.

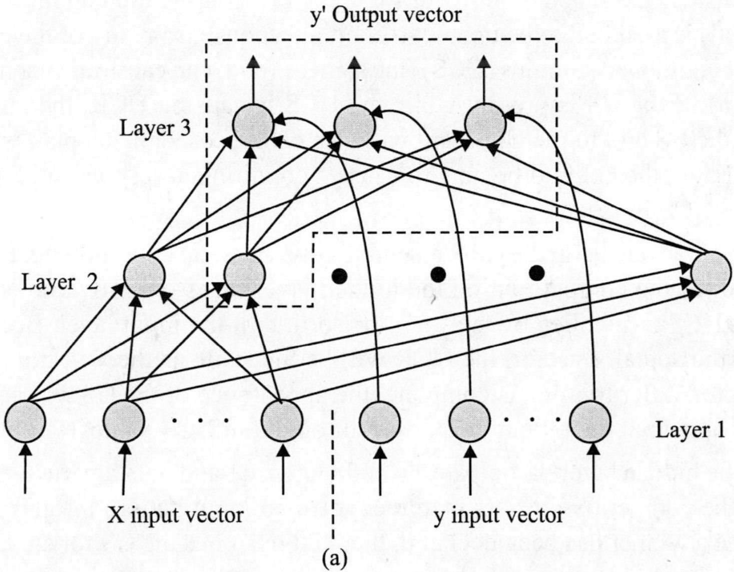

Figure 6.10: This figure illustrates the outstar and its relationship to the CPN architecture. (a) The dotted line encompasses one of the outstar structures in the CPN. The line is intentionally drawn through the middle-layer unit to indicate the dual functionality of that unit. Each middle-layer unit combines with the outer layer to form an individual outstar.

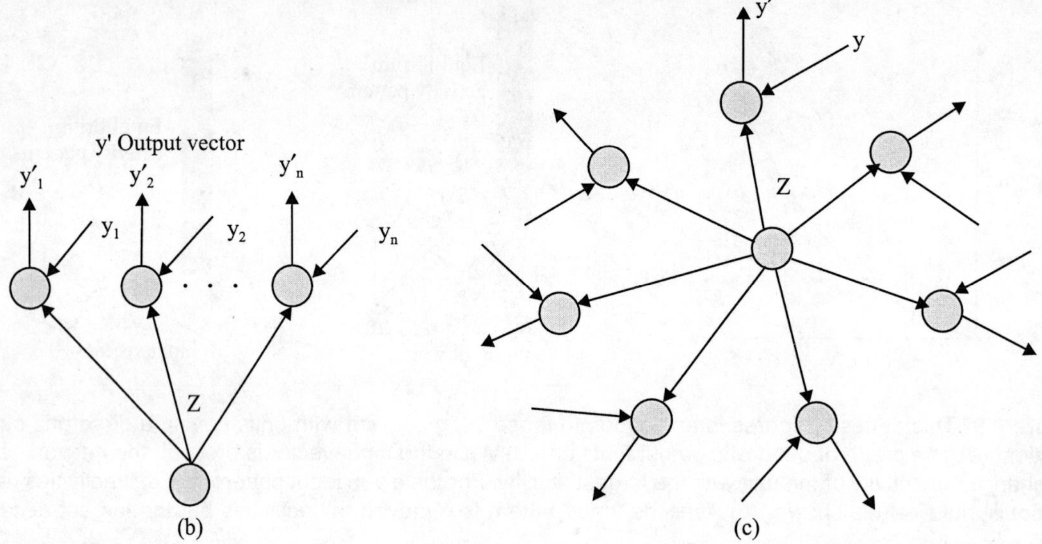

Figure 6.10: (b) A single outstar unit is shown. The output nits of the outstar have two inputs: z, from the connecting unit of the previous layer, and y_i, which is the training input. The training input is present during only the learning period. The output of the outstar is the vector $y' = (y'_1, y'_2, ...y'_n)^t$. (c) The outstar is redrawn in a suggestive configuration. Note that the arrows point outward in a configuration that is complementary to the instar.

Grossberg argues that the outstar is the minimal neural architecture capable of classical conditioning. Consider the outstar shown in Figure 6.11. Intially, the conditioned stimulus (CS) (e.g., a ringing bell) is assumed to be unable to elicit a response from any of the units to which it is connected. An unconditioned stimulus (UCS) (the sight of food) can cause an unconditioned response (UCR) (salivation). If the CS is present while the UCS is causing UCR, then the strength of the connection from the CS unit to the UCR unit will also be increased, in keeping with Hebb's theory (see Chapter 1). Later, the CS will be able to cause a conditioned response (CR) (the same as the UCR), even if the UCS is absent.

The behavior of the outstar in the CPN resembles this classical conditioning. During the training period, the winner of the competition on the hidden layer turns on, providing a single CS to the output units. The UCS is supplied by the y-vector portion of the input layer. Because we want the network to learn the actual y vector, the UCR will be the same as the y vector, within a constant multiplicative factor. After training is complete, the appearance of the CS will cause the CR value (the y' vector) to appear at the output units, even through the UCS values will be all zero.

In the CPN, the hidden layer participates in both the instar and outstar structures of the network. The function of the competitive instars is to recognize an input pattern through a winner-take-all competition. Once a winner has been declared, that unit becomes the CS for an outstar. The outstar associates some value or identity with the input pattern. The instar and outstar complement each other in this fashion: The instar recognizes an input pattern and classifies it; the outstar identifies or names the selected class. This behavior led one researcher to note that the instar is dumb, whereas the outstar is bind.

$$y_I = -ay_i + by_i + c\,net_i$$

which is similar to Eq. (6.4) for the instar except for the additional term due to the training input, y_i. The parameters a, b and c, are all assumed to be positive. The value of net_i is calculated in the usual way as the sum of products of weights and input values from the connecting units. For the outstar and the CPN, only a single connecting unit has a nonzero output at any given time. Even though each output unit of the outstar has an entire weight vector associated with it, the net input reduces to a single term, $w_{ij}z$, where z is the output of the connecting unit. In the case of the CPN, z = 1. Therefore, we can write

$$y_I = -ay_i + by_i + cw_{ij} \tag{6.8}$$

where the jth unit on the hidden layer is the connecting unit. In its most general form, the parameter a, b, and c in Eq. (6.8) are functions of time. Here, we shall consider them to be constants for simplicity. For the remainder of this discussion, we shall drop the subscript from the weight.

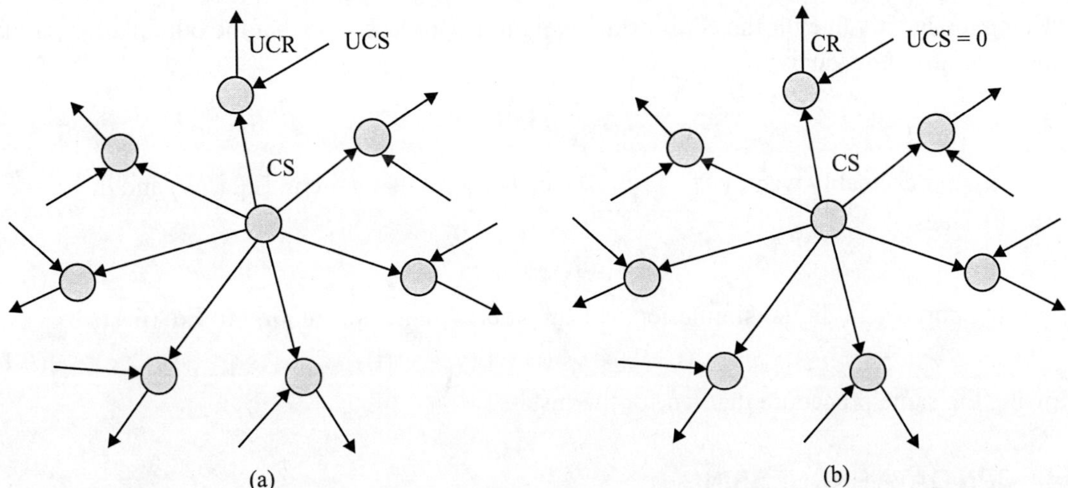

Figure 6.11: This figure shows an implied classical-conditioning scenario. (a) During the conditioning period, the CS and the UCS excite one of the output units simultaneously. (b) After conditioning, the presence of the CS alone can excite the CR without exciting any of the other output units.

After training is complete, no further changes in w_i take place and the training inputs, y_i, are absent. Then, the output of the outstar is

$$y_I = -ay_i \quad cw_i^{eq} \tag{6.9}$$

where w^{eq}_i is the fixed weight value found during training. The weights evolve according to an equation almost identical for the instar:

$$w_i = (-dw_i + ey_i z)U\,(z) \tag{6.10}$$

Notice that the second term in Eq. (6.10) contains the training input, y_i, not the unit output, y'_1. The U(z) function ensures that no unlearning takes place when there is no training input present, or when the connecting unit is off (z = 0). Since both z and U(z) are 1 for the middle-layer unit that wins the competition, Eq. (6.10) becomes

$$w_i = -dw_i + ey_i \tag{6.11}$$

for the connections from the winning, middle-layer unit. Connections from other middle-layer units do not participate in the learning.

Recall that a given instar can learn to recognize a cluster of input vectors. If the desired CPN outputs (the y_is) corresponding to each vector in the cluster are all identical, then the weights eventually reach the equilibrium values:

$$w_i^{eq} = \frac{e}{d} yi$$

If, on the other hand, each input vector in the cluster has a slightly different output value associated with it, then the outstar will learn the average of all of the associated output values:

$$w_i^{eq} = \frac{e}{d} \{yi\}$$

Using the latter value for the equilibrium weight, Eq. (6.9) shows that the output after training reaches a steady state value of

$$y_i^{leq} = \frac{c}{a} \frac{e}{d} \{yi\}$$

Since we presumably want $y_i^{leq} = \{y_i\}$, we can require that a = c in Eq. (6.9) and that d = e in Eq. (6.10) Then,

$$y_i^{leq} = \{y_i\} = w_i^{eq} \tag{6.12}$$

For the purpose of digital simulation, we can approximate the solution to Eq. (6.11) by

$$w_i (t + 1) = w_i (t) + \beta(y_i - w_i(t)) \tag{6.13}$$

following the same procedure that led for the instar.

6.4 CPN DATA PROCESSING

We are now in a position to combine the component structures from the previous section into the complete CPN. We shall still consider only the forward-mapping CPN for the moment. Moreover, we shall assume that we are performing a digital simulation, so it will now be necessary to model explicitly the interconnect for the input layer or the competitive layer.

6.4.1 Forward Mapping

Assume that all training has occurred and that the network is now in a production mode. We have an input vector, I, and we would like to find the corresponding y vector. the proçessing is depicted in Figure 6.12 and proceeds according to the following algorithm:

1. Normalize the input vector, $x_i = I_i/\sqrt{(\ _n I_n^2)}$. .
2. Apply the input vector to the x-vector portion of layer 1. Apply a zero vector to the y-vector to the y-vector portion of layer 1.

3. Since the input vector is already normalized, the input layer only distributes it to the units on layer 2.
4. Layer 2 is a winner-take-all competitive layer. The unit whose weight vector most closely matches the input vector wins and has an output value of 1. All other units have outputs of 0. The output of each unit can be calculated according to

$$z_i = \begin{matrix} 1 & \|net_i\| > \|net_j\| \text{ for all } j \quad i \\ 0 & \text{otherwise} \end{matrix} \qquad (6.14)$$

5. The single winner on layer 2 excites an outstar.

Each unit in the outstar quickly reaches an equilibrium value equal to the value of the weight on the connection from the winning layer 2 unit [see Eq. (6.12)]. If the ith unit wins on the middle layer, then the output layer produces an output vector $y' = (w_{1i}, w_{2i}, \ldots w_{mi})^t$, where m represents the number of units on the output layer. A simple way to view this processing is to realize that the equilibrium output of the outstar is equal to the outstar's net input.

$$y_k^{leq} = \quad \underset{j}{} w_{kj} z_j \qquad (6.15)$$

Since $z_j = 0$ unless $j = i$, then $y_k^{leq} = w_{ki} z_i = w_{ki}$, which is consistent with the results obtained in Section 6.1.

This simple algorithm used equilibrium, er asymptotic, values of node activities and outputs. We thus avo the need to solve numerically all the corresponding differential equations.

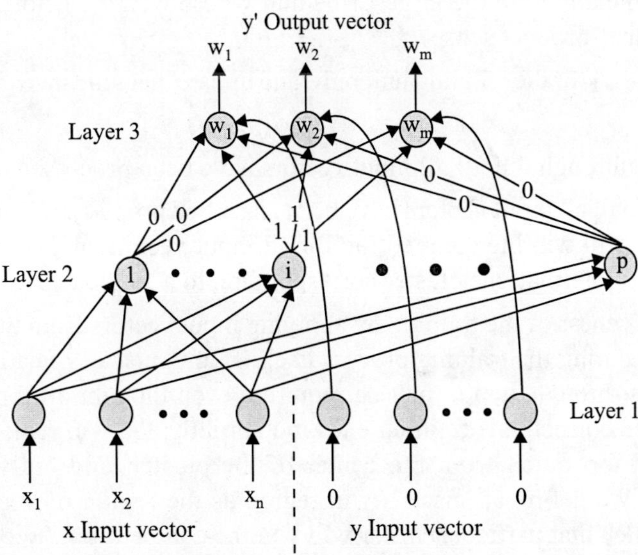

Figure 6.12: This figure shows a summary of the processing done on an input vector by the CPN. The input vector $(x_1, x_2, \ldots, x_n)^t$ is distributed to all units on the competitive layer. The ith unit wins the competition and has an output of 1; all other competitive units have an output of 0. This competition effectively selects te proper output vector by exciting a single connection to each of the outstar units on the output layer.

6.4.2 Training the CPN

Here again, we assume that we are performing a digital simulation of the CPN. Although this assumption does not eliminate the need to find numerical solutions to the differential equations, we can still take advantage of prenormalized input vectors and an external judge to determine winners on the competitive layer. We shall also assume that a set of training vectors has been defined adequately. We shall have more to say on that subject in a later section.

Because there are two different learning algorithms in use in the CPN, we shall look at each one independently. In fact, it is a good idea to train the competitive layer completely before beginning to train the output layer.The competitive-layer units train according to the instar learning algorithm described in Section 6.2. Since there will typically be many instars on the competitive layer, the iterative training process described earlier must be amended slightly. Here, as in Section 6.2, we assume that a cluster of input vectors forms a single class. Now, however, we have the situation where we may have several clusters of vectors, each cluster representing a different class. Our learning procedure must be such that each instar learns (wins the competition) for all the vectors in a single cluster. To accomplish the correct classification for each class of input vectors, we must proceed as follows:

1. Select an input vector from among all the input vectors to be used for training. The selection should be random according to the probability distribution of the vectors.
2. Normalize the input vector and apply it to the CPN competitive layer.
3. Determine which unit wins the competition by calculating the net-input value for each unit and selecting the unit with the largest (the unit whose weight vector is closest to the input vector in an inner-product sense).
4. Calculate $\alpha(x - w)$ for the winning unit only, and update that unit's weight vector according to
$$w(t + 1) = w(t) + \alpha(x - w)$$
5. Repeat steps 1 through 4 until all input vectors have been processed once.
6. Repeat step 5 until all input vectors have been classified properly. When this situation exists, one instar unit will win the competition for all input vectors in a certain cluster. Note that there might be more that one cluster corresponding to a single class of input vectors.
7. Test the effectiveness of the training by applying input vectors from the various classes that were not used during the training process itself. If any misclassifications occur, additional training passes through step 6 may be required, even thought all the training vectors are being classified correctly. If training ends too abruptly, the win region of a particular unit may be offset too much from the center of the cluster, and outlying vectors may be misclassified. We define an instar's win region as the region of vector space containing vectors for which that particular instar will win the competition. (See Figure 6.13)

An issue that we have overlooked in out discussion is the question of initialization of the weight vectors. For all but the simplest problems, random initial weight vectors will not be adequate. We already hinted at an initialization method earlier: Set each weight vector equal to a representative of one of the clusters. We shall have more to say on this issue in the next section.

Once satisfactory results have been obtained on the competitive layer, training of the outstar layer can occur. There are several ways to proceed based on the nature of the problem.

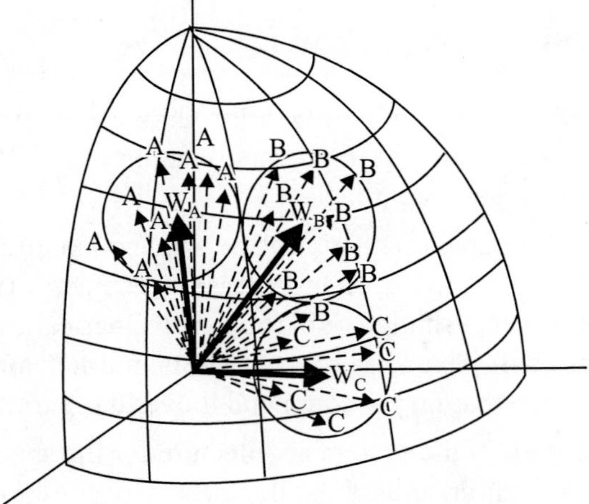

Figure 6.13: In this drawing, three clusters of vectors represent three distinct classes: A, B and C. Normalized, these vectors end on the unit hypersphere. After training, the weight vectors on the competitive layer have settled near the centroid of each cluster. Each weight vector has a in region represented, although not accurately, by the circles drawn on the surface of the sphere around each cluster. Note that one of the B vectors encroaches into C's win region indicating that erroneous classification is possible in some cases.

Suppose that each cluster of input vectors represents a class, and all of the vectors in a cluster map to the identical output vector. In this case, no iterative training algorithm is necessary. We need only to determine which hidden unit wins for a particular class. Then, we simple assign the weight vector on the appropriate connections to the output layer to be equal to the desired output vector. that is, if the ith hidden unit wins for all input vectors of the call for which A is the desired output vector, then we set $w_{ki} = A_k$, where w_{ki} is the weight on the connection from the ith hidden unit to the kth output unit.

If each input vector in a cluster maps to a different output vector, then the outstar learning procedure will enable the outstar to reproduce the average of those output vectors when any member of the class is presented to the inputs of the CPN. If the average output vector for each class is known or can be calculated in advance, then a simple assignment can be made as in the previous paragraph: Let $w_{ki} = (A_k)$.

If the average of the output vectors is not known, then an iterative procedure can be used based on Eq. (6.13).

1. Apply a normalized input vector, x_k, and its corresponding output vector, y_k, to the x and y inputs of the CPN, respectively.
2. Determine the winning competitive-layer unit.
3. Update the weights on the connections from the winning competitive unit to the output units according to Eq. (6.13):

$$w_i(t+1) = w_i(t) + \beta(y_{ki} - w_i(t))$$

4. Repeat steps 1 through 3 until all vectors of all classes map to satisfactory outputs.

6.5 AN IMAGE-CLASSIFICATION EXAMPLE

In this section, we shall look at an example of how the CPN can be used to classify images into categories. In addition, we shall see how a simple modification of the CPN will allow the network to perform some interpolation at the output layer.

The problem is to determine the angle of rotation of the principal axis of an object in tow dimensions, directly from the raw video image of the object. In this case, the object is a model of the Space Shuttle that can be rotated 360 degrees about a single axis of rotation. Numerical algorithms as well as pattern-matching techniques exist that will solve this problem. The neural-network solution possesses some interesting advantages, however, that may recommend it over these traditional approaches.

Figure 6.14 shows a diagram of the system architecture for the spacecraft orientation system. The video camera, television monitor, and robot all interface to a desktop computer that simulates the neural network and hoses a video frame-grabber board. The architecture is an example of how a neural network can be embedded as a part of an overall system.

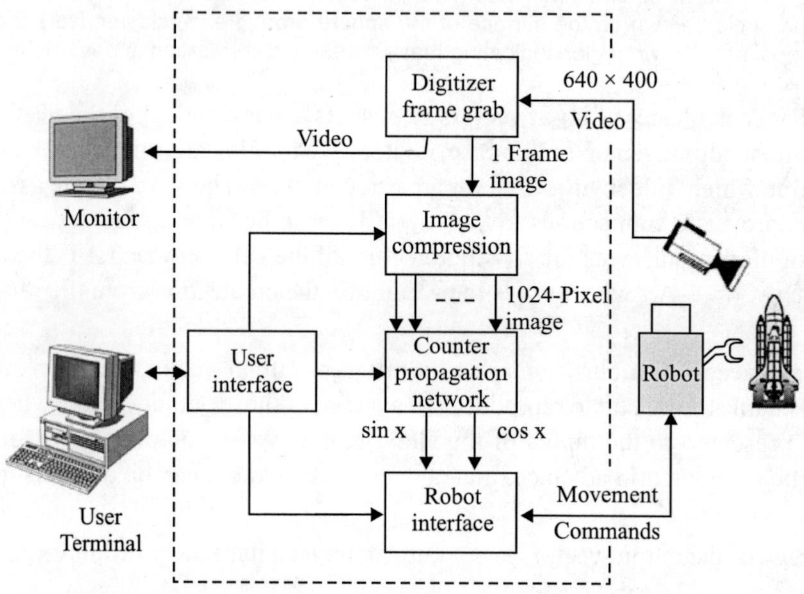

Figure 6.14: The system architecture for the spacecraft orientation system is shown. The video camera and frame-grabber capture a 256-by-256-pixel image of the model. That image is reduced to 32-by-32 pixels by a pixel-averaging technique and is then threshold to produce a binary image. The resulting 1024-component vector is used as the input to the neural network, which responds by giving the sine and cosine of the rotation angle of the principal axis of the model. These output values are converted to an angle that is sent as part of a command string to a mechanical robot assembly. The command sequence causes the robot to reach out and pick up the model. The angle is used to roll the robot's wrist to the proper orientating, so that the robot can grasp the model perpendicular to the long axis.

The system uses CPN having 1026 input units (1024 for the image and 2 for the training inputs), 12 hidden units, and 2 output units. The units on the middle layer learn to divide the input vectors into different classes. There are 12 units in this layer, and 12 different input vectors are used to train the network. These 12 vectors represent images of the shuttle at 30-degree increments (0°, 30°, ...330°). Since there are 12 categories and 12 training vectors, training of the competitive layer consists of setting each unit's weight equal to one of the (normalized) input vectors. The output layer units learn to associate the correct sine and cosine values with each of the classes represented on the middle layer.

It would seem that this network is limited to classifying all input patterns into only one of 12 categories. An input pattern representing a rotation of 32 degrees, for example, probably would be classified as a 30-degree pattern by this network. One way to remedy this deficiency would be to add more units on the middle layer, allowing for a finer categorization of the input images. An alternative approach is to allow the output units to perform an interpolation for patterns that do not match one of the training patterns to within a certain tolerance. For this intrpolative scheme to be accomplished, more than one unit on the competitive layer must share in winning for each input vector.

Recall that the output-layer units calculate their output values according to Eq. (6.15): $y^1_k = \Sigma_j w_{kj} z_j$. In the normal case, where the ith hidden unit wins, $y^1_k = w_{ki}$, since $z_j = 0$ otherwise. Suppose two competitive units shared in winning-the ones with the two closest matching patterns. Further, let the output of those units be proportional to how close the input pattern is; that is $z_j \propto \cos \theta_j$ for the two wining units. If we restrict the total outputfrom the middle layer to unity, then the output values from the output layer would be

$$y^1_k = w_{ki} z_i + w_{kj} z_j$$

where the ith and jth units on the middle layer were the winners, and

$$z_i + z_j = 1$$

The network output is a linear interpolation of the output that would be obtained from the two patterns that exactly matched the two hidden units that shared the victory.

Using the technique, the network will classify successfully input patterns representing rotation angles it had never seen during the training period. In our experiments, the average error was approximately ± 3°. However, since a simple linear interpolation scheme is used, the error varied from almost 0 to as mush as 10 degrees. Other interpolation schemes could result in considerably higher accuracy over the entire range of input patterns.

One of the benefits of using the neural-network approach to pattern matching is robustness in the presence of noise or of contradictory data. An example is shown in Figure 6.15, where the network was able to respond correctly, even though a substantial portion of the image was obscured.

It is unlikely that someone would use a neural network for a simple orientation determination. The methodology can be extended to more realistic cases, however, where the object can be rotated in three dimensions. In such cases, the time required to construct and train a neural network may be significantly less than the time required for development of algorithms that perform the identical tasks.

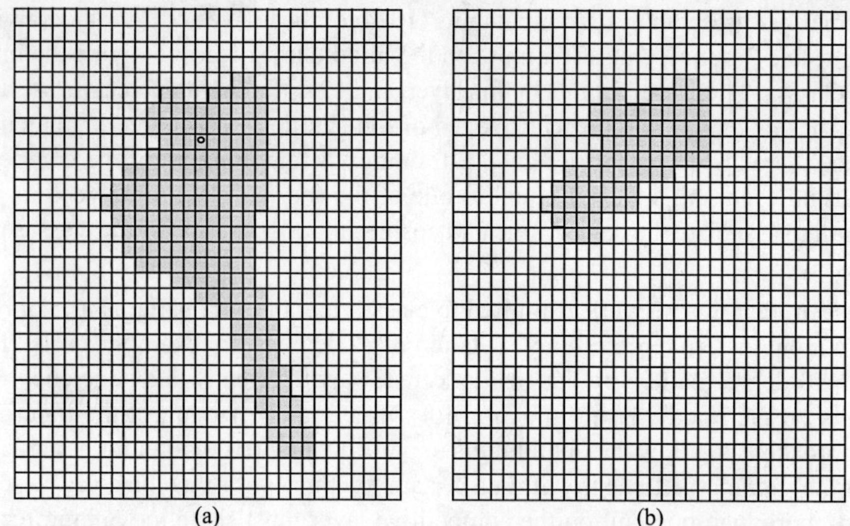

Figure 6.15: These figures show 32-by-32-pixel arrays of two different input vectors for the spacecraft orientation system. (a) This is a bit-mapped image or the space-shuttle model at an angle of 150° as measured clockwise from the vertical. (b) The obscured image was used as an input vector to the spacecraft-orientation system.

EXERCISES

1. What is counter propagation network?
2. Explain the architecture of CPN?
3. Draw the spider like diagram of CPN architecture and explain it?
4. Explain the CPN building block in detail?
5. What is instar?
6. What is outstar? Explain the function of outstar in CPN building block with the help of diagram?
7. Explain the processing of CPN data?
8. How we can train the Counter propagation network?
9. How CPN can be use to classify images of different categories?
10. Explain the system architecture for the space craft orientation system?

CHAPTER 7

Adaptive Resonance Theory

7.1 INTRODUCTION

One of the nice features of human memory is its ability to learn many new things without necessarily forgetting things learned in the past. A frequently cited example is the ability to recognize your parents even if you have not seen them for some time and have learned many new faces in the interim. It would be highly desirable if we could impart this same capability to an Artificial Neural Networks. Most neural networks will tend to forget old information if we attempt to add new information incrementally. When developing an artificial neural network to perform a particular pattern-classification operation, we typically proceed by gathering a set of exemplars, or training patterns, then using these exemplars to train the system.

During the training, information is encoded in the system by the adjustment of weight values. Once the training is deemed to be adequate, the system is ready to be put into production, and no additional weight modification is permitted. This operational scenario is acceptable provided the problem domain has well-defined boundaries and is stable. Under such conditions, it is usually possible to define an adequate set of training inputs for whatever problem is being solved. Unfortunately, in many realistic situations, the environment is neither bounded nor stable. Consider a simple example. Suppose you intend to train a backpropagation to recognize the silhouettes of a certain class of aircraft. The appropriate images can be collected and used to train the network, which is potentially a time-consuming task depending on the size of the network required. After the network has learned successfully to recognize all of the aircraft, the training period is ended and no further modification of the weights is allowed. If, at some future time, another aircraft in the same class becomes operational, you may wish to add its silhouette to the store of knowledge in your neural network. To do this, you would have to retrain the network with the new pattern plus all of the previous patterns. Training on only the new silhouette could result in the network learning that pattern quite well, but forgetting previously learned patterns. Although retraining may not take as long as the initial training, it still could require a significant investment.

The adaptive resonance theory (ART) has been developed to avoid the stability-plasticity dilemma in competitive networks learning. The stability-plasticity dilemma addresses how a learning system can preserve its previously learned knowledge while keeping its ability to learn new patterns.

ART architecture models can self-organize in real time pro-ducing stable recognition while getting input patterns beyond those originally stored. ART is a family of different neural architectures. The first and most basic architec-ture is ART1 (Carpenter and Grossberg, 1987). ART1 can learn and recognize binary patterns. ART2 (Carpenter and Grossberg, 1987) is a class of architectures categorizing arbitrary sequences of analog input patterns. ART is used in modeling such as invariant visual pattern recognition (Carpenter et al 1989) where biological equivalence is dis-cussed (Carpenter and Grossberg 1990).

An ART system consists of two subsystems, an attentional subsystem and an orient-ing subsystem. The stabilization of learning and activation occurs in the attentional sub-system by matching bottom-up input activation and top-down expectation. The orienting subsystem controls the attentional subsystem when a mismatch occurs in the attentional subsystem. In other words, the orienting subsystem works like a novelty detector.

An ART system has four basic properties. The first is the self-scaling computational units. The attentional subsystem is based on competitive learning enhancing pattern fea-tures but suppressing noise. The second is self-adjusting memory search. The system can search memory in parallel and adaptively change its search order. Third, already learned patterns directly access their corresponding category. Finally, the system can adaptively modulate attentional vigilance using the environment as a teacher. If the environment disapproves the current recognition of the system, it changes this parameter to be more vigilant.

7.2 MOTIVATION

Adaptive resonance theory nets are designed to allow the user to control the degree of similarity of patterns placed on the same cluster. However, since input pattern may differ in their level of detail (number of components that are nonzero), the relative similarity of an input pattern to the weight vector for a cluster unit, rather then the absolve difference between the vector, is used. (A difference in one component is more significant in patterns that have very few nonzero components than it is in patterns with many nonzero components). As the net trained, each training pattern may be presented several times. A patterns may be placed on one cluster unit the first time it is presented and then placed on a different cluster when it is presented later (due to changes in the weights for the first cluster if it has learned other patterns in the meantime). A stable net will not return a pattern to a previous cluster, in other words, a pattern oscillating among different cluster unit at different stages of training indicated an unstable net.

Some nets achieves stability by reducing the learning rate as the same set of training patterns is presented many times. However, this does not allow the net to learn readily a new pattern that is presented for the first time after a number of training epochs have already taken place. The ability of a net to respond to (learn) a new pattern equally well at any stage of learning is called plasticity. Adaptive resonance theory nets are designed to be both stable and plastic.

Also, attention has been paid to structuring ART nets so that neural processes can control the rather intricate operation of these nets. This requires a number of neurons in addition to the input units, cluster unit's, and unit for the comparison of the input signal with the cluster unit's weights.

7.3 BASIC ARCHITECTURE

The basic architecture of an adaptive resonanceneural net involves three groups of neurons; an it processing field (called the F_1 layer), the cluster units (the F_2layer), and a mechanism to control the degree of similarity of patterns placed on the same cluster (a reset mechanism). The F_1 layer can be considered to consist of two parts; the input portion (especially in ART2). The interface portion combines signal from the input portion and the F_2 layer, for use in comparing the similarity of the input signal to the weight vector for the cluster unit that has been selected as a candidate for learning.. We Shall denote the input portion of the $F_{1,}$ layer as F_2 (a) and the interface portion as F_1 (b).

To control the similarity of patterns placed on the same cluster, there are two sets of connection (each with its own weight) between each unit.in the interface portion of the input field and each cluster unit. The F_1 (b) layer is connected to theF_2 layer by bottom-up weights; the bottom-up weight on the connection from the ithF_1 unit to the jth F_2 unit is designated b_{ji}. The F_2 layer is connected to the F_1(b) layer by top-down weight; the top-down weight on the connection from the jth F_2 unit to the jth F_1 unit is designated t_{ji}.

The F_2 layer is a competitive layer: The cluster unit with the largest net becomes the candidate to learn the input pattern. The activation of all other F_2 unit are set to zero, the interface units now combine information from the input and cluster units Whether or not this cluster unit is allowed to learn the input pattern depends on how similar it top-down weight vector is to the input vector. This decision is made by the reset unit. based on signals it receives from the input (a) and interface (b) portions of the F_1 layer. If the cluster unit is not allowed to learn, it is inhibited and a new cluster unit is selected as the candidate.

The supplemental units needed to control the processing of information in the ART nets described forART1 and ART2 in sections 7.4 and 7.5 respectively..

7.3.1 Basic Operation

It is difficult to describe even the basic architecture of adaptive resonance theory nets without discussing the operation of the nets. Details of the operation of ART1 and ART2 are presented later in this chapter.

A learning trial in ART consist of the presentation of one input pattern. Before the pattern is presented, the activations of all units in the net are set to zero. All F_2 units are inactive. (Any F_2 units that had been inhibited on the previous learning trial are again available to complete.) Once a pattern is presented, it continues to send its input signal

until the learning trial is completed. The degree of similarity required for pattern to be assigned to the same cluster unit is controlled by a user-specified parameter, known as the vigilance parameter.

Although the detail of the reset mechanism for ART21 and ART2 differ, its function is to control the state of each node in the F_2 layer. At any time, an F_2 node is in one of three states.

Active ("on ," activation = d; d = 1 for ART1, $0 < d < 1$ for ART2),

Inactive ("off," activation = 0, but available to participate in competition or

Inhibited ("off," activation = 0, and prevented from participating in any further competition during the presentation of the current input vector).

A summary of the steps that occur in ART nets in general is as follows.

Step 0: Initialize parameters.

Step 1: While stopping condition is false, do steps 2-9,

Step 2: For each input vector, do steps 3-8.

Step 3: Process F_1 layer.

Step 4: While reset condition is true, do steps 5-7

Steps 5: Find candidate unit to learn the current input pattern F_2 units (which is not inhibited) with largest input.

Step 6: F_1 (b) units combine their input from F_1 (a) and F_2.

Step 7: Test reset condition (detail differ for ART1 and ART2):

If reset is true, then the current candidate unit is rejected (inhibited) ; return to step 4.

If reset is false, then the current candidate unit is accepted for learning; proceed to step 8.

Sec. 7.1 Introduction

Step 8: Learning Weights change according to different equations.

Step 9: Text stopping condition.

The calculations in Step 2 constitute a "learning trial," i.e., one presentation of one pattern. Although ART does not require that all training patterns be presented in the same prodder, or even that all patterns be presented with the same frequency, we shall refer to the calculations of step 1 (one presentation of each training pattern) as an epoch. Thus, foregoing algorithmic structure, while convenient, is not the most general from for ART. The learning process may involve many weight updates and/or many epochs.

7.3.2 Learning

In adaptive resonance theory, the change in the activations of units and in weights are governed y coupled differential equations. The net is a continuously changing (dynamical) system, but the process can be simplified because the activations are assumed to change much more rapidly than the weights. Once an acceptable cluster unit has been selected for learning, the bottom-up and top-down signals are maintained for an extended period, during which time the weight changes occur. This is the "reasonable" that gives the net its name.

Two types of learning that differ both in their theoretical assumptions and n their performance characteristics can be sued for ART nets. In the fast learning mode, it is assumed that weight updates during resonance occur rapidly, relative to the length of time a pattern is presented on any particular trail. Thus, in fast learning, the weights reach equilibrium on each trail. In the slow learning mode the weight changes occur slowly relative to the duration of a learning trail; the weights do not reach equilibrium on a particular trail. Many more presentations of the patterns are required for slow learning that for fast learning, but fewer calculations occur on each learning trail in slow learning. In order to achieve the performance characteristics of slow learning to the fullest extent, we shall assume that only one weight update, with a relatively small learning rate, occurs on each learning trial in the slow learning mode.

In fast learning, the net is considered stabilized when each pattern chooses the correct cluster unit when it is presented (without causing any unit to reset). For ART1, because the patterns are binary, the weights associated with each cluster unit also stabilize in the fast learning mode. The resulting weight vectors are appropriate for the type of input patterns used in ART1. Also, the equilibrium weights are easy to determine, and the iterative solution of the differential equations that control the weight updates is not necessary. This is the form of learning that is typically used for ART1 and is the nly algorithm we consider.

In general, for ART2, the weights produced by fast learning continue to change each time a pattern is presented. The net stabilizers after only a few presentations of each training pattern. However, since the differential equations for the weight updates depend on the activation of units whose activations change during the resonance process, it is not as straightforward to find the equilibrium weights immediately for ART2 as it is for ART1. The process of solving the weight update equations by letting the net iterate as resonance occurs is illustrated in several examples.

In the slow learning mode, weight changes do not reach equilibrium during any particular learning trial and more trials are required before the net stabilizes [Carpenter & Gross berg, 1987a, 1987b].Although slow learning is theoretically possible for ART1, it is not typically used in this form. For ART2, however, the weight produced by slow learning may be much more appropriate than those produced by fast learning for certain types of data.

7.4 ART1

ART1 is designed to cluster binary input vectors, following for great variation the number of nonzero components, and direct user control of the degree of similarity among patterns placed on the same cluster unit. The architecture of an ART1 net consists of two field units—the F_1 unit and the F_2 (cluster) units— together with a reset unit to control the degree of similarity of patterns placed on the same cluster unit. (For convenience, we have expanded the description of the F_1 units from the original presentation of the net in Carpenter and Grossberg (1987a) to include an explicit set of input units, the F_1(a) units, as well as the F_1(b) units, which exchange information with the F_2 units.) The F_1 and F_2 layers are connected by two sets of weighted pathways, In addition, several supplemental units are included in the net to provide for neural control of the learning process.

The learning process is designed so that it is not required either that patterns be presented in a fixed order or that the number of patterns to be clustered be known in advance (i.e., more patterns can be added to the data set during the training process if desired) . Updates for both the bottom-up and top-down weight are controlled by differential equations. However, it is assumed that the ART1 net is being operated in the fast learning mode, in which the weights reach equilibrium during each learning trial (presentation of a pattern).Since the activation of the F_1units do not change during this resonance phase, the equilibrium weights can be determined exactly, and the iterative solution of the differential equations is not necessary.

7.4.1 Architecture

The architecture of ART1 consists of computational units and supplemental units.

7.4.2 Computational Units

The architecture of the computational units for ART1 consists of F_1 units (input and interface units), F_2 units (cluster units), and a reset unit that implements user control over the degree of similarity of patterns placed on the same cluster. This main portion of the ART1 architecture is illustrated in Figure 7.1.

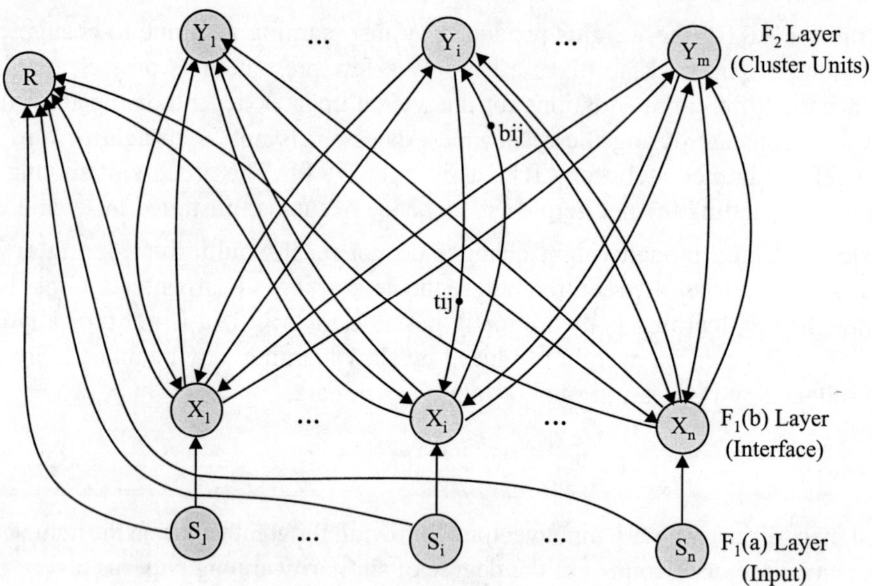

Figure 7.1: Basic structure of ART1

Each unit in the F_1(a) (input) layer is connected to the corresponding unit in the F_1 (b) (interface) layer. Each unit in the F_1 (a) and F_1(b) layer is connected to the reset unit, which in turn is connected to every F_2 unit. Each unit in the F_1(b) layer is connected to each unit the F_2 (cluster) layer by two weighted pathways. The F_1 (b) unit X_i is connected to the F_2 unit Y_j by bottom-up weights b_{ij}. Similarly, unit Y_j is connected to unit X_i by top-down weights t_{ij}. Only one representative weight b_{ij} is indicated on the connections between the F_1 and F_2 layer; similarly, t_{ji} is a representative weight for the connections between the F_2 and F_1 layer. The F_2 layer is a competitive layer in which only the uninhibited node with the largest net input has a nonzero activation.

7.4.3 Supplementary Units

The supplemental units shown in Figure 7.2 are important from a theoretical point of view. They provide a mechanism by which the computations performed by the algorithm in Section 7.2.2 can be accomplished using neural network principles. However, this theoretical discussion of the necessary supplemental units is not required to be able to use the computational algorithm. The reader may proceed directly to the algorithm if desired.

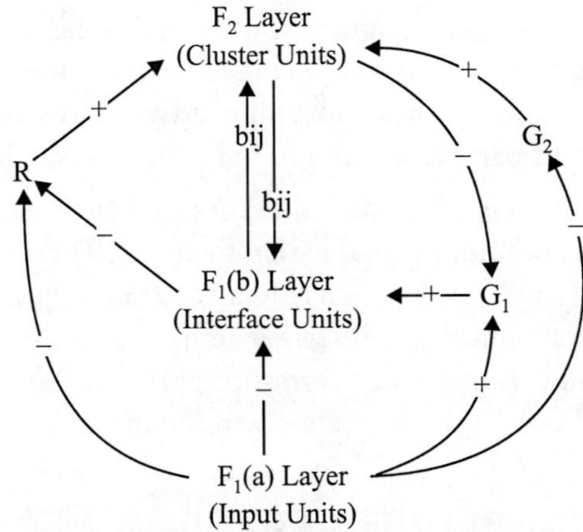

Figure 7.2: The supplemental units for ARTI.

The computational algorithm for ARTI represents a more involved neural process than can be represented in terms of just the F_1 units, the F_2 units, and the reset unit in Figure7.1. The difficulty is that these units are required to respond differently at different stages of the process, and a biological neuron does not have a method for deciding what to do when. For example, units in the F_1 interface region (F_1 (b) units) should be "on" when an input signal is received (from F_1 (a)) and no F_2 units are active however, when an F_2 unit is active, an F_1 (b) unit should remain "on" only if it receives (nonzero) signals from both the F_2 layer and the input units.

The operation of the reset mechanism also poses a challenge in terms of implementation within a neural processing system. F_2 units must be inhibited (and prevented from competing) under certain conditions, but returned to availability on subsequent learning trails.

Both of these problems can be solved by introducing two supplemental units (called gain control units) G_1 and G_2, in addition to the reset unit R shown in Figure7.1. Each of these three special units receives signals from, and sends its signal to, all of the units in the layers indicated in Figure 7.2. Excitatory signals are indicated by "+" and inhibitory signals by " –", A signal is sent whenever any unit in the designated layer is "on."

Each unit in either the F_1 (b) (interface region) or F_2 layer of the ART1 net has three sources from which it can receive a signal. F_1 (b) interface units can receive signals from an F_1 (a) unit (an input signal), from an F_2 node (a top-down signal), or from the G_1 unit. Similarly, an F_2 unit can receive signal from the F_1 interface units, unit R, r the G_2 unit. An F_1 (b) (interface) or F_2 unit must receive two excitatory signals in order to be "on." Since there are three possible sources of signals, this requirement is called the two-thirds rule.

The F_1 (b) (interface) nodes are required to send a signal (to the F_2 nodes and the reset unit) whenever an input vector is presented and no F_2 node is active. However, after an F_2 node has been chosen in the competition, it is necessary that only the F_1 (b) nodes whose top-down signal and input signal match remain active. This is accomplished through the use of the G_1 and G_2 units and the two-thirds rule. The G_1 unit is inhibited whenever any F_2 units is on. When no F_2 unit is on, each F_1 interface unit receives a signal from the G_1 unit; in this case, all of the units that receive a positive input signal from the input vector that is presented will fire. In a similar manner, the G_2 unit controls the firing of the F_2 units; they must obey a two-thirds rule, too. The two-thirds rule also plays a role in the choice of parameters and initial weights, considered in Section 7.2.4.

The reset unit R controls the vigilance matching. As indicated in Figure 7.2 when any unit in the F_1 (a) input layer is on, an excitatory signal is sent to unit R. The strength of that signal depends on how many F_1 (input) units are on. However, R also receives inhibitory signals from the F_1 interface units that are on. If enough F_1 (b) interface units are on (as determined by the vigilance parameter set by the user), unit R is prevented from firing. If unit R does fire, it inhibits any F_2 unit that is on. This forces the F_2 layer to choose a new winning node.

7.4.4 Algorithm

In the first two parts of this section, we provide a description of the training process for ART1 (using fast learning) and a step-by-step algorithm for the training. A discussion of the choice of parameter values and initial weights follows the training algorithm. the notation we use is as follows:

- n number of components in the input vector.
- m maximum number of clusters that can be formed.
- b_{ij} bottom-up weights (from F_1 (b) unit X_i to F_2 unit Y_j).
- t_{ji} top-down weights (from F_2 unit Y_j to F_1 unit X_i).
- p vigilance parameter.
- s binary input vector (an n-tuple).
- x activation vector for F_1 (b) layer (binary).
- $||x||$ norm of vector x, defined as the sum of the components x_i.

7.4.5 Description

A binary input vector s is presented to the F_1 (a) layer, and the signals are sent to the corresponding X units. These F_1 (b) units then broadcast to the F_2 layer over connection pathways with bottom-up weights. Each F_2 unit computes its net input, and the units compete for the right to be active. The unit with the largest net input sets its activation to 1; all other have an activation of 0. We shall denote the index of the winning unit as J. this winning unit becomes the candidate to learn the input pattern. A signal is then sent down from F_2 to F_1 (b) (multiplied by the top-down weights). The X units (in the interface portion of the F_1 layer) remain "on" only if they receive nonzero signals from both the F_1 (a) and F_1 units.

The norm of the vector x (the activation vector for the interface portion of F_1) gives the number of components in which the top-down weight vector for the winning F_2 unit t_j and the input vector s are both 1. (This quantity is sometimes referred to as the match.) If the ratio of $||x||$ to $||s||$ is greater than r equal to the vigilance parameter, the weights (top down and bottom up) for the winning cluster unit are adjusted.

However, if the ratio is less than the vigilance parameter, the candidate unit is rejected, and another candidate unit must be chosen. The current winning cluster unit becomes inhibited, so that it cannot be chosen again as a candidate on this learning trail, and the activations of the F_1 units are reset to zero. The same input vector again sends its signal to the interface units, which again sent this as the bottom-up signal to the F_2 layer, and the competition is repeated (but without the participation of any inhibited units).

The process continues until either a satisfactory match is found (a candidate is accepted) or all units are inhibited. The action to be taken if all units are inhibited must be specified by the user. It might be appropriate to reduce the value of the vigilance parameter, allowing less similar patterns to be placed on the same cluster, or to increase the number cluster units, or simply to designate the current input pattern as an outlier that could not be clustered.

In the theoretical formulation of the ART process, learning occurs during the resonance phase, in which the signals continue t flow throughout the net Care is taken in setting the parameter values so that a reset cannot suddenly occur as the weights change, nor will a new winning unit be chosen after a candidate unit is accepted for learning (see Section 7.2.4). The algorithm given shortly uses these equilibrium values in Step 8.

At the end of each presentation of a pattern (normally, after the weights have been adjusted), all cluster units are returned to inactive status (zero activations, but available to participate in the next competition).

The use of the ratio of the match to the norm of the input vector in the reset calculations described allows an ART1 net to respond to relative differences. This reflects the fact that a difference of one component in vector with only a few nonzero components is much more significant than a difference of one component in vectors with many nonzero components.

7.4.6 Training Algorithm

The training algorithm for an ART1 net is presented next. A discussion of the role of the parameters and an appropriate choice of initial weights follows.

Step 0: Initialize parameters:

$$L > 1,$$

$$0 < p \leq 1.$$

Initialize weights:

$$0 < b_{ij}(0) < \frac{L}{L \quad 1 \quad n},$$

$$t_{ij}(0) = 1.$$

Step 1: While stopping condition is false, do steps 2-13.

Step 2: For each training input, do Steps 3-12.

Step 3: Set activations of all F_2 units to zero.
Set activations of $F_1(a)$ units to input vector s.

Step 4: Compute the norm of s:

$$\|s\| = \underset{i}{\quad} s_i$$

Step 5: Send input signal from F_1 (a) to the F_1 (b) layer:

$$x_i = s_i.$$

Step 6. For each F_2 node that is not inhibited:

If $\quad y_j \neq -1$, then

$$y_j = \underset{i}{\quad} b_{ij} x_i$$

Step 7: While reset is true, do Steps 8-11.

Step 8: Find J such that $y_j \geq y_j$ for all nodes j.
If $y_j = -1$, then all nodes are inhibited and this pattern cannot be clustered.

Step 9: Recomputed activation x of F_1 (b):

$$x_i = d_i t_{ji}.$$

Step 10: Compute the norm of vector x:

$$\|x\| = \underset{i}{\quad} x_i$$

Step 11: Test for reset:

If $\quad \frac{\|x\|}{\|s\|} < p$, then

$y_j = -1$ (inhibit node J) (and continue, executing Step 7 again).

If $\quad \frac{\|x\|}{\|s\|} \geq p,$

Step 12: Update the weights for node J (fast learning):

$$b_{ij}\text{ (new)} = \frac{Lx_i}{L \quad 1 \quad \|x\|},$$

$$t_{ji}\text{(new)} = x_i.$$

Step 13: Test for stopping condition.

Comments:

Step 3 removes all inhibitions from the previous learning trail (presentation of a pattern).

Setting y = – 1 for an inhibited node (in step 6) will prevent that node from being a winner. Since all weights and signals in the net are nonnegative a unit with a negative activation can never have the largest activation.

In step 8, in case of a tie, take J to be the smallest such index.

In step 9, unit X_i is "on" only if it receives both an external signal s_i and a signal sent down from F_2 to F_1, t_{ji}.

The stopping condition in Step 13 might consist of any of the following:

No weight changes,

No units reset, or

Maximum number of epochs reached.

The ART1 training process is often described in terms of setting the activation of the winning F_2 unit 1 and all others to 0. However, it is easy to implement the algorithm without making explicit use of those activations, so in the interest of computational simplicity, they are omitted here.

The user must specify the desired action to be taken in the event that all the F_2 nodes are inhibited in Step 8. The possibilities include adding more cluster units, reducing the vigilance, and classifying the pattern as an outlier that cannot be clustered (with the given parameters).

Notes that t_{ij} is either 0 or 1, and once it is set to 0 during learning, it can never be set back to 1 (which provides the stable learning mentioned before).

7.4.7 Parameters

User-defined parameters with restrictions indicated for permissible values [Carpenter & Grossberg, 1987a] and sample values [Lippmann, 1987] are as follows:

Parameter	Permissible Range	Sample Value
L	$L > 1$	2
p	$0 < p \le 1$ (vigilance parameter)	.9
b_{ij}	$0 < b_{ij}(0) < \frac{L}{L \quad 1 \quad n}$, (bottom-up weights)	$\frac{1}{1 \quad n}$
t_{ji}	$t_{ji}(0) = 1$ (top-down weights)	1

The derivation of the restrictions on the initial bottom-up and top-down weights is given in Section 7.2.4. Larger values for the initial bottom-up weights may encourage the net to form more clusters. The sample values of $b_{ij}(0)$ (one-half of the maximum allowed value for L = 2) are used in the examples of Section 7.2.3.

The equilibrium weights, which are used in the ART1 algorithm are derived in Section 7.2.4. The algorithm uses fast learning, which assumes that the input pattern is presented for the long enough period of time for the weights to reach equilibrium. Since none of the activations of the F_{1-} units change during resonance, it is not necessary actually to perform the iterations to solve the weight-update differential equations numerically.

Several values of p are illustrated in the examples of Section 7.2.3.

7.5 ART2

ART2 is designed to perform for continuous-valued input vectors the same type of tasks as ART1 does for binary-valued input vectors. The differences between ART2 and ART1 reflect the modifications needed to accommodate patterns with continuous-valued components. The more complex F_1 field f ART2 is necessary because continuous-valued input vectors may be arbitrarily close together. The F_1 field in ART2 includes a combination of normalization and noise suppression, in addition to the comparison of the bottom-up and top-down signals needed for the reset mechanism. The learning process for ART2 is summarized in Section 7.3.2 and discussed in more detail in 7.3.4.

There are two types of continuous-valued inputs for which ART2 may be used. The first might be called "noisy binary" signals. These consist of patterns whose information is conveyed primarily by which components are "on" or "virtually off," rather than by the differences in the magnitude of the components that are positive. The equilibrium weights found by the fast learning mode are suitable for this type of data. However, it is not as easy to find equilibrium weights in ART2 as it is for ART1, because the differences equations for the weight updates depend on activations in the F_1 layer, which are changing as learning progress.

For patterns in which the range of values of the components carries significant information and the weight vector for a cluster unit is to be interpreted as an exemplar for the patterns placed on that unit, the slow learning mode may be more appropriate. We can think of this second type of data as "truly continuous." Both forms of learning are included in the algorithm in Section 5.3.2.

7.5.1 Architecture

A typical ART2 architecture [Carpenter & Grossberg, 1987b] is illustrated in Figure 7.3. The F_1 layer consists of six types of units (the W, X, U, V, P, and Q units). There are n units of each of these types (where n is the dimension of an input pattern). Only one unit of each type is shown in the figure. A supplemental unit between the W and X units receives signals from all of the W units, computes the norm of the vector w, and sends this (inhibitory0 signal to each of the X units. Each of these also receives an excitatory signal from the corresponding W unit. Detail of this portion of the net is shown in Figure 7.4.

A similar supplemental unit performs the same role between the P and Q units, and another does so between the V and U units. Each X unit is connected to the corresponding V unit, and each Q unit is connected to the corresponding V unit also. The symbols on the connection paths between the various units in the F_1 layer in Figure 7.3 indicate the transformation that occurs to the signal as it passes from one type of unit to the next; they do not indicate multiplication by the given quantity. However, the connections between units $P\text{-}_i$ (of the F_1 layer) and Y_j (0f the F_2 layer) do show the weights that multiply the signal transmitted over those paths. The activation of the winning F_2 unit is d, where $0 < d < 1$. The activation function applied to x and q will be discussed later. The symbol $\rightarrow$ indicates normalization; i.e. the vector q of activations of the Q units is just the vector p of activations of the P units,, normalized to approximately unit length.The action of the F_2 layer (units Y_j in Figure 7.3) is essentially unchanged from the action in ART1. The units complete in a winner-take-all mode for the right to learn each input pattern. As in ART1, learning occurs only if the top-down weight vector for the winning unit is sufficiently similar to the input vector. The test for reset in ART1 and ART 2 differ. (See the algorithm in Section 7.3.2 for details of the test used in ART2.)

The U units perform a similar role to the input phase of the F_1 layer in ART1. However, in ART2 some processing of the input vector is necessary because the magnitudes of the real-values input vectors may vary more than for the binary input vectors of ART1. ART2 treats small components as noise and does not distinguish between patterns that are merely scaled versions of each other. The P units play the role of the interface F_1 units in the ART1 architecture. The role of the supplemental units in ART1 has been incorporated within the F_1 layer.

Figure 7.5 presents an expanded diagram of the F_1 layer of the ART2 net illustrated in Figure 7.3. In keeping with the diagrams for other nets (in other chapters), only weights are shown on the connections between units. (IF no weight is indicated, the signal transverses that pathway without modification.)

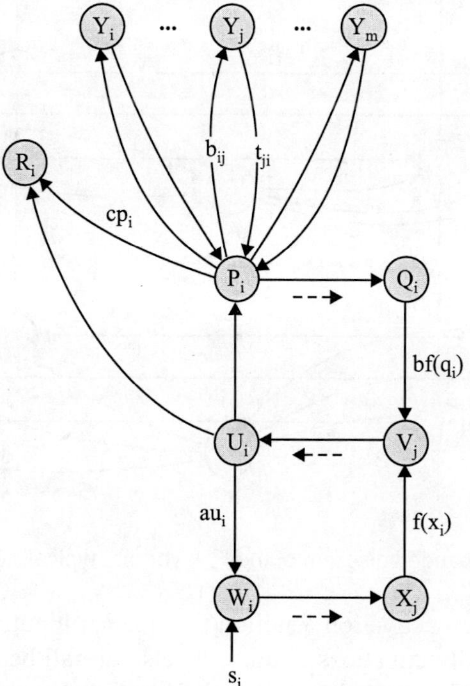

Figure 7.3: Typical ART2 architecture [Carpenter & Grossberg, 1987b]

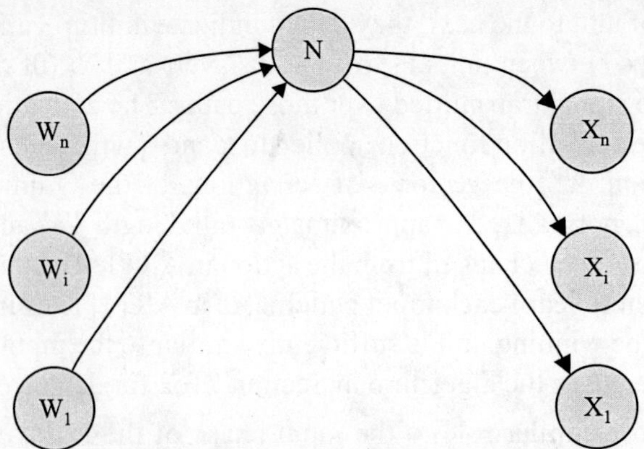

Figure 7.4: Detail of connections from W units to X units, showing the supplemental unit N to perform normalization.

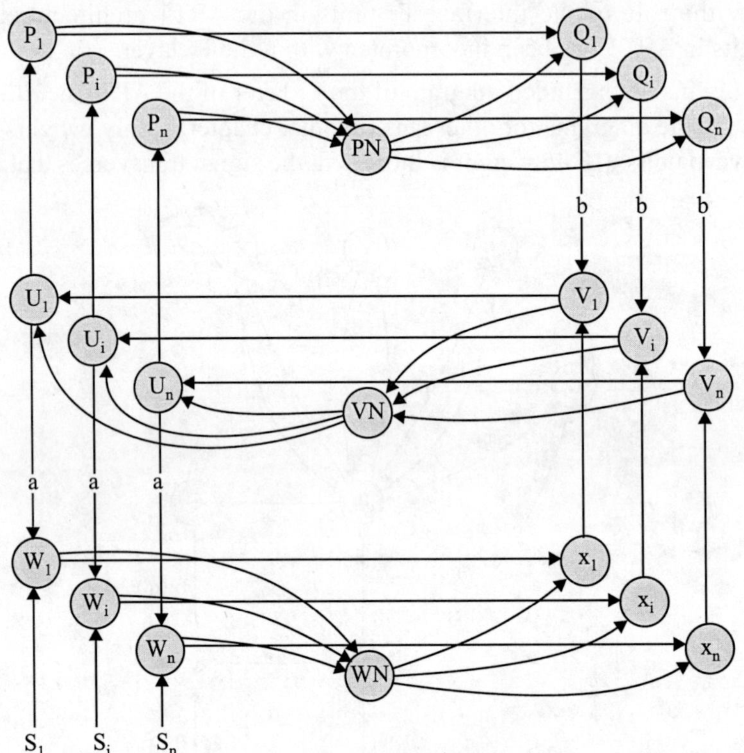

Figure 7.5: Expanded diagram of the F_1 layer of a typical ART2 architecture.

Units X_i and Q_i apply an activation function to their net input; this function suppresses any components of the vectors of activations at those levels that fall below the user-selected value q. The connection paths from U to W and from Q to V have fixed weights a and b, respectively.

7.5.2 Algorithm

This section provides a description of the training algorithm for ART2 (for both fast and slow learning), a step-by-step statement of the algorithm, and a summary of the basic information about the parameters and choice of initial weights necessary to implement the algorithm. Examples in Section 7.3.3 illustrate the influence of some of these parameters. Derivations of the restrictions on the choice of parameter values and initial weights are given in Section 7.3.4.

7.5.3 Description

A learning trial consists of one presentation of one input pattern. The input signal $s = (s_1,\ldots,s_i,\ldots s_n)$ continues to be sent while all of the actions to be described are performed. At the beginning of a learning trial, all activations are set to zero.

The computation cycle (for a particular learning trial) within the F_1 layer can be thought of as originating with the computation of the activation of unit U_i (the activation of unit V_i normalized to approximately unit length). Next, a signal is sent from each unit U_i to its associated units W_i and P_i. The activations of units W_i and P_i are then computed. Unit W_i sums the signal it receives from U_i and the input signal s_i. P_i sums the signal it receives from U_i and the top-down signal it receives if there is an active F_2 unit. The activations of X_i and Q_i are normalized versions of the signals at W_i and P_i, respectively. An activation function is applied at each of these units before the signal is sent to V_i, V_i then sums the signals it receives concurrently from X_i and Q_i; this completes one cycle of updating the F_1 layer.

The activation function is used in examples in Carpenter and Grossberg's (1987b)

$$f(x) = \begin{matrix} x & \text{if } x \\ 0 & \text{if } x\ \theta \end{matrix}$$

original paper and here. With this function, the activations of the U and P units reach equilibrium after two updates of the F_1 layer. This function treats any signal that is less than θ as noise and suppresses it (sets it to zero). The value of the parameter q is specified by the user. Noise suppression helps the net achieve stable cluster formation. The net is stable when the first cluster unit chosen for each input pattern is accepted and no reset occurs. For slow learning, the weight vectors for the clusters will also converge to stable values.

After the activations of the F_1 units have reached equilibrium, the P units send their signals to the F_2 layer, where a winner-take-all competition chooses the candidate cluster unit to learn the input pattern. (It is not important how fast this competition takes place relative to iterations in the F_1 layer, since the activations of the U and P units there will not change until the top-down signal from the winning F_2 unit is received by the P units.)

The units U_i and P_i in the F_1 layer also send signals to the corresponding reset unit R_i. The reset mechanism can check for a reset each time it receives a signal from P_i, since the necessary computations are based on the value of that signal and the most recent signal the unit R_i had received from U_i. However, this needs to be done only when P_i first receives a top-down signal, since parameter values are chosen such that no reset will occur if no F_2 unit is active, or after learning has started.

The reset mechanism will be considered in more detail in Section 7.3.4.

After the conditions for reset have been checked, the candidate cluster unit either will be rejected as not similar enough to the input pattern or will be accepted. If the cluster unit is rejected, it will become inhibited (prevented from further participation in the current learning trial), and the cluster unit with the next largest net input is chosen as the candidate. This process continues until an acceptable cluster unit is chosen (or the supply of available cluster units is exhausted). When a candidate cluster unit is chosen that passes the reset conditions, learning will occur.

In slow learning, only one iteration of the weight update equations occurs on each learning trial. A large number of presentations of each pattern is required, but relatively little computation is done on each trial. For convenience, these repeated presentations are treated as epochs in the algorithm that follows. However, there is no requirement that the patterns be presented in the same order or that exactly the same patterns be presented on each cycle through them.

In the fast learning mode, the weight updates (alternating with updates of the F_1 layer activations) continue until the weights reach equilibrium on each trial. Only a few epochs are required, but a large number of iterations through the weight-update-F_1-update portion of the algorithm must be performed on each learning trial (presentation of a pattern). In fast learning, the placement of the patterns on clusters stabilizers (no reset occurs), but the weights will change for each pattern presented.

7.5.4 Training Algorithm

The algorithm that follows can be used for either fast learning or slow learning. In fast learning, iterations of weight change followed by updates of F_1 activations proceed until equilibrium is reached. In slow learning, only one iteration of the weight-update step is performed, but a large number of learning trial is required in order for the net to stabilize,. [Carpenter & Grossberg, 1987b]. Fast learning and slow learning are compared in the examples in Section 7.3.3.

Calculations for Algorithm. The following calculation are repeated at several steps of eh algorithm and will be referred to as "update F_1 activations." Unit J is the winning F_2 node after competition. If no winning unit has been chosen, d will be zero of all units. Note that the calculations for w_i and p_i can be done in parallel, as can the calculations for x_i and q_i.

The update F_1 activations are:

$$u_i = \frac{v_i}{e + \|v\|},$$

$$w_i = s_i + au_{\ i}, \quad p_i = u_i\, dt_{\ j\, i},$$

$$x_i = \frac{w_i}{e + \|w\|}, \quad q_i = \frac{p_i}{e + \|p\|}$$

$$v_i = f(x_i) + bf(q_i).$$

The activation function is

$$f(x) = \begin{matrix} x & \text{if } x \\ 0 & \text{if } x\,\theta \end{matrix}$$

Algorithm

Step 0: Initialize parameters:

$$a, b, \theta, c, d, e, \alpha, \rho.$$

Step 1: Do Steps 2-12 N_EP times.

(Perform the specified number of epochs of training.)

Step 2: For each input vector s, do Steps 3-11.

Step 3: Update F_1 unit activations:

$$u_i = 0, \quad x_i = \frac{s_i}{e + ||s||},$$

$$w_i = s_i, \quad q_i = 0,$$

$$p_i = 0, \quad v_i = f(x_i).$$

Update F_1 unit activations again:

$$u_i = \frac{v_i}{e + ||v||},$$

$$w_i = s_i + au_i,$$

$$p_i = u_i,$$

$$x_i = \frac{w_i}{e + ||w||}$$

$$q_i = \frac{p_i}{e + ||p||},$$

$$v_i = f(x_i) + bf(q_i).$$

Step 4: Compute signals to F_2 units:

$$y_i = \underset{i}{\ } b_{ij}p_i.$$

Step 5: While reset is true, do Steps 6-7.

Step 6: Find F_2 unit Y_j with largest signal. (Define J such that $Y_j \geq y_j$ for $j = 1,\ldots.m.$)

Step 7: Check for reset:

$$u_i = \frac{v_i}{e + ||v||},$$

$$p_i = u_i + dt_{ji},$$

$$r_i = \frac{u_i + cp_i}{e + ||u|| + c\,||p||}$$

If $||r|| < p - e$, then

$$y_j = -1 \text{ (inhibit J)}$$

(reset is true; repeat Step 5);

If $\|r\| \geq p - e$, then

$$w_i = s_i + au_i,$$

$$x_i = \frac{w_i}{e + \|w\|},$$

$$q_i = \frac{p_i}{e + \|p\|},$$

$$v_i = f(x_i) + bf(q_i).$$

Reset is false; proceed to Step 8.

Step 8: Do steps 9-11 N_IT times.

(Perform the specified number of learning iterations.)

Step 9: Update weights for winning unit J:

$$t_{ji} = \alpha du_i + \{1 + \alpha d(d-1)\}t_{ji}$$
$$b_{ij} = \alpha du_i + \{1 + \alpha d(d-1)\}b_{ij}$$

Step 10: Update F_i activations:

$$u_i = \frac{v_i}{e + \|v\|},$$

$$w_i = s_i + au_i,$$

$$p_i = u_i\, dt_{ji},$$

$$x_i = \frac{w_i}{e + \|w\|},$$

$$q_i = \frac{p_i}{e + \|p\|},$$

$$v_i = f(x_i) + bf(q_i).$$

Step 11: Test stooping condition for weight updates.

Step 12: Test stopping condition for number of epochs.

Comments. In the preceding algorithms, we have made use of the following facts:

1. Reset cannot occur during resonance (Step 8).
2. A new winning unit cannot be chosen during resonance.

We have not used the facts that:

1. Typically, in slow learning N_IT = 1, and Step 10 can be omitted.
2. In fast learning, for the pattern learned by a cluster, u will be parallel to t throughout the training cycle and the equilibrium weights will be

$$t_{ji} = \frac{1}{1\quad d} u_i;$$

$$b_{ij} = \frac{1}{1\quad d} u_i;$$

Other possible stopping conditions are as follows:

Repeat Step 8 until the weight changes are below some specified tolerance. For slow learning, repeat Step 1 until the weight changes are below some specified tolerance. For fast learning, repeat Step 1 until the placement of patterns on the cluster units does not change from on epoch to next.

Steps 3 through 11 constitute on learning trial (one presentation of a pattern). It will be convenient (especially in describing the implementation of fast learning and slow learning using this algorithm) to refer to the performance of a learning trial for each input pattern as an epoch. It is not necessary that the patterns be presented in the same order on each epoch. Note that the action of updating the F_1 activations during the extended resonance phase of the fast learning mode (the computations in Step 8) causes the values of the u_i that appear in the weight update equations to change as learning progress.

7.5.5 Choices

Parameters. A summary of the role of the various parameters used in the algorithm is given here. Derivations of some of these restrictions are given in Section 7.3.4. The parameters and their roles are as follows:

- n — Number of input units (F_1 layer);
- m — number of cluster units (F_2 layer);
- a, b — fixed weights in the F_1 layer; sample values are a = 10. Setting either a = 0 or b = 0 produces instability in the net; other than that, the net is not particularly sensitive to the values chosen.
- c — fixed weight used in testing for reset; a sample value is c = 1. A small c gives larger effective range of the vigilance parameter (see Section 7.3.4).
- d — activation of winning F_2 unit; a sample value is d = .9. Note that c and d must be chosen to satisfy the inequality

$$\frac{cd}{1\quad d} \leq 1$$

  (in order to prevent a reset from occurring during a learning trial). The ratio should be chosen close to 1 to achieve a larger effective range for vigilance (see Section 7.3.4).
- e — a small parameter introduced to prevent division by zero when the norm of a vector is zero. This value prevents the normalization to unity from being exact. A value of zero is typically used in the hand computations and derivations that follow and may be used in the algorithm if the normalization step is skipped when the vector is zero.

θ noise suppression parameter, a sample value is $\theta = 1/\sqrt{n}$. The sample value may be larger than desired in some applications. Components of the normalized input vector (and other vector in the F_1 loop) that are less than this value are set to zero.

α learning rate. A smaller value will slow the learning in either the fast or the slow learning mode. However, a smaller value will ensure that the weights (as well as the placement of patterns on clusters) eventually reach equilibrium in the slow learning mode.

ρ vigilance parameter. Along with the initial bottom-up weights, this parameter determines how many clusters will be formed. Although theoretically, values from 0 to 1 are allowed, only values between approximately 0.7 and 1 perform any useful role in controlling the number of clusters. (Any value less than 0.7 will have the same effect as setting ρ to zero.) Some choices of vales for c and d will restrict the effective range of values for r even further.

Initial Weights. The initial weights for the ART2 net are as follows:

$t_{ij}(0)$ initial top-down weights (must be small to ensure that no reset will occur for the first pattern placed on a cluster unit);

$$t_{ji}(0) = 0.$$

$b_{ij}(0)$ intial bottom-up weights; must be chosen to satisfy the inequality

$$b_{ij}(0) \leq \frac{1}{1 \quad d\sqrt{n}}$$

to prevent the possibility of a new winner being chosen during "resonance" as the weights change. Larger values of b_{ij} encourage the net to form more clusters.

Learning Mode. Fast learning and slow learning differ not only in the theoretical assumption on which they are based (in terms of the speed of learning relative to the duration of presentation of a pattern during any one learning trial), but also in the performance characteristics of the clusters and weight vectors formed when they are used. Some differences in the performance of fast and slow learning are summarized here and are illustrated in the examples of the next section.

Fast learning results in weight vectors that have some of the same characteristics as the weights found by ART1. Typically, a component of the weight vector for a particular cluster unit that is set to zero during a learning trial will not become nonzero during a subsequent learning trial. Furthermore, if a pattern being learned by a cluster has one or more components that are zero after noise suppression is applied, the corresponding components of the weight vector will be set to zero during learning. However, the weights of the nonzero components will change on each learning trial to reflect the relative magnitudes of the nonzero components of the current input vector. this suggest that fast learning may be more appropriate for data in which the primary information is contained in the pattern of components that are "small" or "large," rather than for data in which the relative sizes of the nonzero components is important.

Slow learning requires many epochs of training, with only one weight update iteration performed on each learning trial. The weight vector for each cluster is the average of the pattern it has learned, which may make the weight vector a more suitable exemplar for the cluster for certain types of applications. The weights reach equilibrium (to within a tolerance determined by the learning rate). In some applications, slow learning may also produce clustering that is less influenced by the order of presentation of the pattern than the clustering produced by fast learning.

7.6 SIMPLE ARCHITECTURE OF ART

Grossberg introduced a model for explaining biological phenomena. The model has three crucial properties: a normalization of the total network activity. Biological systems are usually very adaptive to large changes in their environment. For example, the human eye can adapt itself to large variations in light intensities; contrast enhancement of input patterns. The awareness of subtle differences in input patterns can mean a lot in terms of survival. Distinguishing a hiding panther from a resting one makes all the difference in the world. The mechanism used here is contrast enhancement;

Short-term memory (STM) storage of the contrast-enhanced pattern. Before the input pattern can be decoded, it must be stored in the short-term memory. The long-term memory (LTM) implements an arousal mechanism (i.e., the classi cation), whereas the STM is used to cause gradual changes in the LTM.

The system consists of two layers, F1 and F2, which are connected to each other via the LTM

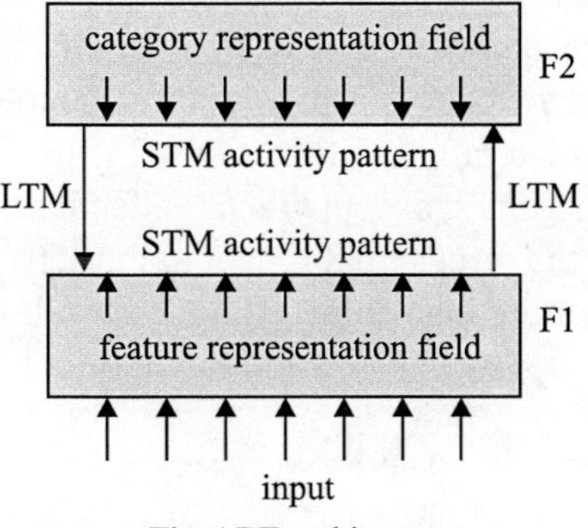

The ART architecture

Figure 7.6: Simple architecture of ART

The input pattern is received at F1, whereas classi cation takes place in F2. As mentioned before, the input is not directly classified. First a characterisation takes place by means of extracting features, giving rise to activation in the feature representation field. The expectations, residing in the LTM connections, translate the input pattern to a categorisation in the category representation field. The classi cation is compared to the expectation of the network, which resides in the LTM weights from F2 to F1. If there is a match, the expectations are strengthened, otherwise the classification is rejected.

7.7 ART: THE SIMPLIFIED NEURAL NETWORK MODEL

The ART simplified model consists of two layers of binary neurons (with values 1 and 0), called F1 (the comparison layer) and F2 (the recognition layer)

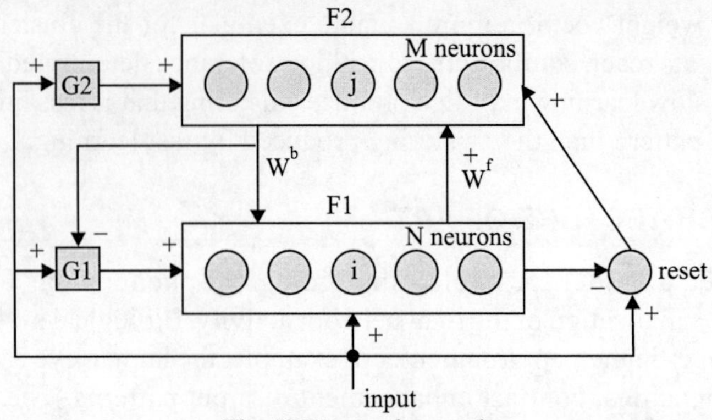

Figure 7.7: ART Simplified model consists of f1 (the comparison layer) and f2 (the recognition Layer)

Each neuron in F1 is connected to all neurons in F2 via the continuous-valued forward long term memory (LTM) Wf , and vice versa via the binary-valued backward LTM Wb. The other modules are gain 1 and 2 (G1 and G2), and a reset module. Each neuron in the comparison layer receives three inputs: a component of the input pattern, a component of the feedback pattern, and a gain G1. A neuron outputs a 1 if and only if at least three of these inputs are high: the 'two-thirds rule.' The neurons in the recognition layer each compute the inner product of their incoming (continuous-valued) weights and the pattern sent over these connections. The winning neuron then inhibits all the other neurons via lateral inhibition. Gain 2 is the logical 'or' of all the elements in the input pattern x. Gain 1 equals gain 2, except when the feedback pattern from F2 contains any 1; then it is forced to zero. Finally, the reset signal is sent to the active neuron in F2 if the input vector x and the output of F1 differ by more than some vigilance level.

7.8 OPERATION

The network starts by clamping the input at F1. Because the output of F2 is zero, G1 and G2 are both on and the output of F1 matches its input.The pattern is sent to F2, and in F2 one neuron becomes active. This signal is then sent back over the backward LTM, which reproduces a binary pattern at F1. Gain 1 is inhibited, and only the neurons in F1 which receive a 'one' from both x and F2 remain active. If there is a substantial mismatch between the two patterns, the reset signal will inhibit the neuron in F2 and the process is repeated.

1. Initialisation:

$$w_{ji}^{b}(0) = 1$$

$$w_{ji}^{f}(0) = \frac{1}{1+N}$$

where N is the number of neurons in F1, M the number of neurons in F2, $0 < i < N$, and $0 \leq j < M$. Also, choose the vigilance threshold ρ, $0 \leq \rho \leq 1$;

2. Apply the new input pattern x:
3. compute the activation values y0 of the neurons in F2:

$$y_i \qquad \overset{N}{\underset{j\ 1}{}} \; w^f_{ij}(t)x_i;$$

4. select the winning neuron k $(0 \le k < M)$:
5. vigilance test: if

$$\frac{w^b_k(t) \cdot x}{x \cdot x} \quad ,$$

where $\cdot$ denotes inner product, go to step 7, else go to step 6. Note that w^b_k essentially is the inner product $x^* \cdot x$,which will be large if x^* and xnear to each other;

6. neuron k is disabled from further activity. Go to step 3;
7. Set for all l, $0 \le l < N$:

$$w^b_{kl}(t \quad 1) = w^b_{kl}(t)x_l,$$

$$w^f_{lk}(t \quad 1) = \frac{w^b_{kl}(t)x_l}{\frac{1}{2} \qquad \overset{N}{\underset{i\ 1}{}} \; w^b_{ki}(t)x_i}$$

8. re-enable all neurons in F2 and go to step 2.

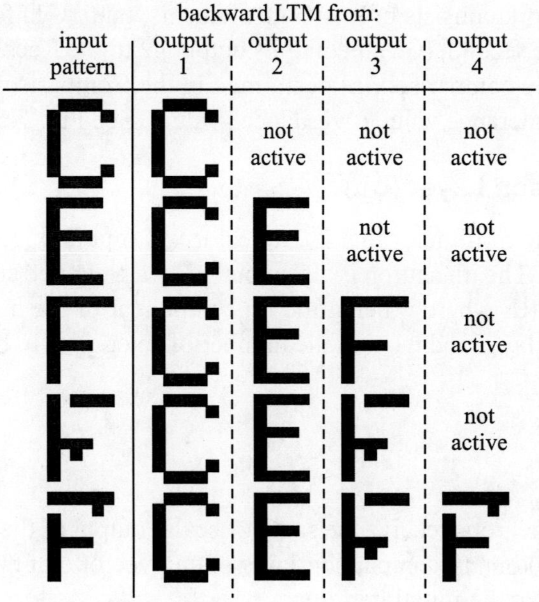

input pattern	backward LTM from: output 1	output 2	output 3	output 4
		not active	not active	not active
			not active	not active
				not active
				not active

Figure 7.8: Carpenter grossberg network for letter patterns

An example of the behaviour of the Carpenter Grossberg network for letter patterns. The binary input patterns on the left were applied sequentially. On the right the stored patterns (i.e., the weights of Wb for the first four output units) are shown.

7.9 ART: THE ORIGINAL MODEL

In later work, Carpenter and Grossberg (Carpenter & Grossberg, 1987a, 1987b) present several neural network models to incorporate parts of the complete theory. We will only discuss the first model, ART1. The network incorporates a follow-the-leader clustering algorithm (Hartigan, 1975). This algorithm tries to fit each new input pattern in an existing class. If no matching class can be found, i.e., the distance between the new pattern and all existing classes exceeds some threshold, a new class is created containing the new pattern. The novelty in this approach is that the network is able to adapt to new incoming patterns, while the previous memory is not corrupted. In most neural networks, such as the backpropagation network, all patterns must be taught sequentially; the teaching of a new pattern might corrupt the weights for all previously learned patterns. By changing the structure of the network rather than the weights, ART1 overcomes this problem.

7.10 THE ART NETWORK STRUCTURE

The ART network consists of 2 layers:

(i) a Comparison Layer (CL)

(ii) a Recognition Layer (RL), which are interconnected.

In addition, the network consists of two Gain elements, one, (G1) feeding its output g1 to the Comparison layer and the second, (G2) feeding its output g2 to the Recognition Layer, and thirdly, a Reset element where the comparison, as performed in the Comparison Layer, is evaluated with respect to a preselected tolerance value ("vigilance" value). See Fig. 7.6.

7.10.1 The Comparison Layer (CL)

A binary element x_j of the m-dimensional input vector x is inputted into the jth (j = 1 .... m; m = dim(x)) neuron of the CL. The jth neuron is also inputted by a weighted sum. (p_j) of the recognition-output vector r from the RL where r_i being the ith component of the m-dimensional recognition-output vector r of the RL layer and n being the number of categories to be recognized. (See Figure 7.9 on next page.)

$$p_j = \sum_{i=1}^{m} t_{ij} r_i \tag{7.1}$$

Furthermore, all CL neurons receive the same g1 scalar output of the same element G1. The m-dimensional (m = dim(x)) binary comparison-layer output vector c of the CL layer initially equals the input vector, namely, at the initial iteration

$$c_j(0) = x_j(0) \tag{7.2}$$

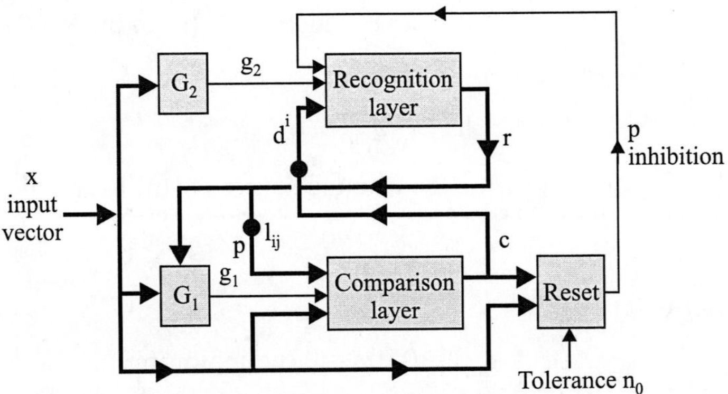

Figure 7.9: ART network schematic.

Also, initially:

$$g_1(0) = 1 \tag{7.3}$$

The CL's output vector c satisfies a (two-thirds) majority rule requirement s.t. its output is

$$c_j = 1$$

only if at least two of this (CL) neuron's three inputs are 1. Hence, Eqs. (7.2), (7.3) imply, by the "two-thirds majority" rule, that initially

$$c(0) = x(0) \tag{7.4}$$

since initially no feedback exists from the RL layer, while g1 (0) = 1.

7.10.2 The Recognition Layer (RL)

The RL layer serves as a classification layer. It receives as its input an n-dimensional weight vector d with elements dj, which is the weighted form of the CL's output vector c; s.t.

$$d_j = \sum_{i=1}^{m} b_{ji}c_i = b_j^T c; \quad b_j = \begin{bmatrix} b_{j1} \\ \vdots \\ b_{jm} \end{bmatrix}; \tag{7.5}$$

$$i = 1, 2, \ldots m;$$

$$j = 1, 2, \ldots n;$$

$$m = \dim(x)$$

$$n = \text{number of categories}$$

where b_{ij} are real numbers,

The RL neuron with the maximal (winning) dj will output a "1" as long as g2 = 1. All others will output a zero. Hence, the RL layer serves to classify its input vector. The weights b_{ij} of the jth (winning) RL neuron that fires (having maximal output dj) constitute an exemplar of the pattern of vector c, in similarity to the properties of the BAM memory discussed earlier (Sec. 9.3), noting that an output d_j satisfies

$$d_j = c^T c \text{ at maximum (as in the Kohonen layer)} \quad (7.6)$$

d_j being the maximal possible outcome of Eq. (7.5),

since $$b_j = c; \ d_{i \neq j} = 0$$

We achieve the locking of one neuron (the winning neuron) to the maximal output by outputting a winner-take-all (as in Sec. 7.2):

$$r_j = 1 \quad (7.7)$$

while all other neurons yield

$$r_{i \neq j} = 0 \text{ if } p = 0 \text{ (no inhibition)} \quad (7.8)$$

For this purpose an interconnection scheme is employed in the RL that is based on lateral inhibition. The lateral inhibition interconnection is as in Fig. 7.7, where the output r of each neuron (i) is connected via an inhibitory (negative) weight matrix $L = \{l_{ij}\}$, $i \neq j$, where $l_{ij} < 0$ to any other neutron (j). Hence, a neuron with a

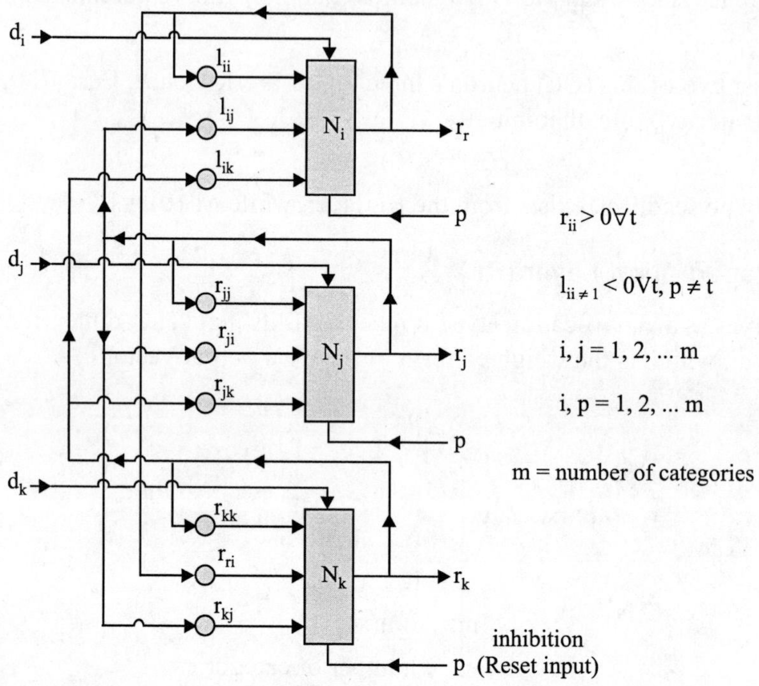

Figure 7.10: Lateral inhibition in an RL layer of an ART network.

large output inhibits all other neurons. Furthermore, positive feedback ljj > 0 is employed such that each neuron's output rj is fed back with a positive weight to its own input to reinforce its output if it is to fire (to output a "one"). This posi-tive reinforcement is termed as adaptive resonance to motivate the resonance term in "ART".

7.10.3 Gain and Reset Elements

The gain elements feed the same scalar output to all neurons concerned as in Fig. 7.9, g1 being inputted to the CL neurons and g2 to RL neurons, where:

$$g_2 = OR(x) = OR(x_1 \ldots. x_N$$

$$g_1 = \overline{OR(r)} \cap OR(x)$$

$$= \overline{OR(r_1 \ldots\ldots r_N)} \cap OR\,(x_1 \ldots x_N) = g_2 \cap \overline{OR(r)} \quad (7.9)$$

Hence, if at least one element of x is 1 then g2 = 1. Also, if any element of g2 = 1 but also no elements of r is 1 then gl = 1, else gl = 0. (See Table5.1). Note that the overhead bar denotes negation, whereas fl denotes a logical "and" (intersection). Also, note that if OR(x) is zero, then OR(r) is always zero, by the derivation of r as above.

OR(x)	OR(r)	$\overline{OR(r)}$	g1
0	0	1	0
1	0	1	1
1	1	0	0
0	1	0	0
R(x)	OR(r)	$\overline{OR(r)}$	g1
0	0	1	0
1	0	1	1
1	1	0	0
0	1	0	0

Finally, the reset element evaluates the degree of similarity between the input vector x and the CL output vector c in terms of the ratio η, where:

$$\eta = \frac{\text{No. of "1"s in c}}{\text{No. of "1"s in x}} \quad (7.10)$$

Subsequently, if

$$\eta < \eta_o \quad (7.11)$$

η_0 being a pre-set initial tolerance (vigilance) value, then a reset signal (p) is out-putted to inhibit the particular RL neuron that has fired at the given iteration. See Fig. A reset factor based of the Hamming distance between vectors c and x can also be considered.\

7.11 SETTING-UP OF THE ART NETWORK

7.11.1 Initialization of Weights

The CL weight matrix B is initialized [Carpenter and Grossberg, 1987a] as follows:

$$b_{ij} < \frac{E}{E+m-1} \quad ij \quad (7.12)$$

Where

$$m = \dim(x)$$

E > 1 (typically E = 2)

The RL weight matrix T is initialized such that

$$t_{ij} = 1 \quad i, j \tag{7.13}$$

The tolerance level η_0 (vigilance) is chosen as

$$0 < \eta_0 < 1 \tag{7.14}$$

A high η_O yields fine discrimination whereas a low η_O allows grouping of more dissimilar patterns. Hence, one may start with lower η_O and raise it gradually.

7.11.2 Training

The training involves the setting of the weight matrices B (of the RL) and T (of the CL) of the ART network.

Specifically, the network may first be exposed for brief periods to successive input vectors, not having time to converge to any input vector but only to approach some settings corresponding to some averaged x.

The parameters b_{ij} of vector bj of B are set according to:

$$b_{ij} = \frac{Ec_i}{E \quad 1 \quad 1 \quad \underset{k}{c_k}} \tag{7.15}$$

where E > 1 (usually, E = 2)

c_i = the ith component of vector c where j corresponds to the winning neuron. Furthermore, the parameter t_{ij} of T are set such that

$$t_{ij} = c_i \quad {}_i = 1\ldots m; \; m = \dim(x) \tag{7.16}$$

j denoting the winning neuron.

7.12 NETWORK OPERATION

Initially, at iteration 0, x = 0. Hence, by Eq. (7.9), g2(0) = 0 and

g1(0) = 0 Consequently c(0) = 0 by Eq. (4).

Also, since g2(0) = 0, the output vector r to the CL is, by the majority 2/3 rule that governs both layers is: r(0) = 0.

Subsequently, when a vector x ≠ 0 is being applied, no neuron has an advantage on any other.

Since now x ≠ 0 then g2 = 1 and thus also gl = 1 (due to r(0) = 0). Hence by the majority rule described earlier.

$$c = x \tag{7.17}$$

Subsequently, by Eqs. (7.5), (7.6) and the properties of the RL, the jth of the RL neuron, which best matches vector c will be the only RL neuron to fire (to output a one). Hence $r_j = 1$ and $r_{i \neq j} = 0$ to determine vector r at the output of the RL. Note that if several neurons have same d then the first one will be chosen (lowest j).

Now r as above is fed back to the CL such that it is inputted to the CL neurons via weights t_{ij}. The m-dimensional weight vector p at the input of the CL thus satisfies namely

$$p_j = t_{j\,;}\ t_j \text{ denoting a vector of T} \tag{7.18a}$$

for winning neuron, and

$$p_j = 0 \tag{7.18b}$$

otherwise

Notice that $r_j = 1$ and t_{ij} are binary values. The values t_{ij} of T of the CL are set by the training algorithm to correspond to the real weight matrix B (with elements b_{ij}) of the RL.

Since now $r \neq 0$, then g1 becomes 0 by Eq. (7.9) and by the majority rule, the CL neurons which receive that non-zero components of x and of p will fire (to output a "one" in the CL's output vector c). Hence, the outputs of the RL force these components of c to zero where x and p do not have matching "ones".

If classification is considered by the reset element to be adequate, then classifi-cation is stopped. Go to (f), else: A considerable mismatch between vectors p and x will result in a considerable mismatch (in terms of "one's") between vectors x and c. This will lead to a low η as in Eq. (7.10) as computed by the reset element of the network such that $\eta < \eta o$. This, in turn, will inhibit the firing neuron of the

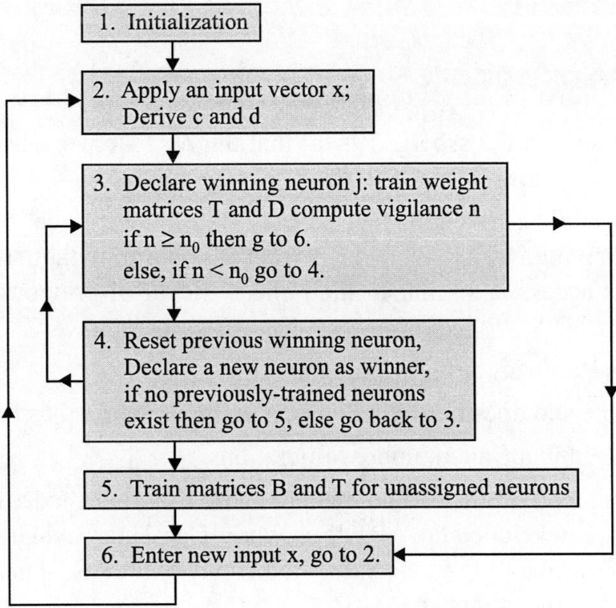

Figure 7.11: Flow-chart of ARToperation.

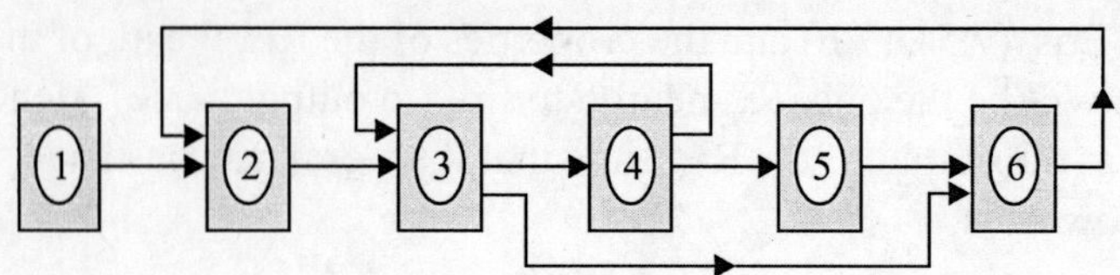

Figure 7.12: Simplified ART flow chart (encircled numbers: as in Fig. 7.8).

RL. Since now $\eta < \eta_{O}$, then also all elements of r = 0. Hence, g1 = 1 and x = c by the majority rule. Consequently, as long as neurons that are weighted still exist, a different neuron in the RL will win (the last winner being now inhibited), go to (c). (If at this iteration the reset element still considers the fit (classification) to be inadequate, the cycle is repeated. Now either a match will eventually be found:

In that case the network will enter a training cycle where the weights vectors t_j and b_j associated with the firing RL neuron are modified to match the input x considered.) Alternatively, if no neuron matches the input within the tolerance, then go to (e).

Now, a previously unassigned neuron is assigned weights vectors t_j, and b_j to match the input vector x. In this manner, the network does not lose (forget) previously learned patterns, but is also able to learn new ones, as does a biological network.

Apply new input vector.

The procedure above is summarized in Figure 7.8. The categories (classes, patterns) which have been trained to be recognized are thus in terms of vectors (columns t_j) of the weights matrix T; j denoting the particular category (class) considered, and j = 1, 2,...., n, where n is the total number of classes considered.

7.13 PROPERTIES OF ART

One can show [Carpenter and Grossberg, 1987a] that the ART network has several features that characterize the network, as follows:

Once the network stabilizes (weights reach steady state), the application of an input vector x, that has been used in training, will activate the correct RL neuron without any search (iterations). This property of direct access is similar to the rapid retrieval of previously learned patterns in biological networks.

The search process stabilizes at the winning neuron.

The training is stable and does not switch once a winning neuron has been identified.

The training stabilizes in a finite number of iterations.

To proceed from binary patterns (0/1) to patterns with different shades of gray, the authors of the ART-I network above developed the ART-II network [Carpenter and Grossberg, 1987b] which is not discussed here but which follows the basic philosophy of the ART-I network described above while extending it to continuous inputs.

The above indicates that the ART network; have many desirable features of biological networks, such as its being unsupervised, plastic, stable and of a finite number of iterations, and having immediate recall of previously learned patterns. The main shortcoming of the ART-I network is that a missing neuron destroys the whole learning process (since x and c must be of the same dimension). This contrasts an important property of biological neural networks. Whereas many of the properties of the ART network outlined above were missing in the previous networks, the latter shortcoming is not fundamental to the networks of the earlier chapters. It also leads us to consider the neural network designs of the next chapters, specifically, the Cognitron/Neocognitron neural network design and the LAMSTAR network design, which (among other things) avoid the above shortcoming.

EXERCISES

1. What do you mean by Adaptive resonance theory?
2. What are the various motivation of ART?
3. Explain the basic architecture of Adaptive resonance theory in detail?
4. Explain the basic operation of ART nets?
5. What is ART1? Explain the architecture of ART?
6. Write steps to train the ART1 network?
7. What is ART2? How it is different from ART1?
8. Explain the architecture of ART2 and also draw its diagram?
9. Write steps to train a ART network?
10. Explain the simple architecture of ART having LTM and STM activity pattern?
11. Draw the ART simplified model consist of comparison layer and recognition layer?
12. Explain the basic operation of two layer ART network?
13. Explain the structure of ART network?
14. How we can set up ART network?
15. Draw flow chart of ART operation?
16. What are the various properties of ART networks?

CHAPTER 8

Neocognitron

8.1 INTRODUCTION

Artificial neural network architectures such as backpropagation tend to have general applicability. We can use a single network type in many different applications by changing the network's size, parameters, and training sets. In contrast, the developers of the neocognitron set out to tailor architecture for a specific application: recognition of handwritten characters. Such a system has a great deal of practical application, although, judging from the introductions to some of their papers, Fukushima and his coworkers appear to be more interested in developing a model of the brain .To that end, their design was based on the seminal work performed by Hubel and Weisel elucidating some of the functional architecture of the visual cortex. We could not begin to provide a complete accounting of what is known about the anatomy and physiology of the mammalian visual system. Nevertheless, we shall present a brief and highly simplified description of some of that system's features as an aid to understanding the j basis of the neocognitron design. (See figure 8.1 on next page)

Some nerve fibers from each eye cross over into the opposite hemisphere of the brain, where they meet nerve fibers from the other eye at the LGN. From the LGN, neurons project back to area 17. From area 17, neurons project into other cortical areas, other areas deep in the brain, and also back to the LGN.

Figure shows the main pathways for neurons leading from the retina back to the area of the brain known as the viiual, or striate, cortex. This area is also known as area 17. The optic nerve ii made up of axons from nerve cells called retinal ganglia. The ganglia receive stimulation indirectly from the light-receptive rods and cones through several intervening neurons. Hubel and Weisel used an amazing technique to discern the function of the various nerve cells in the visual system. They used microelectrodes to record the response of individual neurons in the cortex while stimulating the retina with light. By applying a variety of patterns and shapes, they were able to determine the particular stimulus to which a neuron was most sensitive. The retinal ganglia and the cells of the lateral geniculate nucleus (LGN) appear to have circular receptive fields.

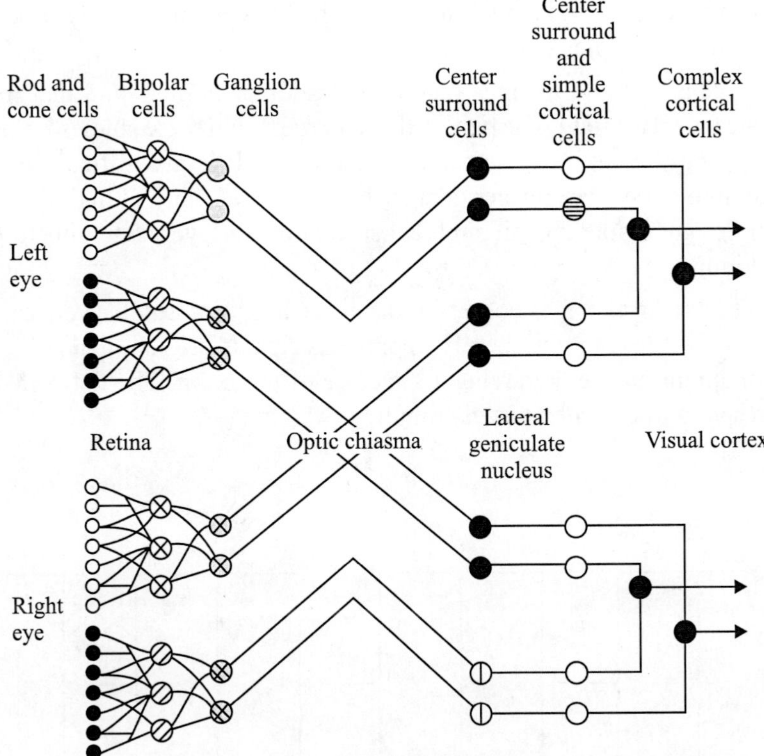

Figure 8.1: Visual pathways from the eye to the primary visual cortex are shown

They respond most strongly to circular spots of light of a particular size on a particular part of the retina. The part of the retina responsible for stimulating a particular ganglion cell is called the receptive field of the ganglion. Some of these receptive fields give an excitatory response to a centrally located spot of light, and an inhibitory response to a larger, more diffuse spot of light. These fields have an on-center off-surround response characteristic. Other receptive fields have the opposite characteristic, with an inhibitory response to the centrally located spot—an off-center on-surround response characteristic.

The visual cortex itself is composed of six layers of neurons. Most of the neurons from the LGN terminate on cells in layer IV. These cells have circularly symmetric receptive fields like the retinal ganglia and the cells of the LGN. Further along the pathway, the response characteristic of the cells begins to increase in complexity. Cells in layer IV project to a group of cells directly above called simple cells. Simple cells respond to line segments having a particular orientation. Simple cells project to cells called complex cells. Complex cells respond to lines having the same orientation as their corresponding simple cells, although complex cells appear to integrate their response over a wider receptive field.

In other words, complex cells are less sensitive to the position of the line on the retina than are the simple cells. Some complex cells are sensitive to line segments of a particular orientation that are moving in a particular direction. Cells in different layers of area 17 project to different locations of the brain. For example, cells in layers II and III project to cells in areas 18 and 19. These areas contain cells called hypercomplex cells.

Hypercomplex cells respond to lines that form angles or corners and that move in various directions across the receptive field. The picture that emerges from these studies is that of a hierarchy of cells with increasingly complex response characteristics. It is not difficult to extrapolate this idea of a hierarchy into one where further data abstraction takes place at higher and higher levels. The neocognitron design adopts this hierarchical structure in a layered architecture, as illustrated schematically in Figure.

Each box represents a level in the neocognitron comprising a simplecell layer, usi, and a complex-cell layer, Ua, where i is the layer number. U_0 represents signals originating on the retina. There is also a suggested mapping to the hierarchical structure of the brain. The network concludes with single cells that respond to complex visual stimuli.

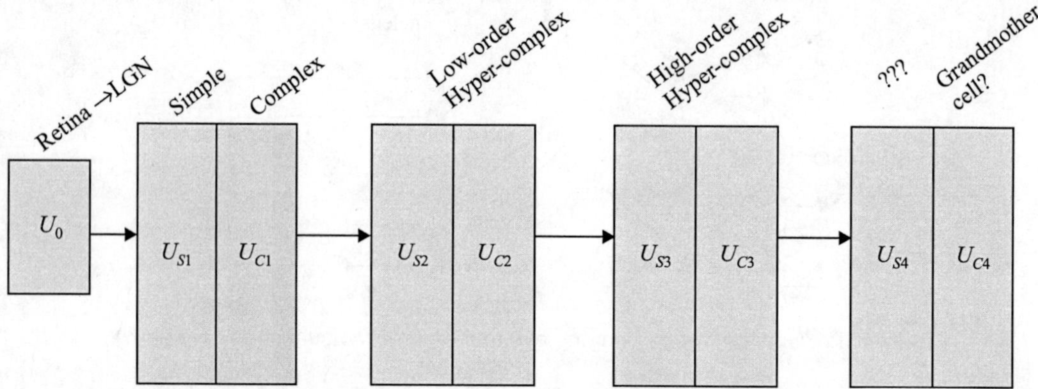

Figure 8.2: The neocognitron hierarchical structure is shown

These final cells are often called grandmother cells after the notion that there may be some cell in your brain that responds to complex visual stimuli, such as a picture of your grandmother. We remind you that the description of the visual system that we have presented here is highly simplified. There is a great deal of detail that we have omitted. The visual system does not adhere to a strict hierarchical structure as presented here. Moreover, we do not subscribe to the notion that grandmother cells per se exist in the brain. We know from experience that strict adherence to biology often leads to a failed attempt to design a system to perform the same function as the biological prototype: Flight is probably the most significant example. Nevertheless, we do promote the use of neurobiological results if they prove to be appropriate. The neocognitron is an excellent example of how neurobiological results can be used to develop a new network architecture.

8.2 NEOCOGNITRON ARCHITECTURE

The neocognitron design evolved from an earlier model called the cognitron, and there are several versions of the neocognitron itself. The one that we shall describe has nine layers of PEs (Processing elements), including the retina layer. The system was designed to recognize the numerals 0 through

9, regardless of where they are placed in the field of view of the retina. Moreover, the network has a high degree of tolerance to distortion of the character and is fairly insensitive to the size of the character. This first architecture contains only feedforward connections.

The PEs of the neocognitron are organized into modules that we shall refer to as levels. A single level is shown in Figure 8.3. Each level consists of two layers: a layer of simple cells, or S-cells, followed by a layer of complex cells, or C-cells. Each layer, in turn, is divided into a number of planes, each of which consists of a rectangular array of PEs. On a given level, the S-layer and the C-layer may or may not have the same number of planes. All planes on a given layer will have the same number of PEs; however, the number of PEs on the S-planes can be different from the number of PEs on the C-planes at the same level. Moreover, the number of PEs per plane can vary from level to level. There are also PEs called Vs-cells and Vc-cells that are not shown in the figure. These elements play an important role in the processing, but we can describe the functionality of the system without reference to them.

We construct a complete network by combining an input layer, which we shall call the retina, with a number of levels in a hierarchical fashion, as shown in Figure 8.3.

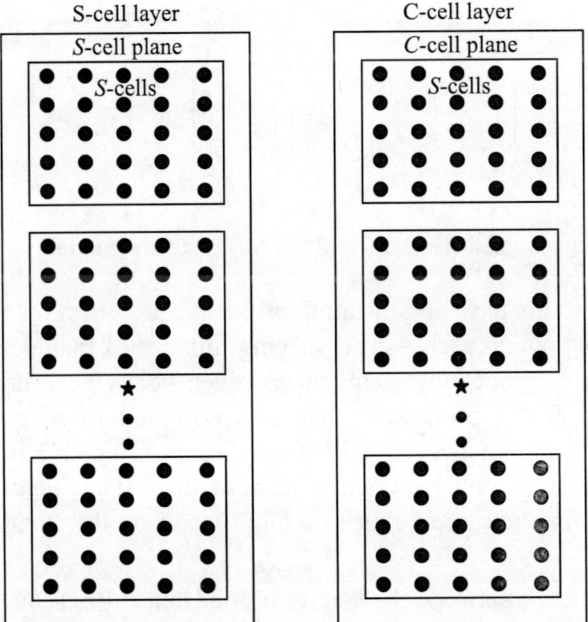

Figure 8.3: A single level of a neocognitron is shown

Each level consists of two layers, and each layer consists of a number of planes. The planes contain the PEs in a rectangular array. Data pass from the S-layer to the C-layer through connections that are not shown here. In neocognitrons having feedback, there also will be connections from the C-layer to the S-layer. That figure shows the number of planes on each layer for the particular implementation that we shall describe here. We call attention to the fact that there is nothing, in principle, that dictates a limit to the size of the network in terms of the number of levels.

The interconnection strategy is unlike that of networks that are fully interconnected between layers, such as the backpropagation network.

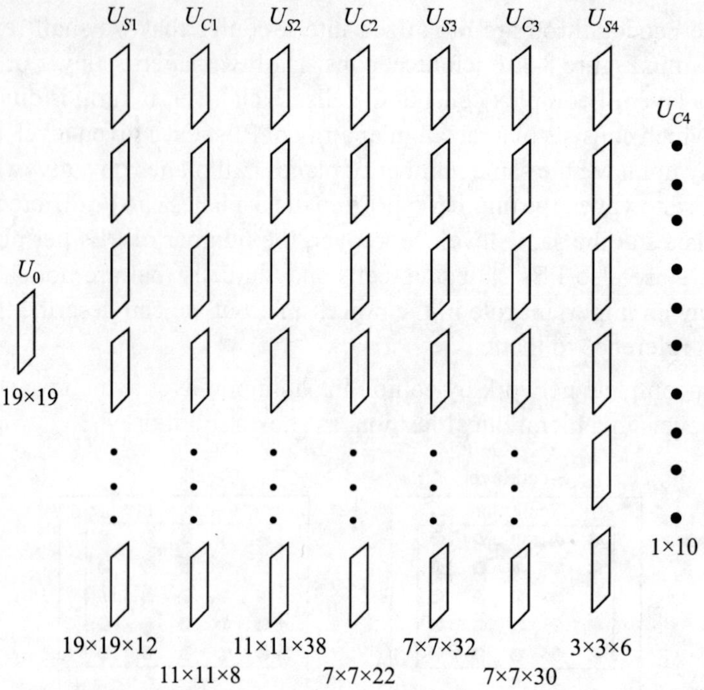

Figure 8.4: Shows a schematic illustration of the way units are connected in the neocognitron

The figure 8.4 shows the basic organization of the neocognitron for the numeral-recognition problem. There are nine layers, each with a varying number of planes. The size of each layer, in terms of the number of processing elements, is given below each layer. For example, layer Uc2 has 22 planes of 7 × 7 processing elements arranged in a square matrix. The layer of C-cells on the final level is made up of 10 planes, each of which has a single element. Each element corresponds to one of the numerals from 0 to 9. The identification of the pattern appearing on the retina is made according to which C-cell on the final level has the strongest response.

As we look deeper into the network, the S-cells respond to features at higher levels of abstraction; for example, corners with intersecting lines at various angles and orientations. The C-cells integrate the responses of groups of Scells. Because each S-cell is looking for the same feature in a different location, the C-cells' response is less sensitive to the exact location of the feature on the input layer. This behavior is what gives the neocognitron its ability to identify characters regardless of their exact position in the field of the retina. By the time we have reached the final layer of C-cells, the effective receptive field of each cell is the entire retina. Figure 8.6 shows the character identification process schematically.

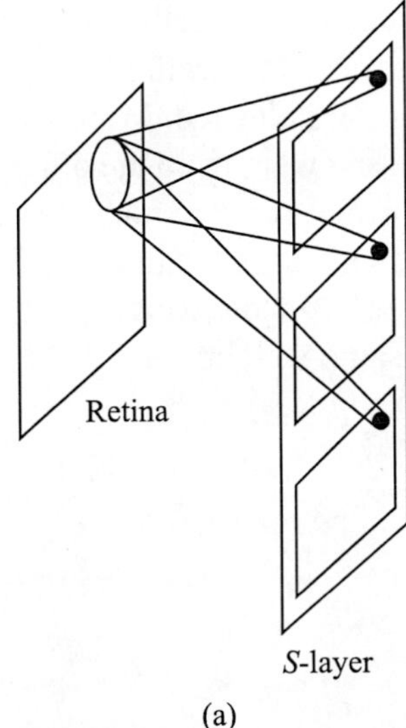

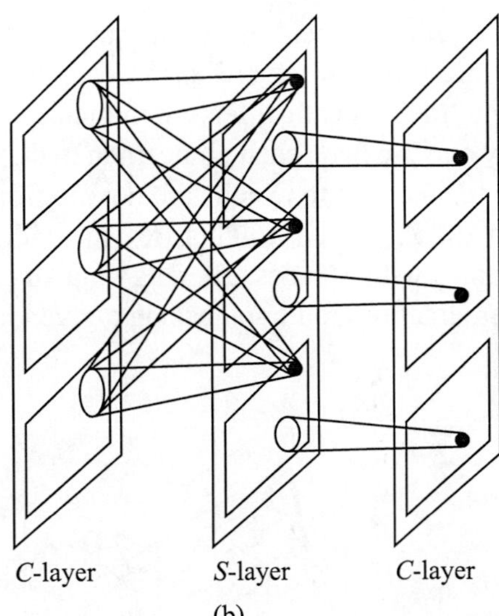

Figure 8.5: This diagram is a schematic representation of the interconnection strategy of the neocognitron. (a) On the first level, each S unit receives input connections from a small region of the retina. Units in corresponding positions on all planes receive input connections from the same region of the retina. The region from which an S-cell receives input connections defines the receptive field of the cell, (b) On intermediate levels, each unit on an s-plane receives input connections from corresponding locations on all C-planes in the previous level. C-cells have connections from a region of S-cells on the S level preceding it. If the number of C-planes is the same as that of S-planes at that level, then each C-cell has connections from S-cells on a single s-plane. If there are fewer C-planes than S-planes, some C-cells may receive connections from more than one S-plane

Each cell in a plane on the first S-layer receives inputs from a single input layer—namely, the retina. On subsequent layers, each S-cell plane receives inputs from each of the C-cell planes immediately preceding it. The situation is slightly different for the C-cell planes. Typically, each cell on a C-cell plane examines a small region of S-cells on a single S-cell plane. For example, the first C-cell plane on layer 2 would have connections to only a region of S-cells on the first S-cell plane of the previous layer. Reference back to Figure D reveals that there is not necessarily a one-to-one correspondence between C-cell planes and S-cell planes at each layer in the system. This discrepancy occurs because the system designers found it advantageous to combine the inputs from some S-planes to a single C-plane if the features that the S-planes were detecting were similar. This tuning process is evident in several areas of the network architecture and processing equations. (See figure 8.6 on next page.)

The neocognitron decomposes the input pattern into elemental parts consisting of line segments at various angles of rotation. The system then integrates these elements into higher-order structures at each successive level in the network. Cells in each level integrate the responses of cells in the previous level over a finite area. This behavior gives the neocognitron its ability to identify characters regardless of their exact position or size in the field of view of the retina. The weights on connections to S-cells are determined by a training process. Unlike in many other network architectures (such as backpropagation), where each unit has a different weight vector, all S-cells on a single plane share the same weight vector. Sharing weights in this manner means that all S-cells on a given plane respond to the identical feature in their receptive fields, as we indicated. Moreover, we need to train only one S-cell on each plane, then to distribute the resulting weights to the other cells. The weights on connections to C-cells are not modifiable in the sense that they are not determined by a training process. All C-cell weights are usually determined by being tailored to the specific network architecture. As with Splanes, all cells on a single C-plane share the same weights. Moreover, in some implementations, all C-planes on a given layer share the same weights.

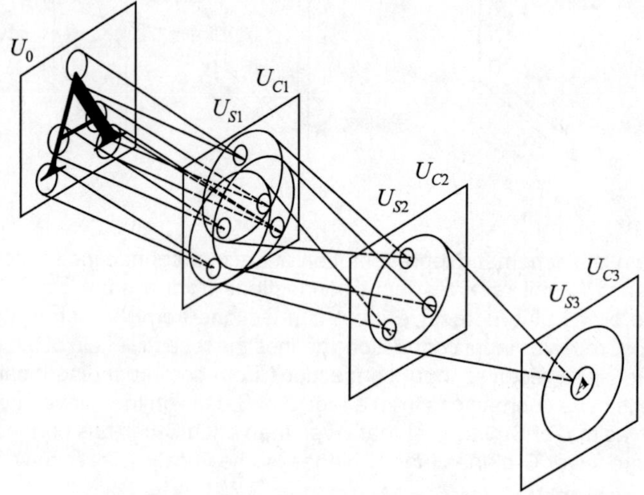

Figure 8.6: This figure illustrates how the neocognitron performs its character-recognition function

8.2.1 Algorithm

The output signal of a unit in an S-type cell (a cell in any of the 5-layers) is a function of the excitatory signals it receives from units in the previous layer and the inhibitory signals it receives from those same units. The mechanism is described in terms of an intermediate, or auxiliary, unit (denoted here as a V unit) whose signal to the S unit is proportional to the (weighted) Euclidean norm of the signal sent by the input units. We adopt the following notation:

- c_i output from C unit
- s_i output from S unit
- v output from v unit
- w_i adjustable weight from C unit to S unit
- w_0 adjustable weight from V unit to S unit
- t_i fixed weight from c unit to V unit
- u_i fixed weight from S unit to C unit

The signal sent by the inhibitory unit V is

$$v = \sqrt{\quad t_i c_i^2},$$

where the summations are over all units that are connected to V in any array and over all arrays. The input layer is treated as the C0 level.

Thus, a typical S unit forms its scaled input,

$$x = \frac{1 \quad e}{1 \quad vw_0} \quad 1,$$

where

$$e = \quad c_i w_i$$

is the net excitatory input from c units, and v w_0 is the net input from the V unit. The output signal is

$$S = \begin{matrix} x \text{ if } x \quad 0 \\ 0 \text{ if } x < 0. \end{matrix}$$

The inhibitory signal serves to normalize the response of the S unit in a manner somewhat similar to that used in ART2.

The output of a C layer unit is a function of the net input it receives from all of the units, in all of the S arrays that feed into it. As was shown in the description of the architecture, that input is typically from 9 or 25 units in each of one, two, or three S arrays. The input is

$$c\_in = \underset{i}{\quad} s_i u_i$$

The output is

$$c = \begin{matrix} \dfrac{c\_in}{a \quad c\_in} \text{ if } c\_in \quad 0 \\ 0 \end{matrix}$$

The parameter a depends on the level and is 0.25 for Levels 1, 2, and 3 and 1.0 for Level 4.

8.3 NEOCOGNITRON DATA PROCESSING

In this section we shall discuss the various processing algorithms of the neocognitron cells. First we shall look at the S-cell data processing including the method used to train the network. Then, we shall describe processing on the C-layer.

8.3.1 S-Cell Processing

We shall first concentrate on the cells in a single plane , as indicated in Figure 8.7

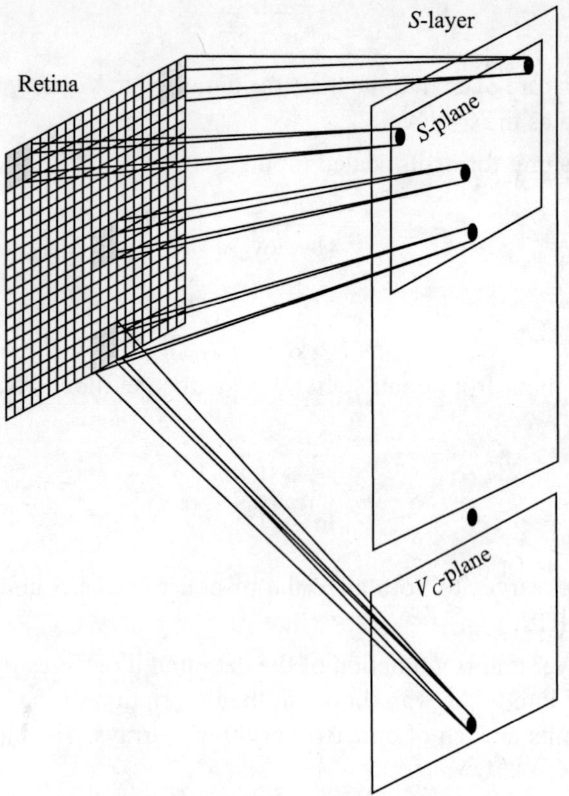

Figure 8.7: The retina, layer U0, is a 19-by-19-pixel array, surrounded by inactive pixels to account for edge effects as described in the text

One of the S-planes is shown, along with an indication of the regions of the retina scanned by the individual cells. Associated with each S-layer in the system is a plane of vrcells. These cells receive input connections from the same receptive field as do the S-cells in corresponding locations in the plane. The processing done by these Vc-cells is described in the text.

We shall assume that the retina, layer Uo, is an array of 19 by 19 pixels. Therefore, each Usi plane will have an array of 19 by 19 cells. Each plane scans the entire retina for a particular feature. As indicated in the figure, each cell on a plane is looking for the identical feature but in a different location on the retina. Each S-cell receives input connections from an array of 3 by 3 pixels on the retina. The receptive field of each S-cell corresponds to the 3 by 3 array centered on the pixel that corresponds to the cell's location on the plane. When building or simulating this network, we must make allowances for edge effects. If we surround the active retina with inactive pixels (outputs always set to zero), then we can automatically account for cells whose fields of view are centered on edge pixels. Neighboring S-cells scan the retina array displaced by one pixel from each otlier. In this manner, the entire image is scanned from left to right and top to bottom by the cells in each Splane.

A single plane of Vc-cells is associated with the S-layer, as indicated in Figure 8.7 . The Vc-plane contains the same number of cells as does each Splane. Vc-cells have the same receptive fields as the S-cells in corresponding locations in the plane. The output of a Vc-cell goes to a single S-cell in every plane in the layer. The S-cells that receive inputs from a particular Vc-cell are those that occupy a position in the plane corresponding to the position of the Vc-cell. The output of the Vc-cell has an inhibitory effect on the S-cells. Figure 8.8 shows the details of a single S-cell along with its corresponding inhibitory cell.

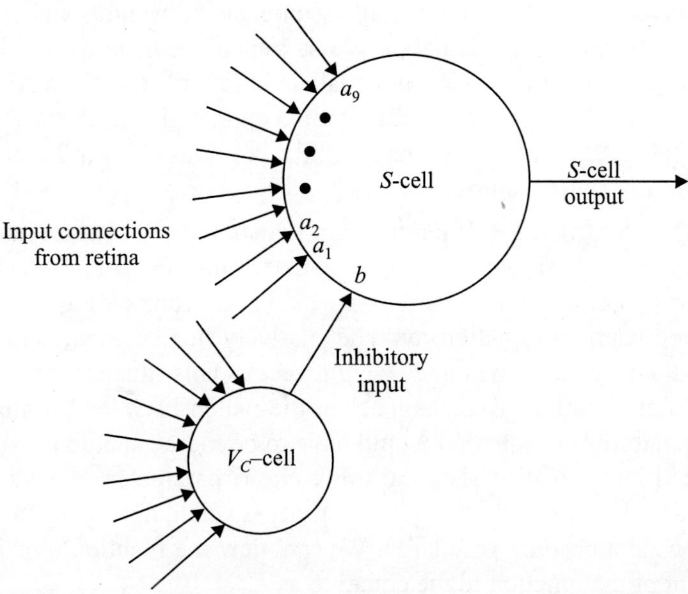

Figure 8.8: A Single 5-Cell And Corresponding Inhibitory Cell On The Us\ Layer Are Shown

Each unit receives the identical nine inputs from the retina layer. The weights, a,, on the S-cells determine the feature for which the cell is sensitive. Both the a, weights on connections from the retina, and the weight, b, from the Vr-cells are modifiable and are determined during a training process, as described in the text.Up to now, we have been discussing the first S-layer, in which cells receive input connections from a single plane (in this case the retina) in the previous layer. For what follows, we shall generalize our discussion to include the case of layers deeper in the network where an S-cell will receive input connections from all the planes on the previous C-layer. Let the index k refer to the kth plane on level: 1. We can label each cell on a plane with a two-dimensional vector, with n indicating its position on the plane; then, we let the vector v refer to the relative position of a cell in the previous layer lying in the receptive field of unit n. With these definitions, we can write the following equation for the output of any 5-cell:

$$U_{Sl}(k_i, n) = \cdot \frac{1 + {}^{K_{l\ 1}}_{k_{l\ 1}} \quad {}_{v\ A_l} a_l(k_{l\ 1}, v, k_l) \cdot U_{C_{l\ 1}}(k_{l\ 1}, n \quad v)}{1 \quad \frac{r_l}{1 \quad r_l} b_l(k_t) \quad V_{Ct(n)}}$$

where the function Φ is a linear threshold function given by

$$\phi(x) = \begin{matrix} x & x & 0 \\ 0 & x < 0. \end{matrix}$$

Let's dissect these equations in some detail. The inner summation of first equation is the usual sum-of-products calculation of inputs, UCi-1(ki-1,n+v), and weights, ai(ki-1, v. ki). The sum extends over all units in the previous Clayer that lie within the receptive field of unit n. Those units are designated by the vector n + v. Because we shall assume that all weights and cell output values are nonnegative, the sum-of-products calculation yields a measure of how closely the input pattern matches the weight vector on a unit.2 We have labeled the receptive field Ai, indicating that the geometry of the receptive field is the same for all units on a particular layer. The outer summation of the equation extends over all of the ki-1planes of the previous C-layer. In the case of Us1 , there would be no need for this outer summation.

The product, bi(ki) · Vc,(n), in the denominator of Equation, represents the inhibitory contribution of the Vc-cell. The parameter ri, where 0 < ri < ∞, determines the cell's selectivity for a specific pattern. The factor ri/(1 + ri) goes from zero to one as ri goes from zero to infinity. Thus, for small values of r;, the denominator of Equation could be relatively small compared to the numerator even if the input pattern did not exactly match the weight vector. This situation could result in a positive argument to the Φ function. If ri were large, then the match between the input pattern and the weights in the numerator of the equation would have to be more exact to overcome the inhibitory effects of the Vc-cell input. Notice also that this same ri parameter appears as a multiplicative factor of the 0 function. If ri is small, and cell selectivity is small, this factor ensures that the output from the cell itself cannot become very large. We can view the function of r; in another way. We rewrite the argument of the function in the equation as

$$\frac{e - [r_l/(1 \quad r_l)]h}{1 \quad [r_l/(1 + r_l)]h}$$

where e is the net excitatory term and h is the net inhibitory term. According to function

$$\phi(x) = \begin{matrix} x & x & 0 \\ 0 & x < 0. \end{matrix}$$

the S-cell output will be nonzero only if

$$e \quad \frac{r_l}{1 \quad r_l} h > 0$$

or

$$\frac{e}{h} > \frac{r_l}{1 \quad r_l}$$

Thus, the quantity ri determines the minimum relative strength of excitation versus inhibition that will result in a nonzero output of the unit. As r; increases, ri/(l + ri) ! 1. Therefore, a larger ri requires a larger excitation relative to inhibition for a nonzero output.

Notice that neither of the weight expressions, ai(ki-1,v,ki), or bi(ki) depend explicitly on the position, n, of the cell. Remember that all cells on a plane share the same weights, even the bi(ki) weights, which we did not discuss previously.

We must now specify the output from the inhibitory nodes. The Vc-cell at position n has an output value of

$$V_{C_l(n)} = \sqrt{\sum_{k_{l-1}}^{K_{l-1}} \sum_{v \in A_l} c_l v \cdot U^2_{C_{l-1}}(k_{l-1}, n+v)}$$

where ci(v) is the weight on the connection from a cell at position v of the Vc -cell's receptive field. These weights are not subject to training. They can take the form of any normalized function that decreases monotonically as the magnitude of v increases.

8.3.2 Training Weights on the S-layers

In principle, training proceeds as it does for many networks. First, an input pattern is presented at the input layer and the data are propagated through the network. Then, weights are allowed to make incremental adjustments according to the specified algorithm. After weight updates have occurred, a new pattern is presented at the input layer, and the process is repeated with all patterns in the training set until the network is classifying the input patterns properly.In the neocognitron, sharing of weights on a given plane means that only a single cell on each plane needs to participate in the learning process. Once its weights have been updated, a copy of the new weight vector can be distributed to the other cells on the same plane. To understand how this works, we can think of the 5-planes on a given layer as being stacked vertically on top of one another, aligned so that cells at corresponding locations are directly on top of one another. We can now imagine many overlapping columns running perpendicular to this stack. These columns define groups of S-cells, where all of the members in a group have receptive fields in approximately the same location of the input layer.

8.3.2.1 Unsupervised training

With this model in mind, we now apply an input pattern and examine the response of the S'-cells in each column. To ensure that each 5-cell provides a distinct response, we can initialize the a; weights to small, positive random values. The bi weights on the inhibitory connections can be initialized to zero. We first note the plane and position of the S-cell whose response is the strongest in each column. Then we examine the individual planes so that, if one plane contains two or more of these S-cells, we disregard all but the cell responding the strongest. In this manner, we will locate the S-cell on each plane whose response is the strongest, subject to the condition that each of those cells is in a different column. Those S-cells become the prototypes, or representatives, of all the cells on their respective planes. Likewise, the strongest responding Vf-cell is chosen as the representative for the other cells on the Vc-plane. Once the representatives are chosen, weight updates are made according to the following equations:

$$a_l(k_{i-1}, v, \hat{k}i) = ql c_{i-1}(v) U_{C_{i-1}}(k_{i-1}, \hat{n}+v)$$

$$b_1(\hat{k}i) = q_1 V_{C_{i\ 1}}(\hat{n})$$

where qi is the learning rate parameter, ci–1(v), is the monotonically decreasing function as described in the previous section, and the location of the representative for plane ki is A. Notice that the largest increases in the weights occur on those connections that have the largest input signal, Uci–1(ki–1, n + v). Because the 5-cell whose weights are being modified was the one with the largest output, this learning algorithm implements a form of Hebbian learning.

Notice also that weights can only increase, and that there is no upper bound on the weight value. Once the cells on a given plane begin to respond to a certain feature, they tend to respond less to other features. l\fter a short time, each plane will have developed a strong response to a particular feature. Moreover, as we look deeper into the network, planes will be responding to more complex features.

8.4 EXAMPLE - ABILITIES OF THE NEOCOGNITRON

On this simple example we will demonstrate abilities of the neocognitron at recognition of presented patterns. The black-box in this example contains neocognitron network which can distinguish between two different types of patterns (between digit zero and digit one). For the learning of the network we have used patterns shown in Figure 8.9.

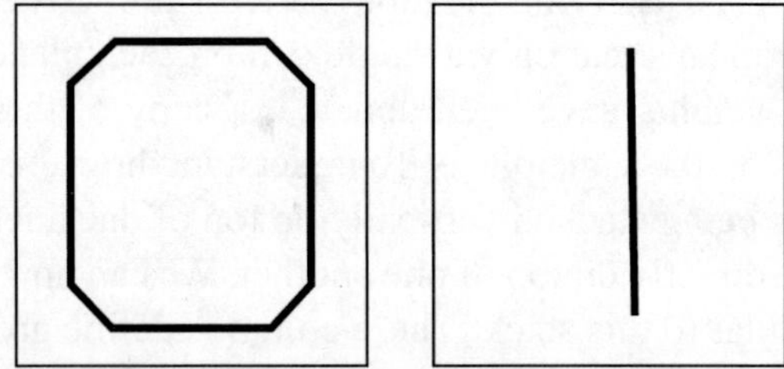

Figure 8.9: Patterns 0 and 1 used for learning

By the learning of the neocognitron to distinguish between these two types of patterns we have created two different categories in the network. In the future the network will respond on every presented pattern with a pair of values. Each of these values is a measure of belonging of presented pattern into one of two created categories. Click on one of the prepared patterns. The network processes it and assigns it to one of the categories. Notice, that the network assigns patterns which have not been presented during learning to the correct category, too. These patterns were produced by distortion of patterns used for learning, shown in Figure 8.9.

8.4.1 Basic Principle of the Neocognitron

Hierarchical feature extraction is the basic principle of the neocognitron. For easier understanding of this principle we will explain terms feature and feature extraction firstly.

Hierarchical feature extraction consists in distribution of extracted features to several stages. The simplest features (usually only rotated lines) are extracted in the first stage and in each of the following stages the more complex features are extracted. In this process it is important fact that only informations obtained in the previous stage are used for feature extraction in the certain stage. Hierarchy of features which we can use for recognition of digit zero in the neocognitron is illustrated schematically in figure 8.10. Joining between features in adjoining stages represents what features from previous layer are used during extraction of the certain feature.

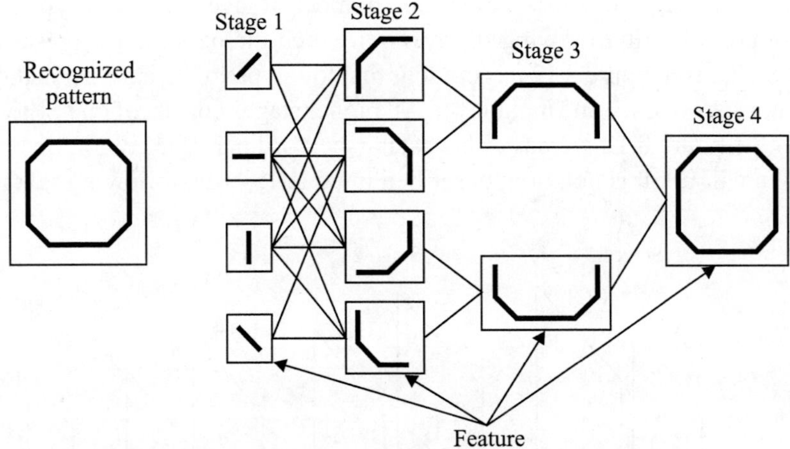

Figure 8.10: Principle of the hierarchical feature extraction

8.4.2 Network Structure-Stages

Structure of the neocognitron arises from a hierarchy of extracted features. One appropriate stage of the neocognitron is created for each stage of the hierarchy of extracted features. The network however contains one additional stage, labeled as stage 0, which is not used, in contrast to higher stages, for feature extraction.

All the stages of the neocognitron and a part of features extracted by them, which corresponds to hierarchy in Figure 8.10, are shown in Figure 8.11.

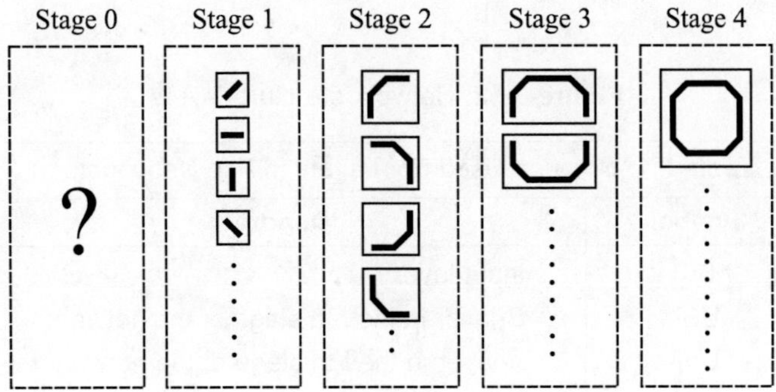

Figure 8.11: Network structure-stages

Total number of stages of the neocognitron depends on the complexity of recognized patterns. The more complex recognized patterns are, the more stages of hierarchy of extracted features we need and the higher number of stages of the neocognitron is.

8.4.3 Network Structure-Layers

Each stage of the neocognitron consists of certain number of layers of given type. Structure of the network from figure 8.11 after drawing of layers of which the particular stages are assembled is shown in figure 8.12. From figure 8.12 it is obvious that four types of layers exist in the neocognitron. Stage 0 always consists of only one input layer. All higher stages consist of one S-layer, one V-layer and one C-layer. In figure 8.12 we have also established ordinarily used notation of layers in the neocognitron. We will use this notation, described in table 1, in the following text as well.

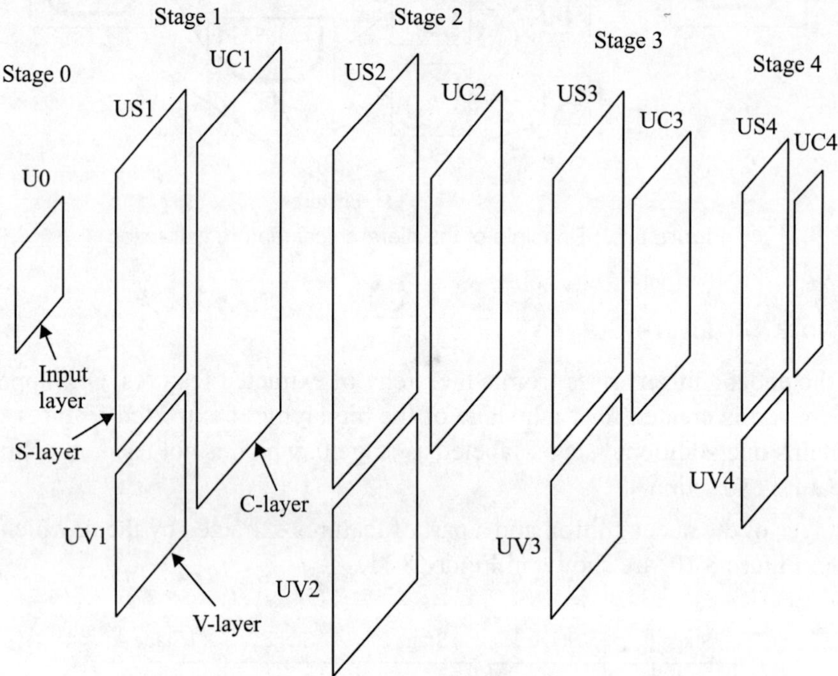

Figure 8.12: Network structure-layers

Table 8.1: Notation Used For Layers In The Neocognitron

Symbol	Denotes
U0	input layer
USl	S-layer in the l-th stage of the network
UVl	V-layer in the l-th stage of the network
UCl	C-layer in the l-th stage of the network

8.4.4 Network Structure-Cell Planes

Each layer in the neocognitron consists of certain number of cell planes of the same type. Input layer is exception from this rule. For the input layer the term cell plane is not established. Number of cell planes in each S-layer and C-layer depends on the number of features extracted in corresponding stage of the network. Each V-layer always consists of only one cell plane. Structure of the network from figure 8.12 after drawing of cell planes from which the particular layers are assembled is shown in figure 8.13. From figure 8.13 it is obvious that three types of cell planes exist in the neocognitron - S-planes, V-planes and C-planes.

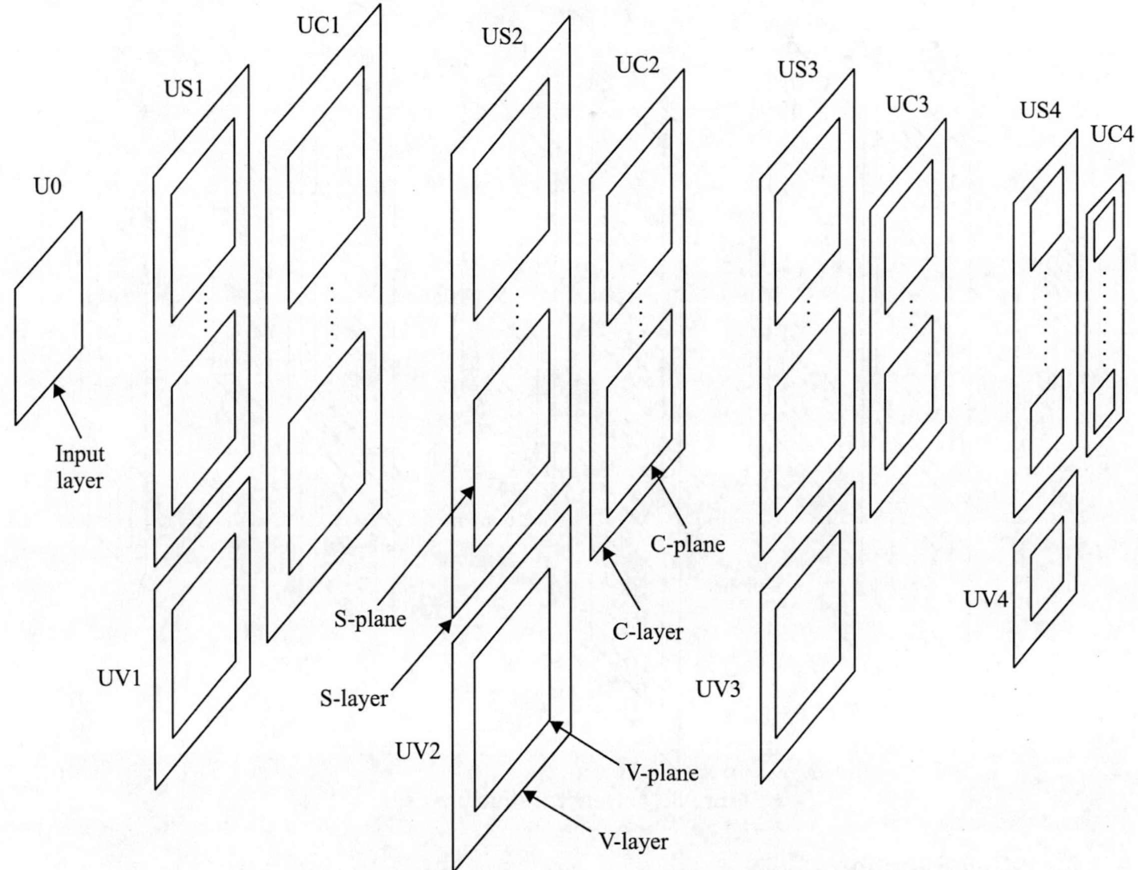

Figure 8.13: Network structure-cell planes

8.4.5 Network Structure-Cells

Now we have come to the ground of the neocognitron which is cell. The neocognitron is made of large amount of cells of several distinct types which are organized in cell planes, layers and stages. All the cells, regardless of their type, process and generate analog values. From figure 8.14 it is obvious that each S-plane, V-plane, C-plane and input layer consists of array of cells of the certain type. Size of cell arrays is the same for all cell planes in one layer and it decreases with increasing of the network stage. Each C-plane in the highest stage of the network contains only one cell. Its output value indicates a measure of belonging of presented pattern into the category represented by this cell. Size of cell array in each V-plane is the same as size of cell arrays in S-planes in the same stage of the network.

From figure 8.14 it is obvious that four types of cells exist in the neocognitron - receptor cells, S-cells, V-cells and C-cells.

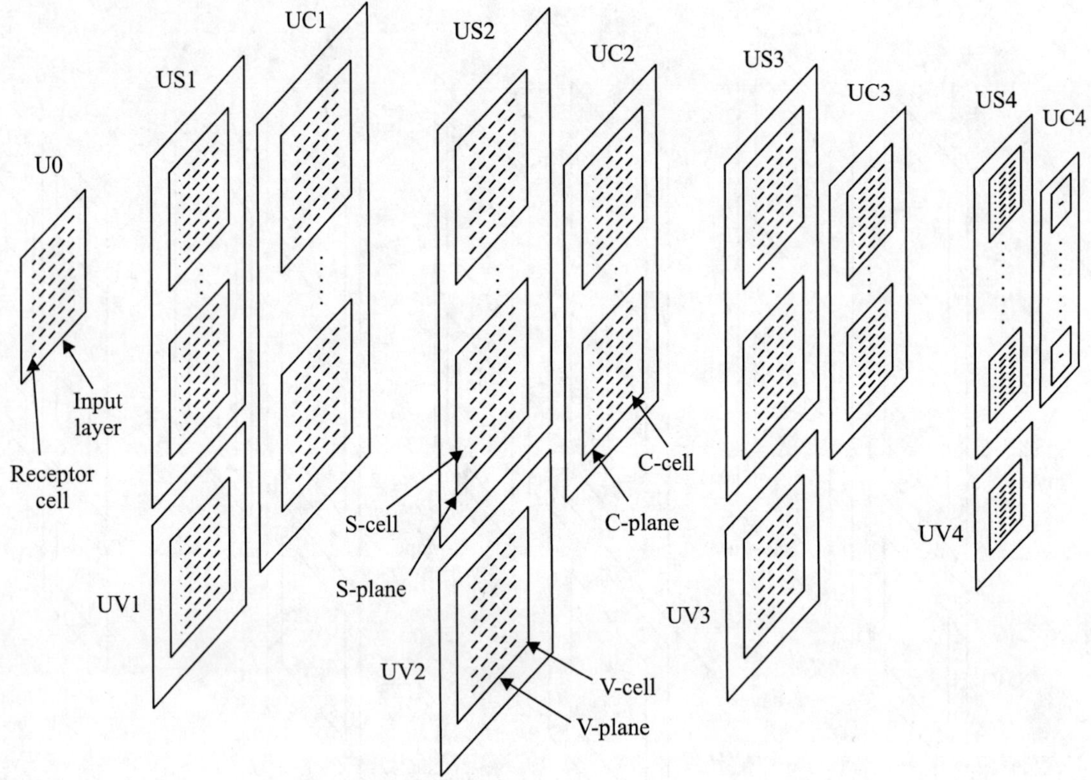

Figure 8.14: Network structure-cells

8.4.6 V-Cell Function

Each V-cell in the neocognitron evaluates outputs of C-cells (or receptor cells) from the certain connection areas from previous C-layer (or input layer). Size of connection areas is the same for all V-cells and S-cells in one stage of the network and it is determined at construction of the network. One V-cell connection areas of size 3 by 3 cells are shown in figure 8.15.

V-cell output value represents average activity of cells from connection areas and it is used for inhibition of corresponding S-cell activity. Exact specification of V-cell function is described in mathematical description of its behaviour.

8.4.7 S-Cell Function

Each S-cell in the neocognitron evaluates outputs of C-cells (or receptor cells) from the certain connection areas from previous C-layer (or input layer). Size of connection areas is the same for all S-cells in one S-layer and it is determined at construction of the network. One S-cell connection areas of size 3 by 3 cells are shown in Figure 8.16 (on next page).

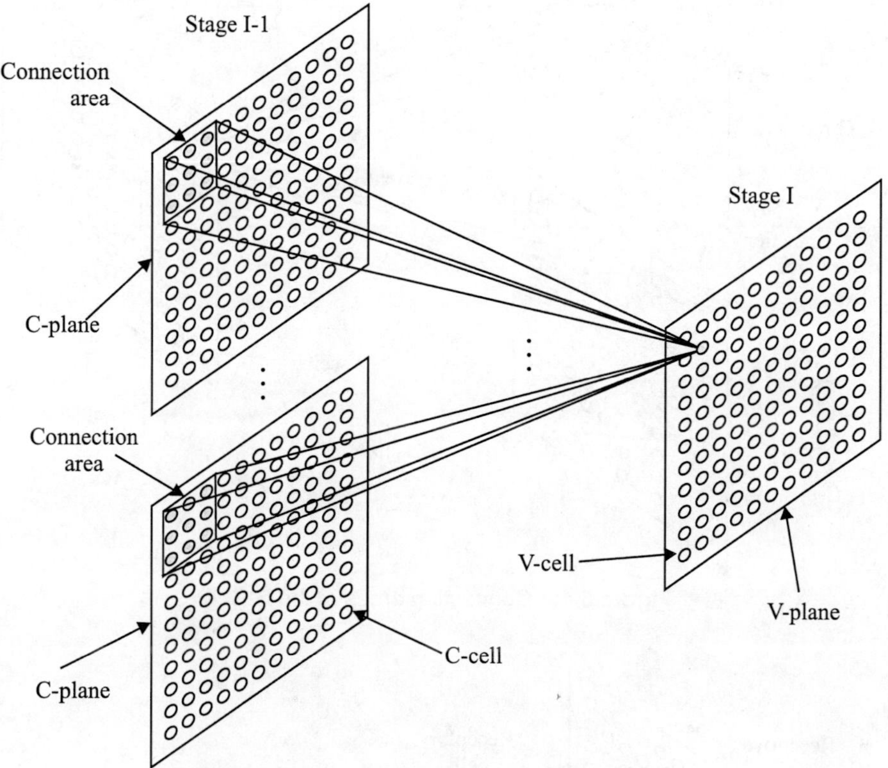

Figure 8.15: Connection areas of the V-Cell

Function of each S-cell is to extract the certain feature at the certain position in the input layer (i.e. in its receptive field). For extraction of this feature an S-cell uses only informations obtained from its connection areas and information about average activity in these areas obtained from corresponding V-cell. All S-cells in one S-plane always extract the same feature.

The feature extracted by S-cell is determined by weights for this cell. Weights and method for their adjusting will be described later in detail. For a better conception about function of weights we can compare them to a mask which is used at determination about feature presence for now. The meaning of weights is obvious best for cells from layer US1.

Each S-cell in this layer has only one connection area and this area is S-cell's receptive field at the same time. So weights (mask if you want) contain directly representation of the certain feature. In higher S-layers correspondency between extracted feature and its representation by the weights is already not so obvious. Cell plane of S-cells designated for extraction of feature corresponding to vertical line is shown in Figure 8.17.

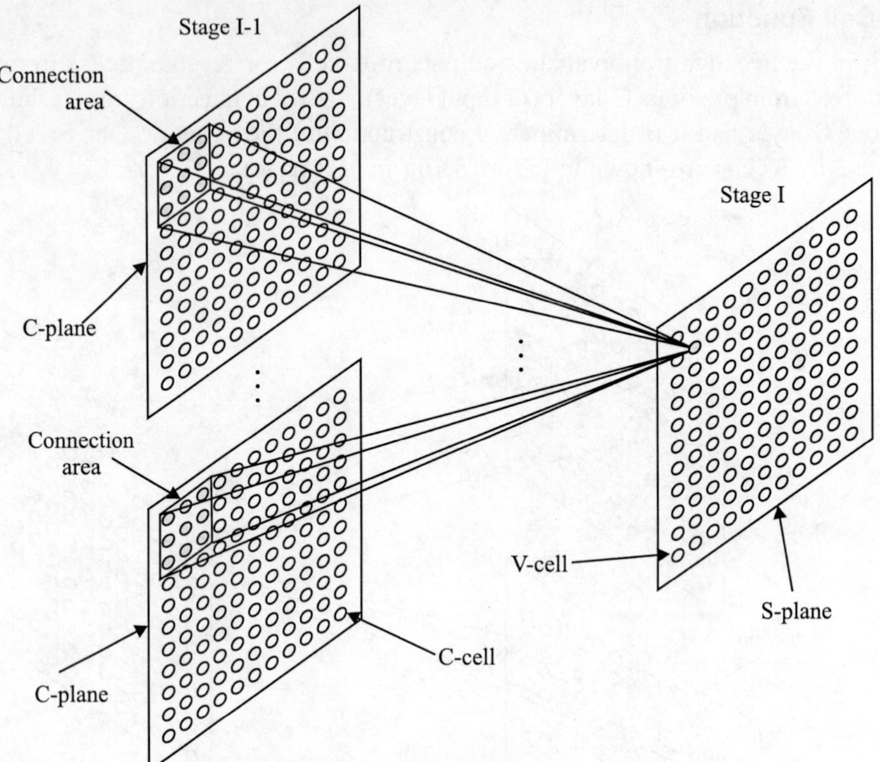

Figure 8.16: Connection areas of the S-Cell

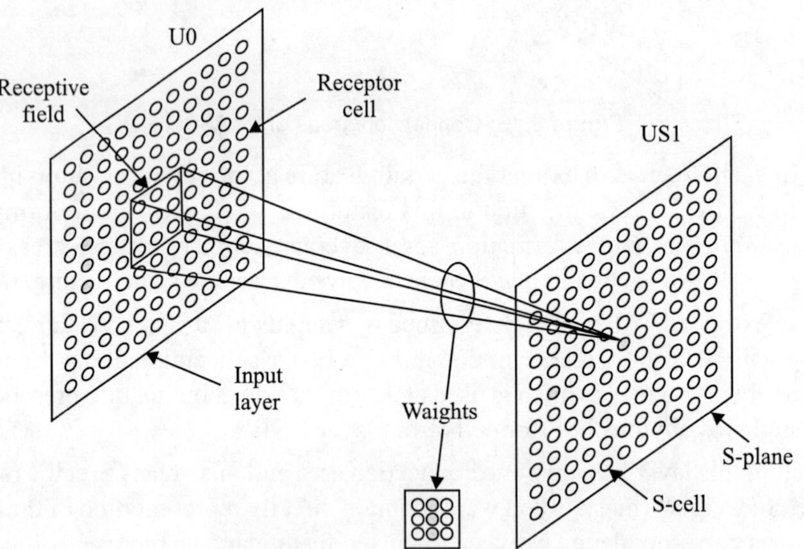

Figure 8.17: S-Cell Function

S-cell is activated only if this feature is present in S-cell's receptive field (it is identical with connection area here). When incorrect feature is presented the cell becomes inactive.

S-cell output value is determined exactly by the equation described in mathematical description. However, for understanding of S-cell function simplified equation is sufficient:

$$u_s \quad * \ \frac{E(a, u_c)}{I(r, b, u_v)}$$

The symbols used in this equation have the following meaning : Symbol Denotes

us S-cell output value

ϕ* non-linear function

E excitatory part

a a-weights

uc output values of C-cells from connection areas

I inhibitory part

r selectivity

b b-weight

uv V-cell output value

The S-cells ability to extract not only learned features but also deformed representations of these features is influenced by the choice of parameter denoted as selectivity to a great extent. On the following example we will demonstrate how selectivity affects the process of feature extraction in the neocognitron.

8.5 EXAMPLE-SELECTIVITY

The process of feature extraction is influenced by selectivity to a great extent. For each S-layer in the neocognitron we can set different amount of selectivity at construction of the network. By the change of selectivity we change the effect of inhibitory part on the S-cell output value. Decreasing of selectivity causes decreasing of effect of inhibition part. Decreased S-cell ability to distinguish learned feature exactly is the result of it. In other words it means that S-cell considers also more deformed features to be correct.

Example represents one S-cell from layer US1 and its connection area which is its receptive field here as well. This S-cell extracts feature corresponding to vertical line in the centre of the receptive field. Select one of the prepared patterns with using of mouse, set up desired amount of selectivity and observe the effect on excitatory part E, inhibitory part I and S-cell output value as well. We reminder that S-cell output value is exactly determined by equation described in mathematical description of its behaviour but simplified form of this equation will suffice for us :

$$u_s \quad * \ \frac{E(a, u_c)}{I(r, b, u_v)}$$

8.5.1 C-Cell Function

Each C-cell in the neocognitron evaluates outputs of S-cells from the certain connection area from one of S-planes from previous S-layer. Number of S-planes, however, can be greater in some cases. Size of connection areas is the same for all C-cells in one C-layer and it is determined at construction of the network. One C-cell connection area of size 5 by 5 cells is shown in figure 8.18. C-cell output value depends on activity of S-cells from connection area. The greater number of active S-cells is or the greater their activities are the greater C-cell output value is.

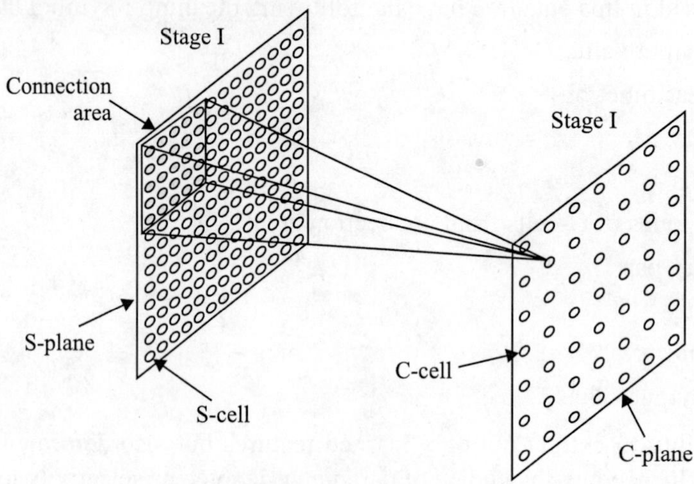

Figure 8.18: Connection area of the C-Cell

C-cell function is exactly described in mathematical description. For C-cell to be active it is sufficient that at least one active S-cell is present in its connection area. With regard to overlapping of neighbouring C-cell connection areas activity of one S-cell affects activity of greater number of C-cells. In consequence of that C-plane contains a blurred representation of S-plane content. This is obvious from Figure 8.19 as well where one active S-cell and all C-cells influenced by it are marked.

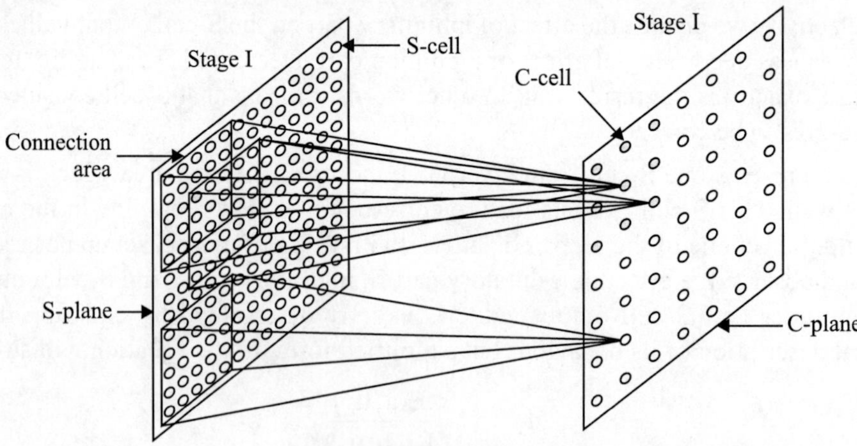

Figure 8.19: C-Cell function

Ability of C-cell to compress content of connection area in the certain way is the next consequence of C-cell function. Hence we can decrease the density of cells in C-layer to the half of density of cells in previous S-layer in some cases. On the following example we will show the last and probably the most important consequence of C-cell function which is ensuring of the neocognitron's tolerance of feature shifts.

8.6 EXAMPLE-TOLERANCE OF FEATURE SHIFTS

This important property of the neocognitron is ensured by C-cells. Connection area of one of C-cells is marked in S-plane in figure 8.20. This C-cell is active only if there is an active S-cell in its connection area. It corresponds to presence of correct feature at the certain position in the input layer. When this feature is shifted to another position another S-cell is activated. If the activated S-cell belongs to the marked connection area again our C-cell remains active.

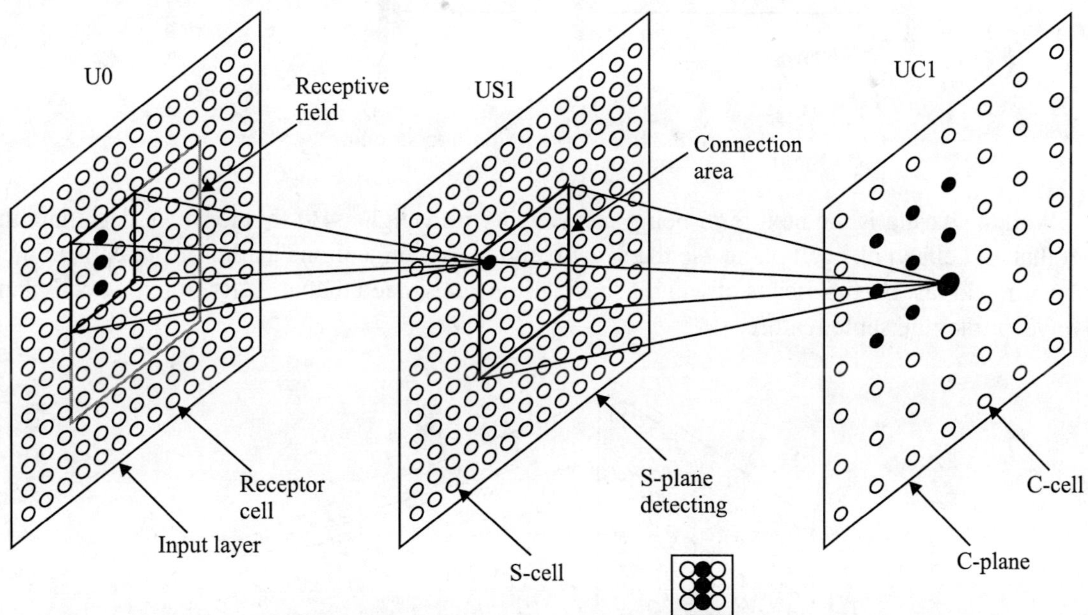

Figure 8.20: Tolerance of feature shifts

Receptive field of observed C-cell is marked in the input layer U0. It is obvious that C-cell is activated only if any S-cell detects correct feature in this field.

8.7 WEIGHTS AND CONNECTIONS

The neocognitron is characteristic not only by large number of cells but also by large number of connections. These connections serve for transfer of informations between cells in adjoining layers. Particular cell obtains by means of connections informations from all cells which are located in its connection areas.For each connection there is a weight by means of it we can affect amount of transferred information. If we imagine a connection as a pipeline with a valve we can compare weight assigned to the connection to a degree of opening of this valve. Four types of weights (a-weights, b-weights, c-weights and d-weights) exist in the neocognitron. Each of these types of weights is used for connections between two layers of different types. It is shown schematically in Figure 8.21.

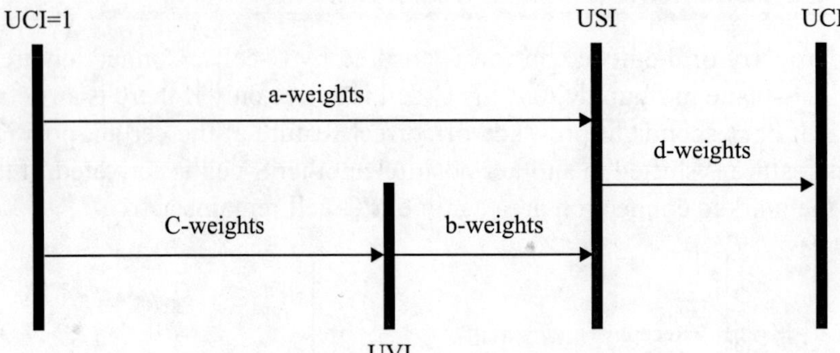

Figure 8.21: Weights in the neocognitron

Weight sharing is the next term being connected with weights. By this term we designate the fact that all cells in one cell plane use the same weights for connections leading from cells in their connection areas. By the means of weight sharing it is guaranteed that all cells from one cell plane always extract the same feature.

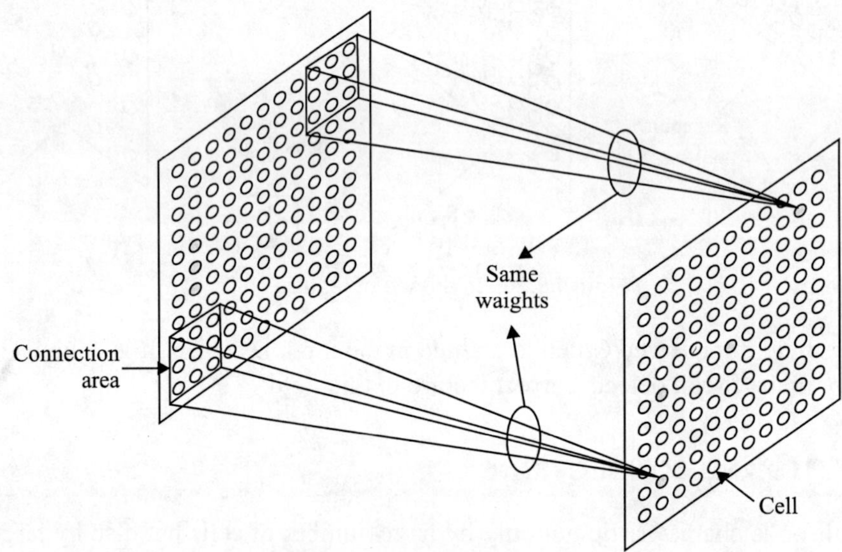

Figure 8.22: Weight sharing

We can split the weights shown in Figure 8.21 according to the way which they are adjusted :

weights modified by learning

1. a-weights
2. b-weights

Fixed Weights

3. c-weights
4. d-weights

1. a-weights

The a-weights are the first type of weights modified by learning. These weights are used for connections between S-cells and C-cells which belong to their connection areas. Features extracted by S-cells are encoded in these a-weights. Adjusting of a-weights is performed during learning of the network according to the presented training patterns.

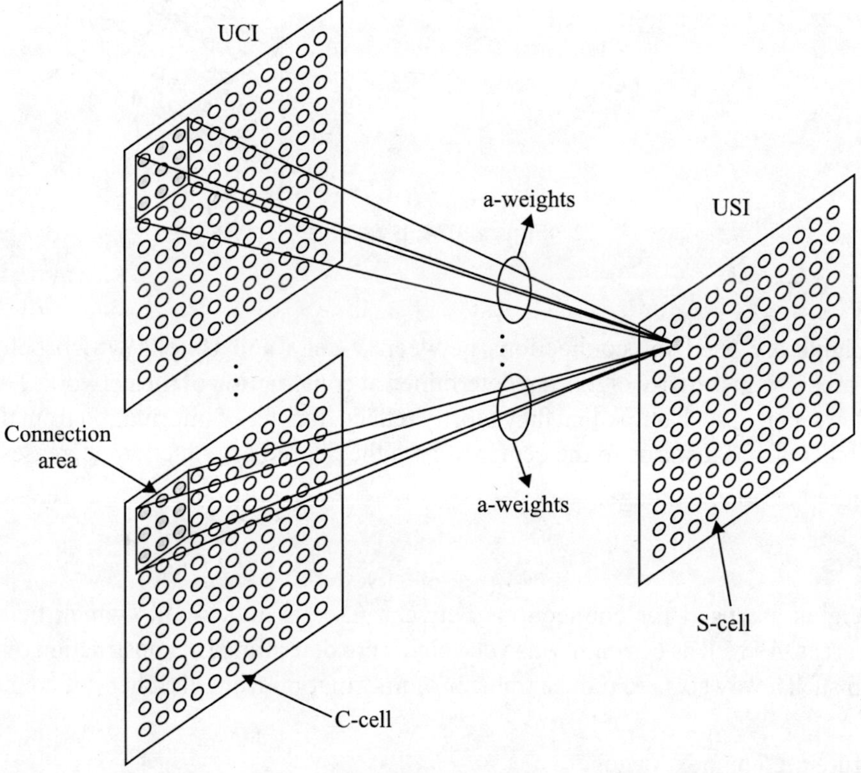

Figure 8.23: a-weights

2. b-weights

The b-weights are the second type of weights modified by learning. These weights are used for connections between S-cells and corresponding V-cells. Adjusting of b-weights is performed during learning of the network according to the presented training patterns as well.

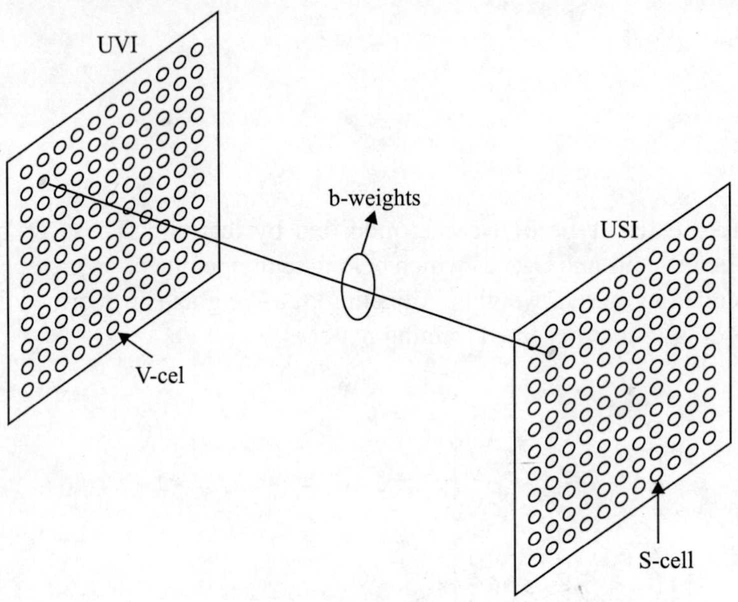

Figure 8.24: b-weights

3. c-weights

Fixed c-weights are used for connections between V-cells and C-cells which belong to their connection areas. Values of c-weights are determined at construction of the network. These weights are most often set up in such a way that they mostly reduce transfer of information from the periphery of connection area and towards to the center of area the degree of reduction decreases.

See Figure 8.25 on next page.

4. d-weights

Fixed d-weights are used for connections between C-cells and S-cells which belong to their connection areas. As well as c-weights also d-weights are determined at construction of the network and again in such a way so as to reduce transfer of information from periphery of connection areas mostly.

See Figure 8.26 on next page.

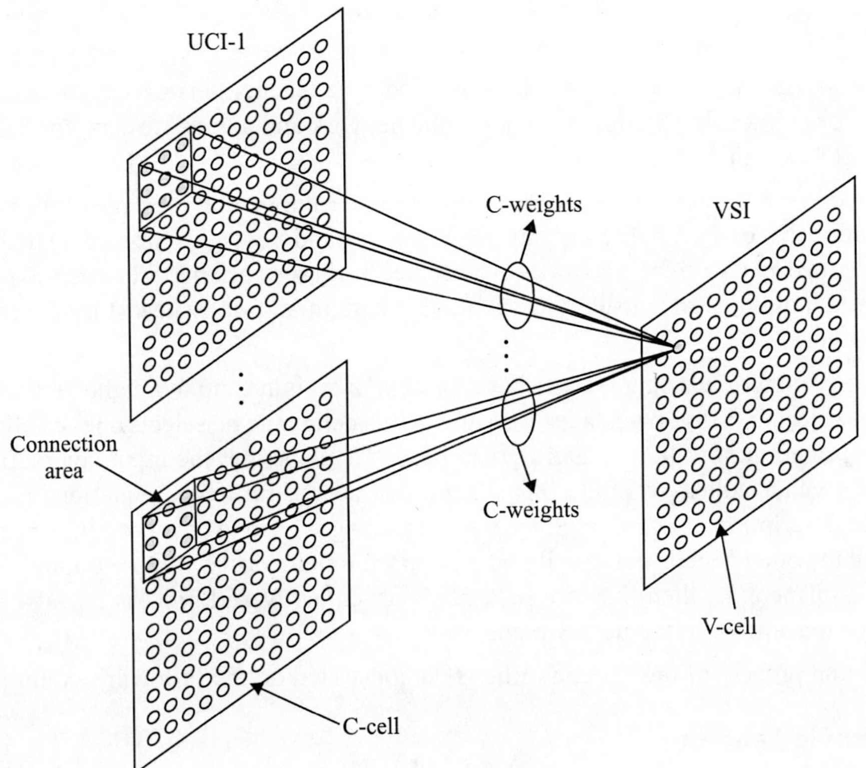

Figure 8.25: c-weights

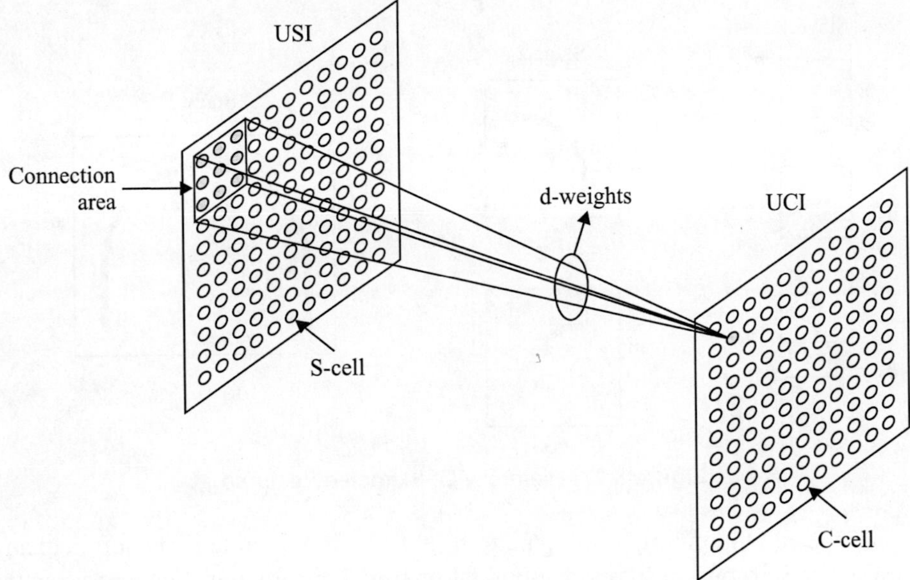

Figure 8.26: d-weights

8.8 LEARNING

Learning in this version of the network is controlled by a teacher. His task is to determine what features shall be extracted in particular stages of the network and to prepare corresponding training patterns before beginning of learning.

Learning of the neocognitron proceeds stage by stage from the lowest stage of the network and it inheres in adjusting of modifiable weights (i.e. a-weights and b-weights) according to the response of already learned parts of the network to presented training patterns. For each S-plane in the network one training pattern is usually used and this pattern is usually necessary to present to the network only once.

On the beginning of learning teacher have to set all a-weights and b-weights in the network to zero. Then he selects S-plane from layer US1 and in this cell plane he selects one of cells, so-called seed cell. Presentation of training pattern given for this S-plane into the input layer U0 is the next step. Finally teacher adjusts weights of the seed cell according to the equations mentioned in mathematical description of learning. Since weight sharing is used in the neocognitron adjusting of weights of all the other S-cells in the cell plane occurs simultaneously. If more training patterns for the selected S-plane exist then they are presented subsequently and process repeats. In opposite case we move to learning of the next S-plane.

The learning process of the neocognitron is demonstrated on the following example in detail.

8.8.1 Example-Learning

In this example we will demonstrate learning of the simple version of the neocognitron network. We want that our network will extract features shown in figure 8.27.

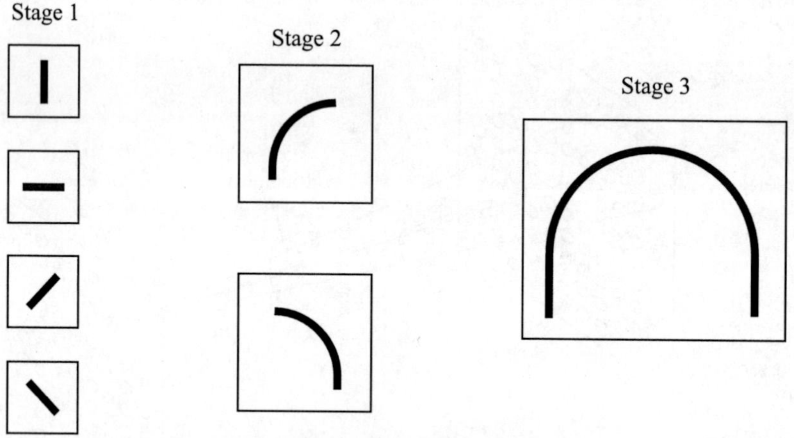

Figure 8.27: Hierarchy Of Extracted Features

We prepare the corresponding training pattern set (it is shown quite in the left in example) and we start learning by Start button.In our demonstration b-weights are not shown because the way of their modification is not so important for us now. Remember however that both a-weights and b-weights are adjusted during learning. Notice that together with seed cell selecting their connection areas and receptive field are selected as well.

8.8.2 Recall

Recall in the neocognitron inheres in evaluation of output values of all cells stage by stage. The result of this process is a decision to which of learned categories presented pattern belongs. The process of recall begins with presentation of pattern intended for recognition to the input layer U0. Then output values of V-cells in the layer UV1 are evaluated. S-cells from the layer US1 can extract the simplest features and C-cells from layer UC1 ensure decreasing of effect of extracted features shifts. The whole process repeats analogically for all the following layers of the network. After completion of recall output values of C-cells from the highest layer of the network correspond to measures of belonging presented pattern to categories which the particular C-cells represent.

In figure 8.28 the process of recall in the neocognitron is demonstrated schematically.

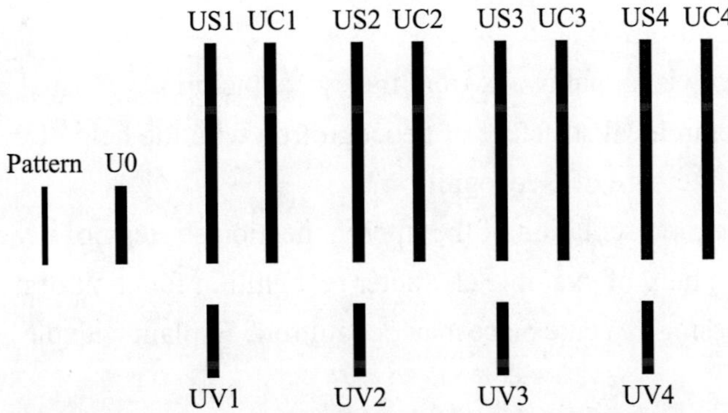

Figure 8.28: Process Of Recall In The Neocognitron

On the following example we will examine recall on the simulator of the neocognitron in detail.

8.9 EXAMPLE-SIMULATOR OF THE NEOCOGNITRON

At the end, we have prepared simulator of the neocognitron network mentioned in the first example.

Each quadrangle in the simulator represents one certain cell plane in the network. For simplicity V-planes are not shown here because their content is not so important for us. Output values of cells in cell planes are expressed by different intensity of color. The higher the output value of cell the darker the color is. After clicking on any cell in any cell plane all its connection areas and receptive field are marked.

In control panel select one of patterns and observe state of the network after its presentation. Examine what features are extracted in particular S-planes and in detailed view how these features are encoded in a-weights.

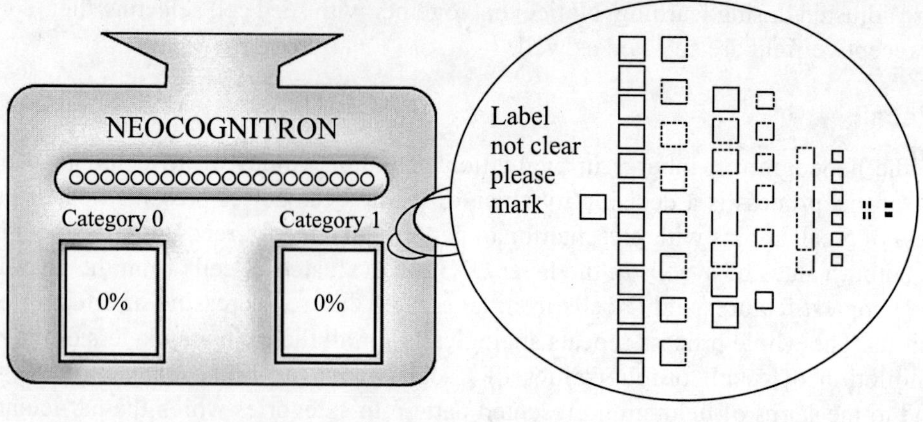

EXERCISES

1. What is Neocognitron?
2. Draw diagram of visual pathways from the eye to the primary visual cortex and explain it?
3. Explain the Hierarchical structure of neocognitron with the help of the diagram?
4. Explain the architecture of Neocognitron?
5. Draw schematic representation of the interconnection strategy of neocognitron?
6. Explain with the help of example character recognition function of neocognitron?
7. How data processing can take place in neocognitron? Explain with the help of cell processing diagrams?
8. How we can train weights on the S layer?
9. How pattern 0 and 1 used for learning in neocognitron?
10. Explain the basic principal of the hierarchical feature extraction?
11. Explain the various stages of neocognitron network?
12. Explain the various layers of neocognitron network?
13. Explain S- plane, V- plane, C-plane of neocognitron network?
14. Explain S-cell, V-cell, C-cell of neocognitron network?
15. Explain the example of selectivity in feature extraction with the help of diagram?
16. Explain the example of tolerance of feature shifts with the help of diagram?
17. Explain the concept of weights and connection in neocognitron?
18. Demonstrate learning of the simple version of neocognitron network?
19. Explain the process of recall in the neocognitron?
20. Discuss the implementation of simulator of neocognitron?

CHAPTER 9

Bidirectional Associative Memory

9.1 INTRODUCTION

Bidirectional Associative Memory usually referred to as **BAM** is a type of recurrent neural network. BAM was introduced by Bart Kosko in 1988. There are two types of associative memory, auto-associative and hetro-associative. BAM is hetro-associative, meaning given a pattern it can return another patten which is potentially of a different size. It is similar to the Hopfield network in that they are both forms of associative memory. However, Hopfield nets return patterns of the same size.

BAM has 2 layers: input and output and information can go in both directions - from input to output and back from output to input. This page presents some demo that can demonsrate learning of BAM. A BAM stores a set of pattern associations by summing bipolar correlation matrices (an n by m outer product matrix for each pattern to be stored). The architecture of the net consists of two layers of neurons, connected by directional weighted connection paths. The net iterates, sending signals back and forth between the two layers until all neurons reach equilibrium. Bidirectional associative memory neural nets can respond to input to either layer. Because the weights are bidirectional and the algirithm alternates between updating the activations for each layer, we shall refer to the layer as the X-layer and the Y-layer.

Three varities of BAM—binary, bipolar, and continuous—are considered here. Several other variations exist. The architecture for each is same and is illustrated in figure9.1.

9.2 ARCHITECTURE

The single-layer nonlinear feedback BAM network (with heteroassociative content-addressable memory) has n units in its X-layer and m units in its Y-layer. The connections between the layers are bidirectional; i.e., if the weight matrix for signals sent from the X-layer to the Y-layer is W, the weight matrix for signals sent from the Y-layer to the X-layer is W^T.

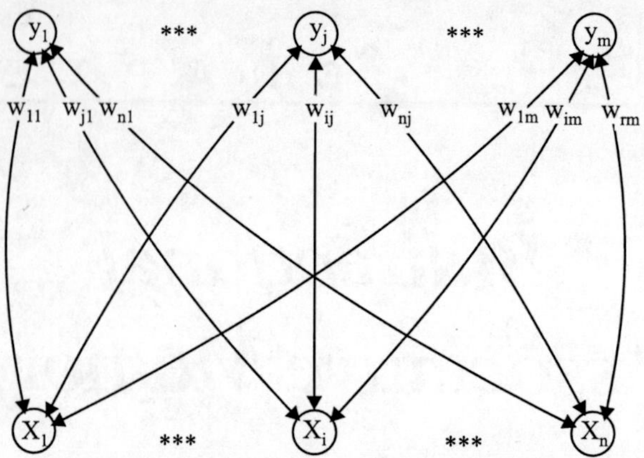

Figure 9.1: Bidirectional associative memory

9.3 ALGORITHM

9.3.1 Discrete BAM

The two bivalent (binary or bipolar) forms f BAM are closely related. In each, the weights are found from the sum f the outer products of the bipolar form of the training vectors pairs. Also, the activation function is a step function, with the possibility of a nonzero threshold. It has been shown that bipolar vectors improve the performance of the net.

Setting the Weights. The weight matrix to store a set of input and target vectors s(p): t(p), p = 1,..., P, where

$$s(p) = (s_1(p),\ldots, s_i(p),\ldots s_n(p))$$

and

$$t(p) = (t_1(p),\ldots, t_j(p),\ldots t_m(p))$$

can be determined by the Hebb rule. The formulas for the entries depend on whether the training vectors are binary or bipolar. For binary input vectors, the weight matrix $W = \{w_{ij}\}$ is given by

$$w_{ij} = \underset{p}{} (2s_i(p) - 1)(2t_j(p) - 1).$$

For bipolar input vectors, the weight matrix $W = \{w_{ij}\}$ is given by

$$w_{ij} = \underset{p}{} s_i(p)t_{ij}(p).$$

Activation Functions. The activation function for the discrete BAM is the appropriate step function, depending on whether binary or bipolar vectors are used.

For binary input vectors, the activation function for the Y-layer is

$$y_j = \begin{matrix} 1 & \text{if } y\_in_j > 0 \\ y_i & \text{if } y\_in_j = 0 \\ 0 & \text{if } y\_in_j < 0 \end{matrix}$$

and the activation function for the X-layer is

$$x_i = \begin{cases} 1 & \text{if } x\_in_i > 0 \\ x_i & \text{if } x\_in_i = 0 \\ 0 & \text{if } x\_in_i < 0 \end{cases}$$

For bipolar input vectors, the activation function for the Y-layer is

$$y_j = \begin{cases} 1 & \text{if } y\_in_j > \ _j \\ y_i & \text{if } y\_in_j = \ _j \\ -1 & \text{if } y\_in_j < \ _j \end{cases}$$

and the activation function for the X-layer is

$$x_i = \begin{cases} 1 & \text{if } x\_in_i > \ _j \\ x_i & \text{if } x\_in_i = \ _j \\ -1 & \text{if } x\_in_i < \ _j \end{cases}$$

Note that if the net input is exactly equal to the threshold value, the activation function "decides" to leave the activation of that unit at its previous value. For that reason, the activations of all units are initialized to zero in the algorithm that follows. The algorithm is written for the first signal to be sent from the X-layer to the Y-layer. However, if the input signal for the X-layer is the zero vector, the input signal to the Y-layer will be unchanged by the activation function, and the process will be the same as if the first piece of information had been sent from the Y-layer to the X-layer. Signals are sent only from one layer to the other at any step of the process, not simultaneously in both directions.

Algorithm

Step 0: Initialize the weights to store a set of P vectors;

Initialize all activations to 0.

Step 1: For each testing input, do Steps 2-6.

Step 2a: Present input pattern x to the X-layer

(i.e., set activations of X-layer to current input pattern).

Step 2b: Present input pattern y t the Y-layer.

(Either of the input patterns may be the zero vector.)

Step 3: While activation are not converged, do Steps 4-6.

Step 4: Update activations of units in Y-layer.

Compute net inputs:

$$y\_in_j = \ _i \ w_{ij} x_i .$$

Compute activations:

$$y_j = f(y\_in_j).$$

Send signal to X-layer.

Step 5: Update activations of units in X-layer.

Compute net inputs:

$$x\_in_i = \sum_j w_{ij}x_j.$$

Compute activations:

$$x_i = f(x\_in_i).$$

Send signal to Y-layer.

Step 6: Test for convergence:

If the activation vectors x and y have reached equilibrium, then stop; otherwise, continue.

9.3.2 Continuous BAM

A continuous bidirectional associative memory transforms input smoothly and continuously into output in the range [0, 1] using he logistic sigmoid function as the activation function for all units.

For binary input vectors (s(p), t(p)), p = 1, 2,…., P, the weights are determined by the aforementioned formula

$$w_{ij}\Sigma(2s_i(p) - 1)(2t_j(p) - 1).$$

The activation function is the logistic sigmoid

$$f(y\_in_j) = \frac{1}{1 + \exp(-y\_in_j)},$$

where a bias is included in calculating the net input to any unit

$$y\_in_j = b_i \sum_i x_i w_{ij}$$

and corresponding formulas apply for the units n the X-layer.

A number of other forms of BAMs have been developed. In some, the activations change based on a differential equation known as Cohen-Grossberg activation dynamics [Cohen & Grossberg, 1983]. Note, however, that Kosko uses the term "activation" to refer to the activity level of a neuron before the output function (such as the logistic sigmoid function) is applied.

9.4 APPLICATIONS

Example 9.1: A BAM net to associate letters with simple bipolar codes.

Consider the possibility of using a (discrete) BAM network (with bipolar vectors) to map to simple letters (given by 5 × 3 patterns) to the following bipolar codes:

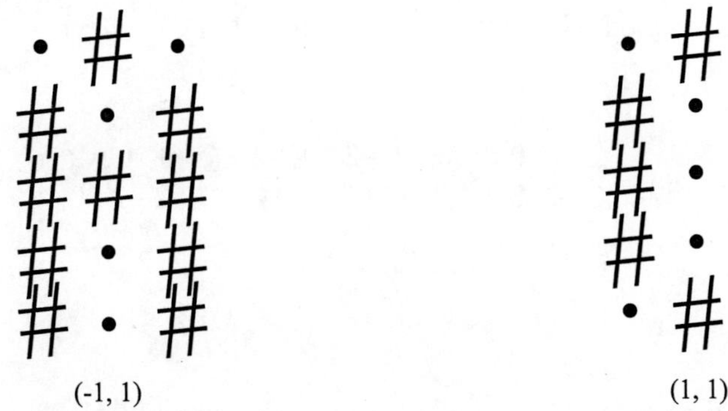

(-1, 1) (1, 1)

The weight matrices are:

to store A	– 11)	(C	11)	(W, to store both)
1	–1	–1	1	0–2
–1	1	1	1	0 2
1	–1	1	1	2 0
–1	1	1	1	0 2
1	–1	–1	–1	0 –2
–1	1	–1	–1	–2 0
–1	1	1	1	0 2
–1	1	–1	–1	–2 0
–1	1	–1	–1	–2 0
–1	1	1	1	0 2
1	–1	–1	–1	0–2
–1	1	–1	–1	–2 0
–1	1	–1	–1	–2 0
1	–1	1	1	2 0
–1	1	1	1	0 2

To illustrate the use of a BAM, we first demonstrate that the net gives the correct Y vector when presented with the x vector for either the pattern A or the pattern C:

Input Pattern A

$$(-1\ 1 - 1\ 1 - 1\ 1\ 1\ 1\ 1\ 1 - 1\ 1\ 1 - 1\ 1)W = (-14, (16) \rightarrow (-1, 1)$$

Input Pattern C

$$(-1\ 1\ 1\ 1 - 1 - 1\ 1 - 1 - 1\ 1 - 1 - 1 - 1\ 1\ 1)\ W = (14, 16) \rightarrow (1, 1).$$

To see the bidirectional nature of the net, observe that the Y vectors can also be used as input. For signals sent from the Y-layer to the X-layer, the weight matrix is the transpose of the matrix W, i.e.,

$$W^T = \begin{matrix} 0 & 0 & 2 & 0 & 0 & -2 & 0 & -2 & -2 & 0 & 0 & -2 & -2 & 2 & 0 \\ -2 & 2 & 0 & 2 & -2 & 0 & 2 & 0 & 0 & 2 & -2 & 0 & 0 & 0 & 2 \end{matrix}$$

For the input vector associated with pattern A, namely, (-1, 1), we have

$$(-1, 1)\, W^T =$$

$$(-1, 1) = \begin{matrix} 0 & 0 & 2 & 0 & 0 & -2 & 0 & -2 & -2 & 0 & 0 & -2 & -2 & 2 & 0 \\ -2 & 2 & 0 & 2 & -2 & 0 & 2 & 0 & 0 & 2 & -2 & 0 & 0 & 0 & 2 \end{matrix}$$

$$= (-2\ 2\ -2\ 2\ -2\ 2\ 2\ 2\ 2\ 2\ -2\ 2\ 2\ -2\ 2)$$

$$\rightarrow (-1\ 1\ -1\ 1\ -1\ 1\ 1\ 1\ 1\ 1\ -1\ 1\ 1\ -1\ 1).$$

This is pattern A.

Similarly, if we input the vector associated with pattern C, namely, (1, 1), we obtain

$$(1, 1)\, W^T =$$

$$(-1, 1) = \begin{matrix} 0 & 0 & 2 & 0 & 0 & -2 & 0 & -2 & -2 & 0 & 0 & -2 & -2 & 2 & 0 \\ -2 & 2 & 0 & 2 & -2 & 0 & 2 & 0 & 0 & 2 & -2 & 0 & 0 & 0 & 2 \end{matrix}$$

$$= (-2\ 2\ 2\ 2\ -2\ -2\ 2\ -2\ -2\ 2\ -2\ -2\ -2\ 2\ 2)$$

$$\rightarrow (-1\ 1\ 1\ 1\ -1\ -1\ 1\ -1\ -1\ 1\ -1\ -1\ -1\ 1\ 1),$$

which is pattern C.

The net can also be used with noisy input for the x vector, the y vector, or both, as is shown in the next example.

Example 9.2: Testing a bam net with noisy input.

In this example, the net is given a y vector as input that is a noisy version of one of the training y vectors and no information about the corresponding x vector (i.e., the x vector is identically 0). The input vector is (0,1); the response of the net is

$$(0.1)\, W^T =$$

$$(0, 1) = \begin{matrix} 0 & 0 & 2 & 0 & 0 & -2 & 0 & -2 & -2 & 0 & 0 & -2 & -2 & 2 & 0 \\ -2 & 2 & 0 & 2 & -2 & 0 & 2 & 0 & 0 & 2 & -2 & 0 & 0 & 0 & 2 \end{matrix}$$

$$= (-2\ 2\ 0\ 2\ -2\ 0\ 2\ 0\ 0\ 2\ -2\ 0\ 0\ 0\ 2)$$

$$\rightarrow (-1\ 1\ 0\ 1\ -1\ 0\ 1\ 0\ 0\ 1\ -1\ 0\ 0\ 0\ 1).$$

Note that the units receiving 0 net input have their activations left at that value, since the initial x vector is 0. This x vector is then sent back to the Y-layer, using the weight matrix W:

$$(-1\ 1\ 0\ 1\ -1\ 0\ 1\ 0\ 0\ 1\ -1\ 0\ 0\ 0\ 1)\begin{matrix} 0 & -2 \\ 0 & 2 \\ 2 & 0 \\ 0 & 2 \\ 0 & -2 \\ -2 & 0 \\ 0 & 2 \\ -2 & 0 \\ -2 & 0 \\ 0 & 2 \\ 0 & -2 \\ -2 & 0 \\ -2 & 0 \\ 2 & 0 \\ 0 & 2 \end{matrix} \to (0\ 1).$$

This result is not too surprising, since the net had no information to give it a preference for either A or C. The net has converged (since, obviously, no further changes in the activations will take place) to a spurious stable state, i.e., the solution is no is not one of the stored pattern pairs.

If, on the other hand, the net was given both the input vector y, as before, and some information about the vector, x for example,

$$y = (0\ 1),\ x = (0\ 0\ -1\ 0\ 0\ 1\ 0\ 1\ 1\ 0\ 0\ 1\ 1\ -1\ 0).$$

the net would be able to reach a stable set of activations corresponding to one of the stored pattern pairs.

Note that the x vector is a noisy version of

$$A = (-1\ 1\ -1\ 1\ -1\ 1\ 1\ 1\ 1\ 1\ -1\ 1\ 1\ -1\ 1),$$

where the nonzero components are those that distinguish A from

$$C\ (-1\ 1\ 1\ 1\ -1\ -1\ 1\ -1\ -1\ 1\ -1\ -1\ -1\ 1\ 1).$$

Now, since the algorithm specifies that if the net input to a unit is zero, the activation of that unit remains unchanged, we get

$$(0, 1)W^T =$$

$$(0, 1) = \begin{matrix} 0 & 0 & 2 & 0 & 0 & -2 & 0 & -2 & -2 & 0 & 0 & -2 & -2 & 2 & 0 \\ -2 & 2 & 0 & 2 & -2 & 0 & 2 & 0 & 0 & 2 & -2 & 0 & 0 & 0 & 2 \end{matrix}$$

$$= (-2\ 2\ 0\ 2\ -2\ 0\ 2\ 0\ 0\ 2\ -2\ 0\ 0\ 0\ 2)$$

$$\to (-1\ 1\ -1\ 1\ -1\ 1\ 1\ 1\ 1\ 1\ -1\ 1\ 1\ -1\ 1).$$

which is pattern A.

Since this example is fairly extreme, i.e., every component that distinguishes A from C was given an input value for A, let us try something with less information given concerning x.

For example, let y = (0 1) and x = (0 0 –1 0 0 1 0 1 0 0 0 0 0 0 0). Then

$$(0, 1)W^T =$$

$$(0,1) = \begin{matrix} 0 & 0 & 2 & 0 & 0 & -2 & 0 & -2 & -2 & 0 & 0 & -2 & -2 & 2 & 0 \\ -2 & 2 & 0 & 2 & -2 & 0 & 2 & 0 & 0 & 2 & -2 & 0 & 0 & 0 & 2 \end{matrix}$$

$$= (-2\ 2\ 0\ 2\ -2\ 0\ 2\ 0\ 0\ 2\ -2\ 0\ 0\ 0\ 2)$$

$$\rightarrow (-1\ 1\ -1\ 1\ -1\ 1\ 1\ 1\ 0\ 1\ -1\ 0\ 0\ 0\ 1),$$

which is not quite pattern A.

So we try iterating, sending the x vector back to the Y-layer using the weight matrix W:

$$(-1\ 1\ 0\ 1\ -1\ 0\ 1\ 0\ 0\ 1\ -1\ 0\ 0\ 0\ 1)$$

$$\begin{matrix} 0 & -2 \\ 0 & 2 \\ 2 & 0 \\ 0 & 2 \\ 0 & -2 \\ -2 & 0 \\ 0 & 2 \\ -2 & 0 \\ -2 & 0 \\ 0 & 2 \\ 0 & -2 \\ -2 & 0 \\ -2 & 0 \\ 2 & 0 \\ 0 & 2 \end{matrix}$$

$$\rightarrow (-6, 10) \rightarrow (-1, 1).$$

If this pattern is fed back to the X-layer one more time, the pattern A will be produced.

9.5 HAMMING DISTANCE

The number of different bits in two binary or bipolar vectors x_1 and x_2 is called the Hamming distance between the vectors and is denoted by $H[x_1, x_2]$. The average Hamming distance between the vectors is 1 $H[x_1, x_2]$, where n is the number of n components is each vector. The x vectors in Examples 9.1 and 9.2, namely, differ in the 3rd, 6th, 8th, 9th, 12th, 13th, and 14th positions. This gives an average Hamming distance between these vectors of 7/15. The average Hamming distance between the corresponding y vectors is 1/2.

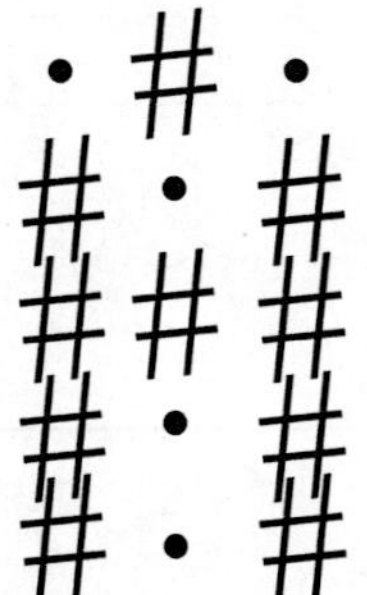

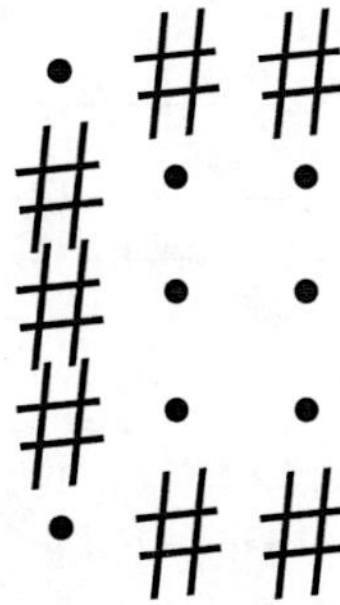

Kosko (1988) has observed that "correlation encoding" (as is used in the BAM neural net) is improved to the extent that the average Hamming distance between paris of input patterns is comparable to the average Hamming distance between the corresponding pairs of output patterns. If that is the case, input patterns that are separated by a small Hamming distance are mapped to output vectors that are also so separated, while input vectors that are separated while input vectors that are separated by a large Hamming distance go to correspondingly distant (dissimilar) output patters. This is analogous to the behavior of a continuous function.

9.6 ERASING A STORED ASSOCIATION

The complement of a bipolar vector x is denoted x^e; it is the vector formed by changing all of the 1's in vector x to -1's and vice versa. Encoding (storing the pattern pair s^c:t^c stores the same information as encoding s:t; encoding s^c:t or s:t^c will erase the encoding of s:t [Kosko, 1988].

9.7 STORAGE CAPACITY

Kosko (1988) has shown that the upper limit on the no. p of pattern pairs which can be stored and successfully retrieved is min (m, n). The substantiation for this estimate is rather heuristic. The memory storage capacity of BAM is

$$P \leq \min (m,n)$$

A more conservative heuristic capacity measure is used in a literature,

$$P = \sqrt{\min(m,n)}$$

9.8 RESULTS

The network has 49 neurons in first layer and five neurons in the second layer. With this configuration the network is capable of storing six alphabets. The alphabets have been represented as a pattern grid of size 7 × 7. From the pattern grid each alphabet is obtained in the form of a vector with entries 1 and -1. All the alphabets in the form vector **a** and its associated output as vector **b** is stored. Weight matrix is obtained by taking inner product of **a** and **b**. The network has been tested for A, I, L, M, X, and P. The network gives the correct associated output when these characters are given at the time of testing. The result has been shown in table 9.1.

Table 9.1

Character	Input	Output
A	a = [–1–1111–1–1–11–1–11–11–1–1–1–1–111111111–1–1–1–1–111–1 –1–1–1–111–1–1–1–1–11] b = [–1–1–1–11]	–1–1–1–11
I	a = [–111111–1–1–1–11–1–1–1–1–1–11–1–1–1–1–1–11–1–1–1–1–1–11 –1–1–1–1–1–11–1–1–1–111111-1] b = [–11–1–11]	–11–1–11
L	a = [1–1–1–1–1–1–11–1–1–1–1–1–11–1–1–1–1–1–11–1–1–1–1–1–11–1 –1–1–1–1–11–1–1–1–1–1–1111111] b = [–111–1–1]	–111–1–1
M	a = [1–1–1–1–1–1111–1–1–1111–11–11–111–1–11–1–111–1–1–1–1–11–1 –1–1–1–111–1–1–1–1–11] b = [–111–11]	–111–11
P	a = [11111–1–11–1–1–1–11–11–1–1–1–1–111–1–1–1–11–111111–1–11–1 –1–1–1–1–11–1–1–1–1–1–1] b = [1–1–1–1–1]	1–1–1–1–1
x	a = [1–1–1–1–1–11–11–1–1–11–1–1–11–11–1–1–1–1–11–1–1–1–1–11-11 –1–1–11–1–1–11–11–1–1–1–1–11] b = [11–1–1–1]	11–1–1–1

9.9 MERITS AND DEMERITS

In BAM, a distorted input pattern may also cause correct heteroassociation at the output. The logical symmetry of interconnection severely hampers the efficiency of BAM in pattern storage and recall capability. It also limits their use for knowledge representation and inference. There is limitation on number of pattern pairs, which can be stored and successfully retrieved.

EXERCISES

1. What is bidirectional associative memory?
2. Explain the architecture of BAM network?
3. Write an algorithm for discrete BAM?
4. Write an algorithm for continuous BAM?
5. Explain various application of BAM network?
6. What do you mean by hamming distance?
7. Explain the memory storage of BAM?
8. What are the merits and demerits of BAM?

CHAPTER 10

Case Studies

CASE STUDY 1–SPEECH RECOGNITION

10.1 INTRODUCTION

Speech is a natural mode of communication for people. We learn all the relevant skills during early childhood, without instruction, and we continue to rely on speech communication throughout our lives. It comes so naturally to us that we don't realize how complex a phenomenon speech is. The human vocal tract and articulators are biological organs with nonlinear properties, whose operation is not just under conscious control but also affected by factors ranging from gender to upbringing to emotional state. As a result, vocalizations can vary widely in terms of their accent, pronunciation, articulation, roughness, nasality, pitch, volume, and speed; moreover, during transmission, our irregular speech patterns can be further distorted by background noise and echoes, as well as electrical characteristics (if telephones or other electronic equipment are used). All these sources of variability make speech recognition, even more than speech generation, a very complex problem.

What makes people so good at recognizing speech? Intriguingly, the human brain is known to be wired differently than a conventional computer; in fact it operates under a radically different computational paradigm. While conventional computers use a very fast & complex central processor with explicit program instructions and locally addressable memory, by contrast the human brain uses a massively parallel collection of slow & simple processing elements (neurons), densely connected by weights (synapses) whose strengths are modified with experience, directly supporting the integration of multiple constraints, and providing a distributed form of associative memory.

The brain's impressive superiority at a wide range of cognitive skills, including speech recognition, has motivated research into its novel computational paradigm since the 1940's, on the assumption that brainlike models may ultimately lead to brainlike performance on many complex tasks. This fascinating research area is now known as connectionism, or the study of artificial neural networks.

What is the current state of the art in speech recognition? This is a complex question, because a system's accuracy depends on the conditions under which it is evaluated: under sufficiently narrow conditions almost any system can attain human-like accuracy, but it's much harder to achieve good accuracy under general conditions. The conditions of evaluation - and hence the accuracy of any system - can vary along the following dimensions:

1. **Vocabulary size and confusability**: As a general rule, it is easy to discriminate among a small set of words, but error rates naturally increase as the vocabulary size grows. For example, the 10 digits "zero" to "nine" can be recognized essentially perfectly , but vocabulary sizes of 200, 5000, or 100000 may have error rates of 3%, 7%, or 45%. On the other hand, even a small vocabulary can be hard to recognize if it contains confusable words. For example, the 26 letters of the English alphabet (treated as 26 "words") are very difficult to discriminate because they contain so many confusable words (most notoriously, the E-set: "B, C, D, E, G, P, T, V, Z"); an 8% error rate is considered good for this vocabulary
2. **Speaker dependence vs. independence:** By definition, a speaker dependent system is intended for use by a single speaker, but a speaker independent system is intended for use by any speaker. Speaker independence is difficult to achieve because a system's parameters become tuned to the speaker(s) that it was trained on, and these parameters tend to be highly speaker-specific.
3. **Isolated, discontinuous, or continuous speech:** Isolated speech means single words; discontinuous speech means full sentences in which words are artificially separated by silence; and continuous speech means naturally spoken sentences. Isolated and discontinuous speech recognition is relatively easy because word boundaries are detectable and the words tend to be cleanly pronounced.
4. **Task and language constraints:** Even with a fixed vocabulary, performance will vary with the nature of constraints on the word sequences that are allowed during recognition. Some constraints may be task-dependent (for example, an airlinequerying application may dismiss the hypothesis "The apple is red"); other constraints may be semantic (rejecting "The apple is angry"), or syntactic (rejecting "Red is apple the"). Constraints are often represented by a grammar, which ideally filters out unreasonable sentences so that the speech recognizer evaluates only plausible sentences. Grammars are usually rated by their perplexity, a number that indicates the grammar's average branching factor (i.e., the number of words that can follow any given word). The difficulty of a task is more reliably measured by its perplexity than by its vocabulary size.
5. **Read vs. spontaneous speech:** Systems can be evaluated on speech that is either read from prepared scripts, or speech that is uttered spontaneously. Spontaneous speech is vastly more difficult, because it tends to be peppered with disfluencies like "uh" and "um", false starts, incomplete sentences, stuttering, coughing, and laughter; and moreover, the vocabulary is essentially unlimited, so the system must be able to deal intelligently with unknown words (e.g., detecting and flagging their presence, and adding them to the vocabulary, which may require some interaction with the user).

6. **Adverse conditions:** A system's performance can also be degraded by a range of adverse conditions. These include environmental noise (e.g., noise in a car or a factory); acoustical distortions (e.g, echoes, room acoustics); different microphones (e.g., close-speaking, omnidirectional, or telephone); limited frequency bandwidth (in telephone transmission); and altered speaking manner (shouting, whining, speaking quickly, etc.).

In order to evaluate and compare different systems under well-defined conditions, a number of standardized databases have been created with particular characteristics. For example, one database that has been widely used is the DARPA Resource Management database - a large vocabulary (1000 words), speaker-independent, continuous speech database, consisting of 4000 training sentences in the domain of naval resource management, read from a script and recorded under benign environmental conditions; testing is usually performed using a grammar with a perplexity of 60. Under these controlled conditions, state-of-the-art performance is about 97% word recognition accuracy (or less for simpler systems).

10.2 FUNDAMENTALS OF SPEECH RECOGNITION

Speech recognition is a multileveled pattern recognition task, in which acoustical signals are examined and structured into a hierarchy of subword units (e.g., phonemes), words, phrases, and sentences. Each level may provide additional temporal constraints, e.g., known word pronunciations or legal word sequences, which can compensate for errors or uncertainties at lower levels. This hierarchy of constraints can best be exploited by combining decisions probabilistically at all lower levels, and making discrete decisions only at the highest level.

The structure of a standard speech recognition system is illustrated in Figure. The elements are as follows:

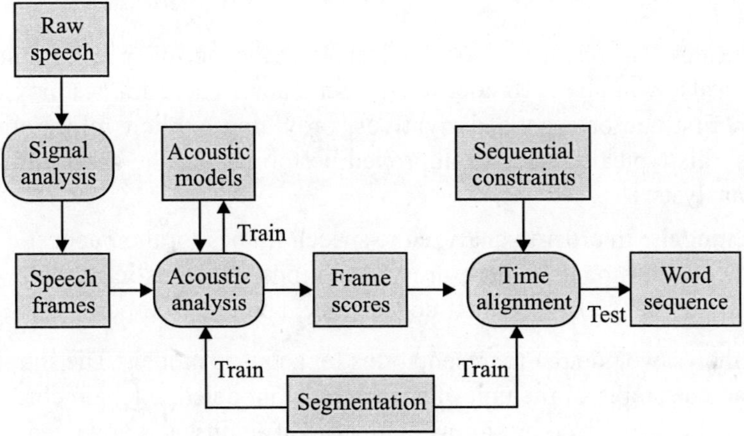

Figure10.1: Structure of a standard speech recognition system.

- **Raw speech:** Speech is typically sampled at a high frequency, e.g., 16 KHz over a microphone or 8 KHz over a telephone. This yields a sequence of amplitude values over time.
- **Signal analysis:** Raw speech should be initially transformed and compressed, in order to simplify subsequent processing. Many signal analysis techniques are available which can extract useful features and compress the data by a factor of ten without losing any important information. Among the most popular:
- Fourier analysis (FFT) yields discrete frequencies over time, which can be interpreted visually. Frequencies are often distributed using a Mel scale, which is linear in the low range but logarithmic in the high range, corresponding to physiological characteristics of the human ear.
- Perceptual Linear Prediction (PLP) is also physiologically motivated, but yields coefficients that cannot be interpreted visually.
- Linear Predictive Coding (LPC) yields coefficients of a linear equation that approximate the recent history of the raw speech values.
- Cepstral analysis calculates the inverse Fourier transform of the logarithm of the power spectrum of the signal.

  In practice, it makes little difference which technique is used1. Afterwards, procedures such as Linear Discriminant Analysis (LDA) may optionally be applied to further reduce the dimensionality of any representation, and to decorrelate the coefficients.

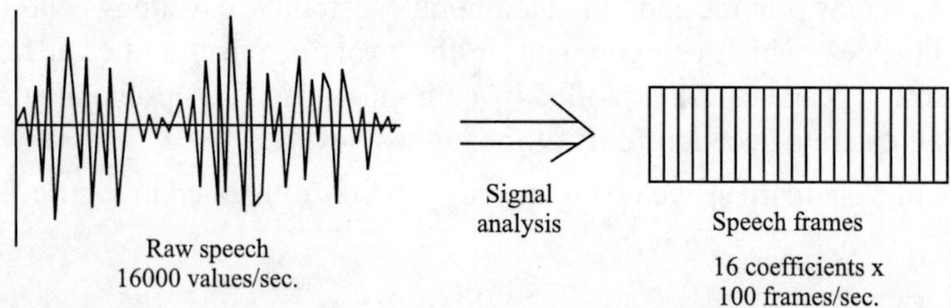

- **Speech frames:** The result of signal analysis is a sequence of speech frames, typically at 10 msec intervals, with about 16 coefficients per frame. These frames may be augmented by their own first and/or second derivatives, providing explicit information about speech dynamics; this typically leads to improved performance. The speech frames are used for acoustic analysis.
- **Acoustic models:** In order to analyze the speech frames for their acoustic content, we need a set of acoustic models. There are many kinds of acoustic models, varying in their representation, granularity, context dependence, and other properties.

Figure 10.2 shows two popular representations for acoustic models. The simplest is a template, which is just a stored sample of the unit of speech to be modeled, e.g., a recording of a word. An unknown word can be recognized by simply comparing it against all known templates, and finding the closest match. Templates have two major drawbacks: (1) they cannot model acoustic variabilities,

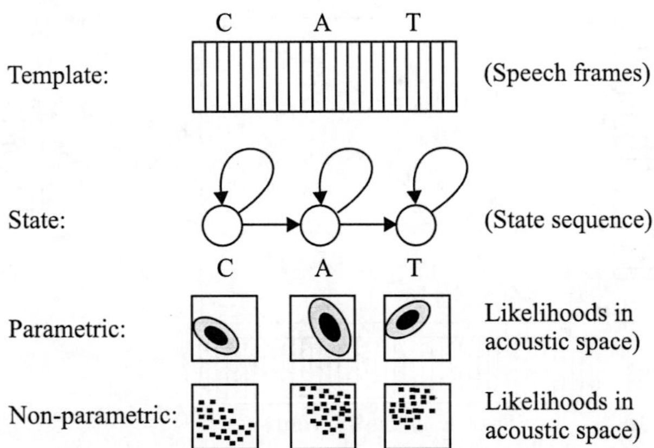

Figure 10.2: Acoustic models: template and state representations for the word "cat".

except in a coarse way by assigning multiple templates to each word; and (2) in practice they are limited to whole-word models, because it's hard to record or segment a sample shorter than a word - so templates are useful only in small systems which can afford the luxury of using whole-word models. A more flexible representation, used in larger systems, is based on trained acoustic models, or states. In this approach, every word is modeled by a sequence of trainable states, and each state indicates the sounds that are likely to be heard in that segment of the word, using a probability distribution over the acoustic space. Probability distributions can be modeled parametrically, by assuming that they have a simple shape (e.g., a Gaussian distribution) and then trying to find the parameters that describe it; or non-parametrically, by representing the distribution directly (e.g., with a histogram over a quantization of the acoustic space, or, as we shall see, with a neural network).

10.3 DYNAMIC TIME WARPING

In this section we motivate and explain the Dynamic Time Warping algorithm, one of the oldest and most important algorithms in speech recognition.

The simplest way to recognize an isolated word sample is to compare it against a number of stored word templates and determine which is the "best match". This goal is complicated by a number of factors. First, different samples of a given word will have somewhat different durations. This problem can be eliminated by simply normalizing the templates and the unknown speech so that they all have an equal duration. However, another problem is that the rate of speech may not be constant throughout the word; in other words, the optimal alignment between a template and the speech sample may be nonlinear. Dynamic Time Warping (DTW) is an efficient method for finding this optimal nonlinear alignment.

DTW is an instance of the general class of algorithms known as dynamic programming. Its time and space complexity is merely linear in the duration of the speech sample and the vocabulary size. The algorithm makes a single pass through a matrix of frame scores while computing locallyoptimized segments of the global alignment path.

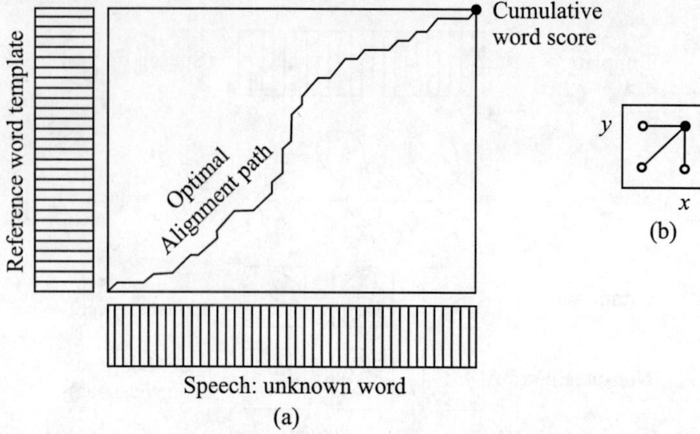

Figure 10.3: Dynamic time warping (speech recognition)

If D(x,y) is the Euclidean distance between frame x of the speech sample and frame y of the reference template, and if C(x,y) is the cumulative score along an optimal alignment path that leads to (x,y), then

$$C(x, y) = \text{MIN}\,(C(x-1,y)\,,\,C(x-1,y-1)\,,\,C(x, y-1)\,) + D(x, y)$$

The resulting alignment path may be visualized as a low valley of Euclidean distance scores, meandering through the hilly landscape of the matrix, beginning at (0, 0) and ending at the final point (X, Y). By keeping track of backpointers, the full alignment path can be recovered by tracing backwards from (X, Y). An optimal alignment path is computed for each reference word template, and the one with the lowest cumulative score is considered to be the best match for the unknown speech sample.

There are many variations on the DTW algorithm. For example, it is common to vary the local path constraints, e.g., by introducing transitions with slope 1/2 or 2, or weighting the transitions in various ways, or applying other kinds of slope constraints (Sakoe and Chiba 1978). While the reference word models are usually templates, they may be state-based models (as shown previously in Figure). When using states, vertical transitions are often disallowed (since there are fewer states than frames), and often the goal is to maximize the cumulative score, rather than to minimize it.

A particularly important variation of DTW is an extension from isolated to continuous speech. This extension is called the One Stage DTW algorithm (Ney 1984). Here the goal is to find the optimal alignment between the speech sample and the best sequence of reference words. The complexity of the extended algorithm is still linear in the length of the sample and the vocabulary size. The only modification to the basic DTW algorithm is that at the beginning of each reference word model (i.e., its first frame or state), the diagonal path is allowed to point back to the end of all reference word models in the preceding frame. Local backpointers must specify the reference word model of the preceding point, so that the optimal word sequence can be recovered by tracing backwards from the final point of the word W with the best final score. Grammars can be imposed on continuous speech recognition by restricting the allowed transitions at word boundaries.

10.4 NEURAL NETWORK APPROACHES

Because speech recognition is basically a pattern recognition problem, and because neural networks are good at pattern recognition, many early researchers naturally tried applying neural networks to speech recognition. The earliest attempts involved highly simplified tasks, e.g., classifying speech segments as voiced/unvoiced, or nasal/fricative/plosive. Success in these experiments encouraged researchers to move on to phoneme classification; this task became a proving ground for neural networks as they quickly achieved world-class results.

There are two basic approaches to speech classification using neural networks: static and dynamic, as illustrated in Figure. In static classification, the neural network sees all of the input speech at once, and makes a single decision. By contrast, in dynamic classification, the neural network sees only a small window of the speech, and this window slides over the input speech while the network makes a series of local decisions, which have to be integrated into a global decision at a later time. Static classification works well for phoneme recognition, but it scales poorly to the level of words or sentences; dynamic classification scales better.

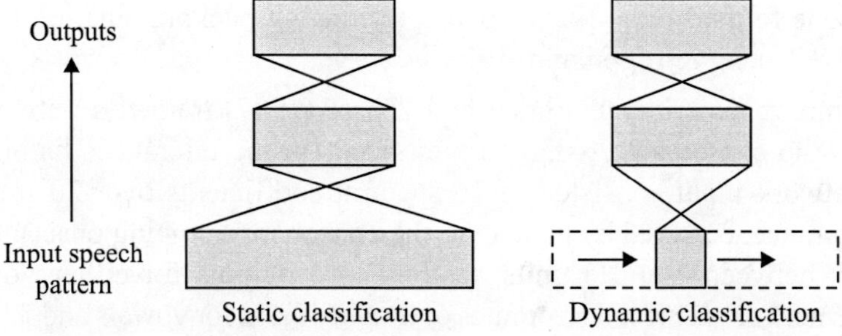

Figure 10.4: Static and dynamic approaches to classification.

Either approach may make use of recurrent connections, although recurrence is more often found in the dynamic approach.

10.4.1 Phoneme Classification

Phoneme classification can be performed with high accuracy by using either static or dynamic approaches. Here we review some typical experiments using each approach.

10.4.2 Static Approaches

A simple but elegant experiment was performed by Huang & Lippmann (1988), demonstrating that neural networks can form complex decision surfaces from speech data. They applied a multilayer perceptron with only 2 inputs, 50 hidden units, and 10 outputs, to Peterson & Barney's collection of vowels produced by men, women, & children, using the first two formants of the vowels as the input speech representation. After 50,000 iterations of training, the network produced the decision regions shown in Figure below. These decision regions are nearly optimal, resembling the decision regions that would be drawn by hand, and they yield classification accuracy comparable to that of more L

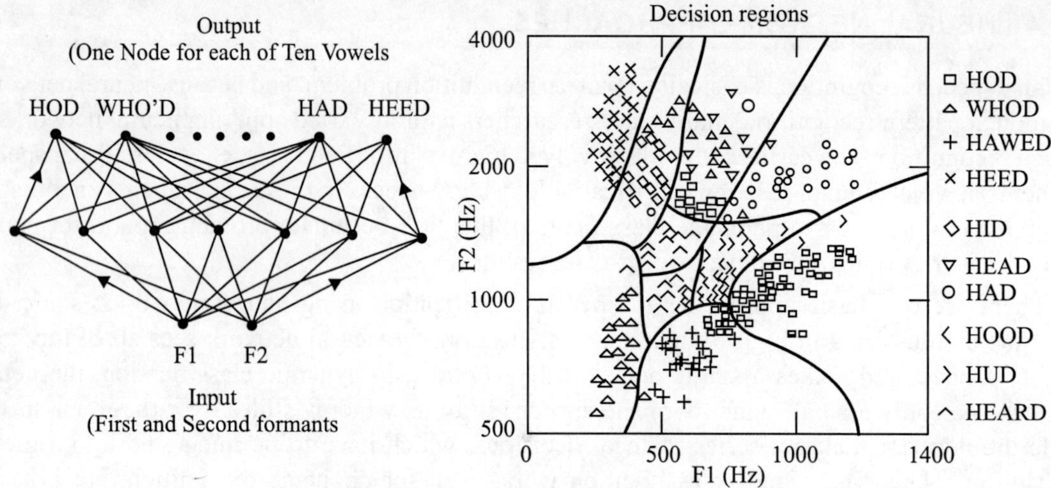

Figure 10.5: After 50,000 Iterations of training

Decision regions formed by a 2-layer perceptron using backpropagation training and vowel formant data. (From Huang & Lippmann, 1988.)

In a more complex experiment, Elman and Zipser (1987) trained a network to classify the vowels /a,i,u/ and the consonants /b,d,g/ as they occur in the utterances ba,bi,bu; da,di,du; and ga,gi,gu. Their network input consisted of 16 spectral coefficients over 20 frames (covering an entire 64 msec utterance, centered by hand over the consonant's voicing onset); this was fed into a hidden layer with between 2 and 6 units, leading to 3 outputs for either vowel or consonant classification. This network achieved error rates of roughly 0.5% for vowels and 5.0% for consonants. An analysis of the hidden units showed that they tend to be feature detectors, discriminating between important classes of sounds, such as consonants versus vowels.

Among the most difficult of classification tasks is the so-called E-set, i.e., discriminating between the rhyming English letters "B, C, D, E, G, P, T, V, Z". Burr (1988) applied a static network to this task, with very good results. His network used an input window of 20 spectral frames, automatically extracted from the whole utterance using energy information. These inputs led directly to 9 outputs representing the E-set letters. The network was trained and tested using 180 tokens from a single speaker. When the early portion of the utterance was oversampled, effectively highlighting the disambiguating features, recognition accuracy was nearly perfect.

10.4.3 Dynamic Approaches

In a seminal paper, Waibel et al (1987=1989) demonstrated excellent results for phonemean classification using a Time Delay Neural Network (TDNN), shown in Figure 10.6.

This architecture has only 3 and 5 delays in the input and hidden layer, respectively, and the final output is computed by integrating over 9 frames of phoneme activations in the second hidden layer. The TDNN's design is attractive for several reasons: its compact structure economizes on weights and forces the network to develop general feature detectors; its hierarchy of delays optimizes these feature detectors by increasing their scope at each layer; and its temporal integration at the output layer makes the network shift invariant (i.e., insensitive to the exact positioning of the speech). The TDNN was trained and tested on 2000 samples of / b,d,g/ phonemes manually excised from a database of 5260 Japanese words. The TDNN achieved an error rate of 1.5%, compared to 6.5% achieved by a simple HMM-based recognizer.

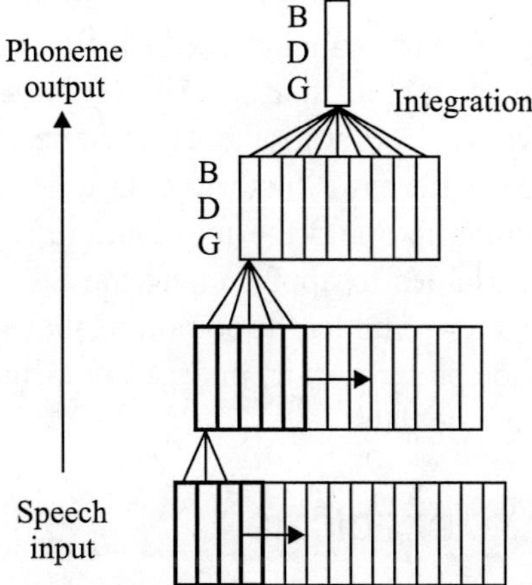

Figure 10.6: Time delay neural network

CASE STUDY 2 – STOCK MARKET PREDICTION

10.5 INTRODUCTION

It is nowadays a common notion that vast amounts of capital are traded through the Stock Markets all around the world. National economies are strongly linked and heavily influenced of the performance of their Stock Markets. Moreover, recently the Markets have become a more accessible investment tool, not only for strategic investors but for common people as well. Consequently they are not only related to macroeconomic parameters, but they influence everyday life in a more direct way. Therefore they constitute a mechanism which has important and direct social impacts. The characteristic that all Stock Markets have in common is the uncertainty, which is related with their short and long-term future state. This feature is undesirable for the investor but it is also unavoidable whenever the Stock Market is selected as the investment tool. The best that one can do is to try to reduce this uncertainty. Stock Market Prediction (or Forecasting) is one of the instruments in this process.

The Stock Market prediction task divides researchers and academics into two groups those who believe that we can devise mechanisms to predict the market and those who believe that the market is efficient and whenever new information comes up the market absorbs it by correcting itself, thus there is no space for prediction (EMH). Furthermore they believe that the Stock Market follows a Random Walk, which implies that the best prediction you can have about tomorrow's value is today's value.

In literature a number of different methods have been applied in order to predict Stock Market returns. These methods can be grouped in four major categories: (i) Technical Analysis Methods, (ii) Fundamental Analysis Methods, (iii) Traditional Time Series Forecasting and (iv) Machine Learning Methods. Technical analysts, known as chartists, attempt to predict the market by tracing patterns that come from the study of charts which describe historic data of the market. Fundamental analysts study the intrinsic value of an stock and they invest on it if they estimate that its current value is lower that its intrinsic value. In Traditional Time Series forecasting an attempt to create linear prediction models to trace patterns in historic data takes place. These linear models are divided in two categories: the univariate and the multivariate regression models, depending on whether they use one of more variables to approximate the Stock Market time series. Finally a number of methods have been developed under the common label Machine Learning these methods use a set of samples and try to trace patterns in it (linear or non-linear) in order to approximate the underlying function that generated the data.

10.6 STOCK MARKETS AND PREDICTION

Investment Theories: An investment theory suggests what parameters one should take into account before placing his (or her) capital on the market. Traditionally the investment community accepts two major theories: the Firm Foundation and the Castles in the Air. Reference to these theories allows us to understand how the market is shaped, or in other words how the investors think and react. It is this sequence of 'thought and reaction' by the investors that defines the capital allocation and thus the level of the market.

There is no doubt that the majority of the people related to stock markets is trying to achieve profit. Profit comes by investing in stocks that have a good future (short or long term future). Thus what they are trying to accomplish one way or the other is to predict 16 the future of the market. But what determines this future? The way that people invest their money is the answer; and people invest money based on the information they hold. Therefore we have the following schema:

INformation ! Investor ! Market Level

The factors that are under discussion on this schema are: the content of the 'Information' component and the way that the 'Investor' reacts when having this info.

On the other hand, according to the Castles in the Air theory the investors are triggered by information that is related to other investors' behavior. So for this theory the only concern that the investor should have is to buy today with the price of 20 and sell tomorrow with the price of 30, no matter what the intrinsic value of the firm he (or she) invests on is.

Prediction Methods: The prediction of the market is without doubt an interesting task. In the literature there are a number of methods applied to accomplish this task. These methods use various approaches, ranging from highly informal ways (e.g. the study of a chart with the fluctuation of the market) to more formal ways (e.g. linear or non-linear regressions). We have categorized these techniques as follows:

- Technical Analysis Methods
- Fundamental Analysis Methods
- Traditional Time Series Prediction Methods
- Machine Learning Methods

The criterion to this categorization is the type of tools and the type of data that each method is using in order to predict the market. What is common to these techniques is that they are used to predict and thus benefit from the market's future behavior.

Technical Analysis: "Technical analysis is the method of predicting the appropriate time to buy or sell a stock used by those believing in the castles-in-the-air view of stock pricing". The idea behind technical analysis is that share prices move in trends dictated by the constantly changing attributes of investors in response to different forces. Using technical data such as price, volume, highest and lowest prices per trading period the technical analyst uses charts to predict future stock movements. Price charts are used to detect trends, these trends are assumed to be based on supply and demand issues which often have cyclical or noticeable patterns. From the study of these charts trading rules are extracted and used in the market environment. The technical analysts are known and as 'chartists'. Most chartists believe that the market is only 10 percent logical and 90 percent psychological. The chartist's belief is that a careful study of what the other investors are doing will shed light on what the crowed is likely to do in the future.

This is a very popular approach used to predict the market, which has been heavily criticized. The major point of criticism is that the extraction of trading rules from the study of charts is highly subjective therefore different analysts might extract different trading rules by studying the same charts. Although it is possible to use this methodology to predict the market on daily basis we will not follow this approach on this study due to its subjective character.

Fundamental Antalysis: "Fundamental analysis is the technique of applying the tenets of the firm foundation theory to the selection of individual stocks". The analysts that use this method of prediction use fundamental data in order to have a clear picture of the firm (industry or market) they will choose to invest on. They are aiming to compute the 'real' value of the asset that they will invest in and they determine this value by studying variables such as the growth, the dividend payout, the interest rates, the risk of investment, the sales level, the tax rates an so on. Their objective is to calculate the intrinsic value of an asset (e.g. of a stock). Since they do so they apply a simple trading rule. If the intrinsic 21 value of the asset is higher than the value it holds in the market, invest in it. If not, consider it a bad investment and avoid it. The fundamental analysts believe that the market is defined 90 percent by logical and 10 percent by physiological factors. This type of analysis is not possible to fit in the objectives of our study. The reason for this is that the data it uses in order to determine the intrinsic value of an asset does not change on daily basis. Therefore fundamental analysis is helpful for predicting the market only in a long-term basis.

Traditional Time Series Prediction: The Traditional Time Series Prediction analyzes historic data and attempts to approximate future values of a time series as a linear combination of these historic data. In econometrics there are two basic types of time series forecasting: univariate (simple regression) and multivariate (multivariate regression). These types of regression models are the most common tools used in econometrics to predict time series. The way they are applied in practice is that firstly a set of factors that influence (or more specific is assumed that influence) the series under prediction is formed. These factors are the explanatory variables xi of the prediction model.

Then a mapping between their values xit and the values of the time series yt (y is the to-be explained variable) is done, so that pairs {xit , yt} are formed. These pairs are used to define the importance of each explanatory variable in the formulation of the to-be explained variable. In other words the linear combination of xi that approximates in an optimum way y is defined. Univariate models are based on one explanatory variable (I = 1) while multivariate models use more than one variable (I > 1). Regression models have been used to predict stock market time series.

Machine Learning Methods: Several methods for inductive learning have been developed under the common label "Machine Learning". All these methods use a set of samples to generate an approximation of the underling function that generated the data. The aim is to draw conclusions from these samples in such way that when unseen data are presented to a model it is possible to infer the to-be explained variable from these data. The methods we discuss here are: The Nearest Neighbor and the Neural Networks Techniques.

10.7 PREDICTION USING NEURAL NETWORKS

The experiment consisted of three phases. In the first phase a genetic algorithm (GA) searched the space of NNs with different structures and resulted a generation with the fittest of all networks searched based on a metric which was either: TheilA or TheilB or TheilC or MAE. The GA search was repeated three times for each metric. Then the best three networks were selected from each repetition of the GA search and for each one of the metrics.

The output of the first phase was a set of thirtysix network structures. In the second phase for each one of the thirty-six resulting network structures we applied the following procedure. We trained (on Training1 set) and validated (on Validation1 set) the network. Then we used the indicated number of epochs from the validation procedure and based on it we retrained the network on the Training1 plus the Validation1 set. Finally we tested the performance of the network on unseen data (Validation2 set).

This procedure was repeated 50 times for each network structure for random initializations of its weights. From the nine networks for each performance statistic, we selected the most stable in terms of standard deviation of their performance. Thus the output of the second phase was a set of four network structures. During the third phase for each one of these four networks we applied the following procedure 50 times. We trained each network on the first half of the Training Set and we used the remaining half for validation. Then, using the indicated epochs by the validation procedure, we retrained the network on the complete Training Set. Finally we tested the network on the Test Set calculating all four metrics.The performance for each network on each metric was measured again in terms of standard deviation and mean of its performance over 50 times that it was trained, validated and tested.

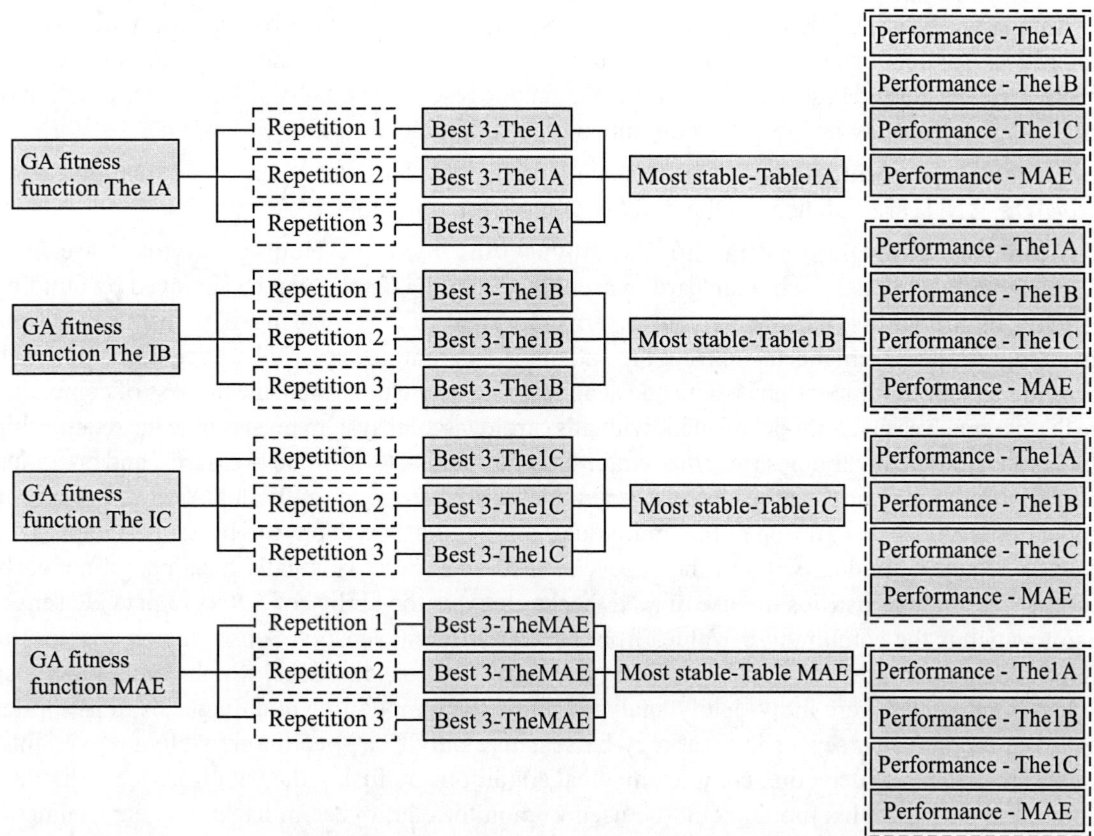

10.8 NEURAL NETWORKS IN MEDICINE

Medicine has always benefited from the forefront of technology. Technology advances like computers, lasers, ultrasonic imaging, etc. have boosted medicine to extraordinary levels of achievement. Artificial Neural Networks (ANN) is currently the next promising area of interest. It is believed that neural networks will have extensive application to biomedical problems in the next few years. Already, it has been successfully applied to various areas of medicine, such as diagnostic systems, biochemical analysis, image analysis, and drug development.

Diagnostic systems: ANNs are extensively used in diagnostic systems. They are normally used to detect cancer and heart problems. The benefits of using ANNs is that they are not affected by factors such as fatigue, working conditions and emotional state.

Biochemical Analysis: ANNs are used in a wide variety of analytical chemistry applications. In medicine, ANNs have been used to analyse blood and urine samples, track glucose levels in diabetics, determine ion levels in body fluids, and detect pathological conditions such as tuberculosis.

Image analysis: ANNs are used in the analysis of medical images from a variety of imaging modalities. Applications in this area include tumour detection in ultra-sonograms, classification of chest x-rays, tissue and vessel classification in magnetic resonance images (MRI), determination of skeletal age from x-ray images, and determination of brain maturation.

Drug development: ANNs are used as tools in the development of drugs for treating cancer and AIDS. ANNs are also used in the process of modelling biomolecules.

Modeling and Diagnosing the Cardiovascular System: Neural Networks are used experimentally to model the human cardiovascular system. Diagnosis can be achieved by building a model of the cardiovascular system of an individual and comparing it with the real time physiological measurements taken from the patient. If this routine is carried out regularly, potential harmful medical conditions can be detected at an early stage and thus make the process of combating the disease much easier. A model of an individual's cardiovascular system must mimic the relationship among physiological variables (i.e., heart rate, systolic and diastolic blood pressures, and breathing rate) at different physical activity levels. If a model is adapted to an individual, then it becomes a model of the physical condition of that individual. The simulator will have to be able to adapt to the features of any individual without the supervision of an expert. This calls for a neural network. Another reason that justifies the use of ANN technology, is the ability of ANNs to provide sensor fusion which is the combining of values from several different sensors. Sensor fusion enables the ANNs to learn complex relationships among the individual sensor values, which would otherwise be lost if the values were individually analysed. In medical modelling and diagnosis, this implies that even though each sensor in a set may be sensitive only to a specific physiological variable, ANNs are capable of detecting complex medical conditions by fusing the data from the individual biomedical sensors. This model could be used to monitor employees in hazardous environments like fire-fighters. The system could be used to determine whether firemen have recovered sufficiently from the last inhalations of smoke to be allowed to enter smoke-filled environments again.

The advantages that such a system can offer are obvious. People can be checked for heart diseases quickly and painlessly and thus detecting any disease at an early stage. Of course, the system doesn't eliminate the need for doctors since a human expert is more reliable.

Electronic Noses: ANNs are used experimentally to implement electronic noses. Electronic noses have several potential applications in telemedicine. Telemedicine is the practice of medicine over long distances via a communication link. The electronic nose would identify odours in the remote surgical environment. These identified odours would then be electronically transmitted to another site where an odour generation system would recreate them. Because the sense of smell can be an important sense to the surgeon, telesmell would enhance telepresent surgery.

Pattern Recognition of Pathology Images: Pathology is an imaging technique in medicine which deals with the nature of disease (structural and functional changes in tissue). Its need of colour and high resolution makes the use of digital image technology very difficult to implement.

Pattern recognition is an idea of classifying input data into identifiable classes by use of significant feature attributes of the data (sample), where the feature attributes are extracted from a background of irrelevant detail.

Neural Networks are used in pattern recognition because of their ability to learn and to store knowledge. Because of their 'parallel' nature can achieve, ANNs can achieve very high computation rates which is vital in application like telemedicine.

Instant physician: An application developed in the mid-1980s called the "instant physician" trained an autoassociative memory neural network to store a large number of medical records, each of which includes information on symptoms, diagnosis, and treatment for a particular case. After training, the net can be presented with input consisting of a set of symptoms; it will then find the full stored pattern that represents the "best" diagnosis and treatment.

Conclusion: ANNs have a lot to offer to modern medicine. At the moment they are mainly used for pattern recognition using images but experiments are being done in using ANNs to model parts of the human body. The high computation rates of ANNs are vital to telemedicine which is a 'hot' research area at the moment. Neural networks will never replace human experts but they can help in screening and can be used by experts to double-check their diagnosis.

PART - II
Fuzzy Logic and Genetic Algorithm

11. Introduction to Fuzzy System
12. Fuzzy Logic
13. Classical Sets and Fuzzy Sets
14. Fuzzy Relations, Fuzzy Graphs, and Fuzzy Arithmetic
15. Fuzzy If-then Rules
16. Applications of Fuzzy Logic
17. Neuro-fuzzy Systems
18. Genetic Algorithm

CHAPTER 11

Introduction to Fuzzy System

11.1 INTRODUCTION

The past few years have witnessed a rapid growth in the number and variety of applications of fuzzy logic (FL). FL techniques have been used in image-understanding applications such as detection of edges, feature extraction, classification, and clustering. Fuzzy logic poses the ability to mimic the human mind to effectively employ modes of reasoning that are approximate rather than exact. In traditional hard computing, decisions or actions are based on precision, certainty, and vigor. Precision and certainty carry a cost. In soft computing, tolerance and impression are explored in decision making. The exploration of the tolerance for imprecision and uncertainty underlies the remarkable human ability to understand distorted speech, decipher sloppy handwriting, comprehend nuances of natural language, summarize text, and recognize and classify images. With FL, we can specify mapping rules in terms of words rather than numbers. Computing with the words explores imprecision and tolerance. Another basic concept in FL is the fuzzy if–then rule. Although rule-based systems have a long history of use in artificial intelligence, what is missing in such systems is machinery for dealing with fuzzy consequents or fuzzy antecedents. In most applications, an FL solution is a translation of a human solution. Thirdly, FL can model nonlinear functions of arbitrary complexity to a desired degree of accuracy. FL is a convenient way to map an input space to an output space. FL is one of the tools used to model a multiinput, multioutput system.

Soft computing includes fuzzy logic, neural networks, probabilistic reasoning, and genetic algorithms. Today, techniques or a combination of techniques from all these areas are used to design an intelligence system. Neural networks provide algorithms for learning, classification, and optimization, whereas fuzzy logic deals with issues such as forming impressions and reasoning on a semantic or linguistic level. Probabilistic reasoning deals with uncertainty. Although there are substantial areas of overlap between neural networks, FL, and probabilistic reasoning, in general they are complementary rather than competitive. Recently, many intelligent systems called neuro fuzzy systems have been used. There are many ways to combine neural networks and FL techniques. Before doing so, however, it is necessary to understand basic ideas in the design of FL techniques. In this chapter, we will introduce FL concepts such as fuzzy sets and their properties, FL operators, hedges, fuzzy proposition and rule-based systems, fuzzy maps and inference engine, defuzzification methods, and the design of an FL decision system.

Fuzzy logic is a form of multi-valued logic derived from fuzzy set theory to deal with reasoning that is approximate rather than precise. In contrast with binary sets having binary logic, also known as crisp logic, the fuzzy logic variables may have a membership value of only 0 or 1. Just as in fuzzy set theory with fuzzy logic the set membership values can range (inclusively) between 0 and 1, in fuzzy logic the degree of truth of a statement can range between 0 and 1 and is not constrained to the two truth values {true (1), false (0)} as in classic propositional logic. And when linguistic variables are used, these degrees may be managed by specific functions. Fuzzy logic is an approach to computing based on "degrees of truth" rather than the usual "true or false" (1 or 0) Boolean logic on which the modern computer is based. The idea of fuzzy logic was first advanced by Dr. Lotfi Zadeh of the University of California at Berkeley in the 1960s. Dr. Zadeh was working on the problem of computer understanding of natural language. Natural language (like most other activities in life and indeed the universe) is not easily translated into the absolute terms of 0 and 1. (Whether everything is ultimately describable in binary terms is a philosophical question worth pursuing, but in practice much data we might want to feed a computer is in some state in between and so, frequently, are the results of computing.)

Fuzzy logic includes 0 and 1 as extreme cases of truth (or "the state of matters" or "fact") but also includes the various states of truth in between so that, for example, the result of a comparison between two things could be not "tall" or "short" but ".38 of tallness." Fuzzy logic seems closer to the way our brains work. We aggregate data and form a number of partial truths which we aggregate further into higher truths which in turn, when certain thresholds are exceeded, cause certain further results such as motor reaction. A similar kind of process is used in artificial computer neural network and expert systems.

11.2 THE CASE FOR IMPRECISION

Our understanding of most physical processes is based largely on imprecise human reasoning. This imprecision (when compared to the precise quantities required by computers) is nonetheless a form of information that can be quite useful to humans. The ability to embed such reasoning in hitherto intractable and complex problems is the criterion by which the efficacy of fuzzy logic is judged. Undoubtedly this ability cannot solve problems that require precision – problems such as shooting precision laser beams over tens of kilometers in space; milling machine components to accuracies of parts per billion; or focusing a microscopic electron beam on a specimen the size of a nanometer. The impact of fuzzy logic in these areas might be years away, if ever. But not many human problems require such precision – problems such as parking a car, backing up a trailer, navigating a car among others on a freeway, washing clothes, controlling traffic at intersections, judging beauty contestants, and a preliminary understanding of a complex system. Requiring precision in engineering models and products translates to requiring high cost and long lead times in production and development. For other than simple systems, expense is proportional to precision: more precision entails higher cost. When considering the use of fuzzy logic for a given problem, an engineer or scientist should ponder the need for exploiting the tolerance for imprecision. Not only does high precision dictate high costs but also it entails low tractability in a problem. For example the "traveling sales representative" problem. In this classic optimization problem a sales representative wants to minimize total distance traveled by considering various itineraries and schedules between a series of cities on a particular trip. For a small number of cities, the problem is a trivial exercise in enumerating all the possibilities and choosing the shortest route. As the number of cities continues to grow, the problem quickly approaches a combinatorial explosion impossible to solve through an exhaustive search, even with a computer. For example, for 100 cities there are $100 \times 99 \times 98 \times 97 \times \cdots \times 2 \times 1$, or about 10200, possible routes to consider! No computers exist today that can solve this problem through a brute-force enumeration of all the possible routes. There are real, practical problems analogous to the traveling sales representative problem. For example, such problems arise in the fabrication of circuit boards, where precise lasers drill hundreds of thousands of holes in the board. Deciding in which order to drill the holes (where the board moves under a stationary laser) so as to minimize drilling time is a traveling sales representative problem. Thus, algorithms have been developed to solve the traveling sales representative problem in an optimal sense; that is, the exact answer is not guaranteed but an optimum answer is achievable – the optimality is measured as a percent accuracy, with 0% representing the exact answer and accuracies larger than zero representing answers of lesser accuracy. Suppose we consider a signal routing problem analogous to the traveling sales representative problem where we want to find the optimum path (i.e., minimum travel time) between 100,000 nodes in a network to accuracy within 1% of the exact solution; this requires significant CPU time on a supercomputer. If we take the same problem and increase the precision requirement a modest amount to accuracy of 0.75%, the computing time approaches a few months! Now suppose we can live with an accuracy of 3.5% (quite a bit more accurate than most problems we deal with), and we want to consider an order-of-magnitude more nodes in the network, say 1,000,000; the computing time for this problem is on the order of several minutes. This remarkable reduction in cost (translating time to dollars) is due solely to the acceptance of a lesser degree of precision in the optimum solution. Can humans live with a little less precision? The answer to this question depends on the situation, but for the vast majority of problems we deal with every day the answer is a resounding yes.

11.3 AN HISTORICAL PERSPECTIVE

From an historical point of view the issue of uncertainty has not always been embraced within the scientific community. In the traditional view of science, uncertainty represents an undesirable state, a state that must be avoided at all costs. This was the state of science until the late nineteenth century when physicists realized that Newtonian mechanics did not address problems at the molecular level. Newer methods, associated with statistical mechanics, were developed which recognized that statistical averages could replace the specific manifestations of microscopic entities. These statistical quantities, which summarized the activity of large numbers of microscopic entities, could then be connected in a model with appropriate macroscopic variables. Now, the role of Newtonian mechanics and its underlying calculus which considered no uncertainty was replaced with statistical mechanics which could be described by a probability theory – a theory which could capture a form of uncertainty, the type generally referred to as random uncertainty. After the development of statistical mechanics there has been a gradual trend in science during the past century to consider the influence of uncertainty on problems, and to do so in an attempt to make our models more robust, in the sense that we achieve credible solutions and at the same time quantify the amount of uncertainty. Of course, the leading theory in quantifying uncertainty in scientific models from the late nineteenth century until the late twentieth century had been probability theory. However, the gradual evolution of the expression of uncertainty using probability theory was challenged, first in 1937 by Max Black, with his studies in vagueness, then with the introduction of fuzzy sets by Lotfi Zadeh in 1965.

Zadeh's work [1965] had a profound influence on the thinking about uncertainty because it challenged not only probability theory as the sole representation for uncertainty, but the very foundations upon which probability theory was based: classical binary (two-valued) logic. Probability theory dominated the mathematics of uncertainty for over five centuries. Probability concepts date back to the 1500s, to the time of Cardano when gamblers recognized the rules of probability in games of chance. The concepts were still very much in the limelight in 1685, when the Bishop of Wells wrote a paper that discussed a problem in determining the truth of statements made by two witnesses who were both known to be unreliable to the extent that they only tell the truth with probabilities p1 and p2, respectively.

The Bishop's answer to this was based on his assumption that the two witnesses were independent sources of information [Lindley, 1987]. Probability theory was initially developed in the eighteenth century in such landmark treatises as Jacob Bernoulli's Ars Conjectandi (1713) and Abraham DeMoiver's Doctrine of Chances (1718, 2nd edition 1738). Later in that century a small number of articles appeared in the periodical literature that would have a profound effect on the field. Most notable of these were Thomas Bayes's "An essay towards solving a problem in the doctrine of chances" (1763) and Pierre Simon Laplace's formulation of the axioms relating to games of chance, "Memoire sur la probabilite des causes par les evenemens" (1774). Laplace, only 25 years old at the time he began his work in 1772, wrote the first substantial article in mathematical statistics prior to the nineteenth century. Despite the fact that Laplace, at the same time, was heavily engaged in mathematical astronomy, his memoir was an explosion of ideas that provided the roots for modern decision theory, Bayesian inference with nuisance parameters (historians claim that Laplace did not know of Bayes's earlier work), and the asymptotic approximations of posterior distributions [Stigler, 1986].

By the time of Newton, physicists and mathematicians were formulating different theories of probability. The most popular ones remaining today are the relative frequency theory and the subjectivist or personalistic theory. The later development was initiated by Thomas Bayes (1763), who articulated his very powerful theorem for the assessment of subjective probabilities. The theorem specified that a human's degree of belief could be subjected to an objective, coherent, and measurable mathematical framework within subjective probability theory. In the early days of the twentieth century Researcher developed a formal framework for a conditional probability theory.

The twentieth century saw the first developments of alternatives to probability theory and to classical Aristotelian logic as paradigms to address more kinds of uncertainty than just the random kind. Jan Lukasiewicz developed a multivalued, discrete logic (circa 1930). In the 1960's Arthur Dempster developed a theory of evidence which, for the first time, included an assessment of ignorance, or the absence of information. In 1965 Lotfi Zadeh introduced his seminal idea in a continuous-valued logic that he called fuzzy set theory. In the 1970s Glenn Shafer extended Dempster's work to produce a complete theory of evidence dealing with information from more than one source, and Lotfi Zadeh illustrated a possibility theory resulting from special cases of fuzzy sets. Later in the 1980s other investigators showed a strong relationship between evidence theory, probability theory, and possibility theory with the use of what was called fuzzy measures [Klir and Wierman, 1996], and what is now being termed monotone measures.

Uncertainty can be thought of in an epistemological sense as being the inverse of information. Information about a particular engineering or scientific problem may be incomplete, imprecise, fragmentary, unreliable, vague, contradictory, or deficient in some other way [Klir and Yuan, 1995]. When we acquire more and more information about a problem, we become less and less uncertain about its formulation and solution. Problems that are characterized by very little information are said to be ill-posed, complex, or not sufficiently known. These problems are imbued with a high degree of uncertainty. Uncertainty can be manifested in many forms: it can be fuzzy (not sharp, unclear, imprecise, approximate), it can be vague (not specific, amorphous), it can be ambiguous (too many choices, contradictory), it can be of the form of ignorance (dissonant, not knowing something), or it can be a form due to natural variability (conflicting, random, chaotic, unpredictable). Many other linguistic labels have been applied to these various forms, but for now these shall suffice. Zadeh [2002] posed some simple examples of these forms in terms of a person's statements about when they shall return to a current place in time. The statement "I shall return soon" is vague, whereas the statement "I shall return in a few minutes" is fuzzy; the former is not known to be associated with any unit of time (seconds, hours, days), and the latter is associated with an uncertainty that is at least known to be on the order of minutes. The phrase, "I shall return within 2 minutes of 6pm" involves an uncertainty which has a quantifiable imprecision; probability theory could address this form.

Vagueness can be used to describe certain kinds of uncertainty associated with linguistic information or intuitive information. Examples of vague information are that the data quality is "good," or that the transparency of an optical element is "acceptable." Moreover, in terms of semantics, even the terms vague and fuzzy cannot be generally considered synonyms, as explained by Zadeh [1995]: "usually a vague proposition is fuzzy, but the converse is not generally true."

Discussions about vagueness started with a famous work by the philosopher Max Black. Black [1937] defined a vague proposition as a proposition where the possible states (of the proposition) are not clearly defined with regard to inclusion. For example, consider the proposition that a person is young. Since the term "young" has different interpretations to different individuals, we cannot decisively determine the age(s) at which an individual is young versus the age(s) at which an individual is not considered to be young. Thus, the proposition is vaguely defined. Classical (binary) logic does not hold under these circumstances, therefore we must establish a different method of interpretation. Max Black, in writing his 1937 essay "Vagueness: An exercise in logical analysis" first cites remarks made by the ancient philosopher Plato about uncertainty in geometry, then embellishes on the writings of Bertrand Russell (1923) who emphasized that "all traditional logic habitually assumes that precise symbols are being employed." With these great thoughts as a prelude to his own arguments, he proceeded to produce his own, now-famous quote:

It is a paradox, whose importance familiarity fails to diminish, that the most highly developed and useful scientific theories are ostensibly expressed in terms of objects never encountered in experience. The line traced by a draftsman, no matter how accurate, is seen beneath the microscope as a kind of corrugated trench, far removed from the ideal line of pure geometry. And the "point-planet" of astronomy, the "perfect gas" of thermodynamics, or the "purespecies" of genetics are equally remote from exact realization. Indeed the unintelligibility at the atomic or subatomic level of the notion of a rigidly demarcated boundary shows that such objects not merely are not but could not be encountered. While the mathematician constructs a theory in terms of "perfect" objects, the experimental scientist observes objects of which the properties demanded by theory are and can, in the very nature of measurement, be only approximately true.

More recently, in support of Black's work, Quine [1981] states:

Diminish a table, conceptually, molecule by molecule: when is a table not a table? No stipulations will avail us here, however arbitrary. If the term 'table' is to be reconciled with bivalence, we must posit an exact demarcation, exact to the last molecule, even though we cannot specify it. We must hold that there are physical objects, coincident except for one molecule, such that one is a table and the other is not.

Bruno de Finetti [1974], publishing in his landmark book Theory of Probability, gets his readers' attention quickly by proclaiming, "Probability does not exist; it is a subjective description of a person's uncertainty. We should be normative about uncertainty and not descriptive." He further emphasizes that the frequentist view of probability (objectivist view) "requires individual trials to be equally probable and stochastically independent." In discussing the difference between possibility and probability he states, "The logic of certainty furnishes us with the range of possibility (and the possible has no gradations); probability is an additional notion that one applies within the range of possibility, thus giving rise to graduations ('more or less' probable) that are meaningless in the logic of uncertainty."

In his book, de Finetti gives us warnings:

"The calculus of probability can say absolutely nothing about reality," and in referring to the dangers implicit in attempts to confuse certainty with high probability, he states We have to stress this point because these attempts assume many forms and are always dangerous. In one sentence: to make a mistake of this kind leaves one inevitably faced with all sorts of fallacious arguments and contradictions whenever an attempt is made to state, on the basis of probabilistic considerations, that something must occur, or that its occurrence confirms or disproves some probabilistic assumptions.

In a discussion about the use of such vague terms as "very probable" or "practically certain," or "almost impossible," de Finetti states:

The field of probability and statistics is then transformed into a Tower of Babel, in which only the most naive amateur claims to understand what he says and hears, and this because, in a language devoid of convention, the fundamental distinctions between what is certain and what is not, and between what is impossible and what is not, are abolished. Certainty and impossibility then become confused with high or low degrees of a subjective probability, which is itself denied precisely by this falsification of the language. On the contrary, the preservation of a clear, terse distinction between certainty and uncertainty, impossibility and possibility, is the unique and essential precondition for making meaningful statements (which could be either right or wrong), whereas the alternative transforms every sentence into a nonsense.

11.4 UNCERTAINTY AND INFORMATION

Only a small portion of the knowledge (information) for a typical problem might be regarded as certain, or deterministic. Unfortunately, the vast majority of the material taught in engineering classes is based on the presumption that the knowledge involved is deterministic. Most processes are neatly and surreptitiously reduced to closed-form algorithms – equations and formulas. When students graduate, it seems that their biggest fear upon entering the real world is "forgetting the correct formula." These formulas typically describe a deterministic process, one where there is no uncertainty in the physics of the process (i.e., the right formula) and there is no uncertainty in the parameters of the process (i.e., the coefficients are known with impunity). It is only after we leave the university, it seems, that we realize we were duped in academe, and that the information we have for a particular problem virtually always contains uncertainty. For how many of our problems can we say that the information content is known absolutely, i.e., with no ignorance, no vagueness, no imprecision, no element of chance? Uncertain information can take on many different forms.

There is uncertainty that arises because of complexity; for example, the complexity in the reliability network of a nuclear reactor. There is uncertainty that arises from ignorance, from various classes of randomness, from the inability to perform adequate measurements, from lack of knowledge, or from vagueness, like the fuzziness inherent in our natural language. The nature of uncertainty in a problem is a very important point that engineers should ponder prior to their selection of an appropriate method to express the uncertainty.

Fuzzy sets provide a mathematical way to represent vagueness and fuzziness in humanistic systems. For example, suppose you are teaching your child to bake cookies and you want to give instructions about when to take the cookies out of the oven. You could say to take them out when the temperature inside the cookie dough reaches 375°F, or you could advise your child to take them out when the tops of the cookies turn light brown. Which instruction would you give? Most likely, you would use the second of the two instructions. The first instruction is too precise to implement practically; in this case precision is not useful. The vague term light brown is useful in this context and can be acted upon even by a child. We all use vague terms, imprecise information, and other fuzzy data just as easily as we deal with situations governed by chance, where probability techniques are warranted and very useful. Hence, our sophisticated computational methods should be able to represent and manipulate a variety of uncertainties. Other representations of uncertainties due to ambiguity, nonspecificity, beliefs, and ignorance are introduced in the next chapters.

11.5 FUZZY SYSTEMS

Fuzzy system was first proposed by an American professor, Lotfi A. Zadeh, in 1965 when he presented his seminal paper on "fuzzy sets." Zadeh showed that fuzzy logic unlike classical logic can realize values between false (0) and true (1). Basically, he transformed the crisp set into the continuous set. Fuzzy sets thus have movable boundaries, i.e., the elements of such sets not only represent true or false values but also represent the degree of truth or degree of falseness for each input.

In the literature sources, we can find different kinds of justification for fuzzy systems theory. Human knowledge nowadays becomes increasingly important – we gain it from experiencing the world within which we live and use our ability to reason to create order in the mass of information (i.e., to formulate human knowledge in a systematic manner). Since we are all limited in our ability to perceive the world and to profound reasoning, we find ourselves everywhere confronted by uncertainty which is a result of lack of information (lexical impression, incompleteness), in particular, inaccuracy of measurements. The other limitation factor in our desire for precision is a natural language used for describing/sharing knowledge, communication, etc. We understand core meanings of word and are able to communicate accurately to an acceptable degree, but generally we cannot precisely agree among ourselves on the single word or terms of common sense meaning. In short, natural languages are vague.

Our perception of the real world is pervaded by concepts which do not have sharply defined boundaries – for example, many, tall, much larger than, young, etc. are true only to some degree and they are false to some degree as well. These concepts (facts) can be called fuzzy or gray (vague) concepts – a human brain works with them, while computers may not do it (they reason with strings of 0s and 1s). Natural languages, which are much higher in level than programming languages, are fuzzy whereas programming languages are not. The door to the development of fuzzy computers was opened in 1985 by the design of the first logic chip by Masaki Togai and Hiroyuki Watanabe at Bell Telephone Laboratories. In the years to come fuzzy computers will employ both fuzzy hardware and fuzzy software, and they will be much closer in structure to the human brain than the present-day computers are. The entire real world is complex; it is found that the complexity arises from uncertainty in the form of ambiguity. According to Dr. Lotfi Zadeh, Principle of Compatability, the complexity, and the imprecision are correlated and adds, The closer one looks at a real world problem, the fuzzier becomes its solution (Zadeh 1973) The Fuzzy Logic tool was introduced in 1965, also by Lotfi Zadeh, and is a mathematical tool for dealing with uncertainty. It offers to a soft computing partnership the important concept of computing with words'. It provides a technique to deal with imprecision and information granularity.

The fuzzy theory provides a mechanism for representing linguistic constructs such as "many," "low," "medium," "often," "few." In general, the fuzzy logic provides an inference structure that enables appropriate human reasoning capabilities. On the contrary, the traditional binary set theory describes crisp events, events that either do or do not occur. It uses probability theory to explain if an event will occur, measuring the chance with which a given event is expected to occur. The theory of fuzzy logic is based upon the notion of relative graded membership and so are the functions of mentation and cognitive processes. The utility of fuzzy sets lies in their ability to model uncertain or ambiguous data, Figure 11.1, so often encountered in real life.

It is important to observe that there is an intimate connection between Fuzziness and Complexity. As the complexity of a task (problem), or of a system for performing that task, exceeds a certain threshold, the system must necessarily become fuzzy in nature. Zadeh, originally an engineer and systems scientist, was concerned with the rapid decline in information afforded by traditional mathematical models as the complexity of the target system increased. As he stressed, with the increasing of complexity our ability to make precise and yet significant statements about its behavior diminishes. Realworld problems (situations) are too complex, and the complexity involves the degree of uncertainty – as uncertainty increases, so does the complexity of the problem. Traditional system modeling and analysis techniques are too precise for such problems (systems), and in order to make complexity less daunting we introduce appropriate simplifications, assumptions, etc. (i.e., degree of uncertainty or Fuzziness) to achieve a satisfactory compromise between the information we have and the amount of uncertainty we are willing to accept.In this aspect, fuzzy systems theory is similar to other engineering theories, because almost all of them characterize the real world in an approximate manner.

Figure 11.1: A fuzzy logic system which accepts imprecise data and vague statements such as low, medium, high and provides decisions

Fuzzy sets provide means to model the uncertainty associated with vagueness, imprecision, and lack of information regarding a problem or a plant, etc. Consider the meaning of a "short person." For an individual X, the short person may be one whose height is below 4.25. For other individual Y, the short person may be one whose height is below or equal to 3.90. This "short" is called as a linguistic descriptor. The term "short" informs the same meaning to the individuals X and Y, but it is found that they both do not provide a unique definition. The term "short" would be conveyed effectively, only when a computer compares the given height value with the preassigned value of "short." This variable "short" is called as linguistic variable, which represents the imprecision existing in the system.

The uncertainty is found to arise from ignorance, from chance and randomness, due to lack of knowledge, from vagueness (unclear), like the fuzziness existing in our natural language. Lotfi Zadeh proposed the set membership idea to make suitable decisions when uncertainty occurs. Consider the "short" example discussed previously. If we take "short" as a height equal to or less than 4 feet, then 3.90 would easily become the member of the set "short" and 4.25 will not be a member of the set "short." The membership value is "1" if it belongs to the set or "0" if it is not a member of the set. Thus membership in a set is found to be binary i.e., the element is a member of a set or not.

It can be indicated as,

$$x_A(x) \quad \begin{matrix} 1\,, x & A \\ 0\,, x & A' \end{matrix}$$

where $\chi A(x)$ is the membership of element x in set A and A is the entire set on the universe.

This membership was extended to possess various "degree of membership" on the real continuous interval [0,1]. Zadeh formed fuzzy sets as the sets on the universe X which can accommodate "degrees of membership." The concept of a fuzzy set contrasts with a classical concept of a bivalent set (crisp set), whose boundary is required to be precise, i.e., a crisp set is a collection of things for which it is known whether any given thing is inside it or not. Zadeh generalized the idea of a crisp set by extending a valuation set { 1, 0} (definitely in/definitely out) to the interval of real values (degrees of membership) between 1 and 0 denoted as [0,1]. We can say that the degree of membership of any particular element of a fuzzy set express the degree of compatibility of the element with a concept represented by fuzzy set. It means that a fuzzy set

A contains an object x to degree a(x), i.e., a(x) = Degree ($x \in A$), and the map $a : X \rightarrow$ {Membership Degrees} is called a set function or membership function. The fuzzy set A can be expressed as $A = \{(x, a(x))\}$, $x \in X$, and it imposes an elastic constrain of the possible values of elements $x \in X$ called the possibility distribution. Fuzzy sets tend to capture vagueness exclusively via membership functions that are mappings from a given universe of discourse

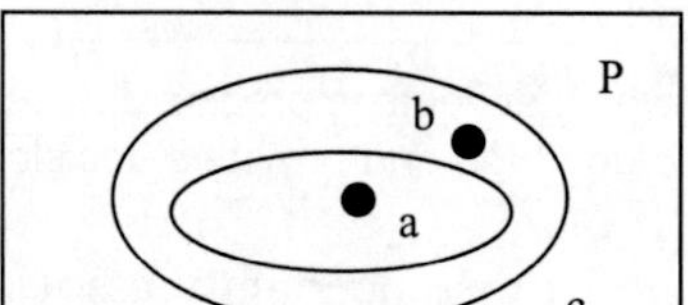

Figure 11.2: Boundary Region of a Fuzzy Set

X to a unit interval containing membership values. It is important to note that membership can take values between 0 and 1. Fuzziness describes the ambiguity of an event and randomness describes the uncertainty in the occurrence of an event. It can be generally seen in classical sets that there is no uncertainty, hence they have crisp boundaries, but in the case of a fuzzy set, since uncertainty occurs, the boundaries may be ambiguously specified. From the Figure 11.2, it can be noted that a is clearly a member of fuzzy set P, c is clearly not a member of fuzzy set P, but the membership of b is found to be vague. Hence a can take membership value 1, c can take membership value 0 and b can take membership value between 0 and 1 [0 to 1], say 0.4, 0.7, etc. This is set to be a partial member ship of fuzzy set P.

The membership function for a set maps each element of the set to a membership value between 0 and 1 and uniquely describes that set. The values 0 and 1 describe "not belonging to" and "belonging to" a conventional set respectively; values in between represent "fuzziness." Determining the membership function is subjective to varying degrees depending on the situation.

It depends on an individual's perception of the data in question and does not depend on randomness. This is important, and distinguishes fuzzy set theory from probability theory (Figure 11.3). In practice fuzzy logic means computation of words. Since computation with words is possible, computerized systems can be built by embedding human expertise articulated in daily language. Also called a fuzzy inference engine or fuzzy rule-base, such a system can perform approximate reasoning somewhat similar to but much more primitive than that of the human brain.

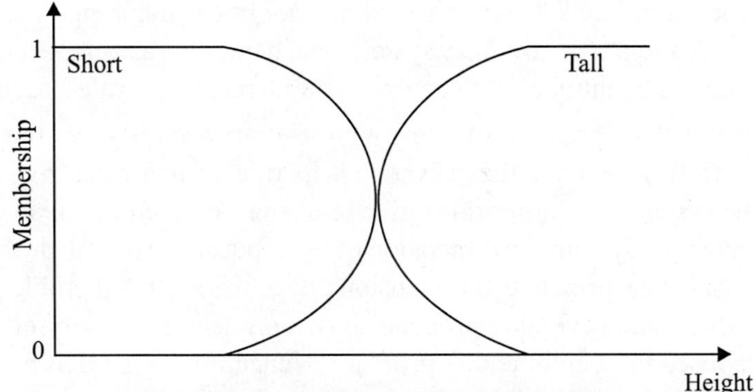

Figure 11.3: The fuzzy sets "tall" and "short".

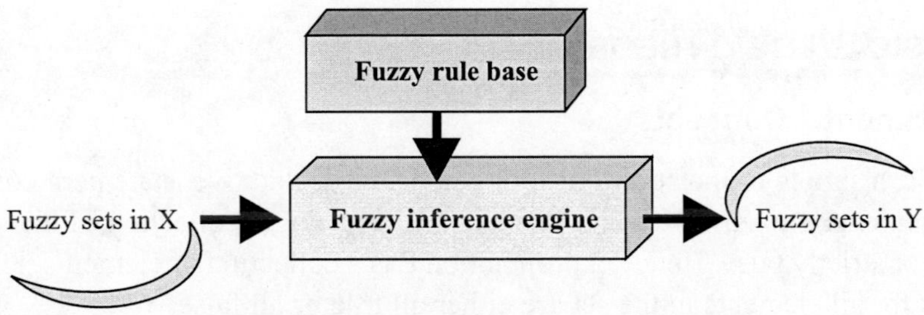

Figure 11.4: Configuration of a Pure Fuzzy Set

Computing with words seems to be a slightly futuristic phrase today since only certain aspects of natural language can be represented by the calculus of fuzzy sets, but still fuzzy logic remains one of the most practical ways to mimic human expertise in a realistic manner. The fuzzy approach uses a premise that humans do not represent classes of objects (e.g. class of bald men, or the class of numbers which are much greater than 50) as fully disjoint but rather as sets in which there may be grades of membership intermediate between full membership and non-membership. Thus, a fuzzy set works as a concept that makes it possible to treat fuzziness in a quantitative manner. Fuzzy sets form the building blocks for fuzzy IF–THEN rules which have the general form "IF X is A THEN Y is B," where A and B are fuzzy sets. The term "fuzzy systems" refers mostly to systems that are governed by fuzzy IF– THEN rules. The IF part of an implication is called the antecedent whereas the second, THEN part is a consequent. A fuzzy system is a set of fuzzy rules that converts inputs to outputs. The basic configuration of a pure fuzzy system is shown in Figure 11.4. The fuzzy inference engine (algorithm) combines fuzzy IF–THEN rules into a mapping from fuzzy sets in the input space X to fuzzy sets in the output space Y based on fuzzy logic principles. From a knowledge representation viewpoint, a fuzzy IF–THEN rule is a scheme for capturing knowledge that involves imprecision. The main feature of reasoning using these rules is its partial matching capability, which enables an inference to be made from a fuzzy rule even when the rule's condition is only partially satisfied.

Fuzzy systems, on one hand, are rule-based systems that are constructed from a collection of linguistic rules; on the other hand, fuzzy systems are nonlinear mappings of inputs (stimuli) to outputs (responses), i.e., certain types of fuzzy systems can be written as compact nonlinear formulas. The inputs and outputs can be numbers or vectors of numbers. These rule-based

systems in theory model represents any system with arbitrary accuracy, i.e., they work as universal approximators. The Achilles' heel of a fuzzy system is its rules; smart rules give smart systems and other rules give smart systems and other rules give less smart or even dumb systems. The number of rules increases exponentially with the dimension of the input space (number of system variables). This rule explosion is called the principle of dimensionality and is a general problem for mathematical models. For the last five years several approaches based on decomposition (cluster) merging and fusing have been proposed to overcome this problem. Hence, Fuzzy models are not replacements for probability models. The fuzzy models sometimes found to work better and sometimes they do not. But mostly fuzzy is evidently proved that it provides better solutions for complex problems.

11.6 CLASSICAL LOGIC THEORY

11.6.1 Fundamental Concepts

In classical logic, a simple proposition P is a linguistic, or declarative, statement contained within a universe of elements, say X, which can be identified as being a collection of elements in X that are strictly true or strictly false. Hence, a proposition P is a collection of elements, i.e., a set, where the truth values for all elements in the set are either all true or all false.

To introduce the basic concepts in the classical logic theory, we consider a typical example of a process (a system, or a plant) that is operated by a console consisting of a lock (with a key) and an ON-OFF switch as shown in Figure 11.5

For this console, we use L to denote the situation of the lock:

$$L \quad \begin{matrix} 1 & \text{if the console is unlocked,} \\ 0 & \text{if the console is locked,} \end{matrix}$$

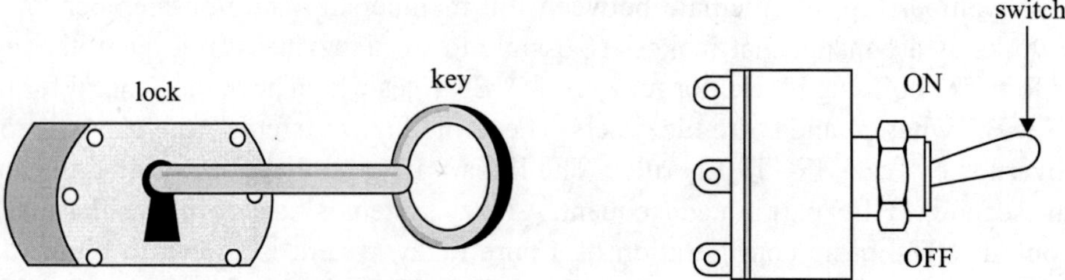

Figure 11.5: A Console Lock with a Switch

Table 11.1: Truth table for console controlled process

Inputs			Outputs
L	S	P	P
0	0	0	0
0	0	1	1
1	0	0	0
1	0	1	0
0	1	0	0
0	1	1	1
1	1	0	1
1	1	1	1

The two digits, 0 and 1, are used here to represent the two states of the logical variables. L, S, and P are logical functions, which only assume one of these two values, 0 or 1. After the logical variables and functions are defined, it is common practice to establish a truth table for their relationships and possible outcomes of the relations. This truth table displays all rules of the two-valued logic for the particular problem in consideration. For this console example, we have the truth table shown as in Table 11.1, which is sometimes called a look-up table. On the other hand, we use S to denote the state of the switch:

$$S \quad \begin{matrix} 1 & \text{if the switch is ON,} \\ 0 & \text{if the switch is OFF} \end{matrix}$$

Moreover, we use P to denote the status of the process:

$$P \quad \begin{matrix} 1 & \text{if the process is running} \\ 0 & \text{if the process is shutdown} \end{matrix}$$

In Table 11.1, it is important to point out that the process P is an input (the current status) as well as an output (the resulting status), where its current status may affect its future status. For example, if L = 0 (the key is not in the lock, or the console is locked), then the process will remain its current status, regardless of the state of the ON-OFF switch. A truth table is interpreted row by row.

For instance, the fourth row of Table 11.1 is interpreted as follows:

IF the key is in the lock (the console is unlocked)

AND the switch is turned to OFF

AND the process is currently running

THEN the process will be shutdown.

This is a rule. In general, a rule may have any number of inputs and outputs like

IF (input 1) AND (input 2) AND ... AND (input n)

THEN (output 1) AND (output 2) AND ... AND (output m).

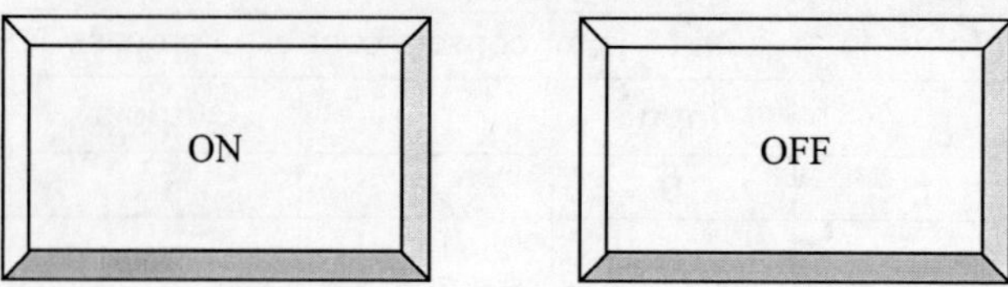

Figure 11.6: A Push Button Switch

From this simple example, one can see that a classical logic string consists of several two-valued inputs, several rules, and several two-valued outputs. It will be seen later that fuzzy logic has the same structure except that both the inputs and outputs are n-valued, with $n \geq 2$ (probably, $n = \infty$).

As a second example, let us consider the push-button switch shown in Figure 11.6. For this push-button switch, we use L to denote the situation of the ON button:

$$L \quad \begin{matrix} 1 & \text{if the ON button is depressed,} \\ 0 & \text{if the ON button is released} \end{matrix}$$

On the other hand, we use S to denote the state of the OFF button:

$$S \quad \begin{matrix} 1 & \text{if the OFF button is depressed,} \\ 0 & \text{if the OFF button is released} \end{matrix}$$

Finally, we use P to denote the status of the process under control:

$$P \quad \begin{matrix} 1 & \text{if the current process is running,} \\ 0 & \text{if the current process is shutdown.} \end{matrix}$$

Then, one can easily establish the truth table for this push-button control process, as shown in Table 11.2.

It is important and interesting to compare Tables 11.1 and 11.2. The most significant difference can be seen from the last rows of the two tables, in

Table 11.2: Truth table for the console-controlled process

Inputs			Outputs
L	**S**	**P**	**P**
0	0	0	0
0	0	1	1
0	1	0	0
0	1	1	0
1	0	0	1
1	0	1	1
1	1	0	0
1	1	1	0

Table 11.3: Logic functions of two variables

x_1 x_2	1 0 1 0 1 1 0 0	**Name of Function**	**Symbol**
y_1	0 0 0 0	Zero function	0
y_2	0 0 0 1	nor(not-or)function	$x_1 \quad x_2$
y_3	0 0 1 0	Proper inequality	$x_1 \leftarrow x_2$
y_4	0 0 1 1	negation	$\overline{x}_2$
y_5	0 1 0 0	proper inequality	$x_1 \rightarrow x_2$
y_6	0 1 0 1	negation	$\overline{x}_1$
y_7	0 1 1 0	nonquivalence	$x_1 \quad x_2$
y_8	0 1 1 1	nand(not-and)function	$x_1 - x_2$
y_9	1 0 0 0	and function	$x_1 \wedge x_2$
y_{10}	1 0 0 1	equivalence	$x_1 \Leftrightarrow x_2$
y_{11}	1 0 1 0	identity	x_1
y_{12}	1 0 1 1	implication	$x_1 \Leftarrow x_2$
y_{13}	1 1 0 0	identity	x_2
y_{14}	1 1 0 1	implication	$x_1 \Rightarrow x_2$
y_{15}	1 1 1 0	or function	$x_1 \vee x_2$
y_{16}	1 1 1 1	unity	1

which the three inputs (1,1,1) produce an output 1 in Table 11.1 but an output 0 in Table 11.2. The reason is that S = 1 means "ON" in Table 11.1 but it means "OFF" in Table 11.2, due to the nature of the two different switches.

11.6.2 Logical Functions of the Two-Valued Logic

Suppose that we are given n logical variables, $x_1, ..., x_n$. These n variables can have 2^n different combinations of truth values. Hence, there are a total of 2^{2n} possible logical functions defining these variables. For example, for n = 2, there are $2^2 = 4$ combinations of logical variables: (1, 1), (1, 0), (0, 1), and (0, 0). The $2^4 = 16$ logical functions are listed in Table 11.3, where the resulting logical variables are denoted by $y_1, ..., y_{16}$. Logical functions of one or two variables are usually called logical operations.

It can be seen from Table 11.3 that the number of logic functions of n variables grows extremely rapidly with increasing values of n. However, it is known that the logical functions listed in Table 11.3, and those created from them, can be obtained from a set of few primary logical functions. Two sets of primary logical functions are:

(i) negation, and function, and or function;

(ii) negation and the two implications. Using either set of primary logical functions, we can form any other logical functions via appropriate algebraic expressions, called logical formulas. For example, using the first set of primary logical functions, namely, negation – , and function , and or function , logical formulas can be defined recursively as follows:

(a) The truth values 0 and 1 are logical formulas.

(b) If x is a logical variable, then both x and $\overline{x}$ are logical formulas.

(c) If x_1 and x_2 are logical formulas, then both $x_1 \quad x_2$ and $x_1 \quad x_2$ are logical formulas.

(d) The only logical formulas are those defined by (a), (b), and (c). Then, every logical formula of this type defines a logical function by composing it from the three primary logical functions –, , and . To define a unique function, the composition order must be specified, say using parentheses. For example,

$$(x_1 \quad x_2) \quad (x_1 \quad x_3) \quad (x_2 \quad x_3)$$

defines a unique logical function of three variables. When two logical formulas a and b are equivalent, we usually write a = b. For instance, one has

$$(x_1 \quad x_2) \quad (x_1 \quad x_3) \quad (x_2 \quad x_3) = (x_2 \quad x_3) \quad (x_1 \quad x_3) \quad (x_1 \quad x_2).$$

This equivalence can be verified by evaluating each of the two formulas for all eight combinations of truth values of the logical variables x_1, x_2, and x_3. The Boolean algebra to be studied in the next section can help simplify such verifications.

11.6.3 Multi-valued Logic

(i) Three-Valued Logic

The classical two-valued logic can be extended to a three-valued logic in various ways, each having its own rationale. In a typical three-valued logic, we denote the truth, falsity, and indeterminacy by values of 1, 0, and 1/2, respectively. The negation a of a proposition a is usually defined to be 1-a. Thus, in this three-valued logic, we have $\overline{1}$ 0, $\overline{0}$ 1, and $\overline{(1/2)}$ 1/2

Other primary logical operations, such as , , ⇒, and ⇔ will differ from one logic to another. A commonly used three-valued logic is shown in Table 11.4.

Comparing the three-valued logic shown in Table 11.4 with the twovalued logic, one can see that the only new operations are those involving the new truth value 1/2. It should also be clear that the three-valued logic does not satisfy many basic operation laws of the two-valued logic, such as

$$a \quad \overline{a} \quad 0 \text{ and } a \quad \overline{a} \quad 1.$$

Table 11.4: A Three-Valued Logic

a	b	∧	∨	⇒	⇔
0	0	0	0	1	1
0	1/2	0	1/2	1	1/2
0	1	0	1	1	0
1/2	0	0	1/2	1/2	1/2
1/2	1/2	1/2	1/2	1	1
1/2	1	1/2	1	1	1/2
1	0	0	1	0	0
1	1/2	1/2	1	1/2	1/2
1	1	1	1	1	1

(ii) n-Valued Logic

Once a three-valued logic is accepted as a meaningful and useful tool for applications, it is not difficult to further extend it to an n-valued logic, for $3 < n < n < \infty$ For a given finite positive integer, $n > 3$, an n-valued logic assumes a rational truth value in the range [0,1], defined by the following equally spaced partition:

$$0 \quad \frac{0}{n\ \ 1}, \frac{1}{n\ \ 1}, \frac{2}{n\ \ 1}, \ldots., \frac{n\ \ 2}{n\ \ 1}, \frac{n\ \ 1}{n\ \ 1} \quad 1.$$

Each of these truth values describes a degree of truth. The commonly used n-valued logic, particularly in fuzzy set and fuzzy systems theories, is the Lukasiewicz-Zadeh n-valued logic. Lukasiewicz developed an n-valued logic in the 1930s, using only the negation and the implication Þ logical operations. Based on that, one can define

$$a \vee b = (a \Rightarrow b) \Rightarrow b,$$

$$a \wedge b = \overline{(\bar{a} \quad \bar{b})},$$

$$a \Leftrightarrow b = (a \Rightarrow b) \wedge (b \Rightarrow a).$$

The fuzzy set theory was developed by Zadeh in 1960s, which has been thoroughly studied in Chapter 2. To develop an n-valued logic, with $2 \leq n \leq \infty$, such that it is isomorphic to the fuzzy set theory in the same way as the two-valued logic is isomorphic to the classical set theory, Zadeh modified the Lukasiewicz logic and established an infinite-valued logic, by defining the following primary logic operations:

$$\bar{a} = 1 - a$$

$$a \wedge b = \min\{a, b\},$$

$$a \vee b = \max\{a, b\},$$

$$a \Rightarrow b = \min\{1, 1 + b - a\},$$

$$a \Leftrightarrow b = 1 - |a - b|$$

It has been shown, in logic theory, that all these logical operations become the same as those for the two-valued logic when $n = 2$, and the same as those for the three-valued logic shown in Table 11.4 when $n = 3$. More importantly, when $n = \infty$, this logic does not restrict the truth values to be rational: they can be any real numbers in [0,1]. It has also been shown that this infinite-valued logic is isomorphic to the fuzzy set theory that employs the min, max, and 1-a operation for fuzzy set intersection, union, and complement, respectively, in the same way as the classical two-valued logic is isomorphic to the crisp set theory. These verifications are beyond the scope of this text and, hence, are omitted.

11.7 FUZZY LOGIC THEORY

Fuzzy logic is the part of artificial intelligence or machine learning which interprets a human's actions. Computers can interpret only true or false values but a human being can reason the degree of truth or degree of falseness. Fuzzy models interpret the human actions and are also called intelligent systems.

Fuzzy logic is a form of multi-valued logic derived from fuzzy set theory to deal with reasoning that is approximate rather than precise. In contrast with binary sets having binary logic, also known as crisp logic, the fuzzy logic variables may have a membership value of only 0 or 1. Just as in fuzzy set theory with fuzzy logic the set membership values can range (inclusively) between 0 and 1, in fuzzy logic the degree of truth of a statement can range between 0 and 1 and is not constrained to the two truth values {true (1), false (0)} as in classic propositional logic and when linguistic variables are used, these degrees may be managed by specific functions, as discussed below.

The term "fuzzy logic" emerged as a consequence of the development of the theory of fuzzy sets by Lotfi Zadeh[2]. A paper introducing the concept without using the term was published by R.H. Wilkinson in 1963[3] and thus preceded fuzzy set theory. Wilkinson was the first one to redefine and generalize the earlier multivalued logics in terms of set theory. The main purpose of his paper, following his first proposals in his 1961 Electrical Engineering master thesis, was to show how any mathematical function could be simulated using hardwired analog electronic circuits. He did this by first creating various linear voltage ramps which were then selected in a "logic block" using diodes and resistor circuits which implemented the maximum and minimum Fuzzy Logic rules of the INCLUSIVE OR and the AND operations respectively. He called his logic "analog logic".

In 1965 Lotfi Zadeh axiomatized fuzzy set theory, thereby creating the set-theoretical equivalent of the "analog logic" of Wilkinson (without recourse to electrical circuits), not giving Wilkinson any credit.[4] Fuzzy logic has been applied to diverse fields, from control theory to artificial intelligence, yet still remains controversial among most statisticians, who prefer Bayesian logic,[citation needed] and some control engineers, who prefer traditional two-valued logic.

Fuzzy logic provides an inference morphology that enables approximate human reasoning capabilities to be applied to knowledge-based systems. The theory of fuzzy logic provides a mathematical strength to capture the uncertainties associated with human cognitive processes, such as thinking and reasoning. The conventional approaches to knowledge representation lack the means for representing the meaning of fuzzy concepts. As a consequence, the approaches based on first order logic and classical probability theory do not provide an appropriate conceptual framework for dealing with the representation of commonsense knowledge, since such knowledge is by its nature both lexically imprecise and noncategorical. The development of fuzzy logic was motivated in large measure by the need for a conceptual frame-4 work which can address the issue of uncertainty and lexical imprecision.

Some of the essential characteristics of fuzzy logic relate to the following (Zadeh, 1992):

- In fuzzy logic, exact reasoning is viewed as a limiting case of approximate reasoning.
- In fuzzy logic, everything is a matter of degree.
- In fuzzy logic, knowledge is interpreted a collection of elastic or, equivalently, fuzzy constraint on a collection of variables.
- Inference is viewed as a process of propagation of elastic constraints.
- Any logical system can be fuzzified.

There are two main characteristics of fuzzy systems that give them better performance for specific applications.

- Fuzzy systems are suitable for uncertain or approximate reasoning, especially for the system with a mathematical model that is difficult to derive.
- Fuzzy logic allows decision making with estimated values under incomplete or uncertain information.

Fuzzy logic is a logic. Logic refers to the study of methods and principles of human reasoning. Classical logic, as common practice, deals with propositions (e.g., conclusions or decisions) that are either true or false. Each proposition has an opposite. This classical logic, therefore, deals with combinations of variables that represent propositions. As each variable stands for a hypothetical proposition, any combination of them eventually assumes a truth value (either true or false), but never is in between or both (i.e., is not true and false at the same time).

The main content of classical logic is the study of rules that allow new logical variables to be produced as functions of certain existing variables. Suppose that n logical variables, $x_1, ..., x_n$, are given, say

x_1 is true; x_2 is false;

x_n is false.

Then a new logical variable, y, can be defined by a rule as a function of $x_1, ..., x_n$ that has a particular truth value (again, either true or false).

One example of a rule is the following:

Rule: IF x_1 is true AND x_2 is false AND ... AND x_n is false

THEN y is false.

Because one, and only one truth value (either true or false) is assumed by a logical function of a (finite) number of logical variables (hypothetical propositions), the classical logic is also called a two-valued logic.

The fundamental assumption upon which the classical logic is based is that every proposition is either true or false. This principle has been questioned by many philosophers, ever since Aristotle (in his treatise On Interpretation). It is now well understood and well accepted that many propositions are both partially true and partially false. To describe such partial truth values by some new rules, in a way to extend and generalize the two-valued logic, multivalued logics were proposed and developed. As the first attempt, several three-valued logics have now been well established, with their own rationale.

It is common in these logics to introduce a "neither" in between "true" and "false." It has turned out that three-valued logics are successful both logically and mathematically. Motivated by the useful three-valued logics, n-valued logics were developed in the 1930s. In particular, the n-valued logic of Lukasiewicz even allows $n = \infty$.

It has lately been understood that there exists an isomorphism between the two-valued logic and the crisp set theory, and, similarly, there is an isomorphism between the Lukasiewicz logic and the fuzzy set theory. In fact, the isomorphism for the former is the standard characteristic function

$$y = x_A(x) \begin{cases} 1 & \text{if } x \quad A \\ 0 & \text{ifx} \quad A' \end{cases}$$

Where can be interpreted as

$$y = \begin{cases} \text{ture} & \text{if x is true,} \\ \text{false} & \text{if x is false;} \end{cases}$$

and the next is a fuzzy membership function, which has been thoroughly studied in Chapter 3.

In this chapter, we study in somewhat detail the classical two-valued logic and its operations (the Boolean algebra), a three-valued logic, an n-valued logic (the Zadeh-Lukasiewicz logic with n = ∞), and the fuzzy logic. Since the ultimate goal of developing the fuzzy logic is to provide foundations for approximate reasoning, approximate reasoning using fuzzy logic will also be discussed briefly in this chapter. Finally, two important topics, fuzzy relation and fuzzy logic rule base, are studied. In particular, fuzzy logic rule base is the core for fuzzy systems and fuzzy control – the main subjects to be studied in detail in the rest of the book.

11.7.1 Advantages

Following are the advantages of fuzzy logic:

1. Use rules that express the imprecision and approximations of the real world.
2. Easy to understand, test and maintain
3. Easy to be prototyped
4. Robust. They operate even when there is lack of rules or wrong rules.
5. Need less rules
6. Parallel evaluation of rules
7. Accumulate evidences in favour and against

11.7.2 Disadvantages

Following are the disadvantages of fuzzy logic:

1. Need more tests and simulation
2. Do not learn easily
3. Difficult to establish correct rules
4. Lack of precise mathematical model

11.8 THE VOCABULARY OF FUZZY LOGIC

Fuzzy logic suffers from a rich vocabulary of unfamiliar terms and reluctance among its researchers and developers to adhere to a standard vocabulary. It also suffers from an overuse of obscure mathematical symbolism in place of simple and explanatory narrative (but that is another issue). The literature of fuzzy logic and fuzzy systems is filled with a nomenclature derived from its own private world of continuous logic. We find ourselves speaking about fuzzification and defuzzification, hedges, membership functions, and linguistic variables. Before moving on to a more comprehensive and detailed exploration of fuzzy logic, fuzzy systems, and how they work, we need to understand the principal nomenclatures and how they are related to the elements of fuzzy systems.

Although not a complete dictionary of terms associated with fuzzy logic, a preview of the basic vocabulary at the beginning of this chapter will make reading and understanding the material in the chapter 2 much easier. It is not always possible, while maintaining an uncluttered and coherent discussion of fuzzy systems, to ensure that every term is introduced before it is used. Many of these terms, of course, will be discussed in greater depth later in this and subsequent chapters.

11.8.1 Alpha Cut Threshold

An alpha cut threshold truncates the membership function of a fuzzy set or the truth value of a fuzzy rule's predicate at a specific truth value. Any value that falls below the alpha cut threshold is equivalent to zero. Alpha cuts come in two forms: strong (the comparison is less than) and weak (the comparison is less than or equal).

11.8.2 Boolean Logic

Boolean logic is a logic of crisp sets. A crisp set has two truth values: 1 and 0. Propositions in Boolean logic are either true or false, and membership in Boolean sets is either fully inclusive or fully exclusive. Boolean logic was initially formalized by George Boole (1815–1864). In 1854, he published An Investigation into the Laws of Thought, on Which Are Founded the Mathematical Theories of Logic and Probabilities, which unified the mathematical concepts of algebra and logic.

11.8.3 Crisp Set

Boolean sets are often called crisp sets as a way of distinctly differentiating them from fuzzy sets, as well as a way of indicating the sharpness or crispness of their membership function.

11.8.4 Domain

Often confused with the term universe of discourse, the domain of a fuzzy set is the explicit range of values over which the fuzzy set's membership function is defined. For vocabulary fuzzy sets (e.g., the term set of a variable), the domain is generally the same as the support set.

11.8.5 Expectancy

The width of a fuzzy number, usually measured from the center of the fuzzy set, is called the expectancy (a measure of the number's elasticity). The larger the expectancy the more imprecision is built into the fuzzy number. However, we should not confuse imprecision with a lack of accuracy. In many fuzzy models, relaxing the precision of a number increases the model's fault tolerance and reduces its brittleness, thereby making the model more precise over a wider range of values.

11.8.6 Fuzzy Logic

Fuzzy logic is a logic of fuzzy sets. A fuzzy set has, potentially, an infinite range of truth values between one (1) and zero (0). Propositions in fuzzy logic have a degree of truth, and membership in fuzzy sets can be fully inclusive, fully exclusive, or some degree in between. Fuzzy logic was initially formalized by Lotfi Zadeh (1921–) in his seminal 1965 paper "Fuzzy Sets" (see "Further Reading") followed in 1973 with "Outline of a New Approach to the Analysis of Complex Systems and Decision Process" (see "Further Reading").

11.8.7 Fuzzy Number

A bell-shaped, triangular-shaped, or trapezoidal-shaped fuzzy set represents a central value and is, in essence, a fuzzy number. Fuzzy numbers give fuzzy models a great deal of robustness and flexibility. The width of a fuzzy number is a measure of its overall expectancy (the degree to which it corresponds to a crisp number).

11.8.8 Fuzzy Quantifier

Fuzzy sets that are not numbers are fuzzy quantifiers. These sets generally have linear or sigmoid shapes. Concepts such as Tall, Fast, Heavy, and Large are examples of fuzzy quantifiers.

11.8.9 Fuzzy Set

A fuzzy set is distinct from a crisp or Boolean set in that it allows its elements to have a degree of membership. The core of a fuzzy set is its membership function: a surface or line that defines the relationship between a value in the set's domain and its degree of membership. The relationship (Expression 11.1) is functional because it returns a single degree of membership for any value in the domain.

$$t = f(s, x) \tag{11.1}$$

Here, t is a truth membership value (degree of membership in fuzzy set) s is the fuzzy set x is a value from the underlying domain (universe of discourse) Fuzzy sets provide a means of defining a series of overlapping concepts for a model variable, thus permitting rules to address the state of a model in terms of these fuzzy set names. Such names are called linguistic variables. They allow fuzzy sets to represent the underlying semantics of a variable (that is, the concept represented by a variable).

11.8.10 Hedge

Hedges act like adjectives or adverbs in the English language. They modify the shape of the fuzzy set's underlying membership function to or dilute the membership relationships, and they convert scalars (crisp numbers) into fuzzy sets through a process called approximation. They can be used in rules to modify the evaluation of both the premise and the consequent. The following is an example.

if a is very Z,

then b is somewhat Y

Here, very and somewhat are intensifier and dilution hedges.

11.8.11 Linguistic Variable

A fuzzy set that forms part of the term set for a variable and is used in fuzzy rules as part of a fuzzy relation is called a linguistic variable. For example, in the rule **if** height is Tall **then** weight is Heavy both Tall and Heavy are linguistic variables representing one of the possible partitions of height and weight. Fuzzy sets used in this way are called linguistic variables because they are used in place of numbers and allow rules to be cast in form of linguistic statements (such as height is Tall).

11.8.12 Membership Function

The core of a fuzzy set is the membership function. See "Fuzzy Set" for a more complete description.

11.8.13 Overlap

Because fuzzy sets represent degrees of membership, values from the complete universe of discourse for a variable can have memberships in more than one fuzzy set. For example, consider the variable height with a term set of Short, Medium, and Tall. An individual's height can be, to some degree, both Short and Medium. This is because the Short and Medium fuzzy sets overlap (as the values for height increase, they become less Short and more Medium, but the transition is gradual, not abrupt).

11.8.14 Support Set

The region of the membership function in which the truth values are greater than zero is called the support set. The support set plays an important part in the evaluation of a fuzzy model because only within the support set region can a set actually contribute to the outcome of a model.

11.8.15 Term Set

The collection of fuzzy sets that define the semantics of a variable is called the variable's term set. Each variable used in a fuzzy rule must have a term set. The individual fuzzy sets in a term set are the linguistic variables associated with the variable. Thus, Tall in the rule **if** height is Tall **then** weight is Heavy is part of the term set for the variable height and Heavy is part of the term set for the variable weight.

11.8.16 Universe of Discourse

The complete range of values over which a variable can assume values is called the universe of discourse (UoD). Although this term is often applied to the range of values in a fuzzy set, the proper term for the fuzzy set is its domain. The Universe of discourse for a variable is decomposed into a collection of fuzzy sets (the term set), each set of which has a domain that overlays part of the universe of discourse.

11.9 FUZZY LOGIC AND APPROXIMATE REASONING

Fuzzy logic is logic; its ultimate goal is to provide foundations for approximate reasoning using imprecise propositions based on fuzzy set theory, in a way similar to the classical reasoning using precise repositions based on the classical set theory. To introduce this notion, we first recall how the classical reasoning works, using only precise propositions and the two-valued logic. The following syllogism is an example of such reasoning in linguistic terms:

(i) Everyone who is 40 years old or older is old.

(ii) David is 40 years old and Mary is 39 years old.

(iii) David is old but Mary is not.

This is a very precise deductive inference, correct in the sense of the two valued logic.

In this classical (precise) reasoning using the two-valued logic, when the (output) logical variable represented by a logical formula is always true regardless of the truth values of the (input) logical variables, it is called a tautology. If, on the contrary, it is always false, then it is called a contradiction. Various tautologies can be used for making deductive inferences, which are referred to as inference rules. The four frequently used inference rules in classical reasoning are:

modus ponens: $(a \wedge (a \Rightarrow b)) \Rightarrow b;$

modus tollens: $(\bar{b} \quad (a \quad b)) \quad \bar{a};$

syllogism: $(a \Rightarrow b) \wedge (b \Rightarrow c) \Rightarrow (a \Rightarrow c);$

contrapositions: $(a \quad b) \quad (\bar{b} \quad \bar{a}).$

These inference rules are very easily understood and, indeed, have been commonly used in one's daily life. For example, the modus ponens is interpreted as follows:

IF "a is true" AND the statement "IF a is true THEN b is true" is true THEN "b is true."

Using this logic, we see that the deductive inference IF "40 years old or older is old" AND "IF 40 years old or older is old THEN David is old" THEN "David is old" is a modus ponens, and the deductive inference

IF "Mary is not old" AND "IF Mary is 40 years old or older then Mary is old" THEN "Mary is not 40 years old nor older" is a modus tollens.

With the above discussion in mind, we now consider the following example of approximate reasoning in linguistic terms that cannot be handled by the classical (precise) reasoning using two-valued logic:

(i) Everyone who is 40 to 70 years old is old but is very old if he (she) is 71 years old or above; everyone who is 20 to 39 years old is young but is very young if he (she) is 19 years old or below.

(ii) David is 40 years old and Mary is 39 years old.

(iii) David is old but not very old; Mary is young but not very young.

This is of course a meaningful deductive inference, which indeed has been frequently used in one's daily life. This is an example of what is called approximate reasoning. In order to deal with such imprecise inference, fuzzy logic can be employed. Briefly, fuzzy logic allows the imprecise linguistic terms such as:

- fuzzy predicates: old, rare, severe, expensive, high, fast
- fuzzy quantifiers: many, few, usually, almost, little, much
- fuzzy truth values: very true, true, unlikely true, mostly false, false, definitely false

Example 11.1: Let P be the proposition "The structural beam is an 18WF45" and let Q be the proposition "The structural beam is made of steel." Let X be the universe of structural members comprised of girders, beams, and columns; x is an element (beam), A is the set of all wide-flange (WF) beams, and B is the set of all steel beams. Hence,

P: x is in A

Q: x is in B

The five logical connectives already defined can be used to create compound propositions, where a compound proposition is defined as a logical proposition formed by logically connecting two or more simple propositions. Just as we are interested in the truth of a simple proposition, classical logic also involves the assessment of the truth of compound propositions. For the case of two simple propositions, the resulting compound propositions are defined next in terms of their binary truth values.

Given a proposition $P : x \quad A, \overline{P} : x \quad A$, we have the following for the logical connectives:

Disjunction

$$P \vee Q : x \in A \text{ or } x \in B$$

Hence, $$T(P \vee Q) = \max\,(T(P), T(Q)) \tag{11.1a}$$

Conjunction

$$P \wedge Q : x \in A \text{ or } x \in B$$

Hence, $$T(P \wedge Q) = \min\,(T(P), T(Q)) \tag{11.1b}$$

Negation

If $$T(P) = 1\ T(\overline{p}) = 0; \text{ if } T(P) = 0, \text{ then } T(\overline{P}) = 1. \tag{11.1c}$$

Implication

$$(P \to Q) : x \notin A \text{ or } x \in B$$

Hence, $$T(P \to Q) = T(\overline{P} \cup Q) \tag{11.1d}$$

Equivalence

$$(P \leftrightarrow Q) : (P \leftrightarrow Q) = \begin{matrix} 1 & \text{for } T(P) \quad T(Q) \\ 0 & \text{for } T(P) \quad T(Q) \end{matrix} \tag{11.1e}$$

The logical connective implication, i.e., P ‡Q (P implies Q), presented here is also known as the classical implication, to distinguish it from an alternative form devised in the 1930s by Lukasiewicz, a Polish mathematician, who was first credited with exploring logics other than Aristotelian (classical or binary logic) [Researcher, 1969], and from several other forms (see end of this chapter). In this implication the proposition P is also referred to as the hypothesis or the antecedent, and the proposition Q is also referred to as the conclusion or the consequent. The compound proposition $P \to Q$ is true in all cases except where a true antecedent P appears with a false consequent, Q, i.e., a true hypothesis cannot imply a false conclusion.

Example 11.2: Consider the following four propositions:

1. If $1 + 1 = 2$, then $4 > 0$.
2. If $1 + 1 = 3$, then $4 > 0$.
3. If $1 + 1 = 3$, then $4 < 0$.
4. If $1 + 1 = 2$, then $4 < 0$.

The first three propositions are all true; the fourth is false. In the first two, the conclusion $4 > 0$ is true regardless of the truth of the hypothesis; in the third case both propositions are false, but this does not disprove the implication; finally, in the fourth case, a true hypothesis cannot produce a false conclusion.

Hence, the classical form of the implication is true for all propositions of P and Q except for those propositions that are in both the truth set of P and the false set of Q, i.e.,

$$T(P \quad Q) = \overline{T(P) \quad T(\overline{Q})} \tag{11.2}$$

This classical form of the implication operation requires some explanation. For a proposition P defined on set A and a proposition Q defined on set B, the implication "P implies Q" is equivalent to taking the union of elements in the complement of set A with the elements in the set B (this result can also be derived by using De Morgan's principles on Eq. (11.2)). That is, the logical implication is analogous to the set-theoretic form

$$(P \quad Q) = (\overline{A} \quad B \text{ is true}) \quad (\text{either "not in} \quad \text{" or " in} \quad \text{"})$$

so that

$$T(P \to Q) = (\bar{\ } \quad Q) \quad (T(\bar{\ }), T(Q)) \tag{11.3}$$

This expression is linguistically equivalent to the statement, "$P \to Q$ is true" when either "not A" or "B" is true (logical or). Graphically, this implication and the analogous set operation are represented by the Venn diagram in Figure 11.7. As noted in the diagram, the region represented by the difference $A \mid B$ is the set region where the implication $P \to Q$ is false (the implication "fails"). The shaded region in Figure 11.7 represents the collection of elements in the universe where the implication is true; that is, the set

$$\overline{\quad \mid B} \quad \bar{\ } \quad \bar{\bar{B}} \quad \overline{\quad \bar{\bar{B}}}$$

If x is in A and x is not in B, then

$$A \to B \text{ fails a} \cdot A \mid B \text{ (difference)}$$

Now, with two propositions (P and Q) each being able to take on one of two truth values (true or false, 1 or 0), there will be a total of $2^2 = 4$ propositional situations. These situations are illustrated, along with the appropriate truth values, for the propositions P and Q and the various logical connectives between them in Table 11.5.

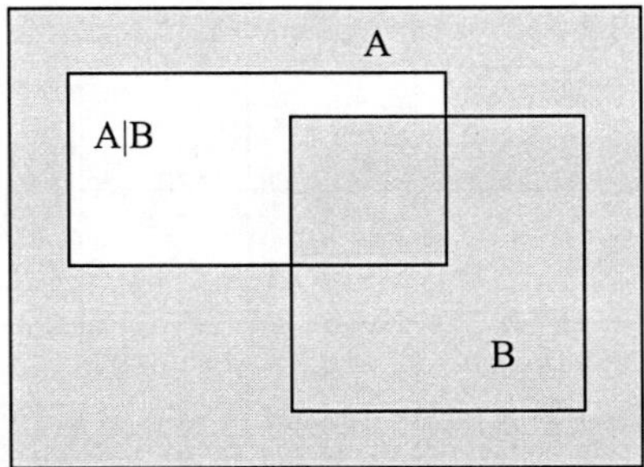

Figure 11.7: Graphical analog of the classical implication operation; gray area is where implication holds.

Table 11.5: Truth table for various compound propositions

P	Q	P	$P \vee Q$	$P \wedge Q$	$P \rightarrow Q$	$P \leftrightarrow Q$
T(1)	T(1)	F(0)	T(1)	T(1)	T(1)	T(1)
T(1)	F(0)	F(0)	T(1)	F(0)	F(0)	F(0)
F(0)	T(1)	T(1)	T(1)	F(0)	T(1)	F(0)
F(0)	F(0)	T(1)	F(0)	F(0)	T(1)	T(1)

The values in the last five columns of the table are calculated using the expressions in Eqs. (11.1) and (11.3). In Table 11.5 T (or 1) denotes true and F (or 0) denotes false. Suppose the implication operation involves two different universes of discourse; P is a proposition described by set A, which is defined on universe X, and Q is a proposition described by set B, which is defined on universe Y. Then the implication $P \rightarrow Q$ can be represented in set-theoretic terms by the relation R, where R is defined by

$$R = (A \times B) \quad (\bar{\ } \quad Y) \quad \text{If} \quad , \text{THEN B}$$

IF $x \in A$ where $x \in X$ and $A \subset X$ (11.4)

THEN $y \in B$ where $y \in Y$ and $B \subset Y$

This implication, Eq. (11.4), is also equivalent to the linguistic rule form, IF A, THEN B. The graphic shown in Figure 11.8 represents the space of the Cartesian product $X \times Y$, showing typical sets A and B; and superposed on this space is the set-theoretic equivalent of the implication. That is,

$P \rightarrow Q$: IF $x \in A$, THEN $y \in B$, or $P \rightarrow Q \quad \bar{A} \quad B$

The shaded regions of the compound Venn diagram in Figure 11.8 represent the truth domain of the implication, IF A, THEN B ($P \rightarrow Q$). Another compound proposition in linguistic rule form is the expression IF A, THEN B, ELSE C

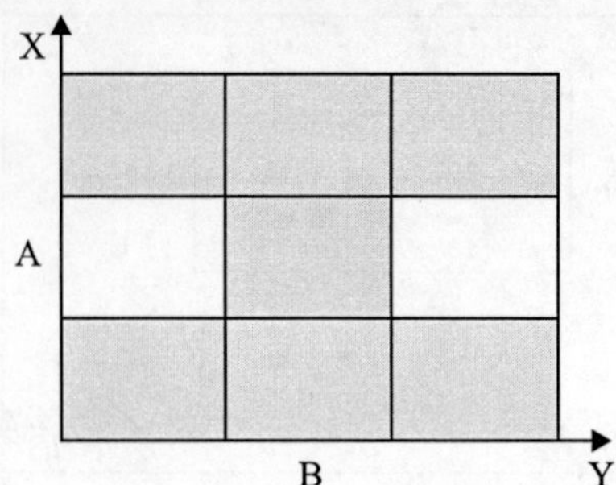

Figure 11.8: The cartesian space showing the implication IF A, THEN B.

11.9.1 Mathematical Fuzzy Logic

In mathematical logic, there are several formal systems of "fuzzy logic"; most of them belong among so-called t-norm fuzzy logics.

11.9.2 Propositional Fuzzy Logics

The most important propositional fuzzy logics are:

Monoidal t-norm-based propositional fuzzy logic MTL is an axiomatization of logic where conjunction is defined by a left continuous t-norm, and implication is defined as the residuum of the t-norm. Its models correspond to MTL-algebras that are prelinear commutative bounded integral residuated lattices.

Basic propositional fuzzy logic BL is an extension of MTL logic where conjunction is defined by a continuous t-norm, and implication is also defined as the residuum of the t-norm. Its models correspond to BL-algebras.

Łukasiewicz fuzzy logic is the extension of basic fuzzy logic BL where standard conjunction is the Łukasiewicz t-norm. It has the axioms of basic fuzzy logic plus an axiom of double negation, and its models correspond to MV-algebras.

Gödel fuzzy logic is the extension of basic fuzzy logic BL where conjunction is Gödel t-norm. It has the axioms of BL plus an axiom of idempotence of conjunction, and its models are called G-algebras.

Product fuzzy logic is the extension of basic fuzzy logic BL where conjunction is product t-norm. It has the axioms of BL plus another axiom for cancellativity of conjunction, and its models are called product algebras.

Fuzzy logic with evaluated syntax (sometimes also called Pavelka's logic), denoted by EVŁ, is a further generalization of mathematical fuzzy logic. While the above kinds of fuzzy logic have traditional syntax and many-valued semantics, in EVŁ is evaluated also syntax. This means that each formula has an evaluation. Axiomatization of EVŁ stems from Łukasziewicz fuzzy logic. A generalization of classical Gödel completeness theorem is provable in EVŁ.

11.9.3 Predicate Fuzzy Logics

These extend the above-mentioned fuzzy logics by adding universal and existential quantifiers in a manner similar to the way that predicate logic is created from propositional logic. The semantics of the universal resp. existential quantifier in t-norm fuzzy logics is the infimum resp. supremum of the truth degrees of the instances of the quantified subformula.

11.9.4 Higher-order Fuzzy Logics

These logics, called fuzzy type theories, extend predicate fuzzy logics to be able to quantify also predicates and higher order objects. A fuzzy type theory is a generalization of classical simple type theory introduced by B. Russell and mathematically elaborated by A. Church and L. Henkin.

11.9.5 Decidability Issues for Fuzzy Logic

The notions of a "decidable subset" and "recursively enumerable subset" are basic ones for classical mathematics and classical logic. Then, the question of a suitable extension of such concepts to fuzzy set theory arises. A first proposal in such a direction was made by E.S. Santos by the notions of fuzzy Turing machine, Markov normal fuzzy algorithm and fuzzy program. Successively, L. Biacino and G. Gerla showed that such a definition is not adequate and therefore proposed the following one. U denotes the set of rational numbers in [0,1]. A fuzzy subset s : S [0, 1] of a set S is recursively enumerable if a recursive map h : S × N U exists such that, for every x in S, the function h(x, n) is increasing with respect to n and s(x) = lim h(x,n). We say that s is decidable if both s and its complement –s are recursively enumerable. An extension of such a theory to the general case of the L-subsets is proposed in Gerla 2006. The proposed definitions are well related with fuzzy logic. Indeed, the following theorem holds true (provided that the deduction apparatus of the fuzzy logic satisfies some obvious effectiveness property).

Theorem: Any axiomatizable fuzzy theory is recursively enumerable. In particular, the fuzzy set of logically true formulas is recursively enumerable in spite of the fact that the crisp set of valid formulas is not recursively enumerable, in general. Moreover, any axiomatizable and complete theory is decidable.

It is an open question to give supports for a Church thesis for fuzzy logic claiming that the proposed notion of recursive enumerability for fuzzy subsets is the adequate one. To this aim, further investigations on the notions of fuzzy grammar and fuzzy Turing machine should be necessary (see for example Wiedermann's paper). Another open question is to start from this notion to find an extension of Godel's theorems to fuzzy logic.

EXERCISES

1. What do you mean by fuzzy system?
2. Explain the concepts of imprecision?

3. Explain the historical point of view of uncertainty?
4. Explain the concept of uncertainty and information?
5. Why we use fuzzy system?
6. What do you mean by pure fuzzy set?
7. Explain the concept of classical logical theory?
8. Explain the logic function for :
   (i) Two valued logic
   (ii) Multi-valued logic
9. What do you mean by fuzzy logic theory?
10. What are the various characteristic of fuzzy logic?
11. What are the advantages and disadvantages of fuzzy logic?
12. Explain the vocabulary of fuzzy logic?
13. Explain the relationship between fuzzy logic and approximate reasoning?
14. What do you mean by mathematical fuzzy logic?
15. Explain the following:
    (i) Propositional fuzzy logic
    (ii) Predicate fuzzy logic
    (iii) Higher order fuzzy logic

CHAPTER 12

Fuzzy Logic

12.1 INTRODUCTION

Fuzzy logic means inexact reasoning, data granulation, computing with words and so on. Haziness is always present in any realistic process. This vagueness may come up from the analysis of the data inputs and in the directives used to describe the relationships between the informative attributes. Fuzzy logic grants an inference structure that allows the human reasoning capacities to be applied to artificial knowledge-based structures. Fuzzy logic gives a means for adapting linguistic strategy into control actions and thus offers a high-level computation.

A definition of fuzzy logic systems set mathematical determination to the emulation of certain perceptual and lingual attributes related with human cognition, where the science of neural networks provides a new computing tool with learning and adaptation capabilities. The theory of fuzzy logic gives an inference method under cognitive uncertainty, computational neural networks, fuzzy logic offer exciting benefits such as learning, adaptation, fault tolerance, parallelism, and generalization.

In the literary texts sources, we can find different kinds of explanation for fuzzy systems theory. Human knowledge these days becomes more and more important – we increase it from living through the world after only which we live and use our capability to reason to create an order in the mass of information (i.e., to formulate human knowledge in a organized manner). As we are all limited in our ability to perceive the world and to deep reasoning, we find ourselves everywhere faced by uncertainty that is a result of lack of information, in particular, miscalculation of measurements.

The other restriction factor in our request for precision is a natural language used for describing/sharing knowledge, communication, etc. We understand core meanings of word and are able to communicate without error to an adequate degree, but generally we cannot precisely agree among ourselves on the singular word or terms of communal sense meaning. In other words, ordinary languages are unclear.

Our impression of the real world is pervaded by concepts, which do not have severely defined boundaries – for example, many, tall, much larger than, young, etc. are true only to some degree, and they are false to some extent as well. These concepts can be called fuzzy or vague concepts –

a human brain works with them, while computers may not do it (they reason with strings of 0s and 1s). Natural languages, which are much higher in level than programming languages, are fuzzy, while programming languages are not. The door to the development of fuzzy computers was opened in 1985 by the design of the first logic chip by Masaki Togai and Hiroyuki Watanabe at Bell Telephone Laboratories. In the years to come fuzzy computers will employ both fuzzy hardware and fuzzy software, and they will be much closer in structure to the human brain than the present-day computers are.

The Fuzzy Logic tool was introduced in 1965 by Lotfi Zadeh. It is a mathematical tool for dealing with uncertainty. It offers to a software computing system the important concept of computing with words'. It grants a technique to deal with vagueness and information granularity. The fuzzy theory provides a mechanism for representing linguistic constructs such as "many," "low," "medium," "often," "few."

Basically, the fuzzy logic provides an inference organization that enables proper human reasoning capabilities that machines do not have. In the other hand, the traditional binary set theory describes crisp events, events that have two options: one or zero. It uses probability theory to explain whether an event is about to happen, measuring the chance with which a given event is expected to come about. The premise of fuzzy logic is based leading the concept of relative graded connection and so are the functions of awareness and cognitive processes.

It is important to keep in mind that there is a close connection between *Fuzziness* and *Complexity*. As the complexity of a task, or of a system for performing that task, exceeds a certain limit, the system must unavoidably become fuzzy in nature. Zadeh, initially an engineer and systems scientist, was concerned with the fast turn down in information afforded by common mathematical models as the complexity of the target system increased.

As he stressed, with the increasing of complexity our skill to make accurate and yet major statements about its behavior diminishes. Real world problems are too complex, and the difficulty involves the degree of vagueness – as uncertainty increases, so does the involvedness of the problem. Habitual system modeling and analysis techniques are too precise for such problems, and in order to make complexity less daunting we set up appropriate simplifications, assumptions, etc. to accomplish a reasonable compromise between the information we have and the amount of uncertainty we are willing to accept. In this aspect, fuzzy systems theory is similar to other engineering theories, because almost all of them describe the real world in an approximate manner.

Engineers define fuzzy logic as a useful tool with diverse applications; especially on solving problems that linear computing is not able to do. A good example of this functionality is the capability for image recognition, since human brain is capable to distinguish an object from an image even if is blur, meanwhile linear computing is able to read just pixels as set of colors. There is an analog factor: vagueness, images may have fuzzy maps.

Fuzzy sets grants means to model the ambiguity associated with vagueness, imprecision, and lack of information concerning a dilemma or a plant, etc. Consider the significance of a "short person." For an entity X, the short person may be one whose height is below 4.20. For another individual Y, the short person may be one whose height is beneath or equal to 3.9. This "short" is called as a linguistic descriptor. The term "short" informs the same meaning to the individuals X and Y, but it is establish that they both do not supply a unique definition. The term "short" would be conveyed successfully, only when a computer compares the given height value with the pre-assigned value of "short." This variable "short" is called as *linguistic variable*, which represents the elusiveness existing in the system.

12.2 FUZZY LOGIC

Fuzzy logic has been used in two different senses. It is important to clarify the distinctions between these two different usages of the term.

1. **In a narrow sense:** Fuzzy logic refers to a logical system that generalizes classical two-valued logic for reasoning under uncertainly.
2. **In a board sense:** fuzzy logic refers to all of the theories and technologies that employ fuzzy sets, which are classes with unsharp boundaries.

Definition:

"Fuzzy logic is used for solving problems with expert systems and real-time systems that must react to an imperfect environment of highly variable, volatile or unpredictable conditions."

For instance, the concept of "warm room temperature" may be expressed as an interval (e.g., [75° F]) in classical set theory. However, the concept does not have a well-defined natural boundary. A representation of the concept closer to human interpretation is to allow a gradual transition from "not warm" to "warm". In order to achieve this, the notion of membership in a set needs to become a matter of degree. This is the essence of fuzzy sets. An example of a classical set and a fuzzy set is shown in Figure 12.1, where the vertical axis represents the degree of membership in a set.

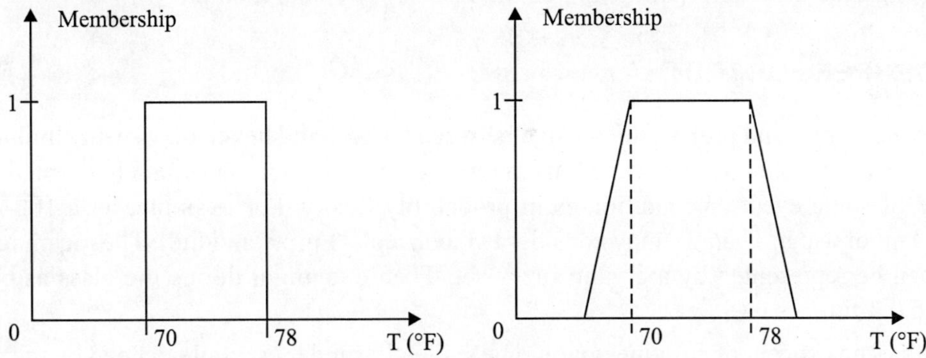

Figure 12.1: Representation of a classical set and a fuzzy set "warm room temperature".

The board sense of fuzzy logic includes the narrow sense of fuzzy logic as a branch. Other areas include fuzzy control, fuzzy pattern recognition, fuzzy arithmetic, fuzzy math, fuzzy probability theory, fuzzy decision analysis, fuzzy neural networks theory, and fuzzy topology, etc. In all these areas, a conventional black-and-white concept is generalized to a matter of degree.

By doing this, one accomplishes two things:

1. Ease of describing human knowledge involving vague concepts
2. Enhanced ability to develop a cost-effective solution to real-world problems.

The term fuzzy logic in this book is most frequently used in the broad sense. Whenever it is used in the narrow sense, we will explicitly state so.

12.3 MOTIVATIONS

Fuzzy logic was motivated by two objectives. First, it aims to alleviate difficulties in developing and analyzing complex systems encountered by conventional mathematics tools. Second, it is motivated by observing that human reasoning can utilize concepts and knowledge that do not have well-defined, sharp boundaries (i.e. vague concepts). The first motivation is directly related to solving **real-world problems**, while the second motivation is related to **artificial intelligence**-the discipline in computer science involved with developing computer systems that exhibit intelligent behaviors similar to those of human beings. The former motivation requires fuzzy logic to work in qualitative and numeric domains, while the latter motivation enables fuzzy logic to have a descriptive and qualitative form because vague concepts are often described qualitatively by words.

These two motivations together not only make fuzzy logic unique and different from other technologies that focus on only one of these goals but also enable fuzzy logic to be a natural bridge between the quantitative world and the qualitative world. As will become clear at a later point, this unique characteristic of fuzzy logic allows this technology to offer an important benefit-it not only provides a cost-effective way to model complex systems involving numeric variables bus also offers a qualitative description of the system that is easy to comprehend.

12.4 DEGREES OF TRUTH

Both degrees of truth and probabilities range between 0 and 1 and hence may seem similar at first. However, they are distinct conceptually; truth represents membership in vaguely defined sets, not likelihood of some event or condition as in probability theory. For example, let a 100-ml glass contain 30 ml of water. Then we may consider two concepts: Empty and Full. The meaning of each of them can be represented by a certain fuzzy set. Then one might define the glass as being 0.7 empty and 0.3 full.

Note that the concept of emptiness would be subjective and thus would depend on the observer or designer. Another designer might equally well design a set membership function where the glass would be considered full for all values down to 50 ml. It is essential to realize that fuzzy logic uses truth degrees as a mathematical model of the vagueness phenomenon while probability is a mathematical model of randomness.

A probabilistic setting would first define a scalar variable for the fullness of the glass, and second, conditional distributions describing the probability that someone would call the glass full given a specific fullness level. This model, however, has no sense without accepting occurrence of some event, e.g. which after a few minutes, the glass will be half empty. Note that the conditioning can be achieved by having a specific observer that randomly selects the label for the glass, a distribution over deterministic observers, or both.

Consequently, probability has nothing in common with fuzziness, these are simply different concepts which superficially seem similar because of using the same interval of real numbers [0, 1]. Still, since theorems such as De Morgan's have dual applicability and properties of random variables are analogous to properties of binary logic states, one can see where the confusion might arise.

12.4.1 Applying Truth Values

A basic application might characterize subranges of a continuous variable. For instance, a temperature measurement for anti-lock brakes might have several separate membership functions defining particular temperature ranges needed to control the brakes properly. Each function maps the same temperature value to a truth value in the 0 to 1 range. These truth values can then be used to determine how the brakes should be controlled.

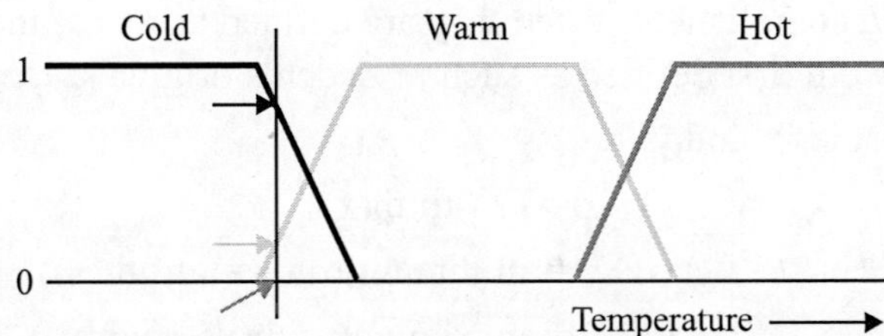

In this image, the meaning of the expressions cold, warm, and hot is represented by functions mapping a temperature scale. A point on that scale has three "truth values" — one for each of the three functions. The vertical line in the image represents a particular temperature that the three arrows (truth values) gauge. Since the red arrow points to zero, this temperature may be interpreted as "not hot". The orange arrow (pointing at 0.2) may describe it as "slightly warm" and the blue arrow (pointing at 0.8) "fairly cold".

12.5 LINGUISTIC VARIABLES

While variables in mathematics usually take numerical values, in fuzzy logic applications, the non-numeric linguistic variables are often used to facilitate the expression of rules and facts.

A linguistic variable such as age may have a value such as young or its antonym old. However, the great utility of linguistic variables is that they can be modified via linguistic hedges applied to primary terms. The linguistic hedges can be associated with certain functions. For example, L. A. Zadeh proposed to take the square of the membership function. This model, however, does not work properly. For more details, see the next sections.

12.6 AN EXAMPLE OF FUZZY REASONING

Fuzzy Set Theory defines Fuzzy Operators on Fuzzy Sets. The problem in applying this is that the appropriate Fuzzy Operator may not be known. For this reason, Fuzzy logic usually uses IF-THEN rules, or constructs that are equivalent, such as fuzzy associative matrices.

Rules are usually expressed in the form:

IF variable IS property THEN action

For example, an extremely simple temperature regulator that uses a fan might look like this:

IF temperature IS very cold THEN stop fan

IF temperature IS cold THEN turn down fan

IF temperature IS normal THEN maintain level

IF temperature IS hot THEN speed up fan

Notice there is no "ELSE". All of the rules are evaluated, because the temperature might be "cold" and "normal" at the same time to different degrees.

The AND, OR, and NOT operators of boolean logic exist in fuzzy logic, usually defined as the minimum, maximum, and complement; when they are defined this way, they are called the Zadeh operators, because they were first defined as such in Zadeh's original papers.

So for the fuzzy variables x and y:

$$\text{NOT } x = (1 - \text{truth}(x))$$

$$x \text{ AND } y = \text{minimum}(\text{truth}(x), \text{truth}(y))$$

$$x \text{ OR } y = \text{maximum}(\text{truth}(x), \text{truth}(y))$$

There are also other operators, more linguistic in nature, called hedges that can be applied. These are generally adverbs such as "very", or "somewhat", which modify the meaning of a set using a mathematical formula.

In application, the programming language Prolog is well geared to implementing fuzzy logic with its facilities to set up a database of "rules" which are queried to deduct logic. This sort of programming is known as logic programming.

Once fuzzy relations are defined, it is possible to develop fuzzy relational databases. The first fuzzy relational database, FRDB, appeared in Maria Zemankova's dissertation. Later, some other models arose like the Buckles-Petry model, the Prade-Testemale Model, the Umano-Fukami model or the GEFRED model by J.M. Medina, M.A. Vila et al. In the context of fuzzy databases, some fuzzy querying languages have been defined, highlighting the SQLf by P. Bosc et al. and the FSQL by J. Galindo et al. These languages define some structures in order to include fuzzy aspects in the SQL statements, like fuzzy conditions, fuzzy comparators, fuzzy constants, fuzzy constraints, fuzzy thresholds, linguistic labels and so on.

Other examples

If a male is 1.8 meters, consider him as tall:

IF male IS true AND height > = 1.8 THEN is_tall IS true; is_short IS false

The fuzzy rules do not make sharp distinction between tall and short:

IF height < = medium male THEN is_short IS agree somewhat

IF height > = medium male THEN is_tall IS agree somewhat

In the fuzzy case, there are no such heights as 1.83 meters, but there are fuzzy values, like the following assignments:

dwarf male = [0, 1.3] m

short male = [1.3, 1.5] m

medium male = [1.5, 1.8] m

tall male = [1.8, 2.0] m

giant male > 2.0 m

For the consequent, there are may also be more than two values:

agree not = 0

agree little = 1

agree somewhat = 2

agree a lot = 3

agree fully = 4

In the binary (or "crisp") case, a person of 1.79 meters is considered of medium height, while another person who is 1.8 meters or 2.25 meters tall is considered tall.

The crisp example differs deliberately from the fuzzy one. The antecedent was not given fuzzy values:

IF male > = agree somewhat AND ... as gender is often considered binary information.

12.7 APPLICATION AREAS OF FUZZY LOGIC

Following are the various application areas of fuzzy logic:

1. Automobile and other vehicle subsystems, such as :automatic transmissions, ABS, cruise control (e.g. Tokyo monorail)
2. Air conditioners
3. Cameras
4. Digital image processing, such as edge detection -
5. Rice cookers
6. Dishwashers
7. Elevators
8. Washing machines and other home appliances

9. Video game artificial intelligence
10. Language filters on message boards and chat rooms for filtering out offensive text
11. Pattern recognition in Remote Sensing
12. Hydrometeor classification algorithms for polarimetric weather radar
13. Fuzzy logic has also been incorporated into some microcontrollers and microprocessors

12.8 WHY USE FUZZY LOGIC FOR CONTROL?

One common answer to this question is that fuzzy logic can be used for controlling a process (i.e., a plant in control engineering terminology) that is too nonlinear or too ill-understood to use conventional control designs. Another answer is that fuzzy logic enables control engineers to easily implement control strategies used by human operators. The first answer echoes the first motivation for fuzzy logic – to deal with complex, systems – while the second answer is related to the second motivation – the ease of describing human knowledge.

We will illustrate these points using a real-world application below. Before we do that, though, we would like to point out that fuzzy logic control broadens the range of applications of control engineering tools and methods. It is not meant to replace but rather to augment existing methodologies for control design.

12.9 FUZZY LOGIC FOR CONTROL

A fuzzy control system is a control system based on fuzzy logic - a mathematical system that analyzes analog input values in terms of logical variables that take on continuous values between 0 and 1, in contrast to classical or digital logic, which operates on discrete values of either 0 and 1 (true and false). Fuzzy logic is widely used in machine control. The term itself inspires a certain skepticism, sounding equivalent to "half-baked logic" or "bogus logic", but the "fuzzy" part does not refer to a lack of rigour in the method, rather to the fact that the logic involved can deal with fuzzy concepts - concepts that cannot be expressed as "true" or "false" but rather as "partially true". Although genetic algorithms and neural networks can perform just as well as fuzzy logic in many cases (in fact, certain neural networks can be shown to be mathematically equivalent to certain fuzzy logic systems), fuzzy logic has the advantage that the solution to the problem can be cast in terms that human operators can understand, so that their experience can be used in the design of the controller. This makes it easier to mechanize tasks that are already successfully performed by humans.

Although an American professor introduced the fuzzy logic theory, it was first implemented in the control of cement kilns in Denmark in 1977. The Japanese were successful in applying fuzzy logic in commercial goods like automobiles and washing machines and their current fuzzy logic market is estimated around 2 billion dollars. America has been left behind in the implementation of fuzzy logic to real world problems.

Fuzzy logic has mostly been applied to control systems. Fuzzy control systems interpret the expert human and replace them for performing certain tasks such as control of a power plant. Fuzzy controllers apply decision rules (if-then rules) by making use of critical variables to interpolate the output between the crisp boundaries.

Some typical examples where fuzzy logic has been implemented are:

1. Railway (Sendai Railways in Japan)
2. Automobile industries (transmission and braking)
3. Heating and cooling systems
4. Copy machines
5. Washing machines

Fuzzy logic has rapidly become one of the most successful of today's technologies for developing sophisticated control systems. The reason for which is very simple. Fuzzy logic addresses such applications perfectly as it resembles human decision making with an ability to generate precise solutions from certain or approximate information. It fills an important gap in engineering design methods left vacant by purely mathematical approaches (e.g. linear control design), and purely logic-based approaches (e.g. expert systems) in system design.

While other approaches require accurate equations to model real-world behaviors, fuzzy design can accommodate the ambiguities of real-world human language and logic. It provides both an intuitive method for describing systems in human terms and automates the conversion of those system specifications into effective models.

12.10 WHAT DOES IT OFFER?

The first applications of fuzzy theory were primaly industrial, such as process control for cement kilns. However, as the technology was further embraced, fuzzy logic was used in more useful applications. In 1987, the first fuzzy logic-controlled subway was opened in Sendai in northern Japan. Here, fuzzy-logic controllers make subway journeys more comfortable with smooth braking and acceleration. Best of all, all the driver has to do is push the start button! Fuzzy logic was also put to work in elevators to reduce waiting time. Since then, the applications of Fuzzy Logic technology have virtually exploded, affecting things we use everyday. Take for example, the fuzzy washing machine . A load of clothes in it and press start, and the machine begins to churn, automatically choosing the best cycle. The fuzzy microwave, Place chili, potatoes, or etc in a fuzzy microwave and push single button, and it cooks for the right time at the proper temperature. The fuzzy car, manuvers itself by following simple verbal instructions from its driver. It can even stop itself when there is an obstacle immedeately ahead using sensors. But, practically the most exciting thing about it, is the simplicity involved in operating it.

12.11 WHAT DO YOU MEAN FUZZY?

Before illustrating the mechanisms which make fuzzy logic machines work, it is important to realize what fuzzy logic actually is. Fuzzy logic is a superset of conventional(Boolean) logic that has been extended to handle the concept of partial truth- truth values between "completely true" and "completely false". As its name suggests, it is the logic underlying modes of reasoning which are approximate rather than exact. The importance of fuzzy logic derives from the fact that most modes of human reasoning and especially common sense reasoning are approximate in nature.

The essential characteristics of fuzzy logic as founded by Zader Lotfi are as follows:

1. In fuzzy logic, exact reasoning is viewed as a limiting case of approximate reasoning.
2. In fuzzy logic everything is a matter of degree.
3. Any logical system can be fuzzified.
4. In fuzzy logic, knowledge is interpreted as a collection of elastic or, equivalently, fuzzy constraint on a collection of variables.
5. Inference is viewed as a process of propagation of elastic constraints.

12.12 INTELLIGENCE, CONTROL AND INFORMATION (ICI)

Fuzzy logic is a technology for developing intelligent control and information systems. We summarize below three facets of fuzzy logic from the viewpoint of machine intelligence, control systems, and information technology.

Fuzzy logic achieves machine intelligence by offering a way for representing and reasoning about human knowledge that is imprecise by nature. Even though representing and reasoning about human knowledge that is imprecise by nature. Even though fuzzy logic is not the only technique for developing AI systems, it is unique in its approach for explicit representation of the impreciseness in human knowledge and problem solving technique s. this facet of fuzzy logic will be revealed throughout the book. In addition to achieving artificial intelligence, fuzzy logic also benefits from machine learning techniques because they can be used to construct fuzzy systems automatically. Neural networks and genetic algorithms are two machine learning techniques that are particularly useful for this purpose.

Fuzzy logic offers a practical way for designing nonlinear control systems. It achieves nonlinearity through piece-wise linear approximation. The basic building block of a fuzzy logic control system is set of fuzzy if-then rules (i.e., fuzzy rule-based models) that approximate a functional mapping. In fact, fuzzy rule-based models are useful not only for control systems, but also for decision making and pattern recognition. The basics of fuzzy rule-based models will be introduced in next Chapters.

Fuzzy logic is becoming increasingly important in advanced <$no page> information systems. In addition to its potential for developing intelligent software agents, it has been used for storing and retrieving imprecise information from databases and information sources, as well as for extracting interesting patterns from a large amount of data. The latter can be applied to medical image analysis, computer vision, and data mining.

Like facets of a diamond, the three facets of fuzzy logic technology shed light on each other and create brilliant and vivid colors. We hope that the remaining Chapters of this book help you to visualize such an exciting image.

12.13 BASIC CONCEPTS OF FUZZY LOGIC

Even though the broad sense of fuzzy logic introduced in the previous chapter covers a wide range of theories and techniques, its core technique is based on four basic concepts:

1. **Fuzzy sets:** Sets having smooth boundaries;
2. **Linguistic variables:** Variables whose values are both qualitatively and quantitatively described by a fuzzy set;
3. **Possibility distribution:** Constraints on the value of a linguistic variable imposed by assigning it a fuzzy set; and
4. **Fuzzy if-then rules:** A knowledge representation scheme for describing a functional mapping or a logic formula that generalizes an implication in two-valued logic.

The first three concepts are fundamental for all sub areas in fuzzy logic. The fourth concept is also important because it is the basis for most industrial applications of fuzzy logic developed to date, including many fuzzy logic control systems.

12.14 TWO PROBLEMS ARE GIVEN RELATED TO FUZZY LOGIC

Problem 1: Rudimentary Air Flows Mixing Control

The first problem is the control of air flow mixing for room temperature control. It is a "rudimentary" control problem because no feedback about the current room temperature is provided. We choose it for its simplicity and its connection no fuzzy logic control. The given task of this problem is to control the amount of hot air flow and cold air flow based on a set target temperature. In this rudimentary version of the problem, we assume that there is no feedback signal about the current room temperature. The amount of hot air flow and cold air flow is controlled by adjusting the voltage to the pump in the mixing stage. The lowest and highest voltage settings are denoted by $\underline{V}$ and $\overline{V}$. If the voltage is set at $\underline{V}$, maximal cold air flow will be allowed. If the voltage is set at $\overline{V}$, maximal hot air flow will be generated. A voltage between $\underline{V}$ and mixes the hot flow and the cold flow proportionally. This problem is depicted in Figure 12.2.

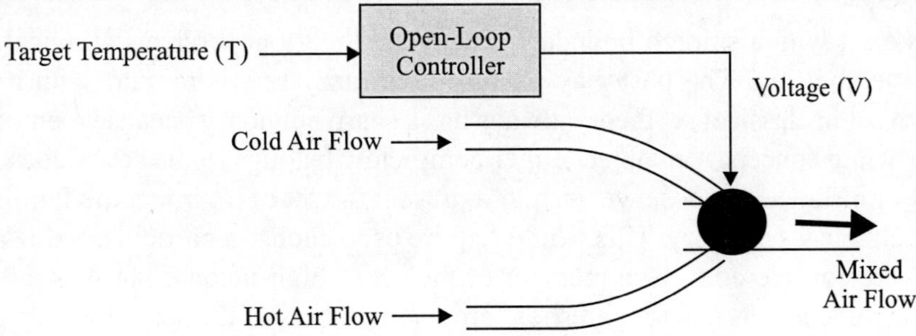

Figure 12.2: Rudimentary Air Flow Mixing Controller.

Problem 2: Automated Washing Machine Control

The second problem is about the automatic selection of cycles and washing time for a washing machine. This problem allows us to illustrate certain fuzzy logic techniques that cannot be demonstrated using the first problem. We chose to use this problem among many candidate applications for two additional reasons. First, the nature of human decision making involved in this problem is easy to understand due to out familiarity with the tasks in our daily lives. Second, a fuzzy logic approach to problem developed by Matsushita Electric Industrial Co. [the automatic washing machine is called "Aisai-go (beloved wife) Day Fuzzy"], as mentioned in previous section, generated a fuzzy vogue in 1990 which triggered the introduction of many other successful consumer products using fuzzy logic. The word "fuzzy" even won the 1990 gold prize for a new word in Japan. This application therefore has an additional historical significance.

The goal of this problem is to simplify the operation of the washing machine while ensuring high-quality results. More specifically, we wish to automate the selection of the wash cycle and wash time based on the quality and the softness of the laundry. To simplify our discussion, we assume that the quantity and the softness of the laundry are provided directly by two sensing techniques. In reality, however, these measures are not measurable directly. They are often inferred from other sensor inputs. Figure 12.3 depicts the problem graphically.

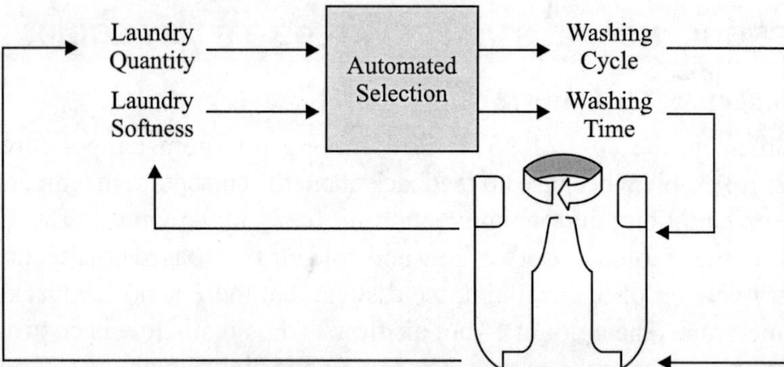

Figure 12.3: Fully automatic washing machine.

12.15 FUZZY SETS

A fuzzy set is a set with a smooth boundary. Fuzzy set theory generalizes classical set theory to allow partial membership. The best way to introduce fuzzy sets is to start with a limitation of classical sets. A set in classical set theory always has a sharp boundary because membership in a set is a black-and-white concept – an object either completely belongs to the set or does not belong to the set at all. For instance, suppose we wish to represent the set of high-income families within the framework of classical set theory. This would require us to choose a particular value as a threshold (say \$90,000) are considered to be a member of the set of high-income families, and all families with a yearly income lower than the threshold are not members of the set. However, the fact that a family with a yearly income of \$89,999 is not considered high income whereas a family with \$1 more yearly income is considered high income is counterintuitive, to say the least. Even through unnatural and sometimes disturbing, such artificially created sharp boundaries have often been used in defining classical sets, primarily due to a lack of a better methodology.

Even through some sets do have sharp boundaries (e.g., the set of married people), many others do not have sharp boundaries (e.g., the set of happily married couples, the set of good graduate schools). Fuzzy set theory directly addresses this limitation by allowing membership in a set to be a matter of degree. The degree of membership in a set is expressed by a number between 0 and 1; 0 means entirely not in the set, 1means completely in the set, and a number in between means partially in the set. This way, a smooth and gradual transition from the regions outside the set can be described. A fuzzy set is thus defined by a function that maps objects in a domain of concern to their membership value in the set. Such a function is called the membership function and is usually denoted by the Greek symbol u for ease of recognition and consistency. For example a more realistic representation of the high-income family can now be expressed by the membership function in Figure 12.4. The membership function of a fuzzy set A is denoted as u_A, and the membership value of x in A is denoted as $u_{A(x)}$. The domain of the membership function, which is the domain of concern from which elements of the set are drawn, is called the universe of discourse. For instance, the universe of discourse of the fuzzy set High Income can be the positive real line [0, ∞).

12.16 DESIGNING MEMBERSHIP FUNCTIONS

A membership function can be designed in three ways:

1. Interview those who are familiar with underlying concept and later adjust it based on a tuning strategy.
2. Construct it automatically from data;
3. Learn it based on feedback from the system performance.

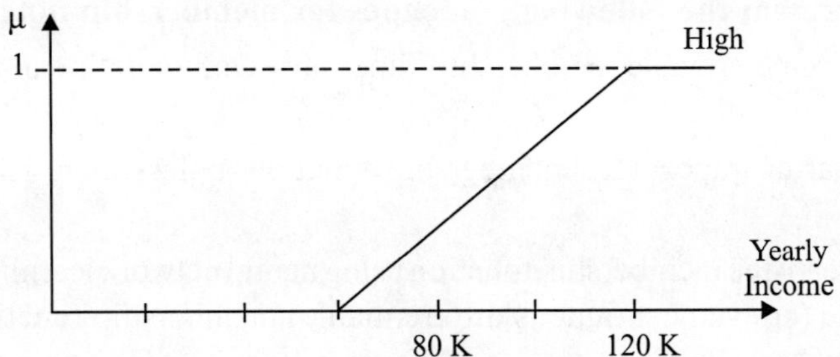

Figure 12.4: Membership function represents the high annual income.

We strongly recommend the use of parameterizable functions that can be defined by a small number of parameters. Using parameterized membership functions cannot only reduce the system design time, it can also facilitate the automated tuning of the system because desired changes to the membership function (e.g., widening vs. narrowing a membership function) can be directly related to corresponding changes in the related parameters.

The parameterizable membership functions most commonly used in practice are the triangular membership function and the trapezoid function. The former has three parameters and the latter has four parameters. An example of these two kinds of membership function and their parameters are shown in Figure 12.5 and 12.6.

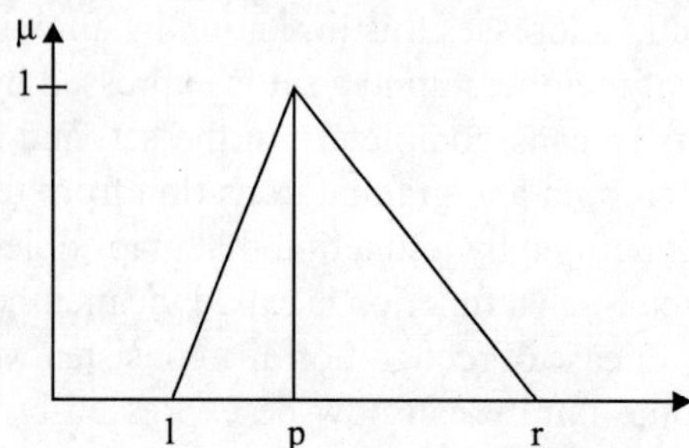

Figure 12.5: A triangular membership function having different parameters.

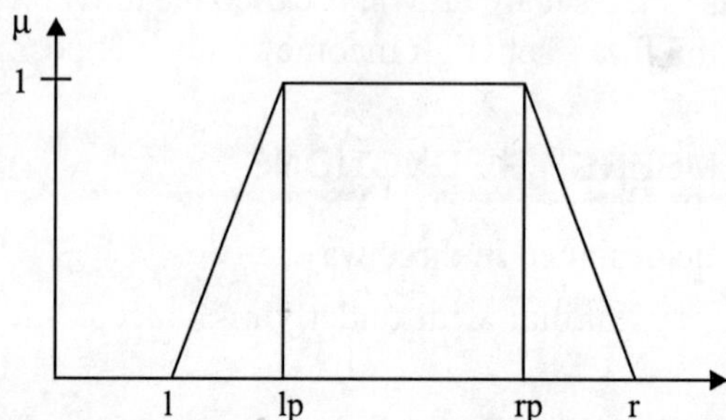

Figure 12.6: A trapezoid membership function having different parameters

To summarize, we present the following guidelines for membership function design:

1. Always use parameterizable membership functions. Do not define a membership function point by point.
2. Use a triangular or trapezoidal membership function, unless there is a good reason to do otherwise.
3. If you want to learn the membership function using neural network learning techniques, choose a differentiable (or even continuous differentiable) membership function (e.g., Gaussian).

12.17 BASIC OPERATIONS IN FUZZY SETS

The three fundamental operations in classical sets are union, intersection, and complement. The union of two sets A and B (denoted $A \cup B$) is the collection of those objects that belong to either A or B. The intersection A and B (denoted $A \cap B$) is the collection of those objects that belong to both A and B. The complement of a set A (denoted as A^c or $\overline{A}$) is the collection of objects not belonging to A. For instance, let A and B be two sets of annual personal income defined as below:

$$A = \{x \mid 100K \leq x \leq 200K, x \in U\}$$
$$B = \{x \mid 80K \leq x \leq 140K, x \in U\}$$

where U is the universe of discourse [0, 1000K]. We get

$$A \cap B = \{x \mid 100K \leq x \leq 140K, x \in U\}$$
$$A \cup B = \{x \mid 80K \leq x \leq 200K, x \in U\}$$
$$A^C = \{x \mid 0 \leq x < 100K \text{ or } 200K \leq x \leq 1000 K\}$$

These operations are illustrated in Figure 12.7.

A statement in classical logic has only two possible truth values: T (true) or F (false). Two logic statements can be combined using logic connectives such as AND (conjunction, denoted by $\wedge$), OR (disjunction, denoted by $\vee$), NOT (negation, denoted by $\neg$) and IMPLY (implication, denoted by $\rightarrow$). The truth values of these compound statements are listed in Table 12.1 for all possible cases. We use p and q in the table to denote two arbitrary logic statements (called propositions).

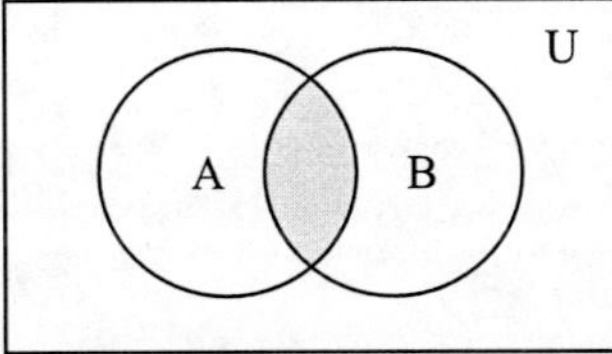

(a) Intersection of Two Sets

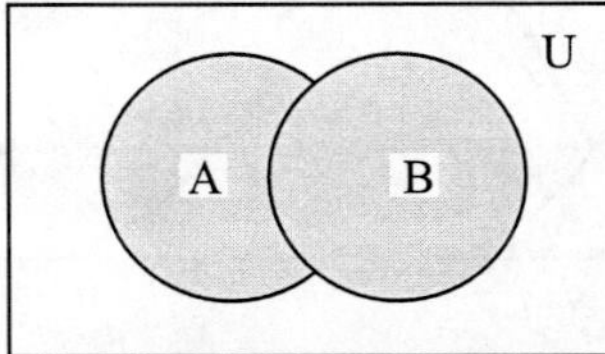

(b) Union of Two Sets

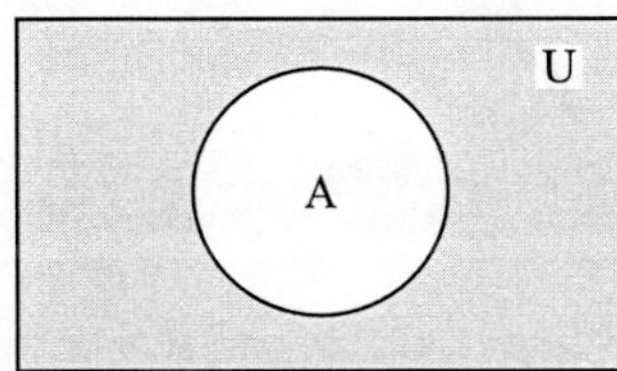

(c) Complement of a Set

Figure 12.7: Basic Set Operations in Fuzzy Logic.

Table 12.1: Truth table of classical logic connectives

p	q	¬p	p∧q	p∨q	p→q
F	F	T	F	F	T
F	T	T	F	T	T
T	F	F	F	T	F
T	T	F	T	T	T

A conjunctive composite statement p∧q is true if and only if both p and q are true. A disjunctive composite statement p∨q is true if and only if either statement is true. A negated statement is true if and only if the original statement is false. We will discuss the implication statement in Section possibility distribution because it is related to fuzzy rules.

Suppose we use the proposition p to represent the sentence "x is in the set A," i.e.,

$$p \text{ is true iff } x \in A$$

and another proposition to represent the sentence "x is in the set B," i.e.,

$$q \text{ is true iff } x \in B$$

where iff stands for "if and only if". It is easy to see that p and q are both true when x is in the intension of A and B, i.e.,

$$(p \wedge q) \text{ is true iff } x \in A \cap B$$

and that p or q is true when x is in the union of A and B, i.e.,

$$(p \vee q) \text{ is true iff } x \in A \cup B$$

Finally, p is false when x is in A's complement, i.e., is true iff

$$\neg p \text{ is true iff } x \in A^C$$

Hence, intersection, union and complement operations in set theory are similar to conjunction, and negation in logic. A common fuzzy disjunction operator is the maximum operator. Hence, fuzzy union is often defined as

$$\mu_{A \cup B}(x) = \max\{\mu_A(x), \mu_B(x)\} \qquad \text{(Eq 12.1)}$$

and is illustrated in Figure 12.8.

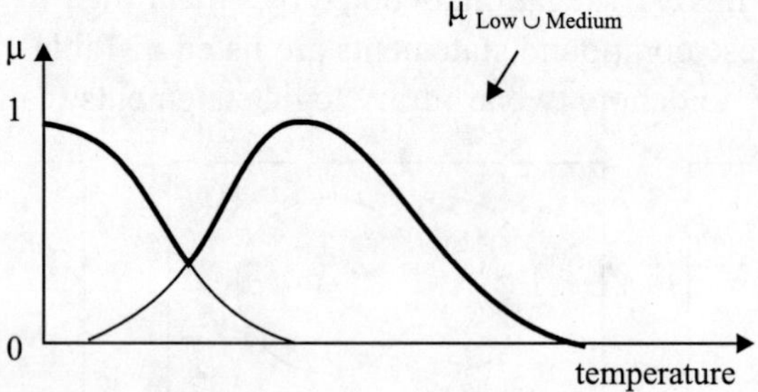

Figure 12.8: Fuzzy Set: Union

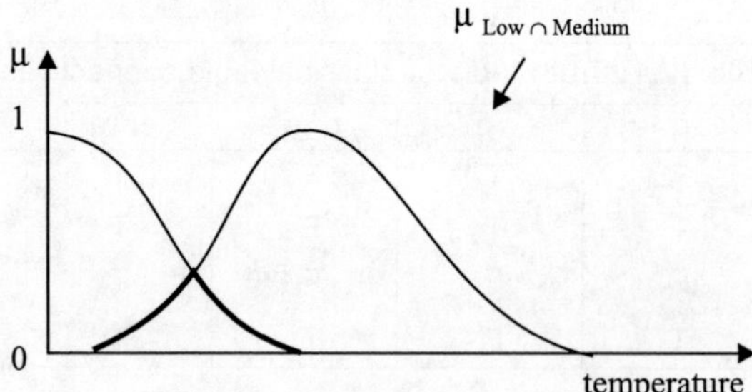

Figure 12.9: Fuzzy Set; Intersection

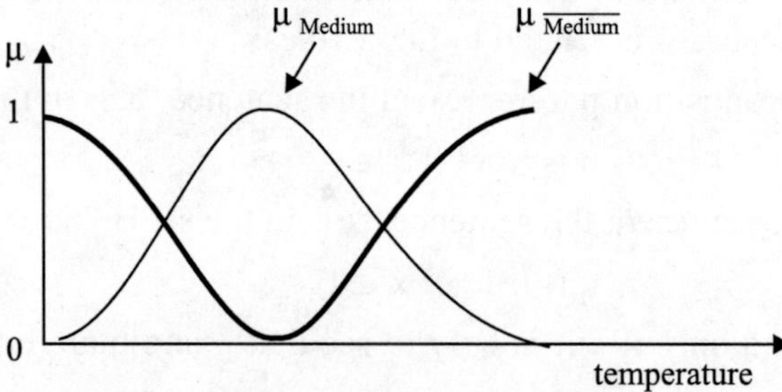

Figure 12.10: Complement of a Fuzzy Set.

A common fuzzy conjunction (AND) operation is the minimum operator. Figure 12.9 shows the result of using min to form the intersection of two fuzzy sets, i.e.,

$$\mu_{A \cap B}(x) = \min \{\mu_A(x), \mu_B(x)\} \qquad \text{(Eq. 12.2)}$$

The complement of a fuzzy set A is defined by the difference between one and the membership degree in A. This is illustrated in Figure 12.10 using the fuzzy set Medium.

$$\mu_A{}^c(x) = 1 - \mu_A(x) \qquad \text{(Eq. 12.3)}$$

12.18 LINGUISTIC VARIABLES

A fuzzy set can be used to describe the value of a variable. For example, the sentence "The amount of trading is heavy" uses a fuzzy set "Heavy" to describe the quantity of the stock market trading in one day. More formally, this is expressed as

Trading Quantity is Heavy

The variable Trading Quantity in this example demonstrates an important concept in fuzzy logic: the linguistic variable. A linguistic variable enables its value to be described both qualitatively by linguistic term (i.e., a symbol serving as the name of a fuzzy set) and quantitatively by a corresponding membership function (which expresses the meaning of the fuzzy set). The linguistic term is used to express concepts and knowledge in human communication, whereas membership function is useful for processing numeric input data.

A linguistic variable is like a composition of a symbolic variable (a variable whose value is a symbol) and a numeric variable (a variable whose value is a number). An example of a symbolic variable is

Shape = Rectangular

where Shape is a variable indicating the shape of an object. An example of numeric variable is

Height = 6‘

Numeric variables are frequently used in science, engineering, mathematics, medicine, and many other disciplines.

In our example about stock market trading activities, there are certainly many other linguistic descriptions about the trading quantity such as "light," "moderate," "somewhat heavy," "very heavy," and so on. One of the important concepts in fuzzy logic is that instead of enumerating all these different descriptions, they can be generated from a core set of linguistic terms (called a term set) using modifiers (e.g., "very," "more or less") and connectives (e.g., "and," "or"). In fuzzy logic, we call these modifiers hedges.

12.19 POSSIBILITY THEORY

Possibility theory is an uncertainty theory devoted to the handling of incomplete information. As such, it complements probability theory. It differs from the latter by the use of a pair of dual set-functions (possibility and necessity measures) instead of only one.

A **possibility distribution** is a mapping π from a set of states of affairs S to a totally ordered scale such as the unit interval [0, 1]. The function π represents the knowledge of an agent (about the actual state of affairs) distinguishing what is plausible from what is less plausible, what is the normal course of things from what is not, what is surprising from what is expected. It represents a flexible restriction on what the actual state of affairs is, with the following conventions:

- $\pi(s) = 0$ means that state s is rejected as impossible;
- $\pi(s) = 1$ means that state s is totally possible (= plausible or unsurprizing).

If the state space is exhaustive, at least one of its elements should be the actual world, so that at least one state is totally possible (normalization). Distinct values may simultaneously have a degree of possibility equal to 1.

Assigning a fuzzy set to a linguistic variable contains the value of the variable, just as a crisp set does. The difference between the two, however, is that the notion of possible versus impossible values becomes a matter of degree. We will illustrate this using the following example. Suppose the police report that the suspect of a bombing is a terrorist, between 20 and 30 years old. This can be expressed by assigning the interval [20, 30] to a variable representing the suspect's age:

$$\text{Age(suspect)} = [20, 30].$$

This interval-valued assignment constrains the age of the suspect. More specifically, it states that the suspect's age can be 20, 21,..., 29, or 30. It is, on the other hand, impossible for the suspect to be 19, 31 or any other age not included in the set [20, 30]. Thus, the assignment above introduces a sharp boundary between possible values and impossible values. For situations where such a sharp boundary is undesirable, fuzzy logic offers an appealing alternative – it generalizes the binary distinction between possible vs. impossible to a matter of degree called the possibility. For instance, if we assign the fuzzy set YOUNG, whose membership function is shown in Figure 12.11, to the age of the suspect, we obtain a distribution about the possibility degree of the suspect's age (e.g., the possibility that the suspect is 19 years old is 0.7, while the possibility of 21 through 28 is 1), i.e.,

$$\Pi_{\text{Age(Suspect)}}(x) = \mu_{\text{Young}}(x) \quad \text{(Eq. 12.4)}$$

where Π denotes a possibility distribution of the suspect's age, and x is a variable representing a person's age. In general, when we assign a fuzzy set A to a variable X, the assignment results in a possibility distribution of X, which is defined by A's membership function:

$$\Pi_x(x) = \mu_A(x) \quad \text{(Eq. 12.5)}$$

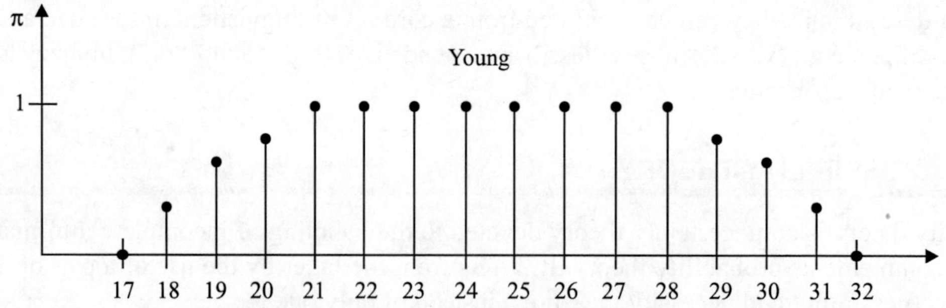

Figure 12.11: Possibility distribution of the fuzzy set (young)

12.20 FUZZY RULES

Fuzzy if-then rules have been applied to many disciplines such as control systems, decision making, pattern recognition, and system modeling. Fuzzy if-then rules also play a critical role in industrial applications ranging from consumer products, robotic, manufacturing, process control, medical imaging, to financial trading.

Let us consider an ancient kingdom in which only seven masters have knowledge about calculating the square root of a real number. Unfortunately, none of them knows a general procedure for calculating the square root of an arbitrary real number. Each one of them, nevertheless, is specialized in solving the problem for a fuzzy region of a real number. For instance, one is an expect for calculating the square root of numbers around 100. One day, the king is challenged to solve a square root square problem by his enemy. He immediately assembles the seven masters in his place. Each master will provide a solution to the king, which is attached with a confidence measure between 0 and 1 (1 means most confident, 0 means no confidence at all). The king will combine all their solutions, each weighted by their confidence measure, into a final solution, which he will present to his enemy. Even though the king and the masters do not know about fuzzy logic, this process turns out to be very close to fuzzy rule-based inference. Each master is like a fuzzy rule; the confidence measure of a master's solution corresponds to the degree a fuzzy rule's condition is satisfied; and the way the masters' recommendations are combined by the king is similar to the way conclusions of multiple fuzzy rules are combined in fuzzy logic.

Mathematically, fuzzy rule-based inference can be viewed as an interpolation scheme because it enables the fusion of multiple fuzzy rules when their conditions are all satisfied to a degree. The degree to which each rule is satisfied determines the weight of the rule's conclusion. Using these weights, fuzzy rule-based inference combines the conclusions of multiple fuzzy rules in a manner similar to linear interpolation. From a logical viewpoint, fuzzy rule-based inference is a generalization of a logical reasoning scheme called modus ponens.

In classical logic, if we know a rule is true and we also know the antecedent of the rule is true, then it can be inferred that the consequent of the rule is true. This is referred to as modus ponens. For example, suppose we know that rule R1 below is true:

R1: IF the annual income of a person of a person is greater that 100,000
THEN the person is rich

we also know that the following statement is true:

Harry annual income is 100,001K

Bases on modus ponens, classical logic can deduce that the following statement is also true;

Harry is rich.

One limitation of modus ponens is that it cannot deal with partial matching. To illustrate this, let us consider rule R1 and a different case:

Robin annual income is $99,999.

People would usually say that Robin is somewhat rich. However modus ponens cannot infer whether Robin is rich or not using rule R1, because Robin annual income does not satisfy the antecedent (i.e., the "IF" part) of R1, even though it is only one dollar short!

The problem has two causes:

1. The antecedent of R1 does not represent a smooth transition into the rich category that is often exhibited in human reasoning.
2. Modus ponens cannot deal with a situation where the antecedent of a rule is partially satisfied.

Viewing such a limitation, fuzzy rule-based inference generalizes modus ponens to allow its inferred conclusion to be modified by the degree to which the antecedent is satisfied. This is the essence of fuzzy rule-based inference.

12.20.1 Structure of Fuzzy Rules

A fuzzy rule is the basic unit for capturing knowledge in many fuzzy systems. A fuzzy rule has two components: an if-part (also referred to as the antecedent) and a then-part (also referred to as the consequent):

IF < antecedent > THEN < consequent >

The antecedent describes a condition, and the consequent describes a conclusion that can be drawn when the condition holds. We introduce the basics of these two components below.

(i) The Antecedent of Fuzzy Rules

For instance, consider the two rules below:

R1: IF the annual income of a person is greater than 120K.

THEN the person is rich.

R2: IF the annual income of a person is high.

THEN the person is Rich.

where High is a fuzzy set defined by the membership function shown in Figure 12.4.

The rule R1 is a conventional one, because its condition is rigid. In contrast, R2 is a fuzzy rule because its condition can be satisfied to a degree for those people whose income lies in the boundary of the fuzzy set High representing high annual income. Like conventional rules, the antecedent of a fuzzy rule may combine multiple simple conditions into a complex one using three logic connectives: AND (conjunction), OR (disjunction), and NOT (negation). For instance, a loan approval system may contain the following fuzzy rule:

IF the annual income of a person is High AND

(the credit report of the person is Fair OR

the person has a Valuable real estate asses) AND

the amount of the loan requested is NOT Jumbo

THEN recommend approving the loan.

(ii) The Consequent of Fuzzy Rules

The consequent of fuzzy rules can be classified into three categories:

1. **Crisp Consequent:** IF....THEN y = a (where a is nonfuzzy numeric value or symbolic value.)
2. **Fuzzy Consequent:** IF.... THEN y is A (where A is a fuzzy set.)
3. **Functional Consequent:** IF x_1 is A_1 AND x_2 is A_2 AND ... x_n is A_n

THEN
$$y = a_0 \quad \overset{n}{\underset{i\ 1}{}} \quad a_i \quad x_i$$

where $a_0, a_1, \ldots, a_n$ are constants.

Each type of rule consequent has its merit. Generally speaking, fuzzy rules with a crisp consequent can be processed more efficiently. A rule with a fuzzy consequent is easier to understand and more suitable for capturing imprecise human expertise. Finally, rules with a functional consequent can be used to approximate complex nonlinear models using only a small number of rules.

One possible approach to problem 1 in Section 12.14 is to program a rudimentary controlled pump controller to enact the following fuzzy rules:

R1: IF the target temperature T is Low,
THEN set the voltage to $\underline{V}$ (i.e., turn on the cold flow).

R2: IF the target temperature T is High,
THEN set the voltage to $\overline{V}$ (i.e., turn on the hot flow).

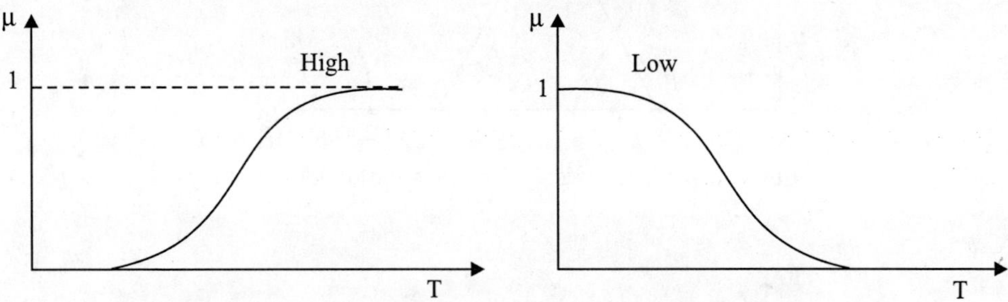

Figure 12.12: Membership functions for target temperature.

For the automatic washing machine problem, rules should combine conditions on laundry quantity and laundry softness using conjunction (AND). Two rules for selecting the wash cycle are listed below:

R1: IF Laundry Quantity is Normal AND
Laundry Softness is Hard
THEN Washing Cycle is Strong

R2: IF Laundry Quantity is Large AND

Laundry Softness is Normal Hard

THEN Washing Cycle is Normal

The membership functions for fuzzy conditions about laundry softness and laundry quantity are depicted in Figure 12.13 and 12.14 respectively. The membership function for fuzzy decisions regarding the wash cycle are shown in Figure 12.15. A complete set of fuzzy rules for the selection of a cycle is shown in Table 12.2.

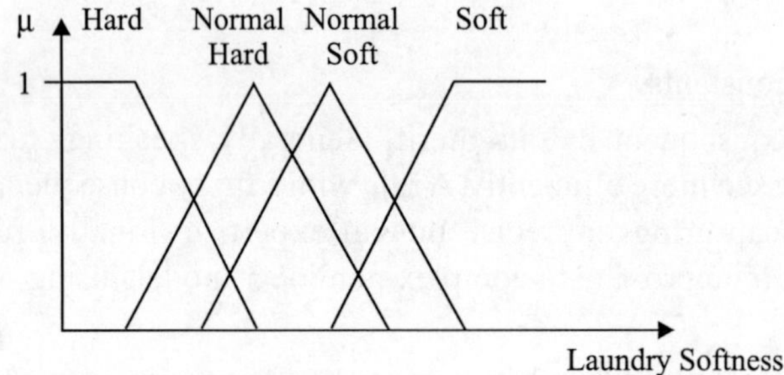

Figure 12.13: Membership functions represents for softness

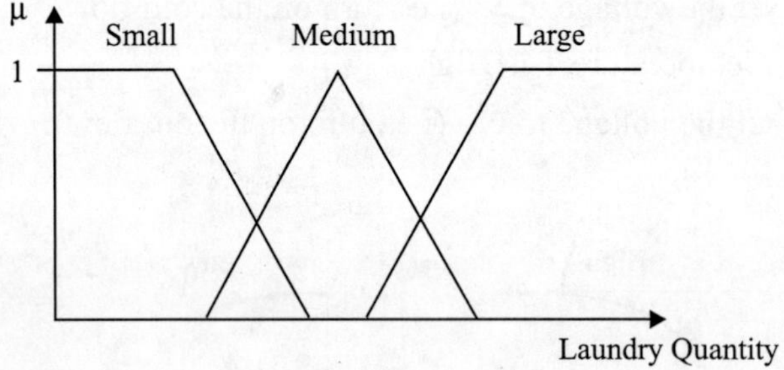

Figure 12.14: Membership functions for laundry quantity

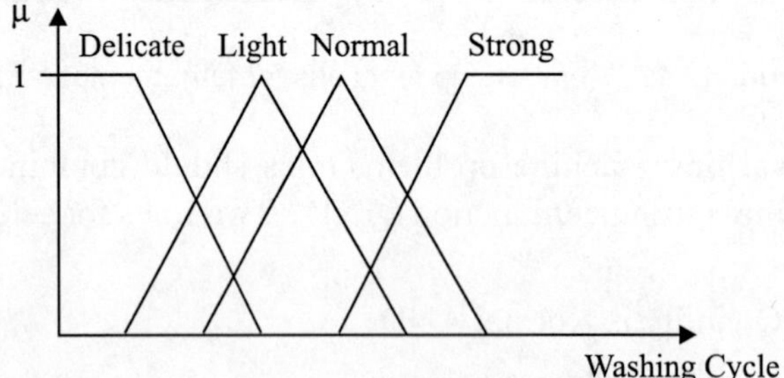

Figure 12.15: Membership functions for washing cycles

Table 12.2: Fuzzy rules for washing cycle			
Laundry Quantity → **Laundry Softness ↓**	**Small**	**Medium**	**Large**
Soft	Delicate	Light	Normal
Normal Soft	Light	Normal	Normal
Normal Hard	Light	Normal	Strong
Hard	Light	Normal	Strong

12.21 FUZZY RULE-BASED INFERENCE

The algorithm of fuzzy rule-based inference consists of three basic steps and an additional optional step.

1. **Fuzzy Matching:** Calculate the degree to which the input data match the condition of the fuzzy rules.
2. **Inference:** Calculate the rule's conclusion based on its matching degree.
3. **Combination:** Combine the conclusion inferred by all fuzzy rules into a final conclusion.
4. **Defuzzification (optional):** For applications that need a crisp output (e.g., in control systems), an additional step is used to convert a fuzzy conclusion into a crisp one.

We will illustrate the basics of these four steps using the flow mixing problem and the automatic washing machine problem.

12.21.1 Fuzzy Matching

Let us first consider fuzzy matching for the flow mixing control rules. The rudimentary flow mixing control is described in Section 12.20.1. The degree to which the input target temperature satisfies the condition of rule R3 "target temperature is Low" is the same as the degree to which the input target temperature T belongs to the fuzzy set Low. For the convenience of our discussion, we denote the degree of matching between input data d and rule r as Matching Degree (d, r). Thus, we summarize the discussion above as

$$\text{Matching Degree}(T, R3) = \mu_{\text{Low}}(T)$$

where "=" represents assignment (not equality test). Similarly, we have

$$\text{Matching Degree}(T, R4) = \mu_{\text{High}}(T)$$

Figure 12.16 illustrates this step for the case of input target temperature T = 80° F.

When a rule has multiple conditions combined using AND (conjunction), we simply use a fuzzy conjunction operator to combine the matching degree of each condition. One of the most commonly used fuzzy conjunction operators is the min operator. Another fuzzy conjunction operator used for this purpose is the product (i.e., multiplication) operator.

In Figure 12.17, the use of min operator for combining the degree of matching of conjunction conditions for washing cycle selection rules.

For the first rule in the figure the condition "Laundry Quantity is Heavy" matches the sensor input 0.5 degree; and the condition "Laundry Softness" matches the sensor input 0.2 degree. Combining the two matching degrees using min, we obtain 0.2 as the degree to which the input data match the antecedent of the following rule:

IF Laundry Quantity is Heavy AND

Laundry Softness is Hard

THEN ....

Similarly, we can find that the degree the input data match the second rule in figure 12.17 is 0.5.

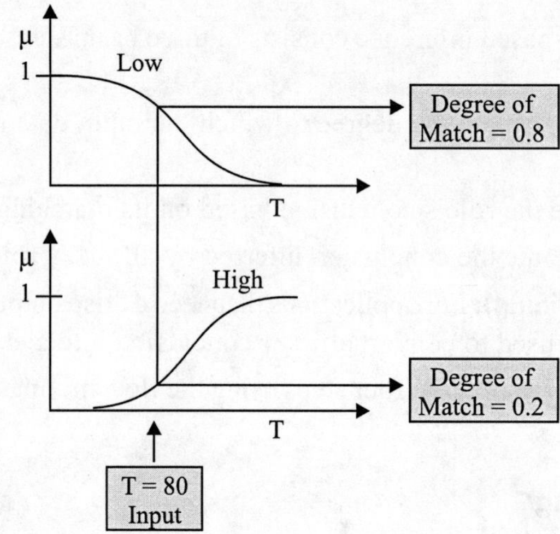

Figure 12.16: Fuzzy Matching for Simple Conditions

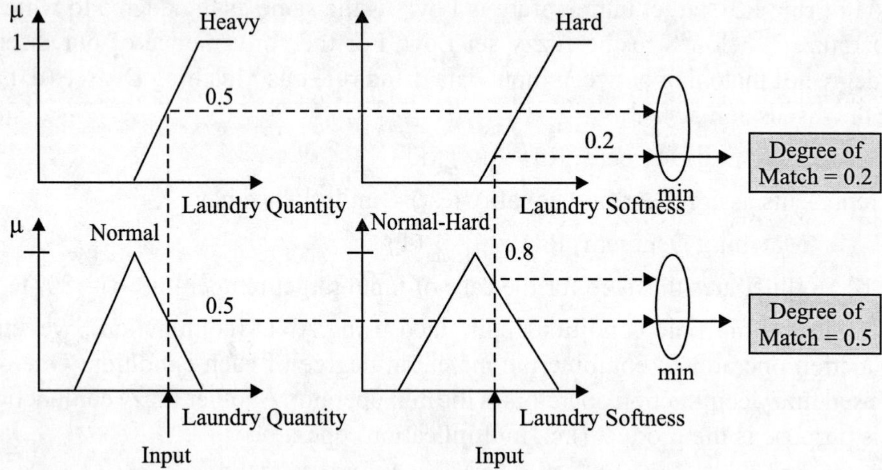

Figure 12.17: Fuzzy Matching for Conjunctive Conditions

In general, the degree to which a rule in the form of

IF X_1 is $A^1_{i_1}$ AND X_2 is $A^2_{i_2}$ AND .... X_n is A^1_{in} THEN.......

matches the input data

$$X_1 = x^0_1, X_2 = x^0_2, ... X_n = x^0_n$$

is computed by the following formula:

$$\text{Matching Degree} = \min \{ A^1_{i_1}(x^0_1), \quad A^2_{i_2}(x^0_2), ... \; x^1_{i_n}(x^0_n)\} \quad \text{(Eq 12.6)}$$

If the antecedent of a rule includes conditions connected by OR (disjunction), we use a fuzzy disjunction operator (e.g., max) to combine matching degree accordingly.

12.21.2 Inference

After the fuzzy matching step, a fuzzy inference step is invoked for each of the relevant rules to produce a conclusion based on their matching degree. How should the conclusion be produced?

There are two methods:

1. The clipping method
2. The scaling method

Both methods generate an inferred conclusion by suppressing the membership function of the consequent.

The clipping and scaling methods produce their inferred conclusion by suppressing the membership function of the consequent differently. The clipping method cuts off the top of the membership function whose value is higher than the matching degree. The scaling method scales down the membership function in proportion to the matching degree. These two methods are illustrated in Figure 12.18 and 12.19 using a hypothetical fuzzy consequent "Y is A." It is easy to see that both methods are consistent with modus ponens in classical logic:

- When the matching degree is (i.e., the antecedent is completely satisfied), the inferred conclusion is identical to the rule's consequent.
- When the matching degree is 0 (i.e., the antecedent is not satisfied at all), no conclusion can be inferred from the rule.

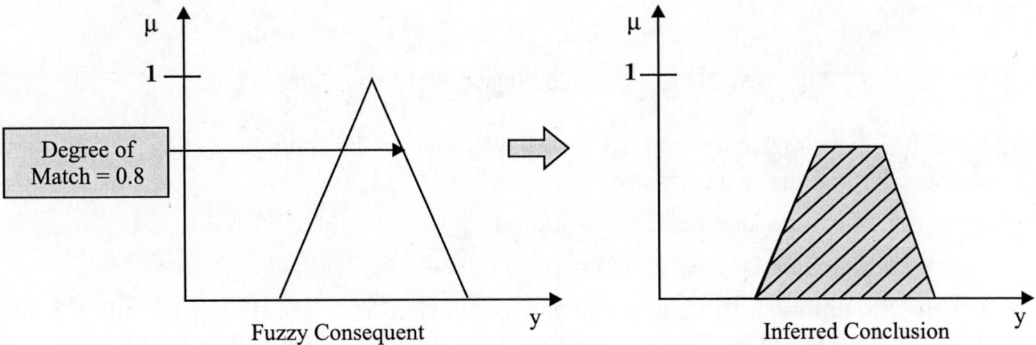

Figure 12.18: Clipping Method for the Fuzzy Inference

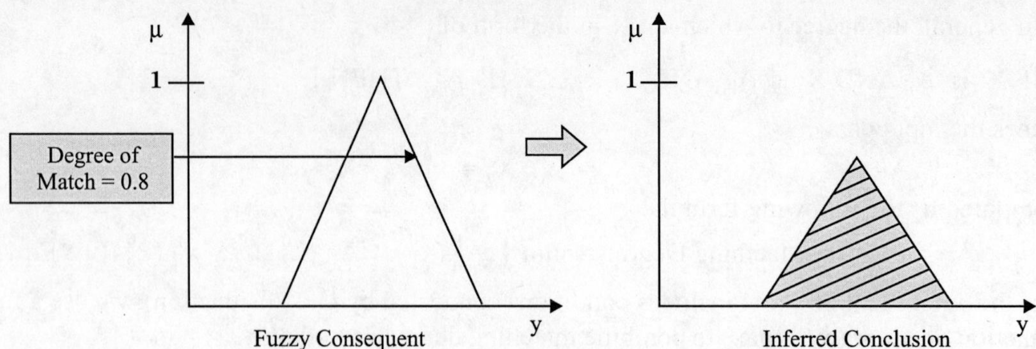

Figure 12.19: Scaling Method for the Fuzzy Inference

In the case of a crisp consequent, the two methods degenerate into an identical one. We will use the air flow mixing control problem to illustrate this. Recall that the rules for this problem are

R3: If T is Low THEN $V = \underline{V}$.

R4: If T is High THEN $V = \overline{V}$.

To apply fuzzy inference to these rules with crisp consequents, we need to first convert them into an equivalent fuzzy set representation. For instance, the crisp value $\underline{V}$ is equivalent to a membership function that assigns value 1 to $\underline{V}$, and 0 to all other values as shown in Figure 12.20(a). Similarly, we can construct the membership function of crisp value $\overline{V}$ as shown in Figure 12.20(b).

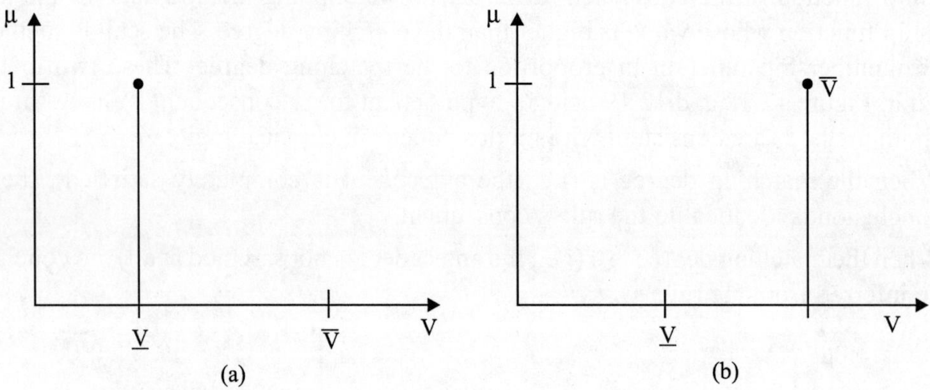

Figure 12.20: Membership Functions of Crisp Consequents

Suppose the input target temperature is T we have shown in the previous section that the matching degrees between T and the two rules are

$$\text{Matching Degree}(T, R3) = \mu_{Low}(T)$$

$$\text{Matching Degree}(T, R4) = \mu_{High}(T)$$

It is then straightforward to show that the conclusion V = V' inferred by rule R3 and the conclusion V = V" inferred by R4 have the following membership function for both the clipping method and the scaling method:

$$\mu_{V'}(V) = \begin{cases} {}_{\text{LOW}}(T) & V = \underline{V} \\ 0 & V = \bar{V} \end{cases} \qquad \text{(Eq. 12.7)}$$

$$\mu_{V'}(V) = \begin{cases} 0 & V = \underline{V} \\ {}_{\text{LOW}}(T) & V = \bar{V} \end{cases} \qquad \text{(Eq. 12.8)}$$

Figure 12.21 illustrates this for R3 and a target temperature that is 0.8 degree in the fuzzy set Low. Hence, the conclusion inferred by R3 in this case is

$$\mu_{V'}(V) = \begin{cases} 0.8 & V = \underline{V} \\ 0 & V = \bar{V} \end{cases} \qquad \text{(Eq. 12.9)}$$

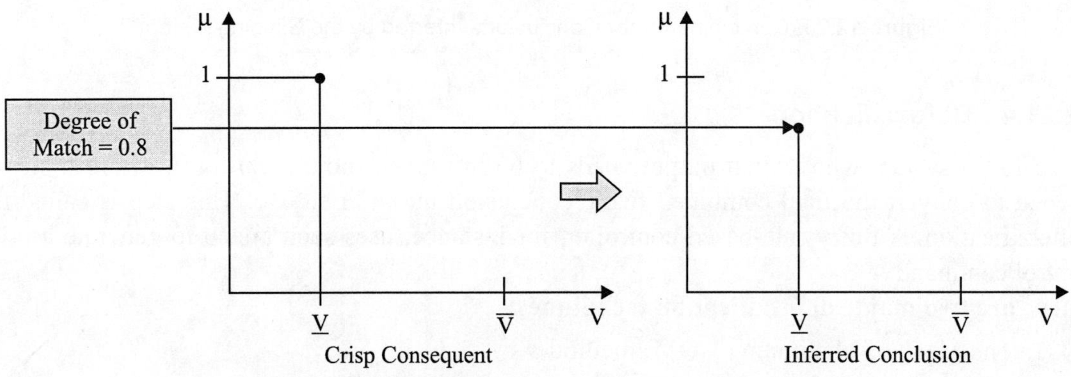

Figure 12.21: A Fuzzy Inference for a Crisp Consequent

12.21.3 Combining Fuzzy Conclusions

A third step is needed to combine the inference results of these rules. This is accomplished typically by superimposing all fuzzy conclusions about a variable. This is illustrated in Figure 12.22 for combining two fuzzy conclusions obtained using the scaling method, and in Figure 12.23 for combining fuzzy conclusions inferred using the clipping method.

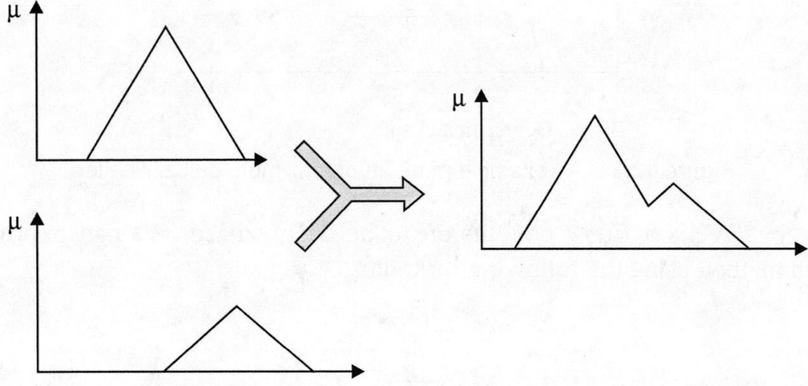

Figure 12.22: Combining Fuzzy Conclusions Inferred by the Scaling Method

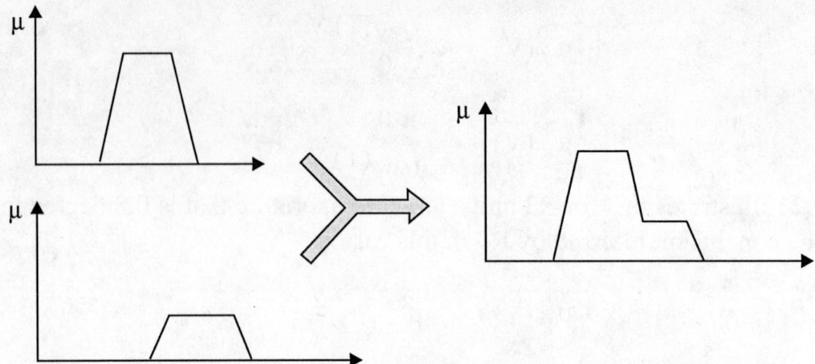

Figure 12.23: Combining Fuzzy Conclusions Inferred by the Clipping Method

12.21.4 Defuzzification

For a fuzzy system whose final output needs to be in a crisp (nonfuzzy) form, a fourth step is needed to convert the final combined fuzzy conclusion into a crisp one. This step is called the defuzzification. A fuzzy rule-based controller, for instance, uses such a step to generate a crisp control command.

There are two major defuzzification techniques:

1. The Mean of Maximum (MOM) method
2. The Center of Area (COA) or the centroid method

The mean of maximum defuzzification calculates the average of all variable values with maximum membership degrees. Figure 12.24 shows the result of applying MOM defuzzification to a combined fuzzy conclusion.

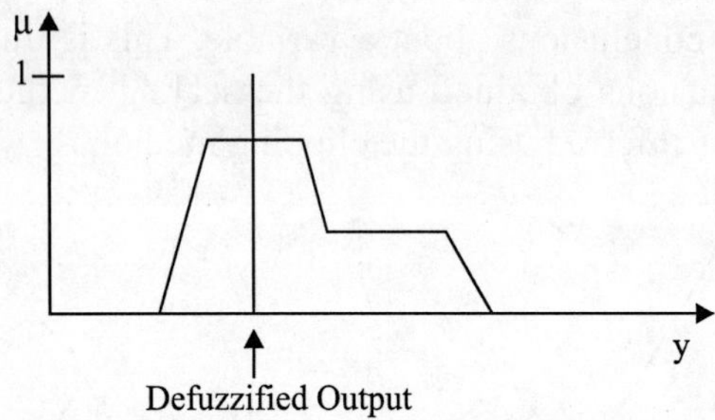

Figure 12.24: An example of mean of maximum defuzzification

Suppose "y is A" is a fuzzy conclusion to be deffuzzified. We can express the MOM defuzzification method using the following formula:

$$y^*$$

$$\text{MOM}(A) = \frac{y^{*}\ p}{|P|} \qquad \text{(Eq 12.10)}$$

where P(A) is the set of output values y with the highest membership degree in A, i.e.,

$$P = \{y^* \mid \mu_A(y^*)\ \sup_y \mu_A(y)\} \qquad \text{(Eq 12.11)}$$

where sup is an operator that returns the maximum value of a continuous function (i.e., the continuous version of the max operator).

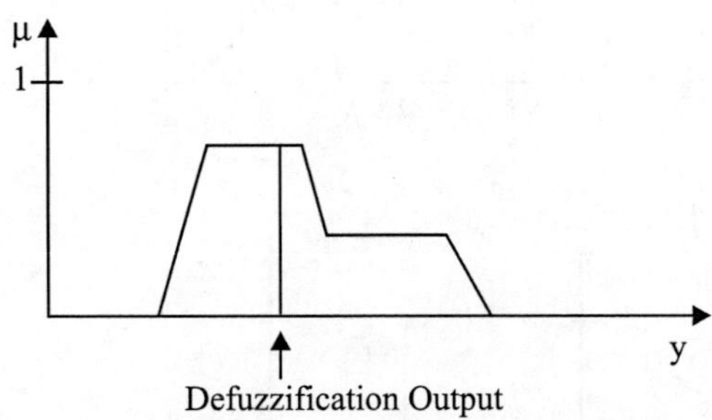

Figure 12.25: An Example of Center of Area Defuzzification

The centroid (or COA) defuzzification method calculates the weighted average of a fuzzy set. The result of applying COA defuzzification to a fuzzy conclusion "Y is A" can be expressed by the formula

$$y = \frac{\underset{i}{}\ {}_A(y_i)\quad y_i}{\underset{i}{}\ {}_A(y_i)} \qquad \text{(Eq 12.12)}$$

if y discrete, and by the formula

$$y = \frac{{}_A(y_i)\quad y_i dy}{{}_A(y_i) dy} \qquad \text{(Eq. 12.13)}$$

if y is continuous.

12.21.5 Putting All Four Steps Together

Figure 12.26 and 12.27 show the result of combining all four steps for the flow mixing controller and the automatic washing machine, respectively. The clipping inference method and the centroid defuzzification technique are used in these two examples.

The defuzzified output for the flow mixing controller can be expressed as a function of the input target temperature using the formula below:

$$V = \frac{{}_{LOW}(T) \times \underline{V} + {}_{HIGH}(T) \times \overline{V}}{{}_{LOW}(T) + {}_{HIGH}(T)} \qquad \text{(Eq. 12.14)}$$

This formula clearly shows that fuzzy rule-based inference indeed performs a kind of interpolation, as we explain in earlier sections.

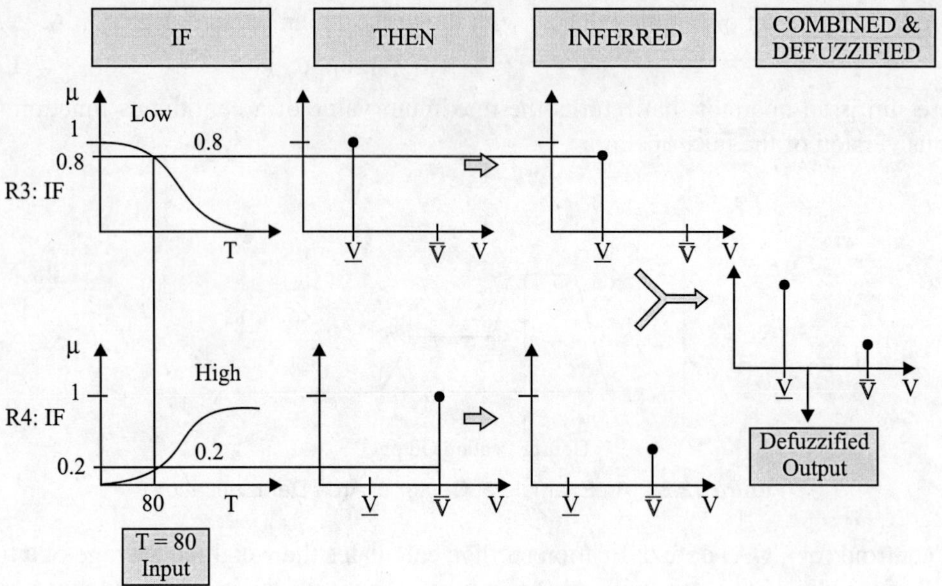

Figure 12.26: Fuzzy Rule-based Inference Rudimentary Flow Mixing Controller

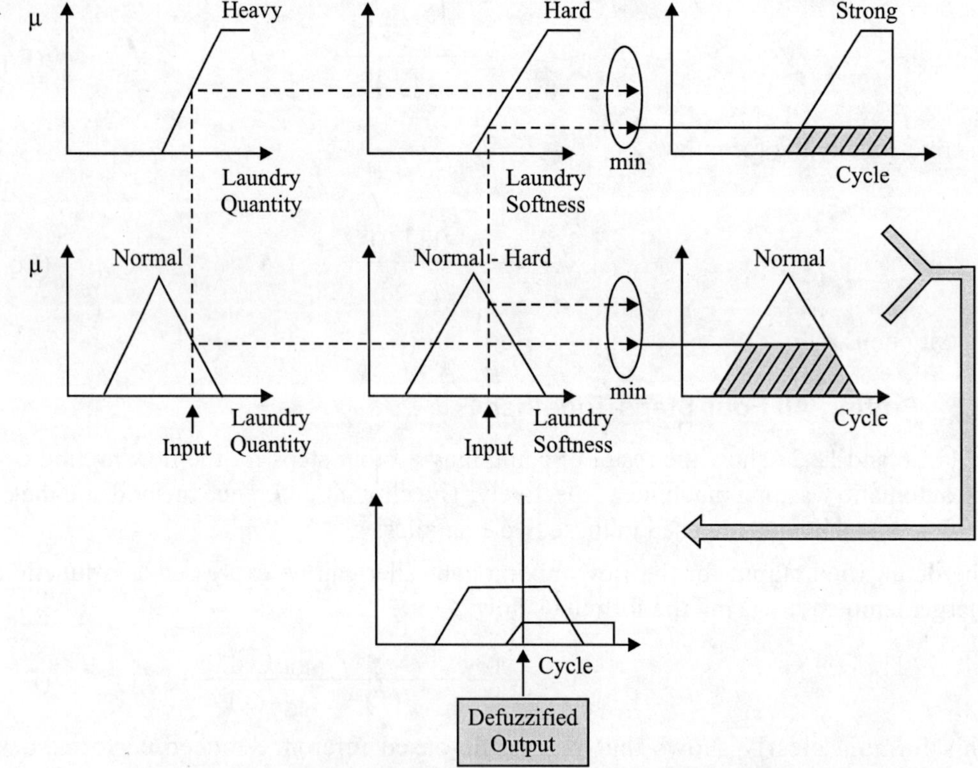

Figure 12.27: Fuzzy Inference of Fuzzy Logic Automatic Washing Machine

EXERCISES

1. What do you understand by fuzzy logic?
2. Why we use the concept of fuzzy logic? Explain with the help of example?
3. What are the various objectives of fuzzy logic?
4. What do you mean by degrees of truth?
5. How we can apply truth values?
6. What do you mean linguistic variables?
7. Explain the concept of fuzzy reasoning?
8. What are the various applications areas of fuzzy logic?
9. Why we use fuzzy logic for control?
10. What do you mean by fuzzy?
11. Why we call fuzzy as ICI?
12. Explain the basic concepts of fuzzy logic with the help of examples?
13. What do you mean by fuzzy sets?
14. Difference between sharp boundaries and smooth boundaries?
15. How we can design membership function?
16. What are the basic operations in fuzzy sets?
17. What do you mean by possibility theory?
18. What do you mean by fuzzy rules?
19. Explain the structures of fuzzy rules?
20. Explain the concept of fuzzy rule based inference?

CHAPTER 13

Classical Sets and Fuzzy Sets

13.1 INTRODUCTION

The theory on classical sets and the basic ideas of the fuzzy sets are discussed in detail in this chapter. The various operations, laws and properties of fuzzy sets are introduced along with that of the classical sets. The classical set we are going to deal is defined by means of the definite or crisp boundaries. This means that there is no uncertainty involved in the location of the boundaries for these sets. But whereas the fuzzy set, on the other hand is defined by its vague and ambiguous properties, hence the boundaries are specified ambiguously. The crisp sets are sets without ambiguity in their membership. The fuzzy set theory is a very efficient theory in dealing with the concepts of ambiguity. The fuzzy sets are dealt after reviewing the concepts of the classical or crisp sets.

The universe of discourse is the universe of all available information on a given problem. Once this universe is defined we are able to define certain events on this information space. We will describe sets as mathematical abstractions of these events and of the universe itself. Figure 13.1 a shows an abstraction of a universe of discourse, say X, and a crisp (classical) set A somewhere in this universe. A classical set is defined by crisp boundaries, i.e., there is no uncertainty in the prescription or location of the boundaries of the set, as shown in Figure 13.1a where the boundary of crisp set A is an unambiguous line. A fuzzy set, on the other hand, is prescribed by vague or ambiguous properties; hence its boundaries are ambiguously specified, as shown by the fuzzy boundary for set $\underset{\sim}{}$ in Figure 13.1b.

We introduced the notion of set membership, from a one-dimensional viewpoint. Figure 13.1 again helps to explain this idea, but from a two-dimensional perspective. Point a in Figure 13.1a is clearly a member of crisp set A; point b is unambiguously not a member of set A. Figure 13.1b shows the vague, ambiguous boundary of a fuzzy set on the same universe X: the shaded boundary represents the boundary region of $\underset{\sim}{}$. In the central (unshaded) region of the fuzzy set, point a is clearly a full member of the set.

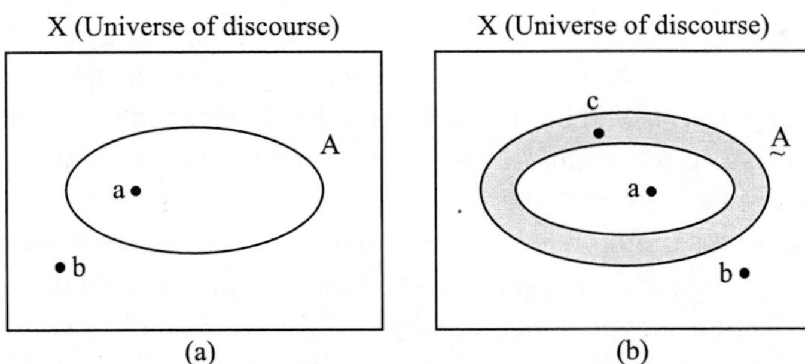

Figure: 13.1 Diagrams for (a) crisp set boundary and (b) fuzzy set boundary.

Outside the boundary region of the fuzzy set, point b is clearly not a member of the fuzzy set. However, the membership of point c, which is on the boundary region, is ambiguous. If complete membership in a set (such as point a in Figure 13.1b) is represented by the number 1, and no-membership in a set (such as point b in Figure 13.1b) is represented by 0, then point c in Figure 13.1b must have some intermediate value of membership (partial membership in fuzzy set $_{\sim}$) on the interval [0, 1]. Presumably the membership of point c in $_{\sim}$ approaches a value of 1 as it moves closer to the central (unshaded) region in Figure 13.1b of $_{\sim}$, and the membership of point c in $_{\sim}$ approaches a value of 0 as it moves closer to leaving the boundary region of $_{\sim}$.

It will be shown that fuzzy set theory is a mathematically rigorous and comprehensive set theory useful in characterizing concepts (sets) with natural ambiguity. It is instructive to introduce fuzzy sets by first reviewing the elements of classical (crisp) set theory.

13.2 SET THEORY

The problem of capturing the vagueness present in the real world is difficult to overcome using classical set theory alone. As a result several extensions to set theory have been proposed that deal with different aspects of uncertainty. Some of the most popular methods for this are fuzzy set theory, rough set theory, and their hybridization, fuzzy-rough set theory. This chapter starts with a quick introduction to classical set theory, using a simple example to illustrate the concept. Then an introduction to fuzzy sets is given, covering the essentials required for a basic understanding of their use. There are many useful introductory resources regarding fuzzy set theory, for example. Following this, rough set theory is introduced with an example dataset to illustrate the fundamental concepts. Finally, fuzzy-rough set theory is detailed.

13.3 CLASSICAL SETS

A classical set is a collection of objects in a given domain. An object either belongs to the set or does not belong to the set. Therefore, these is a sharp boundary between members of the set and those not in the set. The difficulty in expressing sets with smooth boundaries motivated the development of fuzzy sets.

A set may defined in two ways: (1) by enumerating its elements, or (2) by describing the common properties of its elements. The former is called an extensional definition and the latter, an intentional definition. An intentional definition is usually preferred to an extensional definition for three major reasons. First, an intentional. Definition of a set is usually more concise than the set's extensional definition. In fact, enumerating all elements of a set is sometimes impossible (e.g., the set of real numbers between 1 and 10 has an infinite number of elements). Second, an intentional definition explicitly expresses the meaning of a set, Third, an in tensional definition can be used to recognize new elements of a set when the properties of the element change or when the definition properties change.

Suppose we wish to represent the set of universities in Texas whose total student population is greater than 40,000. Let the universe of discourse U be the set of universities in the United States. The extensional definition would list to such universities: Universities of Texas at Austin (UTA), and Texas A&M Universities (TAMU).

$$A = (\text{UTA, TAMU})$$

An intensional definition of the set is given below for comparison.

$$A = \{u \mid \text{total-student-population}(u) > 40{,}000 \text{ AND state}(u) = \text{Texas}\}$$

Membership of an element in a set is denoted by the symbol $\in$. For instance, the fact that Texas A&M Universities is a member of set a can be expressed as

$$\text{TAMU} \in A$$

In contrast, the nonmembership relation is denoted by $\notin$. For instance, Rice $\notin$ A because the student population of Rice University is less than 40,000.

A set S_1, is a subset of set is a subset of set S_2, denoted as $S_1 \subset S_2$, if every element of S_1 is also an element S_2. For instance, let us define a set B to be the set of public universities in Texas. Since both UTA and TAMU are public universities in Texas, set A is a subset of B, i.e., $A \subset B$. The inverse of the subset relation is a superset, also referred to as inclusion. The set B defined earlier includes (is a superset of) the set A, denoted as $B \supset A$. A set without any elements is an empty set, denoted by the symbol ϕ. The empty set is a subset of any set.

The cardinality of a set, denoted as [S], is the number of elements in the set. For instance, the set of Texas universities having at least 40,000 students has exactly two elements. Therefore, its cardinality is 2, i.e., $|A| = 2$.

13.3.1 Classical Set Theory

In classical set theory, elements can belong to a set or not at all. For example, in the set of old people, defined here as {Rod, Jane, Freddy}, the element Rod belongs to this set whereas the element George does not. No distinction is made within a set between elements; all set members belong fully. This may be considered to be a source of information loss for certain applications. Returning to the example, Rod may be older than Freddy, but by this formulation both are considered to be equally old. The order of elements within a set is not considered. More formally, let U be a space of objects, referred to as the universe of discourse, and x an element of U. A classical (crisp) set A, $A \subseteq U$, is defined as a collection of elements $x \in U$, such that each element x can belong to the set or not belong. A classical set A can be represented by a set of ordered pairs (x, 0) or (x, 1) for each element, indicating $x \notin A$ or $x \in A$, respectively. Two sets A and B are said to be equal if they contain exactly the same elements; every element of A is an element of B and every element of B is an element of A. The cardinality of a set A is a measure of the number of elements of the set, and is often denoted |A|. For example, the set {Rod, Jane, Freddy} has a cardinality of 3 (|{Rod, Jane, Freddy}| = 3). A set with no members is called the empty set, usually denoted " and has a cardinality of zero.

Define a universe of discourse, X, as a collection of objects all having the same characteristics. The individual elements in the universe X will be denoted as x. The features of the elements in X can be discrete, countable integers or continuous valued quantities on the real line.

Examples of elements of various universes might be as follows:

The clock speeds of computer CPUs

The operating currents of an electronic motor

The operating temperature of a heat pump (in degrees Celsius)

The Richter magnitudes of an earthquake

The integers 1 to 10

Most real-world engineering processes contain elements that are real and non-negative. The first four items just named are examples of such elements. However, for purposes of modeling, most engineering problems are simplified to consider only integer values of the elements in a universe of discourse. So, for example, computer clock speeds might be measured in integer values of megahertz and heat pump temperatures might be measured in integer values of degrees Celsius. Further, most engineering processes are simplified to consider only finite-sized universes. Although Richter magnitudes may not have a theoretical limit, we have not historically measured earthquake magnitudes much above 9; this value might be the upper bound in a structural engineering design problem. As another example, suppose you are interested in the stress under one leg of the chair in which you are sitting. You might argue that it is possible to get an infinite stress on one leg of the chair by sitting in the chair in such a manner that only one leg is supporting you and by letting the area of the tip of that leg approach zero.

Although this is theoretically possible, in reality the chair leg will either buckle elastically as the tip area becomes very small or yield plastically and fail because materials that have infinite strength have not yet been developed. Hence, choosing a universe that is discrete and finite or one that is continuous and infinite is a modeling choice; the choice does not alter the characterization of sets defined on the universe. If elements of a universe are continuous, then sets defined on the universe will be composed of continuous elements. For example, if the universe of discourse is defined as all Richter magnitudes up to a value of 9, then we can define a set of "destructive magnitudes," which might be composed (1) of all magnitudes greater than or equal to a value of 6 in the crisp case or (2) of all magnitudes "approximately 6 and higher" in the fuzzy case.

A useful attribute of sets and the universes on which they are defined is a metric known as the cardinality, or the cardinal number. The total number of elements in a universe X is called its cardinal number, denoted n_x, where x again is a label for individual elements in the universe. Discrete universes that are composed of a countably finite collection of elements will have a finite cardinal number; continuous universes comprised of an infinite collection of elements will have an infinite cardinality. Collections of elements within a universe are called sets, and collections of elements within sets are called subsets. Sets and subsets are terms that are often used synonymously, since any set is also a subset of the universal set X. The collection of all possible sets in the universe is called the whole set. For crisp sets A and B consisting of collections of some elements in X, the following notation is defined:

$X \in X \Rightarrow$ x belongs to X

$X \in A \Rightarrow$ x belongs to A

$X \notin A \Rightarrow$ x does not belong to the A

For sets A and B on X, we also have

$A \subset B \Rightarrow$ A is fully contained in B(if $x \in A$, then $x \in B$)

$A \subseteq B \Rightarrow$ A is contained in or is equivalent to B

$A \leftrightarrow B \Rightarrow A \subseteq B$ and $B \subseteq A$ (A is equivalent to B)

We define the null set, $\varnothing$, as the set containing no elements, and the whole set, X, as the set of all elements in the universe. The null set is analogous to an impossible event, and the whole set is analogous to a certain event. All possible sets of X constitute a special set called the power set, P(X). For a specific universe X, the power set P(X) is enumerated in the following example.

Example 13.1: We have a universe comprised of three elements, X = {a, b, c}, so the cardinal number is $n_x = 3$. The power set is

$$P(X) = \{\varnothing, \{a\}, \{b\}, \{c\}, \{a, b\}, \{a, c\}, \{b, c\}, \{a, b, c\}\}$$

The cardinality of the power set, denoted $n_{P(x)}$, is found as $n_{P(x)} = 2^n x = 2^3 = 8$

Note that if the cardinality of the universe is infinite, then the cardinality of the power set is also infinity, i.e., $n_X = \infty \Rightarrow n_{P(X)} = \infty$

Example 13.2: Let universe comprised of four elements X = {1, 2, 3, 4} find cardinal number, power set, and cardinality of the power set.

Solution: The cardinal number is the number of elements in the defined set.

The defined set X consists of four elements 1, 2, 3, and 4. Therefore, the Cardinal number = η_x = 4. The power set consists of all possible sets of X. It is given by,

Power set P(x) = {$\varnothing$, {1}, {2}, {3}, {4}, {1, 2}, {1, 3}, {1, 4}, {2, 3}, {2, 4}, {3, 4}, {1, 2, 3}, {2, 3, 4}, {1, 3, 4}, {1, 2, 4}, {1, 2, 3, 4}} Cardinality of the power set is given by, $n_{P(x)} = 2^n x = 2^4 = 16$

13.4 OPERATIONS ON CLASSICAL SETS

There are various operations that can be performed in the classical or crisp sets. The results of the operation performed on the classical sets will be definite. The operations that can be performed on the classical sets are dealt in detail below:

Let A and B be two sets on the universe X. The union between the two sets, denoted A U B, represents all those elements in the universe that reside in (or belong to) the set A, the set B, or both sets A and B. (This operation is also called the logical or; another form of the union is the exclusive or operation. The exclusive or will be described in the next sections.) The intersection of the two sets, denoted $A \cap B$, represents all those elements in the universe X that simultaneously reside in (or belong to) both sets A and B. The complement of a set A, denoted $\bar{A}$, is defined as the collection of all elements in the universe that do not reside in the set A. The difference of a set A with respect to B, denoted A | B, is defined as the collection of all elements in the universe that reside in A and that do not reside in B simultaneously. These operations are shown below in set-theoretic terms.

Union $A \cup B = \{x | x \in \text{ or } x \in B\}$

Intersection $A \cap B = \{x | x \in A \text{ and } x \in B\}$

Complement $\bar{A} = \{x | x \notin A, x \in X\}$

Difference $A | B = \{x | x \in A \text{ and } x \notin B\}$

These four operations are shown in terms of Venn diagrams in Figures 13.2–13.5.

13.4.1 UNION

The Union of two classical sets A and B is denoted by AUB. It represents all the elements in the universe that reside in either the set A, the set B or both sets A and B. This operation is called the logical OR. In set theoretic form it is represented as

$$A \cup B = \{x/x \in A \text{ or } x \in B\}.$$

In Venn diagram form it can be represented as shown in Figure 13.2.

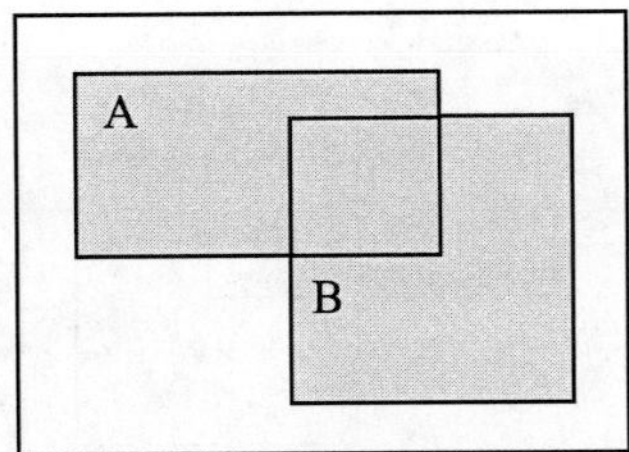

Figure 13.2: Union of Sets A and B (logical or).

13.4.2 Intersection

The intersection of two sets A and B is denoted $A \cap B$. It represents all those elements in the universe X that simultaneously reside in (or belongs to) both sets A and B. In set theoretic form it is represented as $A \cap B = \{x/x \in A \text{ and } x \in B\}$.

In Venn diagram form it can be represented as shown in Figure 13.13.

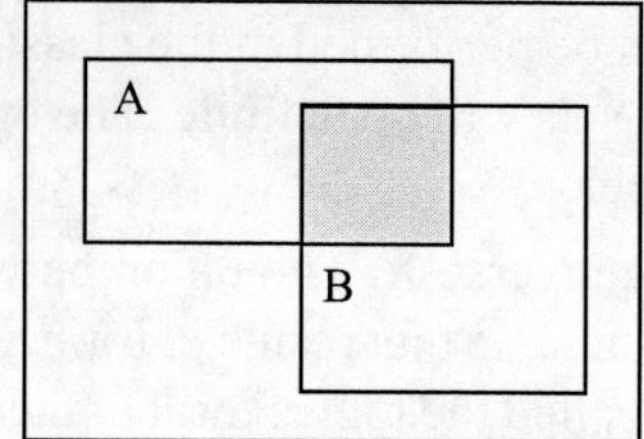

Figure 13.3: Intersection of Sets A and B.

13.4.3 Complement

The complement of set A denoted $\overline{A}$, is defined as the collection of all elements in the universe that do not reside in the set A. In set theoretic form it is represented as $\overline{A} = \{x/x \,/\!\in A, x \in X\}$ .In Venn diagram form it is represented as shown in Figure 13.4.

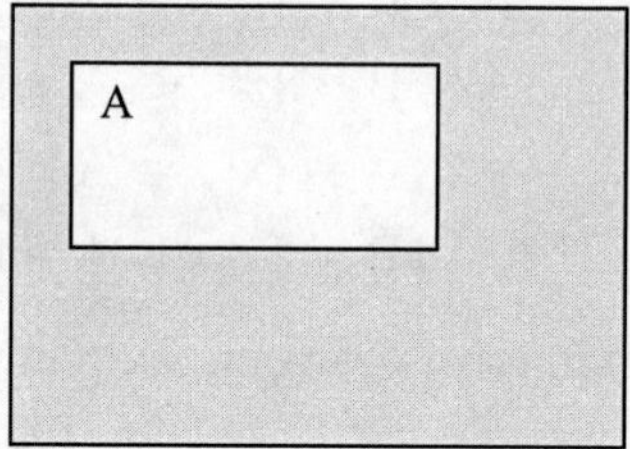

Figure 13.4: Complement of Set A.

13.4.4 Difference

The difference of a set A with respect to B, denoted A|B is defined as collection of all elements in the universe that reside in A and that do not reside in B simultaneously. In set theoretic form it is represented as $A|B = \{x/x \in A \text{ and } x \in B\}$.

In Venn diagram form it is represented as shown in Figure 13.5.

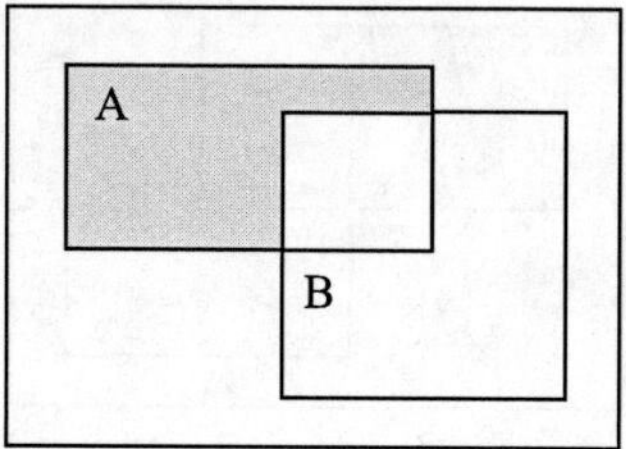

Figure 13.5: Difference operation A | B.

13.4.5 Properties of Classical (Crisp) Sets

In any mathematical operations the properties plays a major role. Based upon the properties, the solution can be obtained for the problems. The following are the important properties of classical sets:

Commutativity $A \cup B = B \cup A$

$A \cap B = B \cap A$

Associativity $A \cup (B \cup C) = (A \cup B) \cup C$

$A \cap (B \cap C) = (A \cap B) \cap C$

Distributivity $A \cup (B \cap C) = (A \cup B) \cap (A \cup C)$

$A \cap (B \cup C) = (A \cap B) \cup (A \cap C)$

Idempotency $A \cup A = A$

$A \cap A = A$

$A \cup \phi = A$

$A \cap X = A$

$A \cap \phi = \phi$

$A \cup X = X$

Transitivity If $A \subseteq B$ and $B \subseteq C$, then $A \subseteq C$

Involution $\bar{\bar{A}} = A$

The double-cross-hatched area in Figure 13.6 is a Venn diagram example of the associativity property for intersection, and the double-cross-hatched areas in Figures 13.7 and 13.8

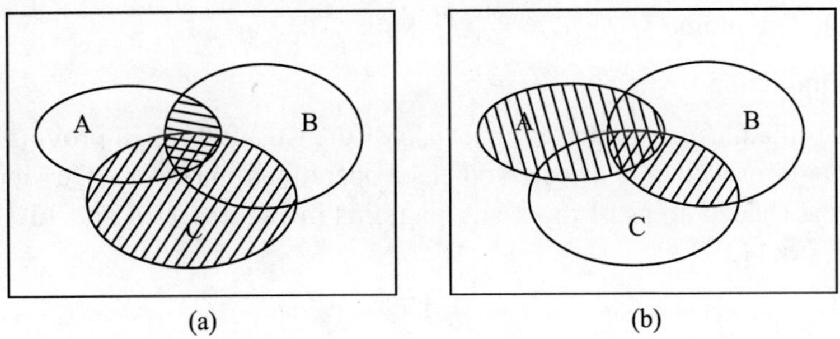

Figure 13.6: Venn Diagrams for (a) $(A \cap B) \cap C$ and (b) $A \cap (B \cap C)$.

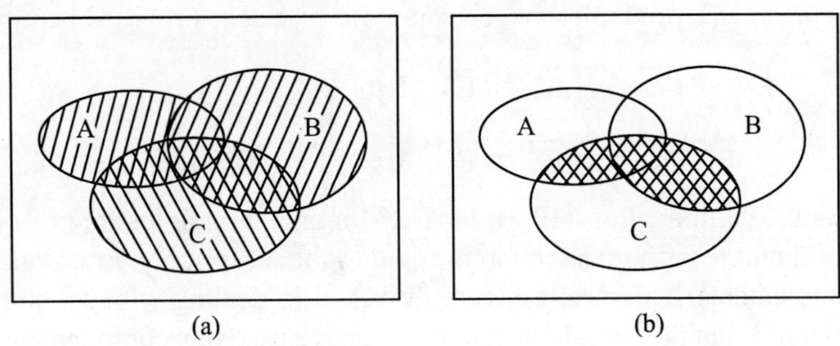

Figure 13.7: Venn diagrams for (a) $(A \cup B)) \cap C$ and (b) $(A \cap C) \cup (B \cap C)$.

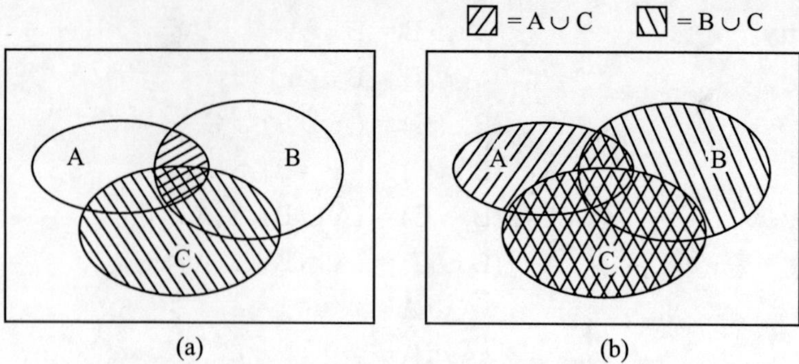

Figure 13.8: Venn Diagrams for (a) $(A \cap B) \cup C$ and (b) $(A \cup C) \cap (B \cup C)$.

are Venn diagram examples of the distributivity property for various combinations of the intersection and union properties. Two special properties of set operations are known as the excluded middle axioms and De Morgan's principles. These properties are enumerated here for two sets A and B. The excluded middle axioms are very important because these are the only set operations described here that is not valid for both classical sets and fuzzy sets. There are two excluded middle axioms (given in Eqs. (13.1)). The first, called the axiom of the excluded middle, deals with the union of a set A and its complement; the second, called the axiom of contradiction, represents the intersection of a set A and its complement.

Axiom of the excluded middle $\quad \overline{A} = X \quad$ (13.1a)

Axiom of the contradiction $\quad \overline{A} = \phi \quad$ (13.1b)

De Morgan's principles are important because of their usefulness in proving tautologies and contradictions in logic, as well as in a host of other set operations and proofs. De Morgan's principles are displayed in the shaded areas of the Venn diagrams in Figures 13.9 and 13.10 and described mathematically in Eq. (13.2).

$$\overline{\qquad} = \overline{\ } \ \overline{\ } \qquad (13.2a)$$

$$\overline{\qquad} = \overline{\ } \ \overline{\ } \qquad (13.2b)$$

In general, De Morgan's principles can be stated for n sets, as provided here for events, E_i:

$$\overline{E_1 \quad E_2 \quad \ldots\ldots \quad E_n} = \overline{E}_1 \quad \overline{E}_2 \quad \ldots\ldots \quad \overline{E}_n \qquad (13.3a)$$

$$\overline{E_1 \ E_2 \ \ldots\ldots \ E_n} = \overline{E}_1 \quad \overline{E}_2 \quad \ldots\ldots \quad \overline{E}_n \qquad (13.3b)$$

From the general equations, Eqs. (13.3), for De Morgan's principles we get a duality relation: the complement of a union or an intersection is equal to the intersection or union, respectively, of the respective complements. This result is very powerful in dealing with set structures since we often have information about the complement of a set (or event), or the complement of combinations of sets (or events), rather than information about the sets themselves.

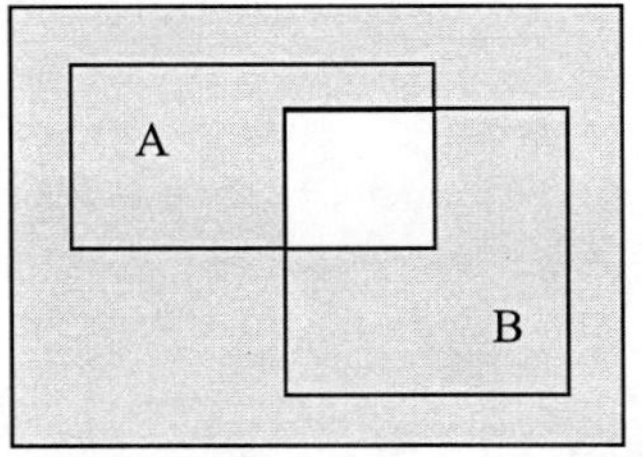

Figure 13.9: De Morgan's Principle $(\overline{A \quad B})$.

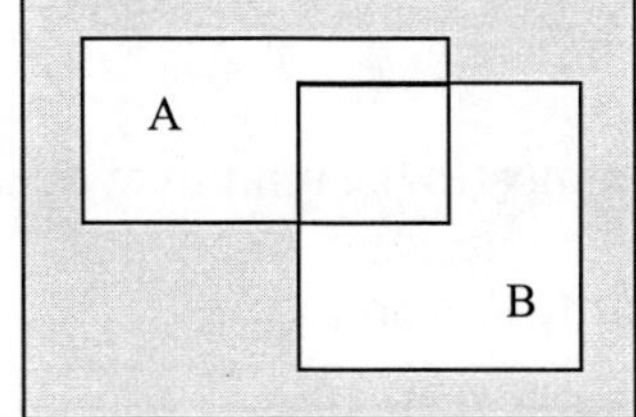

Figure 13.10: De Morgan's Principle $(\overline{A \quad B})$.

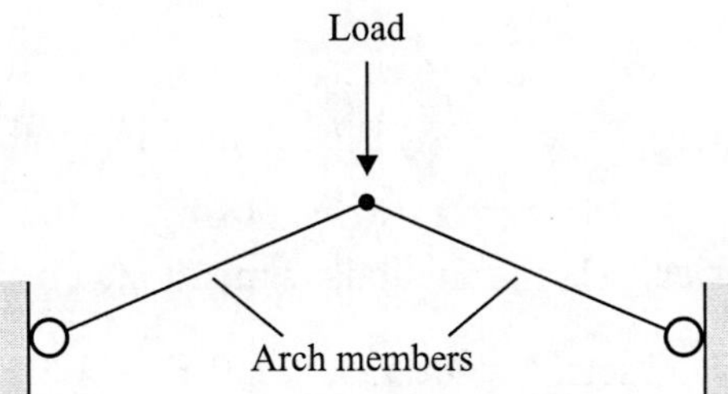

Figure 13.11: A Two-member Arch.

13.5 MAPPING OF CLASSICAL SETS TO A FUNCTION

Mapping of set theoretic forms to function theoretic forms is an important concept. In general it can be used to map elements or subsets on one universe of discourse to elements or sets in another universe. Suppose X and Y are two different universe of discourse. If an element x is contained in X and corresponds to an element y contained in Y, it is generally represented as f: $X \rightarrow Y$, which is said as the mapping from X to Y. The characteristic function χ_A is defined by

$$\chi_A(x) = \begin{matrix} 1 & x \quad A, \\ 0 & x \quad A, \end{matrix}$$

where χ_A represents the membership in set a for the elements x in the universe. The membership mapping for the crisp set A is shown in Figure 13.6. Let us define two sets A and B on the Universe X.

13.5.1 Union

The union of these two sets in terms of function theoretic form is given as follows:

$$A \cup B \rightarrow \chi_{A \cup B}(x) = \chi_A(x) V \chi_B(x)$$
$$= \max(\chi_A(x), \chi_B(x)).$$

Here V indicates the maximum operator.

13.5.2 Intersection

The intersection of two sets in function theoretic form is given as

$$A \cap B \rightarrow \chi_{A \cap B}(x) = \chi_A(x) \Lambda \chi_B(x)$$
$$= \max(\chi_A(x), \chi_B(x)).$$

Here Λ indicates the minimum operator.

13.5.3 Complement

The complement of single set on universe X, say A is given by

$$\bar{A} \rightarrow \ _{\bar{A}}(x) = 1 - \chi_A(x).$$

13.5.4 Containment

The two sets A and B in universe, if one set (A) is contained in another set B, then

$$A \subseteq B \rightarrow \chi_A(x) \leq \chi_B(x).$$

Thus, the mapping of classical sets to functions is mentioned here.

Example 13.3: Given the classical sets, A = {9, 5, 6, 8, 10} B = {1, 2, 3, 7, 9} C = {1, 0} defined on universe X = { Set of all 'n' natural no} Prove the classical set properties associativity and distributivity.

Solution: The associative property is given by

1. A U (B U C) = (A U B) U C.

   LHS

   A U (B U C)

   (a) U C = {2, 3, 7, 9, 1, 0}.

   (b) A U (B U C) = {5, 6, 8, 10, 2, 3, 7, 9, 1, 0}. (13.4)

   RHS

   (A U B) U C

   (a)(A U B) = {9, 5, 6, 8, 10, 1, 2, 3, 7}.

   (b) (A U B) U C = {9, 5, 6, 10, 8, 1, 2, 3, 7, 0}. (13.5)

   From (13.4) and (13.5)

   LHS = RHS

   A U (B U C) = (A U B) U C.

2. $(A \cap (B \cap C) = (A \cap B) \cap C$

   LHS

   (a) $(B \cap C) = \{1\}$.

   (b) $A \cap (B \cap C) = \{\varphi\}$. (13.6)

   RHS

   $(A \cap B) \cap C$

(a) $(A \cap B) = \{9\}$.

(b) $(A \cap B) \cap C = \{\varphi\}$. (13.7)

From (13.6) and (13.7)

LHS = RHS

$A \cap (B \cap C) = (A \cap B) \cap C$.

Thus associative property is proved.

The distributive property is given by,

1. $A \cup (B \cap C) = (A \cup B) \cap (A \cup C)$

LHS

(a) $B \cap C = \{1\}$.

(b) $A \cup (B \cap C) = \{9, 5, 6, 8, 10, 1\}$ (13.8)

RHS

$(A \cup B) \cap (A \cup C)$

(a) $(A \cup B) = \{9, 5, 6, 8, 10, 1, 2, 3, 7\}$.

(b) $(A \cup C) = \{9, 5, 6, 8, 10, 1, 0\}$.

(c) $(A \cup B) \cap (A \cup C) = \{9, 5, 6, 8, 10, 1\}$. (13.9)

From (13.8) and (13.9)

LHS = RHS

$A \cup (B \cap C) = (A \cup B) \cap (A \cup C)$.

2. $A \cap (B \cup C) = (A \cap B) \cup (A \cap C)$

LHS

(a) $(B \cup C) = \{1, 2, 3, 7, 9, 0\}$.

(b) $A \cap (B \cup C) = \{9\}$. (13.10)

RHS

(a) $A \cap B = \{9\}$.

(b) $A \cap C = \{\varphi\}$.

(c) $(A \cap B) \cup (A \cap C) = \{9\}$. (13.11)

From (13.10) and (13.11),

LHS = RHS

$A \cap (B \cup C) = (A \cap B) \cup (A \cap B)$.

Hence distributive property is proved.

13.6 FUZZY SETS

A fuzzy set is a set with a smooth (unsharp) boundary. It generalizes the notion of membership from a black and white binary categorization in classical set theory into one that allows partial membership. The notion of membership in fuzzy sets thus becomes a matter of degree, which is a number between 0 and 1. A membership degree of 0 represents complete non-membership, while a membership degree of 1 represents a complete membership. Mathematically speaking, a fuzzy set is characterized by a mapping from its universe of discourse into the interval, [0, 1]. This mapping is the membership function of the set. Usually, the membership or characteristic function is denoted by the Greek lower-case latter m.(For instance, we may define the fuzzy set High Temperature using the membership function shown in Figure 13.12).

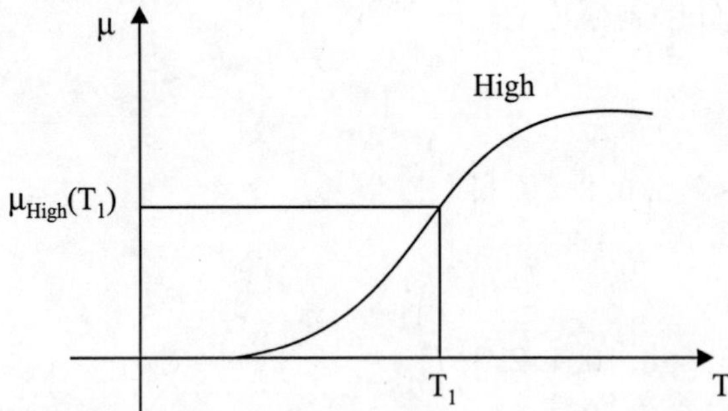

Figure 13.12: Membership Function of High Temperature

A set of core fuzzy sets about a variable forms a term set, which is the basis for generating composite fuzzy sets using hedges. For instance, Low, Medium, and High whose membership functions are shown in Figure 13.13 form a complete term set for the temperature T process. We say that a term set is complete if, for any element in the given universe of discourse, there is at least one term in the term set that covers the given element.

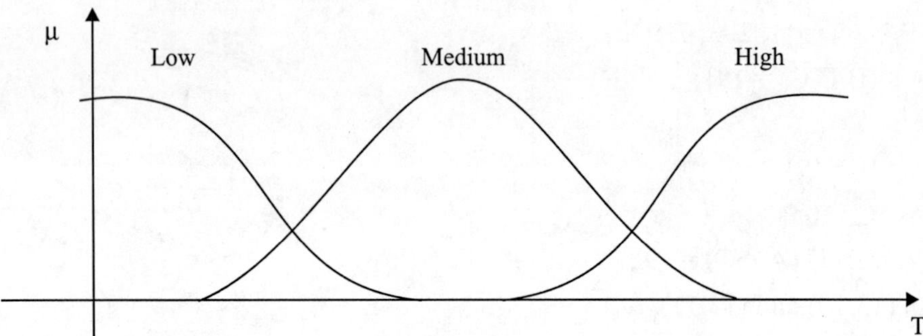

Figure 13.13: A complete Term Set for Temperature.

13.6.1 Definition

A fuzzy set can be defined as a set of ordered pairs A = {x, μA(x)|x ∈ U}. The function μA(x) is called the membership function for A, mapping each element of the universe U to a membership degree in the range [0, 1]. The universe may be discrete or continuous. Any fuzzy set containing at least one element with a membership degree of 1 is called normal. It may be better to represent the set of old people as a fuzzy set, Old. The membership function for this set is given in Figure 13.14, defined over a range of ages (the universe). Given that the age of Rod is 74, it can be determined that this element belongs to the set Old with a membership degree of 0.95. Similarly, if the age of Freddy is 38, the resulting

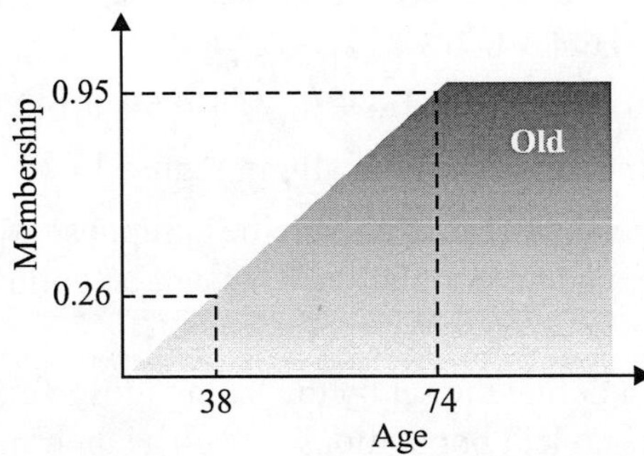

Figure 13.14: Fuzzy Set Representing the Concept Old.

degree of membership is 0.26. Here, both Rod and Freddy belong to the (fuzzy) set of old people, but Rod has a higher degree of membership to this set. The specification of membership functions is typically subjective, as can be seen in this example. There are many justifiable definitions of the concept Old. Indeed people of different ages may define this concept quite differently. One way of constructing the membership function is by using a voting model, and this way the generated fuzzy sets can be rooted in reality with clear semantics. An alternative to this is the integration of the probability distribution of variables. For example, integrating the probability distribution of height gives a possible version of the tall fuzzy set. This does not help with hedges and sets such as very tall, and so although the integration of the distribution gives a voting model, it needs more to arrive at the hedges. In fuzzy logic the truth value of a statement is linguistic (and no longer Boolean), of the form very true, true, more or less true, not very false, false. These logic values are themselves fuzzy sets; some may be compounded fuzzy sets from other atomic ones, by the use of certain operators. As with ordinary crisp sets, different operations can be defined over fuzzy sets.

13.6.2 Representation of Fuzzy Sets

A fuzzy set can be defined in two ways: (1) by enumerating membership values of those elements in the set (completely or partially), or (2) by defining the membership function mathematically.

Obviously, the first approach is possible only if the set is discrete, because a continuous fuzzy set has an infinite number of elements. Generally speaking, a fuzzy set A can be defined through enumeration using the expression

$$A = \underset{i}{} \ {}_{A}(x_i)/x_i \qquad (13.12)$$

where the summation and addition operators refer to the union(disjunction) operation and the notation $\mu_A(x_i) / x_i$ refers to a fuzzy set containing exactly one(partial) element x with a membership degree $\mu_A(x_i)$. For brevity, we do not list those elements x_i whose membership degree in set A is zero.

Example 13.4: Given the discrete universe of discourse, U = {1, 2,…., 20}, Small and Medium are fuzzy subsets of U characterized by the following membership functions:

Small = 1/1+ 1/2 + 0.9/3 + 0.6/4 + 0.3/5 + (0.1/6),

Medium = 0.1/2 + 0.3/3 + 0.7/4 + 1/5 + 1/6 + 0.7/7 + 0.5/8 + 0.2/9

The two fuzzy sets are also depicted graphically in Figure 13.15.

Let us return to the example about Texas universities. Suppose we wish to represent the set of Texas universities with a large student population. This can be defined using the two approaches described above.

1. By enumeration: We can define the set by the listing those Texas universities considered to have, to an extent, large student populations as well as their membership degrees.

   LargeTexasUniv = 1/UT + 1/TAMU + 0.5/UH + 0.3/Rice

2. Alternatively, we can define the set by explicitly describing its characteristics: Texas Universities with Large total student population:

$$\mu_{LargeTexasUniv}(x) = \mu_{Large}(\text{TotalStudentPopulation}(x))$$

$$= \begin{cases} 0 & P \quad 20000 \\ \dfrac{(P \quad 20000)}{20000} & 20000 \quad P \quad 40000 \\ 1 & P \quad 40000 \end{cases}$$

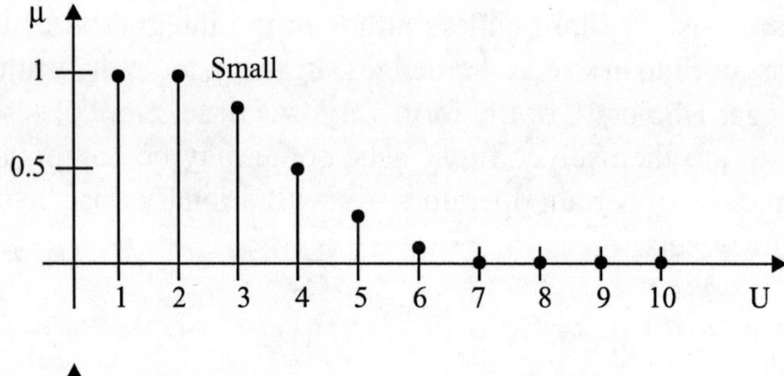

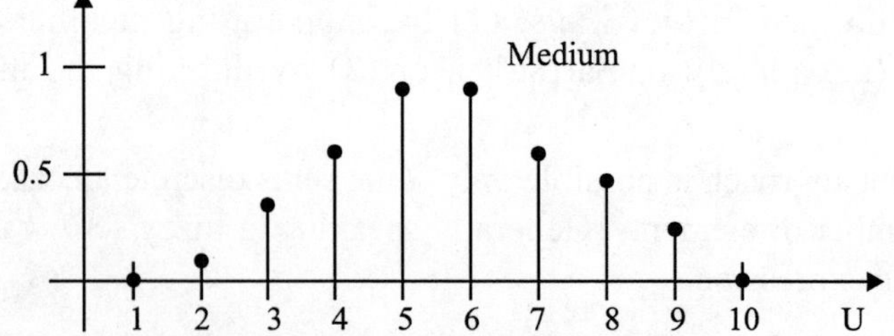

Figure 13.15: Definitions of the Terms Small and Medium

In the example above, the first approach is an extensional definition of the set, while the second approach is an intensional definition of the set.

13.6.3 Simple Example of Fuzzy Sets

An example should help with the understanding of the basic concepts and operators introduced above. Suppose that the universe of discourse, X, is a class of students and that a group, A, of students within this class are said to be tall in height. Thus A is a fuzzy subset of X (but X itself is not fuzzy), since the boundary between tall and not tall cannot be naturally defined with a fixed real number. Rather, describing this vague concept using a gradual membership function as characterized in Figure 13.16. is much more appealing. Similarly the fuzzy term very tall can be represented by another fuzzy (sub-) set as also shown in this figure. Given such a definition of the fuzzy set A = tall, a proposition like "student x is tall" can be denoted by $\mu_{A(x)}$. Assume that Andy is a student in the class and that he has a 80% possibility of being considered as a tall student. This means that

$$\mu_A(\text{andy}) = 0.8. \text{ Also}$$

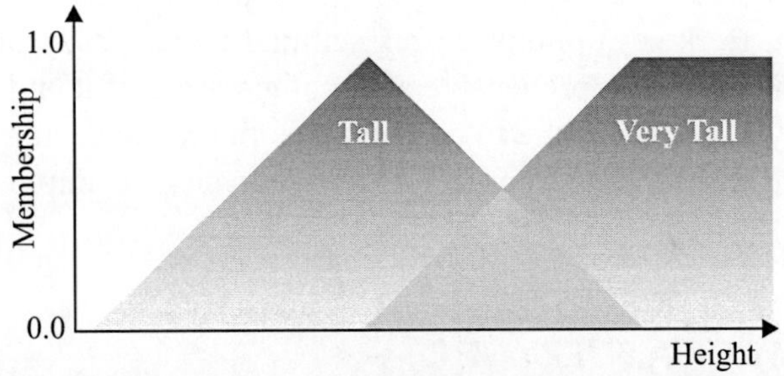

Figure 13.16: Representation of Fuzzy Sets "Tall" and "Very Tall"

suppose that another fuzzy set B is defined on the same universe X, whose members are said to be young in age, and that $\mu_B(\text{andy}) = 0.7$, meaning that Andy is thought to be young with a possibility of 70%. From this, using the operations defined above, the following can be derived that is justifiable with respect to common-sense intuitions:

- $\mu_{\neg A}(\text{Andy}) = 1 - 0.8 = 0.2$, indicating the possibility of Andy being not
- $\mu_{A \cup B}(\text{Andy}) = \max(\mu_A(\text{Andy}), \mu_B(\text{Andy})) = \max(0.8, 0.7) = 0.8$, including the possibility of Andy being tall of young
- $\mu_{A \cap B}(\text{Andy}) = \min(\mu_A(\text{Andy}), \mu_B(\text{Andy})) = \min(0.8, 0.7) = 0.7$, including the possibility being both tall and young

Not only having an intuitive justification, these operations are also computationally very simple. However, care should be taken not to explain the results from the conventional Boolean logic point of view. The laws of excluded-middle and contradiction do not hold in fuzzy logic anymore. To make this point clearer, let us attempt to compare the results of $A \cup \neg A$ and $A \cap \neg A$ obtained by fuzzy logic with those by Boolean probabilistic logic (although such a comparison is itself a common source for debate in the literature). Applying fuzzy logic to the case above of Andy gives that

- $\mu_{A \cup \neg A}(\text{Andy}) = \max(\mu_A(\text{Andy}), \mu_{\neg A}(\text{Andy})) = \max(0.8, 0.2) = 0.8$
- $\mu_{A \cap \neg A}(\text{Andy}) = \min(\mu_A(\text{Andy}), \mu_{\neg A}(\text{Andy})) = \min(0.8, 0.2) = 0.8$

However, using the theory of probability, different results would be expected such that

- p("Andy is tall" or "Andy is not tall") = 1
- p("Andy is tall" and "Andy is not tall") = 0

This important difference is caused by the deliberate avoidance of the excluded-middle and contradiction laws in fuzzy logic. This avoidance enables fuzzy logic to represent vague concepts that are difficult to capture otherwise. If the memberships of x belonging to A and ¬A are neither 0 nor 1, then it should not be surprising that x is also of a nonzero membership belonging to A and ¬A at the same time.

13.7 HISTORY OF FUZZY SETS

In 1965, professor Lotfi Zadeh (Electrical Engineering and Electronics Research Laboratory, University of California, Berkeley) published his seminal paper on the idea of fuzzy sets, thus establishing the foundation of a comprehensive and mathematically sound logic of imprecisely or ambiguously defined sets. This has come to be known as fuzzy logic, first given full treatment in Zadeh's 1973 paper "Outline of a New Approach to the Analysis of Complex Systems and Decision Process".

13.8 THE ANATOMY OF A FUZZY SET

The core idea of fuzzy logic rests with the concept of a fuzzy set. These sets are not fuzzy in the conventional English-language sense of the word: blurred, hazy, out of focus, or indistinct. Rather, they are fuzzy in the way they treat their set boundaries. Fuzzy sets have a semipermeable membrane. In a fuzzy set, an element can be in three states: not a member of the set, a full member of the set, or a partial member of the set. Set membership is thus represented as a continuous range of values in the interval [0, 1] with [0] indicating no set membership, [1] indicating complete set membership, and values in the range [> 0, < 1] indicating a partial degree of membership.

Fuzzy logic is a superset of Boolean logic. Consequently, fuzzy sets are, in many respects, supersets of Boolean sets. A fuzzy set incorporates as part of its structure the intrinsic degrees of membership associated with each element. Figure 13.17 illustrates schematically the general components of a fuzzy set.

A fuzzy set has three principal components: a degree of membership measure along the vertical (Y) axis, the possible domain values for the set along the horizontal (X) axis, and the set membership function (a continuous curve that connects a domain value to its degree of membership in the set). The connecting curve is the crucial part of the fuzzy set. It defines the set membership relations. In addition to an underlying domain or universe of discourse, a fuzzy set also has a support set. This is the region of the domain at which the membership values are greater than zero.

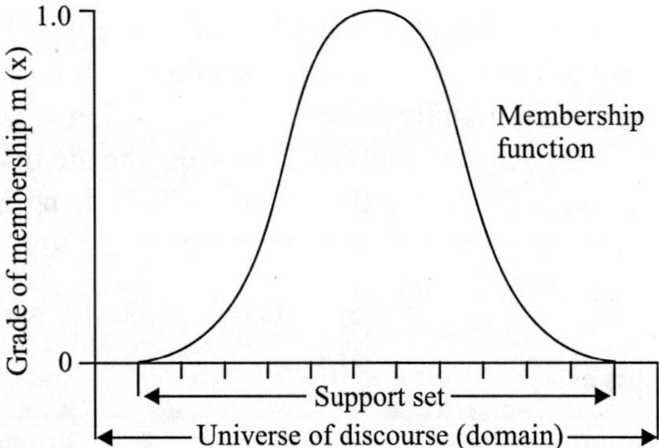

Figure 13.17: General Components of a Fuzzy Set.

13.9 THE TAXONOMY OF FUZZY SETS

Comparing the crisp set Tall (see Figure 13.18) with its fuzzy counterpart will illustrate these differences and expose the structure of a basic fuzzy set. Figure 13.19 shows one possible fuzzy set representation for the concept Tall.

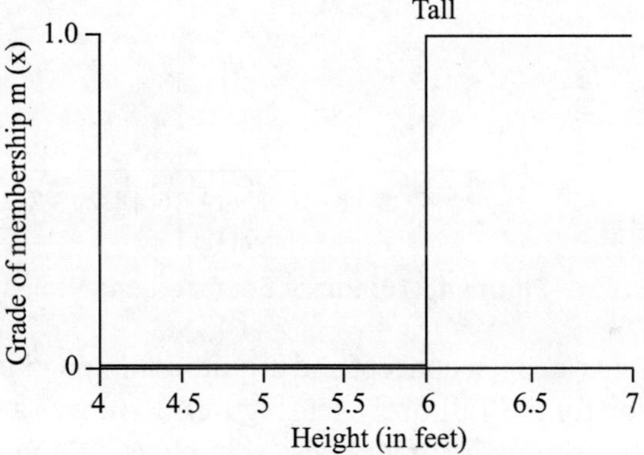

Figure 13.18: The Boolean Tall Set.

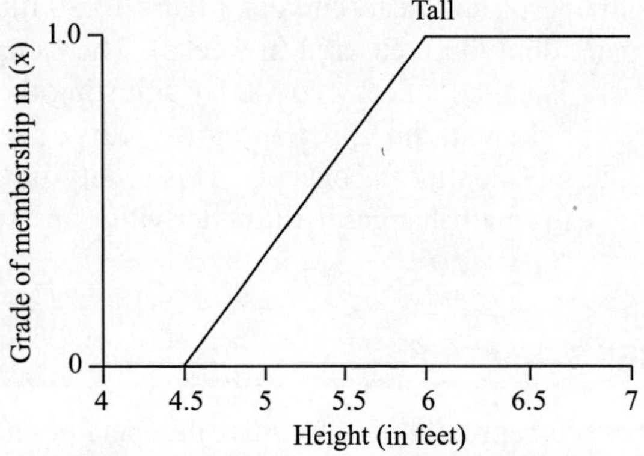

Figure 13.19: The Fuzzy Set Tall (for Men).

The Tall fuzzy set defines how heights are related to the concept of Tall. All heights below 4.5 feet have zero membership values (and are outside the support set). From 4.5 to 6 feet, the degree of membership in the fuzzy set Tall gradually increases. At 6 feet it reaches [1.0] (all heights above 6 feet are fully members of the set). Alternatively, we can view the membership value as the degree of compatibility between the value of height and the concept Tall. As heights increase they become more and more compatible with the idea of Tall. At 6 feet and above all values of Height are completely compatible with the idea of Tall.

13.10 FUZZY QUANTIFIERS

The fuzzy set Tall represents a class of fuzzy sets known as quantifiers. These are sets whose structure is not built around a central value (see the next section "Fuzzy Numbers").

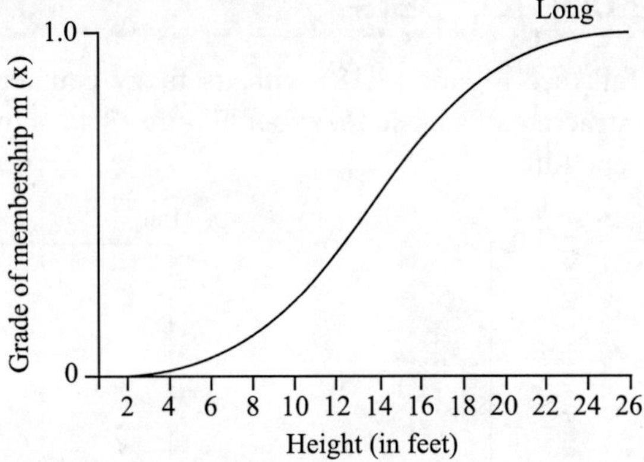

Figure 13.20: Fuzzy Set for a Long Project.

A quantifier represents an open concept and is quite common in fuzzy expert systems. Although the membership function for the Tall fuzzy set (Figure 13.20) was a straight line, implying a linear relationship, quantifier sets more commonly use sigmoid (left- and right-facing S-shaped) curves. Sigmoid curves, with inflection points and attenuated surfaces, can model a wide variety of growth curves (such as logistics, Gompertz, and Pearl curves). Figure 13.20 illustrates the fuzzy set for a Long project (with the project duration measured in weeks). The Long fuzzy set uses a growth curve. The left-facing S-curve is called a decay curve. By adjusting the inflection point on an S-curve, as well as the degree of skew in the upper and lower curve segments, decay and growth curves can represent many highly nonlinear concepts. This ability is very important in types of fuzzy models that are sensitive to small changes in the underlying data (such as risk assessment and sustainability models).

13.11 FUZZY NUMBERS

A much larger class of fuzzy sets represents approximate numbers of one type or another. Some of these fuzzy sets are explicitly "fuzzified" numbers, whereas others simply represent fuzzy numeric intervals over the domain of a particular variable (see the section "Fuzzy Term Sets"). Fuzzy numbers can take many shapes: bell curves, triangles, and trapezoids. Within each of these shapes the actual meaning of the fuzzy set depends on the width or spread of the set itself. Figure 13.21 illustrates a typical bell-shaped fuzzy number. This is a numeric quantity, About 20.

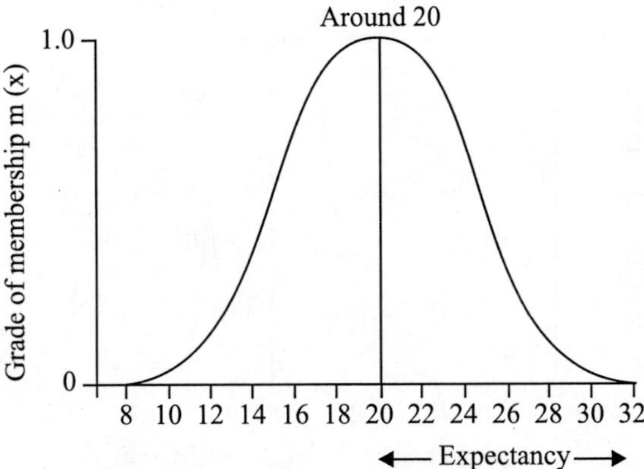

Figure 13.21: The Fuzzy Number about 20.

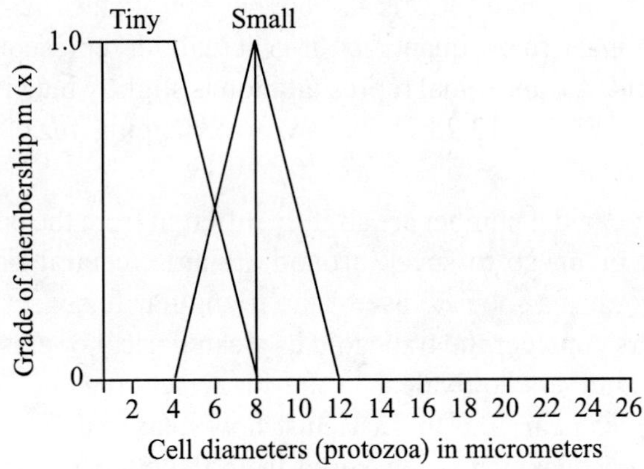

Figure 13.22: The Fuzzy Number Small.

The fuzzy set About 20 shows two principal attributes of fuzzy numbers: a central value and a degree of spread2 around the value. This degree of spread is called the expectancy (e) of the fuzzy number and is an important property. When e = 0, the fuzzy number is a single point and corresponds to a normal scalar value (called a singleton). As the expectancy increases, the number becomes fuzzier. This fuzziness is directly connected to the robustness or brittleness of a fuzzy model as well as to the separation of related concepts in the model. And, because expectancy increases confusion over the exact value of a fuzzy number, a wide expectancy also increases information entropy. Another very common fuzzy number shape is the triangle. Due primarily to the low computational cost of creating and interrogating triangular fuzzy sets they are used extensively in control applications. In general, a triangular fuzzy number is more brittle and therefore less robust than a bell-shaped fuzzy number. Figure 13.22 illustrates a triangular fuzzy set for the concept Small and shows that fuzzy numbers are often used to represent the underlying numbers in terms of a particular concept. In this instance, the cell diameter of a protozoa is taken to be Small (to some degree) when it lies between 4 and 12 micrometers.

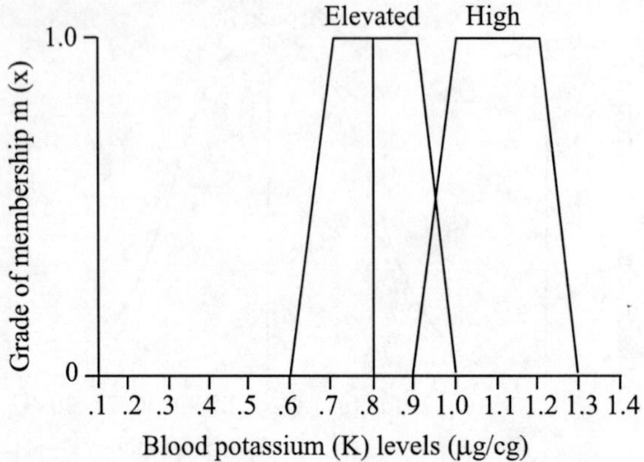

Figure 13.23: The Fuzzy Numbers for Elevated and High.

The fuzzy number Small in Figure 13.22 is also bounded by another fuzzy number, Tiny. Although this might appear to be a linear fuzzy quantifier, it is actually a representative of the third type of fuzzy number, the trapezoid. A trapezoidal representation is slightly but crucially different from the bell and triangle numbers. Figure 13.23 shows two overlapping fuzzy numbers represented as trapezoids.

The semantics of a trapezoidal number are slightly different from the bell and triangular numbers because the set does not pivot, so to speak around a single, central number. Although we can continue to treat a trapezoid as a special case of the triangular fuzzy set (with a plateau width of zero), some model builders consider the trapezoid as a categorical or class fuzzy set—interpreting the plateau as a class of numbers equivalent to the fuzzy set concept. In this case, for example, Elevated is a class of values near {0.6 to 1.0}. Just how near is determined by the width of the trapezoid's expectancy spread (which is measured from the edge, not the center, of the plateau). The existence of a plateau means that a set of values in the fuzzy set has maximum membership values in the set. In both the bell and the triangular sets only a single value is completely compatible with the set concept. On either side of this single number, the fuzzy membership values can (and usually do) drop off rather rapidly. By introducing plateaus into the fuzzy number, we establish a class of values that in a fuzzy model tends to create local areas of concentration.

13.11.1 A Symmetric Fuzzy Numbers

Unlike crisp numbers that have a precise value, fuzzy numbers have a certain amount of ambiguity or spread around them. This spread or expectancy is actually measured in two directions, to the left and the right of the central value (or, for a trapezoid, the edges of the plateau of values). Having two measures of fuzziness allows fuzzy numbers to have asymmetric shapes. A fuzzy number can have both a kurtosis and a skew (although these are not computed or measured as the equivalent concepts in statistics). Figure 13.24 illustrates several asymmetric fuzzy numbers in a robotic arm controller.

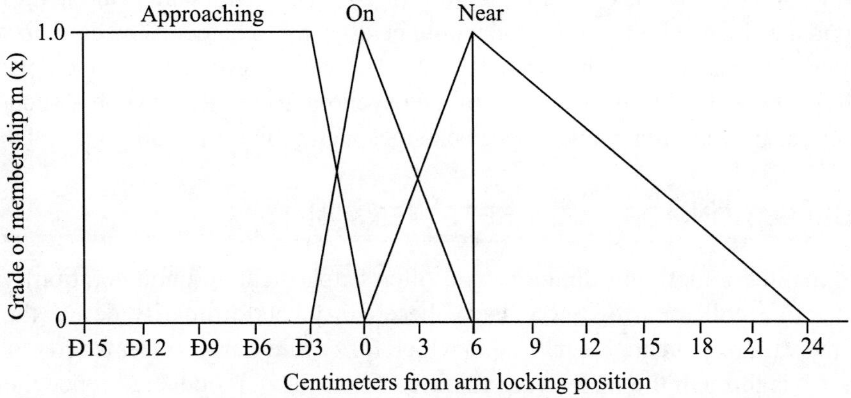

Figure 13.24: Asymmetric fuzzy numbers.

Nonsymmetric fuzzy sets are frequently encountered in control systems (such as the robotic arm controller) but they also play important roles in both the development of complex nonlinear expert systems as well as in the automatic, genetic tuning of rule-based fuzzy systems.

13.12 PSYCHOMETRIC FUZZY SETS

In the previous fuzzy set examples the underlying domains were drawn from a measurement associated with the property of data. Tall is a concept overlaid on the measured values of Height. Long is a concept overlaid on the measured values of project duration. Many models, however, use or produce fuzzy sets that correspond to concepts unsupported by any measured data. Such fuzzy sets often represent subjective mappings between a concept and its intensity or degree of realization. Hence, these fuzzy sets use a psychometric scaling for their domain. Psychometric (or nonmeasured) fuzzy sets include a broad range of concepts, such as Risk, Aptitude, Aggression, Sustainability, Indicated, Acceptable, and Compatible. Figure 13.25 shows a fuzzy set representation for Risk.

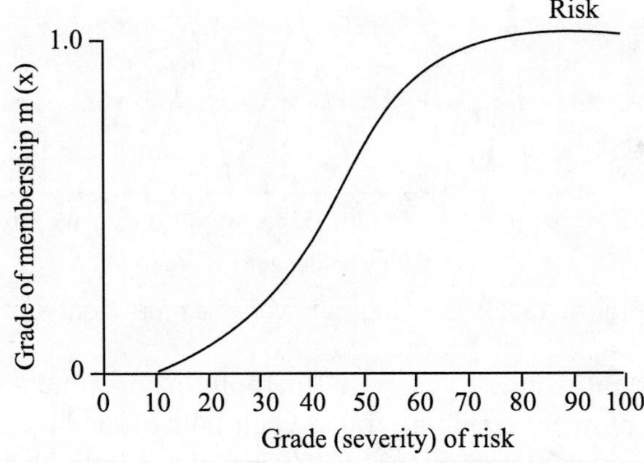

Figure 13.25: The Psychometric Risk Fuzzy Set.

The underlying domain must correspond to the granularity of the model. The wider the domain, the larger the degree of evident separation (a matter of resolution or discrimination) between the relative domain points. In the Risk example (Figure 13.24), a small movement along the membership function around the slope at them[.5] region would be difficult to detect if the domain were [0, 10], would be moderately easy to see with range [0, 100], and would produce a large displacement with range [0, 1000]. At the same time, the range of the psychometric scale must be associated with the model's objectives in resolving small or large changes along the horizontal axis.

13.13 COLLECTIONS OF FUZZY SETS (TERM SETS)

In fuzzy systems, the underlying numeric (and often categorical and enumeration) variables are broken down into a collection of fuzzy sets. These fuzzy sets ordinarily define the underlying semantics of the variable and are the names by which fuzzy rule-based systems refer to the variable itself. Because it is through the underlying fuzzy sets that fuzzy models reference their variables, these sets are often called linguistic variables. As an example, Figure 13.26 shows the variable Client_Age with its set of underlying fuzzy sets. Each underlying fuzzy set defines a portion of the variable's domain. But this portion is not uniquely defined. Fuzzy sets overlap as a natural consequence of their elastic boundaries. Such an overlap not only implements a realistic and functional semantic mechanism for defining the nature of a variable when it assumes various data values but provides a smooth and coherent transition from one state to another. This transition from one semantic state to another can be seen, for example, for the YoungAdult and MiddleAged fuzzy sets (Figure 13.26).

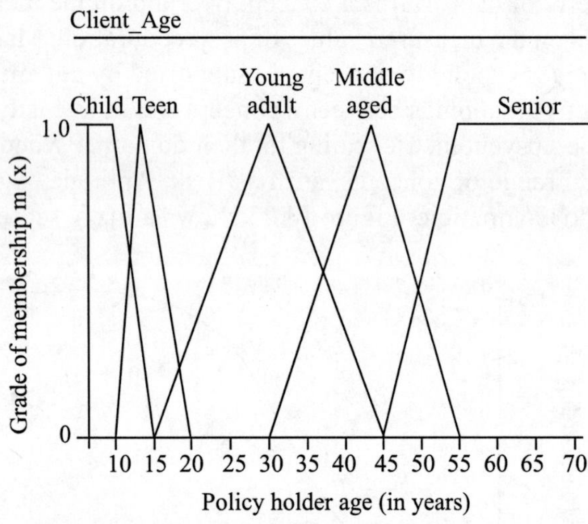

Figure 13.26: The Linguistic Variables for Client Age

As we move to the right from 30 years old (the point of maximum grade of membership in YoungAdult), the degree of membership in YoungAdult falls off and the degree of membership in MiddleAged begins to increase. Between 30 and 45 years old an individual is, to some degree, both a young adult and middle aged. When they are close to 30, their membership in the middle-aged concept is very small, and when then they are close to 45 their membership in the young adult concept is very small (and goes to zero at both of these end points). As we move further to the right, the individual's compatibility with the idea of middle aged begins to fall off and they become more and more representative of a senior citizen.

13.14 FUZZY SET OPERATIONS

Define three fuzzy sets $\underset{\sim}{}$, $\underset{\sim}{B}$ and $\underset{\sim}{C}$ on the universe X. For a given element x of the universe, the following function-theoretic operations for the set-theoretic operations of union, intersection, and complement are defined for $\underset{\sim}{}$, $\underset{\sim}{B}$ and $\underset{\sim}{C}$ on X:

Union $\quad {}_{\underset{\sim}{}\,\underset{\sim}{B}}(x) = {}_{\underset{\sim}{}}(x) \quad {}_{\underset{\sim}{B}}(x)$ (13.13)

Intersection $\quad {}_{\underset{\sim}{}\,\underset{\sim}{B}}(x) = {}_{\underset{\sim}{}}(x) \quad {}_{\underset{\sim}{B}}(x)$ (13.14)

Complement $\quad {}_{\bar{A}}(x) = 1 \quad {}_{\underset{\sim}{A}}(x)$ (13.15)

Venn diagrams for these operations, extended to consider fuzzy sets, are shown in Figures 13.27–13.29. The operations given in Eqs. (13.13) – (13.15) are known as the standard fuzzy operations. There are many other fuzzy operations, and a discussion of these is given later in this chapter. Any fuzzy set $\underset{\sim}{}$ defined on a universe X is a subset of that universe. Also by definition, just as with classical sets, the membership value of any element x in the null set ∅ is 0, and the membership value of any element x in the whole set X is 1. Note that the null set and the whole set are not fuzzy sets in this context (no tilde understrike).

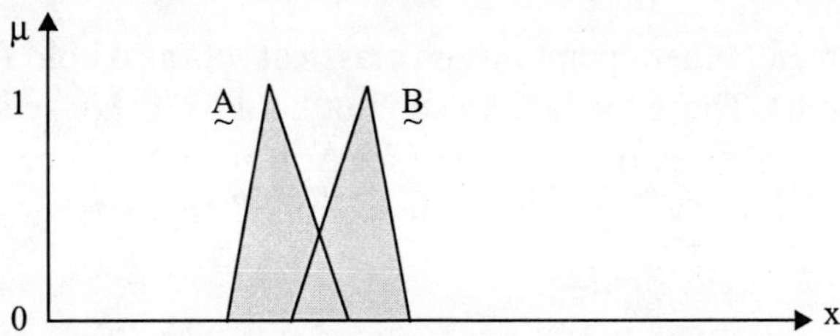

Figure 13.27: Union of Fuzzy Sets $\underset{\sim}{}$ and $\underset{\sim}{B}$.

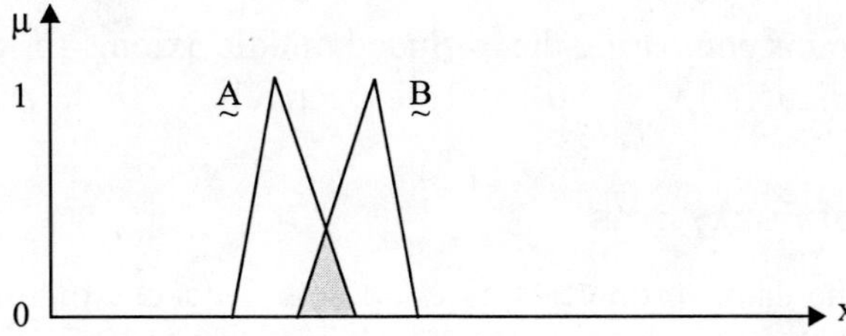

Figure 13.28: Intersection of Fuzzy Sets $\underset{\sim}{}$ or $\underset{\sim}{B}$.

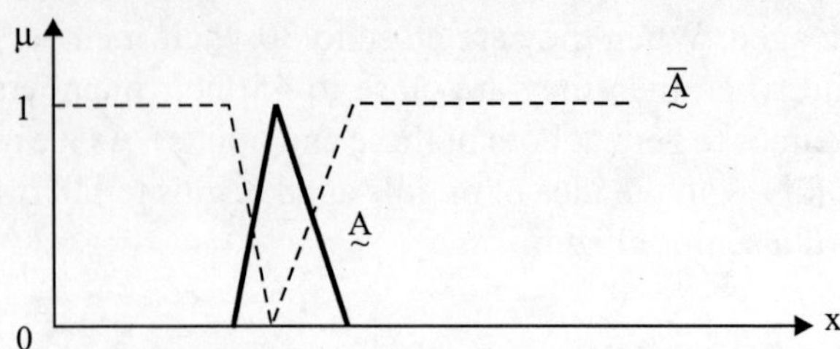

Figure 13.29: Complement of Fuzzy Set $\underset{\sim}{}$.

The appropriate notation for these ideas is as follows:

$$\underset{\sim}{A} \quad X \Rightarrow \quad {}_{\underset{\sim}{A}}(x) \quad {}_{X}(x) \tag{13.16a}$$

For all $\quad x \in X, \mu_{\phi}(x) = 0$ (13.16b)

For all $\quad x \in X, \mu_{X}(x) = 1$ (13.17c)

The collection of all fuzzy sets and fuzzy subsets on X is denoted as the fuzzy power set $P(\underset{\sim}{X})$.

It should be obvious, based on the fact that all fuzzy sets can overlap, that the cardinality, $n_{p(x)}$, of the fuzzy power set is infinite; that is, $n_{p(x)} = \infty$. De Morgan's principles for classical sets also hold for fuzzy sets, as denoted by these expressions:

$$\overline{\underset{\sim}{A} \quad \underset{\sim}{B}} = \overline{\underset{\sim}{A}} \quad \overline{\underset{\sim}{B}} \tag{13.17a}$$

$$\overline{\underset{\sim}{A} \quad \underset{\sim}{B}} = \overline{\underset{\sim}{A}} \quad \overline{\underset{\sim}{B}} \tag{13.17b}$$

As enumerated before, all other operations on classical sets also hold for fuzzy sets, except for the excluded middle axioms. These two axioms do not hold for fuzzy sets since they do not form part of the basic axiomatic structure of fuzzy sets (see Appendix A); since fuzzy sets can overlap, a set and its complement can also overlap. The excluded middle axioms, extended for fuzzy sets, are expressed by

$$\overline{\underset{\sim}{A}} \quad \overline{\underset{\sim}{A}} \neq X \tag{13.18a}$$

$$\overline{\underset{\sim}{A}} \quad \overline{\underset{\sim}{A}} \neq \phi \tag{13.19b}$$

Extended Venn diagrams comparing the excluded middle axioms for classical (crisp) sets and fuzzy sets are shown in Figures 13.30 and 13.31, respectively.

13.14.1 Properties of Fuzzy Sets

Fuzzy sets follow the same properties as crisp sets. Because of this fact and because the membership values of a crisp set are a subset of the interval [0,1], classical sets can be

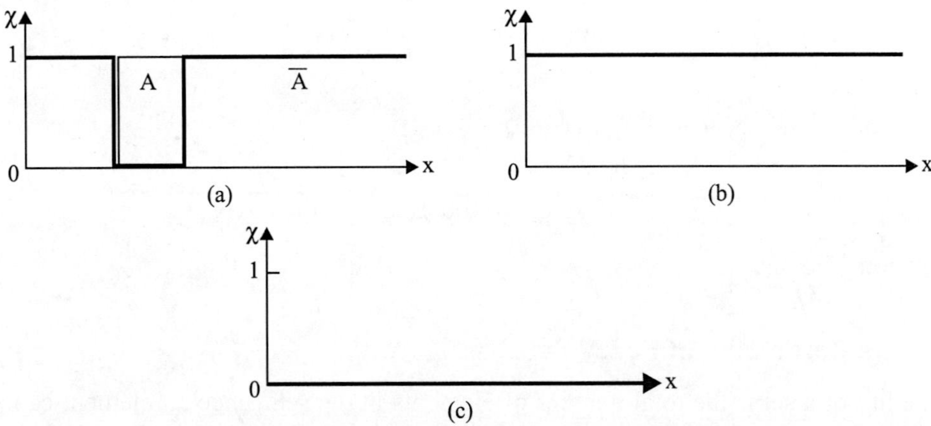

Figure 13.30: Excluded middle axioms for crisp sets. (a) Crisp set A and its complement; (b) crisp (axiom of excluded middle); (c) crisp (axiom of contradiction).

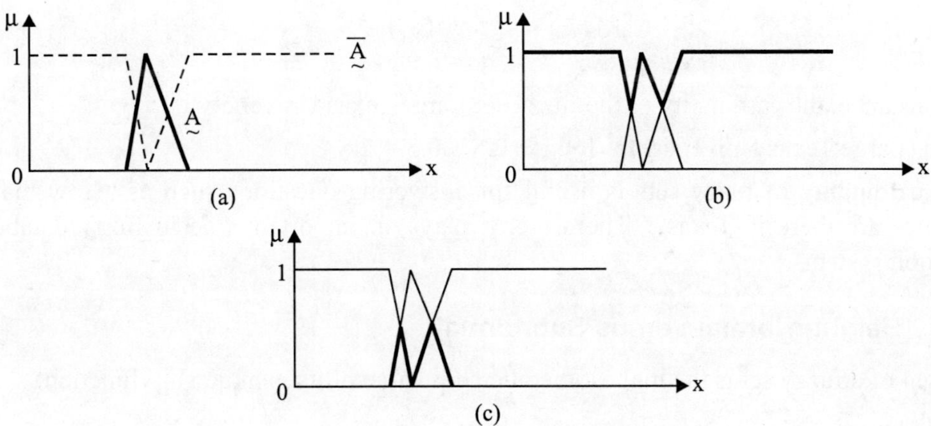

Figure 13.31: Excluded middle axioms for fuzzy sets. (a) Fuzzy set and its complement; (b) fuzzy $\bar{\underset{\sim}{A}}$ X (axiom of excluded middle); (c) fuzzy $\bar{\underset{\sim}{A}}$ (axiom of contradiction). thought of as a special case of fuzzy sets. Frequently used properties of fuzzy sets are listed below.

Commutativity $\underset{\sim}{A} \quad \underset{\sim}{B} = \underset{\sim}{B} \quad \underset{\sim}{A}$

$\underset{\sim}{A} \quad \underset{\sim}{B} = \underset{\sim}{B} \quad \underset{\sim}{A}$

Associativity $\underset{\sim}{A} \quad (\underset{\sim}{B} \quad \underset{\sim}{C}) = (\underset{\sim}{A} \quad \underset{\sim}{B}) \quad \underset{\sim}{C}$

$\underset{\sim}{A} \quad (\underset{\sim}{B} \quad \underset{\sim}{C}) = (\underset{\sim}{A} \quad \underset{\sim}{B}) \quad \underset{\sim}{C}$

Distributivity $\underset{\sim}{A} \quad (\underset{\sim}{B} \quad \underset{\sim}{C}) = (\underset{\sim}{A} \quad \underset{\sim}{B}) \quad (\underset{\sim}{A} \quad \underset{\sim}{C})$

$\underset{\sim}{A} \quad (\underset{\sim}{B} \quad \underset{\sim}{C}) = (\underset{\sim}{A} \quad \underset{\sim}{B}) \quad (\underset{\sim}{A} \quad \underset{\sim}{C}))$

Idempotency $\underset{\sim}{A} \quad \underset{\sim}{A} = \underset{\sim}{A}$

and $\underset{\sim}{A} \quad \underset{\sim}{A} = \underset{\sim}{A}$

$$\underset{\sim}{A} \cup \phi = \underset{\sim}{A}$$

and $$\underset{\sim}{A} \cap X = \underset{\sim}{A}$$

$$\underset{\sim}{A} \cap \phi = \phi$$

and $$A \cup X = X$$

Transitivity If $\underset{\sim}{A} \subseteq \underset{\sim}{B}$ and $\underset{\sim}{B} \subseteq \underset{\sim}{C}$, then $\underset{\sim}{A} \subseteq \underset{\sim}{C}$

Involution $\overline{\overline{\underset{\sim}{A}}} = \underset{\sim}{A}$

13.14.2 The Cardinality of Fuzzy Sets

The cardinality of a set is the total number of elements in the set. Since an element can partially belong to a fuzzy set, a natural generalization of the classical notion of cardinality is to weigh each element by its membership degree, which gives us the following formula for calculating the cardinality of a fuzzy set:

$$\text{Card}(A) = \underset{i}{\quad}(x_i) \qquad (13.20)$$

For instance, the cardinality of the fuzzy set Large Texas University is

Card (Large Texas University) = 1 + 1 + 0.5 + 0.3 = 2.8

The cardinality of fuzzy sets is useful for answering questions such as "How many large universities are there in Texas?" Therefore, it plays an important role in fuzzy databases and information systems.

13.14.3 Height: Normal Versus Subnormal

The height of a fuzzy set is the highest membership value of its membership function:

$$\text{Height}(A) = \max_{X_i} \quad (x_i) \qquad (13.21)$$

For example, the height of the fuzzy set in Figure 13.32 is 0.5. A fuzzy set with height 1 is called a normal fuzzy set. In contrast, a fuzzy set whose height is less than 1 is called a subnormal fuzzy set. The fuzzy in figure 13.32, for example, is subnormal.

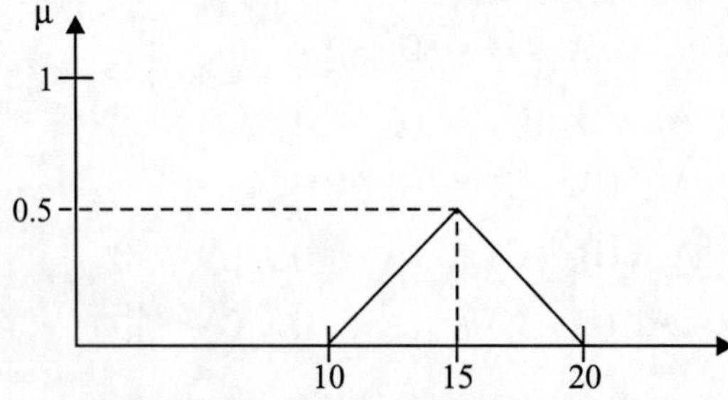

Figure 13.32: A Subnormal Fuzzy Set

13.14.4 Support and Alpha-level Cuts

The support of a fuzzy set A is the set of element whose degree of membership in A is greater than 0. For instance, the support of the fuzzy set in Figure 13.32 is the open interval (10, 20). Let A be a fuzzy set in the universe of discourse U. We can formally define support as follows:

$$Spt = \{x \in U| \mu_A(x) < 0\} \tag{13.22}$$

It should be pointed out that the support of a fuzzy set is a crisp (classical) set.

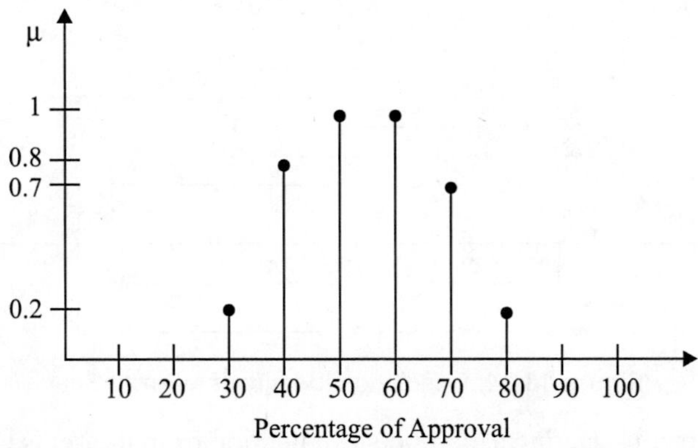

Figure 13.33: The Membership Function of Moderately Approved Presidential Candidate

The notion of α-cut (also called a-level) is more general than that of support. Let α_0 be a number between 0 and 1. The α-cut of a fuzzy set A at α_0, denoted as $A_{\alpha 0}$, is the set of elements whose degree of membership in A is no less than α_0. Mathematically, the a-cut of a fuzzy set A in U is defined as

$$A_{\alpha 0} = \{x \in U \mid \mu_A (x) \geq \alpha_0\} \tag{13.23}$$

For example, let us consider the concept "moderately approved" regarding the public's opinion of a presidential candidate. The universe of discourse is the percentage of those people supporting the candidate in a national poll. To simplify out discussion, we use a discrete universe of discourse: U = {0%, 10%, 20%,...., 100%}. The membership function of the fuzzy set moderately approved is shown in figure 13.33. We can construct the a-cut of the fuzzy set at 0.7 as

Moderately $\text{Approved}_{0.7}$ = {40%, 50%, 60%, 70%}

Similarly, we can construct the following a-cuts:

Moderately $\text{Approved}_{0.2}$ = {30%, 40%, 50%, 60%, 70%, 80%}

Moderately $\text{Approved}_{0.8}$ = {40%, 50%, 60%}

Obviously, as the alpha value increases, the set generated by a-cutting a fuzzy set becomes smaller. It can be shown that if $\alpha_1 < \alpha_2$, we have $A_{\alpha 1} \supseteq A_{\alpha 2}$. Where Êdenotes a crisp superset (i.e. suppositions) relation.

13.14.5 Resolution Identity

Based on the notion of a-cuts, fuzzy set can be decomposed into multiple crisp sets (i.e., a-level sets) using different a values. Intuitively, each a-level specifies a slice of the membership function. Therefore, it is conceivable that the original membership function can be reconstructed by "pilling up" these slices in order.

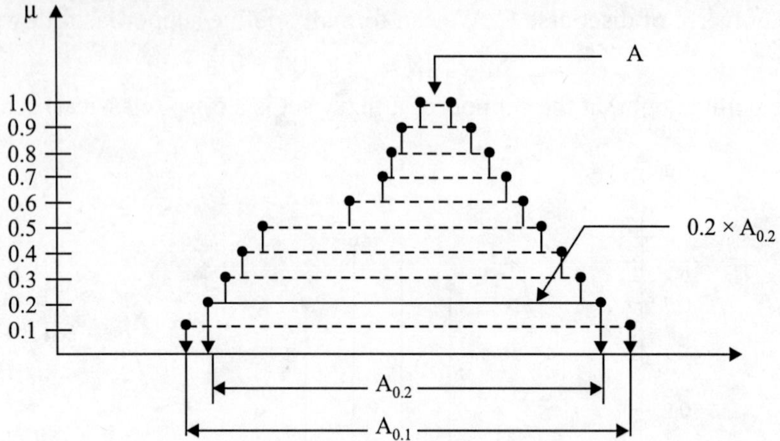

Figure 13.34: Resolution Identify of a Fuzzy Set

The foundation for reconstructing a membership function from its a-cuts is the resolution identity in fuzzy set theory. Let A be a discrete fuzzy set. We can order the Nonzero membership values of the elements in the support set into a list in increasing order (without duplicates): $(\alpha_0, \alpha_1, \ldots, \alpha_n)$. The resolution identity principle in fuzzy set theory states that

$$A = \alpha_0 \text{ X } A_{\alpha 0} + \alpha_1 \text{ X } A_{\alpha 1} + \ldots\ldots + \alpha_n \text{ X } A_{\alpha n} \qquad (13.24)$$

where α_i X $A_{\alpha i}$ represents a fuzzy set such as the one below:

$$_{i}\ _{i} = \begin{matrix} _{i} \text{ if } A \quad _{i} \\ 0 \quad \text{otherwise} \end{matrix} \qquad (13.25)$$

and + represents the disjunction operator. In other words, the original fuzzy set A can be viewed as the union of all those fuzzy sets constructed from an a_i in the list $(\alpha_0, \alpha_1, \ldots, \alpha_n)$ such that (1) their support is the a_i level cut of A, and (2) their membership function is flat at the alpha value a_i. The shape of the membership function α_i X $A_{\alpha i}$ is hence a rectangle with a height of α_i as illustrated in Figure 13.34. Figure 13.35 shows the result of superimposing 0.1 X $A_{0.1}$ and 0.2 X $A_{0.2}$ and so on.

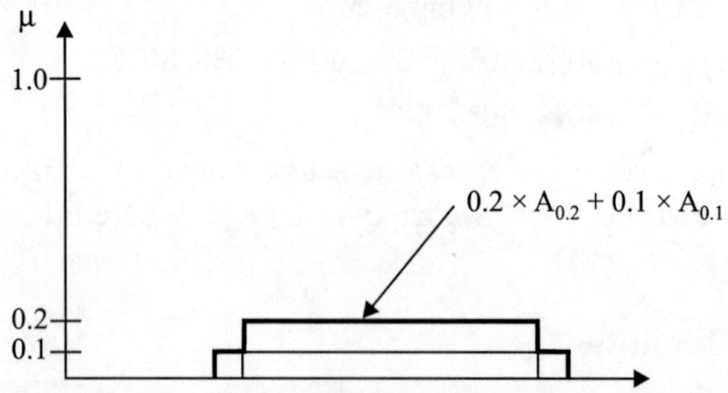

Figure 13.35: Combining Two Scaled α-Cuts.

It should be noted that the a-values in the resolution identity of a discrete fuzzy set may not be equally separated. They are determined by the membership function of the set. For instance, the resolution identity of the fuzzy set in Figure 13.33 consists of four a-cuts with a-values 0.2, 0.7, 0., and 1, respectively, as shown in Figure 13.36.

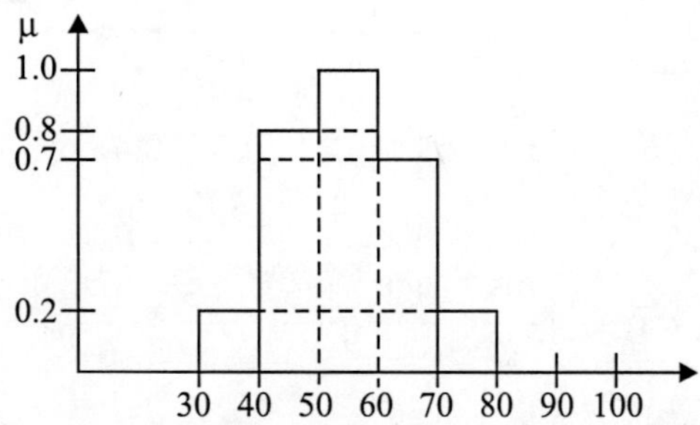

Figure 13.36: Resolution Identity of the Fuzzy Set Moderately Approved.

Example 13.5: Consider two fuzzy sets A and B find Complement, Union, Intersection, Difference, and De Morgan's law.

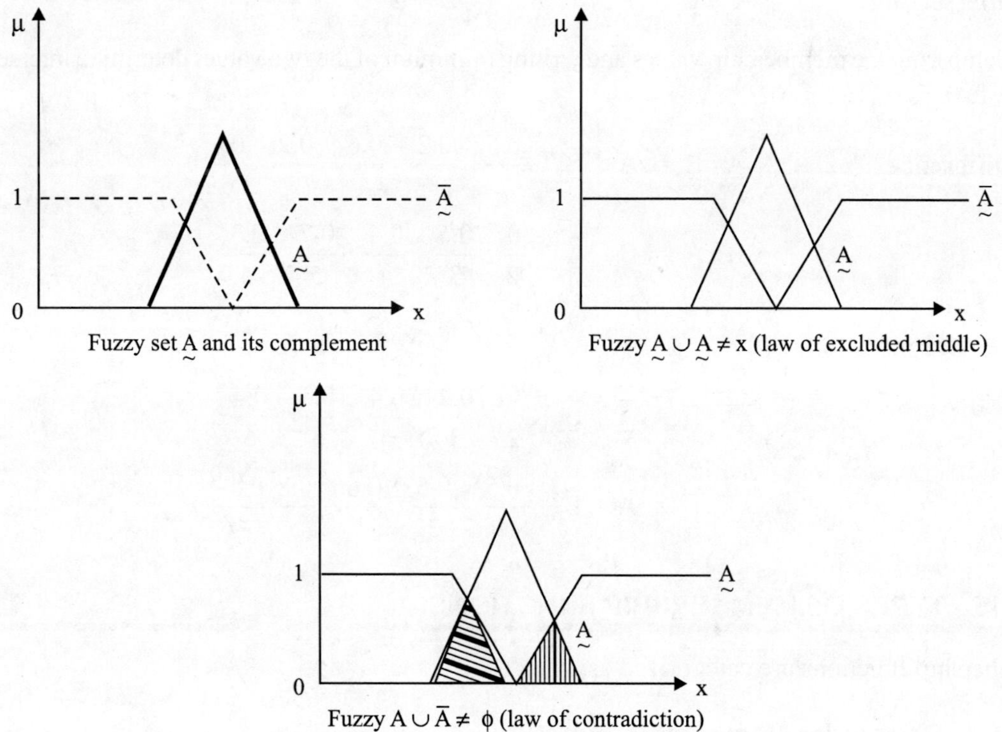

Figure 13.37: Excluded Middle Law for Fuzzy Set

$$\bar{\underset{\sim}{A}} = \frac{1}{2} \quad \frac{0.5}{3} \quad \frac{0.6}{4} \quad \frac{0.2}{5} \quad \frac{0.6}{6},$$

$$\bar{\underset{\sim}{B}} = \frac{0.5}{2} \quad \frac{0.8}{3} \quad \frac{0.4}{4} \quad \frac{0.7}{5} \quad \frac{0.3}{6},$$

Solution:

$$\bar{\underset{\sim}{A}} = \frac{0}{2} \quad \frac{0.5}{3} \quad \frac{0.4}{4} \quad \frac{0.8}{5} \quad \frac{0.4}{6}.$$

Complement $$\bar{\underset{\sim}{B}} = \frac{0.5}{2} \quad \frac{0.2}{3} \quad \frac{0.6}{4} \quad \frac{0.3}{5} \quad \frac{0.7}{6}.$$

Union $$\underset{\sim}{A} \quad \underset{\sim}{B} = \frac{1}{2} \quad \frac{.8}{3} \quad \frac{0.6}{4} \quad \frac{0.7}{5} \quad \frac{0.6}{6}.$$

Comparing the membership values and writing maximum of the two values determine Union of the fuzzy set.

Intersection $$\underset{\sim}{A} \quad \underset{\sim}{B} = \frac{0.5}{2} \quad \frac{0.5}{3} \quad \frac{0.4}{4} \quad \frac{0.2}{5} \quad \frac{0.3}{6}$$

Comparing the membership values and writing minimum of the two values determine intersection of the fuzzy set.

Difference $$\underset{\sim}{A} / \underset{\sim}{B} = \underset{\sim}{A} \quad \bar{\underset{\sim}{B}} \quad \frac{0.5}{2} \quad \frac{0.2}{3} \quad \frac{0.6}{4} \quad \frac{0.2}{5} \quad \frac{0.6}{6}.$$

$$\underset{\sim}{B} / \underset{\sim}{A} = \underset{\sim}{B} \quad \bar{\underset{\sim}{A}} \quad \frac{0}{2} \quad \frac{0.5}{3} \quad \frac{0.4}{4} \quad \frac{0.7}{5} \quad \frac{0.3}{6}.$$

De Morgan's Laws

$$\overline{\underset{\sim}{A} \quad \underset{\sim}{B}} = \bar{\underset{\sim}{A}} \quad \bar{\underset{\sim}{B}} \quad \frac{0}{2} \quad \frac{0.2}{3} \quad \frac{0.4}{4} \quad \frac{0.3}{5} \quad \frac{0.4}{6},$$

$$\overline{\underset{\sim}{A} \quad \underset{\sim}{B}} = \bar{\underset{\sim}{A}} \quad \bar{\underset{\sim}{B}} \quad \frac{0.5}{2} \quad \frac{0.5}{3} \quad \frac{0.6}{4} \quad \frac{0.8}{5} \quad \frac{0.7}{6}.$$

13.15 TYPES OF MEMBERSHIP FUNCTIONS

Membership functions are categorized as:

13.15.1 Triangular Membership Function

A triangular membership function is specified by three parameters {a, b, c}as follows:

$$\text{triangle}(x\text{: a, b, c}) = \begin{cases} 0 \quad x < a \\ (x-a)/(b-a) \; a \quad x \quad b \\ (c-x)/(c-b) \; b \quad x \quad c \\ 0 \quad x > c \end{cases} \tag{13.26}$$

The precise appearance of the function is determined by the choice of parameters a, b and c. Figure 13.38(a) illustrates an example of a triangular membership function defined triangle (x; 20, 60, 80).

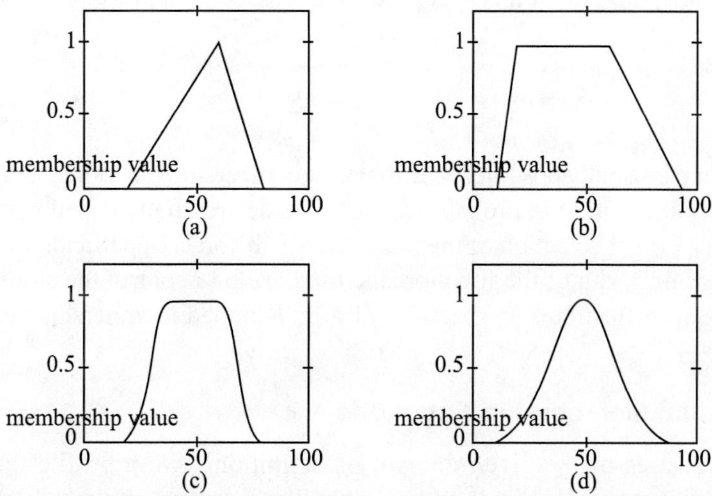

Figure 13.38: Examples of Four types of membership functions: (a) triangle(x; 20, 60, 80); (b) trapezoid(x; 10, 20, 60, 95); (c) Bell(x; 20, 4, 50); (d) gaussian(x; 50, 20)

13.15.2 Trapezoidal Membership Function

A trapezoidal membership function is specified by four parameters {a, b, c, d} as follows:

$$\text{trapezoid}(x\text{: a, b, c, d}) = \begin{cases} 0 \quad x < a \\ (x-a)/(b-a) \; a \quad x \quad b \\ 1 \; b \quad x \quad c \\ (c-x)/(c-b) \; c \quad x \quad c \\ 0 \quad x > d \end{cases} \tag{13.27}$$

Figure 13.38(b) illustrates an example of a trapezoidal membership function defined by trapezoid(x; 10, 20, 60, 95). Obviously, the triangular membership function is a special case of the trapezoidal membership function.

13.15.3 Gaussian Membership Functions

A Gaussian membership function is specified by two parameters {m, s} as follows:

$$\text{Gaussian}(x{:}\ m, \sigma) = \exp \frac{(x - m)^2}{2} \tag{13.28}$$

where m and σ denote the center and width of the function, respectively. We can control the shape of the function by adjusting the parameter σ. A small σ will generate a "thin" membership function, while a big σ will lead to a "flat" membership function.

13.15.4 Bell-shaped Membership Function

A bell-shaped membership function is specified by three parameters {a, b, c} as follows:

$$\text{bell}\ (x{:}\ a, b, c) = \frac{1}{1 \quad \frac{x \quad c}{a}^{2b}} \tag{13.29}$$

where the parameter b is usually positive. Note that this membership function is a direct generalization of the Cauchy distribution used in probability theory. A desired bell-shaped membership function can be obtained by a proper selection of the parameters a, b and c. Specifically, we can adjust c and a to vary the center and width of the function and then use b to control the slopes at the crossover points. Figure 13.38(c) illustrates an example of a bell-shaped membership function defined by bell(x; 20, 4, 50).

13.15.5 Sigmoidal Membership Functions

Terms on the boundaries of the given domain of definition have a profile that is most readily described in terms of a sigmoidal function as shown in the next example.

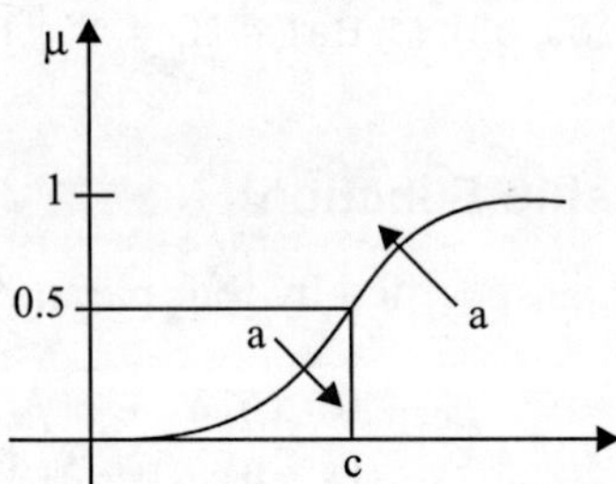

Figure 13.39: Sigmoidal Membership Function

As parameter increases, the transition from 0 to 1 becomes sharper. The function thus approximates the step function as approaches positive infinity. Finally, note that μ(c) = 0.5 for all sigmoidal membership functions, indicating the break-even point of the definition where transition from membership to nonmembership occurs.

13.15.6 S Membership Functions

The S membership function is a smooth membership function with two parameters: a and b. The shape of the function is shown in Figure 13.40. The membership value is 0 for points below a, 1 for points above b, and 0.5 for the midpoint between a and b. The name of this type of membership function, as you may guessed, comes from the "S" shape of the function.

$$S(x: a, b) = \begin{array}{ll} 0 & x < a \\ 2\,\dfrac{x-a}{b-a}^{2} & a \quad x \quad \dfrac{a+b}{2} \\ 1 \quad 2\,\dfrac{x-a}{b-a}^{2} & \dfrac{a+b}{2} \quad x \quad b \\ 1 & x \quad b \end{array} \tag{13.30}$$

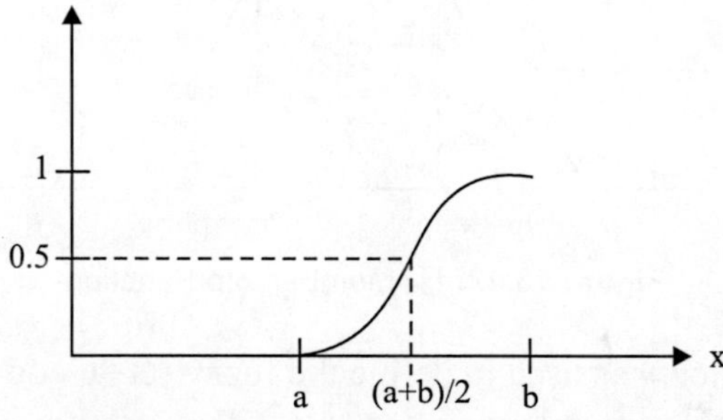

Figure 13.40: S Membership Function

13.15.7 ∏ Membership Function

There are two ∏ membership functions. The first ∏ membership function is defined with two parameters: a and b. The function has a membership value 1 at point a, membership value 0.5 at a – b and a + b, respectively. Unlike the S function, the Õ function decreases toward zero asymptotically as we move away from point a, as shown in Figure 13.41

$$\Pi_1 (x: a, b) = \frac{1}{1 \quad \dfrac{x \quad a}{2}^{2}} \tag{13.31}$$

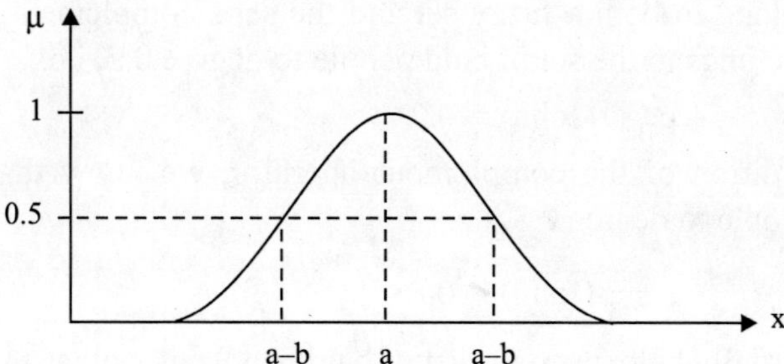

Figure 13.41: Π_1 Membership Function

The other membership function that has the "Π" shape is given in Eq. 13.32 and shown in Figure 13.42. This membership function has four parameters.

$$\Pi_2(x\text{: lw, lp, rp, rw}) = \begin{matrix} \dfrac{lw}{lp + lw - x} \; x < lp \\ 1 \; lp \quad x \quad rp \\ \dfrac{rw}{x - rp + r} \; x > rp \end{matrix} \qquad (13.32)$$

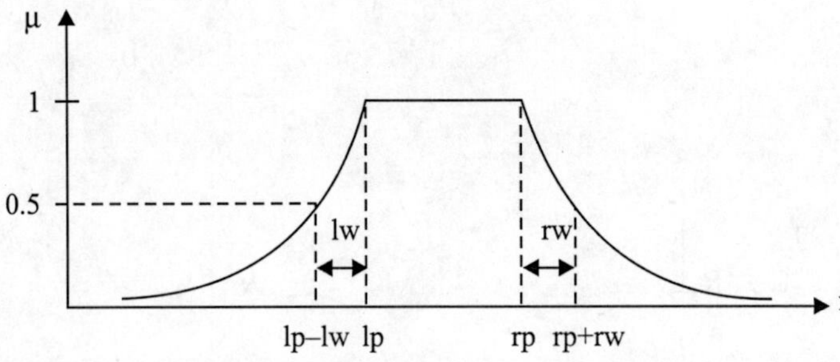

Figure 13.42: Π_2 Membership Function

This membership function was used to define the fuzzy set "Good Stopping Accuracy" in the Sendai Subway Train Control System:

$$\mu_{GoodStoppingAccuracy}(x) = \Pi_2(x; 20, 20, 30, 30)$$

where x is the distance (in cm) between stopping position and target position is considered 100 percent good stopping accuracy, while a train stopped at 50 cm away is considered to satisfy good stopping accuracy up to 50 percent.

13.16 FALLING OF THE LAW OF EXCLUDED MIDDLE AND THE LAW OF CONTRADICTION

Because fuzzy set theory generalizes the black-and-white situations of set membership to allow various "grey areas," it has to violate two fundamental laws of set theory – the law of excluded middle. $A \cup \bar{A} = U$, and the law of contradiction, $A \cap \bar{A} = \phi$. In other words, it is possible for an element to partially belong to both a fuzzy set and the set's complement. For instance, suppose John is a person who belongs to the set of bald people to degree 0.2, i.e.,

$$\mu_{Bald}\,(John) = 0.2$$

Based on the definition of the complement operator, we know that John belongs to the complement of bald people to degree 0.8, i.e.,

$$_{\overline{Bald}}\,(John) = 0.8$$

Therefore, John partially belongs to the set of bald people as well as the set of people who are not bald.

Generally speaking, any element partially belonging to a fuzzy set is also a partial member of its complement. Knowing this difference between classical sets and fuzzy sets is important because it helps us to formally compare and analyze the two theories. Due to the fact that the law of excluded middle and the law of contradiction are not axioms of fuzzy set theory, formula equivalents in classical set theory are not necessarily equivalent in fuzzy set theory.

13.17 HEDGES

A hedge is a modifier to a fuzzy set. It modifies the meaning of the original set to create a compound fuzzy set. "Very" and "More or Less" are two commonly used hedges. Their definitions are listed below.

Very:

$$\mu_{\text{Very A}}(x) = [\mu_A(x)]^2 \tag{13.33}$$

More or Less:

$$\mu_{\text{MoreOrLess A}}(x) = \sqrt{\quad(x)} \tag{13.34}$$

We illustrate these hedges in Figure 13.43 through their application to the concept High temperature. As shown by the figure, "Very" has the effect of narrowing the membership function, while "More or Less" widens the membership function. This is intuitively appealing because the criteria for "Very High" should be more stringent than those for "High", while the criteria for "More or Less high" should be relaxed. In general, we should have

$$\mu_{\text{Very A}}(x) \leq \mu_A(x) \leq \mu_{\text{MoreOrLess A}}(x)$$

In principle, a hedge can be applied to any fuzzy sets.

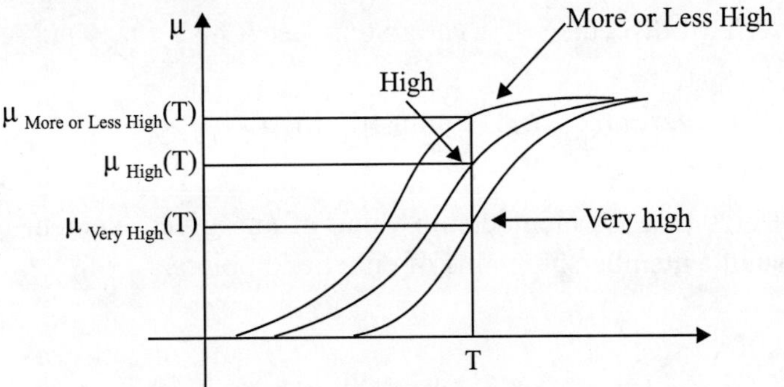

Figure 13.43 Definition of Very High

13.18 COMPLEMENT OF A FUZZY SET

The idea of complement reflects negation. We may define the complement of a fuzzy set in terms of the algebraic complement of its membership function, μ.

Let A be a fuzzy set defined over U. Then its complement, ¬A, is defined, in terms of $\mu_A(u)$, as

$$\mu_{\emptyset A}(u) = 1 - \mu_A(u)$$

Figure 13.44 shows the complement of the membership function High. Note that the above definition overlaps with the definition of the term High. In fact, there exists some T_0 such that $\mu_{NotHigh}(T_0)$, which we may call the break-even point of the membership function. It is easy to see that the break-even point of a fuzzy set A always has 0.5 membership degree in A.

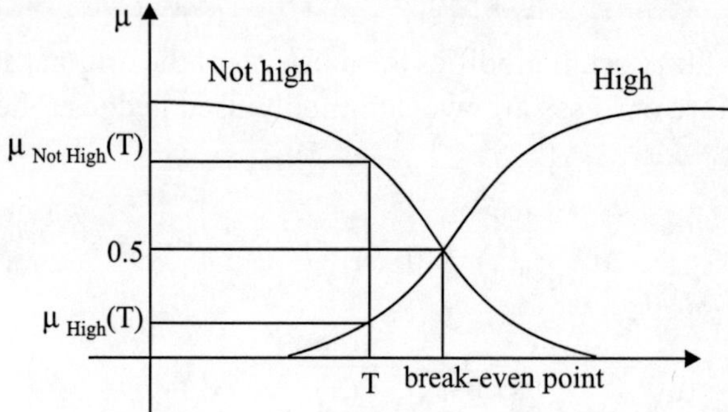

Figure 13.44 Definition of Not High

13.19 CONVEX FUZZY SETS

Another useful concept in fuzzy set theory is the notion of convexity. Intuitively, a fuzzy set is convex if its membership function does not have a "valley". The fuzzy set in Figure 13.45, for example, is not convex because it has a valley around a. Formally, a convex fuzzy set can be described as follows.

Let U be a universe of discourse of a variable x. Let A be a fuzzy subset of U. The set A is convex if and only if

$$\mu_A \lambda\alpha + ((1 - \lambda)b) \geq \min\{\mu_A(a), \mu_A(b)\} \tag{13.35}$$

For all a, b ε U and 0 d∩ λ d∩ 1.

This condition states that the membership value of any given element in the interval [a, b] should be no less than the membership value of either end points.

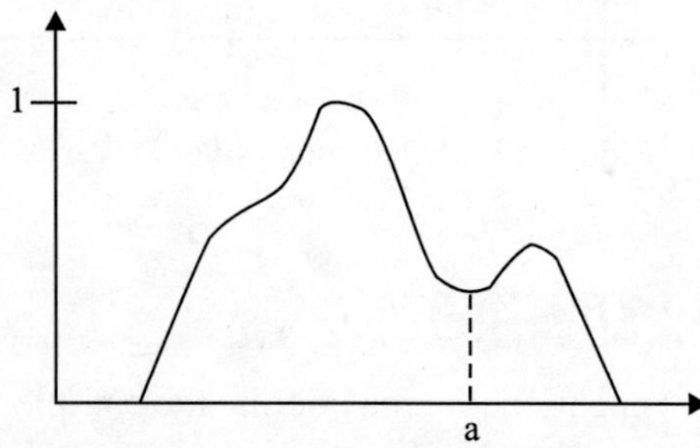

Figure 13.45: A Non-convex Fuzzy Set

13.20 POSSIBILITY THEORY

Possibility distribution states the possible value of the variable or the possibility that the variable takes a certain value. A possibility distribution, π, maps a given domain of definition into the interval [0, 1]. We can view a possibility distribution, as a mechanism for interpreting factual statements involving fuzzy sets. The statement, "Temperature is High," where High is defined as $\mu_{High}: T \rightarrow [0, 1]$, translates into a possibility distribution, $\pi(T) = \mu_{High}(T)$. Complex statements involving more than one fuzzy set translate into possibility distribution as well. In fact this is precisely how we interpret linguistic statements, given a priori or defined through an inference process.

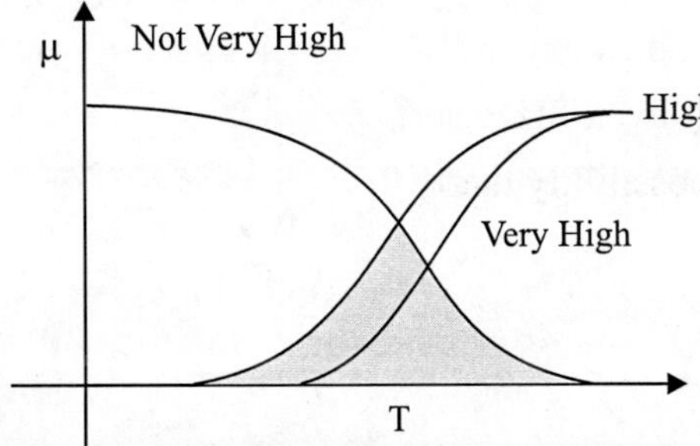

Figure 13.46: A Possibility Distribution of High AND NOT VERY HIGH

The statement, "Temperature is High but not too High," translates into a possibility distribution in terms of conjunction of the terms High and NOT VERY High:

$$\pi(T) = \mu n(\mu_{High}(T), m_{NOT\ VERY\ High}(T)).$$
$$= \min[\mu_{High}(T), 1 - (\mu_{High}(T))^2]$$

EXERCISES

1. Explain the difference between crisp set boundary and fuzzy set boundary?
2. What do you mean by set theory?
3. What do you mean by classical sets?
4. Explain the various operations on classical set?
5. Explain the properties of classical set?
6. How we can map classical sets to a function?
7. What do you mean by fuzzy set? Explain with the help of example.
8. Explain the representation of the fuzzy set?
9. What do you mean by fuzzy quantifiers?
10. What do you mean by fuzzy numbers?

11. Explain the various operations of fuzzy sets?
12. Explain the various properties of fuzzy sets?
13. What do you mean by cardinality of fuzzy set?
14. What do you mean by height of a fuzzy set?
15. Explain the concept of support and alpha level cuts in fuzzy sets?
16. Explain the resolution identify of a fuzzy set?
17. What are the various types of membership functions?
18. Explain the law of excluded middle and law of contradiction?
19. What do you mean by hedges?
20. Explain the complement of fuzzy set?
21. What do you mean by convex fuzzy set?
22. What do you mean by possibility theory?

CHAPTER 14

Fuzzy Relations, Fuzzy Graphs, and Fuzzy Arithmetic

14.1 INTRODUCTION

This chapter introduces the notion of a relation as the basic idea behind operations on sets such as Cartesian products, composition of relations, and equivalence properties. Like a set, a relation is of fundamental importance in all engineering, science, and mathematically based fields Relations can be also be used to represent similarity. Relations are intimately involved in logic, approximate reasoning, rule based systems, nonlinear simulation, synthetic evaluation, classification, pattern recognition, and control. Relations will be referred to repeatedly in this text in many different applications areas. Relations represent mappings for sets just as mathematical functions do; relations are also very useful in representing connectives in logic. This chapter begins by describing Cartesian products as a means of producing ordered relationships among sets. Following this is an introduction to classical (crisp) relations – structures that represent the presence or absence of correlation, interaction, or propinquity between the elements of two or more crisp sets; in this case, a set could also be the universe. There are only two degrees of relationship between elements of the sets in a crisp relation: the relationships "completely related" and "not related," in a binary sense.

Basic operations, properties, and the cardinality of relations are explained and illustrated. Two composition methods to relate elements of three or more universes are illustrated. Fuzzy relations are then developed by allowing the relationship between elements of two or more sets to take on an infinite number of degrees of relationship between the extremes of "completely related" and "not related." In this sense, fuzzy relations are to crisp relations as fuzzy sets are to crisp sets; crisp sets and relations are constrained realizations of fuzzy sets and relations. Both tolerance and equivalence relations are illustrated with some examples. Finally, the chapter concludes with a section on value assignments, which discusses various methods to develop the elements of relations, and a list of additional composition operators.

14.2 CARTESIAN PRODUCT

An ordered sequence of r elements, written in the form $(a_1, a_2, a_3, \ldots, a_r)$, is called an ordered r-tuple; an unordered r-tuple is simply a collection of r elements without restrictions on order. In a ubiquitous special case where r = 2, the r-tuple is referred to as an ordered pair. For crisp sets $A_1, A_2, \ldots, A_r$, the set of all r-tuples $(a_1, a_2, a_3, \ldots, a_r)$, where $a_1 \in A_1$, $a_2 \in A_2$, and $a_r \in A_r$, is called the Cartesian product of $A_1, A_2, \ldots, A_r$, and is denoted by $A_1 \times A_2 \times \ldots \times A_r$. The Cartesian product of two or more sets is not the same thing as the arithmetic product of two or more sets. When the extension principle is introduced. When all the A_r are identical and equal to A, the Cartesian product $A_1 \times A_2 \times \ldots \times A_r$ can be denoted as A_r.

Example 14.1: The elements in two sets A and B are given as A = {0, 1} and B = {e, f, g} find the Cartesian product A × B, B × A, A × A, B × B.

Solution: The Cartesian product for the given sets is as follows:

$$A \times B = \{(0, e), (0, f), (0, g), (1, e), (1, f), (1, g)\},$$

$$B \times A = \{(e, 0), (e, 1), (e, 1), (f, 1), (g, 1)\},$$

$$A \times A = A^2 = \{(0, 0), (0, 1), (1, 0), (1, 1)\},$$

$$B \times B = B^2 = \{(e, e), (e, f), (e, g), (f, e), (f, f), (f, g), (g, e), (g, f), (g, g)\}.$$

14.3 CRISP RELATIONS

A subset of the Cartesian product $A_1 \times A_2 \times \ldots \times A_r$ is called an r-ary relation over $A_1, A_2, \ldots, A_r$. Again, the most common case is for r = 2; in this situation the relation is a subset of the Cartesian product $A_1 \times A_2$ (i.e., a set of pairs, the first coordinate of which is from A_1 and the second from A_2). This subset of the full Cartesian product is called a binary relation from A_1 into A_2. If three, four, or five sets are involved in a subset of the full Cartesian product, the relations are called ternary, quaternary, and quinary, respectively. In this text, whenever the term relation is used without qualification, it is taken to mean a binary relation. The Cartesian product of two universes X and Y is determined as

$$X \times Y = \{x, y) \mid x \in X, y \in Y\} \tag{14.1}$$

which forms an ordered pair of every $x \in X$ with every $y \in Y$, forming unconstrained matches between X and Y. That is, every element in universe X is related completely to every element in universe Y. The strength of this relationship between ordered pairs of elements in each universe is measured by the characteristic function, denoted χ, where a value of unity is associated with complete relationship and a value of zero is associated with no relationship, i.e.,

$$\chi_{X \times Y}(x, y) = \begin{matrix} 1, (x, y) \quad X \;\; Y \\ 0, (x, y) \quad X \;\; Y \end{matrix} \tag{14.2}$$

One can think of this strength of relation as a mapping from ordered pairs of the universe, or ordered pairs of sets defined on the universes, to the characteristic function. When the universes, or sets, are finite the relation can be conveniently represented by a matrix, called a relation matrix. An r-ary relation can be represented by an r-dimensional relation matrix. Hence, binary relations can be represented by two-dimensional matrices (used throughout this text).

An example of the strength of relation for the unconstrained case is given in the Sagittal diagram shown in Figure 14.1. Lines in the Sagittal diagram and values of unity in the relation matrix

$$
\begin{array}{cc|ccc}
 & & a & b & c \\
 & 1 & 1 & 1 & 1 \\
R = & 2 & 1 & 1 & 1 \\
 & 3 & 1 & 1 & 1
\end{array}
$$

correspond to the ordered pairs of mappings in the relation. Here, the elements in the two universes are defined as X = {1, 2, 3} and Y = {a, b, c}.

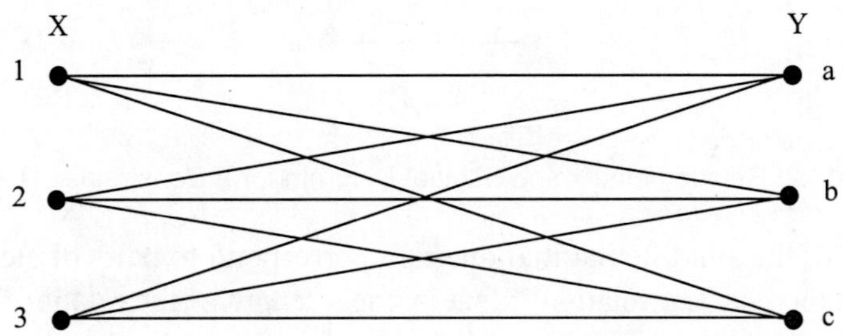

Figure 14.1: Sagittal Diagram of an Unconstrained Relation.

A more general crisp relation, R, exists when matches between elements in two universes are constrained. Again, the characteristic function is used to assign values of relationship in the mapping of the Cartesian space X × Y to the binary values of (0, 1):

$$X_R(x,y) = \begin{array}{l} 1,\ (x,y)\quad R \\ 0,\ (x,y)\quad R \end{array} \qquad (14.3)$$

Example 14.2: Let R be a relation among the three sets
X= {Hindi, English}, Y = {Doxllar, Euro, Pound, Rupees}, and Z ={India, Nepal, United States, Canada} R (x, y, z) = {Hindi, Rupees, India}
{Hindi, Rupees, Nepal}
{English, Dollar, Canada}
{English, Dollar, United States}.

Solution: The relation can be represented as follows:

Hindi

	India	Nepal	US	Canada
Dollar	0	0	0	0
Euro	0	0	0	0
Pound	0	0	0	0
Rupees	1	1	0	0

English

	India	Nepal	US	Canada
Dollar	0	0	1	1
Euro	0	0	0	0
Pound	0	0	0	0
Rupees	0	0	0	0

Example 14.3: In many biological models, members of certain species can reproduce only with certain members of another species. Hence, only some elements in two or more universes have a relationship (nonzero) in the Cartesian product. An example is shown in Figure 14.2 for two two-member species, i.e., for X = {1, 2} and for Y = {a, b}. In this case the locations of zeros in the relation matrix

$$R = \{(1, a), (2, b)\} \quad R \subset X \times Y$$

X Y
1 a
2 b

Figure 14.2: Relation Matrix and Sagittal Diagram for a Constrained Relation.

and the absence of lines in t he Sagittal diagram correspond to pairs of elements between the two universes where there is "no relation"; that is, the strength of the relationship is zero. Special cases of the constrained and the unconstrained Cartesian product for sets where r = 2 (i.e., for A^2) are called the identity relation and the universal relation, respectively.

For example, for A = {0, 1, 2} the universal relation, denoted U_A, and the identity relation, denoted I_A, are found to be

$$U_A = \{(0, 0), (0, 1), (0, 2), (1, 0), (1, 1), (1, 2), (2, 0), (2, 1), (2, 2)\}$$
$$I_A = \{(0, 0), (1, 1), (2, 2)\}$$

Example 14.4: Relations can also be defined for continuous universes. Consider, for example, the continuous relation defined by the following expression:

$$R = \{(x, y) \mid y \geq 2x, x \in X, y \in Y\}$$

which is also given in function-theoretic form using the characteristic function as

$$\chi R(X, Y) = \begin{matrix} 1, \; y \quad 2x \\ 0, \; y \quad 2x \end{matrix}$$

Graphically, this relation is equivalent to the shaded region shown in Figure 14.3.

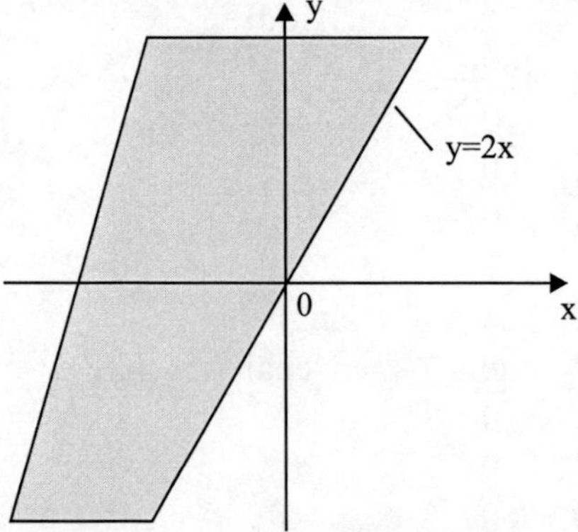

Figure 14.3: Relation Corresponding to the Expression y > 2x.

14.3.1 Cardinality of Crisp Relations

Suppose n elements of the universe X are related (paired) to m elements of the universe Y. If the cardinality of X is n_X and the cardinality of Y is n_Y then the cardinality of the relation, R, between these two universes is $n_{X \times Y}$ $n_X * n_Y$. The cardinality of the power set describing this relation, $P(X \times Y)$, is then $n_{P(\quad)}$ $2^{(n\ n\ )}$.

14.3.2 Operations on Crisp Relations

Define R and S as two separate relations on the Cartesian universe $X \times Y$, and define the null relation and the complete relation as the relation matrices $\underset{\sim}{O}$ and $\underset{\sim}{E}$, respectively. An example of a 4×4 form of the $\underset{\sim}{O}$ and $\underset{\sim}{E}$ matrices are given here:

$$O = \begin{matrix} 0 & 0 & 0 & 0 \\ 0 & 0 & 0 & 0 \\ 0 & 0 & 0 & 0 \\ 0 & 0 & 0 & 0 \end{matrix}$$

$$F = \begin{matrix} 1 & 1 & 1 & 1 \\ 1 & 1 & 1 & 1 \\ 1 & 1 & 1 & 1 \\ 1 & 1 & 1 & 1 \end{matrix}$$

The following function-theoretic operations for the two crisp relations (R, S) can now be defined.

Union	$R \cup S \rightarrow \chi_{R \cup S}(x, y) : \chi_{R \cup S}(x, y) = \max[\chi_R(x, y), \chi_S(x, y)]$
Intersection	$R \cap S \rightarrow \chi_{R \cap S}(x, y) : \chi_{R \cap S}(x, y) = \min[\chi_R(x, y), \chi_S(x, y)]$
Complement	$\overline{R} \rightarrow {}_{\overline{R}}(x, y) : {}_{\overline{R}}(x, y) = 1 - \chi_R(x, y)$
Containment	$R \subset S \rightarrow \chi_R(x, y) : \chi_R(x, y) \leq \chi_S(x, y)$
Identity	$\phi \rightarrow O$ and $X \rightarrow E$

14.3.3 Properties of Crisp Relations

The properties of commutativity, associativity, distributivity, involution, and idempotency all hold for crisp relations just as they do for classical set operations. Moreover, De Morgan's principles and the excluded middle axioms also hold for crisp (classical) relations just as they do for crisp (classical) sets. The null relation, **O**, and the complete relation, **E**, are analogous to the null set, ∅, and the whole set, X, respectively, in the set-theoretic case (see Chapter 3).

14.3.4 Composition

Let R be a relation that relates, or maps, elements from universe X to universe Y, and let S be a relation that relates, or maps, elements from universe Y to universe Z. A useful question we seek to answer is whether we can find a relation, T, that relates the same elements in universe X that R contains to the same elements in universe Z that S contains. It turns out we can find such a relation using an operation known as composition. For the Sagittal diagram in Figure 14.4, we see that the only "path" between relation R and relation S is the two routes that start at x_1 and end at z_2 (i.e., $x_1 - y_1 - z_2$ and $x_1 - y_3 - z_2$). Hence, we wish to find a relation T that relates the ordered pair (x_1, z_2), i.e., $(x_1, z_2) \in$ T. In this example,

$$R = \{(x_1, y_1), (x_1, y_3), (x_2, y_4)\}$$

$$S = \{(y_1, z_2), (y_3, z_2)\}$$

There are two common forms of the composition operation; one is called the max–min composition and the other the max–product composition. (Five other forms of the composition operator are available for certain logic issues; these are described at the end of this chapter.) The ax–min composition is defined by the set-theoretic and membership function-theoretic expressions

$$T = R \circ S$$

$$\chi_T(x, z) = \underset{y\ Y}{\vee} (\ _R(x, y) \qquad _S(y, z)) \tag{14.4}$$

and the max–product (sometimes called max–dot) composition is defined by the set theoretic and membership function-theoretic expressions

$$T = R \circ S$$

$$\chi_T(x, z) = \underset{y\ Y}{\vee} (\ _R(x, y) \qquad _S(y, z)) \tag{14.5}$$

Figure 14.4: Sagittal Diagram Relating Elements of Three Universes.

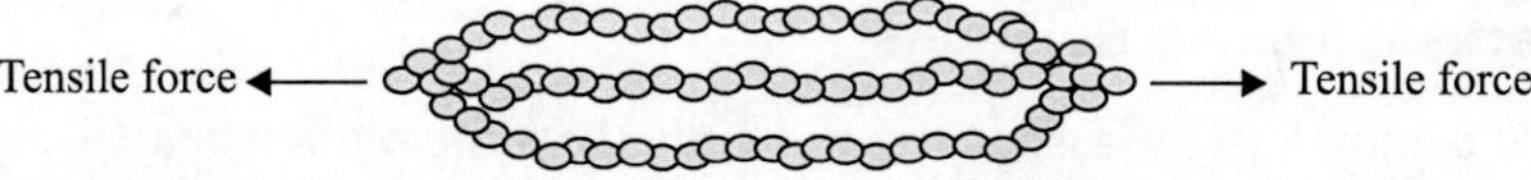

Figure 14.5: Chain Strength Analogy for Max–Min Composition.

There is a very interesting physical analogy for the max–min composition operator. Figure 14.5 illustrates a system comprising several chains placed together in a parallel fashion. In the system, each chain comprises a number of chain links. If we were to take one of the chains out of the system, place it in a tensile test machine, and exert a large tensile force on the chain, we would find that the chain would break at its weakest link. Hence, the strength of one chain is equal to the strength of its weakest link; in other words, the minimum ($\wedge$) strength of all the links in the chain governs the strength of the overall chain.

Now, if we were to place the entire chain system in a tensile device and exert a tensile force on the chain system, we would find that the chain system would continue to carry increasing loads until the last chain in the system broke. That is, weaker chains would break with an increasing load until the strongest chain was left alone, and eventually it would break; in other words, the maximum ($\vee$) strength of all the chains in the chain system would govern the overall strength of the chain system. Each chain in the system is analogous to the min operation in the max–min composition, and the overall chain system strength is analogous to the max operation in the max–min composition.

Example 14.5: The matrix expression for the crisp relations shown in Figure 14.4 can be found using the max–min composition operation. Relation matrices for R and S would be expressed as

$$R = \begin{array}{c|cccc} & y_1 & y_2 & y_3 & y_4 \\ \hline x_1 & 1 & 0 & 1 & 0 \\ x_2 & 0 & 0 & 0 & 1 \\ x_3 & 0 & 0 & 0 & 0 \end{array}$$

and

$$S = \begin{array}{c|cc} & z_1 & z_2 \\ \hline y_1 & 0 & 1 \\ y_2 & 0 & 0 \\ y_3 & 0 & 1 \\ y_4 & 0 & 0 \end{array}$$

The resulting relation T would then be determined by max–min composition, Eq. (14.4), or max–product composition, Eq. (14.5). (In the crisp case these forms of the composition operators produce identical results; other forms of this operator, such as those listed at the end of this chapter, will not produce identical results.) For example,

$$\text{ì}_T(x_1, z_1) = \max[\min(1, 0), \min(0, 0), \min(1, 0), \min(0, 0)] = 0$$
$$\text{ì}_T(x_1, z_2) = \max[\min(1, 1), \min(0, 0), \min(1, 1), \min(0, 0)] = 1$$

and for the rest,

$$T = \begin{array}{c|cc} & z_1 & z_2 \\ \hline x_1 & 0 & 1 \\ x_2 & 0 & 0 \\ x_3 & 0 & 0 \end{array}$$

14.4 FUZZY RELATIONS

A fuzzy relation generalizes the notion of a classical black-and-white relation into one that allows partial membership. For example, a binary relation "friend" will classify all human relationships into either being friend or not being friend. A fuzzy relation "Friend," in contrast, can describe the degree of friendship between tow persons.

The classical notation of relation describes a relationship that holds between two or more objects. A relationship between two objects is represented by a binary relation, a relation with two arguments. For example, the parent relationship between a parent and his/her child can be represented as a binary relation. More generally, we can use an n-ary relation, a relation with n arguments, to describe a relationship between n objects. For instance, we can use an n-ary relation to describe that student X took course Y during semester Z in year W. This relation has four arguments such as took_course (student, course, semester, year). An n-ary relation can be formally defined as set of ordered lists of n objects. Each list describes a case in which the relation holds.

A binary relation on variables x and y, whose domains are X and Y respectively, can be defined as a set of ordered pairs in X × Y. For instance, the binary relation "less than" between two real numbers can be formally defined as

$$R = \{(x, y) \mid x < y, x, y \in R\}$$

It is easy to see that the relation is a subset of X x Y. In general, an n-ary relation on $x_1, x_2, \ldots, x_n$ whose domains are $X_1, X_2, \ldots, X_n$ is a subset of $X_1 \times X_2 \times \ldots \times X_n$.

Since a relation can be viewed as a set, we can easily generalize the classical notion of a relation using fuzzy sets. We will show how to generalize binary relations. First, we can represent a binary relation R on x, y with domains X, Y as a function that maps an ordered pair (x, y) in X × Y to 0 (i.e., the relation does not hold between x and y) or 1 (i.e., the relation holds between x and y), i.e.,

$$R = X \times Y \rightarrow \{0, 1\}$$

A fuzzy relation generalizes the classical notion of relation into a matter of degree. As we mentioned earlier, the fuzzy relation Friend describes the degree of friendship between two persons.

Fuzzy relations also map elements of one universe, say X, to those of another universe, say Y, through the Cartesian product of the two universes. However, the "strength" of the relation between ordered pairs of the two universes is not measured with the characteristic function, but rather with a membership function expressing various "degrees" of strength of the relation on the unit interval [0,1]. Hence, a fuzzy relation $\underset{\sim}{R}$ is a mapping from the Cartesian space X × Y to the interval [0,1], where the strength of the mapping is expressed by the membership function of the relation for ordered pairs from the two universes, or $\underset{\sim}{R}(x, y)$.

Similarly, a fuzzy relation Petite between height and weight of a person describes the degree by which a person with a specific height and weight is considered petite. Formally, fuzzy relation R between variables x and y, whose domains are X and Y, respectively, is defined by a function that maps ordered pairs in X × Y to their degree in the relation, which is a number between 0 and 1, i.e., $R: X \times Y \rightarrow [0, 1]$.

More generally, a fuzzy n-ary relation R in $x_1, x_{2,\ldots,} x_n$ whose domains are $X_1, X_2, \ldots, X_n$, respectively, is defined by a function that maps an n-tuple $< x_1, x_{2,\ldots,} x_n >$ in $X_1 \times, X_2 \times \ldots, \times X_n$, to a number in the interval, i.e., $R: X_1 \times X_2 \times \ldots \times X_n \rightarrow [0, 1]$. Just as a classical relation can be viewed as a set, a fuzzy relation can be viewed as a fuzzy subset. From this perspective, the mapping above is equivalent to the membership function of a multidimensional fuzzy set.

If the possible values of x and y are discrete, we can express a fuzzy relation in a matrix form. For example, suppose we wish to express a fuzzy relation Petite in terms of the height and the weight of a female. Suppose the range of the height and the weight of interest to us are {5' 5'1", 5'2", 5'3", 5'4", 5'5",5'6"}, denoted h,, and {90, 95, 100, 105, 110, 115, 120, 125} (in lb.) denoted w, respectively. We can express the fuzzy relation in a matrix form as shown below:

Each entry in the matrix indicates the degree a female with the corresponding height (i.e., the row

	90	95	100	105	110	115	120	125
5	1	1	1	1	1	1	0.5	0.2
5'1"	1	1	1	1	1	0.9	0.3	0.1
5'2"	1	1	1	1	1	0.7	0.1	0
5'3"	1	1	1	1	0.5	0.3	0	0
5'4"	0.8	0.6	0.4	0.2	0	0	0	0
5'5"	0.6	0.4	0.2	0	0	0	0	0
5'6"	0	0	0	0	0	0	0	0

heading) and weight (i.e., the column heading) is considered to be petite. For instance, the entry corresponding to a height of 5'3" and a weight of 115 lb. has a value 0.3, which is the degree to which such a female person will be considered a petite person; i.e., Petite(5'3", 115 lb) = 0.3.Once we define the Petite fuzzy relation, we can answer two kinds of questions:

- What is the degree that a female with a specific height and a specific weight is considered to be petite?
- What is the possibility that a petite person has a specific pair of height and weight measures?

14.4.1 Composition of Fuzzy Relations

We have shown that once we have a fuzzy relation, we can directly answer two kinds of interesting questions. We can view these question-answer capabilities as inferences (e.g., inferring the possible weight-height combinations knowing that a person is petite). An even more useful king of inference is the following:

- Given a two-dimensional fuzzy relation and the possible values of one variable, infer the possible values of the other variable.

For instance, we may wish to know the possible weight of a petite female called Michelle who is about 5'4" tall where "about" indicates impression. The answer to this question can be obtained through the composition of fuzzy relations, which is also referred to as the compositional rule of inference. To find out the answer, we will then consider whether it is possible for such a person to weigh 90 lb, 95 lb, ..., 120 lb. Because we are interested in finding all possible weights of the person, we may get multiple positive answers. Furthermore, the answer should indicate the degree of possibility for each weight.

How do we find out whether it is possible for Michelle to have a specific weight, say 110 lb?, If we think about this for a moment, it is not difficult to realize that we need to consider all possible heights of a the person and see if petite person with such a height can weigh 110 lb. For example, we may start with 5 feet and check if the following two conditions are both rule:

- What is the possibility that Michelle's height is 5 feet given that she is about 5'4" tall?
- What is the possibility that a petite person is 5 feet tall and weighs 110 lb?

If the answers to both questions are positive, wee infer that 110 lb is a possible weight of Michelle. We can ask two similar questions for the next height, which is 5 feet 2 inches.

- What is the possibility that Michelle's height is 5 feet 2 inches given that she is about 5'4" tall?
- What is the possibility that a petite person is 5 feet 2 inches tall and weighs 110 lb?

The procedure can be repeated for all the remaining height measures (i.e., 5'4", 5'6",..., 6'). We can represent such a procedure in predicate logic. Predicate logic is a logic system that uses "predicate," as building blocks for constructing logic formulae. A predicate is like a function that maps its arguments to either true or false. The arguments of a predicate are usually variables or constants. Predicates are often connected into a logic formula using and (denoted $\wedge$), or (denoted $\vee$), and imply (denoted $\rightarrow$). A bidirectional implication is denoted by $\leftrightarrow$. Variables are quantified by a "for all" quantifier ( ) or a "there exists" quantifier ($\exists$). These notations are summarized in Table 14.1. To help you get familiar with these notations, we will use them in the discussion below.

Table 14.1: Predicate Logic Notations

Symbol	Meaning
$\wedge$	and
$\vee$	or
	for all
$\exists$	there exists
$\leftrightarrow$	if and only if
$\rightarrow$	imply

We use three predicates to describes the reasoning process above in logic:

Possible-height(h_i): The predicate is true if h_i is a possible height of a person.

Possible-height(w_j): The predicate is true if w_j is a possible height of a person.

Petite (h_i, w_j): the predicate is true if a person with height h_i and w_j weight is petite.

Notice that the first two predicates represent crisp (i.e., nonfuzzy) constraints on possible heights and weights, whereas the last predicate represents a crisp binary relation. Therefore, they cannot truly represent the possibility distribution of About 5'4", or the fuzzy relation Petite. However, we will use these predicates to show how the inference procedure above can be expressed in classical logic. We will then generalize such a logic expression to obtain the compositional rule of inference in fuzzy logic. We first represent the inference procedure described earlier in logic as follows:

[(Possible-height (5') $\wedge$ Petite (5', 90)) $\vee$
(Possible-height (5'2") $\wedge$ Petite (5', 90)) $\vee$
$\vdots$
(Possible-height(6') $\wedge$ Petite (6', 90))] $\leftrightarrow$ Possible-weight(90)

Since the same procedure can be used to determine whether it is possible for a person to weigh 95, 100, 105, …., 125 pounds, we can use a more general expression in logic as follows:

w_j [(Possible-height (5') $\wedge$Petite (5', w_j)) $\vee$
(Possible-height (5'2") $\wedge$Petite (5'2", w_j)) $\vee$
$\vdots$
(Possible-height(6') $\wedge$ Petite (6', w_j))] $\leftrightarrow$ Possible-weight(w_j)

This can be rewritten into a more compact form:

$$w_j \text{ Possible-weig ht}(w_j) \quad \bigvee_{h_i} \text{Possible-height}(h_i) \quad \text{Petite}(h_i, w_j) \tag{14.6}$$

In fact, this is a special case (i.e., the binary case) of the composition of a fuzzy relation. In fuzzy logic, as we already know, both the notion of possibility and the notion of relation become matters of degree. Let us return to our original question, "what are the possible weights of a petite female called Michelle who is about 5' 4" tall?" Suppose the meaning of petite is expressed by the fuzzy relation Petite in the previous section. We introduce the following notations to represent about related possibility distributions:

- $\Pi_{height(x)}$ (h_i): The possibility degree for a person's height to be h_i.
- $\Pi_{petite}(h_i, w_j)$: The possibility degree for a petite person to have a height of h_i, and a weight of w_j.

Furthermore, the conjunctions ($\wedge$) and disjunctions ($\vee$) in Equation 14.6 in binary logic need to be generalized to a fuzzy conjunction ($\otimes$) and a fuzzy disjunction ($\otimes$) operator. Therefore, we can infer Michelle's possible weight form her possible height and also the fact that she is petite using a generalized version of Equation 14.6, which is given below:

$$\Pi_{weight(x)} (w_j) = {}_{h_i} (\Pi_{Height(x)} (h_i) \otimes \Pi_{Petite}(h_i, w_j)) \tag{14.7}$$

This is an application of the compositional rule of inference to our example. We define the compositional rule of inference more formally below.

Let X and Y be the universe of discourse for variables x and y, respectively and x_i and y_j be elements of X and Y. Let R be a fuzzy relation that maps X $\times$ Y to [0, 1] and the possibility distribution of X is known to be Π_X (x_i). The compositional rule of inference infers the possibility distribution of Y as follows:

$$\Pi_Y(y_j) = {}_{x_i} (\Pi_X(x_i) \otimes \Pi_R(x_i, y_j)) \tag{14.8}$$

The computation steps for the compositional rule of inference are similar to those of matrix multiplication. The fuzzy conjunction and disjunction operations in Equation 14.8 correspond respectively to the multiplication and summation steps in matrix multiplication.

The compositional rule of inference is not uniquely defined. By choosing different fuzzy conjunction and fuzzy disjunction operators, we get different compositional rules of inference. We list two that are commonly used in practice:

1. max-min composition:

$$\Pi_Y(y_j) = \max_{x_i} (\min(\Pi_x(x_i), \Pi_R(x_i, y_j))) \tag{14.9}$$

2. max-product composition:

$$\Pi_Y(y_j) = \max_{x_i} (\Pi_x(x_i), \Pi_R(x_i, y_j))) \tag{14.10}$$

Returning to our example, let us assume About-5'4" is defined as

About-5'4" = {0/5, 0/5'", 0.4/5'2", 0.8/5'3", 1/5'4", 0.8/5'5", 0.4/5'6"} (14.11)

Using the max-min compositional rule of inference, we can compute the weight possibility distribution of a petite person about 5'4" tall:

$$\Pi_{weight}(90) = (0 \wedge 1) \vee (0 \wedge 1) \vee (0.4 \wedge 1) \vee (0.8 \wedge 1) \vee (1 \wedge 0.8) \vee (0.8 \wedge 0.6) \vee (0.4 \wedge 0) = 0.8 \tag{14.12}$$

Similarly, we can compute the possibility degree for other weights. The final result is

$$\Pi_{weight} = \{0.8/90, 0.8/95, 0.8/100, 0.8/105, 0.5/110, 0.4/115, 0.1/120, 0/125\}$$

Mathematically, the composition of fuzzy relations can be defined using three basic operations: projection, cylindrical extension, and intersection. We introduce the first two concepts before we give a formal definition of the composition of fuzzy relations.

Cylindrical Extension

Cylindrical extension and projection are dual operations. The former extends the dimension of a fuzzy relation while the latter reduces the dimension of a fuzzy relation.

Typically, we apply cylindrical extension to two fuzzy relations so that they have the same dimensionality in order to apply set operations (i.e. intersections and union) to them. For example, we can apply cylindrical extension to the fuzzy set About 5'4" to H × W. The result is

About-5'4" = (14.13)

	90	95	100	105	110	115	120	125
5	0	0	0	0	0	0	0	0
5'1"	0	0	0	0	0	0	0	0
5'2"	0.4	0.4	0.4	0.4	0.4	0.4	0.4	0.4
5'3"	0.8	0.8	0.8	0.8	0.8	0.8	0.8	0.8
5'4"	1	1	1	1	1	1	1	1
5'5"	0.8	0.8	0.8	0.8	0.8	0.8	0.8	0.8
5'6"	0.4	0.4	0.4	0.4	0.4	0.4	0.4	0.4

Figure 14.6 shows graphically the effect of applying cylindrical extension to a fuzzy subset A of U to the extended dimension U × V. As shown in the figure, the membership function of the extended fuzzy set has a cylinder shape from which the operation gets its name.

Definition Let R be a fuzzy subset of $U_{i1} \times U_{i2} \times \ldots \times U_{ik}$, where $(i_1, i_2, \ldots, i_k)$, is a subsequence of (1, 2,…, n). The cylindrical extension of R in $U_1 \times U_2 \times \ldots \times U_n$ is a fuzzy subset of $U_1 \times U_2 \times \ldots \times U_n$, denoted as R, whose membership function is defined as

$$\mu_R(U_1, U_2, \ldots, U_n) = \mu_R(U_{i1}, U_{i2}, \ldots, U_{ik}) \quad (14.14)$$

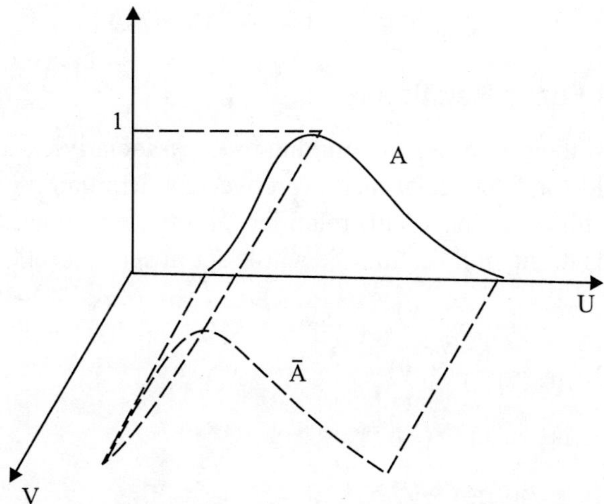

Figure 14.6: An Example of Cylindrical Extension

Projection

The projection operation, as the name suggest projects a fuzzy relation to a subset of selected dimensions. This operation is often used to extract the possibility distribution of a few selected variables from a given fuzzy relation. For instance, the projection of the Petite fuzzy relation to the universe of weight gives us a possibility distribution of a petite female person's weight. Projection to a fuzzy relation is analogous to computing the marginal probability on a joint probability distribution, we perform fuzzy disjunction across a row or a column of a fuzzy relation. Hence, the result of projecting the Petite relation to weight is

$$\text{Proj}_w \text{ Petite} = \{1/90, 1/95, 1/100, 1/105, 1/110, 1/115, 0.5/120, 0.2/125\} \quad (14.15)$$

14.4.2 Cardinality of Fuzzy Relations

Since the cardinality of fuzzy sets on any universe is infinity, the cardinality of a fuzzy relation between two or more universes is also infinity.

14.4.3 Operations on Fuzzy Relations

Let $\underset{\sim}{R}$ and $\underset{\sim}{S}$ be fuzzy relations on the Cartesian space $X \times Y$. Then the following operations apply for the membership values for various set operations:

Union $\quad {}_{\underset{\sim}{R}\ \underset{\sim}{S}}(x, y) = \max(\ {}_{\underset{\sim}{R}}(x, y), \mid {}_{\underset{\sim}{S}}(x, y))$

Intersection $\quad {}_{\underset{\sim}{R}\ \underset{\sim}{S}}(x, y) = \min(\ {}_{\underset{\sim}{R}}(x, y),\ \ {}_{\underset{\sim}{S}}(x, y))$

Complement $\quad \overline{\underset{\sim}{R}}(x, y) = 1 -\ \ {}_{\underset{\sim}{R}}(x, y)$

Containment $\quad \underset{\sim}{R}\ \ \underset{\sim}{S} \Rightarrow\ {}_{\underset{\sim}{R}}(x, y),\ \ \ \ {}_{\underset{\sim}{S}}(x, y)$

14.4.4 Properties of Fuzzy Relations

Just as for crisp relations, the properties of commutativity, associativity, distributivity, involution, and idempotency all hold for fuzzy relations. Moreover, De Morgan's principles hold for fuzzy relations just as they do for crisp (classical) relations, and the null relation, **O**, and the complete relation, **E**, are analogous to the null set and the whole set in set-theoretic form, respectively.

Commutativity $\quad {}_{\underset{\sim}{R}\ \underset{\sim}{S}}(x, y) =\ \ {}_{\underset{\sim}{S}\ \underset{\sim}{R}}(x, y)$.

Associativity $\quad {}_{(\underset{\sim}{R}\ \ \underset{\sim}{S})\ \ \underset{\sim}{T}}(x, y) =\ \ {}_{\underset{\sim}{R}\ \ (\underset{\sim}{S}\ \ \underset{\sim}{T}}(x, y).$

Distributivity $\quad {}_{(\underset{\sim}{R}\ \ \underset{\sim}{S})\ \ \underset{\sim}{T}}(x, y) =\ \ {}_{\underset{\sim}{R}\ \ (\underset{\sim}{S}\ \ \underset{\sim}{T}}(x, y).$

Idempotency $\quad {}_{\underset{\sim}{R}\ \ \underset{\sim}{R}}(x, y) =\ \ {}_{\underset{\sim}{R}}.$

Involtution $\quad {}_{\overline{\overline{\underset{\sim}{R}}}}(x, y) =\ \ {}_{\underset{\sim}{R}}(x, y).$

Fuzzy relations are not constrained, as is the case for fuzzy sets in general, by the excluded middle axioms. Since a fuzzy relation $\underset{\sim}{R}$ is also a fuzzy set, there is overlap between a relation and its complement; hence,

$$\underset{\sim}{R}\ \ \overline{\underset{\sim}{R}} \neq \mathbf{E}$$

$$\underset{\sim}{R}\ \ \overline{\underset{\sim}{R}} \neq \mathbf{O}$$

As seen in the foregoing expressions, the excluded middle axioms for relations do not result, in general, in the null relation, **O**, or the complete relation, **E**.

14.4.5 Fuzzy Cartesian Product and Composition

Because fuzzy relations in general are fuzzy sets, we can define the Cartesian product to be a relation between two or more fuzzy sets. Let $\underset{\sim}{A}$ be a fuzzy set on universe X and $\underset{\sim}{B}$ be a fuzzy set on universe Y; then the Cartesian product between fuzzy sets $\underset{\sim}{A}$ and $\underset{\sim}{B}$ will result in a fuzzy relation $\underset{\sim}{R}$, which is contained within the full Cartesian product space, or

$$\underset{\sim}{A} \quad \underset{\sim}{B} = \underset{\sim}{R} \quad X \quad Y \tag{14.16}$$

where the fuzzy relation $\underset{\sim}{R}$ has membership function

$$\underset{\sim}{R}(x, y) = \quad_{\underset{\sim}{A}\ \underset{\sim}{B}}(x, y) \quad \min(\quad_{\underset{\sim}{A}}(x), \quad_{\underset{\sim}{B}}(y)) \tag{14.17}$$

The Cartesian product defined $\underset{\sim}{A}$ $\underset{\sim}{B}$ $\underset{\sim}{R}$ by, Eq. (14.16), is implemented in the same fashion as is the cross product of two vectors. Again, the Cartesian product is not the same operation as the arithmetic product. In the case of two-dimensional relations (r = 2), the former employs the idea of pairing of elements among sets, whereas the latter uses actual arithmetic products between elements of sets. Each of the fuzzy sets could be thought of as a vector of membership values; each value is associated with a particular element in each set. For example, for a fuzzy set (vector) $\underset{\sim}{A}$ that has four elements, hence column vector of size 4 × 1, and for a fuzzy set (vector) $\underset{\sim}{B}$ that has five elements, hence a row vector size of 1 × 5, the resulting fuzzy relation, ,will be represented by a matrix of size 4 × 5, i.e., $\underset{\sim}{R}$, will have four rows and five columns. This result is illustrated in the following example.

Example 14.6: Suppose we have two fuzzy sets, $\underset{\sim}{A}$ defined on a universe of three discrete temperatures, $X = \{x_1, x_2, x_3\}$, and $\underset{\sim}{B}$ defined on a universe of two discrete pressures, $Y = \{y_1, y_2\}$, and we want to find the fuzzy Cartesian product between them. Fuzzy set $\underset{\sim}{A}$ could represent the "ambient" temperature and fuzzy set $\underset{\sim}{B}$ the "near optimum" pressure for a certain heat exchanger, and the Cartesian product might represent the conditions (temperature–pressure pairs) of the exchanger that are associated with "efficient" operations. For example, let

$$\underset{\sim}{A} = \frac{0.2}{x_1} \quad \frac{0.5}{x_2} \quad \frac{1}{x_3} \text{ and } \quad \underset{\sim}{} \quad \frac{0.3}{y_1} \quad \frac{0.9}{y_2}$$

Note that can be represented as a column vector of size 3 × 1 and $\underset{\sim}{B}$ can be represented by a row vector of 1 × 2. Then the fuzzy Cartesian product, using Eq. (14.17), results in a fuzzy relation $\underset{\sim}{R}$, (of size 3 × 2) representing "efficient" conditions, or

$$\underset{\sim}{A} \quad \underset{\sim}{B} \quad \underset{\sim}{R} = \begin{array}{c|cc} & y_1 & y_2 \\ x_1 & 0.2 & 0.2 \\ x_2 & 0.3 & 0.5 \\ x_3 & 0.3 & 0.9 \end{array}$$

14.5 FUZZY COMPOSITION

Fuzzy composition can be defined just as it is for crisp (binary) relations. Suppose $\underset{\sim}{R}$, is a fuzzy relation on the Cartesian space , $\underset{\sim}{S}$ is a fuzzy relation on Y × Z, and $\underset{\sim}{T}$ is a fuzzy relation on X × Z, then fuzzy max–min composition is defined in terms of the set-theoretic notation and membership function-theoretic notation in the following manner:

$$\tilde{T} = \tilde{R} \circ \tilde{S}$$

$$_{\tilde{T}}(x, z) = \bigvee_{y\ Y} (\ _{\tilde{R}}(x, y) \quad _{\tilde{S}}(y, z)) \tag{14.18a}$$

and fuzzy max–product composition is defined in terms of the membership function theoretic notation as

$$_{\tilde{T}}(x, z) = \bigvee_{y\ Y} (\ _{\tilde{R}}(x, y) \cdot \ _{\tilde{S}}(y, z)) \tag{14.18b}$$

It should be pointed out that neither crisp nor fuzzy compositions are commutative in general; that is,

$$\tilde{R} \circ \tilde{S} \neq \tilde{S} \circ \tilde{R} \tag{14.19}$$

Equation (14.19) is general for any matrix operation, fuzzy or otherwise, that must satisfy consistency between the cardinal counts of elements in respective universes. Even for the case of square matrices, the composition converse, represented by Eq. (14.19), is not guaranteed.

Example 14.7: Let us extend the information contained in the Sagittal diagram shown in Figure 14.4 to include fuzzy relationships for $X \times Y$ (denoted by the fuzzy relation $\tilde{R}$) and $Y \times Z$ (denoted by the fuzzy relation $\tilde{S}$). In this case we change the elements of the universes to, $X = \{x_1, x_2\}$, $Y = \{y_1, y_2\}$, and $Z = \{z_1, z_2, z_3\}$

Consider the following fuzzy relations:

$$\tilde{R} = \begin{array}{c|cc} & y_1 & y_2 \\ x_1 & 0.7 & 0.5 \\ x_2 & 0.8 & 0.4 \end{array}$$

and

$$\tilde{S} = \begin{array}{c|ccc} & z_1 & z_2 & z_3 \\ x_1 & 0.9 & 0.6 & 0.2 \\ x_2 & 0.1 & 0.7 & 0.5 \end{array}$$

Then the resulting relation, $\tilde{T}$, which relates elements of universe X to elements of universe Z, i.e., defined on Cartesian space $X \times Z$, can be found by max–min composition, Eq. (14.18a), to be, for example, $\mu_T(x_1, z_1) = \max[\min(0.7, 0.9), \min(0.5, 0.1)] = 0.7$ and the rest,

$$\tilde{T} = \begin{array}{c|ccc} & z_1 & z_2 & z_3 \\ x_1 & 0.7 & 0.6 & 0.5 \\ x_2 & 0.8 & 0.6 & 0.4 \end{array}$$

and by max–product composition, Eq. (14.18b), to be, for example, $\mu_T(x_2, z_2) = \max[\min(0.8, 0.6), \min(0.4, 0.7)] = 0.48$ and the rest,

$$\underset{\sim}{T} = \begin{array}{c|ccc} & z_1 & z_2 & z_3 \\ x_1 & 0.63 & 0.42 & 0.25 \\ x_2 & 0.72 & 0.48 & 0.20 \end{array}$$

14.6 FUZZY TOLERANCE AND EQUIVALENCE RELATIONS

Relations exhibit various other properties apart from that discussed in previous sections. It is already said that the relation can be used in graph theory. The various other properties that are dealt here include reflexivity, symmetry, and transitivity. These are discussed in detail for the crisp and fuzzy relations and are called as equivalence relation. Apart from these, tolerance relations of both fuzzy and crisp relations are also described.

14.6.1 Crisp Relation: Crisp Equivalence Relation

A relation R is called as an equivalence relation if it satisfies the following properties. They are (1) reflexivity, (2) symmetry, and (3) transitivity.

1. **Reflexivity** When a relation satisfies the reflexive property then every vertex in the graph originates a single loop. This is shown below. For matrix relation reflexivity is given by,

   $(x_i, x_i) \in R$ or $\div_R(x_i, x_i) = 1$.

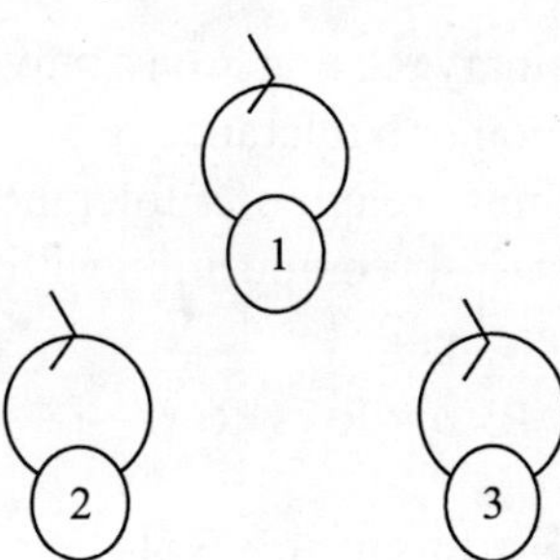

2. **Symmetry** When a relation satisfies symmetric property then in the graph for every edge pointing from vertex i to vertex j there is a edge pointing in the opposite direction, i.e., from vertex j to vertex i. This is shown below. For matrix relation symmetry is given by

   $(x_i, x_j) \in R \rightarrow (x_j, x_i) \in R$ or $\div_R(x_i, x_j) = \div_R(x_j, x_i)$.

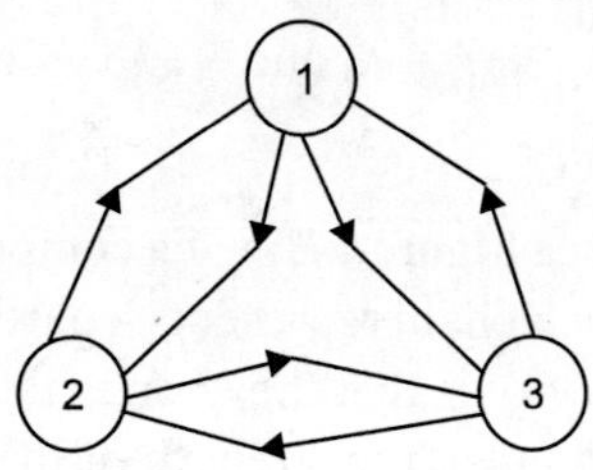

3. **Transitivity** When a relation satisfies transitivity property then every pair of edges in the graph, one pointing from vertex i to vertex j and the other from vertex j to vertex k(i, j, k = 1, 2, 3) there is an edge pointing from vertex i directly to vertex k. This is shown below.
For matrix relation transitivity is given by

$$(x_i, x_j) \in R \text{ and } (x_j, x_k) \in R \rightarrow (x_i, x_k) \in R$$

or

$$\div_R(x_i, x_j) \text{ and } \div_R(x_j, x_k) = 1 \rightarrow \div_R(x_i, x_k) = 1.$$

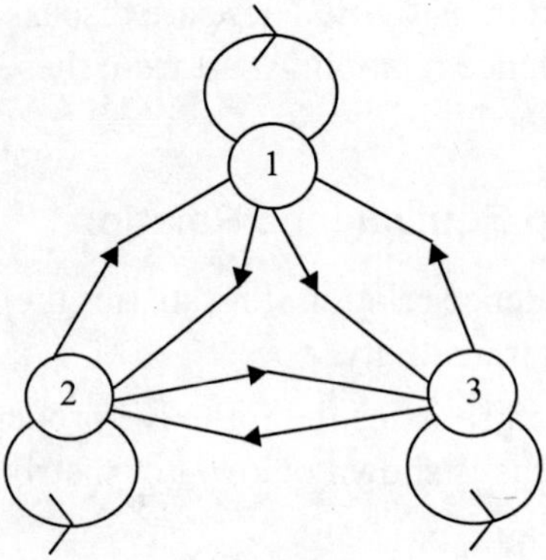

4. **Crisp Tolerance Relation** A binary relation R on a universe X that is reflexive and symmetric is called as compatibility relation or a tolerance relation. When a relation is a reflexive and symmetric it is called as proximity relation. A tolerance relation R can be reformed into an equivalence relation by at most (n–1) composition with itself, where n is the cardinal number of the set defining R, in the case X, i.e.,

$$R^{n-1} = R_1 \circ R_1 \circ \cdots \circ R_1 = R.$$

14.6.2 Fuzzy Relation: Fuzzy Equivalence Relation

A fuzzy relation, $\underset{\sim}{R}$, on a single universe X is also a relation from X to X. It is a fuzzy equivalence relation if all three of the following properties for matrix relations define it:

Reflexivity $\quad \underset{\sim}{R}(x_i, x_i) = 1 \quad$ (4.20a)

Symmetry $\quad \underset{\sim}{R}(x_i, x_j) = \underset{\sim}{R}(x_j, x_i) \quad$ (4.20b)

Transitivity $\quad \underset{\sim}{R}(x_i, x_j) = \lambda_1 \text{ and } \underset{\sim}{R}(x_j, x_k) = \lambda_2 \rightarrow \underset{\sim}{R}(x_i, x_k) = \lambda \quad$ (4.20c)

Where $\lambda \geq \min[\lambda_1, \lambda_2]$.

Looking at the physical analog (see Figure 14.5) of a composition operation, we see it comprises a parallel system of chains, where each chain represents a particular path through the chain system. The physical analogy behind transitivity is that the shorter the chain, the stronger the relation (the stronger is the chain system). In particular, the strength of the link between two elements must be greater than or equal to the strength of any indirect chain involving other elements, i.e., Eq. (14.20c).

It can be shown that any fuzzy tolerance relation, $\underset{\sim}{R}_1$, that has properties of reflexivity and symmetry can be reformed into a fuzzy equivalence relation by at most (n – 1) compositions, just as a crisp tolerance relation can be reformed into a crisp equivalence relation. That is,

$$\underset{\sim}{R}_1^{n-1} = \underset{\sim}{R} \circ \underset{\sim}{R} \circ \ldots \circ \underset{\sim}{R}_1 \quad \underset{\sim}{R} \tag{14.21}$$

Example 14.8: Suppose, in a biotechnology experiment, five potentially new strains of bacteria have been detected in the area around an anaerobic corrosion pit on a new aluminum–lithium alloy used in the fuel tanks of a new experimental aircraft. In order to propose methods to eliminate the biocorrosion caused by these bacteria, the five strains must first be categorized. One way to categorize them is to compare them to one another. In a pairwise comparison, the following "similarity" relation, $\underset{\sim}{R}_1$, is developed. For example, the first strain (column 1) has a strength of similarity to the second strain of 0.8, to the third strain a strength of 0 (i.e., no relation), to the fourth strain a strength of 0.1, and so on. Because the relation is for pairwise similarity it will be reflexive and symmetric. Hence, is reflexive and symmetric. However, it is not transitive, e.g.,

$$\underset{\sim}{R}_1 = \begin{array}{ccccc} 1 & 0.8 & 0.1 & 0.1 & 0.2 \\ 0.8 & 1 & 0.4 & 0 & 0.9 \\ 0 & 0.4 & 1 & 0 & 0 \\ 0.1 & 0 & 0 & 1 & 0.5 \\ 0.2 & 0.9 & 0 & 0.5 & 1 \end{array}$$

is reflexive and symmetric. However, it is not transitive. e.g.,

$$_{\underset{\sim}{R}}(x_1, x_2) = 0.8, \quad _{\underset{\sim}{R}}(x_2, x_5) \quad 0.9 \quad 0.8$$

But

$$_{\underset{\sim}{R}}(x_1, x_5) = 0.2 \quad \min(0.8, 0.9)$$

One composition results in the following relation:

$$\underset{\sim}{R}_1^2 \quad \underset{\sim}{R} \circ \underset{\sim}{R}_1 = \begin{array}{ccccc} 1 & 0.8 & 0.4 & 0.2 & 0.8 \\ 0.8 & 1 & 0.4 & 0.5 & 0.9 \\ 0.4 & 0.4 & 1 & 0 & 0.4 \\ 0.2 & 0.5 & 0 & 1 & 0.5 \\ 0.8 & 0.9 & 0.4 & 0.5 & 1 \end{array}$$

where transitivity still does not result; for example,

$$_{\underset{\sim}{R}^2}(x_1, x_2) \quad 0.8 \quad 0.5, \quad \text{and} \quad _{\underset{\sim}{R}^2}(x_2, x_4) \quad 0.5$$

Finally, after one or two more compositions, transitivity results:

$$\underset{\sim}{R}_1^3 \quad \underset{\sim}{R}_1^4 \quad \underset{\sim}{R} = \begin{array}{ccccc} 1 & 0.8 & 0.4 & 0.5 & 0.8 \\ 0.8 & 1 & 0.4 & 0.5 & 0.9 \\ 0.4 & 0.4 & 1 & 0.4 & 0.4 \\ 0.5 & 0.5 & 0.4 & 1 & 0.5 \\ 0.8 & 0.9 & 0.4 & 0.5 & 1 \end{array}$$

$$\underset{\sim}{R}_1^3(x_1, x_2) = 0.8 \quad 0.5$$

$$\underset{\sim}{R}_1^3(x_2, x_4) = 0.5 \quad 0.5$$

$$\underset{\sim}{R}_1^3(x_1, x_4) = 0.5 \quad 0.5$$

Graphs can be drawn for fuzzy equivalence relations, but the arrows in the graphs between vertices will have various "strengths," i.e., values on the interval [0, 1]. Once the fuzzy relation $\underset{\sim}{R}$ in Example 14.8 is an equivalence relation, it can be used in categorizing the various bacteria according to preestablished levels of confidence. There is an interesting graphical analog for fuzzy equivalence relations. An inspection of a three-dimensional plot of the preceding equivalence relation, $\underset{\sim}{R}_1^3$, is shown in Figure 14.7. In this graph, which is a plot of the membership values of the equivalence relation, we can see that, if it were a watershed, there would be no location where water would pool, or be trapped. In fact, every equivalence relation will produce a surface on which water cannot be trapped; the converse is not true in general, however. That is, there can be relations that are not equivalence relations but whose three-dimensional surface representations will not trap water. An example of the latter is given in the original tolerance relation, $\underset{\sim}{R}_1$, of Example 14.8.

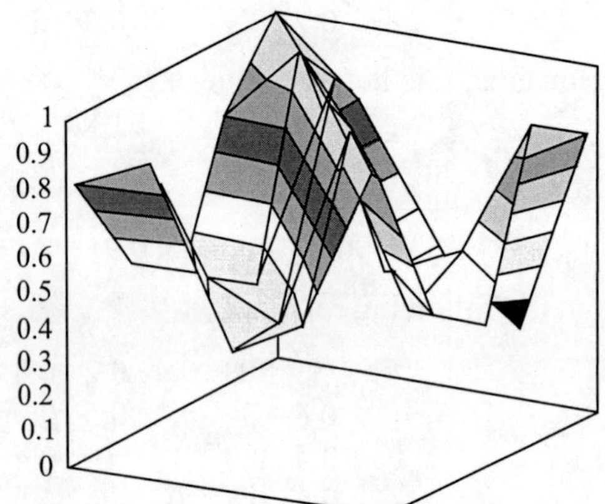

Figure 14.7: Three-dimensional Representation of an Equivalence Relation.

Another way to show this same information is to construct a two-dimensional contour of the relation using various contour levels; these correspond to different degrees of membership. The graphic in Figure 14.8 shows contour plots for the tolerance relation, $\underset{\sim}{R}_1^2$ and the equivalence level, . The contours in Figure 14.8a would trap water (the lightest areas are inside other darker areas), $\underset{\sim}{R}_1^3$ whereas water would not be trapped in the contour diagram of Figure 14.8b.

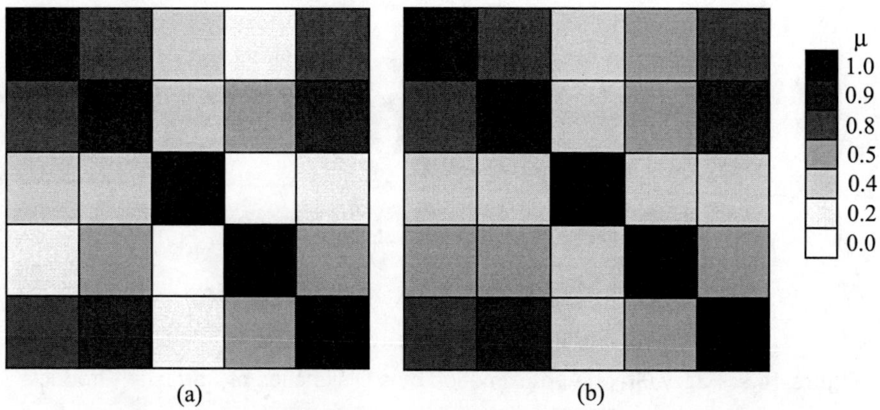

Figure 14.8: Two-dimensional Contours of (a) Tolerance Relation $\underset{\sim}{R}_1^2$ and (b) Equivalence Relation $\underset{\sim}{R}_1^3$.

14.7 FUZZY GRAPHS

A fuzzy relation may not have a meaningful linguistic label such as the petite relation does. In fact, most fuzzy relations used in real-world applications do not represent a concept; rather they represent a functional mapping from a set of input variables to one or more output variables. Often, a set of fuzzy rules used in a fuzzy logic controller describes a fuzzy relation from the observed state variables to a control decision. In other words, a fuzzy relation underlying a fuzzy logic controller can be constructed by a set of if-then fuzzy rules. How is this achieved? To answer this question, we need to introduce fuzzy graphs.

The term "fuzzy graph" has been used for two different concepts in the literature, one introduced by Zadeh, and the other introduced by Rosenfeld. Rosenfeld's fuzzy graph is a generalization of conventional graph theory. In this book, we will discuss only Zadeh's fuzzy graph because it is much more relevant to fuzzy logic control and its industrial applications.

A fuzzy graph describes a functional mapping between a set of input linguistic variables and an output linguistic variable. Assume that a function f: $U \to V$, $X \in U$, $Y \in V$, is approximated by the following fuzzy IF-THEN rules:

f: IF X is small THEN Y is small.
IF X is medium THEN Y is large.
IF X is large THEN Y is small.

which form a fuzzy graph f* (Figure 14.9), where

$$f^* = \text{small} \times \text{small} + \text{medium} \times \text{large} + \text{large} \times \text{small}$$

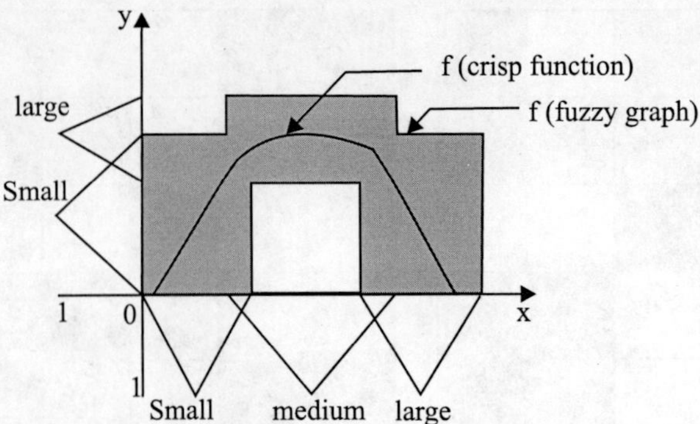

Figure 14.9: Fuzzy Graph Approximation by a Disjunction of Cartesian Products

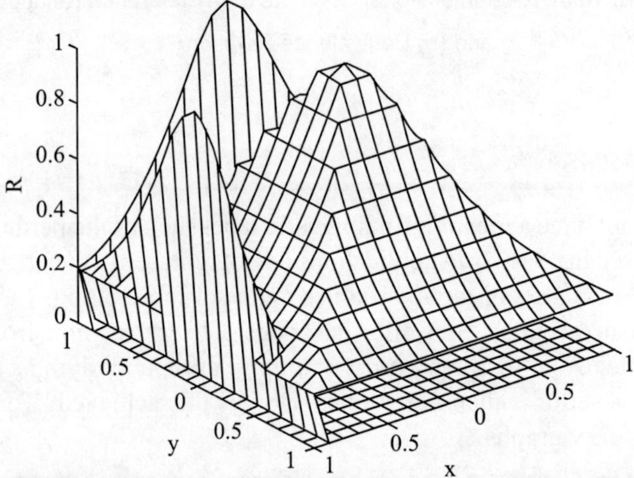

Figure 14.10: A Fuzzy Relation Formed by a Cartesian Product

In f*, + and x denote, respectively, the disjunction and Cartesian product. An expression of the form $A \times B$ where A and B are words (fuzzy sets) is referred as a Cartesian granule.

Suppose that x and y are two variables with universes of discourse X and Y respectively, and A and B are two fuzzy subsets of X and Y. The Cartesian product of A and B denoted by $A \times B$, is defined as

$$\mu_{A \times B}(u, v) = \mu_A(u) \otimes \mu_B(v) \tag{14.22}$$

Figure 14.10 shows a fuzzy relation formed by a Cartesian product using min as the fuzzy conjunction operator. A fuzzy graph f * from X to Y is union of Cartesian products involving linguistic input-output associations (i.e., pairs of "x is A_i" and "y is B_i") i.e.,

$$f^* = \bigcup_i A_i \quad B_i$$

The resulting fuzzy graph is basically a fuzzy relation.

14.8 FUZZY NUMBERS

A fuzzy number is a fuzzy subset of the universe of a numeric number. For instance, a fuzzy real number is a fuzzy subset of the domain of real numbers. A fuzzy integer is a fuzzy subset of the domain of integers. An example of a fuzzy real number, About-10, is shown in Figure 14.11.

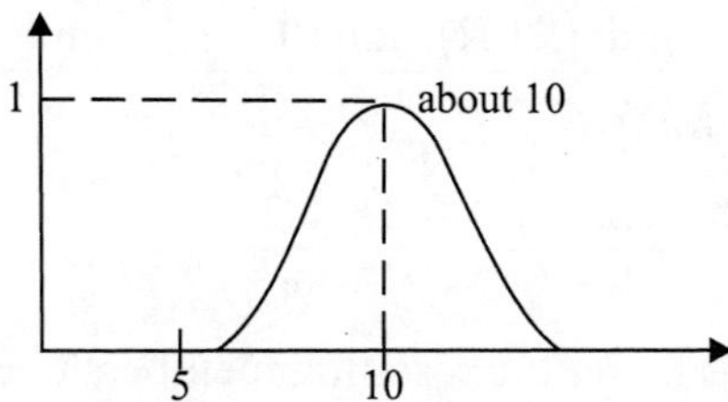

Figure 14.11: A Fuzzy Number

14.9 FUZZY ARITHMETIC

In this chapter we wish to use the extension principle to perform algebraic operations on fuzzy numbers (as illustrated in previous examples in this chapter). We define a normal, convex fuzzy set on the real line to be a fuzzy number, and denote it $\underset{\sim}{I}$.

Let $\underset{\sim}{I}$ and $\underset{\sim}{J}$ be two fuzzy numbers, with $\underset{\sim}{I}$ defined on the real line in universe X and $\underset{\sim}{J}$ defined on the real line in universe Y, and let the symbol "denote a general arithmetic operation, i.e., $* \equiv \{+,-,\times,\div\}$. An arithmetic operation (mapping) between these two number, denoted $\underset{\sim}{I} * \underset{\sim}{J}$, will be defined on universe Z, and can be accomplished using the extension principle, by

$$\underset{\sim}{I} * \underset{\sim}{J}(z) = \bigvee_{x * y \quad z} (\ _{\underset{\sim}{I}}(x) \qquad _{\underset{\sim}{J}}(y)) \qquad (14.23)$$

Equation (14.23) results in another fuzzy set, the fuzzy number resulting from the arithmetic operation on fuzzy numbers $\underset{\sim}{I}$ and $\underset{\sim}{J}$.

Example 14.9: We want to perform a simple addition ($* \equiv +$) of two fuzzy numbers. Define a fuzzy one by the normal, convex membership function defined on the integers,

$$\underset{\sim}{1} = \frac{0.2}{0} \quad \frac{1}{1} \quad \frac{0.2}{2}$$

Now, we want to add "fuzzy one" plus "fuzzy one," using the extension principle, Eq. (14.23), to get

$$\underset{\sim}{1} \quad 1 \quad \underset{\sim}{2} = \frac{0.2}{0} \quad \frac{1}{1} \quad \frac{0.2}{2} \qquad \frac{0.2}{0} \quad \frac{1}{1} \quad \frac{0.2}{2}$$

$$= \frac{\min(0.2, 0.2)}{0} \quad \frac{\max[\min(0.2, 1)\min(1, 0.2)]}{1}$$

$$+ \frac{\max[\min(0.2, 0.2), \min(1, 1), \min(0.2, 0.2]}{2}$$

$$+ \frac{\max[\min(1, 0.2), \min(0.2, 1]}{3} \quad \frac{\min(0.2, 0.2)}{4}$$

$$= \frac{0.2}{2} \quad \frac{0.2}{1} \quad \frac{1}{2} \quad \frac{0.2}{3} \quad \frac{0.2}{4}$$

Note that there are two ways to get the resulting membership value for a 1 (0 + 1 and 1 + 0), three ways to get a 2 (0 + 2, 1 + 1, 2 + 0), and two ways to get a 3 (1 + 2 and 2 + 1). These are accounted for in the implementation of the extension principle.

The support for a fuzzy number, say , is given by

$$\text{supp } \underset{\sim}{I} \{x| \quad _{\underset{\sim}{I}} X > 0\} = I \tag{14.24}$$

which is an interval on the real line, denoted symbolically as I. Since applying Eq. (14.23) to arithmetic operations on fuzzy numbers results in a quantity that is also a fuzzy number, we can find the support of the fuzzy number resulting from the arithmetic operation $\underset{\sim}{I} * \underset{\sim}{J}$ i.e.,.

$$\underset{I*J}{\text{supp}}(z) = I * J \tag{14.25}$$

which is seen to be the arithmetic operation on the two individual supports (crisp intervals), I and J, for fuzzy numbers $\underset{\sim}{I}$ and $\underset{\sim}{J}$, respectively.

The support of a fuzzy set is equal to its ë-cut value at ë = 0^+. In general, we can perform ë-cut operations on fuzzy numbers for any value of ë. General arithmetic operations:

$$(\underset{\sim}{I} * \underset{\sim}{J})_1 = I \quad * J \tag{14.26}$$

Equation 14.26 shows that the ë-cut on a general arithmetic operation (* ≡ {+,–,×, ÷}) on two fuzzy numbers is equivalent to the arithmetic operation on the respective ë-cuts of the two fuzzy numbers. Both $(\underset{\sim}{I} * \underset{\sim}{J})_\lambda$ and I * J are interval quantities; and manipulations of these quantities can make use of classical interval analysis.

Example 14.10: We have two fuzzy sets $\underset{\sim}{A}$ and $\underset{\sim}{B}$, each defined on its own universe as follows:

$$\underset{\sim}{A} = \frac{0.2}{1} \quad \frac{1}{2} \quad \frac{0.7}{4} \quad \text{and } \underset{\sim}{B} \quad \frac{0.5}{1} \quad \frac{1}{2}$$

We wish to determine the membership values for the algebraic product mapping

$$f(\underset{\sim}{A}, \underset{\sim}{B}) = \underset{\sim}{A} \times \underset{\sim}{B} \text{ (arithmetic product)}$$

$$= \frac{\min(0.2, 0.5)}{1} \quad \frac{\max[\min(0.2, 1), \min(0.5, 1)]}{2} + \frac{\max[\min(0.7, 0.5), \min(1,1)]}{4} \quad \frac{\min(0.7, 1)}{8}$$

$$= \frac{0.2}{1} \quad \frac{0.5}{2} \quad \frac{1}{4} \quad \frac{0.7}{8}$$

In this case, the mapping involves two ways to produce a 2 (1×2 and 2×1) and two ways to produce a 4(4×1 and 2×2); hence the maximum operation expressed in Eq.

$$_{\underset{\sim}{B}}(y) = \max_{y \; f(x_1,..x_2...x_n)} \{\min[\ \underset{\sim}{A}_1(x_1),\ \underset{\sim}{A}_2(x_2),...\ \underset{\sim}{A}_n(x_n)]\} \qquad (14.27)$$

is necessary.

The extension principle can also be useful in propagating fuzziness through generalized relations that are discrete mappings of ordered pairs of elements from input universes to ordered pairs of elements in an output universe.

Example 14.11: Suppose we have the integers 1 to 10 as the elements of two identical but different universes; let

$$U_1 = U_2 = \{1, 2, 3, \ldots, 10\}$$

Then define two fuzzy numbers $\underset{\sim}{A}$ and $\underset{\sim}{B}$ on universe U_1 and U_2, respectively:

$$\text{Define } \underset{\sim}{A} \quad \underset{\sim}{2} \quad \text{"approximately 2"} = \frac{0.6}{1} \quad \frac{1}{2} \quad \frac{0.8}{3}$$

$$\text{Define } \underset{\sim}{B} \quad \underset{\sim}{6} \quad \text{"approximately 6"} = \frac{0.8}{5} \quad \frac{1}{6} \quad \frac{0.7}{7}$$

The product of ("approximately 2") × ("approximately 6") should map to a fuzzy number "approximately 12," which is a fuzzy set defined on a universe, say V, of integers, V = {5, 6, . . . , 18, 21}, as determined by the extension principle, Eq. (14.27), or

$$\underset{\sim}{2} \quad \underset{\sim}{6} = \frac{0.6}{1} \quad \frac{1}{2} \quad \frac{0.8}{3} \qquad \frac{0.8}{3} \quad \frac{}{6} \quad \frac{0.7}{7}$$

$$= \frac{\min(0.6, 0.8)}{5} \quad \frac{\min(0.6, 1)}{6} \quad \cdots \quad \frac{\min(0.8, 1)}{18} \quad \frac{\min(0.8, 0.7)}{21}$$

$$= \frac{0.6}{5} \quad \frac{0.6}{6} \quad \frac{0.6}{7} \quad \frac{0.8}{10} \quad \frac{1}{12} \quad \frac{0.7}{14} \quad \frac{0.8}{15} \quad \frac{2.8}{18} \quad \frac{0.7}{21}$$

In this example each of the elements in the universe, V, is determined by a unique mapping of the input variables. For example, $1 \times 5 = 5$, $2 \times 6 = 12$, etc. Hence, the maximum operation expressed in Eq. (14.27) is not necessary. It should also be noted that the result of this arithmetic product is not convex, and hence does not appear to be a fuzzy number (i.e., normal and convex). However, the nonconvexity arises from numerical aberrations from the discretization of the two fuzzy numbers, $\underset{\sim}{2}$ and $\underset{\sim}{6}$, and not from any inherent problems in the extension principle.

14.10 INTERVAL ANALYSIS IN ARITHMETIC

Let I_1 and I_2 be two interval numbers defined by ordered pairs of real numbers with lower and upper bounds:

$$I_1 = [a, b], \text{ where } a \leq b$$
$$I_2 = [c, d], \text{ where } c \leq d$$

When a = b and c = d, these interval numbers degenerate to a scalar real number. We again define a general arithmetic property with the symbol *, where * ≡ {+,–,×, ÷}. Symbolically, the operation

$$I_1 * I_2 = [a, b] * [c, d]$$

represents another interval. This interval calculation depends on the magnitudes and signs of the elements a, b, c, and d. Table 14.2 shows the various combinations of set-theoretic intersection (∩)") and set-theoretic union (∪) for the six possible combinations of these elements (a < b and c < d still hold). Based on the information in Table 14.2, the four arithmetic interval operations associated with above Equation are given as follows:

$$[a, b] + [c, d] = [a + c, + b + d] \quad (4.28)$$
$$[a, b] - [c, d] = [a - d, + b - c] \quad (4.29)$$
$$[a, b] \times [c, d] = [\min(ac, ad, bc, bd), \max(ac, ad, bc, bd)] \quad (4.30)$$
$$[a, b] \div [c, d] = [a,b] \quad \frac{1}{d}, \frac{1}{c} \text{ provided that } 0 \quad [c, d] \quad (4.31)$$
$$\alpha[a, b] = \begin{matrix} [\ a, & b] \text{ for } & 0 \\ [\ b, & a] \text{ for } & 0 \end{matrix} \quad (4.32)$$

where ac, ad, bc, and bd are arithmetic products and 1/d and 1/c are quotients.

The caveat applied to Eq. (14.31) is that the equivalence stated is not valid for the case when c ≤ 0 and d ≥ 0 (obviously the constraint c < d still holds), i.e., zero cannot be contained within the interval [c, d]. Interval arithmetic follows properties of associativity and commutativity for both summations and products, but it does not follow the property of distributivity.

Table 14.2: Set operations on intervals

Cases	Intersection	Union
a > d	ϕ	[c, d] ∪ [a, b]
c > b	ϕ	[a, b] ∪ [c, d]
a > c, b < d	[a, b]	[c, d]
c > a, d < b	[c, d]	[a, b]
a < c < b < d	[c, b]	[a, d]
c < a < d < b	[a, d]	[c, b]

Rather, intervals do follow a special subclass of distributivity known as subdistributivity, i.e., for three intervals, I, J, and K,

$$\mathrm{I} \cdot (\mathrm{J} + \mathrm{K}) \subset \mathrm{I} \cdot \mathrm{J} + \mathrm{I} \cdot \mathrm{K} \tag{14.33}$$

The failure of distributivity to hold for intervals is due to the treatment of two occurrences of identical interval numbers (i.e., I) as two independent interval numbers.

Example 14.12:

$$-3 \cdot [1, 2] = [-6, -3]$$

$$[0, 1] - [0, 1] = [-1, 1]$$

$$[1, 3] \cdot [2, 4] = [\min(2, 4, 6, 12), \max(2, 4, 6, 12)] = [2, 12]$$

$$[1, 2] \div [1, 2] = [1, 2] \cdot [1/2, 1] = [1/2, 2]$$

Consider the following example of subdistributivity.

For I = [1, 2], J = [2, 3],K = [1, 4], then

$$\mathrm{I} \cdot (\mathrm{J} - \mathrm{K}) = [1, 2] \cdot ([2, 3] - [1, 4]) = [1, 2] \cdot [-2, 2] = [-4, 4]$$

$$\mathrm{I} \cdot \mathrm{J} - \mathrm{I} \cdot \mathrm{K} = [1, 2] \cdot [2, 3] - [1, 2] \cdot [1, 4] = [2, 6] - [1, 8] = [-6, 5]$$

Now, $[-4, 4] \neq [-6, 5]$, but $[-4, 4] \quad [-6, 5]$.

Interval arithmetic can be thought of in the following way. When we add or multiply two crisp numbers, the result is a crisp singleton. When we add or multiply two intervals we are essentially performing these operations on the infinite number of combinations of pairs of crisp singletons from each of the two intervals; hence, in this sense, an interval is expected as the result. In the simplest case, when we multiply two intervals containing only positive real numbers, it is easy conceptually to see that the interval comprising the solution is found by taking the product of the two lowest values from each of the intervals to form the solution's lower bound, and by taking the product of the two highest values from each of the intervals to form the solution's upper bound. Even though we can see conceptually that an infinite number of combinations of products between these two intervals exist, we need only the endpoints of the intervals to find the endpoints of the solution.

EXERCISES

1. What do you mean by Cartesian product?
2. What do you mean by crisp relation?
3. Explain the cardinality of crisp relation?
4. Explain the operations performed on crisp relation?
5. Explain the properties of crisp relation?
6. What do you mean by composition operations?
7. What do you mean by fuzzy relations?
8. Explain the composition of fuzzy relation?

9. What do you mean by cardinality of fuzzy relations?
10. What are the basic operations performed on fuzzy relation?
11. What are the properties of fuzzy relation?
12. Explain the concept of fuzzy Cartesian product and composition?
13. Explain the concept of fuzzy tolerance and equivalence relation?
14. What do you mean by fuzzy graph?
15. What do you mean by fuzzy number?
16. What do you mean by fuzzy arithmetic? Explain the various arithmetic operations performed on fuzzy numbers?
17. Explain the interval analysis in fuzzy arithmetic?

CHAPTER 15

Fuzzy If-then Rules

15.1 INTRODUCTION

Rules form the basis for the fuzzy logic to obtain the fuzzy output. The rulebased system is different from the expert system in the manner that the rule comprising the rule-based system originates from sources other than that of human experts and hence is different from expert systems. The rule-based form uses linguistic variables as its antecedents and consequents. The antecedents express an inference or the inequality, which should be satisfied. The consequents are those, which we can infer, and is the output if the antecedent inequality is satisfied. Among all the techniques developed using fuzzy sets fuzzy if-then rules are by far the most visible due to their wide range of successful applications fuzzy if –then rules have been applied to many disciplines. Such as control system, decision making, pattern recognition, and system modeling. Fuzzy if- then rules also play a critical role in industrial applications ranging from consumer products, manufacturing, process control, medical imaging, to financial trading.

A fuzzy if-then rule associates a condition described using linguistic variables and fuzzy sets to a conclusion. From a knowledge representation viewpoint, a fuzzy if-then rule is a scheme for capturing knowledge that involves imprecision. The main feature of reasoning using these rules (i.e., fuzzy rule –based reasoning) is its partial matching capability, which enables an inference to be made from a fuzzy rule even when the rule;s condition is only partially satisfied.

Learning fuzzy if-then rules is both easy and challenging. It is easy to understand the basics of fuzzy if-then and to start building your own application using a commercially available fuzzy logic development tool such as the Matlab Fuzzy Logic Tool Box. It is challenging, however, to master fuzzy if-then rules for two reasons. First, there are two different kinds of fuzzy rules: fuzzy mapping rules and fuzzy implication rules. Understanding the fundamental differences between these two is important for developing their successful application. Second, there are several fuzzy rule-based inference techniques. Understanding the theoretical foundation of these techniques and their relationship to suitable applications can be challenging.

The fuzzy rule-based system uses IF–THEN rule-based system, given by, IF antecedent, THEN consequent. The formation of the fuzzy rules is discussed in this chapter.

15.2 BASICS OF FUZZY RULES

A fuzzy if-then rule is a knowledge representation scheme use for capturing knowledge (typically human knowledge) that is imprecise and inexact by nature. This is achieved by using linguistic variables to describe elastic conditions (i.e. conditions that can be satisfied to a degree) in the "if-part" of fuzzy rules.

The main feature of fuzzy rule-based inference is its capability to perform inference under partial matching. That is, it computes the degree the input data matches the condition of a rule. Figure 15.1 illustrates one way to calculate the matching degree between a fuzzy input A' and a fuzzy condition A that was introduced in Chapter 2.

$$\text{matchingdegree}(A,A') = \sup_{x} \min(\mu_A(x), \mu_{A'}(x)) \tag{15.1}$$

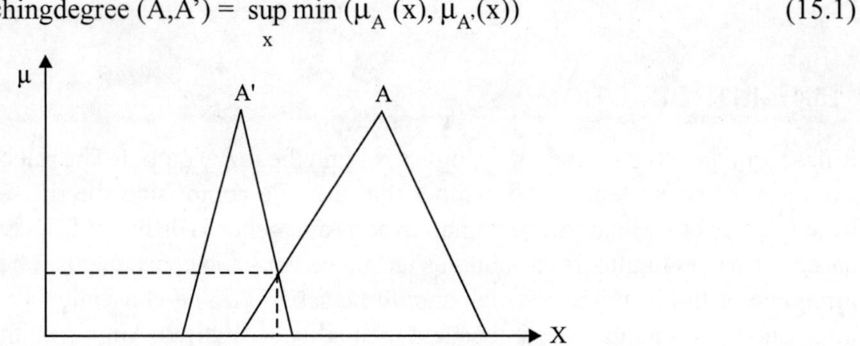

Figure 15.1: Matching Fuzzy Input A' with a Fuzzy Condition A

This matching degree is combined with the consequent (i.e., "then" part) of the rule to form a conclusion inferred by the fuzzy rule. The higher the matching degree, the closer the inferred conclusion to the rule's consequent.

15.3 TWO TYPES OF FUZZY RULES

There are two types of fuzzy rules:

1. **Fuzzy Mapping Rules-** A fuzzy mapping rule describes a functional mapping relationship between inputs and an output using linguistic terms,
2. **Fuzzy Implication Rules-** while a fuzzy implication rule describes a generalized logic implication relationship between two logic formulas involving linguistic variables and imprecise linguistic terms.

15.3.1 Fuzzy Mapping Rules

In many real-world problems, we are interested in finding the functional relationship between a set of observable parameters and one or multiple parameters whose values we do not know. For example, a financial trading broker is interested in the relationship between the history of various financial indices and future stock values. A control engineer is interested in finding an appropriate control law, which can also be viewed as a functional relationship between observable state variables and controllable parameters. Indeed, fuzzy logic controllers use rules of this type to approximate a mapping (typically nonlinear) from the observed state to a desired control action. In fact, most industrial applications of fuzzy logic use fuzzy mapping rules.

The need to approximate a function of interest is often due to one or more of the following reasons.

First, the mathematical structure of the function is not precisely known. Were the structure known, one could use various parameter identification techniques to find the parameters.

Second, the function is so complex that finding its precise mathematical form is either impossible or practically unfeasible due to its high cost.

Third, even if finding the function is not impractical, implementing the function in its precise mathematical form in a product or service may be too costly. This is particularly important for low-cost high volume products. (e.g., automobiles, cameras, and other consumer products.)

15.3.2 Fuzzy Implication Rules

Fuzzy implication rules are a generalization of "implication" in two-valued logic. Their aim is to mimic human reasoning in its ability to reason with ideas or statements that are imprecise by nature. Even though it is obvious that human beings perform certain kinds of approximate reasoning, it is unclear how one can characterize such a reasoning process due to our present limited understanding of the human reasoning process to date. Consequently, there has not been posited a unique set of desired properties for fuzzy implication rules. Rather, several sets of desired properties have been developed, as we shall see later in the next chapter. Even though the set of desired properties is not unique, they are useful for comparing different reasoning schemes using fuzzy implication rules. We want to point out this "nonuniqueness" aspect of fuzzy implication, because it is in sharp contrast with many other techniques in science and engineering that were built on a set of well-defined axioms, properties or principles.

The inference of fuzzy implications generalizes two kinds of logic inference using the implications in classical logic: modus ponens and modus tollens. While we will describe these inferences in detail in the next chapter, we can briefly illustrate here these logic inferences using the following implication:

IF a person's IQ is high THEN the person is smart

Given the implication and the fact that "William's IQ is high", modus ponens enables us to infer that "William is smart," On the other hand, if we are given the implication and the fact that "William is no smart," modus tollens enables us to infer that "William's IQ is not high."

Even though classical logic can perform these two kinds of inferences, they are limited in two ways. First, these inferences insist on perfect matching. If William's IQ is more or less high, for instance, no modus ponens inference can be made from the implication above because "more or less smart" is not identical to "smart". However, our "common-sense reasoning" usually suggests that we can infer that "William is more or less smart." Second these inferences cannot handle uncertainty. For instance, if William told us his IQ is high but cannot provide documents supporting the claim, we may be somewhat uncertain about the claim. Under such a circumstance, however, logic cannot reason about the uncertainty.

These limitations motivated L.A. Zadeh to develop a reasoning scheme that generalizes classical logic so that (1) it can conduct "common-sense" reasoning under partial matching, and (2) it can reason about the certainty degree of a statement. In particular, logic implications are generalized to allow partial matching. In our example, this means that we can infer "William is somewhat smart" from "William's IQ is somewhat high" and the fuzzy implication "If William's IQ is High, then William is smart." as shown below.

Given: William's IQ is High → William is Smart.

William's IQ is somewhat High.

Infer: William is somewhat Smart.

The second limitation of logic (i.e. inability to deal with uncertainty) has motivated another extension to classical logic: multivalues logic. Multivalued logic extends the truth values in logic from binary (i.e., true and false) to multiple (i.e., more than two) so that different degrees of certainty are expressed by different truth values. Since fuzzy logic also generalizes the truth values in classical logic beyond true and false, it is related to multi-multivalued logic in that it also addresses the first limitation of logic (i.e., restricted to a perfect match). The reason that a fuzzy implication can address the first problem is that it uses linguistic variables in its antecedent (i.e., if parts). Consequently, the statement in the antecedent describes an elastic condition that can be partially satisfied. In our example "A person's IQ" is a linguistic variable in the antecedent, and "A person's IQ is high" describes an elastic condition about a person's IQ. This enables a person with a somewhat high IQ to partially match the condition.

The distinctions between fuzzy implication rules and fuzzy mapping rules are subtle, yet important. Prof. Zadeh mentioned in this book's Forward that fuzzy logic has four principle facets:

1. Logical Facet
2. Set-Theoretic Facet
3. Relational Facet
4. Epistemic Facet

Fuzzy implication rules are primarily in the logic facet, whereas fuzzy mapping rules are in the relational facet because functional mapping is a kind of relation. We summarize several major differences between these two types of fuzzy rules in Table 15.1.

Table 15.1: A comparison of two types of fuzzy rules

	Fuzzy Implication Rules	**Fuzzy Mapping Rules**
Purpose	Generalize implications for handling impression	Approximate functional
Desired Inference	generalized modus ponens and modus tollens	Forward only
Application	Diagnostics, high-level decision making	Control, system modeling, and signal processing
Related Disciplines	classical logic, multivalued logic (other extended logic systems)	System ID, piecewise linear interpolation, neural networks
Typical Design Approach	designed individually	Designed as a rule set
Suitable Problem Domains	domains with continuous and discrete variable	Continuous nonlinear domains

The remainder of this chapter will focus on fuzzy mapping rules, because they are central to fuzzy logic control and most industrial applications.

15.4 FORMATION OF RULES

The formation of rules is in general the canonical rule formation. For any linguistic variable, there are three general forms in which the canonical rules can be formed. They are:

1. Assignment statements
2. Conditional statements
3. Unconditional statements

15.4.1 Assignment Statements

These statements are those in which the variable is assignment with the value. The variable and the value assigned are combined by the assignment operator "=." The assignment statements are necessary in forming fuzzy rules. The value to be assigned may be a linguistic term.

The examples of this type of statements are:

y = low,

Sky color = blue,

Climate = hot

a = 5

p = q + r

Temperature = high

The assignment statement is found to restrict the value of a variable to a specific equality.

15.4.2 Conditional Statements

In this statements, some specific conditions are mentioned, if the conditions are satisfied then it enters the following statements, called as restrictions.

If x = y Then both are equal,

If Mark > 50 Then pass,

If Speed > 1, 500 Then stop.

These statements can be said as fuzzy conditional statements, such as If condition C' Then restriction F'

15.4.3 Unconditional Statements

There is no specific condition that has to be satisfied in this form of statements. Some of the unconditional statements are:

Go to F/o

Push the value

Stop

The control may be transferred without any appropriate conditions. The unconditional restrictions in the fuzzy form can be:

R^1 : Output is B^1

AND

R^2 : Output is B^2

AND

. . . , etc.

where B^1 and B^2 are Fuzzy consequents.

Both conditional and unconditional statements place restrictions on the consequent of the rule-based process because of certain conditions. The fuzzy sets and relations model the restrictions.

Table 15.2: Canonical form – fuzzy rule-based system

Rule 1:	If condition C^1 THEN restriction R^1
Rule 2:	If condition C^2 THEN restriction R^2
Rule 3:	If condition C^n THEN restriction R^n

The linguistic connections like "and," "or," "else" connects the conditional, unconditional, and restriction statements. The consequent of rules or output is denoted by the restrictions R^1, R^2, ... , R^n. The rule-based system with a set of conditional rules (canonical form of rules) is shown in Table 15.2.

15.5 DECOMPOSITION OF RULES

There might be a compound rule structure involved in many applications. An example for a compound rule structure is

IF $x = y$ THEN both are equal

ELSE

IF $x \neq y$

THEN

IF $x > y$ THEN X is highest

ELSE

IF $y > x$ THEN Y is highest

ELSE

IF x and y are equal to zero THEN no output is obtained.

By he properties and operations defined on fuzzy sets in Chap. 3, any compound rule structure can be decomposed and reduced to number of simple canonical rules. There are various methods for decomposition of rules. They are:

15.5.1 Multiple Conjunction Antecedents

This uses fuzzy intersection operation. Since it involves linguistic "AND" connective

IF x is $\underset{\sim}{P}^1$ AND $\underset{\sim}{P}^2$ ... AND $\underset{\sim}{P}^n$ THEN y is Q^T,

Where

$$\underset{\sim}{P}^T = \underset{\sim}{P}^1 \text{ AND } \underset{\sim}{P}^2 \ldots \text{ OR } \underset{\sim}{P}^n$$

The membership for this can be

$$\underset{\sim}{P}^r(x) = \min \quad \underset{\sim}{P}^1(x), \ \underset{\sim}{P}^2(x), \ldots., \ \underset{\sim}{P}^n(x) \ .$$

Hence the rule can be

IF x is $\underset{\sim}{P}^r$ THEN $\underset{\sim}{Q}^r$

15.5.2 Multiple Disjunctive Antecedents

This uses fuzzy union operations. It involves linguistic "OR" connections

IF x is $\underset{\sim}{P}^1$ OR $\underset{\sim}{P}^2$ OR $\underset{\sim}{P}^n$ THEN y is Q^T,

Where

$$\underset{\sim}{P}^r = \underset{\sim}{P}^1 \text{ OR } \underset{\sim}{P}^2 \ldots. \text{ OR } \underset{\sim}{P}^n$$

$$= \underset{\sim}{P}^1 \cup \underset{\sim}{P}^2 \ldots. \cup \underset{\sim}{P}^n .$$

The membership for this can be

$$\underset{\sim}{P}^r(x) = \max \quad \underset{\sim}{P}^1(x), \ \underset{\sim}{P}^2(x), \ldots., \ \underset{\sim}{P}^n(x) \ .$$

Hence the rule can be

IF x is $\underset{\sim}{P}^r$ THEN y is $\underset{\sim}{Q}^r$

15.5.3 Conditional Statements with Else

(a) If $\underset{\sim}{P}^1$ THEN ($\underset{\sim}{Q}^1$ ELSE $\underset{\sim}{Q}^2$).

Considering this as one compound statement, splitting this into two canonical form rules, we get

IF $\underset{\sim}{P}^1$ THEN Q^1 OR IF NOT $\underset{\sim}{P}^1$ THEN Q^2.

(b) IF $\underset{\sim}{P}^1$ THEN (Q^1 ELSE $\underset{\sim}{P}^2$ THEN ($\underset{\sim}{Q}^2$)).

The decomposition for this can be of the form

IF $\underset{\sim}{P}^1$ THEN Q^1 OR

IF NOT $\underset{\sim}{P}^1$ THEN $\underset{\sim}{P}^2$ THEN Q^2.

15.5.4 Nested If–Then Rules

IF $\underset{\sim}{P}^1$ THEN (IF $\underset{\sim}{P}^2$ THEN ($\underset{\sim}{Q}^2$)).

This can be decomposed into

IF $\underset{\sim}{P}^1$ AND $\underset{\sim}{P}^2$ THEN Q^1.

Thus the compound rules are decomposed into single canonical rules. Then this rule may be reduced to a series of relations.

15.6 AGGREGATION OF FUZZY RULES

The fuzzy rule-based system may involve more than one rule. The process of obtaining the overall conclusion from the individually mentioned consequents contributed by each rule in the fuzzy rule this is known as aggregation of rule.

There are two methods for determining the aggregation of rules:

15.6.1 Conjunctive System of Rules

The rules that are connected by "AND" connectives satisfy the connective system of rules. In this case, the aggregated output may be found by the fuzzy intersection of all individual rule consequents,

$$Y = y^1 \text{ AND } y^2 \text{ and } \ldots \text{ AND } y^r$$

(or)

$$y = y^1 \wedge y^2 \wedge \ldots. \wedge y^r$$

Then the membership friction is defined as

$$\mu_y(y) = \min \;\; _{y^1}(y), \;\; _{y^2}(y), \ldots., \;\; _{y^n}(y),) \text{ for } y \;\; y.$$

15.6.2 Disjunctive System of Rules

The rules that are connected by "OR" connectives satisfies the disjunctive system of rules. In this case, the aggregated output may be found by the fuzzy union of all individual rule consequents

$$y = y^1 \text{ OR } y^2 \text{ OR } \ldots \text{ OR } y^r$$

(or)

$$y = y^1 \cup y^2 \cup \ldots \cup y^r$$

Then the membership function is defined as

$$\mu_{y(y)} = \min \;\; _{y^1}(y), \;\; _{y^2}(y), \ldots., \;\; _{y^n}(y),) \text{ for } y \;\; y.$$

15.7 PROPERTIES OF SET OF RULES

The properties for the sets of rules are:

(a) Completeness

(b) Consistency

(c) Continuity

(d) Interaction

(a) Completeness A set of IF–THEN rules is complete if any combination of input values result in an appropriate output value.

(b) Consistency A set of IF–THEN rules is inconsistent if there are two rules with the same rules-antecedent but different rule-consequents.

(c) Continuity A set of IF–THEN rules is continuous if it does not have neighboring rules with output fuzzy sets that have empty intersection.

(d) Interaction In the interaction property, suppose that is a rule, "IF x is A THEN y is B," this meaning is represented by a fuzzy relation R2, then the composition of A and R does not deliver B

$$\underset{\sim}{A} \circ \underset{\sim}{R} = \underset{\sim}{B}$$

These are the properties of the fuzzy set of rules

15.8 FUZZY RULE-BASED MODELS FOR FUNCTION APPROXIMATION

There are four major concepts in fuzzy rule-based models thus are:

1. Fuzzy Partition
2. Mapping of Fuzzy Subregions To Local Models
3. Fusion of Multiple Local Models
4. Defuzzification.

These four concepts together enable the construction of a complex global using a set of simpler local models.

15.8.1 Fuzzy Partition

A classical partition of a space is a collection of disjoint subspaces whose union is the entire space. For example, Figure 15.2 shows an example of classical partition for an input space involving two variables: X_1 and X_2. The partition is constructed by first partitioning the range of X_1 into four intervals (i.e., I_1, $I_{2,}$ I_3 and I_4) and the range of X_2 into three intervals (I.e., J_1, J_2 and J_3). Each pair of intervals I_k and J_{l-} specifies a subspace A_{kl} that can be described as

$$zX_1 \in I_k \text{ and } X_2 \in J_1$$

A total of 12 subspaces partition the entire input space in this example.

Figure 15.3 shows a fuzzy partition for a system that controls the contrast of a TV based on two inputs:

1. The distance between the viewer and the TV
2. The brightness of the room.

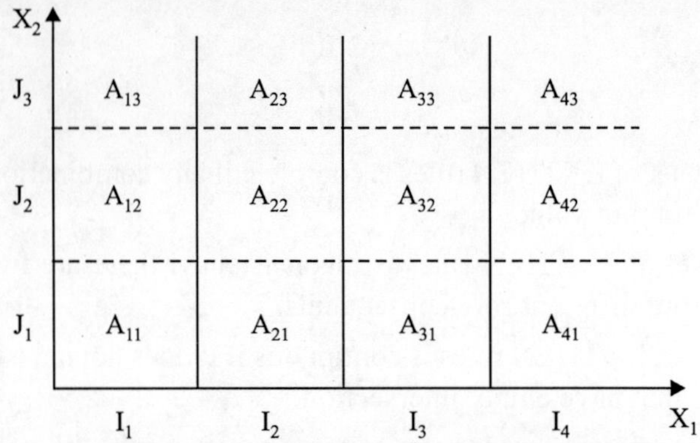

Figure 15.2: An EXample of Classical Partition

In this example, the distance between the viewer and the TV, denoted d, is classified into three fuzzy sets: Near, Medium, and Far. Similarly, the brightness of the room, denoted by b, is classified into two fuzzy sets: Bright and Dark. A fuzzy partition of the entire input space is thus formed by six fuzzy subregions specified by pairs of fuzzy sets (i.e., one for each variable). Fig 15.3 shows two of the six fuzzy subregions:

d is Medium AND b is Dark.

d is Far AND b is Dark.

As shown in the figure, the to fuzzy subregions partially overlap with each other because fuzzy sets Medium and Far partially overlap. Obviously, the same observation can be made for other neighboring fuzzy regions.

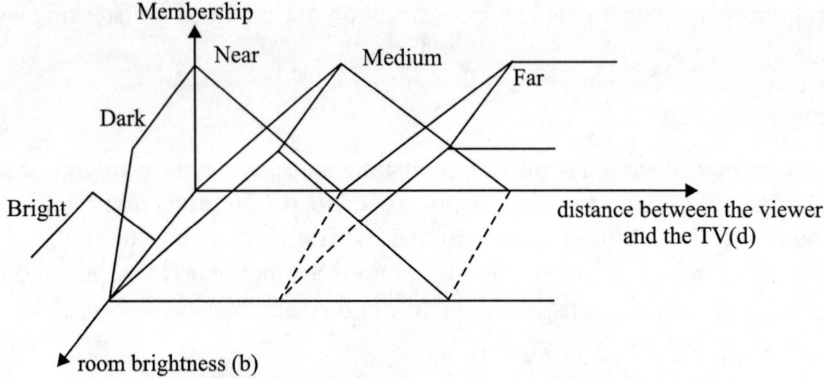

Figure 15.3: An Example of Fuzzy Partition

In a general sense, a fuzzy partition of a space is a collection of fuzzy subspaces whose boundaries partially overlap and whose union is the entire space. Even though there are different operators to choose from for the union operation in fuzzy sets.

15.8.2 Mapping a Fuzzy Subspace To a Local Model

A local model for a subspace of the entire input space describes the system's input-output mapping relationship in the small subspace. In contrast a global model for an input space describes the system's input-output relationship for the entire input space. Because the scope of the local model is smaller than they of a global model, it is usually easier to develop a local model. In particular, a nonlinear global model (i.e., whose input-output mapping function is not linear) can often be approximated by a set of linear local models. This can be understood by remembering the well-known approximation technique called "piecewise linear approximation," which approximates an arbitrary nonlinear function using segments of lines. An example of such an approximation technique is shown in Figure 15.4, where the dotted line indicates the function being approximated.

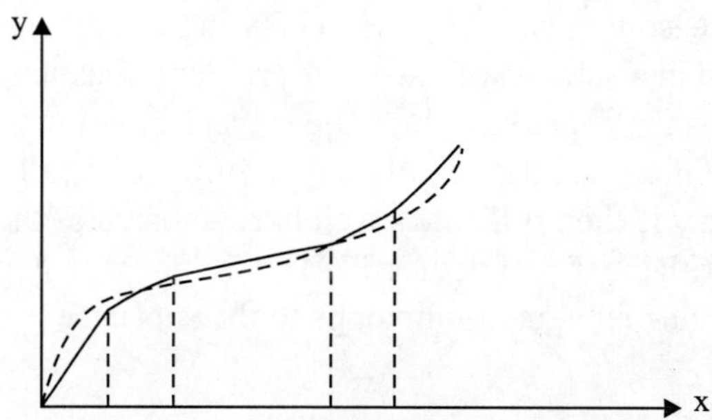

Figure 15.4: Piecewise Linear Approximation

Piecewise linear approximation has two major components:

1. Partitioning the input space to crisp regions.
2. Mapping each partitioned region to a linear local model.

The main difference between fuzzy modeling and piecewise linear approximation is that the transition from one local subregion to a neighboring one is gradual rather than abrupt.

The local model associated with each fuzzy subspace can be of four different types:

1. Crisp constant
2. Fuzzy constant
3. Linear model
4. Nonlinear model

The one that is most frequently used among fuzzy logic applications is the second type: fuzzy constant. We discuss each type of local model below.

1. **Crisp Constant:** This type of local model is simply a crisp (nonvisual) constant (e.g., 4.5), e.g.,

$$\text{IF } x_2 \text{ is Small THEN } y = 4.5$$

2. **Fuzzy Constant:** A local model that is a fuzzy constant (e.g., SMALL) belong to this type. An example is given below:

IF x is Small THEN y is Medium.

3. **Linear Model:** This kind of local model describes the output as a linear function of the input variables, such as in the rule below:

   IF x is small AND x_2 is Large THEN $y = 2x_1 + 5x_2 + 3$.

4. **Nonlinear Model:** Theoretically speaking, a local model can be more complex than a linear model. In practice, however, there is rarely such a need. A fuzzy model that fuses local models of the first three types is often sufficient to approximate an unknown complex plant or system. Nonlinear local models have been introduced in a hybrid neuro-fuzzy system that uses neural networks to represent nonlinear local models associated with the rule.

15.8.3 Fusion of Local Models Through Interpolative Reasoning

Fuzzy models use interpolative reasoning to fuse multiple local models into a global model. The basic behind interpolative reasoning is analogous to drawing a conclusion from a panel of experts, each of whom is specialized in a subarea of the entire problem. Each expert's opinion is associated with a weight, which reflects the degree to which the current situation is in the expert's specialized subarea. These weighted opinions are then combined to form an overall opinion. In this analogy, an expert corresponds to a fuzzy if-then rule, the specialized subarea of the expert corresponds to the fuzzy subspace associated with the if-part of the rule. The weight of an expert's opinion is determined by the degree to which the current situation belongs to the subspace.

15.8.4 Defuzzification

We may interpret a possibility distribution either through linguistic approximation, or through defuzzification.

There are two major defuzzification techniques:

1. The Mean of Maximum (MOM) method
2. The Center of Area (COA) or the centroid method

1. **The Mean of Maximum (MOM) method-** The mean of maximum defuzzification calculates the average of all variable values with maximum membership degrees. Figure 15.5 shows the result of applying MOM defuzzification to a combined fuzzy conclusion.

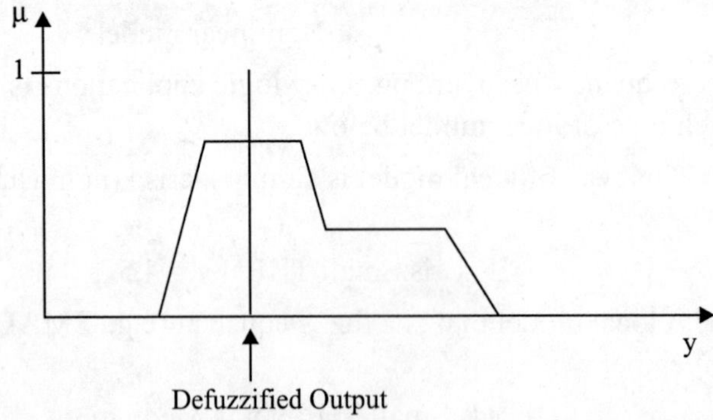

Figure 15.5: An Example of Mean of Maximum Defuzzification

Suppose "y is A" is a fuzzy conclusion to be deffuzzified. We can express the MOM defuzzification method using the following formula:

$$y^*$$

$$\text{MOM}(A) = \frac{y^* \ p}{|P|} \tag{15.2}$$

where P(A) is the set of output values y with the highest membership degree in A, i.e.,

$$P = \{y^* \mid \mu_A(y^*) \ \sup_y \mu_A(y)\} \tag{15.3}$$

where sup is an operator that returns the maximum value of a continuous function (i.e., the continuous version of the max operator).

(2) The Center of Area (COA) or the centroid method- The centroid (or COA) defuzzification method calculates the weighted average of a fuzzy set. The result of applying COA defuzzification to a fuzzy conclusion "Y is A" can be expressed by the formula

$$y = \frac{\underset{i}{} \ {}_A(y_i) \ \ y_i}{\underset{i}{} \ {}_A(y_i)} \tag{15.4}$$

if y discrete, and by the formula]

$$y = \frac{{}_A(y_i) \ \ y_i dy}{{}_A(y_i) dy} \tag{15.5}$$

if y is continuous.

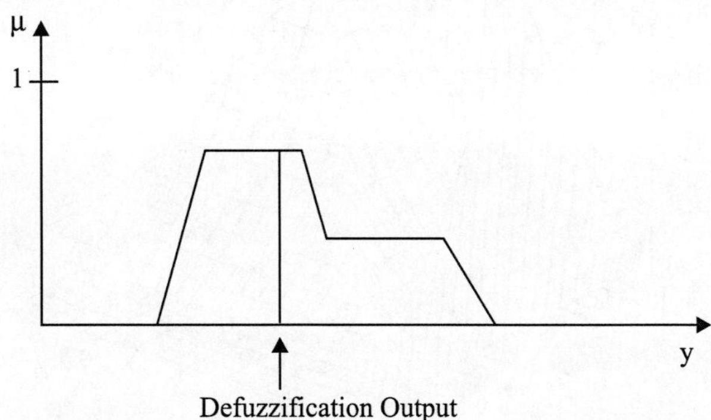

Figure 15.6: An Example of Center of Area Defuzzification

An example of COA defuzzification is shown in Figure 15.6. The main disadvantage of COA method is its high computational cost.

15.9 THE HEIGHT METHOD

The third defuzzification technique is the height method, which can be viewed as a two-step procedure. First, we convert the consequent membership function C_i into crisp consequent $y = c_i$ where C_i is the center of gravity of C_i. The centroid defuzzification is then applied to the rules with crisp consequents, which gives us the following formula:

$$y = \frac{\sum_{i=1}^{M} W_i C_i}{\sum_{i=1}^{M} W_i} \tag{15.6}$$

where w_i is the degree to which the ith rule matches the input data. The main benefit of the height method is its simplicity. The calculation of C_i can be performed during compilation.

15.10 A THEORETICAL FOUNDATION OF FUZZY MAPPING RULES

15.10.1 A Mathematical Representation of Fuzzy Mapping Rules

A fuzzy mapping rule imposes an elastic constraint on possible associations between input and output variables. The constraint is elastic because a fuzzy rule can describe input-output associations that are somewhat possible (i.e., the gray area between totally possible and totally impossible). The degree of possibility of an input-output association imposed by a rule R can be expressed as a possibility distribution, denoted by Π_R.

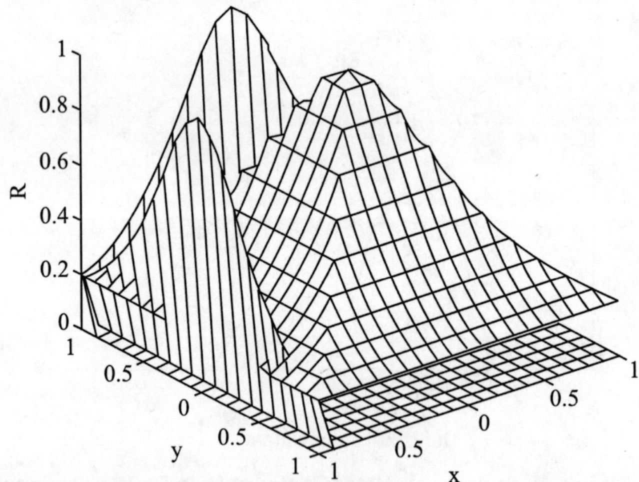

Figure 15.7: A Fuzzy Relation Formed by a Fuzzy Mapping Rule

Since a fuzzy relation is a general way for describing a possibility distribution, it is natural to use it to represent the possibility distribution imposed by a fuzzy rule.

A fuzzy mapping rule is represented mathematically as fuzzy relations formed by the Cartesian product of the variables referred to in the rule's if-part and-then part. For example, the mapping rule

IF x is A, THEN y is B

is mathematically represented as a fuzzy relation R defined as $\mu_R(x, y) = \mu_{A\times B}(x, y)$. If is mathematically represented for the Cartesian product, the fuzzy relation R becomes $\mu_R(x, y) = \min\{\mu_A(x), \mu_B(y)\}$. The two-dimensional membership function of a fuzzy relation constructed this way is depicted in Figure 15.7.

15.11 FUZZY INFERENCE SYSTEM

Fuzzy inference systems (FISs) are also known as fuzzy rule-based systems, fuzzy model, fuzzy expert system, and fuzzy associative memory. This is a major unit of a fuzzy logic system. The decision-making is an important part in the entire system. The FIS formulates suitable rules and based upon the rules the decision is made. This is mainly based on the concepts of the fuzzy set theory, fuzzy IF–THEN rules, and fuzzy reasoning. FIS uses "IF. . . THEN. . . " statements, and the connectors present in the rule statement are "OR" or "AND" to make the necessary decision rules. The basic FIS can take either fuzzy inputs or crisp inputs, but the outputs it produces are almost always fuzzy sets. When the FIS is used as a controller, it is necessary to have a crisp output. Therefore in this case defuzzification method is adopted to best extract a crisp value that best represents a fuzzy set. The whole FIS is discussed in detail in the following subsections.

15.11.1 Construction and Working of Inference System

Fuzzy inference system consists of a fuzzification interface, a rule base, a database, a decision-making unit, and finally a defuzzification interface. A FIS with five functional block described in Figure 15.8. The function of each block is as follows:

- a rule base containing a number of fuzzy IF–THEN rules;
- a database which defines the membership functions of the fuzzy sets used in the fuzzy rules;
- a decision-making unit which performs the inference operations on the rules;

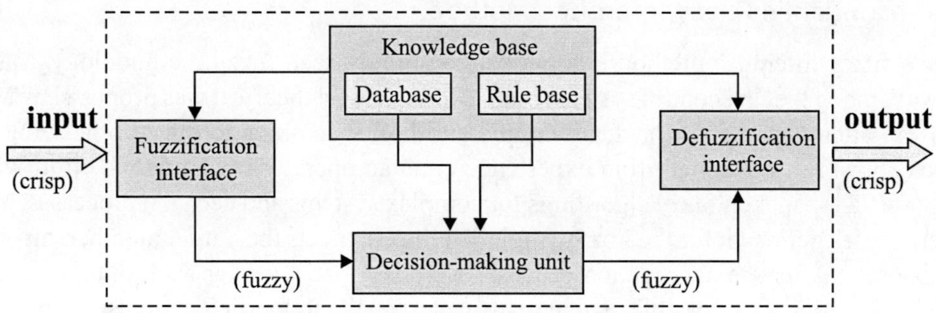

Figure 15.8: Fuzzy Inference System

- a fuzzification interface which transforms the crisp inputs into degrees of match with linguistic values; and
- a defuzzification interface which transforms the fuzzy results of the inference into a crisp output.

The working of FIS is as follows. The crisp input is converted in to fuzzy by using fuzzification method. After fuzzification the rule base is formed. The rule base and the database are jointly referred to as the knowledge base. Defuzzification is used to convert fuzzy value to the real world value which is the output. The steps of fuzzy reasoning (inference operations upon fuzzy IF–THEN rules) performed by FISs are:

1. Compare the input variables with the membership functions on the antecedent part to obtain the membership values of each linguistic label. (this step is often called fuzzification.)
2. Combine (through a specific t-norm operator, usually multiplication or min) the membership values on the premise part to get firing strength (weight) of each rule.
3. Generate the qualified consequents (either fuzzy or crisp) or each rule depending on the firing strength.
4. Aggregate the qualified consequents to produce a crisp output. (This step is called defuzzification.)

15.11.2 Fuzzy Inference Methods

The most important two types of fuzzy inference method are Mamdani's fuzzy inference method, which is the most commonly seen inference method. This method was introduced by Mamdani and Assilian (1975). Another well-known inference method is the so-called Sugeno or Takagi–Sugeno–Kang method of fuzzy inference process. This method was introduced by Sugeno (1985).

This method is also called as TS method. The main difference between the two methods lies in the consequent of fuzzy rules. Mamdani fuzzy systems use fuzzy sets as rule consequent whereas TS fuzzy systems employ linear functions of input variables as rule consequent. All the existing results on fuzzy systems as universal approximators deal with Mamdani fuzzy systems only and no result is available for TS fuzzy systems with linear rule consequent.

15.11.3 Mamdani's Fuzzy Inference Method

Mamdani's fuzzy inference method is the most commonly seen fuzzy methodology. Mamdani's method was among the first control systems built using fuzzy set theory. It was proposed by Mamdani (1975) as an attempt to control a steam engine and boiler combination by synthesizing a set of linguistic control rules obtained from experienced human operators. Mamdani's effort was based on Zadeh's (1973) paper on fuzzy algorithms for complex systems and decision processes. Mamdani type inference, as defined it for the Fuzzy Logic Toolbox, expects the output membership functions to be fuzzy sets. After the aggregation process, there is a fuzzy set for each output variable that needs defuzzification. It is possible, and in many cases much more efficient, to use a single spike as the output membership functions rather than a distributed fuzzy set. This is sometimes known as a singleton output membership function, and it can be thought of as a pre-defuzzified fuzzy set. It enhances the efficiency of the defuzzification process because it greatly simplifies the computation required by the more general Mamdani method, which finds the centroid of a two-dimensional function. Rather than integrating across the two-dimensional function to find the centroid, the weighted average of a few data points. Sugeno type systems support this type of model. In general, Sugeno type systems can be used to model any inference system in which the output membership functions are either linear or constant. An example of a Mamdani inference system is shown in Figure 15.9. To compute the output of this FIS given the inputs, six steps has to be followed:

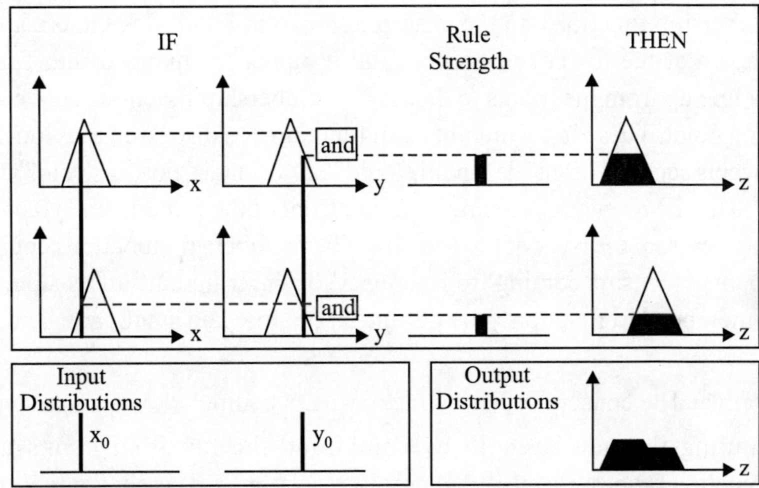

Figure 15.9: A Two Input, Two Rule Mamdani Fis with Crisp Inputs

1. Determining a set of fuzzy rules
2. Fuzzifying the inputs using the input membership functions
3. Combining the fuzzified inputs according to the fuzzy rules to establish a rule strength
4. Finding the consequence of the rule by combining the rule strength and the output membership function
5. Combining the consequences to get an output distribution
6. Defuzzifying the output distribution (this step is only if a crisp output (class) is needed).

The following is a more detailed description of this process

1. **Creating Fuzzy Rules:** Fuzzy rules are a collection of linguistic statements that describe how the FIS should make a decision regarding classifying an input or controling an output. Fuzzy rules are always written in the following form:

   if (input 1 is membership function 1) **and/or** (input 2 is membership function 2) **and/or**. . . **then** (outputn is output membership functionn).

   For example:

   if temperature is high **and** humidity is high **then** room is hot.

There would have to be membership functions that define high temperature (input 1), high humidity (input 2), and a hot room (output 1). This process of taking an input such as temperature and processing it through a membership function to determine "high" temperature is called fuzzification and is discussed in section, "Fuzzification." Also, "AND"/"OR" in the fuzzy rule should be defined. This is called fuzzy combination and is discussed in following section.

2. **Fuzzification:** The purpose of fuzzification is to map the inputs from a set of sensors (or features of those sensors such as amplitude or spectrum) to values from 0 to 1 using a set of input membership functions. In the example shown in Figure 15.9, there are two inputs, x0 and y0 shown at the lower left corner. These inputs are mapped into fuzzy numbers by drawing a line up from the inputs to the input membership functions above and marking the intersection point. These input membership functions, as discussed previously, can represent fuzzy concepts such as "large" or "small," "old" or "young," "hot" or "cold," etc. For example, x0 could be the EMG energy coming from the front of the forearm and y0 could be the EMG energy coming from the back of the forearm. The membership functions could then represent large amounts of tension coming from a muscle or small amounts of tension. When choosing the input membership functions, the definition of large and small may be different for each input.
3. **Consequence:** The consequence of a fuzzy rule is computed using two steps:
   (i) Computing the rule strength by combining the fuzzified inputs using the fuzzy combination process discussed in previous section. This is shown in Figure 15.9. In this example, the fuzzy "AND" is used to combine the membership functions to compute the rule strength.
   (ii) Clipping the output membership function at the rule strength.
4. **Combining Outputs Into an Output Distribution:** The outputs of all of the fuzzy rules must now be combined to obtain one fuzzy output distribution. This is usually, but not always, done by using the fuzzy "OR." Figure 15.9 shows an example of this. The output membership functions on the right-hand side of the figure are combined using the fuzzy OR to obtain the output distribution shown on the lower right corner of the Figure 15.9.
5. **Defuzzification of Output Distribution:** In many instances, it is desired to come up with a single crisp output from an FIS. For example, if one was trying to classify a letter drawn by hand on a drawing tablet, ultimately the FIS would have to come up with a crisp number to tell the computer which letter was drawn. This crisp number is obtained in a process known as defuzzification. There are two common techniques for defuzzifying:
   (i) Center of Mass: This technique takes the output distribution and finds its center of mass to come up with one crisp number. This is computed as follows:

$$z = \frac{\sum_{j=1}^{q} Z_j u_c(Z_j)}{\sum_{j=1}^{q} u_c(Z_j)}$$

where z is the center of mass and u_c is the membership in class c at value z_j. An example outcome of this computation is shown in Figure 15.10.

(ii) Mean of Maximum: This technique takes the output distribution and finds its mean of maxima to come up with one crisp number. This is computed as follows:

$$z = \sum_{j=1}^{l} \frac{Z_j}{l}$$

where z is the mean of maximum, z_j is the point at which the membership function is maximum, and L is the number of times the output distribution reaches the maximum level. An example outcome of this computation is shown in Figure 15.11.

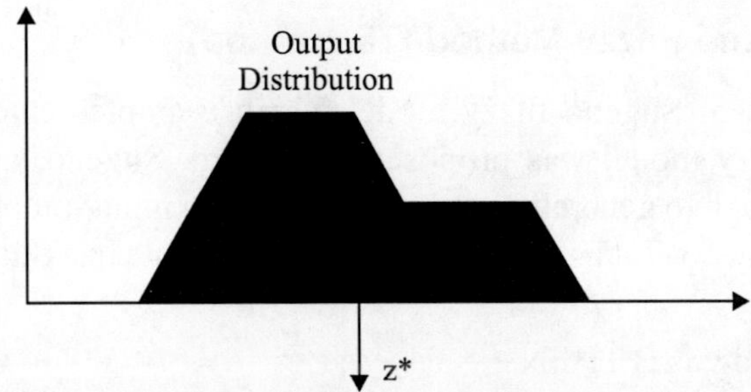

Figure 15.10: Defuzzification Using the Center of Mass

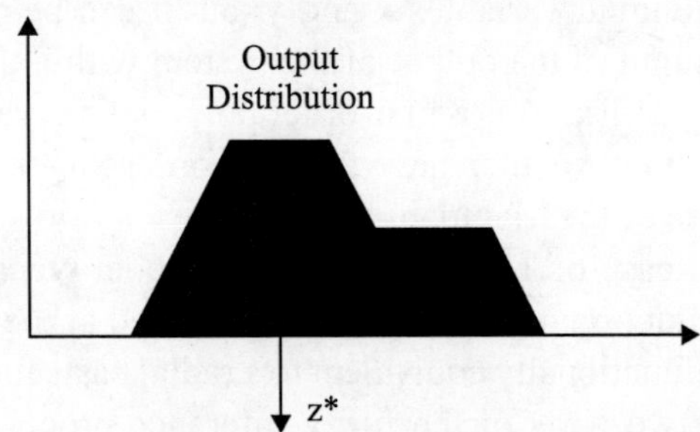

Figure 15.11: Defuzzification Using the Mean of Maximum

6. **Fuzzy Inputs:** In summary, Figure 15.12 shows a two input Mamdani FIS with two rules. It fuzzifies the two inputs by finding the intersection of the crisp input value with the input membership function. It uses the minimum operator to compute the fuzzy AND for combining the two fuzzified inputs to obtain a rule strength. It clips the output membership function at the rule strength. Finally, it uses the maximum operator to compute the fuzzy OR for combining the outputs of the two rules.

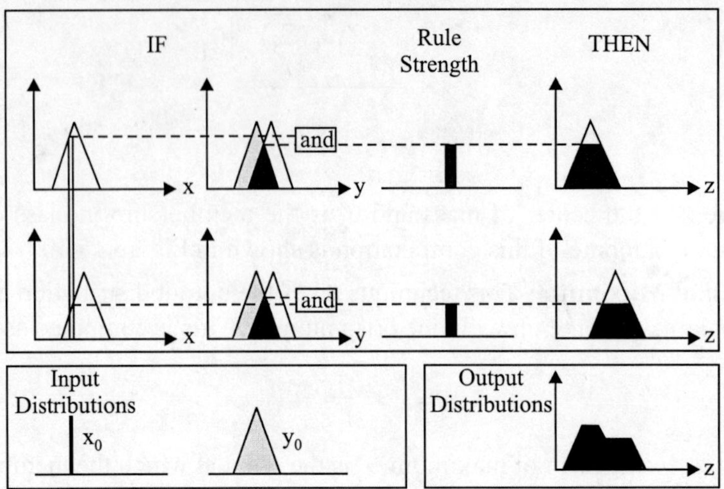

Figure 15.12: A Two Input, Two Rule Mamdani Fis with a Fuzzy Input

15.11.4 Takagi–Sugeno Fuzzy Method (TS Method)

In this section, the basic of Sugeno fuzzy model which is implemented into the neural-fuzzy system. The Sugeno fuzzy model was proposed by Takagi, Sugeno, and Kang in an effort to formalize a system approach to generating fuzzy rules from an input–output data set. Sugeno fuzzy model is also know as Sugeno–Takagi model. A typical fuzzy rule in a Sugeno fuzzy model has the format

IF x is A and y is B THEN z = f(x, y),

where AB are fuzzy sets in the antecedent; Z = f(x, y) is a crisp function in the consequent. Usually f(x, y) is a polynomial in the input variables x and y, but it can be any other functions that can appropriately describe the output of the output of the system within the fuzzy region specified by the antecedent of the rule. When f(x, y) is a first-order polynomial, we have the first-order Sugeno fuzzy model. When f is a constant, we then have the zero-order Sugeno fuzzy model, which can be viewed either as a special case of the Mamdani FIS where each rule's consequent is specified by a fuzzy singleton, or a special case of Tsukamoto's fuzzy model where each rule's consequent is specified by a membership function of a step function centered at the constant. Moreover, a zero-order Sugeno fuzzy model is functionally equivalent to a radial basis function network under certain minor constraints. The first two parts of the fuzzy inference process, fuzzifying the inputs and applying the fuzzy operator, are exactly the same. The main difference between Mamdani and Sugeno is that the Sugeno output membership functions are either linear or constant. A typical rule in a Sugeno fuzzy model has the form

IF Input 1 = x AND Input 2 = y, THEN Output is z = ax + by + c.

For a zero-order Sugeno model, the output level zis a constant (a = b = 0).The output level z_i of each rule is weighted by the firing strength w_i of the rule. For example, for an AND rule with Input 1 = x and Input 2 = y, the firing strength is

$$w_i = \text{AndMethod}\,(F_1\,(x), F_2\,(y)),$$

where F1,2(·) are the membership functions for Inputs 1 and 2. The final output of the system is the weighted average of all rule outputs, computed as

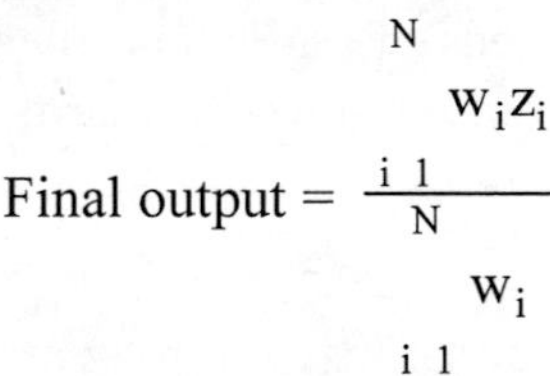

$$\text{Final output} = \frac{\sum_{i=1}^{N} w_i z_i}{\sum_{i=1}^{N} w_i}$$

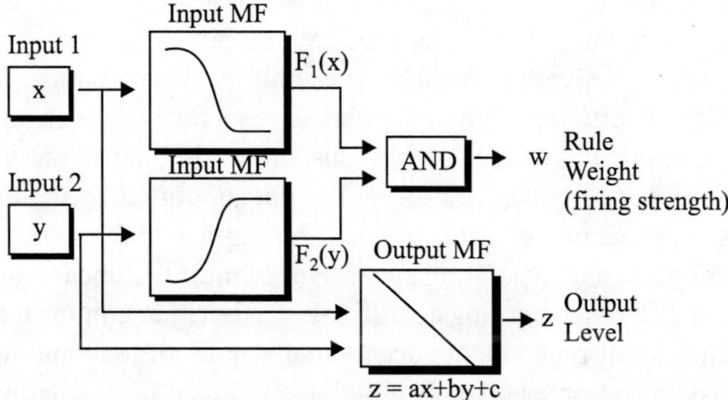

Figure 15.13: Sugeno Rule

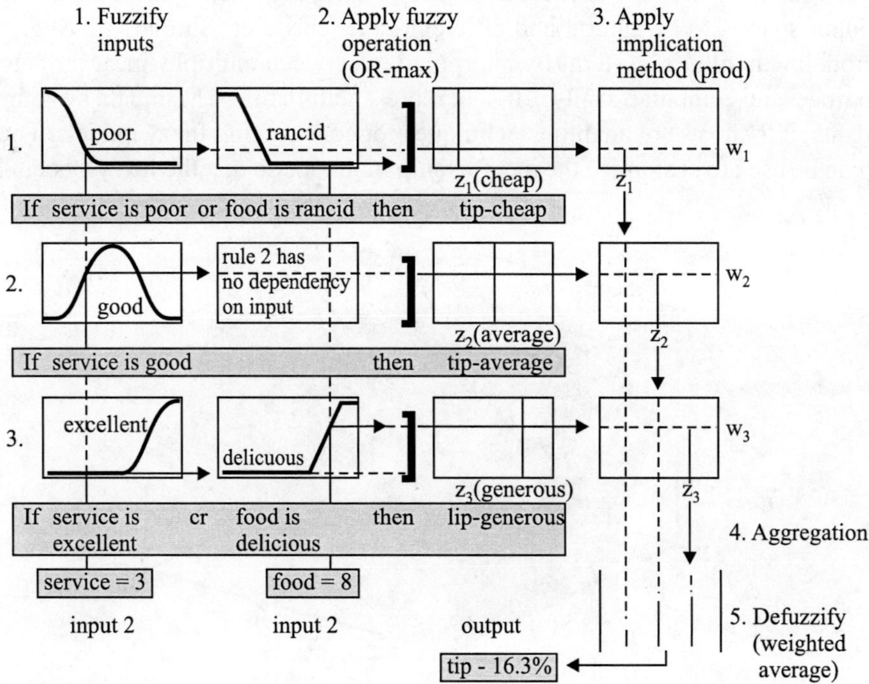

Figure 15.14: Fuzzy Tipping Model

A Sugeno rule operates as shown in Figure 15.13.

Figure 15.14 shows the fuzzy tipping model developed in previous sections of this manual adapted for use as a Sugeno system. Fortunately, it is frequently the case that singleton output functions are completely sufficient for the needs of a given problem. As an example, the system tippersg.fis is the Sugeno type representation of the now-familiar tipping model (Figure 15.14).

- a = readfis('tippersg');

  gensurf(a)

The above command gives the surface view of fuzzy tipping model as shown in Figure 15.15. The easiest way to visualize first-order Sugeno systems is to think of each rule as defining the location of a "moving singleton." That is, the singleton output spikes can move around in a linear fashion in the output space, depending on what the input is. This also tends to make the system notation very compact and efficient. Higher-order Sugeno fuzzy models are possible, but they introduce significant complexity with little obvious merit. Sugeno fuzzy models whose output membership functions are greater than first-order are not supported by the Fuzzy Logic Toolbox. Because of the linear dependence of each rule on the input variables of a system, the Sugeno method is ideal for acting as an interpolating supervisor of multiple linear controllers that are to be applied, respectively, to different operating conditions of a dynamic nonlinear system. For example, the performance of an aircraft may change dramatically with altitude and Mach number. Linear controllers, though easy to compute and well suited to any given flight condition, must be updated regularly and smoothly to keep up with the changing state of the flight vehicle. A Sugeno FIS is extremely well suited to the task of smoothly interpolating the linear gains that would be applied across the input space; it is a natural and efficient gain scheduler. Similarly, a Sugeno system is suited for modeling nonlinear systems by interpolating between multiple linear models. Because it is a more compact and computationally efficient representation than a Mamdani system, the Sugeno system lends itself to the use of adaptive techniques for constructing fuzzy models. These adaptive techniques can be used to customize the membership functions so that the fuzzy system best models the data.

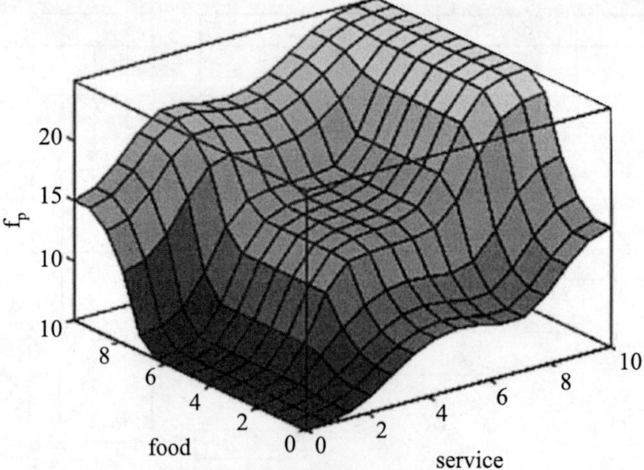

Figure 15.15: Surface View

15.11.5 Comparison Between Sugeno and Mamdani Method

The main difference between Mamdani and Sugeno is that the Sugeno output membership functions are either linear or constant. Also the difference lies in the consequents of their fuzzy rules, and thus their aggregation and defuzzification procedures differ suitably. The number of the input fuzzy sets and fuzzy rules needed by the Sugeno fuzzy systems depend on the number and locations of the extrema of the function to be approximated. In Sugeno method a large number of fuzzy rules must be employed to approximate periodic or highly oscillatory functions. The minimal configuration of the TS fuzzy systems can be reduced and becomes smaller than that of the Mamdani fuzzy systems if nontrapezoidal or nontriangular input fuzzy sets are used.

Sugeno controllers usually have far more adjustable parameters in the rule consequent and the number of the parameters grows exponentially with the increase of the number of input variables. Far fewer mathematical results exist for TS fuzzy controllers than do for Mamdani fuzzy controllers, notably those on TS fuzzy control system stability. Mamdani is easy to form compared to Sugeno method.

15.11.6 Advantages of Sugeno and Mamdani Method

Following are the advantages of sugeno and mamdani methods:

Advantages of the sugeno method

Follow'ing are the advantages of the sugeno method:

1. It is computationally efficient.
2. It works well with linear techniques (e.g., PID control).
3. It works well with optimization and adaptive techniques.
4. It has guaranteed continuity of the output surface.
5. It is well suited to mathematical analysis.

Advantages of the mamdani method

Following are the advantages of the mamdani method:

1. It is intuitive.
2. It has widespread acceptance.
3. It is well suited to human input.

Fuzzy inference system is the most important modeling tool based on fuzzy set theory. The FISs are built by domain experts and are used in automatic control, decision analysis, and various other expert systems.

EXERCISES

1. What do you mean by Fuzzy if then rules?

2. Explain the various types of fuzzy rules?
3. What do you mean by fuzzy mapping rules?
4. What do you mean by fuzzy implication rules?
5. Explain the comparison of two types of fuzzy rules?
6. Explain the formation of rules?
7. Explain the de composition of rules?
8. What do you mean by aggregation of fuzzy rules?
9. Explain the properties of fuzzy rules?
10. Explain the various fuzzy rule based models?
11. What do you mean by defuzzification?
12. What are the two major defuzzification techniques?
13. What do you mean by height method?
14. Explain the mathematical representation of fuzzy mapping rules?
15. What do you mean by fuzzy inference system?
16. Explain the construction and working of fuzzy inference system?
17. Explain the two most important methods of fuzzy inference system?
18. Explain the comparison between sugeno and mamdani method?
19. What are the various advantages of sugeno and mamdani method?
20. Explain in detail mamdani's fuzzy inference method?

CHAPTER 16

Applications of Fuzzy Logic

16.1 INTRODUCTION

This chapter introduces some engineering applications of fuzzy logic and fuzzy control systems. The purpose of this introduction is mainly to illustrate workability and applicability of fuzzy logic and fuzzy control in reaFuzzy If-then Rulesl-life situations, based on the fuzzy systems theories developed in the previous chapters of the book.

Main applications are introduced in the following order: Fuzzy logic in industrial automation, Fuzzy logic supervisory control for coal power plant, Optimization of a water treatment system, Truck speed limiter control by fuzzy logic, Fuzzy logic and neuro-fuzzy in appliances etc. For each application, a description of the functionality of the system is given, followed by the fuzzy logic rules and computer simulation results.

16.2 FUZZY LOGIC IN INDUSTRIAL AUTOMATION

In recent years, fuzzy logic has proven well its broad potential in industrial automation applications. In this application area, engineers primarily rely on proven concepts. For discrete event control, they mostly use ladder logic, a programming language resembling electrical wiring schemes and running on so called programmable logic controllers (PLC). For continuous control, either bang-bang type or PID type controllers are mostly employed.

While PID type controllers do work fine when the process under control is in a stable condition, they do not cope well in other cases:

- The presence of strong disturbances (non-linearity)
- Time-varying parameters of the process (non-linearity)
- Presence of dead times

The reason for this is that a PID controller assumes the process to behave in a strictly linear fashion. While this simplification can be made in a stable condition, strong disturbances can push the process operation point far away from the set operating point. Here, the linear assumption usually does not work any more. The same happens if a process changes its parameters over time.

In these cases, the extension or replacement of PID controllers with fuzzy controllers has been shown to be more feasible more often than using conventional but sophisticated state controllers or adaptive approaches. However, this is not the only area where there is potential for fuzzy logic based solutions.

16.2.1 Multi-variable Control

The real potential of fuzzy logic in industrial automation lies in the straightforward way fuzzy logic renders possible the design of multi-variable controllers. In many applications, keeping a single process variable constant can be done well using a PID or bang-bang type controller. However, set values for all these individual control loops are often still set manually by operators. The operators analyze the process condition, and tune the set values of the PID controllers to optimize the operation. This is called "supervisory control" and mostly involves multiple variables.

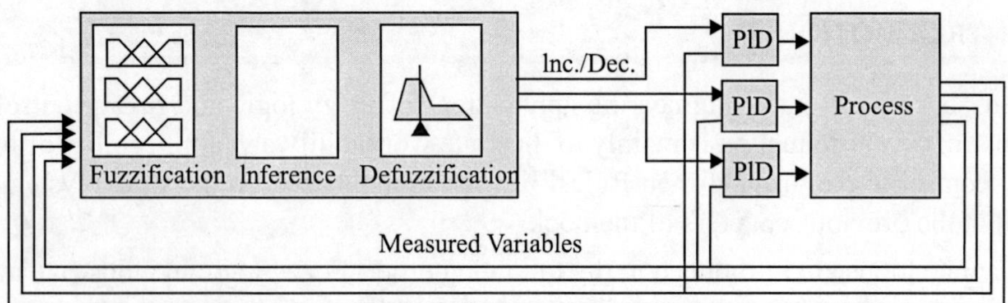

Figure 16.1: Using a Fuzzy Logic Controller to Determine the Set Values for Underlying PID Control Loops

Alas, both PID and bang-bang type controllers can only cope with one variable. This usually results in several independently operating control loops. These loops are not able to "talk to each other". In cases where it is desirable or necessary to exploit interdependencies of physical variables, one is forced to set up a complete mathematical model of the process and to derive differential equations from it that are necessary for the implementation of a solution. In the world of industrial automation, this is rarely feasible:

- Creating a mathematical model for a real-word problem can involve years of work.
- Most mathematical models involve extensive simplifications and linearizations that require "fudge" factors to optimize the resulting controller later on.
- Tuning the fudge factors of a controller derived from a mathematical model is "fishing in the dark", because optimizing the system at one operating point using global factors usually degrades the performance at other operating points.

Also, many practitioners do not have the background required for rigorous mathematical modeling. Thus, the general observation in industry is that single process variables are controlled by simple control models such as PID or bang-bang, while supervisory control is done by human operators.

This is where fuzzy logic provides an elegant and highly efficient solution to the problem.

Fuzzy logic lets engineers design supervisory multi-variable controllers from operator experience and experimental results rather than from mathematical models. A possible structure of a fuzzy logic based control system in industrial automation applications is exemplified by Figure 16.1. Each single process variable is kept constant by a PID controller, while the set values for the PID controller stem from the fuzzy logic system. This arrangement is typical for cases like control of several temperature zones of an oven or control of oxygen concentrations in different zones of a wastewater basin. In other cases, it could be reasonable to develop the complete closed loop control solution in a fuzzy system.

This illustrates why it is very desirable to integrate conventional control engineering techniques, such as ladder logic or instruction list language for digital logic and PID control blocks tightly together with fuzzy logic functionality.

16.2.2 Merging Fuzzy Logic and PICs

In 1990, when more and more successful applications proved the potential of fuzzy logic in industrial automation, the German company Moeller GmbH and the U.S./German company Inform Software created the *fuzzy*PLC based on the observation that fuzzy logic needs tight integration with conventional industrial automation techniques.

The *fuzzy*PLC Hardware and Firmware

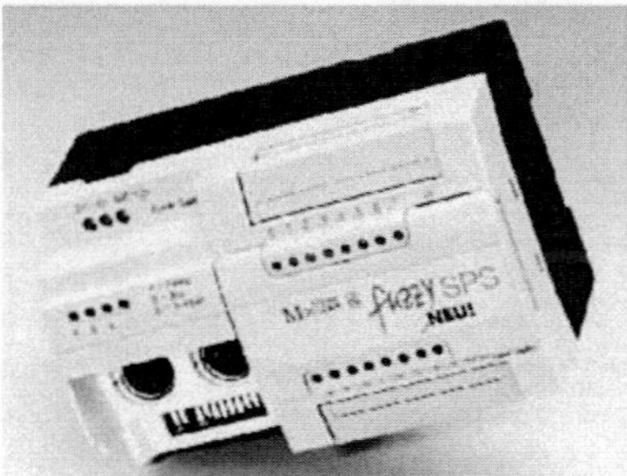

Figure 16.2: The fuzzyPLC contains fuzzy and conventional logic processing capabilities, field bus connections, and interfaces.

To make it available at a low cost, the core of the *fuzzy*PLC uses a highly integrated two-chip solution. An analog ASIC handles the analog/digital interfaces at industry standard 12 bit resolution. Snap-On modules can extend the periphery for large applications of up to about 100 signals. An integrated field bus connection, based on RS485, provides further expansion by networking. The conventional and the fuzzy logic computation is handled by a 16/32 bit RISC microcontroller. The operating system and communication routines, developed by Moeller, are based on a commercial real time multitasking kernel. The fuzzy inference engine, developed by Inform Software, is implemented and integrated into the operating system in a highly efficient manner, so that scan times of less than one millisecond are possible. The internal RAM of 256 KB can be expanded by memory cards using flash technology. Thus, the *fuzzy*PLC is capable of solving quite complex and fast industrial automation problems in spite of its compact and low price design.

The FuzzyPLC Engineering Software

The *fuzzy*PLC is programmed by an enhanced version of the standard fuzzy logic system development software *fuzzy*TECH from Inform Software. *fuzzy*TECH is an all-graphical, design, simulation, and optimization environment with implementation modules for most microcontrollers and industrial computers. To support the complete functionality of the *fuzzy*PLC, *fuzzy*TECH has been enhanced with editors and functions to support the conventional programming of the PLC. Thus, a user only needs one tool to program both conventional and fuzzy logic parts of the solution.

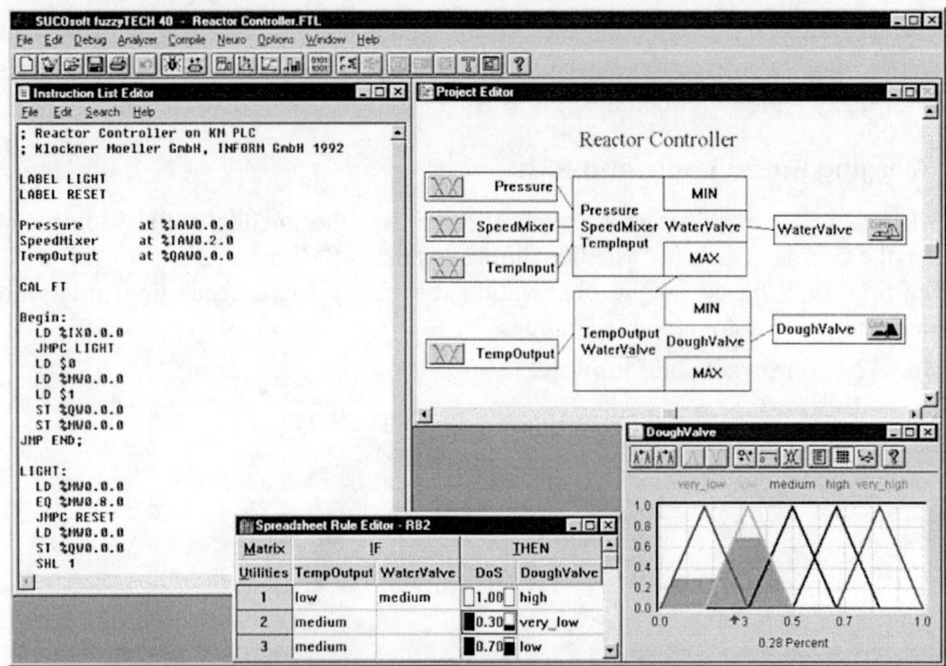

Figure 16.3: Both the Traditional Logic and the Fuzzy Logic System is Programmed by FuzzyTECH 4.0.

The *fuzzy*TECH software combines all necessary editors for membership functions, linguistic variables, rule tables, and system structure with analyzer functions and optimization features. The software runs on a PC and is linked to the *fuzzy*PLC by a standard serial cable (RS232) or the field bus (RS485). Through this link, the developer downloads the designed system to the *fuzzy*PLC. Because fuzzy logic systems often require optimization "on-the-fly", *fuzzy*TECH and the *fuzzy*PLC feature "online-debugging" where the system running on the *fuzzy*PLC is completely visualized by the graphical editors and analyzers of *fuzzy*TECH. Plus, in online-debugging modes, any modification of the fuzzy logic system is instantly translated to the *fuzzy*PLC without halting operation.

16.2.3 Application Case Studies

In this section, we review eight (8) recent highly successful applications of fuzzy logic in industrial automation using the *fuzzy*PLC:

1. Anti-Sway Control of Cranes
2. Fire Zone Control in Waste Incineration Plants
3. Dosing Control in Waste Water Treatment Plants
4. Control of Tunnel Inspection Robots
5. Positioning in Presses
6. Temperature Control in Plastic Molding Machines
7. Climate Control and Building Automation
8. Wind Energy Converter Control

1. Anti-Sway Control of Cranes: In crane control, the objective is to position a load over a target point. While the load connected to the crane head by flexible cables may well sway within certain limits during transportation, the sway must be reduced to almost zero for load release when the target position is reached. Hence, a controller must use at least two input variables, for example position and sway angle. Thus, a simple PID controller cannot be used as it is restricted to one input. Conventional solutions of the problem require highly elaborate approaches, like model based control or state variable controllers that need intensive engineering and hardware resources. These technologies tend to push system costs into regions that make anti-sway systems economically unaffordable. For these reasons, most cranes are still operated manually.

Figure 16.4: The 64 ton crane of Hochtief Corp. uses fuzzyPLC based anti-sway positioning control

In spite of the difficulties involved with automated control, human operators can control cranes quite well in most cases. Because fuzzy logic is a technology that facilitates control system design based directly on such human experiences, it has been used for crane automation for almost a decade. The types of cranes include container cranes in harbors, steel pan cranes, and cranes in a manufacturing environment. Recently, a 64 ton crane that transports concrete modules for bridges and tunnels over a distance of 500 yards has been automated with a *fuzzy*PLC in Germany.

The benefit was a capacity gain of about 20% due to the faster transportation and an increase in safety. Accidents were frequent, because the crane operators walk parallel to the crane during operation with a remote controller. Before, when they had to watch the load to concentrate on the sway angle, they frequently stumbled over parts lying on the ground. The crane was commissioned in Spring 1995 and the fuzzy logic anti-sway controller has been continuously enabled by the crane operator, showing the high degree of acceptance by the operators. This fact is of special importance since not only technological feasibility but also psychological aspects are important for the success of an industrial automation solution.

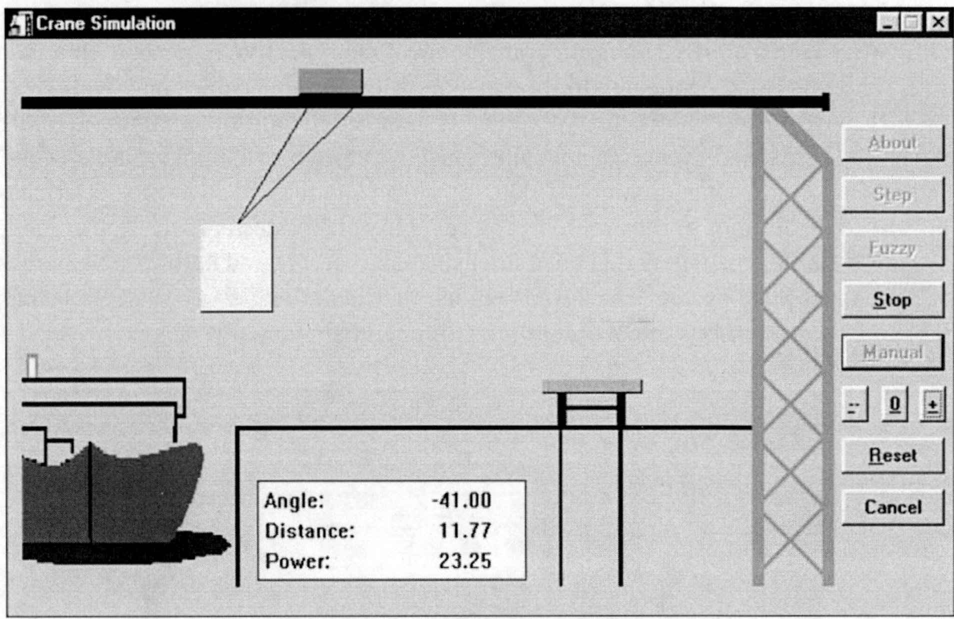

Figure 16.5: A software simulation of the crane controller is contained in [16.4]

A software simulation and a simple example of an anti-sway crane controller for didactic purposes can be found in [16.4]. The real solution uses about 10 inputs, 2 outputs, and 4 rule blocks with a total of 75 rules.

2. Fire Zone Control in Waste Incineration Plants: Maintaining a stable burning temperature in waste incineration plants is important to minimize the generation of toxic gases, such as dioxin and furan, as well as to avoid corrosion in the burning chambers. There are two primary difficulties of this temperature control process:

- The caloric value of the waste fluctuates strongly.
- The fire position and shape cannot be measured directly.

Because the heat generated from the burning process is used to produce electrical energy, a stable incineration process is also of high commercial interest.

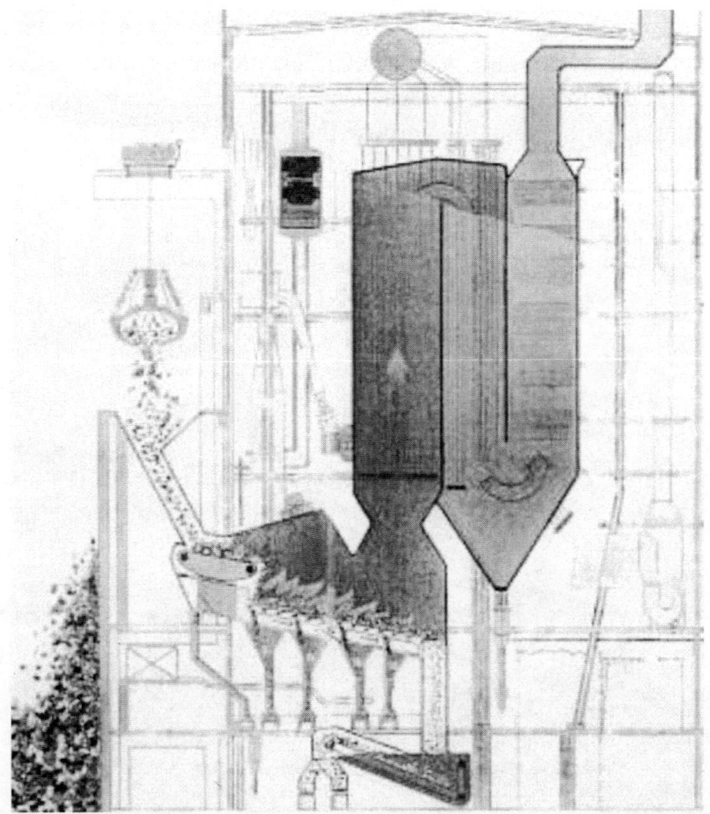

Figure 16.6: In a waste incineration plant, a crane continuously delivers waste from the bunker to the belt running through the burning zone. The exhaust gases are cooled and cleaned.

In recent applications at waste incineration plants in the cities of Hamburg and Mannheim in Germany, fuzzy logic has been successfully applied. In Mannheim, where two *fuzzy*PLCs were used to control the burning process, the steam generation capacity of one furnace is 28 Mg/h. Using the industry standard conventional controller, steam generation fluctuated by as much as 10 Mg/h in just one hour. The fuzzy logic controller was capable of reducing this fluctuation to less than ±1 Mg/h. This dramatically improved robustness and also caused the NOx and SO2 emission to drop slightly, and the CO emission to drop to half.

3. Dosing Control in Waste Water Treatment Plants: Waste water treatment processes are a combination of biological, chemical, and mechanical processes. This makes the creation of a complete mathematical model for their control intractable. However, there is a large amount of human experience that can be exploited for automated controller design. As such operator experience can be efficiently put to work by fuzzy logic, many plants already use this technique.

In a recent application in Bonn, dosing of liquid FeCl3 for phosphate precipitation has been successfully automated using the *fuzzy*PLC. Recently changes in legislation require water treatment plants in Germany to limit the total amount of phosphate in the released water to 1 milligram per liter. To extract the phosphate from the water, FeCl3 is added, which converts the phosphate into FePO4 that is sedimented with the sludge. Because a violation of the legal phosphate limit results in severe penalties, the operators tend to overdose the FeCl3.

Figure 16.7: By injecting FeCl3 into the sludge, dissolved phosphate precipitates from the waste water

To optimize the FeCl3 dosing, a fuzzy logic controller that uses the input variables phosphate concentration, its derivative, water flow, its derivative, and dry substance contents was designed. The output of the fuzzy logic controller is the change of the set variable for the injected FeCl3. An underlying conventional PI type controller stabilizes the FeCl3 flow to this set point. The PI type controller is implemented as a function block in the *fuzzy*PLC as well. This is an example of the combination of fuzzy logic and conventional control engineering techniques.

The total fuzzy logic controller uses 207 rules to express the control strategy based on the five (5) input variables of the fuzzy logic control block. The total implementation time was three (3) staff months and resulted in savings of about 50% of the FeCl3 compared to the manual control before. Taking implementation time and hardware/software costs into consideration with the savings on FeCl3 results a return in investment time of half a year.

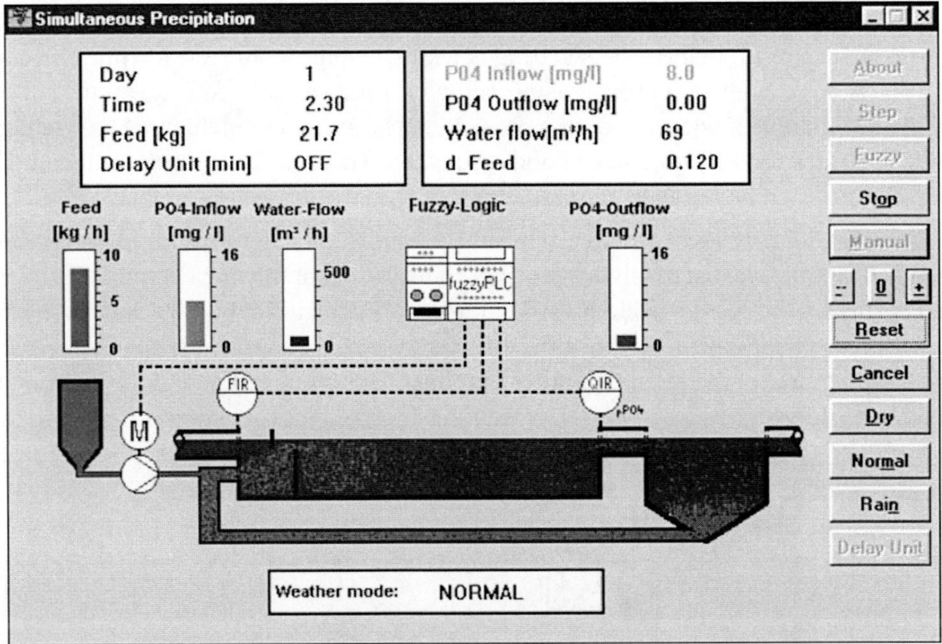

Figure 16.8: A software simulation of a simplified precipitation controller is contained in [4]

4. Control of Tunnel Inspection Robots: The German Aerospace corporation DASA has developed a sewage pipe inspection system using two robot units and a support truck. The objective of the robots is to detect leakage in segments of the pipe by applying air pressure to the sealed space between the two robots. Because the vertical access shafts can be quite far away from each other, the robots have to operate up to 400 yards away from the truck. The robots are connected to each other and the truck by cables that provide air pressure, electrical energy, and control signals to the robots.

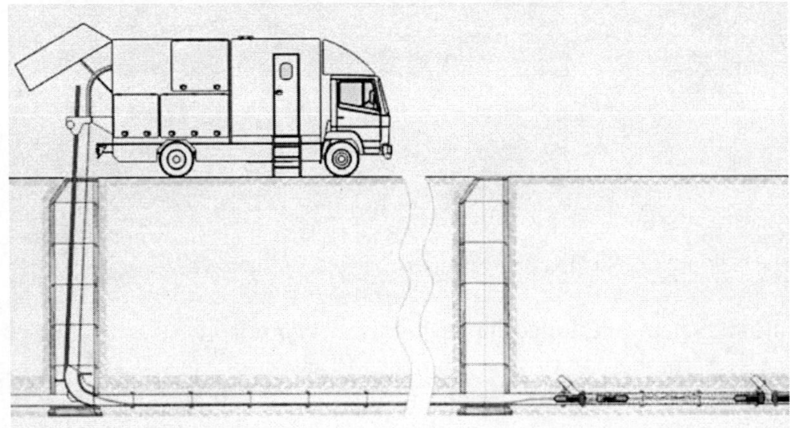

Figure 16.9: The two robot units in the sewage pipe (right) are supplied from a specialized truck by cables

When DASA developed the system, a severe control problem came up. To avoid entanglement of the cables that can result in the robots getting stuck in the pipe, cable tension must be controlled very carefully. A conventional approach using complex state variable controllers turned out to be too costly in terms of both money and design time. A control system implemented on two *fuzzy*PLCs using about 200 rules each showed very good results in a very short engineering time at less than 10% of the costs of a conventional solution.

5. Positioning of Presses: One area with big potential for fuzzy solutions is the control of drives. In this example, we discuss hydraulic axis control. One of the most complex fuzzy projects was done for a hydraulic press used to press laminates, printed circuit boards, and floor coverings. The task was the synchronized control of a 14-axis system. The position control of the axis, a superimposed pressure controller, the parallel running of the steel belt and the synchronization of all axes had to be solved.

Figure 16.10: Control of hydraulic systems is difficult as many non-linearities, Such as the "stick-slip" effect, are involved

The automation system employed has a highly decentralized structure and consists of two large master PLCs, a number of smaller compact PLCs, a PC based supervisory system, and seven *fuzzy*PLCs. All units are networked using the integrated field bus interfaces. Very important for the synchronization of the entire machine is the ability of the field bus network to satisfy the real time requirements. One typical problem involved in the control of hydraulic systems is the so-called "stick slip effect". The transition of an axis from standstill to motion is highly non-linear because of the transition from stick friction to slip friction. This makes designing a good controller for hydraulic systems difficult. In the cited application, fuzzy logic rendered a good solution technique, freeing system design from the burden of the theory of non linear systems synthesis. The overall design time using fuzzy logic was only a third of what a conventional approach had required in past applications of conventional control for similar presses.

6. Temperature Control in Plastic Molding Machines: In plastic molding machines, temperature control is crucial to achieve high and consistent product quality. This requires laborious tuning of the involved control algorithms, because the dead times involved in an extrusion machine are significant and there is significant coupling between the different temperature zones.

Figure 16.11: To achieve high product quality, keeping the temperature constant is critical in molding plastic

To cut down the commission time for these machines, KM corporation has developed a self-tuning controller using the *fuzzy*PLC. At start up time, some parameters are estimated that are used to scale the non linear fuzzy controller. In contrast to conventional tuning algorithms, this controller does not require a cooling down of the machine to room temperature before self tuning can work. Even very difficult temperature zones with big dead times can be handled by this algorithm and the result is a very robust controller. This is important because the temperature properties of an empty machine and one filled with plastic material are extremely different. Compared to conventional systems, the fuzzy logic enhanced temperature controller performs with a faster response time and a significantly smaller overshoot combined with extreme robustness.

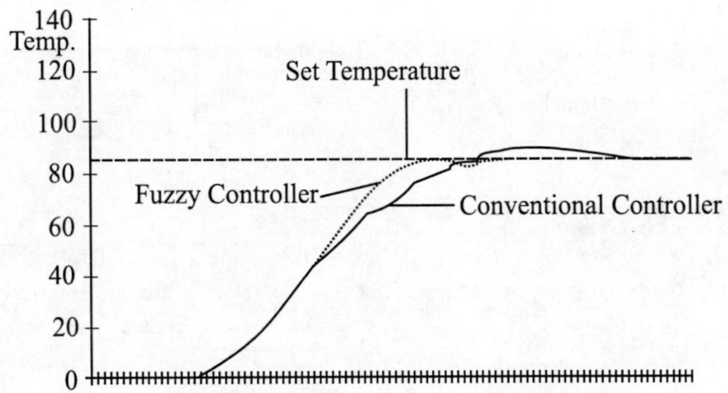

Figure 16.12: The fuzzy logic controller in the molding machine reaches the set point faster and avoids overshoot

7. Climate Control Using Fuzzy Logic: Climate control systems reveal a high potential for energy savings. In a recent application at a major hospital in Europe, the integration of fuzzy logic saves about 25% on electrical energy, equivalent to the amount of 50,000 per year.

Figure 16.13: An application of fuzzy logic in the a/c system of a large hospital in germany saved more than 25% on energy costs

The fuzzy logic controller outputs the set values for the coolant valve, the water heater valve, and the humidifier water valve. The fuzzy logic control strategy uses different temperature and humidity sensors to determine how to operate the air conditioning process in a way that conserves energy. Again, the capability of processing interdependent variables results in significant advantages over conventional solutions. For example, one knows that when temperature rises, relative humidity of the air decreases.

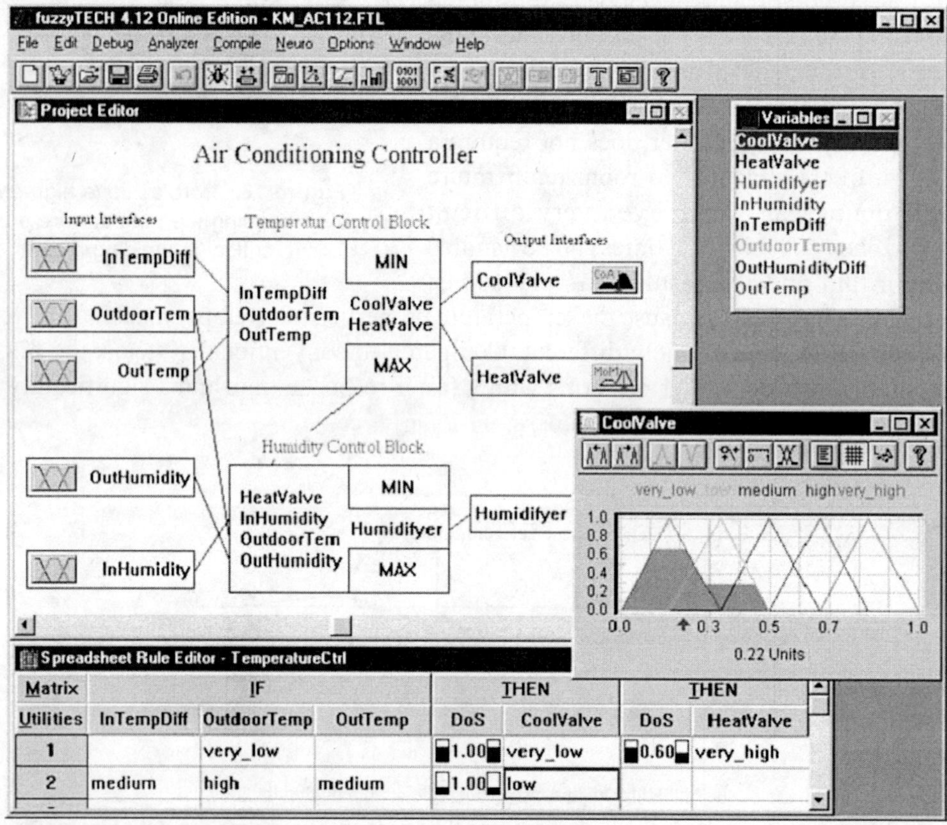

Figure 16.14: Fuzzy Logic allows to increase the energy efficiency of an A/C system by evaluating several process values.

This knowledge can be exploited by implementing a fuzzy logic control strategy that allows the temperature controller "to tell" the humidity controller that it is going to activate the heater valve. The humidity controller now can respond to this before it can detect it by its sensor. The result is an increase in control quality.

8. Wind Energy Converter Control: In recent years, technological advancements made the commercial use of wind energy feasible. A trend to larger plants further improved the cost/performance ratio. However, such large wind energy converters require advanced control systems both to ensure high efficiency and long life. The controller sets the angle of the rotor blades based on the wind situation (pitch control). However, wind is not a one-dimensional figure. Strength, gustiness, and fluctuation of the wind angle must be evaluated to determine the optimal rotor blade angle.

Figure 16.15: To maximize the efficiency of a wind energy converter, the pitch controller must consider many inputs

There is a trade-off between efficiency, safety and wear of the wind energy converter. If the blade angle is set to draw the maximum amount of energy from the wind, the risk of sudden wind gusts causing excessive mechanical stress on the converter increases. For these reasons, an Aerodyn wind energy converter was enhanced with a fuzzy system based on human experience to find the best compromise to this trade-off. The first implemented system is running in a field test and shows quite promising results. The quality of the controller is not only measured in constancy of the delivered power, but also in measures of mechanical stress on the tower, the nacelle and the rotor blades. The next step will be the application of the achieved results to the first 1.2 MW systems that are to be launched in the marketplace in 1996.

16.2.4 Conclusions

As a consequence of the high degree of awareness raised by a large number of publications over the past five years in Europe, a substantial number of successful applications have been generated. Of these, we have presented a selection of eight (8) recent applications in this paper. In all applications, the key to success lies in the clever combination of both conventional automation techniques and fuzzy logic. Fuzzy logic by no means replaces conventional control engineering. Rather, it compliments conventional techniques with a highly efficient methodology to implement multi-variable control strategies. Thus, the major potential for fuzzy logic lies in the implementation of supervisory control loops.

16.3 FUZZY LOGIC SUPERVISORY CONTROL FOR COAL POWER PLANT

The High Temperature Winkler Gasification (HTW) process that was developed by Rheinbraun AG has been used for many years in pilot and demonstration plants to generate synthesis gas and fuel gas out of brown coal. Conventional methods were used before to control the gas throughput. While the conventional control engineering implementation was able to run the process in a stable operating point, improvements were necessary to use the HTW process in a coal power station with integrated coal gasification:

- More precise control of gas throughput under fluctuations of the coal quality
- More robust control in cases of fast load changes
- Automation of supervisory control operation

On top on the existing base level automation, a supervisory fuzzy logic control strategy was implemented on the HTW plant in Berrenrath/Germany. Fuzzy Logic was used because the control problem was strongly non-linear and involves multiple measured and command variables. On the other hand, extensive operator knowledge about the process was available. The implemented fuzzy logic supervisory control strategy successfully improved throughput control quality as well as the adaptation to different coal parameters.

16.3.1 High Temperature Winkler Gasification

The process that is used to gasify the coal is called High Temperature Winkler method (HTW). The HTW Gasification method uses a high temperature fluid bed process to convert brown coal into synthesis gas, a mixture of carbon monoxide (CO) and hydrogen (H_2). This gas mix can be used to produce chemical base products like aldehydes or organic acids. Alternatively it can be used in a power plant gas turbine to generate electricity. The gas produced by the demonstration plant is used for chemical synthesizes. Later in the power plant application the gas will be used to run a gas turbine / steam turbine combination.

The HTW process has been used for the gasification of coal by the German coal company Rheinbraun since 1956. The demonstration plant started operation in 1985. It converts 720 t of coal per day into 900.000 m^3 (iN) synthesis gas. In 1996 Inform added a fuzzy logic supervisory control to enable the process for a power plant application. Figure 6.16 shows a photo of this plant.

Figure 16.16: HTW plant in berrenrath, germany

The main inputs for the HTW process are coal, oxygen and steam. The coal is first ground to small pieces and pre-dried before it is fed into the bottom part of the fluid bed reactor. The steam and the oxygen are fed into the reactor on four different levels, into and above the fluid bed. In the fluid bed the coal reacts with the oxygen and the steam. This reaction takes place at a temperature of around 800°C and at a pressure of 10 bar. After the reaction in the fluid bed the generated gas enters the hot zone above the fluid bed. At temperatures around 1000 °C additional oxygen and steam is added and left over coal particles react with the gases. This way additional gas is produced and by-products like methane and other hydrocarbons are converted to carbon monoxide and hydrogen. The produced gases leave the reactor at the top through the reactor head. At this point the gas is still mixed with a lot of particles. These are filtered out and fed back into the fluid bed with a zyklon filter and a feed back tube.

The coal ashes accumulate at the bottom of the fluid bed reactor. They are removed from there out of the reactor by two conveyor spirals. The hot raw gas is cooled down to 270°C. Its heat is used to generate pressure steam, some of which is recycled back into the process. Ceramic filters remove remaining dust particles out of the gas. The following gas washer removes NH_3, HCL and other gas components. The following CO conversion creates the correct carbon monoxide / hydrogen mix for the methanol synthesis. After a compression to 37 bar the gas is processed in a non-selective rectisol washer ($C0_2/H_2S$ washer). At temperatures below -40°C liquid methanol is used to wash out carbondioxide and sulfuric components. The methanol is used again after recycling it and the purified synthesis gas is used at a nearby chemical plant. Figure 16.17 shows the process diagram of the HTW plant.

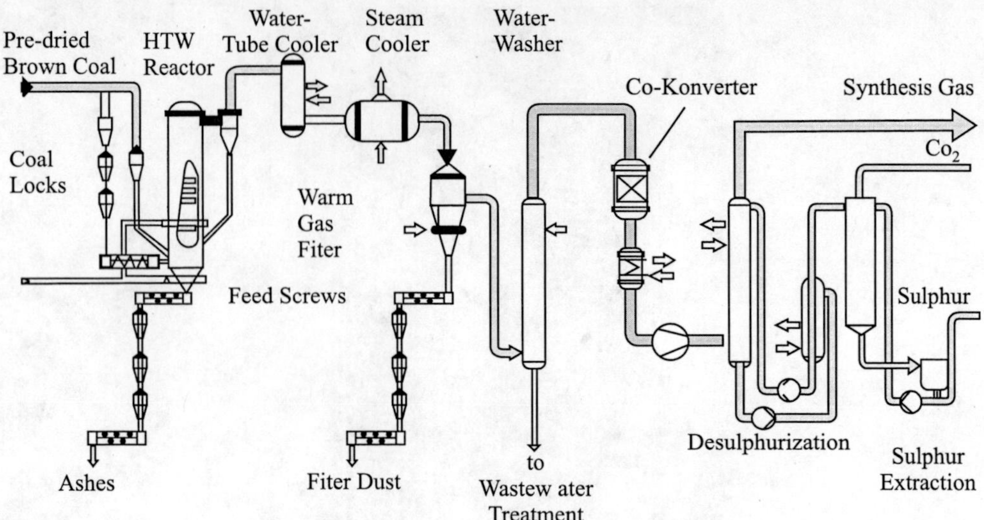

Figure 16.17: Process diagram of HTW plant

The coal input, the oxygen input, the distribution of the oxygen input over the eight different nozzles and the ash removal rate have to be controlled to use the coal efficiently and to generate the correct mixture of gases.

Instead of coal a mixture of coal and plastic refuse can be used in the HTW process. This way the coal consumption is reduced and the plastic refuse is recycled into synthesis gas.

16.3.2 Conventional Control

The HTW demonstration plant is controlled with an Eckhardt PLS-80E DCS system. This system controls over 6000 measurements and actuators. The main control room is equipped with 10 Unix based operator consoles and four real-time servers. So far nearly all the set points of the underlying control circuits are set and adjusted manually by the operators. They constantly monitor the process condition and adjust the set points of the underlying control circuits accordingly (i.e. coal input, oxygen input, ...) A few years ago it was tried to automatically generate some set points using a conventional PID controller But the results were not satisfying. This supervisory control only worked fine when the coal quality was very constant. Otherwise the process quality would deteriorate significantly and the operators had to intervene and switch back to manual operation.

16.3.3 Supervisory Fuzzy Logic Control

Two main tasks have been defin]ed for the supervisory fuzzy logic control: Regulation of the gas throughput and process stabilization.

The fuzzy logic must keep the gas throughput at the set point and it has to respond to set point changes with the correct dynamic speed. The set point can vary from 70% (partial load) to 100% (full load). The fluctuations of the gas throughput result mainly from variations of the coal quality (humidity, ash content and granularity). These effects have to be compensated by the fuzzy logic.

The process stabilization must keep several process parameters in the optimum range. The reactor load influences the optimum of these process parameters. The position of the optimum also depends on the coal quality. The following parameters were used to define the quality of the process:

- Temperature in the post gasification zone
- Height and density of the fluid bed
- Composition of the produced gas (CO, CH_4, H_2)

The process stabilization is especially difficult when the HTW process is fed with a mixture of coal and plastic refuse. This is done because plastic refuse is a very inexpensive fuel. But the addition of plastic to the coal results in drastically different process conditions. The fuzzy logic control uses the regular measurements of the process conditions to detect any addition of plastic to the coal. This will result into an adapted control strategy of the fuzzy logic control.

16.3.4 Fuzzy Logic Control Design

The specification of the control task resulted into a preliminary concept of the fuzzy logic controller. The operator knowledge was than used to specify the control strategy of the fuzzy logic system. Several structured audits took place to evaluate the operator knowledge systematically. The audits focused on the operators' manual control strategies and on the relationships between the inputs and the outputs of the process. This procedure is in accordance with the standardized fuzzy logic design method.

The audits resulted into the following concept for the fuzzy logic control: Deviations of the gas throughput from its set point immediately result into a correction of the oxygen input. The coal input is adjusted accordingly to keep the ratio between coal and oxygen at a constant level. Changes of the reactor pressure predict changes of gas throughput. Therefore the pressure gradient is used as an early warning indicator for changes of the gas throughput.

For process stabilization and for the adaptation to different coal qualities the fuzzy logic controller uses the following parameters to keep the process in a stable operating condition:

- Coal to oxygen ratio
- Distribution of the oxygen between the fluid bed zone and the gasification zone.
- Ash outtake
- Fluidification with steam and inert gas

Sometimes one and the same process input value has to be modified to keep several different critical measurements (temperature, fluid bed height, ...) in the optimum range. This can have conflicting results.

For example: A too low fluid bed is normally corrected with an increase of the coal input. A too low temperature is corrected with a reduction of the coal input and a too low dust output is also corrected with a reduction of the coal input. But a too low temperature can occur together with a too low fluid bed. The ability of the fuzzy controller to weight different conflicting indications based on their significance and to use a lot of inputs to determine the best reaction to each situation is very useful to control complex processes.

The fuzzy logic controller has a total number of 24 inputs and 8 outputs. A preprocessing reduces the 24 inputs to 10 characteristic descriptors. These are fed into the fuzzy logic system. The fuzzy outputs go through a post-processing step to generate the actual set points for the process inputs. Figure 16.18 shows the core structure of the fuzzy logic system.

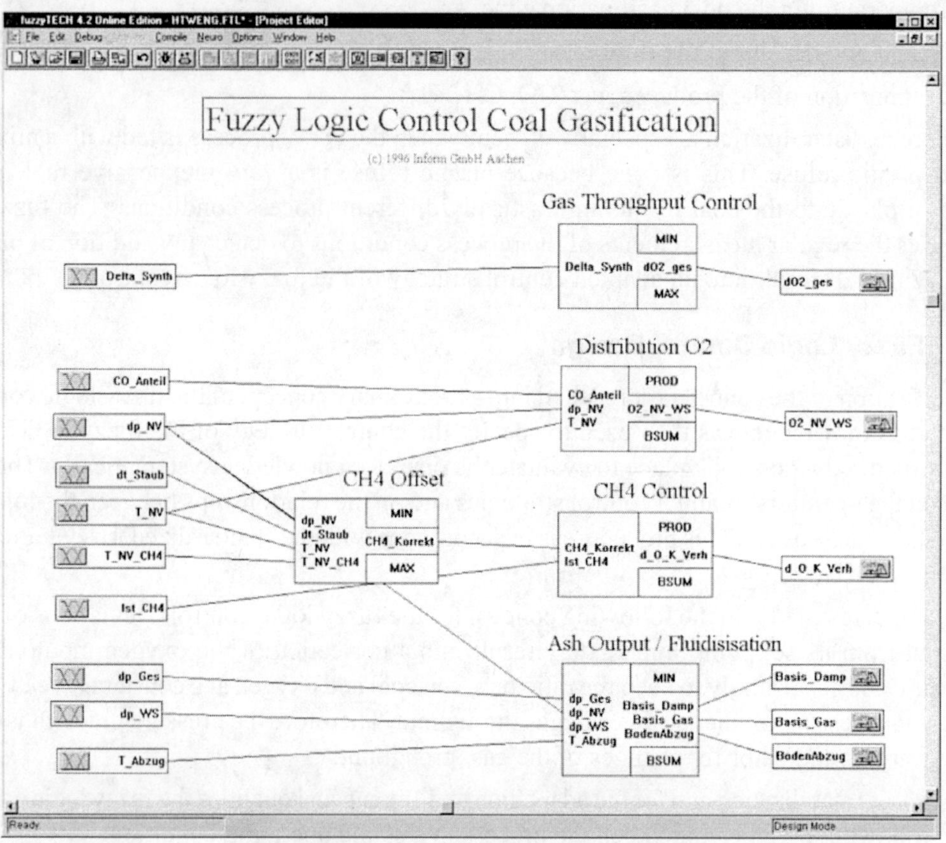

Figure 16.18: Fuzzy controller structure

16.3.5 Integration of Fuzzy Logic Into the DCS

The process measurements are coming to the fuzzy logic control through the Eckhardt DCS. The fuzzy logic system generates set point values for the underlying PID controllers. The fuzzy logic controller was implemented on an OS/2 PC. Therefore the set up of the communication between the DCS and the fuzzy logic controller was an important part of the whole project. The communication was implemented using Factory Link, a well-known SCADA program by US-Data. A factory link application is running on the same OS/2 PC together with the fuzzy logic controller. The fuzzy logic controller reads data out of the Factory Link Real Time DataBase and it also writes data back into it. Another Factory Link task is communicating with the DCS through the Eckhardt DCS bus. This way an image of the process measurements is created in the Factory Link RTDB and the fuzzy outputs are forwarded to the DCS.

Factory Link initiates a new fuzzy logic evaluation every 10 seconds. The DCS either uses the external set points generated by fuzzy logic or the internal set points entered by the operators. The operators can switch from the 'manual mode' to the 'fuzzy logic mode' and back. The 'fuzzy logic mode' can only be activated when all the critical system variables are in a predefined safe range. The DCS automatically switches back into 'manual mode' whenever a system variable exceeds the safe range. The fallback to 'manual mode' also takes place if the communication between the DCS and Factory Link is interrupted.

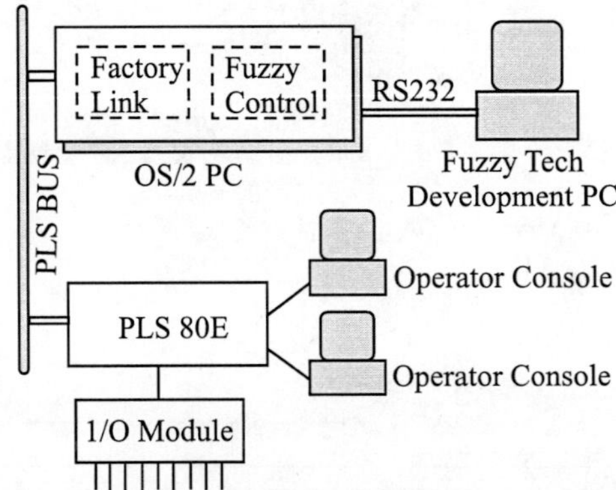

Figure 16.19: Integration of fuzzy logic into DCS

Figure 16.19 shows the integration of the fuzzy logic control into Factory Link and the Eckhardt DCS. The OS/2 PC is also connected with a serial cable to a WIN95 PC, on which the *fuzzy*TECH development system is installed. This program was used to develop the fuzzy logic control and to generate C-Code for the implementation on the OS/2 PC. The WIN95 PC is also used for On-line optimization and visualization of the fuzzy logic controller. The serial link to the OS/2 PC enables the user to modify the fuzzy system on the fly from the *fuzzy*TECH development system on the WIN95 PC while the system is running and controlling the process.

16.3.6 Setting the Fuzzy Logic Control Into Operation

The first design of the fuzzy logic control, the data preprocessing and post-processing were tested using the simulation tool VisSim. This way the concept was checked for any structural errors and an early prototype was presented to the customers. Figure 16.20 shows a test of the fuzzy logic system using simulated data as input.

After the successful completion of the simulations the fuzzy logic was tested off-line with real time data from the DCS. To do this the fuzzy logic control first was implemented on the OS/2 PC. The fuzzy controller than used real time DCS measurement values to generate set points values for the DCS. But during these off-line simulations the DCS was only using the internal manual set points and not the fuzzy logic set points. By comparing the external fuzzy logic set points with the internal operator set points deviations between manual and automatic operation could be detected and if necessary eliminated.

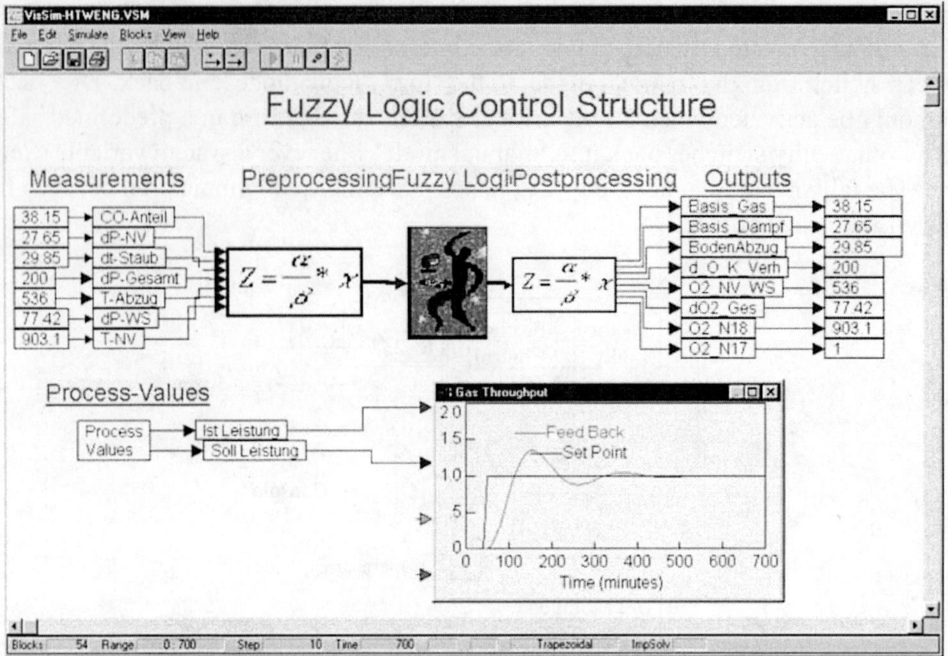

Figure 16.20: Simulation with VisSim

After the off-line testing was finished successfully the on-line testing started. For the on-line tests the DCS activated the external set points and so the closed loop performance of the fuzzy logic controller could be tested. The fuzzy logic controller was optimized while running in the closed loop mode from the *fuzzy*TECH development tool on the WIN 95 PC. To do this the OS/2 PC was connected with a serial cable to the WIN 95 PC. This way the fuzzyfication, inference and defuzzification were visualized in *fuzzy*TECH. Modifications of the rule base or term definitions were also entered in *fuzzy*TECH and than send to the fuzzy logic controller on the OS/2 PC.

16.3.7 Results

The fuzzy controller proved to be working very effectively during the first few on-line tests. After that a long series of evaluation tests started. During these tests the performance of the fuzzy controller was tested using a lot of different coal qualities and different loads (70% to 100%).

1. **Regulation of gas throughput:** The conventional control focussed on process stabilization not keeping the throughput at its set point. The following diagram shows the changes in the gas throughput when fuzzy controller is active. The fuzzy logic control clearly improves the throughput control. It compensates fluctuations in the granulation of the coal.

   Figure 16.21 Shows the fluctuations of the synthesis gas throughput with and without fuzzy logic.

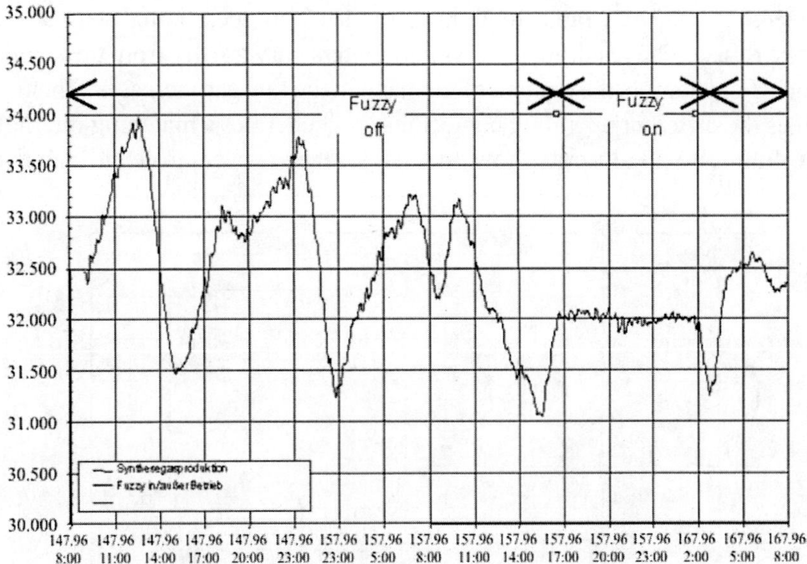

Figure 16.21: Throughput control with and without fuzzy control

2. **Change of Load:** The fuzzy controller has to regulate the gas throughput in the range 70 % to 100 % load with a maximum load gradient of 4% / min.

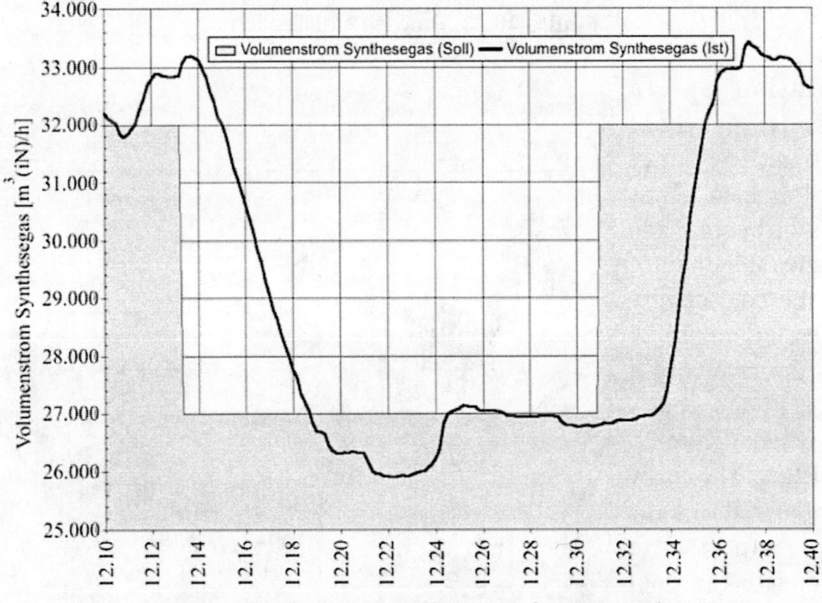

Figure 16.22: Change of load with fuzzy control

Figure 16.22 shows a load change from 94 % to 76 % and back to 94 %. The resulting load gradient was 3,2 % /min. Currently the load change behavior is being improved by using a modified pressure evaluation.

3. **Adaptation to coal add-ons:** Sometimes the HTW process is fed with a mixture of coal and plastic refuse. The resulting process parameters vary greatly from the standard operating conditions. For example the content of methane in the raw gas increases. The fuzzy controller recognizes the different operating conditions and generates a matching internal set point for methane. Figure 16.23 illustrates how this enables the fuzzy controller to stabilize the process.

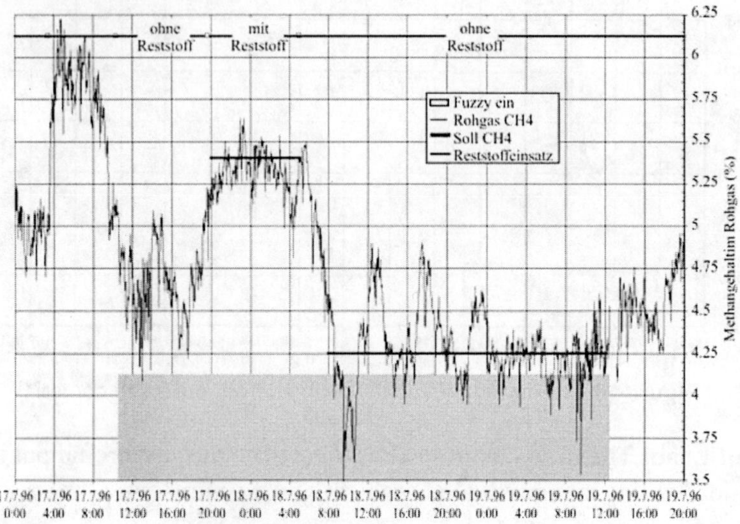

Figure 16.23: Process stabilization

4. **Adaptation to different coal qualities:** The fuzzy controller also keeps the synthesis gas throughput constant when the coal quality changes. Figure 16.24 shows the results of a change of the coal's water content from 18 % to 12 %. The fuzzy controller reduces the coal input to compensate the coal change. Later after switching back to moist coal the coal input is increased accordingly.

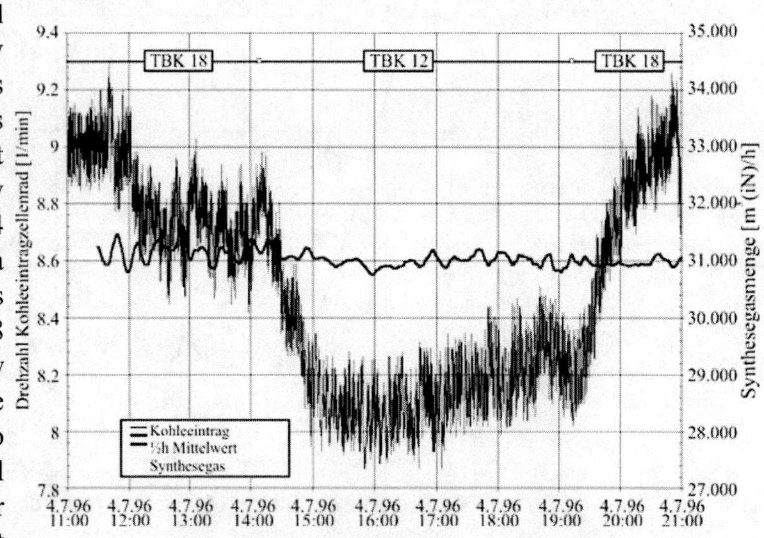

Figure 16.24: Constant Gas Throughput With Different Coal Qualities

16.3.8 Conclusion

The fuzzy controller was implemented very quickly. The transfer of the process know-how into the fuzzy controller and its realization took 15 days. So far over 1100 hours of operating time have been evaluated. In nearly all situations the performance of the fuzzy controller was much superior to the manual control. It was able to keep the process parameters in the optimum range whenever the coal quality changed. It was also able to adjust the gas throughput with the necessary change rate. The average gas throughput was kept at the set point. The operating personal has accepted the fuzzy controller as a helpful component because its transparent integration into the PLS makes it easy for them to use it.

16.4 OPTIMIZATION OF A WATER TREATMENT SYSTEM

This case study is about a fuzzy logic solution in biochemical production at the world's largest oral penicillin production facility in Austria. After extracting the penicillin from the microorganisms that generated it, a waste water treatment system further processes the remaining biomass. Fermentation sludge obtained in the course of this treatment contains microorganisms and remnants of nutrient salts. It is the basic material for a high quality fertilizer and sold as a by-product of the penicillin production. To render the fertilizer, the sludge is concentrated in a decanter and then cleared of the remaining water in a vaporizer. In order to reduce energy costs of the vaporizing process, the separation of water and dry substance in the decanter must be optimized. Before the implementation of the fuzzy logic solution, operators controlled the process manually.

16.4.1 Fuzzy Logic Replaces Manual Control

Due to its complexity, operators control the process of proportioning decanter precipitants manually. Drainage control in the decanter is very crucial. To save energy cost in the vaporizing process, the decanter must extract as much water as possible. However, to achieve optimal results requires an operating point close to the point where the decanter becomes blocked. If blockage occurs the process must be stopped and the decanter manually cleaned, thus operators run the process far away from this optimal point. Alas, this results in high operational energy costs. In this case study, a fuzzy logic system replaced the sub-optimal manual control of the operators.

Picture of a Decanter

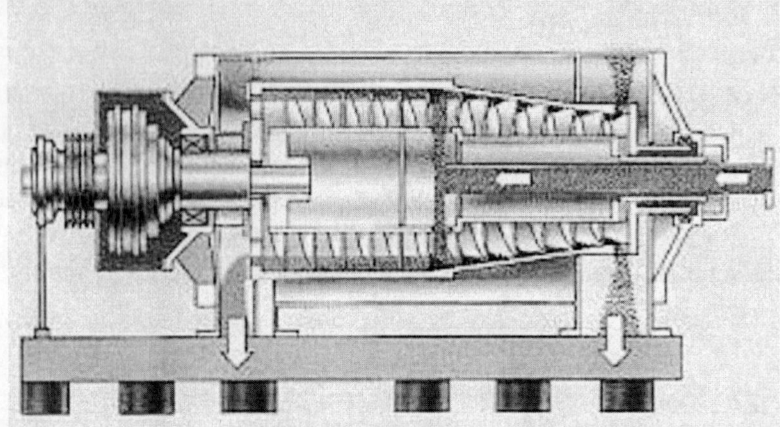

Schematic

16.4.2 Fuzzy Logic Applications in Chemical Industry

A number of conventional control techniques exist to automate continuous processes in chemical industry. To keep single variables of the process constant, PID controllers or the like are very common. Even though, most technical processes are non-linear and PID controllers are a linear model, this works fine. This is because within a continuous process, the behavior of the process can be well-approximated linearly near the operation point. In processes with simple time behavior (no dead times etc.), even P (proportional) controllers and bang-bang controllers often suffice.

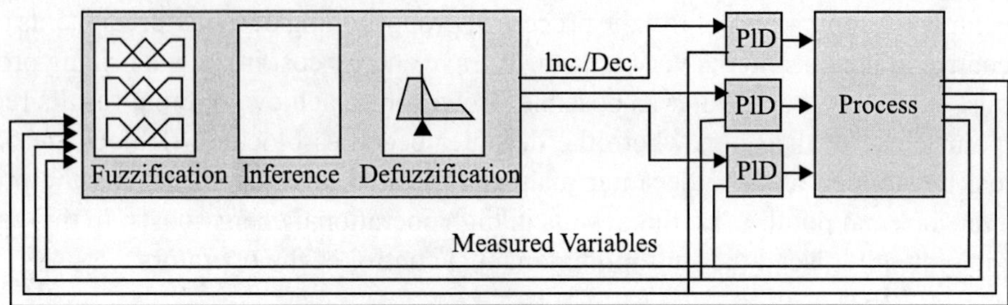

Figure 16.25: Using a fuzzy logic controller to determine the set values for underlying PID control loops

While keeping single process variables at their command values is rather simple, the determination of the optimal operation point as the combination of all set values of the variables is often a complex multi-variable problem. In most cases a solution based on a mathematical model of the process is far beyond acceptable complexity. In some cases, the derivation of a mathematical model of the plant consumes many man years of effort. Hence, in a large number of plants, operators prefer to control the operation point of the process manually.

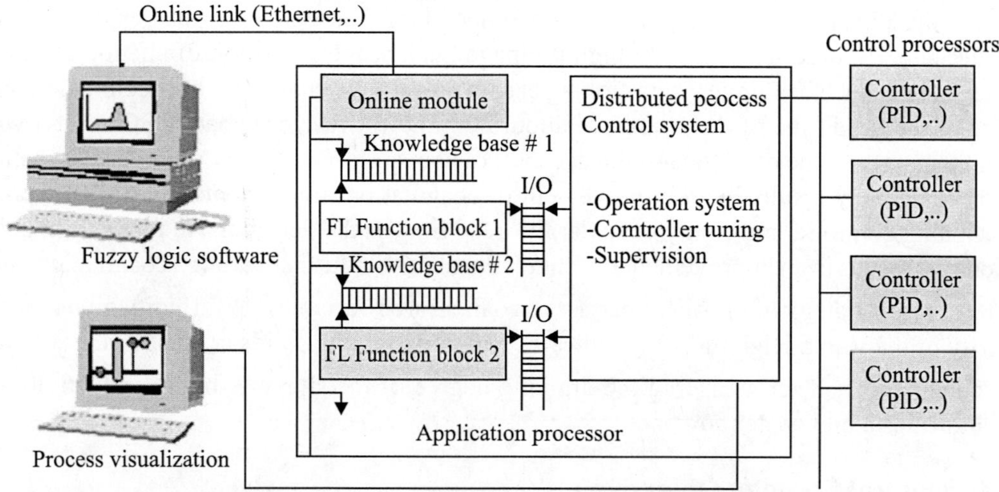

Figure 16.26: Integration of a fuzzy logic component in a distributed control system

In these cases, fuzzy logic provides an efficient technology for putting the operator control strategies into an automation solution with minimum effort. Figure 16.25 shows how to combine the fuzzy logic system with underlying PID controllers. In practical implementations, the PID controllers run on the same Distributed Process Control Systems (DCS) as the fuzzy logic controller. Figure 16.26 shows the technical integration of fuzzy logic into DCS.

16.4.3 Decanter Control

The sewage of the fermenters contains about 2% dry substance. In a first step, milk of lime neutralizes the sewage. Second, a fermenter biologically degrades the sewage. Third, bentonite is added in a large reactor. This results in a pre-coagulation of the sludge. Next, the slurry is enriched with cationic polymer before the water is separated in the decanter. The cationic polymer discharges the surface charge of the sludge particles and hence leads to coagulation.

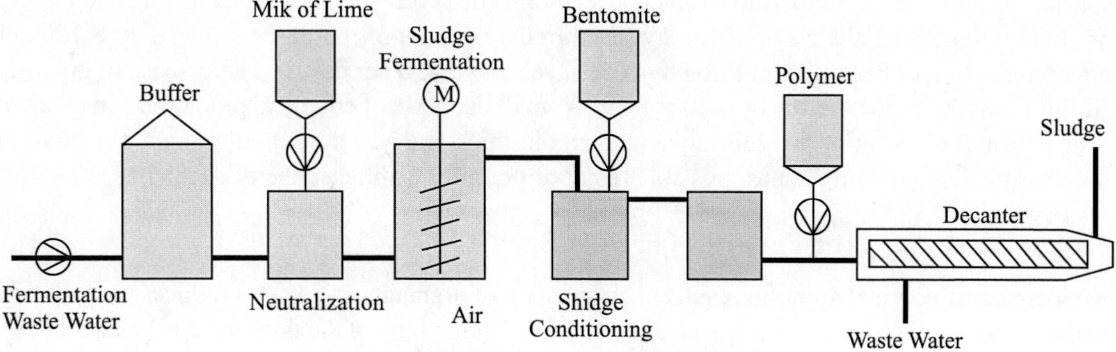

Figure 16.27: Process Diagram of Sludge Draining

Bentonite and polymer addition exert a fundamental influence on the drainage quality obtained in the decanter. In order to achieve a high drainage quality, the gradation of chemicals has to be optimized. A changed bentonite proportioning causes only a slow change in the precipitation process because of the dead time of the reactor of about 20 minutes (reactor capacity 30 m^3 at a volume flow of 90 m^3/h) and the dead time of the decanter of about 5 to 7 minutes. An increase in bentonite addition principally results in an improvement of coagulation. Implementation of just a polymer proportioning controller must only consider the dead time of the decanter. An increase in polymer addition first results in an improvement of coagulation, but with further addition coagulation impairs.

The control strategy of the operators uses two measured variables: A turbidity meter measures the purity of the water. High turbidity indicates a high remaining solids content of the water.

A conductivity meter measured the draining degree of the slurry. A high conductivity of the slurry indicates a high water content.

16.4.4 Control Strategy Objectives

The prime objective of the control strategy is to minimize the operational cost of the total drying process. In particular, the objectives are:

- Minimize amount of precipitants. The polymer used is very expensive.
- Minimize remaining water content. The vaporization of the remaining water consumes large amounts of energy.
- The biological mass content of the sewage water of the decanter should be 0.7 g/l. Exceeding a value of 1.5 g/l reduces the operability of the clarification plant and can even result in a breakdown of the next sewage stage because of its limited capacity to degrade biological mass.

The third objective has an absolute priority, above other objectives, to ensure safe operation. If the biological mass content reaches its upper limits, the control strategy reduces it regardless of economic considerations. Besides the critical biological mass content of the sewage water, only the first two objectives are relevant. A rough cost estimation shows that the most effective way to reduce the expenses of the process is to minimize the energy used in the evaporators. If the dry substance content of the thick slurry is increased by 1% (this corresponds to a change of conductivity of about 0.5 mS/cm), the costs of energy (used in the evaporator) could be reduced by $ 140 per day. A reduction of bentonite addition by 10% saves about $30 per day, and a decrease of polymer addition by 10% reduces costs by $ 40 per day. A small decrease of chemical gradation can result in a significant reduction of dry substance contents in thick slurry. Therefore the main objective of optimization is to obtain the best possible result of draining with least use of chemicals.

16.4.5 Designing The Fuzzy Logic Rule Base

An increase of polymer addition results in an increase of drainage grade. This reduces the turbidity of the sewage water (degree of suspended matter) and conductivity of the thick slurry (water content). Exceeding the optimum polymer gradation, further addition of polymer leads to a decline of the separation power in the decanter. The separation power on polymer gradation L=f(dmpolymer/dt) follows a parabolic curve (Figure 16.28). Conductivity of the slurry is used as an indicator for the separation power obtained. Hence, the control strategy is to find the minimum of conductivity by modifying the polymer addition.

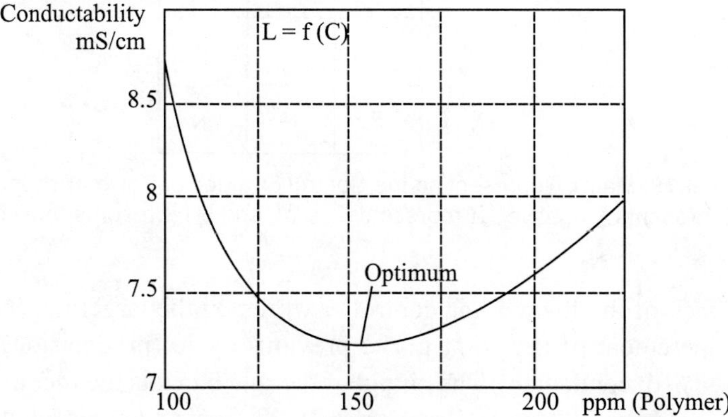

Figure 16.28: Thick slurry conductivity over polymer proportion

The problem with this is that the shape of the curve and hence also the level and position of the minimum may significantly vary over time. The only way to find out the direction to the minimum from the current operating point is to apply a change in the polymer gradation and evaluate its effects. If the draining of thick slurry improves, the conclusion is that this decision was correct and can be repeated. If the decision results in a decline, the fuzzy logic controller pursues the opposite strategy. The stronger the system's reaction to a change in polymer addition is, the greater is the current operation point's distance to the optimum.

Likewise, an increase in bentonite addition leads to an increase in separation power of the decanter until an optimum is reached. If more bentonite is added beyond this point, neither improvement nor decline occurs. Thus, an increase in bentonite addition beyond the optimal point is less critical than an increase in polymer addition. However, bentonite addition should be kept as low as possible to minimize operating cost.

16.4.6 Structure of the Decanter Controller

A change in bentonite addition has a greater long-term effect than a change in polymer addition, due to the larger dead time. As a correlation between bentonite and polymer addition exists, it is sensible to change the polymer addition independent of the separation quality in the short term and to let the bentonite controller run with delay.

Sewage quality is only restricted by an upper limit, whereas slurry quality is of great economical importance. For these reasons, polymer addition is controlled by a first set of rules in correlation to the slurry quality. An absolute point of reference does not exist because of the changing optimum of the polymer addition characteristics. Hence, no absolute input or output values are used. The controller determines its position in the objective function from a prior change in polymer addition and the resulting reaction of conductivity.

Previous Decision (pr _decision) \ Difference in Conductability (d_conductab)	N	Z	P
N	N	Z	P
Z	Z	Z	P
P	P	N	N

Figure 16.29: Matrix Representing the Control Strategy of Polymer Proportion. N Represents "negative", Z represents "zero", and P represents "positive"

The first rule block of the fuzzy logic controller works on the targeting. Input values for this rule block are the increment of set point in the previous cycle (pr_decision) and the resulting change in conductivity (d_conductab). The output of the rule block is the increment (polymer1) on the set point of the polymer PID controller. Figure 16.29 shows the control strategy of this rule block as a matrix. The entries in the matrix represent the output variable polymer1 of the rule block.

A positive change in conductivity implies a decline of the plant's operating state. If the controller in the previous cycle (pr_decision) recommended "negative" (reduce polymer addition) and conductivity increased as a reaction to this, the controller must now operate in the opposite direction and increase polymer addition. If the controller recommended "positive", polymer addition must be reduced. Conductivity may increase although the controller has not given a recommendation in the previous cycle (pr_decision = 0). In this case, the optimum moved by external influence and action must be taken.

As the fuzzy logic controller does not know in which direction the optimum moved, it has to choose one direction. For this, it increases polymer addition to test the reaction of the process. It tests with a polymer increase rather then a decrease, as the curve in the figure rises more gently into the positive direction, and an increased use of polymer is cheaper than the raised energy costs that stem from the evaporation process.

If the test result is favorable, this will be confirmed in the next cycle. If it is negative, the controller will simply change the signs of the output in the subsequent cycle (see matrix in Figure 16.29). This only represents the basic principle of the rule block. The final implementation of the rule block contains additional rules that more finely differentiate the input value. As such, the fuzzy logic controller can differentiate between several cases and thus adapt the size of gradation change to the reaction of the process that is, to the proximity to the optimum.

The turbidity of the sewage water forms a restriction that in some cases forbids the reduction of the precipitant addition. Therefore, a second rule block evaluates the turbidity of the sewage water (turbidity) and the output of the first rule block (polymer1) to determine the final polymer addition increment (polymer2). Figure 16.30 shows the structure of the fuzzy logic system. As long as turbidity units are below 2500 TE/F, the second rule block transfers the first block's recommendation to the output. Starting at about 3000 TE/F, all recommendations of the first rule block are transferred, except recommendations to reduce polymer addition. If about 3500 TE/F are exceeded, the second rule block always recommends an increase of flocculent addition. Only the rate of increase of flocculent addition changes, depending on the recommendation of the first rule block.

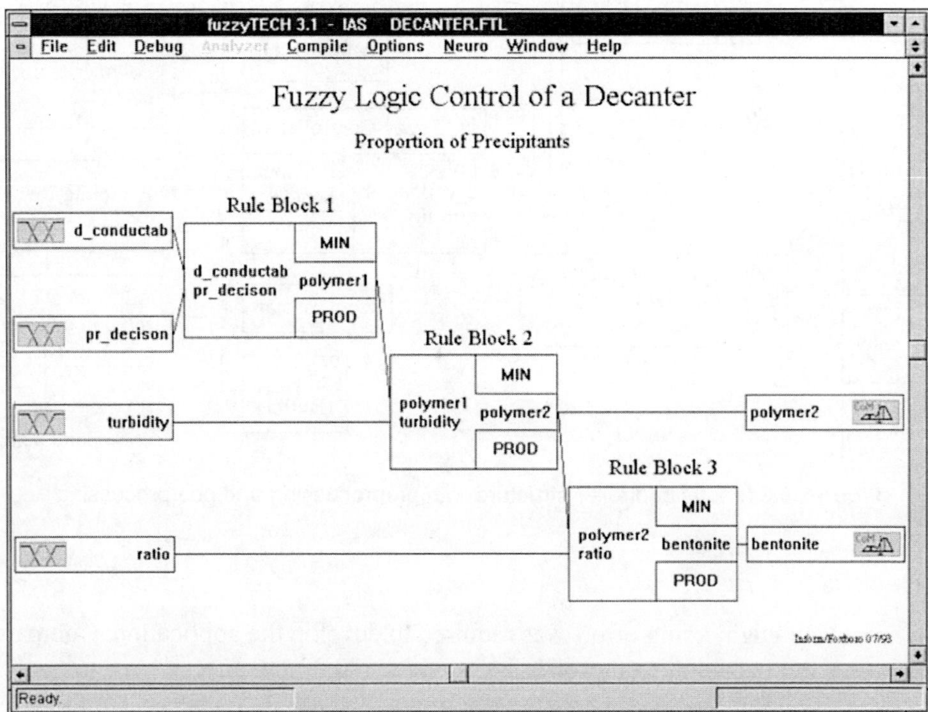

Figure 16.30: Structure of the Fuzzy Logic Controller

To determine the betonite addition, a third rule block uses the output of the second rule block and a fourth input variable, called ration. The ratio is calculated outside the fuzzy logic system.

16.4.7 Integrating the Fuzzy Logic Controller in the System

Figure 16.31 shows the total structure of the entire control system. In addition to the fuzzy logic system, function blocks (CALC, RATIO) provide preprocessing of the sensor signals, ramp generation, and ratio control. The entire control system is implemented using a standard distributed process control system (DCS).

The most important input variable of the controller is the change in the conductivity of the slurry. Alas, the conductivity measurement circuitry is subject to strong signal noise. Hence, a low pass filter is used that determines the average change in conductivity during the last ten minutes at one minute intervals. This forms the input variable d_conductab of the fuzzy logic system. Turbidity, the fuzzy system's second input, uses a similar filter.

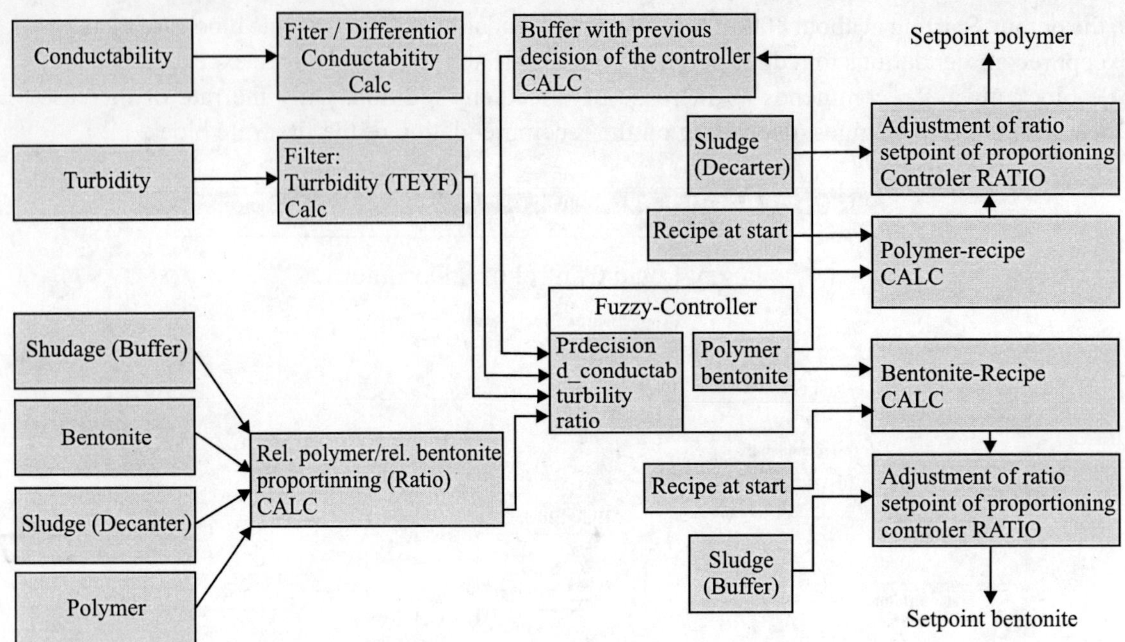

Figure 16.31: Total controller structure with preprocessing and postprocessing

16.4.8 Results

About two months of engineering effort was required to develop the application. Compared to the manual operation, the fuzzy logic controller saves about $70,000 in energy costs per year.

16.5 TRUCK SPEED LIMITER CONTROL BY FUZZY LOGIC

In Europe, commercial trucks in compliance with European legislation, which have a maximum load of more than 12 tons, are required to be equipped with a speed limiter that limits their maximum speed to 53.3 mph (86 km/h). This case study focuses on the electro-pneumatic design of such a speed limiter. In this design, a pneumatic cylinder mechanically limits the throttle opening angle of the fuel pump arm. The cylinder pressure is controlled by a pulse proportional electromechanical valve. This valve is connected to an electronic control unit that uses a microcontroller to drive the valve according to the actual speed of the truck. The design of an algorithm for this control problem proved to be difficult, since the same speed limiter device is used in a variety of different trucks which exhibit different behaviors. In addition to this, the dynamic behavior of a truck differs very much depending on whether it is fully loaded or empty. Conventional control algorithms, such as PID controls, assume a linear model of the process under control and can hence not be used for a solution. A solution using a mathematical model of the truck is first laborious to build and second of prohibitive computational effort for a low-cost 8-bit microcontroller. Hence, fuzzy logic control was used to design the control algorithm.

16.5.1 Speed Limiter Requirements and Conventional Control

Figure 16.32 exemplifies the function of a truck speed limiter. When the truck approaches the maximum velocity, the pneumatic valve reduces the throttle opening angle of the fuel pump arm so that the maximum velocity vs is not surpassed. If the driver pushes down the accelerator pedal even more, the speed limiter has to ensure a smooth ride at the maximum velocity.

However, due to the dead time and non-linearities involved with this control action, an actual overshoot and hunting occurs when using a proportional or on-off controller. Adding a differential and integral part yields a PID controller model. A PID controller generates the command value as a linear combination of the error (P), the derivative of the error with respect to time (D) and the integral of the error with respect to time (I). To tune a PID controller, the combined weights of these three (3) components must be chosen, so that they approximate the nonlinear behavior of the process under control at its operating point. While this works with most processes that are at only one operating point, it fails when the operating point moves. With a truck speed limiter, the operating point moves because of the different load situations, such as driving uphill or downhill, as well as driving empty or with a full load. Furthermore, the characteristic of the pneumatic valve and the truck fuel injection are highly non-linear and vary from one truck to another.

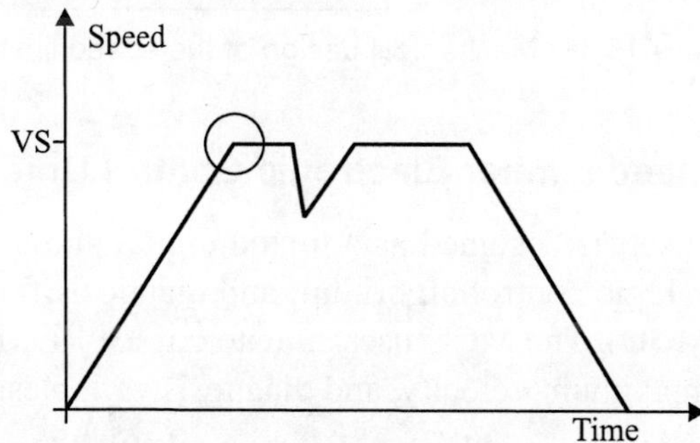

Figure 16.32: The function of as speed Limiter is to stop the truck from driving faster than the maximum allowed speed (vs)

Hence, if a PID control algorithm is used in a truck speed limiter, it can only be tuned well for one operation point and one type of truck. For other operation points and different truck types, overshoot and hunting occurs. The European legislation hence allows operation of the speed limiter within a certain tolerance. Figure 16.33 shows an example of this. When reaching the maximum speed, an initial overshoot of 5 km/h is tolerated. After this, the speed must be kept constant within an interval of ± 1.5 km/h. Even though this overshoot and hunting is tolerated by the European legislation, it causes annoying speed fluctuations when driving.

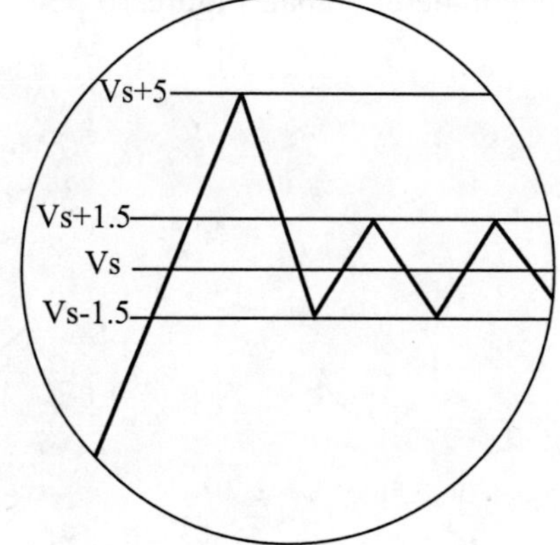

Figure 16.33: Tolerances for the operation of the speed limiter

16.5.2 Mechanical Design of the Speed Limiter

Figure 16.34 sketches the outline of the mechanical design of the speed limiter. An electronic control unit (ECU) compares the digital pulse signal from the speedometer with the maximum speed value pre-set in the device. Based on this, it computes the command value for the pulse proportional valve (PPV) that controls the air pressure in the cylinder. The air stems from the vehicle's pressured air system. In a non-linear but proportional ratio, the cylinder shortens the arm linking the accelerator pedal to the fuel pump so that the fuel pump is throttled.

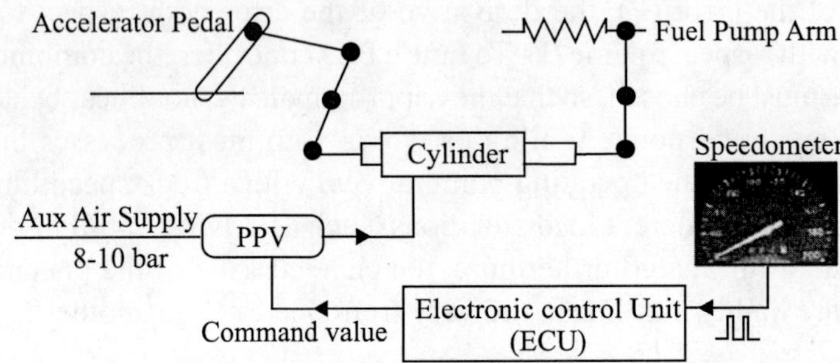

Figure 16.34: Mechanical design of the speed limiter

16.5.3 Design of the Speed Limiter Electronic Control Unit

The electronic control unit itself is designed as a mixed digital and analog circuit. Speedometer signal processing, the fuzzy logic control algorithm, and diagnosis functions are computed by a PIC 8-bit microcontroller (MCU). The MCU uses an external E^2PROM to store parameters of the truck and speedometer, the maximum velocity, and diagnosis variables.

The MCU also generates a pulse-width modulated signal (PWM) that is amplified by a power stage to drive the PPV. The analog part is responsible for the preprocessing and filtering of the speedometer signal. Figure 16.35 shows a photo of the unit.

Figure 16.35: The electronic control unit of the speed limiter using a pic 8-bit microcontroller

16.5.4 The Fuzzy Logic Controller

Fuzzy logic is an innovative technology to design solutions for multi-parameter and non-linear control problems. It uses human experience and experimental results rather than a mathematical model for the definition of a control strategy. As a result, it often delivers solutions faster than conventional control design techniques. In addition, fuzzy logic implementations on microcontrollers are very code space and execution speed efficient.

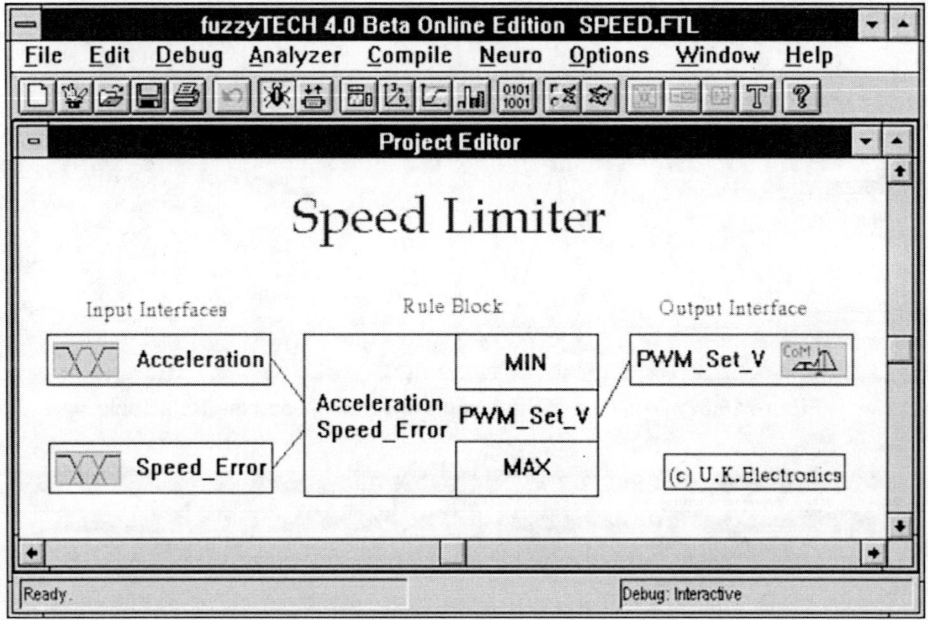

Figure 16.36: Structure of the fuzzy logic speed limiter controller

The entire fuzzy logic algorithm was developed, tested and optimized using the software tool *fuzzy*TECH®. This integrated design environment features automatic assembly code generation on all PIC microcontroller families. Figures 16.36 – 16.38 all show screen shots of the fuzzy logic speed limiter design in various editors and analyzers of *fuzzy*TECH. Figure 16.36 displays the Project Editor featuring the structure of the fuzzy logic system. On the left side, two input interfaces fuzzify the two input variables "Acceleration" and "Speed_Error". The rule block in the middle contains all the fuzzy logic rules that represent the control strategy of the system. On the right side, the output variable "PMV_Set_Value" is defuzzified in an output interface.

Figure 16.37 shows more details of the fuzzy logic system. Each linguistic variable is displayed in a variable editor window and the rules are displayed in the Spreadsheet Rule Editor window. Each linguistic variable contains five (5) terms and membership functions. They are connected by a total of 12 fuzzy logic rules. All membership functions are of Standard types. As a defuzzification method, the Center-of-Maximum (CoM) method is used.

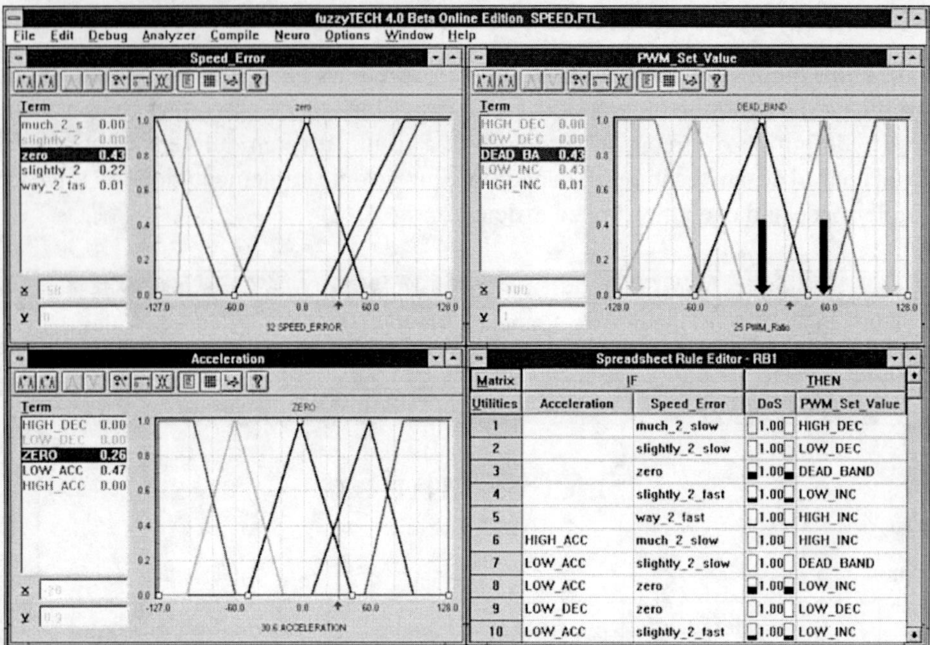

Figure 16.37: Definition of the Linguistic Variables and the Rule Table

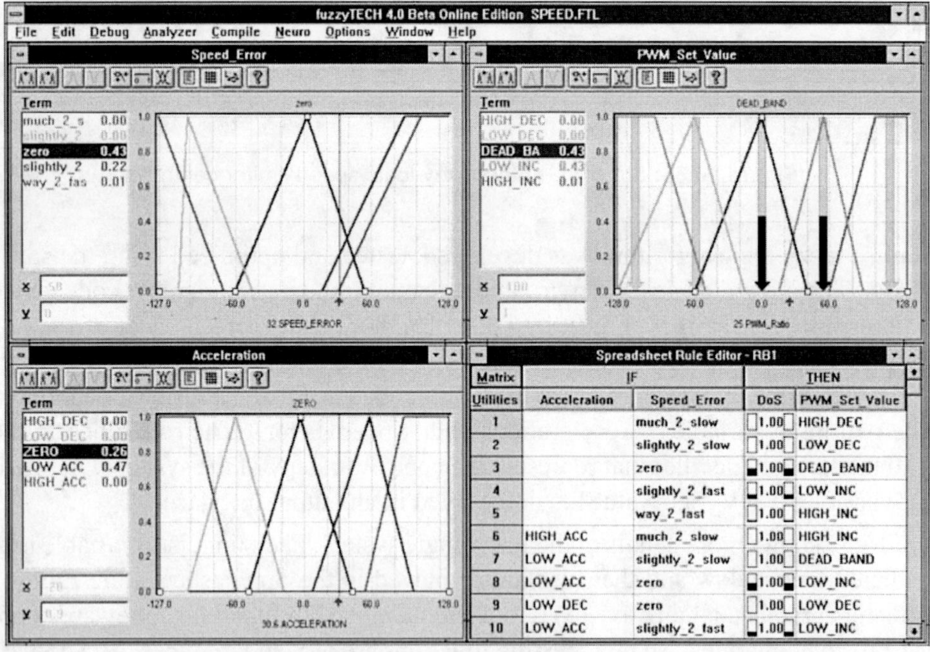

Figure 16.38: Debugging of the fuzzy logic system - transfer characteristics of the fuzzy logic controller under testing

All rules in the fuzzy logic system now let the designer define the best reaction (output variable value) for a given situation. The situation is described by the combination of the input variables. After such a control strategy has been defined by the designer, a number of different analyzer tools can be used to verify the system's performance. Figure 16.38 shows the 3D Plot as an example. In the 3D Plot, the two horizontal axes show the two input variables "Acceleration" and "Speed_Error". The vertical axis plots the output variable, "PWM_Set_Value", the set value for the PWM unit on the microcontroller. Rule 1, as shown in Figure 16.37, indicates:

IF Speed_Error = much_2_slow THEN PWM_Set_Value = HIGH_DEC

This rule represents the engineering knowledge that if the truck is way under the speed limit, no pressure should be applied to the cylinder. The membership function of the term "much_2_slow" is shown also in the respective variable editor in Figure 16.37. The 3D Plot in Figure 16.38 plots the transfer characteristic as a result of this. In the front part of the curve, the value of the output variable is very low (color of surface light). As you proceed to the left along the Acceleration axis, the output variable value gets higher. This is a result of Rule 6 that defines:

IF Acceleration = HIGH_ACC AND Speed_Error = much_2_slow THEN PWM_Set_Value = HIGH_INC

This rule represents the engineering knowledge that if in the same general case of the truck being way slower than the limit, the special case of a high acceleration should result in medium pressure on the cylinder. This ensures that the cylinder is already filled with some pressure if the truck reaches the limit quickly. If this rule would not have been formulated, a speed overshoot would occur as sketched in Figure 16.33.

16.5.5 Optimization and Implementation

A fair deal of optimization was accomplished off-line on the PC since *fuzzy*TECH can simulate the fuzzy logic system without the target hardware. However, final optimization and verification of the system was conducted on real trucks.

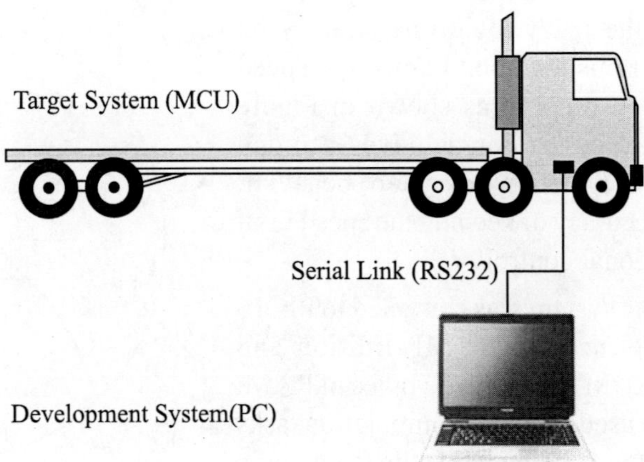

Figure 16.39: Cross optimization of the running fuzzy logic controller by a serial link

Figure 16.39 shows the test and optimization setup. The target system, the MCU of the electronic control unit, is mounted in the truck and connected to the development PC (notebook in the truck's cabin) by a serial cable. Such serial connection allows for modification of the running fuzzy logic controller "on-the-fly". This development technique is very efficient because it allows for the developer to analyze how a certain behavior of the fuzzy logic controller is caused by the membership function definition and the rules. Also, since modifications can be done in real time, the effects can be "felt" on the truck instantly.

One way to enable "on-the-fly" debugging is to link the *fuzzy*TECH RTRCD Module (real-time remote cross debugger) to the fuzzy logic controller that runs on the MCU and connect it to a serial driver. The RTRCD Module consumes about ½ Kbytes of ROM, a few Bytes of RAM, and some computing resources to serve the serial communication on the MCU.

Since the PIC16 MCU used in this application cannot provide such resources, the serial debug mode of *fuzzy*TECH was used rather than the RTRCD Module. In serial debug mode, the values of the input variables are sent from the MCU to *fuzzy*TECH running on the development PC via the serial cable and the results are sent back. *fuzzy*TECH shows the entire fuzzy logic computation in its editor and analyzer windows, and allows for "on-the-fly" modifications. To support serial communication, a piggyback board containing a MAX232 driver IC was mounted on the speed limiter board shown in Figure 16.35.

The advantage of using the serial debug mode of *fuzzy*TECH over the RTRCD Module is that code size and computation effort that previously was required for the fuzzy logic computation on the MCU are now saved and can thus be used for the serial communication. The disadvantage of the serial debug mode of *fuzzy*TECH is that it computes the systems' results on the PC where real-time response cannot be guaranteed. Also, any crash of MS-Windows, the PC, or the serial communication will halt computation in serial debug mode. The RTRCD Module, in contrast, is not affected by this.

16.5.6 Results

After optimization of the fuzzy logic rule strategy on different trucks and various load conditions, the speed limiter showed a response curve as shown in Figure 16.40. The fuzzy logic controller achieves a much smoother response, does not show overshoot behavior, and provides a higher accuracy of keeping the speed limit compared to a conventional controller.

The final fuzzy logic system was compiled to PIC16 assembly code by the *fuzzy*TECH MP-Edition and required 417 words of ROM space and 32 bytes of RAM. The RAM space can be used for other computation tasks such as preprocessing and filtering while the fuzzy logic system is not running. The entire fuzzy logic system needs less than 2 milliseconds to compute on the PIC16 MCU.

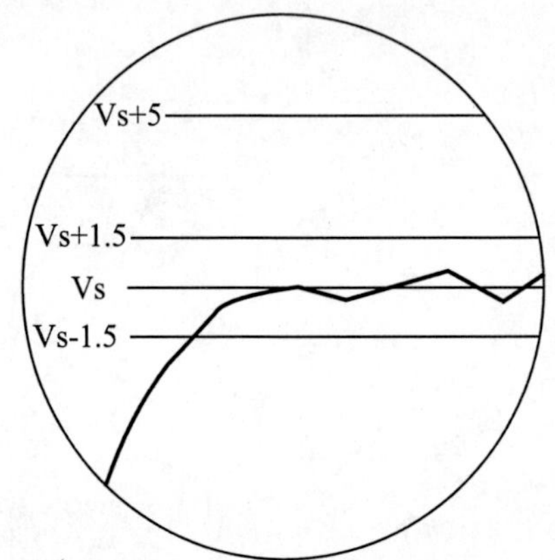

Figure 16.40: Speed limiter performance of the fuzzy logic controller

16.6 FUZZY LOGIC AND NEUROFUZZY IN APPLIANCES

Fuzzy Logic is an innovative technology that enables the implementation of 'intelligent' functions in embedded systems. One of its advantages is that even complicated functions and adaptive control loops can be implemented with the limited resources of low-cost 8 bit microcontrollers. Using three case studies in ABS, engine control, and automatic gearbox control, we will show how superior performance is achieved using fuzzy logic and neural-fuzzy design techniques. We will discuss development methodologies, tools used, and code speed/size requirements of three case studies.

The first case study shows how an existing product is enhanced with new, intelligent functions. In home air conditioners, the enhancement of the thermostat by fuzzy logic control techniques allows for a better adaptation to the requirements of the user. This results in a higher comfort level. Also, detection of low load situations yields energy savings.

The second case study covers the replacement of sensors with fuzzy logic state estimators. In the example of a central heating system control, a 35 outdoor temperature sensor and its installation were replaced. Comparisons show that the fuzzy logic solution better adapts to high and low heat demand periods, thus yielding higher comfort and energy savings at the same time. The presented system is now in production in Germany (350,000 units per year).

The third case study focuses on the automated generation of fuzzy logic systems or parts thereof. For laundry load detection in washing machines, neural-fuzzy technologies are employed that set up a fuzzy logic system using experimental data. The results of washing experiments, evaluated by experts, form this data base. The introduction of the resulting fuzzy logic laundry load detector saves an average of 20% on water and energy. The presented system is now in production in Germany (400,000 units per year).

The following discussion assumes the reader is familiar with basic fuzzy logic design principles.

16.6.1 Energy Saving AC Control

One of the major consumers of the total of all energy produced in the world is the heating and cooling of homes and office buildings. Hence, increasing efficiency of these systems has a great effect on energy savings. These savings can be realized either by constructional improvements, such as better insulation, more efficient heating/cooling systems or by using more intelligent control strategies for the operation of these devices. This case study focuses on the application of fuzzy logic control techniques for air conditioning systems.

Fuzzy logic allows for the formulation of a technical control strategy using elements of everyday language. In this application, fuzzy logic was used to design a control strategy that adapts to the individual user needs, thereby achieving both a higher comfort level and reduced energy consumption at the same time. Using a fuzzy logic software development system, the entire system, containing both conventional code for signal preprocessing and the fuzzy logic system, can be implemented on industry standard 8-bit microcontrollers. Using fuzzy logic on such a low-cost platform enables this solution to be implemented in most air conditioning systems.

1. Fuzzy Logic in AC Control

Quite a few air conditioning systems already use fuzzy logic control. In 1990, Mitsubishi introduced their first line of fuzzy logic controlled home air conditioners. Also, industrial air conditioning systems in Japan have been using fuzzy logic since 1990. Four years later, most Korean, Taiwanese, and European AC controllers also use fuzzy logic as a standard control technique.There are different incentives to use fuzzy logic:

- Industrial AC systems use fuzzy logic to minimize energy consumption. The implementation of complex control strategies optimizes that the set values for the heater, cooler, and humidifier shall be set in a certain load state.
- Car AC systems use fuzzy logic to estimate the temperatures at the head of the driver from multiple indirect sensors.
- Home AC systems are much simpler. They do not contain a humidifier and can only either cool or heat at one time. They use fuzzy logic for robust temperature control.

2. Air Condition Control Thermostats

The application discussed in this case study falls more into the second category. Each AC system has a thermostat that measures the room temperature and compares it with the set temperature that is set on a dial. Figure 16.41 shows the principle of such a thermostat.

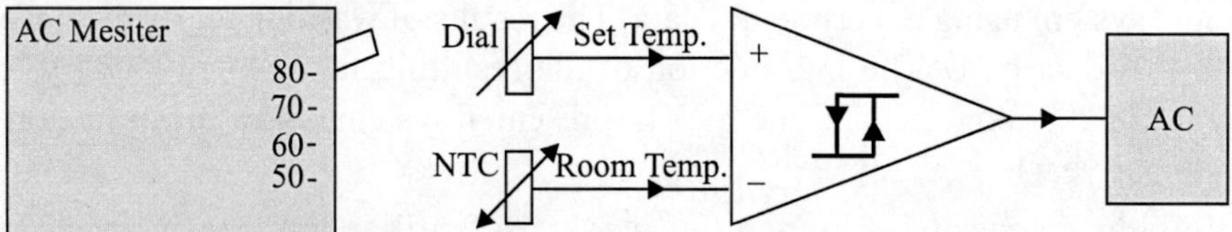

Figure 16.41: A conventional thermostat compares room temperature with the set temperature to turn ac on and off

The thermostat compares the set temperature that is selected on the dial by the user with the actual room temperature. To minimize the number of starts for the AC, a hysterisis is used. Both mechanical and electronic thermostats are used for this. Figure 16.41 shows the principle of an electronic analog AC controller.

3. Intelligent Fuzzy Logic Thermostat

This method works well to maintain a certain temperature level in a room. However, the actual room temperature does not always correspond to the subjective temperature feeling of the people in the room. A certain comfort level is reached with different room temperatures, depending on a number of conditions:

1. During the day, the temperature may be higher than during the night.
2. The same room temperature is perceived warmer if the sun shines.

Empirical analysis on how people adjust the temperature dial on their ACs has shown even more factors:

1. Someone who turns down the set temperature wants a large cooling effect. Due to this, most people tend to put the temperature dial lower than necessary. Usually, people forget to turn the temperature dial up again. Before this is corrected, the increased cooling wastes energy.
2. Someone who turns down the AC just a little bit is not interested in a quick response but rather in an accurate temperature. Reacting too much to this can cause an overshoot in the room temperature.
3. If someone changes the room temperature very often, the control should be sensible.
4. If room temperature varies strongly, the room is often used. Hence, control should be sensible.

The objective in this case study is to design an "intelligent" thermostat that "understands" both different environment conditions and the current needs of the user. For this, knowledge as contained in 16.41.-16.42. and A)-D) must be implemented in the thermostat. Since this kind of knowledge is hard to model mathematically, as well as hard to code in a conventional algorithm, fuzzy logic has been used for implementation.

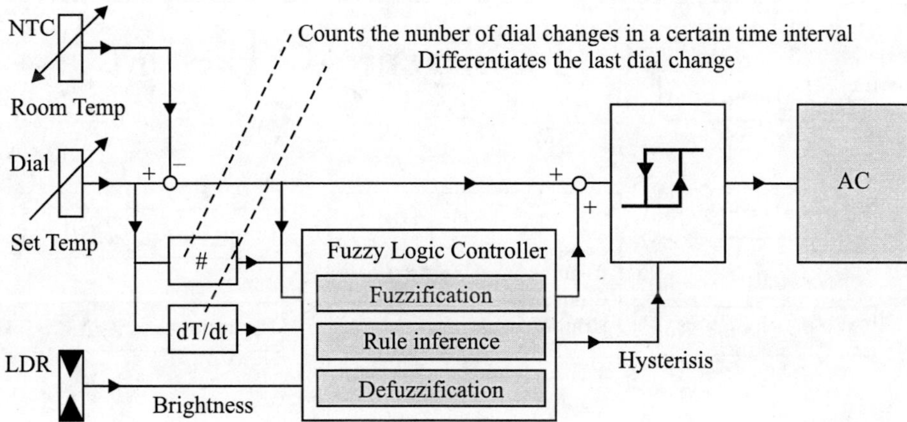

Figure 16.42: Fuzzy thermostat

Figure 16.42 shows the structure of the "intelligent" thermostat. To measure the brightness in the room, a LDR photo sensor is added. The fuzzy logic system corrects the signal before the threshold unit and sets its hysterisis. For that, the fuzzy logic system uses four input variables:

1. Difference between set and room temperature (Temp_Error)

   When the difference between set temperature and room temperature is very large, the fuzzy logic system increases the signal so the desired temperature is reached faster (Rule 5 and 6). At the same time, the hysteresis is set to large, so minor disturbances do not cause unnecessary on/off switches.

2. Time differentiated set temperature (dTemp_by_dt)

   The set temperature signal is differentiated with a time constant of 30 minutes. The fuzzy logic system uses this signal to understand when the user wants the AC to cool down a room quick (Rule 3). Also, the hysterisis is set large, so disturbances do not interrupt the cooling process. As this signal is a differentiated signal, it disappears if the user does not modify the dial.

3. Number of set temperature changes (Changes)

   This input signal is used to identify a user who tries to set the room temperature very precisely (Rule 4). To satisfy such a user, the hysterisis is set to small. This variable counts each time the user moves the dial. Every 6 hours, this variable is counted down until 0 is reached.

4. Brightness in the room (Brightness)

   If direct sunlight hits the room, the set temperature is automatically reduced (Rule 2). During the day or when lights are on in the room, the set temperature is slightly increased (Rule 1) and the hysterisis is set to small.

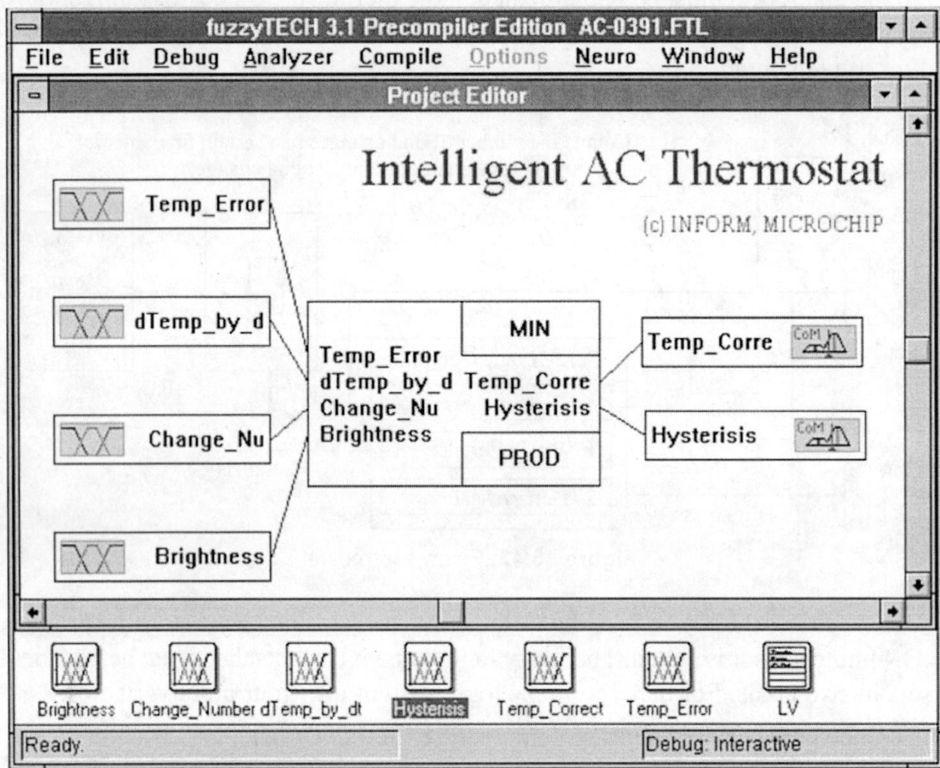

Figure 16.43: Structure of the fuzzy logic system in the thermostat

4. Implementation of a Fuzzy Logic Control Strategy

Figure 16.43 shows the structure of the fuzzy logic system as designed with the *fuzzy*TECH development system. All input variables have three (3) terms with standard membership functions. The output variable "Correction" has five (5) terms and uses Center-of-Maximum defuzzification. The output variable "Hysterisis" has three (3) terms and uses also Center-of-Maximum defuzzification.

Matrix	IF				THEN		THEN	
Utilities	Temp_Error	dTemp_dt	Changes	Brightness	DoS	Correction	DoS	Hysterisis
1				medium	1.00	warmer	1.00	small
2				high	1.00	cooler		
3		negative			1.00	much_cool	1.00	large
4			frequent				1.00	small
5	too_cold				1.00	warmer	1.00	large
6	too_warm				1.00	cooler	1.00	large
7	OK	zero			1.00	zero	1.00	small
8								

Figure 16.44: The fuzzy logic rules represent the knowledge that the thermostat uses to correct the set temperature and the hysterisis

Figure 16.44 shows part of the rule base that defines the strategy of the system. This spread sheet representation is appropriate for small rule bases. Each row represents a rule. The left part of the screen under the [IF] button shows all input variables of the rule block; the right part under the [THEN] button shows all output variables. The column [DoS] that is displayed for each output variable allows for the association of a weight to this conclusion. This enables fine tuning of the fuzzy logic system during optimization.

5. Simulation Results and Comparison

The fuzzy logic system has been tested using data that has been recorded in various rooms under various conditions. This test data has been preprocessed using the spreadsheet software MS-Excel. To test the performance of the fuzzy logic solution, *fuzzy*TECH's Excel link has been used. It allows for MS-Excel cells be linked to fuzzy logic input and output variables. As this link is dynamic, the fuzzy logic system can be monitored and modified using the *fuzzy*TECH analyzers and editors while browsing through the data sets.

As a result, the room temperature as controlled by the fuzzy logic thermostat, results in an increased comfort level. In addition, the fuzzy logic thermostat detected situations where less cooling effort suffices. The simulation revealed that in an average residential house, the average energy consumption was reduced by 3.5%. At the same time, the comfort level was increased, since, depending on the situation, the fuzzy logic thermostat reduced the room temperature 5°F more than the conventional thermostat.

Picture of a Home Air Conditioner

The fuzzy logic thermostat does not require any modification of the AC itself. Hence, by replacing existing temperature controllers, even old ACs can be upgraded. By also controlling the ventilation, an even more improved performance could be reached.

16.6.2 Adaptive Heating System Control

To maximize both the economics and comfort of a private home heating system, fuzzy-logic control has been used by a German company in a new generation of furnace controllers. The fuzzy-logic controller ensures optimal adaptation to changing customer heating demands while using one sensor less than the former generation. Both the fuzzy-logic controller and the conventional control system were implemented on a standard 8-bit microcontroller. Design, optimization and implementation of the fuzzy controller were supported by the software development system *fuzzy*TECH.

1. European Heating Systems

Most European houses have a centralized heating system that uses a furnace for diesel-type fuel to heat the water supply (boiler). From the boiler, the hot water is distributed by a pipe system to individual radiators in the rooms of the house. To meet the different needs of customer heating habits, the temperature of the furnace-heated water must constantly be adjusted in relation to the outdoor temperature (heat characteristic). To measure the outdoor temperature, a sensor is installed on the outside of the house.

Viessmann Home Heating System

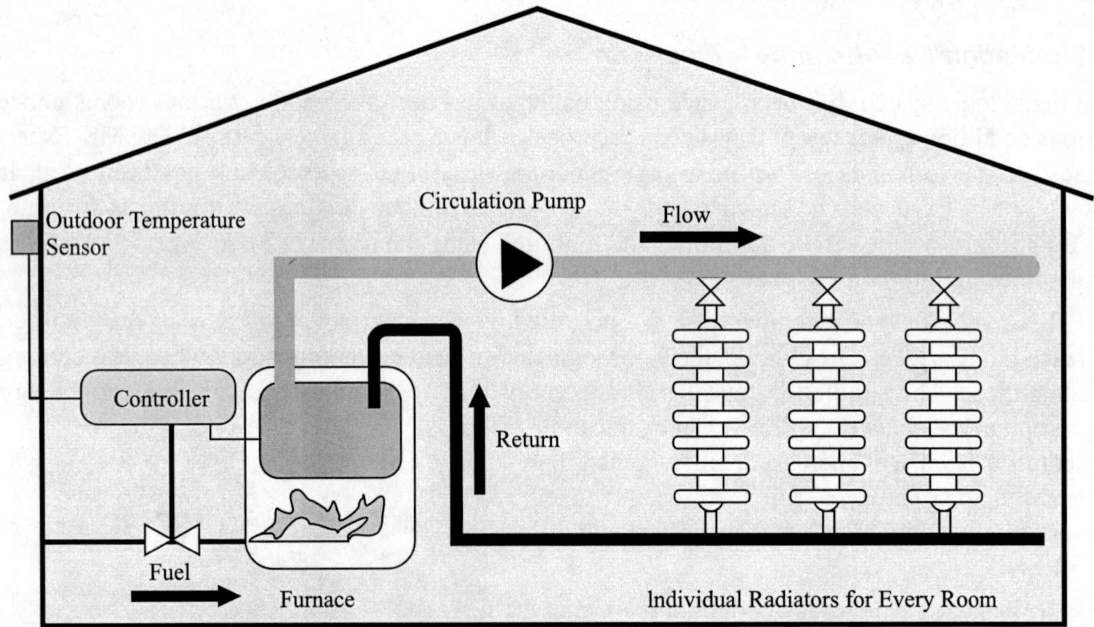

Figure 16.45: Schematic of a Centralized Heating System

The basic structure of a controller for this system is shown in Figure 16.46. The controller itself realizes an on-off characteristic. If the water temperature in the furnace drops to 2 Kelvin below the set temperature, the fuel valve opens and the ignition system starts the burning process. When the water temperature in the boiler itself rises to 2 Kelvin above the set temperature, the fuel valve closes. This on-off control strategy involving hysterisis minimizes the number of starts while assuring that the boiler temperature remains within the desired tolerance.

Although the structure of this control loop is quite simple, the task of determining the appropriate set boiler temperature is not. The maximum heat dissipation of the room radiators depends on the temperature of the incoming water (approximately the boiler temperature). For that, the set point for the water temperature in the boiler must never be set so low that it cannot warm the house when necessary. On the other hand, an excessively high setting of the boiler temperature would result in energy loss in both the furnace and the piping system. Thus the set boiler temperature needs to be carefully set to ensure both user comfort and energy efficiency.

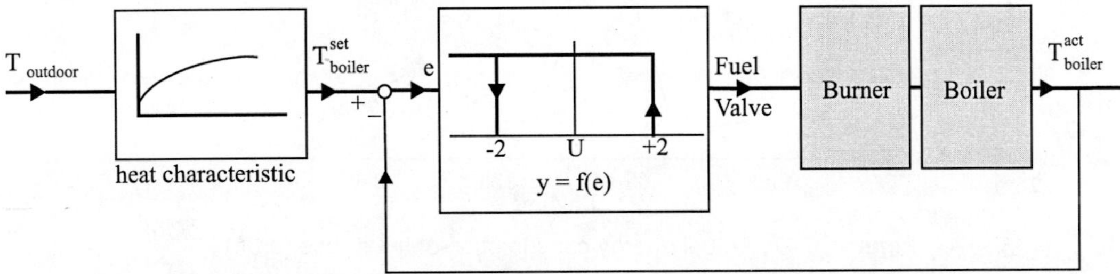

Figure 16.46: Block schematic of the conventional furnace controller

In the 1950's, the German Electrical Engineering Society (VDE) defined a procedure for this. The assumption is that the maximum amount of heat required by the house depends on the outdoor temperature ($T_{outdoor}$). A parametric function $T^{set}_{boiler} = f(T_{outdoor})$ adjusts the set boiler temperature in relation to the outside temperature. This function is also called the "heat characteristic". Parameters are the insulation coefficient of the house and a so-called "comfort parameter". The physical model of this is one in which the maximum amount of available heat equals the amount of heat disposed by the house plus some excess energy to compensate occasional door and window opening.

The assumption that the amount of energy a heating system has to deliver is largely outdoor-temperature dependent, was true back in those days when most houses only had poor thermal insulation. Today, this is obsolete. Due to rising energy costs and environmental concerns, modern houses are built with improved insulation. Therefore, to achieve high efficiency, the outdoor temperature is not the only parameter which reflects the required energy amount. Other factors, such as ventilation, door/window openings and personal lifestyle, have to be considered as well.

2. The Fuzzy Controller

Two approaches for determining the appropriate set boiler temperature for a well-insulated house exist:

- Extensive use of sensors (that is temperature sensors in every room) and use of a mathematical model.

- Definition of engineering heuristics to determine the set boiler temperature based on a knowledge-based evaluation of existing sensor data.

Since the use of extensive sensors is expensive and the construction of a comprising mathematical model is of overwhelming complexity, the second approach has been chosen for realizing the new generation of heating system controllers.

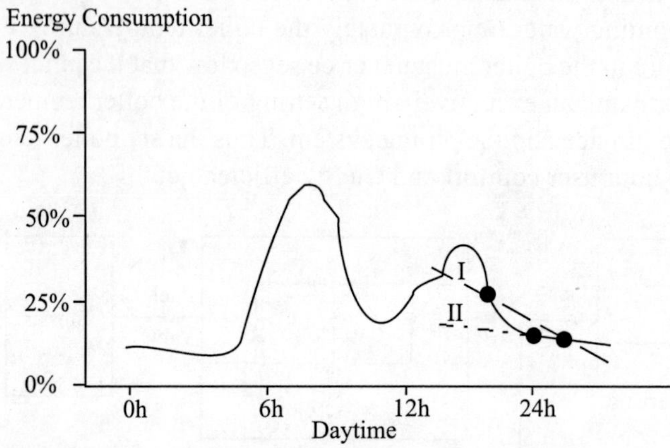

Figure 16.47: Actual energy consumption of the house (draft)

The most important criterion about individual customer heat demand patterns comes from the actual energy consumption curve of the house, which is measured by the on/off-ratio of the burner. An example of such a curve is given in Figure 16.47. From this curve, four descriptive parameters are derived:

- Current energy consumption, indicating current load. <
- Medium term tendency (I), indicating heating-up and heating-down phases.
- Short term tendency (II), indicating disturbances like door/window openings.
- Yesterday average energy consumption, indicating the general situation and house heating level.

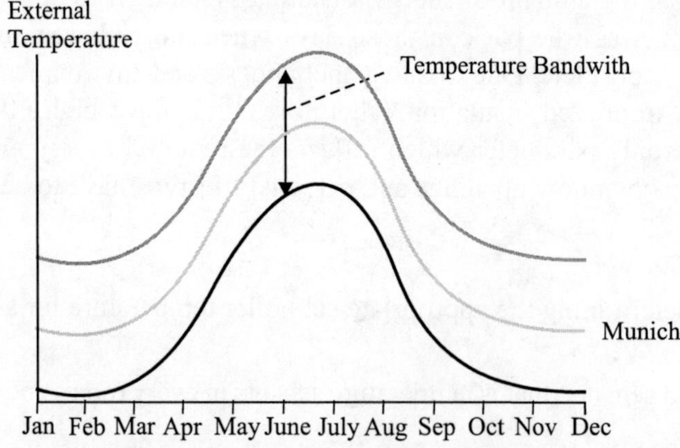

Figure 16.48: Average outside temperatures in munich

These parameters were used to heuristically form rules for the determination of the appropriate set boiler temperature. To allow for the formulation of plausibility rules (such as "temperatures below thirty degrees Fahrenheit are rare in August") the appropriate average outdoor temperature for that season is also a system input parameter. These curves are plotted in Figure 16.48. Since the average temperature curves are given, no outdoor temperature needs to be measured. Hence, the outdoor temperature sensor can be eliminated.

The structure of the new furnace controller is shown in Figure 16.49. The fuzzy controller uses a total of five inputs: four of which are derived from the energy consumption curve using conventional digital filtering techniques; the fifth is the average outdoor temperature. This input comes from a look-up table within the system clock. The output of the fuzzy system represents the estimated heat requirement of the house and corresponds to the $T_{outdoor}$ value in the conventional controller (Figure 16.46).

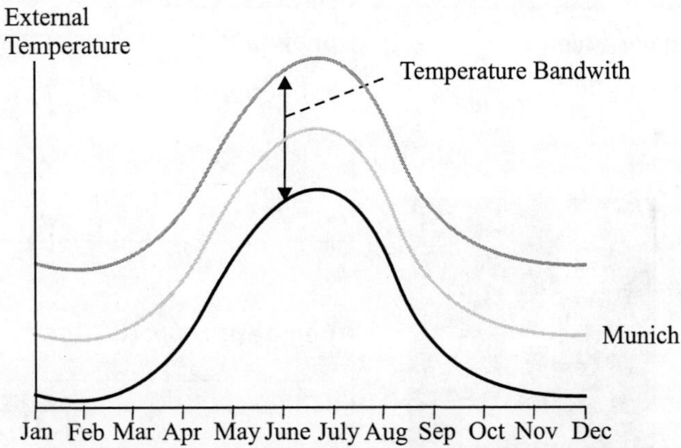

Figure 16.49: Schematic of the new furnace controller

3. Development of the System

The objective of the fuzzy controller is to estimate the actual heat requirement of the house. For this, if-then rules were defined to express the engineering heuristics of this parameter estimation:

IF current_energy_consumption IS low
AND medium_term_tendency IS increasing
AND short_term_tendency IS decreasing
AND yesterday_average IS medium
AND average_outside_temperature IS very_low
THEN estimated_heat_requirement IS medium_high

In total, 405 rules were defined for the parameter estimation. To develop and optimize such a large system efficiently, *fuzzy*TECH's matrix representation was used. This technique enables rule bases to be viewed and defined graphically rather than in text form. Figure 16.50 shows a screen shot of such a rule matrix. In this representation, all linguistic labels of two selected linguistic variables (established heating requirement and yesterday's average energy consumption) are displayed. All other variables (medium term tendency) are kept at a selected label. The matrix may be browsed to show the entire rule base by selecting other terms for these variables.

Within the matrix, a white square indicates rule plausibility whereas a black square indicates rule implausibility (not existent in the rule base). For instance, the highlighted rule in Figure 16.50 is valid. Its textual representation (in the lower part of the window) can be read as:

IF medium_term_tendency IS stable

AND yesterday_avg IS medium

THEN est._heat_req. IS medium.

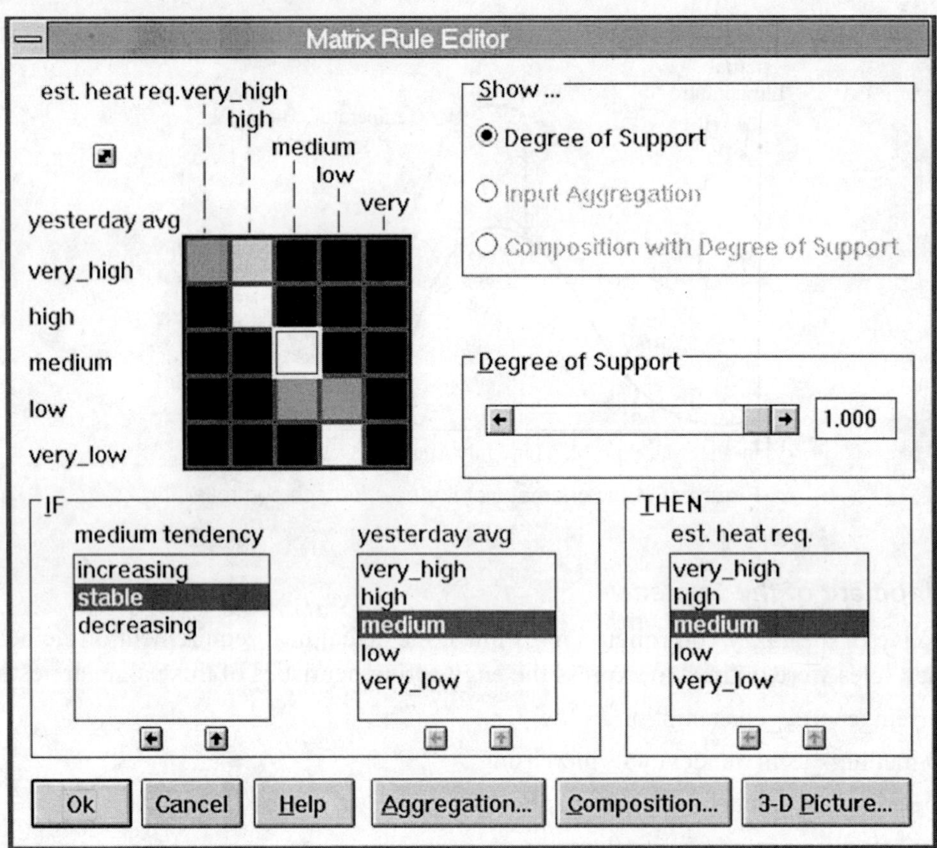

Figure 16.50: Screen shot of rule base as matrix representation

For the formulation of these IF-THEN rules, an initial systems prototype was built. During system optimization, however, it became apparent that some rules were more important than others and that mere rule addition/deletion was too inexact of a system-tuning method. Thus the inference strategy had to be extended to allow rules to be associated with a "degree of support". Such a degree of support is a number between 0 and 1 that expresses the individual importance of each rule with respect to all other rules. The degree of support for each rule is indicated in the matrix by a gray-shaded square. This allows for the expression of rules like:

IF medium_term_tendency IS stable

AND yesterday_avg IS very_high

THEN est_heat_req IS between high and very_high, rather more high.

The inference method used to represent individual degrees of support is based on approximate reasoning and Fuzzy Associative Map (FAM) techniques. After fuzzification, all rule premises are calculated using the minimum operator for the representation of the linguistic AND and the maximum operator for the representation of the linguistic OR. Next, the premise's degree of validity is weighted with the individual degree of support of the rule, resulting in the degree of truth for the conclusion. In the third step, all conclusions are combined using the maximum operator. The result of this is a fuzzy set. The Center-of-Maximum defuzzification method is used to arrive at a real value from a fuzzy output.

The entire structure of the fuzzy controller is shown in Figure 16.51. In this screen shot, the large block in the middle represents the previously described rule base while the small blocks represent input and output interfaces. The icons show the fuzzification/defuzzification methods used in the respective interfaces.

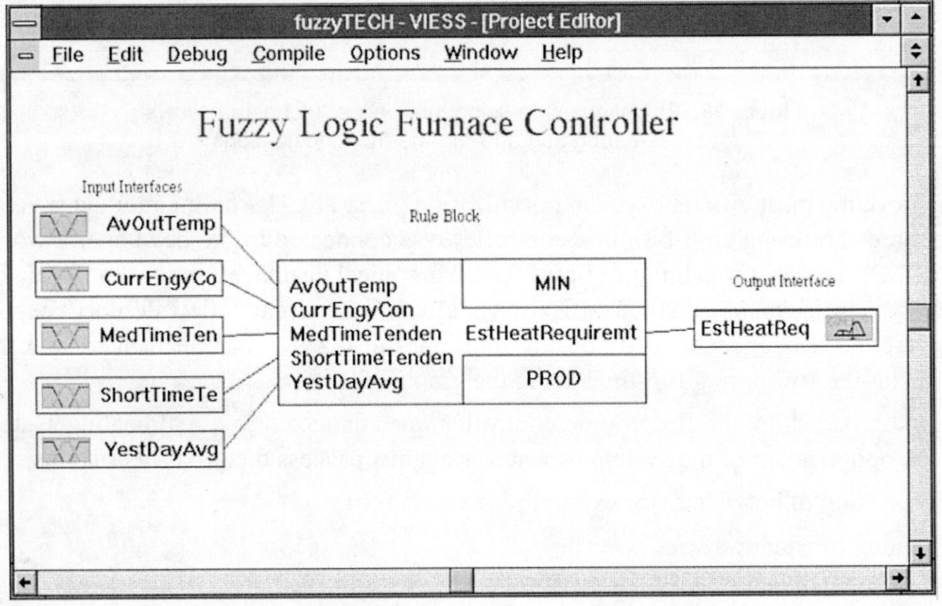

Figure 16.51: Structure of the fuzzy logic controller

4. Implementation and Optimization

After completion of the design of the fuzzy controller and the definition of linguistic variables, membership functions and rules, the system was compiled to the assembly language of the target microcontroller. With this technology, the fuzzy controller only uses 2 KB ROM on a standard 8-bit microcontroller. Once the fuzzy controller had been linked to the entire furnace controller code, the system was optimized.

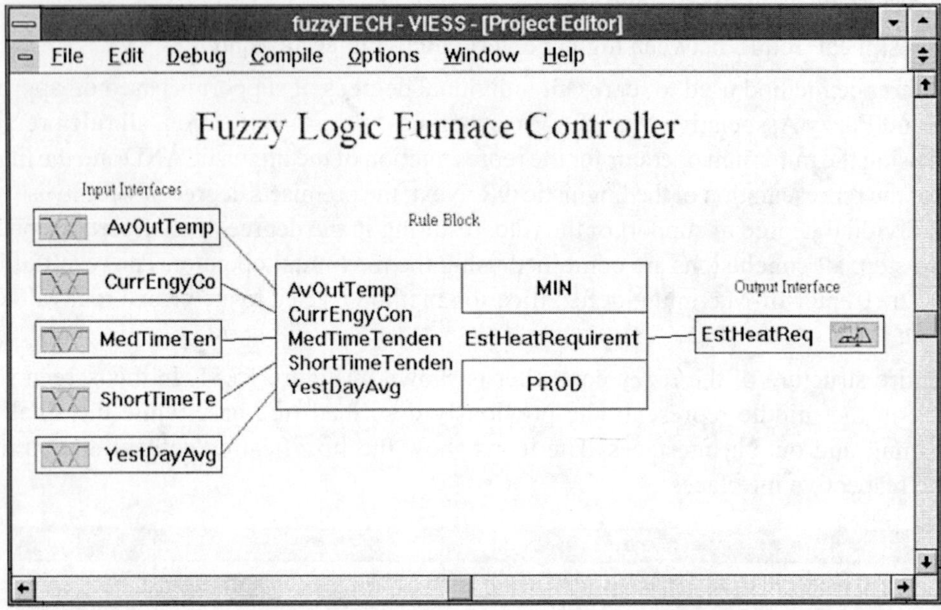

Figure 16.52: Optimization using the "online" technique allows for cross-debugging and "on-the-fly" modifications

To achieve the most efficient system optimization, *fuzzy*TECH's online module was used and the target hardware using an 8-bit microcontroller was connected to the developer's workstation (Windows-PC). The online technique allows for the graphical visualization of the information flow while the system is running. All fuzzification, defuzzification and rule inference steps can be graphically cross-debugged in real-time. In addition, the fuzzy controller can be modified and optimized "on-the-fly" during run-time using the graphical editors.

During optimization, the fuzzy logic controller was connected to a real heating system. This enabled the optimization of the system robustness against process disturbances such as:

- Preparation of hot water (for example for a bath tub)
- Opening of windows
- Extended departure, like for a vacation

5. Performance

To evaluate system performance, both the conventional controller and the fuzzy controller were connected to a test house. One such example is shown in Figure 16.53. Over a period of 48 hours, three graphs were plotted:

- Optimal boiler temperature (calculated from the external/internal house condition).
- Set boiler temperature, as derived from the conventional controller (considering outdoor temperature).
- Set boiler temperature, as derived from the fuzzy controller.

The result of the comparative performance tests showed that the fuzzy controller was highly responsive to the actual heat requirement of the house. It was very reactive to sudden heat demand changes like the return of house inhabitants from vacation. Besides this, the elimination of the outdoor temperature sensor saved about $30 in production costs and even more in installation costs that average about $120. By setting the set boiler temperature beneath the level typically used by a conventional controller in low load periods, the fuzzy controller saves energy. Long-term studies collecting statistical data for quantifying exactly how much energy per house could be saved annually are currently being investigated. In addition to this, the two knobs parameterizing the heat characteristic for the individual house (confer Figure 16.46) used by conventional heating systems, are no longer necessary with the fuzzy logic controller. This eases the use of the heating system, since setting the parameters of the heating curves requires an expertise most home owners do not have.

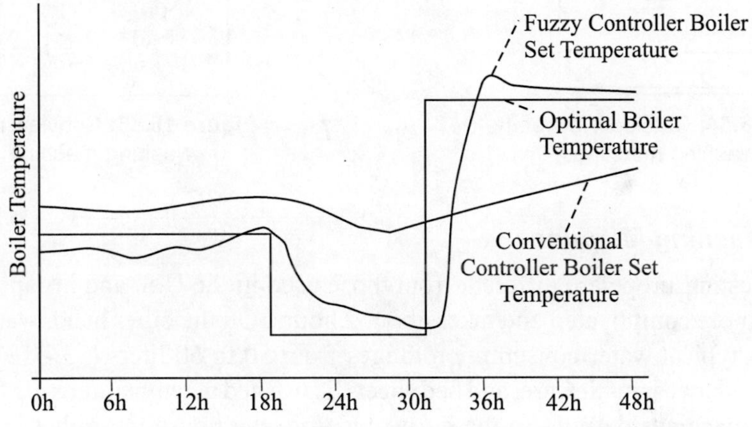

Figure 16.53: Comparative performance test (schematic)

With this new generation of fuzzy logic heating controller, we achieved:

- Improved energy efficiency, since the fuzzy controller reduces heat production at low heat demand periods.
- Improved comfort, due to the detection of sudden heat demand peaks.
- Easy setup, since the heat characteristic does not need to be parameterized manually.
- Savings both in production and installation cost.

Taking into account the benefits of introducing engineering heuristics, formulated using fuzzy logic technologies, the price was rather low. In the product, the fuzzy logic controller only requires 2 KB of ROM. Using matrix rule representation and online development technology, the optimization of a complex fuzzy logic system containing 405 rules was done efficiently. Click here to view the Fuzzy Logic Viessmann Heating System Controller.

16.6.3 Neurofuzzy Signal Analysis in Washing Machines

In some applications, the knowledge about the system solution is contained in sample data. In these cases, NeuroFuzzy is the method of choice. The following case study is a good example to show the potential of NeuroFuzzy technologies. The German home appliance manufacturer AEG used the *fuzzy*TECH NeuroFuzzy Module to design an environment-friendly washing machine. The NeuroFuzzy system analyzes the signal of an existing sensor to estimate the laundry volume and type. This information is used to optimize the washing program. In an average home, this technology saves about 20% on water and energy. Click here for a picture of the AEG NeuroFuzzy washing machine or its presentation at the INFORM Fuzzy Logic User's Conference.

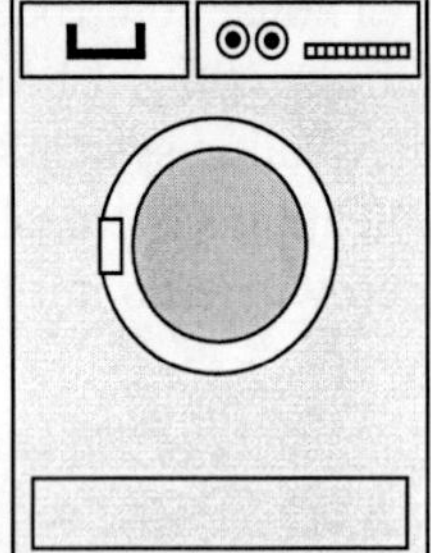

Figure 16.54: Outside View of the washing machine

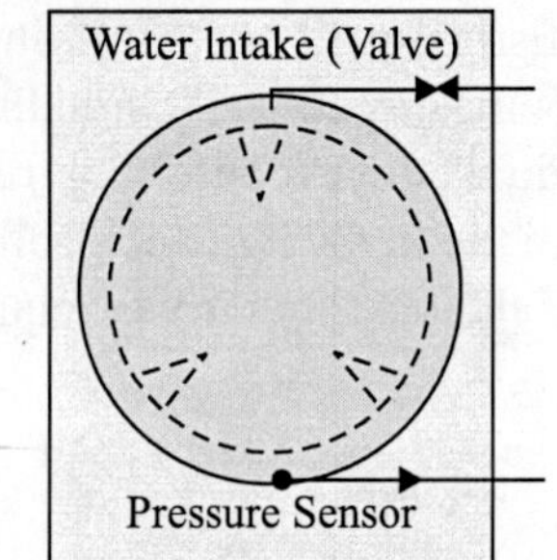

Figure 16.55: Cut view of the washing machine

1. European Washing Machines

Washing machines in Europe are different from those used in the U.S. and in Japan. The washing process is much more complicated and takes about 2 hours. On the other hand, water consumption is much lower. A typical water consumption ranges from 50 to 60 liters (13 - 18 gallons). White laundry, such as underwear, tableware, and bed sheets, is washed at temperatures up to 95°C (203°F). Hence, washing machines do not use the hot water from the house but rather heat up the water electrically.

The complex washing process consists of multiple wash, process, bleach, rinse and spin steps. To control this, today's washing machines use microcontroller hardware and multiple sensors:

- Tachometer for the drum spin.
- Analog pressure sensor for the water level (Figure 16.54, left).
- Digital sensor to detect strong unevenness during spinning.
- Digital sensor to detect excessive foam.

To determine the optimal washing program, actual laundry load (type and volume) of the washing machine must be known. Sensors that could measure these parameters directly are expensive and unreliable. Hence, the objective for AEG was to design a system that estimates the actual laundry load only from the existing sensors.

2. Water Absorption Curves

Figure 16.56 plots the pressure sensor curve over time. The plot starts when the water intake valve first opens.

- The water intake valve opens at T_0. At T_1, the water level reached set value. This duration does not depend much on the laundry load since the laundry in the non-rotating drum does not absorb much water.
- At T_1, the drum starts to rotate in a certain rhythm, causing the laundry to absorb water. Since the weight of the laundry is held by the drum, the water pressure measured by the sensor decreases. At a later time T_2, the new pressure is stored and the difference to the pressure at T_1 gives an indication of the absorption speed.
- At T_2, the current water pressure is stored again. It gives an indication of the absorption volume, as the laundry is mostly saturated at this time. At T_2, the water valve is opened again to fill up the water level to the set point.

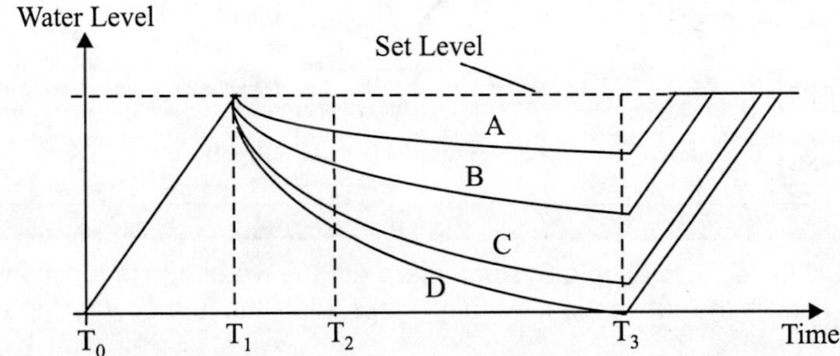

Figure 16.56: Water level in the drum of the washing machine during initial water intake. by interpreting the curves, an estimation of laundry type and volume is possible

As there is no mathematical model on the relation of the water absorption curves to the laundry load, AEG decided to use fuzzy logic to design a solution based on the knowledge of their washing experts. Figure 16.57 shows the structure of the fuzzy logic system that estimates the water requirement in washing and rinse steps. The input variables of the fuzzy logic system stem from the water absorption curve.

The upper fuzzy logic rule block estimates the water requirement during washing (WaterLev1) from absorption speed (AbsorbSp) and absorption volume (AbsorbVol). Both these input variables are calculated from T1 - T0 and T2 - T1. The two lower fuzzy logic rule blocks estimate the water requirement during rinse (WaterLev2). Inputs to the intermediate rule block are water requirement during washing, as determined by the upper rule block, and total absorption volume. These are combined to describe the total absorption characteristic (AbsorbChar). This variable is not an output of the fuzzy logic system, but only used as one input for the lower fuzzy logic rule block.

The lower rule block estimates the water requirement during the rinse step (WaterLev2). Other inputs are the ration of the bounded soap, the number of rinse steps given by the selected washing program, and the selected intensity of the spin step. All membership functions are of Standard type (Z, Lambda, S) and the defuzzification employs Center-of-Maximum (CoM) method.

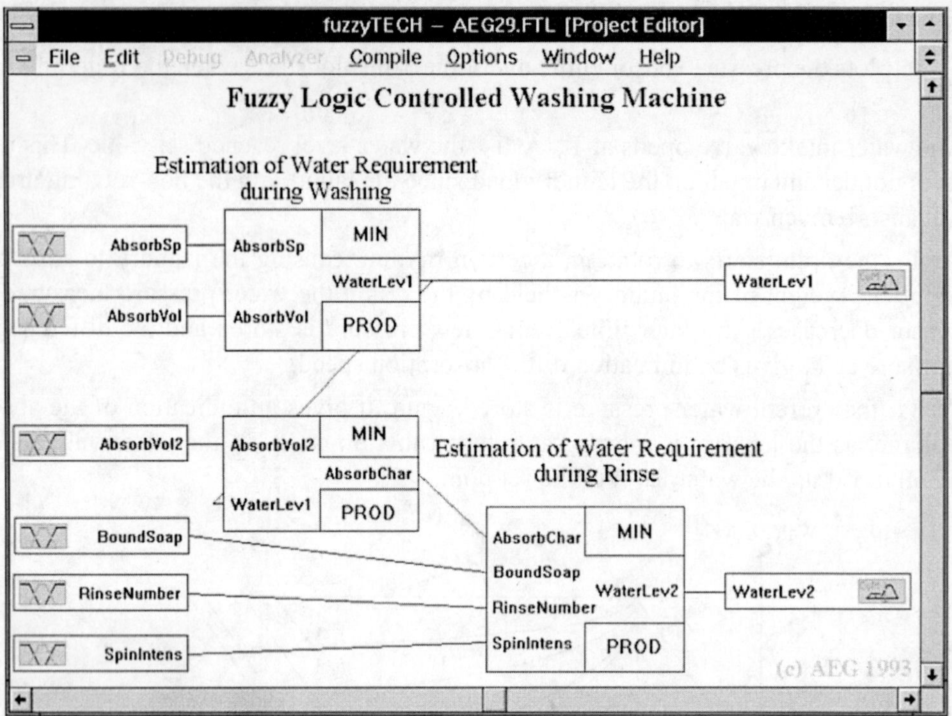

Figure 16.57: The Multi Level Fuzzy Logic System interprets the water intake function and determines the amount of water to be used in the subsequent washing steps. Also, the further washing program is optimized according to the load

3. Fuzzy Logic vs. NeuroFuzzy

The approach of interpreting the water absorption curve to estimate the laundry load is innovative, and hence, not much engineering "know-how" on the interpretation of the curves exists. As engineering "know-how" on the application is essential to building a solution with fuzzy logic, the first try of AEG to find a satisfying set of fuzzy logic rules failed.

On the other hand, AEG already recorded water absorption curves for various known laundry loads. The optimal water requirement for these laundry loads can easily be determined by the washing experts. Using these experimental results as training examples, AEG's next try was to use NeuroFuzzy techniques. Figure 16.58 shows some of these training examples. The left column (Laundry load) lists the materials used for this washing experiment, the next two columns (Water absorption speed and volume) give parameters from the water absorption curve. AEG showed the washing experts the first columns with the actual known load and asked them to recommend the optimum water requirement for this load.

The NeuroFuzzy training used the right column as the desired output and the middle two columns as the respective inputs. The training cannot use the left column as the actual load is not known to the washing machine during operation. The aim of this training is that after training, the fuzzy logic system, which the NeuroFuzzy Module trains, responds with the appropriate water level recommendation determined of the actual values of the input variables.

Laundry load	Water absorption speed	Water absorption volume	Water requirement in subsequent washing steps (from expert)
4 kg Wool / 1 kg Cotton	0.67	2.44	3.5
3 kg Wool / 1 kg Cotton	0.61	2.1	3.1
2 kg Wool / 2kg Cotton	0.62	1.99	2.8
...	...	...	...

Figure 16.58: The Sample Data for the NeuroFuzzy Training Has Been Gained Through Extensive Washing Experiments. In Each Experiment, Different Laundry Types and Volumes Were Used. For Each Experiment, the Washing Expert Gave His Recommendation for the Amount of Water to Be Used in Subsequent Washing Steps.

The NeuroFuzzy learning process created 159 rules in the fuzzy logic system shown in Figure 16.57. The solution was able to estimate the water requirement with a maximum difference from the optimum value of 0.35 liters (0.09 gallons). In an average home, this saves about 20% of the water consumption. As most of the electricity consumed by the washing machine is used to heat up water, 20% of energy is saved too. The fuzzy logic system that the NeuroFuzzy learning process generated, was implemented on a standard 8 bit microcontroller.

16.7 DATA ANALYSIS OF ENVIRONMENTAL DATA FOR TRAFFIC CONTROL

Traffic control is based on the analysis of traffic data and environmental conditions. Particularly bad environmental conditions may cause hazard to drivers. In this paper, we discuss the use of fuzzy logic for the analysis of environmental conditions such as road surface condition, visual range and weather conditions detected by local sensor stations and road sensors. Because detection of environmental conditions involves a number of uncertainties, conventional approaches do not deliver satisfactory solutions. The fuzzy logic solution discussed in this paper in contrast:

- takes into account the different types and quality of equipment used at the different detection stations,
- uses a two-step plausibility check to determine the quality of sensor signals,
- computes substitute values for missing information using sensors from other detection stations,
- leads to more appropriate results for the evaluation of road surface conditions and visual range to indicate slippery road conditions or fog warning.

The discussed fuzzy logic solution was developed for an existing traffic control system of the B27 in Germany, a state highway between Stuttgart city, Stuttgart airport, and Tuebingen. The unit is part of a larger fuzzy logic traffic control system which will be implemented as an additional step in the B27 control system.

16.7.1 Traffic Management

The first traffic management systems used in Germany were implemented on roads with frequent accidents caused by fog or icy road conditions. Later, these system were extended to detect and control traffic to increase the traffic capacity. These traffic control systems use several detection stations along the road. These stations employ magnetic sensors for traffic detection, as well as weather stations transmitting environmental data from road surface and the air layer near the ground.

A central traffic control computer collects the data transmitted from the section stations. A control strategy derives an adequate speed limit for every section. The control objectives are:

- keep traffic flowing in case of peak traffic,
- slow down traffic at the inflow to congestion, and
- warn for bad weather conditions such as fog or ice.

Along the road of such an "intelligent" highway, alterable road signs posted on traffic sign gantries display speed limits for each lane and display non-regular events such as road work, warnings for traffic back-ups, breakdowns, an accident or dangerous weather conditions (Figure 16.59).

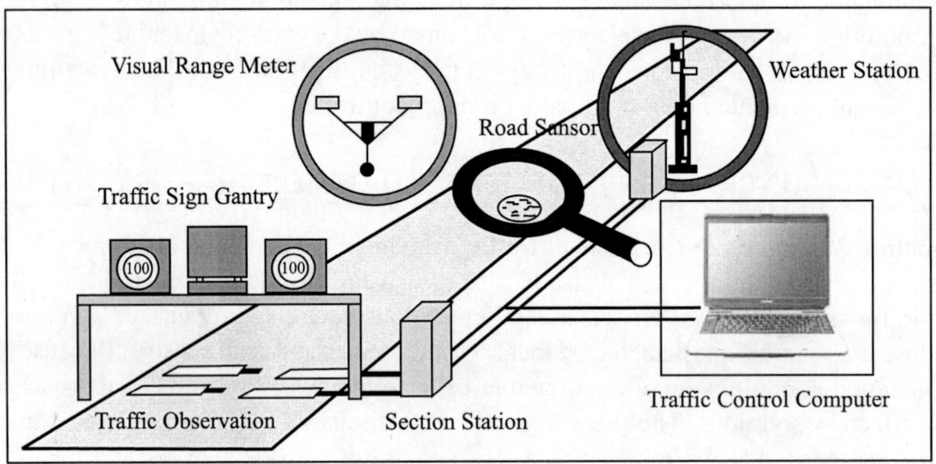

Figure 16.59: Environmental and traffic sensors in a traffic control system

16.7.2 Environmental Data Analysis

The traffic situations depend highly on environmental conditions. An intelligent highway thus should warn drivers of slippery road conditions and low visibility. Sensors are used to indicate and classify icy or wet road pavement and to indicate the visual range.

An ideal weather station uses road sensors measuring road surface temperature, road surface moisture, water film depth, and salt content of water film. Near the road, the ideal weather station detects air and ground temperature, amount of precipitation, type of precipitation, wind velocity and direction, sun beam intensity and illumination.

However, most existing weather stations are not equipped with this full range of sensor equipment. In addition, some sensors do not work reliably under all conditions. For example, a standard salinometer needs a wet road surface to measure the remaining salt content on the road. Besides measurement problems, sensors frequently fail because of "biological attacks" such as spiders or butterflies that cover the surface of visual based detectors. Conventional traffic control systems misinterpret this as high rain intensity or low visual range. This can cause completely wrong traffic warnings. Because sensors often stem from different vendors, conventional systems do not use interrelationships between the signals of different detection stations to identify such implausibilities.

16.7.3 Fuzzy Logic System Architecture

The fuzzy logic data analysis unit was designed as part of a larger traffic control system. As shown in earlier applications, fuzzy logic is well suited to create solutions for traffic control systems. Figure 16.60 shows the architecture of the analysis unit, separating a component to verify the sensor information from components to evaluate the road surface and visual range condition.

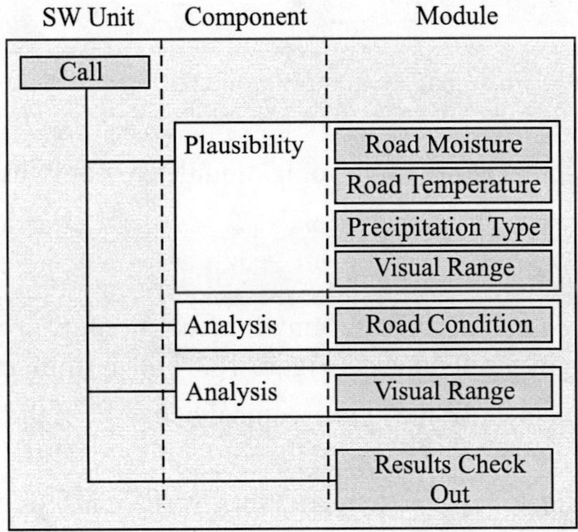

Figure 16.60: Architecture of environmental data analysis

16.7.4 Sensor Plausibility Analysis

A two-step approach was used to verify the sensor signals. The first step utilizes the fact that no weather signal remains constant. In particular, if the signal jumps abruptly or remains completely constant over time, the sensor signal is considered to be faulty.

In this case, the fuzzy logic system regenerates the information from other sensors. To design this fuzzy logic system, meteorological knowledge about the maximum gradients of all sensor signals, a time frame for a required movement of the signals, and maximum jumps of the gradients to identify discontinuity were acquired from experts.

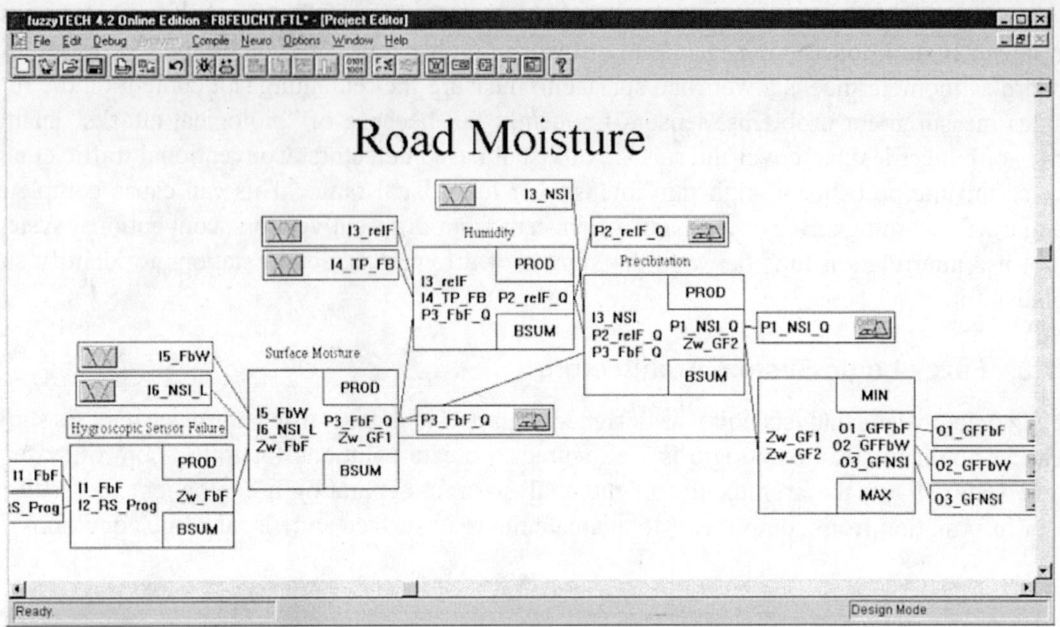

Figure 16.61: Road moisture fuzzy logic module

The second step uses four separate fuzzy logic modules to combine interrelated signals:

A. Road Moisture Module

This module, combines all data, that indicates anything about moisture or water on the road. The fuzzy logic module consists of 5 rule blocks (Figure 16.61) that implement:

1. A compensation rule block for the hygroscopical behavior of the road moisture sensors. For example, if the salt content is very high, the moisture sensor indicates higher values.
2. A cross check rule block between detected road surface moisture, the sensors that detect a water film on the road, and the amount of precipitation ions detected during the last 30 minutes. For example, if strong rain was detected over the past minutes, the road must be wet.
3. A cross check rule block of the humidity sensor using dew point, road temperature, and a moisture sensor. For example, if the dew point is lower than the road temperature and the verified moisture indicates a dry road, the humidity signal must be wrong.
4. A cross check rule block to the precipitation sensor.
5. A diagnosis rule block to derive an error message from the given signal situation.

As result, the module produces verified signals of road moisture, amount of precipitation, and humidity.

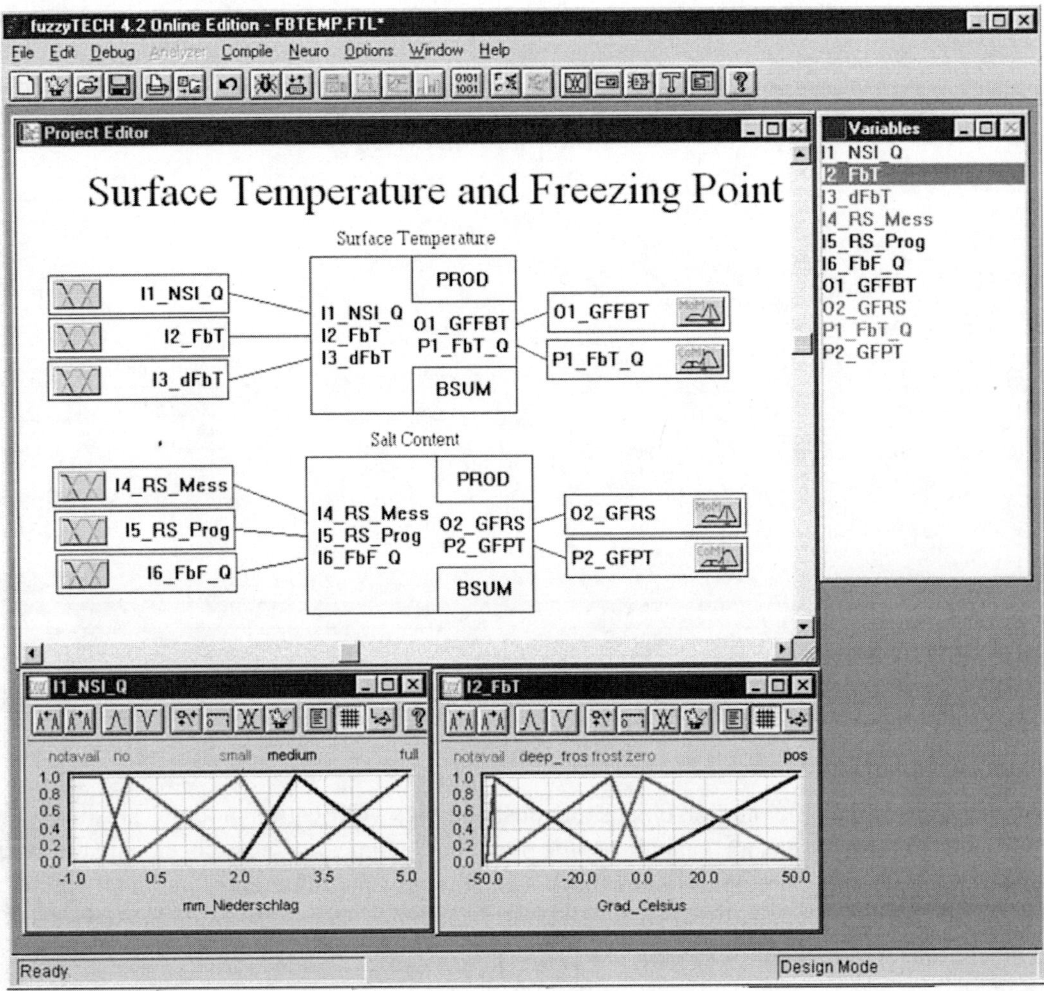

Figure 16.62: Road temperature fuzzy logic module

B. Road Temperature Module

This fuzzy logic module contains two rule blocks (Figure 16.62) to compute:

1. A verified value of the road surface temperature by cross check of the temperature signal, the gradient of this signal, and the precipitation. For example, the temperature signal can only decrease rapidly if a large amount of precipitation is detected.
2. A verified value of the freezing point, taking into account salt content and road surface moisture. Because the salt content sensor does not work with dry road conditions, a salt content forecast is used when the signal is not available.

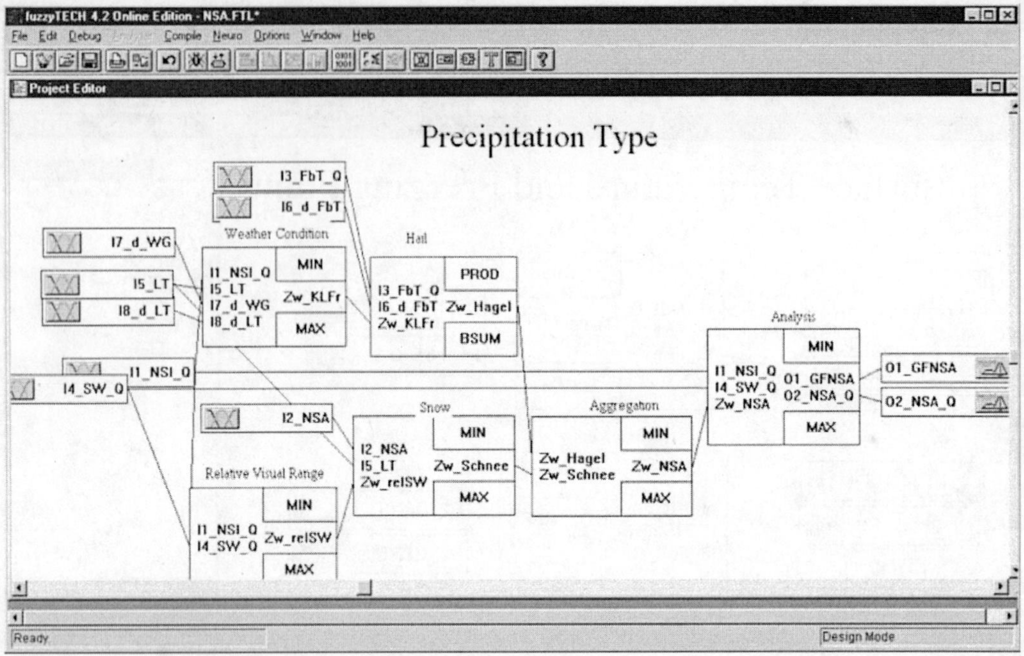

Figure 16.63: Precipitation type fuzzy logic module

C. Precipitation Type Module

The verification of the precipitation type is the most complex verification module. This fuzzy logic module verifies existing sensors that indicate the precipitation type by a cross check with the verified signals of road moisture, precipitation quantity, visual range, and other environmental conditions. If the sensor delivers implausible results or is not available, a substitute value is computed. The module consists of a number of rule blocks that:

1. Indicate if the weather conditions allow for hail or snow. For example, an air temperature level is defined at which snow is implausible.
2. Compare the visual range with the precipitation quantity.
3. Aggregate the information with the precipitation quantity and visual range.

D. Visual Range Module

The visual range fuzzy logic module computes a verified value of the visual range by using two rule blocks (Figure 16.64) that:

1. Cross check the visual range with the precipitation quantity. For example, there is no fog during heavy rain.
2. Cross check the visual range with air humidity. For example, fog only occurs during very high humidity.

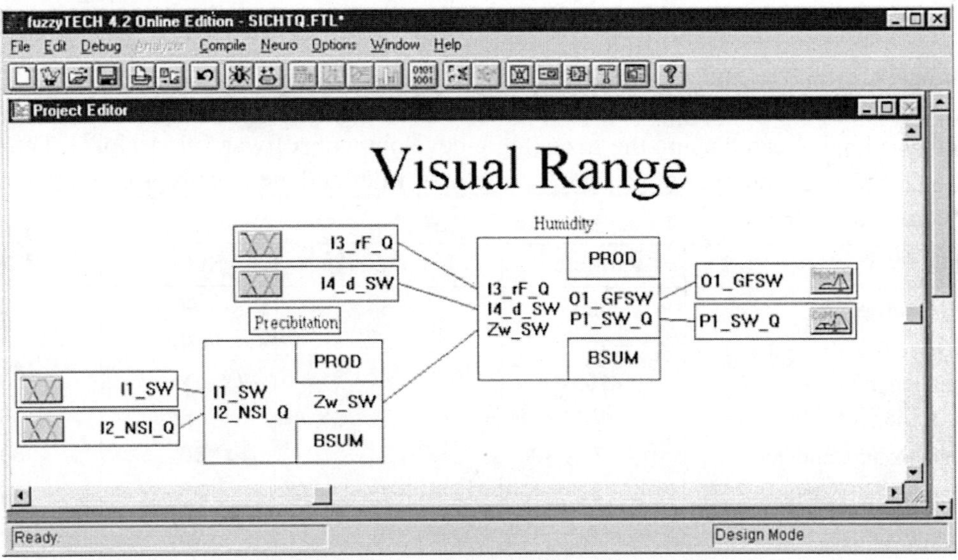

Figure 16.64: Visual Range Fuzzy Logic Module

Using these verified signals, the subsequent two components conclude road and fog conditions. The Road Condition component (Figure 16.65) uses the qualified values of precipitation type and quantity, as well as the road moisture to indicate a dangerously wet road. Precipitation type, freezing point, and road temperature indicate icy conditions. A final rule block aggregates the information to a standardized road condition classification code. An additional component aggregates the verified values of visual range and precipitation type to compute the standardized visual range classification code.

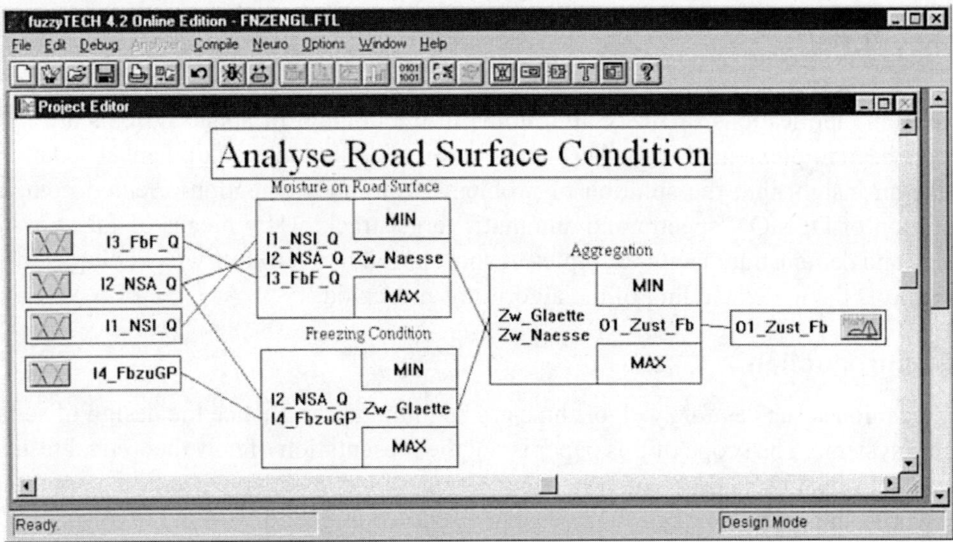

Figure 16.65: Analysis of road surface condition

16.7.5 Results

Conventional traffic systems are susceptible to faulty weather sensor signals. The fuzzy logic approach presented delivers more reliable results using meteorological expertise. The solution discussed was implemented using the fuzzy logic development software *fuzzy*TECH. The table in Figure 16.66 shows the number of variables, structures, rules and memberships of each component and the complete system used.

Module	Variable	Rule blocks	Rules	MBFs
Road Moisture	16	5	489	70
Road Temperature	10	2	130	39
Pricipitation Type	15	6	204	60
Visual Range	7	2	142	36
Analysis Road Condition	7	3	60	33
Analysis Visual Range	3	1	35	14
Complete Unit	**58**	**19**	**1060**	**255**

Figure 16.66: Size of Fuzzy Logic Unit and Its Modules

In day to day operation, the fuzzy logic solution has shown that it can prevent traffic control system malfunction in most sensor breakdown situations. In addition "biological attack" situations were detected and misleading rain or fog detection was avoided.

In a complete traffic control system, analysis of environmental conditions is only one component of its functionality. However, faulty weather detection can cause the entire traffic control system to malfunction. Thus, the enhancement of traffic control systems by fuzzy logic greatly improves the reliability of traffic control.

16.8 FUZZY TECHNOLOGY IMPLEMENTED IN SONAR SYSTEMS

In this section, applications of fuzzy algorithms in the domain of sonar systems are introduced which have been implemented in the latest generation of Atlas sonar equipment. The aim has been to provide an insight into the solution of problems from an application-oriented point of view. Classification of DEMON spectra and automatic target tracking by means of fuzzy systems are introduced and demonstrated with examples. A short introduction to fuzzy technology is also given which supports the understanding of the algorithms presented.

16.8.1 Introduction

Modern techniques such as fuzzy algorithms are beginning to influence the design of sonar signal processing systems. The scope of this paper is not the presentation of new theoretical results in this area but an introduction to problems where such modern methods have been successfully applied. In other words, the applications of fuzzy theory discussed in Sections 16.8.3 and 16.8.4 have been implemented in the latest sonar systems of Atlas Elektronik.

This paper is devoted to two sonar applications of fuzzy theory. The first is concerned with the automatic detection of the propeller shaft rate and number of propeller blades of ships and submarines by analysis of the DEMON spectrum. The second application is an automatic target traking system which incorporates two fuzzy modules. In particular, the main component of the so-called "traking filter" is itself a fuzzy system.

Fuzzy logic and the method of approximate reasoning led to new concepts in control theory and in the design of expert systems. These concepts imitate human thought processes better than do conventional methods. Besides the above-mentioned applications, important notions from fuzzy theory are explained which are needed for the understanding of the fuzzy algorithms considered. Rule-based fuzzy systems can be used if human expert knowledge is available which can be expressed in the form of if-then rules.

16.8.2 Basic Concepts of Fuzzy Theory

Before the applications of fuzzy theory in sonar systems introduced below can be discussed in detail, some basic concepts of this theory have to be considered. Those readers who are familiar with fuzzy systems can skip this section.

The efficiency of knowledge-based expert systems depends on the degree to which human knowledge can be reproduced. Classical mathematical logic, which is the basis of conventional inference machines, can formalise human knowledge and make it computable via algorithms to a very restricted degree only. To overcome the problems of binary logic, the theory of fuzzy logic was developed by Lotfi A. Zadeh. He introduced fuzzy sets in order to describe and process inexact and incomplete data, which is often encountered in real situations. Since fuzzy logic is capable of dealing with linguistic information, it is ideal for serving as a basis for knowledge-based systems.

In contrast to classical logic, which knows only two crisp truth values, yes or no, true or false, 0 or 1, the concept of fuzzy logic is based on so-called "membership functions", which can take arbitrary values from the interval [0, 1]. The membership function describes the degree to which an object belongs to a certain set. Moreover, further important notions from the field of fuzzy systems which are beyond the scope of this paper are discussed in these publications.

Let A, for example, be the set of all possible numbers of spots on a die; we can then define the set "high number of spots" by means of a membership function. In the case of classical logic, the corresponding membership function is depicted in Figure 16.67 where only the two crisp values 0 and 1 are admissible. In contrast to this, the fuzzy set "high number of spots", shown in Figure 16.68, coincides much better with the human concept of "high", since smooth transitions between membership and non-membership are possible.

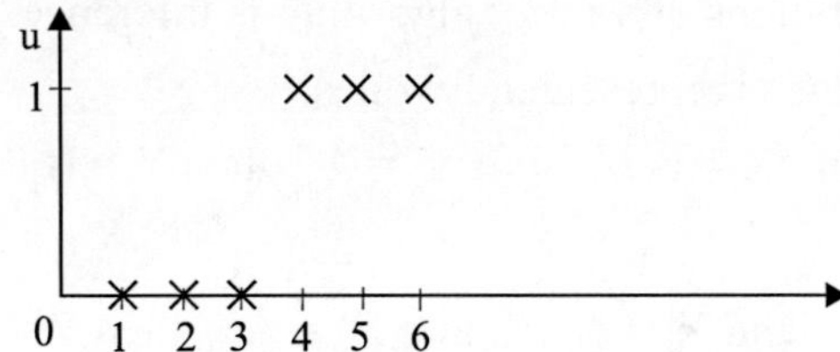

Figure 16.67: Crisp set "high number of spots"

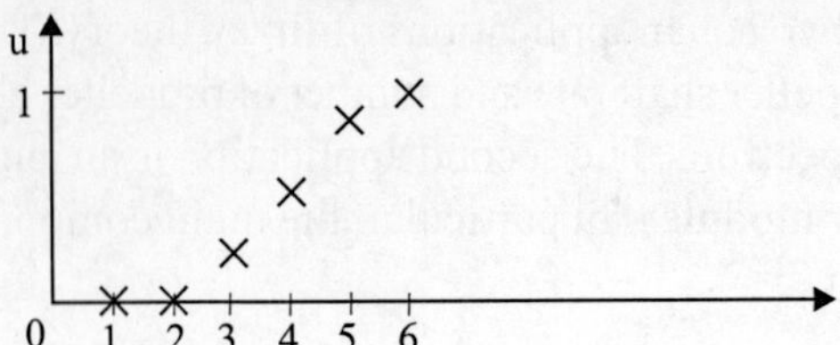

Figure 16.68: Fuzzy set "high number of spots"

The membership function is the essential component of a fuzzy set. Thus, the operations "intersection", "union" and "complement" of fuzzy sets are defined via the membership functions of the sets involved. The number of operators proposed in the literature is large. The reason for the variety of definitions for the operations "AND" (intersection) and "OR" (union) is the context-dependent way in which these operations are performed in human thinking. The choice of the appropriate operator is not trivial in practical situations and needs much experience and a proper analysis of the underlying problem.

Fuzzy inference is the most important operation in fuzzy expert systems and fuzzy controllers. In order to clarify this type of operation we first have to introduce the notion of "linguistic variable". A linguistic variable is a variable whose values are sentences in a natural language. The meaning attached to the values of a linguistic variable are fuzzy sets. This abstract explanation can be illustrated by the following example. We define a linguistic variable "distance". As the domain of interest (universe of discourse) we consider distances between 0 and 100 km. The linguistic variable "distance" can take as values the expressions {very near, near, medium, far, very far}. These expressions are the names of fuzzy sets whose membership functions are depicted in Figure 16.69.

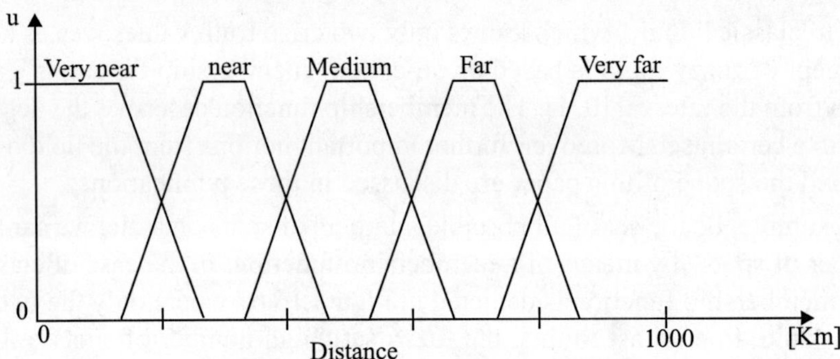

Figure 16.69: Linguistic variable "distance"

One of the essential operations of a fuzzy algorithm is inference.

The underlying knowledge is represented by rules:

Rule 1: If $X_1 = A_{11}$ ... and $X_i = A_{1i}$ ... and $X_n = A_{1n}$ then $Y = B_1$

⋮

Rule m: If $X_1 = A_{m1}$ ... and $X_i = A_{mi}$ ... and $X_n = A_{mn}$ then $Y = B_m$

$X_1,...,X_n$ and Y are linguistic variables, $A_{1i},...,A_{mi}$ are possible values of the variable X_i, i = 1,...,n, and $B_1,...,B_m$ are possible values of the variable Y.

There exist different types of fuzzy inference which can be divided into the following categories:

- MAX-MIN inference
- approximate reasoning
- plausible reasoning.

The terms approximate and plausible reasoning describe techniques which should not be confused with those used in probabilistic concepts. If the MAX-MIN inference is used, then the rules are supposed to be absolutely true, i. e., the consequent term is true to that degree to which the antecedent term is fulfilled. In contrast to this, if approximate reasoning is applied, then not every rule is supposed to be absolutely true. For every rule there is a corresponding number from the interval [0, 1] which represents the degree of confidence in this rule (0 = no confidence, 1 = full confidence). If we operate a fuzzy system, this rule weight is taken into account. If we consider plausible reasoning, then we try, on the basis of additional information, to deduce implications which are not given explicitly.

The mechanism of approximate reasoning will be explained in the following. General fuzzy systems can be described by Figure 16.70. Essentially, they consist of blocks of the types "fuzzification", "rule base", and "defuzzification", which are interconnected. The interfaces with the environment are the fuzzification and defuzzification blocks. The expression "fuzzification" describes the conversion of a crisp value s into a fuzzy set with the special membership function depicted in Figure 16.71. The expression "defuzzification" describes the conversion of a fuzzy set into a crisp value. The latter is often defined as the abscissa of the center of gravity of the area under the membership function of the fuzzy set considered (see Figure 16.72).

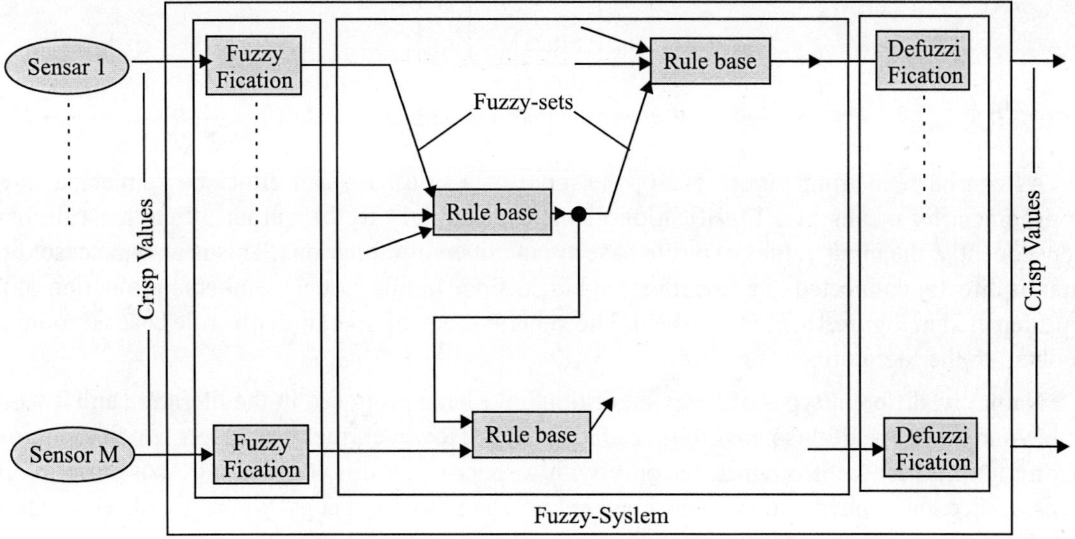

Figure 16.70: General form of a fuzzy system

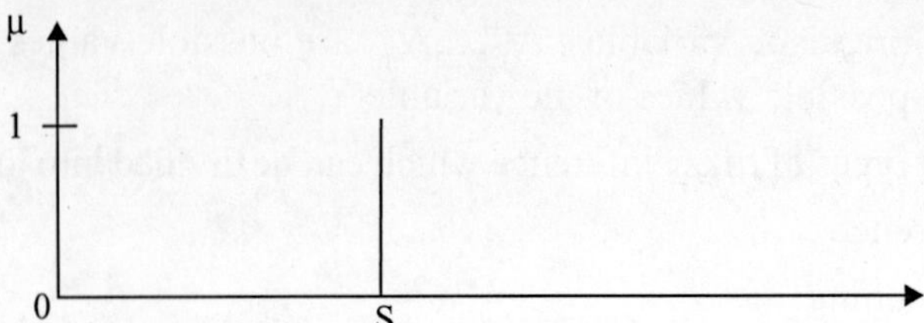

Figure 16.71: Membership function of acrisp value

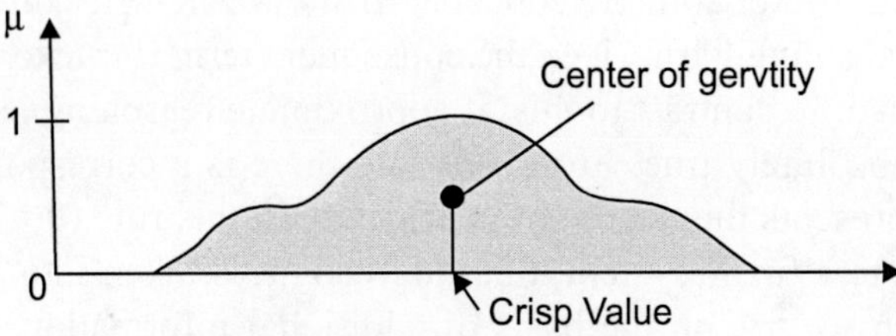

Figure 16.72: Defuzzification

The third element, the rule base, is depicted in Figure 16.73, which comprises the so-called "production rules". The output value and the input values of a rule base are membership functions of fuzzy sets. To the output and to each input of a rule base we assign a linguistic variable (designated here as 0 and $I_1,..., I_N$). The elements of a rule base, the production rules, have already been introduced. The computational method with which such a rule base is processed is called "fuzzy inference".

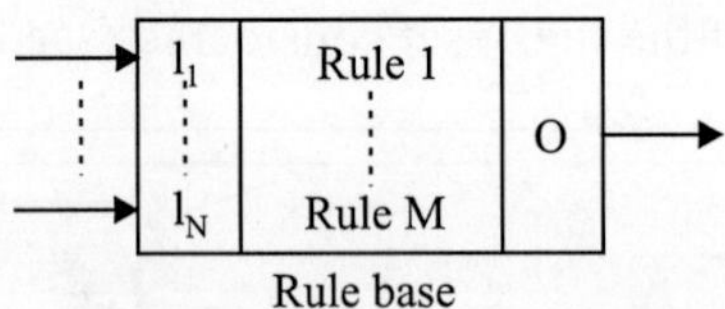

Figure 16.73: The rule base

As can be seen from Figure 16.70, the input of a rule base can either be connected to the environment by means of a fuzzification element or directly to the output of another rule base. Consequently, the input values of a rule base are membership functions. This is also the case if the input is directly connected to a fuzzification block, since in this case a membership function of the type depicted in Figure 16.71 is involved. The general mode of operation of a rule base is explained in detail in the literature.

Naturally, different types of fuzzy algorithm have been proposed in the literature and it would be beyond the scope of this paper to give an overview. However, fuzzy concepts which seem to be distinct at the first sight often differ only with respect to terminology and are based on similar ideas. Hence, our considerations have been restricted to those concepts which are of relevance for the applications introduced in this paper.

16.8.3 Detection of Propeller Shaft Rate and Number of Blades

Passive sonar systems are designed for the reception of underwater sound emitted by unknown vessels. These sound signals are either active pulses or engine noise superimposed on ambient noise. Some of these signals are amplitude-modulated, such as the sound caused by the cavitation of a ship's propeller. The characteristic frequencies of the modulating signal will be the topic of our further considerations.

The sound signals received by a passive sonar system are, on the one hand, used for the determination of target bearing and, on the other hand, for the classification of the sound emitter. One of the components of such a system demodulates the broadband noise signal for the detection of low frequency components of the envelope signal. In this context, the spectrum of the envelope signal (demodulated signal) plays an important role. This component of the signal processing algorithms of a passive sonar system is called DEMON analysis (detection of envelope modulation on noise). In this section, we examine how fuzzy technology has been applied to DEMON processing.

DEMON analysis requires the demodulation of the broadband receiver signal, and is often performed by processing the magnitude of the signal with a low-pass filter, and normalising the resulting spectrum to obtain a constant spectral noise background. The steps for the computation of the DEMON spectrum are summarized in Figure 16.74.

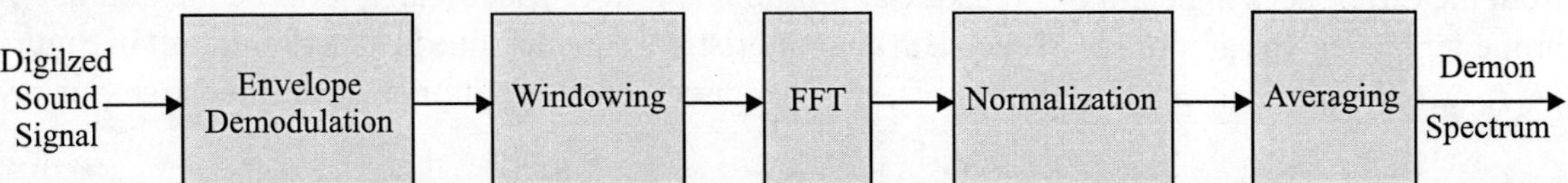

Figure 16.74: Computation of the DEMON spectrum

Human experts usually are able to determine the propeller shaft rate and the number of propeller blades of a detected vessel by analysing the waterfall representation of the DEMON spectrum (see Figure 16.75). Our aim was to replace the human expert with a fuzzy system in order to automate this classification task.

Before the corresponding fuzzy algorithm is introduced, we shall examine the features of the DEMON spectrum which enable the classification task defined above to be accomplished. As already mentioned, cavitation caused by the ship's propeller produces intensity-modulated sound signals. Mathematically, such a signal can be described by

$$s(t) \quad 1 \quad \overset{I}{\underset{i\ 1}{}} A_i \sin(i2 \quad f_s t \mid {}_i)\, n(t) \qquad (1)$$

where the quantities $i * f_s$ are modulation frequencies and n(t) is a broadband noise signal. In other words, the amplitude of the noise signal n(t) is modulated by a set of harmonics. Usually, the amplitudes A_i of these sine signals are much smaller than 1. The determination of the basic frequency f_s from the time signal s(t) is one of the tasks of the DEMON analysis.

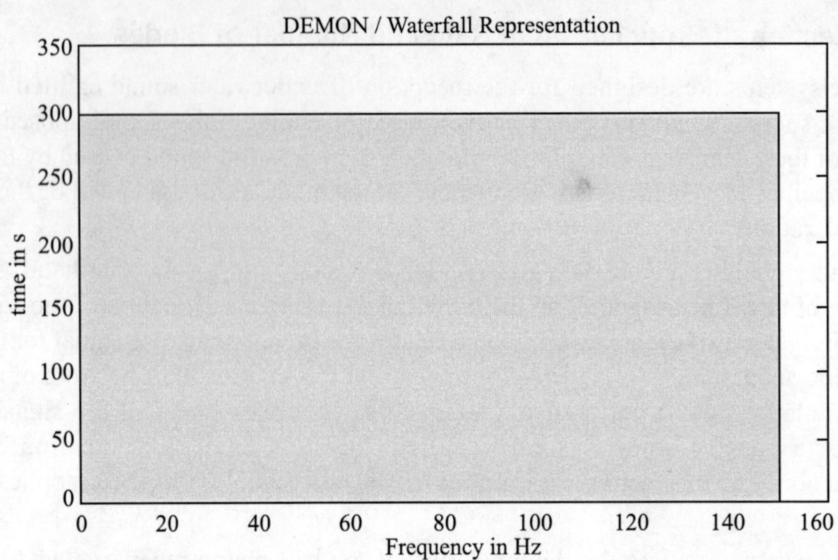

Figure 16.75: Example of the waterfall representation of a DEMON spectrum

The basic frequency f_s in Hz corresponds to the propeller shaft rate expressed in revolutions per second. Hence, f_s has to be determined. Furthermore, the number of propeller blades can be determined from the differences in height between the amplitudes A_i. More specifically, let B be the number of propeller blades; the amplitude of each Bth characteristic frequency line is then dominant. In Figure 16.76 an example is given which implies B = 3. For convenience of notation we define the frequency

$$f_B = B\, f_s. \tag{2}$$

We have developed a fuzzy algorithm that determines the two parameters f_s (propeller shaft rate) and B (number of propeller blades). DEMON spectra can become arbitrarily poor in practice so that even human experts would not be able to classify them correctly. Hence, it is desirable that the quality of the underlying DEMON spectra be indicated by the sonar system. A factor is provided by the fuzzy algorithm which makes it possible to judge the degree of confidence in the displayed values for f_s and B. Such a feature is of great importance for an operator, since nonsensical values can be suppressed by looking at the associated confidence factor.

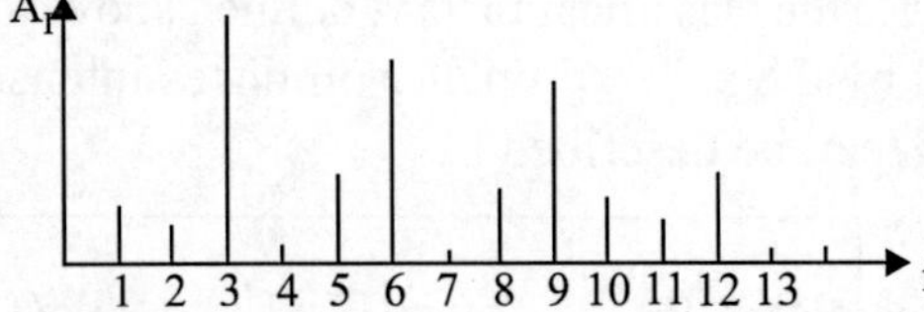

Figure 16.76: Possible distribution of the A_i for B = 3

The algorithm itself is composed of conventional procedures (such as searching for maxima, computing distances between frequency lines, or determining the median of a set of numbers) and fuzzy modules. By using conventional techniques, approximately twenty candidates for f_s are determined. The details of this procedure are of no interest within the context of the topic of this paper.

In a second step, these twenty possible values for the shaft rate are tested by a fuzzy module which calculates a confidence value for each of them. Each of these confidence values is combined with a further confidence factor which has already been determined in the first step. The latter depends on a comparison between the frequency spacing of the largest lines of the DEMON spectrum and the candidate value for f_s. The propeller shaft rate candidate with the greatest resulting confidence factor is accepted and displayed.

The possible values for the number of propeller blades 3, 4, ..., 9 are multiplied by the value just determined for f_s, which provides seven candidates for f_B (see eq. (2)). These seven candidates are tested by a fuzzy module which calculates a confidence value for each of them. The candidate for f_B with the greatest confidence factor is accepted. Finally, the global confidence factor already mentioned is derived from the two confidence factors which have been associated with the accepted values for f_s and B. The number of propeller blades results from the relation $B = f_B/f_s$, where f_B and f_s are the two accepted values.

The two fuzzy systems mentioned above are depicted in Figures 16.77 and 16.78. Obviously, they correspond to the general structure discussed in the last subsection. Both systems are connected to the environment via three input ports and one output port.

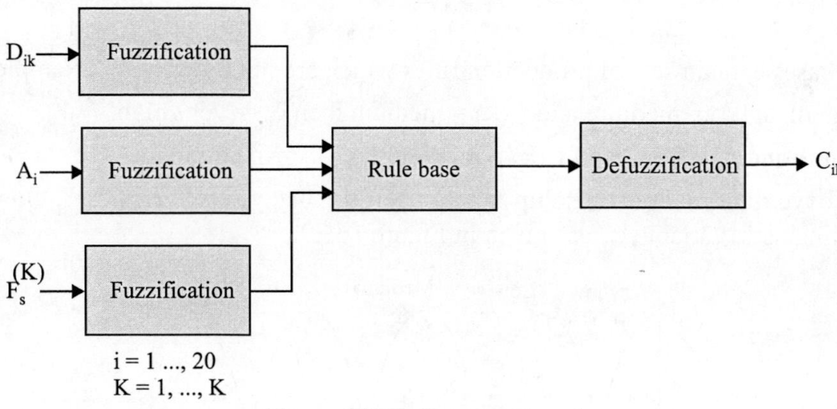

Figure 16.77: Fuzzy system 1

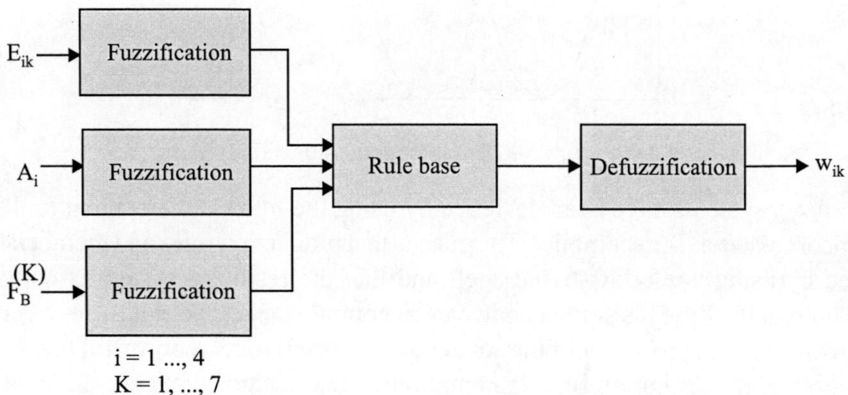

Figure 16.78: Fuzzy system 2

Let $f_s^{(k)}$, k = 1,...,K, be the candidates for f_s, f_i, i = 1,...,20, the frequency locations of the twenty strongest frequency lines of the DEMON spectrum, and A_i, i = 1,...,20, the corresponding amplitudes; we then define

$$\boxed{d_{ik} \quad \min_{q \quad N} \left| f_i - q\, f_s(k) \right|} \tag{3}$$

In other words, d_{ik} is a measure that indicates whether f_i can be interpreted as a harmonic of $f_s^{(k)}$. For each candidate $f_s^{(k)}$, the corresponding confidence factor is the mean of the output values c_{ik} of the fuzzy module, where i = 1,...,20 and k is fixed.

Similarly, $f_B^{(k)}$, k = 1,...,7, are the candidates for f_B, f_i, i = 1,...,4, the frequency locations of the four strongest frequency lines of the DEMON spectrum, and A_i, i = 1,...,4, the corresponding amplitudes.

$$\boxed{e_{ik} \quad \min_{q \quad N} \left| f_i - q\, f_B(k) \right|}$$

The distance is a measure that indicates whether f_i can be interpreted as a harmonic of $f_B^{(k)}$. For each candidate $f_B^{(k)}$, the corresponding confidence factor is the mean of the output values w_{ik} of the fuzzy module, where i = 1,..., 4 and k is fixed.

The rule bases contain sets of production rules which are not listed here. Examples are:

If d_{ik} = small and A_i = medium and $f_S(k)$ = medium then c_{ik} = very high.

If d_{ik} = large and A_i = small and $f_S(k)$ = medium then c_{ik} = medium.

For the above rules, the membership functions of the fuzzy sets "very low", "low", ..., "very high" of the linguistic variable c_{ik} are given in Figure 16.79.

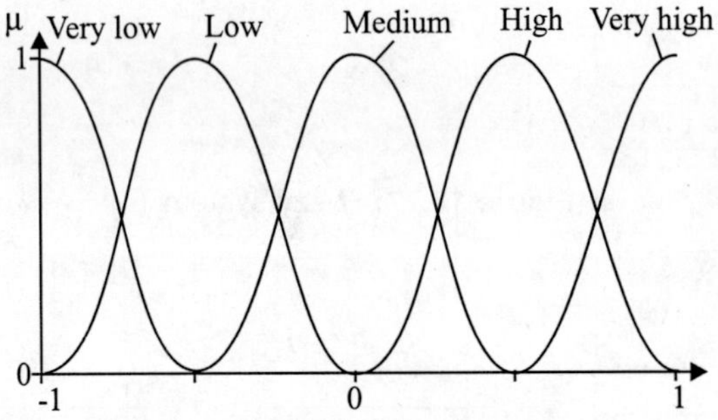

Figure 16.79: Membership functions

The two fuzzy systems have been designed by using the fuzzy development tool "*fuzzy*TECH 2.0" which incorporates a C-precompiler. This means that production rules and membership functions can be edited by using a window-based shell and that the resulting system is converted into C source code automatically. This source code can be compiled and linked into an executable file on the final hardware (signal processor of the sonar equipment). Hence, if powerful fuzzy development tools are available, the design and implementation of fuzzy algorithms are often easier than the implementation of conventional algorithms.

An example of the performance of the algorithm described above for the detection of fs and B from DEMON spectra is given in Figures 16.80 - 16.83. In Figure 16.80 an example of the waterfall representation of DEMON spectra is given where the intensity of the tracks obviously decreases with time. Note that, in contrast to the usual waterfall representations, the time and frequency axes have been interchanged to make the comparison with Figures 16.81 – 16.82 easier.

The corresponding curve of the global confidence factor, which has been determined by the fuzzy algorithm, is shown in Figure 16.81. And indeed, the decrease of the quality of the DEMON spectra with time is indicated by this curve. The propeller shaft rate in revolutions per minute and the number of propeller blades detected by the fuzzy systems are depicted versus time in Figure 16.82 and Figure 16.83, respectively. The correct values are 900 - 920 RPM and 3 blades, respectively. This performance is much better than that which has been achieved by the non-fuzzy algorithm yet used in Atlas sonar systems.

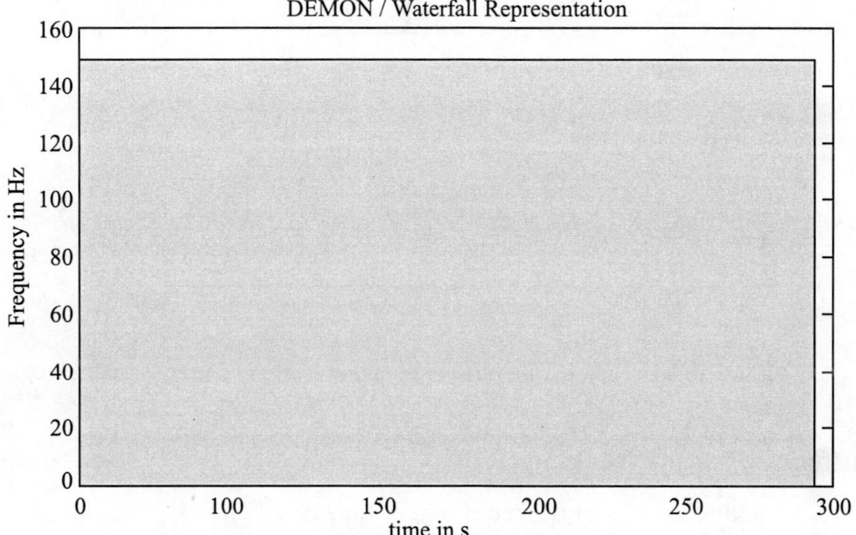

Figure 16.80: Example of the waterfall representation of DEMON spectra

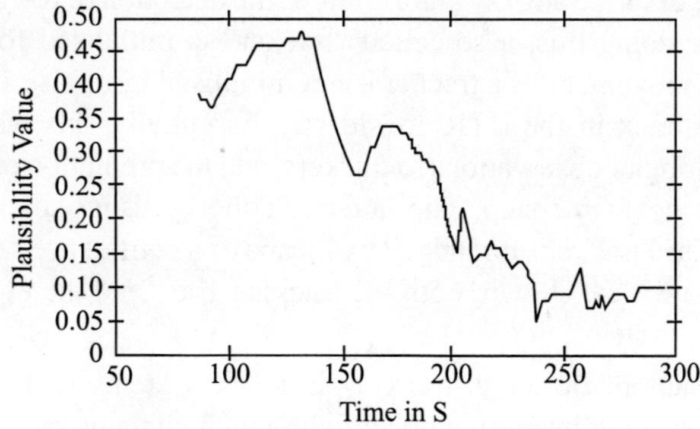

Figure 16.81: Curve of the quality factor

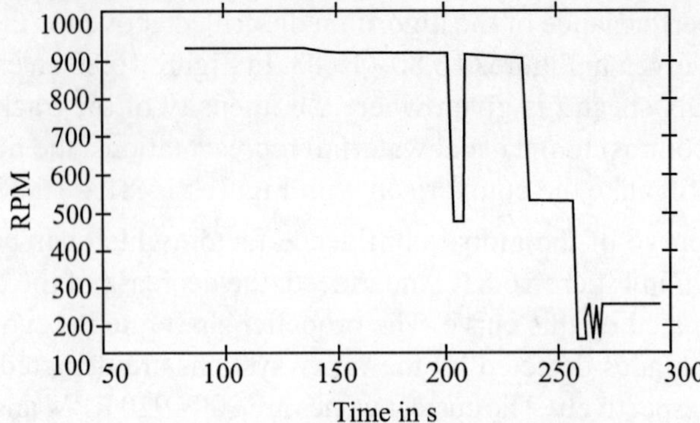

Figure 16.82: Detected propeller shaft rate / correct value » 600 RPM

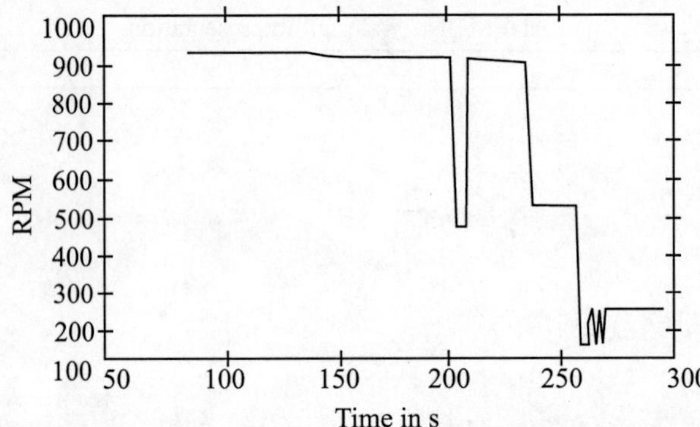

Figure 16.83: Detected number of propeller blades / correct value = 3 blades

16.8.4 Automatic Target Tracking (ATT)

Automatic target tracking is an essential requirement for surveillance systems employing multiple sensors, together with computer subsystems, to interpret an environment that includes both true targets and false alarms.

In the following, we describe a fuzzy algorithm for the detection of tracks (targets) in a bearing/ time record (BTR). For doing this, a so-called "tracker" is initialised for each observed target which tries to follow its movement. If a tracker is not initialised by a false alarm, then its trajectory should correspond to a track in the BTR considered. Essentially, this task is composed of two central features. The pairing of observations to trackers, and the prediction of the bearing of already-detected targets for the next time step. The latter is done by using so-called "tracking filters". Furthermore, the initialised trackers are judged by means of a confidence factor, which is also used for their termination. As will be shown, both the tracking filter and the evaluation of the trackers can be realized by fuzzy systems.

The basic data for automatic target tracking in sonar systems is the integrated magnitude-squared response of a scanning beam in a noise field which contains moving targets. This energy versus bearing representation will be called a "bearing spectrum" and is computed for consecutive time frames of length T (T depends on the integration time). In other words, after time T (e.g. one second) a new bearing spectrum can be analysed. The computation of bearing spectra can be done in several ways; however, a detailed discussion of these various methods would be beyond the scope of this paper.

Usually, the local maxima of the bearing spectra are determined and the corresponding bearings are interpreted as the locations of possible targets. In most cases, preprocessing of the bearing spectra is necessary before local maxima can be searched for. Otherwise, too many false alarms would be accepted. Nevertheless, some of the observations are due to noise and have to be suppressed during the actual tracking phase.

The detection of tracks in the waterfall representation of the bearing spectra can be made more difficult by gaps in the tracks, local maxima of the bearing spectrum which have been caused by noise, and tracks which are not smooth curves but fluctuate randomly around the ideal curve.

The tracking of detected targets is made more difficult by the crossing of tracks. The following situations can occur:

1. The crossing of tracks, i.e., both targets maintain their courses. This does not necessarily lead to collision since two targets having the same bearing can have different ranges. Range is not taken into account by the computation of the waterfall representation of bearing spectra.
2. The touching of tracks, i.e., two tracks converge to the same point and afterwards diverge again without crossing each other. At least one of the two targets undergoes a course change at the point of touching.
3. The merging of tracks. After the tracks have merged, the two targets proceed either close together or one behind the other.

In practice, it is difficult to decide whether case 1 or case 2 is present since the corresponding patterns in the waterfall representation are very similar in both cases. Hence, further features have to be taken into account in order to make these two scenarios distinguishable. An example is given in Figure 16.84 where on the left-hand side the touching of two tracks is shown and in the middle the crossing of two tracks. However, these differences are not visible in Figure 16.84. The white areas next to the tracks are due to the fact that only local maxima have been displayed.

The automation of the target detection and tracking process is the task of the fuzzy system introduced below. It is able to distinguish between the two cases "crossing of tracks" and "touching of tracks". Short gaps in tracks are bridged automatically and the end of a track is recognised within a short time. Naturally, in the case of a poor signal-to-noise ratio, tracks are often blurred and false alarms can consequently occur. Hence, a confidence factor is assigned to each initialised tracker in order to improve the meaningfulness of the displayed results.

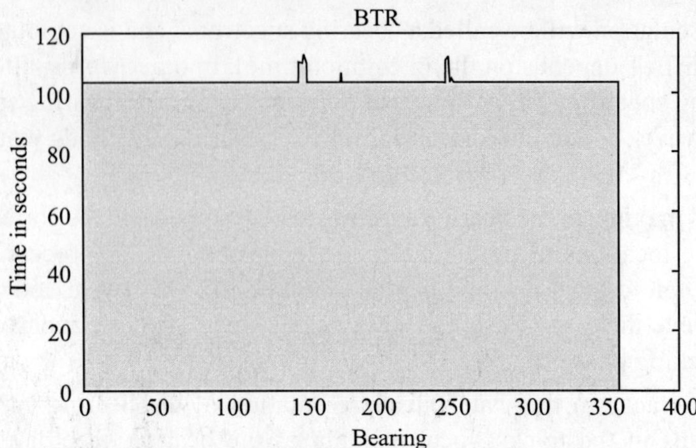

Figure 16.84: Example of the waterfall representation of bearing spectra

In general, batch or sequential approaches for automatic track detection could be considered. In the first case, the bearing spectra could be stored for a certain time interval and afterwards analysed in one step. In other words, the available three-dimensional data record (amplitude versus bearing versus time) could be processed with known pattern recognition algorithms. However, a considerable lag between signal reception and signal analysis would be the result since a time record of approximately 5-10 minutes should be available. In order to be able to respond to the current situation instantaneously, such an approach cannot even be considered. Hence, the sequential approach has been adopted which is outlined in the following. After an initialization procedure has been executed, several possible tracks have been localised, i.e., trackers have been initialised. Their current bearing is stored. By taking into account the latest history of the trackers, the respective bearing for the next time step is predicted by means of tracking filters. Usually, the latter are realised by Kalman or filters. In our approach, however, a fuzzy tracking filter has been realised. As soon as observed data is available for the new time step an observation to tracks assignment has to be performed (data association). If observations occur which cannot be assigned to one of the trackers already initiated, they are considered as the beginning of possible new tracks.

Conversely, if no observation can be associated with a tracker already in existence, then penalty points are added to a score. Two different confidence measures are assigned to each tracker. The local confidence factor describes the short term behaviour and the global confidence factor takes into account the history of the tracker. More precisely, the data association is not performed exclusively, i.e., one observation can be assigned to several trackers in the case of crossings. However, different trackers are not treated equivalently with respect to the assignment of observations. The order in which trackers are processed depends on their current ranks. The latter are newly computed after every 16th time step and depend on the counts of the local confidence factors. These local confidence factors are also newly computed after every 16th time step and additionally increase or decrease the global confidence factors. The global confidence factor of each tracker influences the size of the corresponding gate for data association and terminates the tracker if it drops below a given boundary value. In other words, it represents a measure of the quality of the respective tracker. The computation of the local confidence factors is done by a fuzzy module.

The data association itself obeys the following rules. All existing trackers are processed in the order of their ranks. The tracker currently being considered is associated with that observation from the interior of a gate around its location which has the greatest amplitude. The assigned observation is marked. Observations which cannot be assigned to a tracker already in existence are considered as the locations of new tracks. The tracking filter predicts the bearing of each tracker for the next time step. The main component of the tracking filter is a fuzzy system. The further details of the tracking algorithm are of no interest within the context of this paper. Only the two fuzzy systems should be examined in more detail.

The fuzzy tracking filter estimates the momentary bearing rate of each of the targets already detected and predicts the corresponding bearing for the next time step (see Figure 16.85). In other words, the predicted bearing results from

$$x_p(k+1) = x_p(k) + T\,v(k), \tag{4}$$

where T is the sampling period. The bearing rate v(k) is non-linearly computed from e(k), the difference between predicted, $x_p(k)$, and observed bearing, $x_o(k)$, for the time instant k.

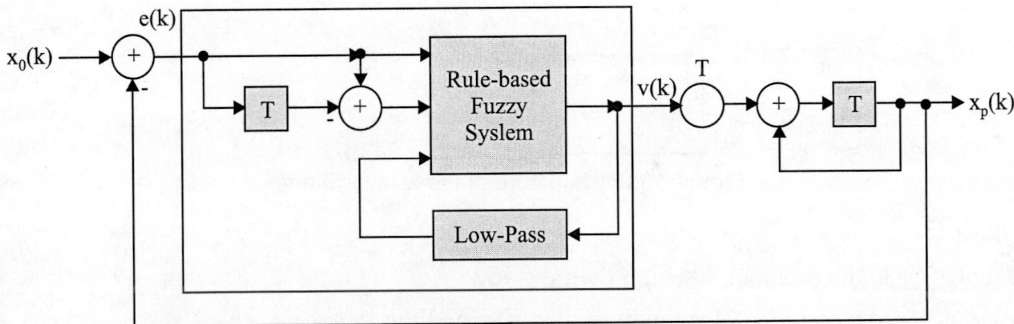

Figure 16.85: The tracking filter

The main component of the tracking filter is the rule-based fuzzy system which has the following input signals:

– prediction error e(k)
– change of e(k)
– low-pass filtered bearing rate v(k).

The use of fuzzy systems for tracking problems has been proposed.

The second fuzzy module computes the increase or decrease of the local certainty factor for each active tracker to which an observation has been assigned. It consists of two rule bases and has the following input signals:

– prediction error e(k) (difference between predicted and observed bearing),
– rank of the assigned observation (position in a list of all observations sorted with respect to the corresponding amplitude of the bearing spectrum),
– magnitude of the difference between the rank of the assigned observation and the rank of the observation assigned in the previous time step,

– magnitude of the difference between the numbers of the frequency bands in which, respectively the present and the previous observation have been localised (the bearing spectrum is computed for different frequency bands of the array signals).

The first input signal is a measure for the likelihood that the assigned observation is indeed the continuation of the track. A low rank of an observation indicates that it might be a false alarm. The third and fourth input signals are measures relating to the continuity of the observations.

Rule base 1 (cf. Figure 16.86) combines input signals 3 and 4 to an intermediate quality variable q which is fed to rule base 2. The latter computes from input signals 1 and 2 and the intermediate variable q a number $v \in [-1, 1]$, which is added to the local confidence factor. Naturally, the whole set of production rules contained in the rule bases cannot be listed here. Examples are:

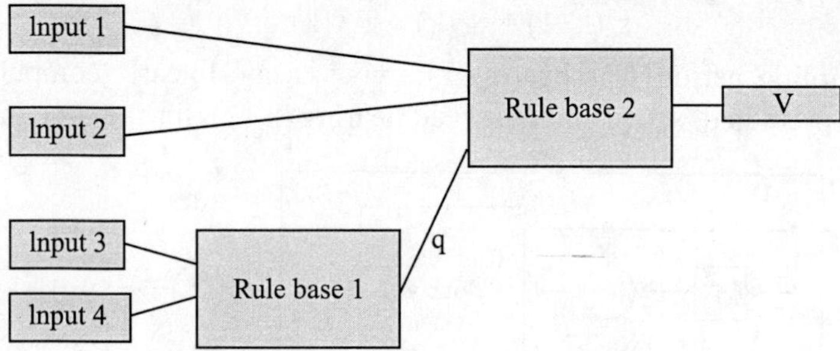

Figure 16.86: Structure of the fuzzy system

Rule base 1:

If input 3 = high and input 4 = high then q = low.

If input 3 = low and input 4 = medium then q = medium.

⋮

Rule base 2:

If input 1 = high and input 2 = high and q = low then v = very low.

If input 1 = high and input 2 = low and q = medium then v = medium.

⋮

Many trackers (usually started by false alarms caused by noise) will be terminated shortly after initialization. Hence, only those trackers whose respective global confidence factor has crossed a certain boundary value will be considered as true targets and the corresponding bearing versus time curves (tracks) will be displayed. All other trackers are suppressed.

In Figure 16.87, a simulated bearing versus time scenario (randomly fluctuating tracks with superimposed noise) is shown which contains (from left to right) the following situations:

– a track which originates at the right-hand side of the scenario,
– the touching of two tracks,
– the crossing of two tracks,
– a track with gaps,

– the touching of two tracks with a long common path,

– the origin of the first track.

The corresponding tracks detected by the automatic tracking algorithm described above are shown in Figure 16.88. Connected branches of a track are marked with the same number which distinguishes between the situations "crossing" and "touching". Obviously, the different situations have been recognised correctly by the algorithm. Only the fifth situation (touching of two tracks with long common path) produced problems in the upper part. Due to the long common path, one of the two trackers had terminated before the bifurcation had been reached. Therefore, a new traker was initialized for the left branch of the bifurcation.

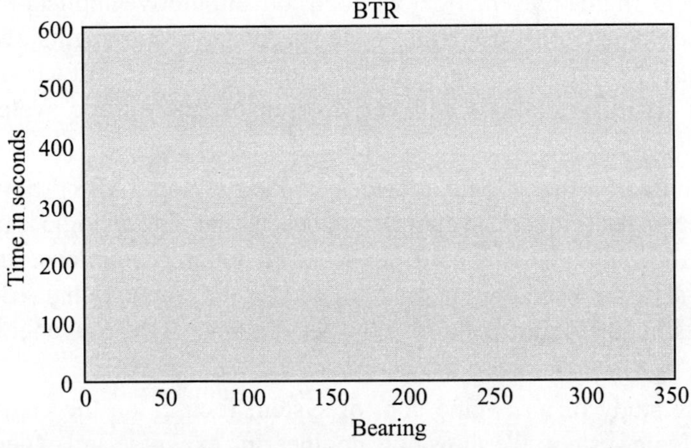

Figure 16.87: Example of the waterfall representation of bearing spectra

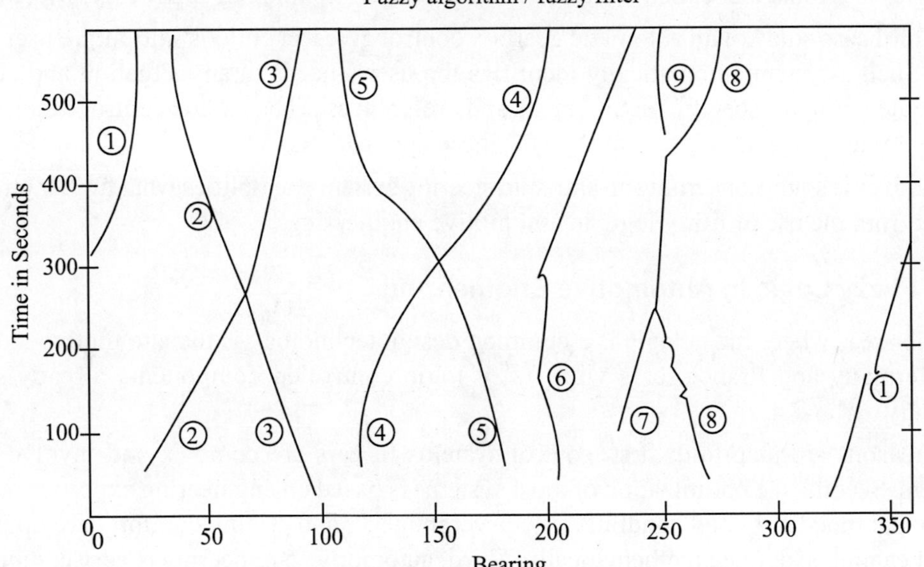

Figure 16.88: Detected tracks

16.8.5 Concluding Remarks

In this paper, rule-based fuzzy systems for classification problems and automatic target tracking have been discussed. Furthermore, a short introduction to fuzzy theory has been given. It should be noted that the above-mentioned applications of fuzzy logic have been already implemented in the latest generation of Atlas sonar equipment.

16.9 FUZZY LOGIC IN AUTOMOTIVE ENGINEERING

Fuzzy Logic is a powerful technology which allows designers to quickly incorporate engineering expertise into products. In this presentation, we focus on automotive applications. We will discuss development methodologies, tools used, and code speed/size requirements of three case studies. Also, we will compare dedicated hardware for fuzzy logic systems to software implementations. A final discussion of stability analysis and verification of fuzzy logic systems concludes the presentation.

The first case study of a fuzzy logic anti-lock braking system (ABS) shows how fuzzy logic and conventional design techniques can complement each other. Fuzzy logic is used to optimize the existing ABS system to achieve a better performance in all braking conditions. An estimation system for the road surface state has been built that parameterizes the conventional ABS. Road tests show that the fuzzy logic estimator is able to improve the performance of the conventional ABS, especially on dry surfaces.

The second case study of an engine control system focuses on the engineering process of building up a fuzzy logic system. We show how engineering expertise and experimental results can be used together with model-based system design to reduce time-to-market. Also, we present design technologies and tools that expedite design and support verification of fuzzy logic systems.

The third case study of an automatic gearbox control gives an outlook into future user adaptive systems. Such a system automatically identifies the user's needs in any situation and adapts the control strategies to his specific requirements and preferences. The gearbox control example shows that fuzzy logic is an enabling technology for these applications.

A fourth case study concerning an anti-skid steering system exemplifies what further innovations can result from the use of fuzzy logic in automotive engineering.

16.9.1 Fuzzy Logic In Automotive Engineering

One of the areas where fuzzy logic is a common design technology is the automotive industry. In Japan, Germany and France, cars with fuzzy logic controlled components already sell very successfully.

The reasons are manifold: first, control systems in cars are complex and involve multiple parameters. Second, the optimization of most systems is based on engineering expertise rather than mathematical models. "Good handling", "Fahrvergnügen", and "riding comfort" are optimization goals that cannot be defined mathematically. Third, automotive engineering is very competitive on an international scale. A technology that provides a competitive advantage is soon commonly used.

The following discussion assumes the reader is familiar with basic fuzzy logic design principles.

16.9.2 Anti-lock Braking Systems with Fuzzy Logic

In 1947, Boeing Corporation developed the first anti-lock braking system for airplanes as a mechanical system. Today, anti-lock braking systems (ABS) are standard equipment with most cars. They use electronic sensors that measure the speed of every wheel and microcontrollers to control the fluid pressure for the brake cylinders. Mathematical models for the braking system of a car do exist, but the interaction of the braking system with the car and the road is by far too complex to model adequately. Hence, today's anti-lock braking systems contain the engineering knowledge of years of testing in different roads and climates.

1. Fuzzy Anti-lock Braking Systems in Production

Fuzzy logic is a very efficient technology for putting engineering knowledge directly into a technical solution. Hence, it is no surprise that already many applications with anti-lock braking systems are on the market. Currently Nissan and Mitsubishi ship cars with fuzzy ABS. Honda, Mazda, Hyundai, BMW, Mercedes-Benz, Bosch and Peugeot are working on solutions.

Another reason why anti-lock braking systems benefit from fuzzy logic is the high computational efficiency of its implementation. In an ABS, the control loop time is in the order of 5 milliseconds. Within this interval, the microcontrollers must fetch all sensor data, preprocess it, compute the ABS algorithm, drive the bypass valves, and conduct the test routines. Any additional functions must be very computationally efficient. Most ABS systems use 16 bit microcontrollers, which can compute a medium size fuzzy logic system in about ½ millisecond using only about 2 KB ROM space.

2. Adapting the ABS to the Road Surface

The implementations of fuzzy logic ABS are very different. The implementation of Nippondenso, which I am now presenting as a case study, also exhibits an intelligent combination of conventional techniques with fuzzy logic. First, some basics of the braking process.

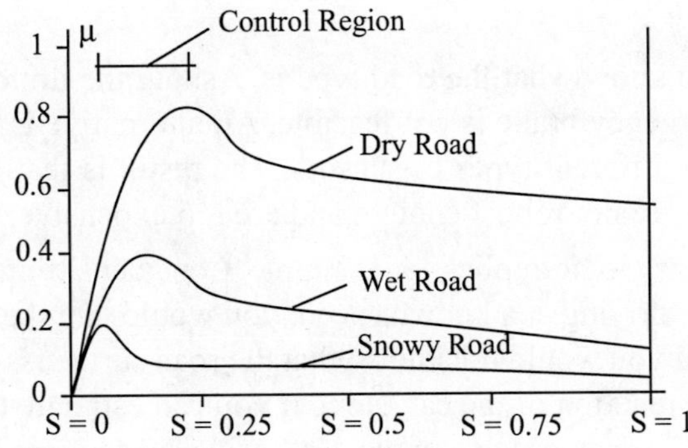

Figure 16.89: Plot of brake effect over the wheel slack s for dry, wet and snowy road surfaces (μ: friction coefficient, measure of brake effect)

If a wheel rotates exactly as fast as it corresponds to the speed of the car, the wheel is experiencing no braking effect at all. If a wheel does not rotate at all, it is blocked. This situation has two disadvantages. First, a car with blocked wheels is impossible to steer. Second, the brake effect is not optimal. The point of optimum brake effect is between these two extremes.

Road condition	Optimum slack
Dry road	0.2
Slippery or wet asphalt	0.12
Ice or Snow	0.05

Figure 16.90: The slack value for maximum brake effect depends on the type of road

The speed difference between the car and the wheel during braking is called "slack". Its definition is:

$$s = (V_{Car} - V_{Wheel}) / V_{Car}$$

where:

s : slack, always between 0 (no braking) and 1 (blocking)

V_{Car} : velocity of the car

V_{Wheel} : velocity of the wheel

Figure 16.89 plots the relation between brake effect and slack for different road surfaces. For s = 0, the speed of the wheel equals the speed of the car. In the case of s = 1, the wheel blocks completely. The curves show that the optimum brake effect lies between these two extremes. However, the point of maximum brake effect depends on the type of road. Figure 16.90 lists typical values.

3. Estimation of Road Surface using Fuzzy Logic

A conventional anti-lock braking system controls the bypass valves of the brake fluid so that the slack equals a set value. Most manufacturers program this set value to a slack of 0.1, because this is a good compromise value for all road conditions. As figures 16.89 and 16.90 show, this set value is not optimal for every road type. By knowing the road type, the braking effect could further be enhanced.

The problem is how to know what the road type is. Asking the driver to push a button on the dash board before an emergency brake is not feasible. An alternative is the use of sensors. Many companies have evaluated different types of sensors. The result is that sensors that deliver good road surface identification are not robust enough and are too expensive.

The idea of the cited fuzzy logic application is simple. Consider sitting in your own car equipped with a standard ABS. After driving at a known speed, you would jam the brake pedal such that the ABS starts to work. Even if you would not know what the road surface is like, you could now have a good guess just from the reaction of the car. Now, if you can estimate the road surface just from the car's reaction, why not implement this in the ABS using fuzzy logic?

This is just what Nippondenso did. When the ABS first detects blocking of a wheel, it starts to control the brake fluid valves so that each wheel rotates with a slack of 0.1. The fuzzy logic system then evaluates the reaction of the car to the braking and estimates the current road surface. Considering this estimation, the ABS then corrects the set value for the slack so that it achieves the best braking effect.

The fuzzy logic system only uses input data that stems from the existing sensors of the ABS. Such input variables are deceleration or speed of the car, deceleration or speed of the wheels and hydraulic pressure of the brake fluid. These input variables are an indirect indicator of the current operation point of the braking (Figure 16.89) and its behavior over time. Experiments showed that a first prototype with just six (6) fuzzy logic rules already improved performance significantly. One test track alternates from snowy to wet road. Here, the fuzzy logic ABS detected the change even during braking.

4. Other Applications of Fuzzy Logic in ABS

Due to the high competition in this area, most manufacturers are reluctant to publish any details about the technologies they use. The cited application only shows results from an experimental fuzzy logic system. The details about the final product are not published.

Also, some companies worry about the negative connotation of the word “fuzzy”. As it implies “imprecision” and “inexact”, manufacturers are afraid drivers could think of a “fuzzy ABS” as something inferior. Others feel threatened by the scenario in which a clever lawyer sues them by suggesting to a laymen’s jury that fuzzy logic ABS is something hazardous. In Japan, where an appreciation for ambiguity lies in the culture, “fuzzy” does not have a negative connotation. In contrast, it is considered an advantage because it enables intelligent systems such as the cited application. Hence, companies are proud of its use and even use it in advertising

In Germany for example, the situation is different. Here, the concepts of fuzziness and engineering masterpiece do not fit in the public perception. Hence, most manufacturers that use fuzzy logic in ABS actually hide the fact. After all, a fuzzy logic system is only a segment of assembly code in a microcontroller once implemented. Who could actually tell that this code implements fuzzy logic? Some engineers already talk about “hidden fuzzy logic”

5. Stability of a Fuzzy ABS

Some engineers, especially those who went to a well-reputed university, argue the stability of fuzzy logic systems. In the case of the Fuzzy ABS shown, this is not an issue. The conventional ABS was considered to be stable for any slack value in the interval from 0.05 to 0.25. Hence, a fuzzy logic road surface estimator that only tunes this value to the optimum can principally not make this system unstable.

16.9.3 Engine Control with Fuzzy Logic

The control of car and truck engines becomes increasingly more complex due to higher emission standards and the constant push for higher fuel efficiency. Twenty years ago, control systems were mechanical (carburetor, distributor and breaker contact). Now, microcontroller based systems control fuel injection and ignition point. Since the control strategy for an engine depends strongly on the current operating point (revolutions, momentum,...), linear control models, such as PID, are not suitable. On the other hand, no mathematical model that describes the complete behavior of an engine exists. Because of this, most engine controllers use a look-up-table to represent the control strategy. The look-up-table is generated from the results of extensive testing and the engineer's experience.

The generation of such a look-up-table, however, is only suitable for three dimensions (2 inputs, 1 output). Also, the generation and interpretation of these look-up-tables is difficult and considered a "black art". Replacing these look-up-tables hence is a potential for fuzzy logic. Alas, most manufacturers are unwilling to publish any details on their fuzzy logic engine control solution. This is due to the fact that the rules of the fuzzy logic system contain the entire engine control knowledge of the company and are completely transparent. Hence, manufacturers are afraid that their competitors could learn too much about the solution by disassembling the fuzzy logic rules.

1. Identification of Driving Condition

The case study of an engine control system by NOK and Nissan illustrates the benefits of using fuzzy logic. Figure 16.91 sketches the components of the engine controller that contains three fuzzy logic modules. The basic idea of the system is that it first identifies the operational condition of the engine by the linguistic variable "Situation" that has the following linguistic terms:

linguistic variable Situation

{

Term 1: Start

Control strategy is that the cold engine runs smooth - ignition is timed early and the mix is fat;

Term 2: Idle

Control ignition timing and fuel injection depending on engine temperature to ensure that the engine runs smooth;

Term 3: Normal drive, low or medium load

Maximize fuel efficiency by meager mix, watch knocking;

Term 4: Normal drive, high load

Fat mix and early ignition to maximize performance - the only constraint is the permitted emission maximum;

Term 5: Coasting

fuel cut-off, depending on situation;

Term 6: Acceleration

Depending on the load, fattening of the mix

}

The determination of the linguistic variable "Situation" is a state estimation of the operation point. As "Situation" is a linguistic variable, more than one term can be valid at the same time. This allows for expressing combinations of the operational points defined by the terms. Hence, a possible value of "Situation" could be: {0.8; 0; 1; 0; 0; 0.3}. Linguistically, this value represents the driving condition *engine started just a short while ago, normal drive condition at medium or low load, slightly accelerating*. From this operation point identification, the individual fuzzy logic modules control injection, fuel cut-off, and ignition.

Similar to ABS systems described in the previous section, engine control requires a very short loop time. Some systems are as fast as 1 millisecond for an entire control loop. For this, some manufacturers design the system using fuzzy logic, but then translate it into a look-up-table for faster processing. Even though, a look-up-table is very fast to compute, the memory requirements may be prohibitive. For a look-up-table with 2 inputs and 1 output, all 8 bit resolution already requires 64 Kbytes of ROM. Restricting the resolution of the input variables to 6 bit each, the look-up-table still requires 4 Kbytes. A look-up-table with 3 inputs and 1 output, all inputs of 6 bit resolution would require ¼ Mbyte. Some engineers tried to implement a look-up-table with a very limited resolution and to use an interpolation algorithm. Comparison, however, shows that the interpolation requires about as much computing time as the fuzzy logic system itself.

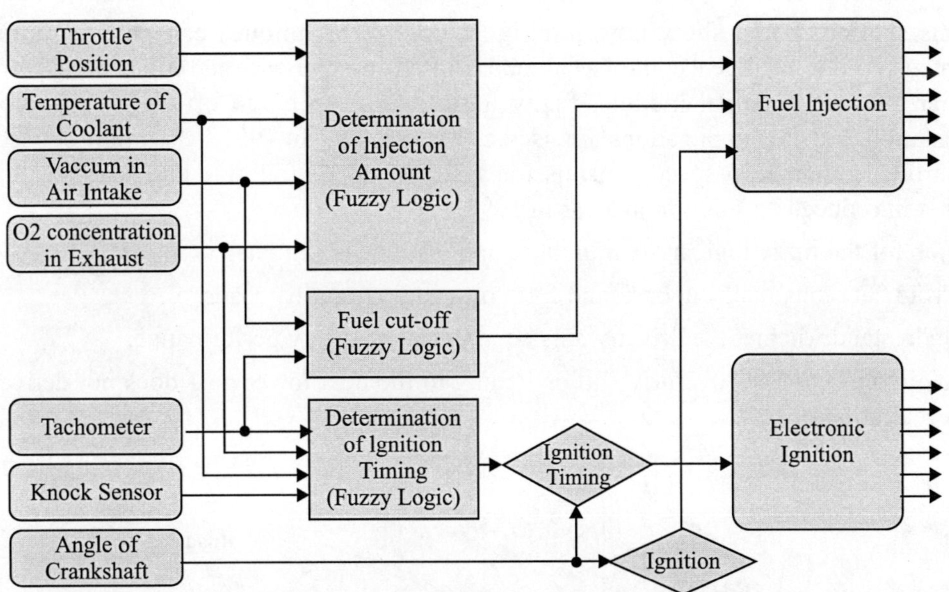

Figure 16.91: Modules of the fuzzy logic engine controller of nok

Another published application of fuzzy logic in engine control is an idle control unit by Ford Motor Corporation.

16.9.4 Adaptive 5-speed Automatic Transmission

When the first 3-speed automatic transmissions appeared on the market about 30 years ago, the engine power of most cars was just sufficient enough to keep the car in pace with traffic. The necessity of getting maximum momentum from the engine determined the shift points for the gears.

Now that most car engines can deliver much more power than necessary to keep the car in pace with traffic, automatic transmission systems have up to five (5) speeds and fuel efficiency is an important issue, plus the control is much more complex.

The higher engine power and five (5) speeds to chose from give the automatic transmission system a much higher degree of freedom. Driving at 35 mph (56 km/h), a 3-speed automatic transmission has no choice but selecting the second gear. A 5-speed automatic transmission with a powerful engine could select the second gear if maximum acceleration is required, the third gear in a normal driving condition, and the fourth gear if only a little acceleration is needed.

1. Acceleration vs. Fuel Efficiency

Unfortunately, the goal for the control strategy is in a dilemma. For maximum fuel efficiency, you must select the next higher gear as early as possible. For maximum performance, you switch to the next higher gear later. If you have a shift gear box, you can choose the strategy depending on the traffic conditions. An automatic gearbox has no understanding of the traffic conditions and the driver's wishes.

In this section, I will show how intelligent control techniques can enhance automatic transmissions. As this intelligent control technique is based on experience and engineering knowledge rather than on mathematical models, fuzzy logic proves to be an efficient technology for implementation. Existing applications are used as case studies. In 1991, Nissan introduced fuzzy logic controlled automatic 5-speed transmission systems. Honda followed one year later and GM/ Saturn first introduced its solution in a car in 1993.

The job for the fuzzy logic system in these applications is similar:

- Avoid "nervous" shifting back and forth on winding or hilly roads.
- Understand whether the driver wants economical or sporty performance.
- Avoid unnecessary "overdrive" if switching to the next lower gear does not deliver more acceleration.

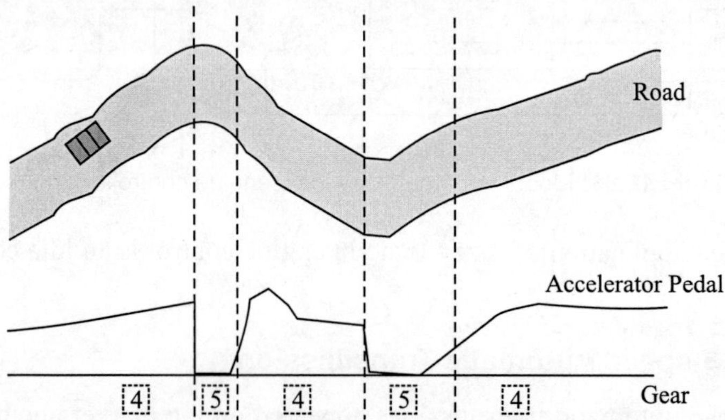

Figure 16.92: A 5-speed automatic transmission with fixed shift points always switches between 4th and 5th gear on a winding road. A driver with a shift gear box would stay in the 4th gear.

Figure 16.92 shows a typical situation on a winding road. While a driver with a shift gear box would stay in the 4th gear, a 5-speed automatic transmission switches between the 4th and the 5th gear.

The fuzzy logic controller in the automatic transmission evaluates more than just the current speed of the car. It also analyzes how the driver accelerates and brakes. To detect the condition of a winding road for instance, the fuzzy logic controller looks at the number of accelerator pedal changes within a certain period. Figure 16.93 shows the definition of the linguistic variable "Accelerator pedal changes". Also, the variance of the accelerator pedal changes is an input to the fuzzy logic controller.

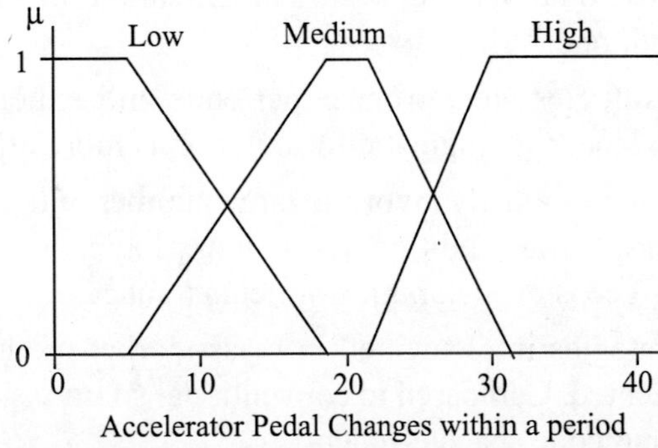

Figure 16.93: Classification of driving condition using a linguistic variable. The variable linguistically interprets the amplitude of accelerator pedal changes within a certain period

Some of the rules that estimate the driving conditions from these input variables are:

- Many pedal changes within a period indicate a fast and winding road
- Few pedal changes within a period indicate a freeway
- Many pedal changes within a period and a very high variance of the pedal changes indicate a slow and winding road
- Medium variance of the pedal changes indicates a fast and winding road
- Low variance of the pedal changes indicates a freeway

The interesting part of this application is that it uses the driver as the actual sensor for the driving condition. The fuzzy logic controller only interprets the driver's reaction to the driving condition and adapts the car's performance accordingly. This could be used as the definition of an intelligent control system. The technical system tries to understand whether the human is satisfied with its performance. If not, the technical system adapts itself to suit the needs of the human that uses it.

2. *"Intelligent" Automatic Transmissions*

Another example of an automatic transmission system, currently under development in Germany, shows this even better. The following situation is typical, if the driver is not satisfied with the acceleration of a car. The driver pushes down the accelerator pedal and within 1 to 1.5 seconds, he pushes the pedal down even a little bit more. This is the subconscious reaction to a non-satisfying acceleration. Most drivers do not even consciously realize that they like the car to accelerate faster. If the automatic transmission system is capable of detecting this, it could move the shift points higher to achieve more acceleration. The opposite case is similar. If the automatic transmission detects that the driver accelerates very carefully and takes the foot off from the accelerator long before red lights, chances are that the driver wants high fuel efficiency.

3. Why Fuzzy Logic?

The question remains, why do you need fuzzy logic to implement these intelligent functions? The answer is, certainly you can use other techniques to implement these control strategies. But fuzzy logic may be the most efficient one:

- Intelligent control strategies stem from experience and experiments rather than from mathematical models. Hence, a linguistic formulation is more efficient.
- Intelligent control strategies mostly involve a large number of inputs. Most of the inputs are only relevant for some specific condition. Using fuzzy logic, this input is only considered in the relevant rule. This keeps even complex systems transparent.
- Intelligent control strategies implemented in mass-market products have to be very cost efficient to be implemented. Compared to conventional solutions, fuzzy logic is often much more computational and code space efficient.

16.9.5 Anti-skid Steering Systems

Active stability control systems in cars have a long history. First, anti-locking brakes (ABS) improved braking performance by reducing the amount of brake force to what the road conditions can handle. This avoids sliding and results in shorter braking distances. Second, traction control systems that do essentially the same thing improved acceleration. Reducing engine power applied to the wheels to what the road can handle, it maximizes acceleration and minimizes tire wear. The next logical step, after skid-controlled braking and skid-controlled acceleration, is skid-controlled steering. Such an anti-skid steering system (ASS) reduces the steering angle to the amount the road can take. As such, it optimizes the steering action and avoids sliding. A sliding car is very hard to stabilize, especially for drivers not used to it.

Figure 16.94: Model car for high-speed driving experiments

Though an anti-skid steering system (ASS) makes a lot of sense from a technical point of view, such a system is hard to market. For an ABS, one can prove that it never performs worse than a traditional brake system. For an ASS, this is very hard to prove. Also, it may be difficult to sell cars that "take over the steering" in emergency situations. Even ABS faced a long period of rejection by customers, because they felt uneasy about a system inhibiting their brake action. For these reasons, it may take a long time before an ASS system is implemented in a production car. All results shown in this section stem from a research project of a German car manufacturer. As this system is one of the most complex fuzzy logic embedded systems, it shows well the potential of the technology.

1. The Test Vehicle

Real experiments were made on a modified Audi sedan and on a 20" model car (Figure 16.94). In the following, I will only present the results derived from the model car experiments. A one-horsepower electric motor powers the car, rendering the power-to-weight-ratio of a race car. This allows it to perform skidding and sliding experiments in extreme situations at high speeds. On a dry surface, the car reaches a velocity of 20 mph in 3.5 seconds with top speed up to 50 mph. The speed for most experiments ranges from 20 to 30 mph. Each wheel features individual suspension and has a separate shock absorber. The car has disk brakes and a lockable differential.

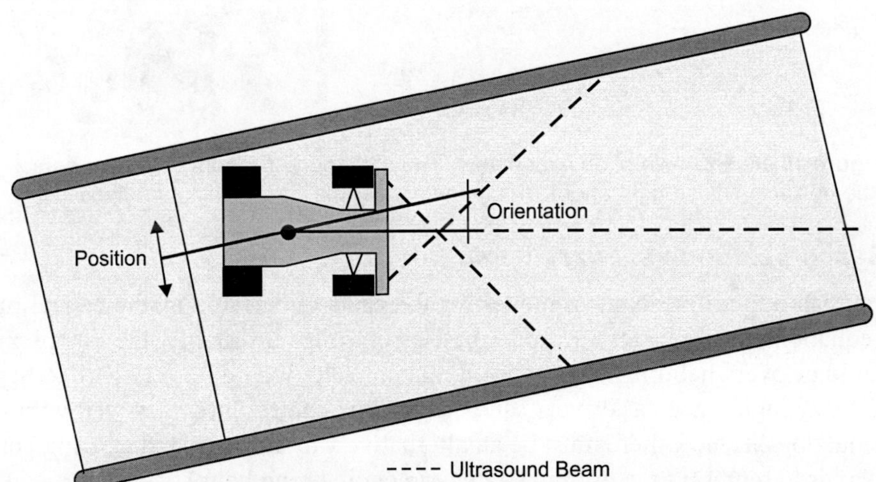

Figure 16.95: Three ultrasound sensors guide the car on the track

The controller of the car uses the motherboard of a 12 MHz notebook 286-PC connected to an interface board that drives actors and sensors. Actors are power steering servo, disk brake servo, and pulse width modulated motor control. Sensors are three ultrasound distance sensors for track guidance and infrared reflex sensors in every wheel for speed. The control loop time, from reading in sensor signals to setting the values for the actors, is 10 milliseconds.

To measure the dynamic state of the car, such as skidding and sliding, infrared sensors measure the individual speed of all four wheels. Evaluating wheel speed differences, the fuzzy logic system interprets the current situation. Three fixed mounted ultrasound sensors measure the distance to the next obstacle to the front, the left and the right. This allows for an autonomous operation of the car. Intentionally, low-cost sensors have been used in this study rather than CCD cameras and picture recognition techniques, to prove that expensive sensors can be replaced by a fuzzy logic control strategy.

Figure 16.96 shows the example of an experiment involving the model car. The obstacle (block) is placed right after the curve, so that the ultrasound sensors of the car will "see" the obstacle too late. To not hit the obstacle, the car has to decide for a very rapid turn. To optimize the steering effect, the anti-skid controller has to reduce the desired steering angle to the maximum the road can take, avoiding both sliding and hitting the obstacle.

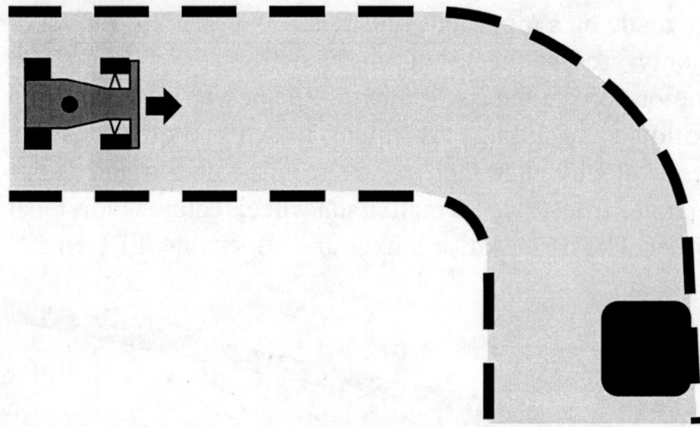

Figure 16.96: Example of an experiment. The ultrasound sensors of the car detect the obstacle placed right after the curve very late, making a quick turn necessary

2. Model Based Solution vs. Fuzzy Logic Control

In theory, you can build a mechanical model for the car and derive a mathematical model with differential equations to implement a model based controller. In reality, the complexity of this approach would be overwhelming and the resulting controller would be very hard to tune. Here is the point for fuzzy logic: race car drivers can perform this control task very well without solving differential equations. Hence, there must be an alternative way for anti-skid steering control. This alternative way is to represent the driving strategy in engineering heuristics.

Though there are multiple ways of expressing engineering heuristics, fuzzy logic has proven to be very effective, due to the following reasons:

- You can often formulate engineering heuristics in "if-then" causalities. The "if" part usually represents a certain state of a process while the "then" part represents the action to be taken in this case.
- In contrast to other methods of expressing "if-then" causalities, such as expert systems, the computation in a fuzzy logic system is quantitative rather than symbolic. In a fuzzy logic system, you use a few rules to express general situations, then the fuzzy logic algorithm deduces decisions for the real occurring situations. A conventional expert system would need a rule for each possible situation.

- In a fuzzy logic system, every element is self-explanatory. Linguistic variables are very close to the human representation of continuous concepts. Fuzzy inference and fuzzy operators combine these concepts very much the way humans do.
- Fuzzy logic is non-linear and multi-parametric by nature. So it can better cope with complex control problems that are also non-linear and involve multiple parameters.
- Fuzzy logic can efficiently be implemented in embedded control applications. Even on a standard microcontroller, a fuzzy logic system can outperform a comparable conventional solution both by code size and computing speed.

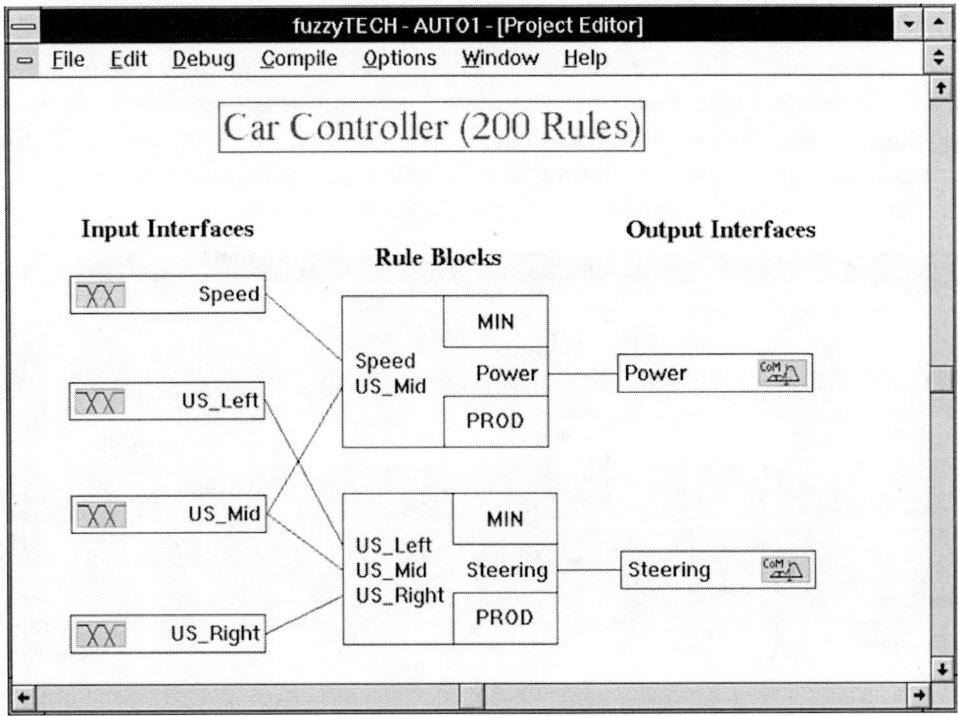

Figure 16.97: First version with 200 rules in two rule blocks. The four left boxes indicate input interfaces for sensors; the two right boxes indicate output interfaces for the actors and the two large boxes in the middle represent fuzzy logic rule blocks

3. Design and Implementation of a Fuzzy Logic Controller

Figure 16.97 shows the first version of a fuzzy logic controller for the car. The objective for this controller was autonomous guidance of the car in the track at slow speed, where no skidding and sliding occurs. In Figure 16.98, the lower rule block uses the distances measured by the three ultrasound sensors to determine the steering angle. The upper rule block implements a simple speed control by using the distance to the next obstacle measured by the front ultrasound sensor and the speed of one front wheel only. Due to the slow speeds, no skidding or sliding occurs. Hence, all wheel speeds are the same. The first version contains about 200 rules and took only a few hours to implement.

The second version of a fuzzy logic controller implements a more complex fuzzy logic system for dynamic stability control. It includes anti-locking brakes, traction and anti-skid steering control (Figure 16.99). This 600 rule fuzzy logic controller has two stages of fuzzy inference. The first stage, represented by the three left rule blocks, estimates the state variables of the dynamic situation of the car out of sensor data. The two lower rule blocks estimate skidding and sliding states out of speed sensor signals, while the upper rule block estimates position and orientation of the car in the test track. Note, the output of the left three rule blocks is linguistic rather than numerical. An estimated state of the car therefore could be: "the position is rather left, while the orientation is strongly to the right, and the car skids over the left front wheel".

The second stage, represented by the three right rule blocks, uses these estimations as inputs to determine the best control action for this situation. The upper rule block determines the steering angle, the middle one the engine power to be applied, and the lower one controls the brake. Such a two-stage control strategy is similar to the human behavior, which first analyzes the situation and then determines the action. Also, this allows for efficient optimization, since the total of 600 rule structures into 6 rule blocks that can be designed and optimized independently.

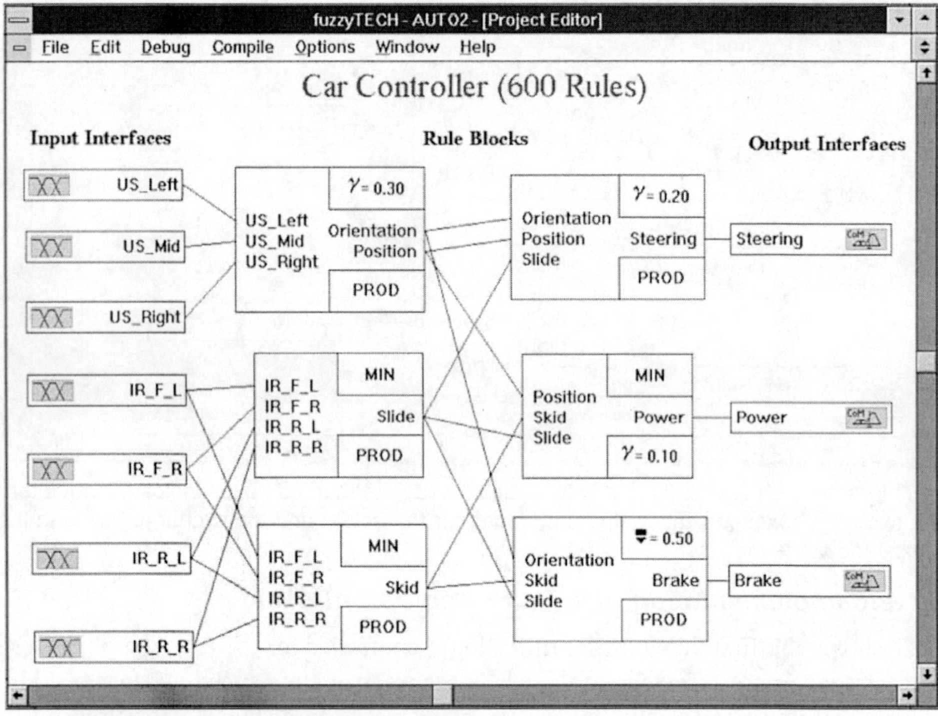

Figure 16.98: Second version of the fuzzy logic controller. the controller uses advanced fuzzy logic design technologies and contains a total of 600 rules

The first version of the controller was only able to guide the car for autonomous cruising (Figure 16.97). The second version also succeeded to dynamically stabilize the car's cruising with anti-locking brakes, traction control, and anti-skid steering. However, this version required a lot longer design time before the results were completely satisfactory. The second version also uses advanced fuzzy logic technologies, such as FAM inference and the Gamma aggregational operator.

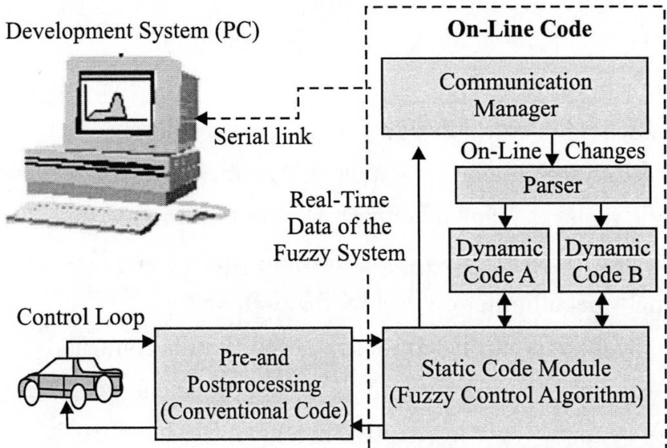

Figure 16.99: The fuzzyTECH Online Edition features both visualization of the running system and modifications "on-the-fly"

4. Online Development

The development of the fuzzy logic system involved the *fuzzy*TECH Online Edition. After the graphical definition of the system structure (Figure 16.97 and 16.98), the linguistic variables and the rule bases, then the compiler of *fuzzy*TECH generated the system as C code. This code was compiled and implemented on the PC mounted in the car. Figure 16.99 shows how the running fuzzy logic system was modified "on-the-fly" for optimization. The fuzzy logic code is separated into two segments. One contains all "static" code, which is code that does not need to be modified for system modifications. The other one contains all "dynamic" code, which is the code containing the membership functions of the linguistic variables, the inference structure, and the rules. The "dynamic" segment is doubled with only one of the segments active at a time. As such, the parser, linked to the development PC via a communications manager, can modify the inactive code segment. This allows for modifications of the running system without halting or compiling. At the same time, the entire inference flow inside the fuzzy logic controller is graphically visualized on the PC, since the communications manager also transfers all real-time data.

On the example of a anti-skid steering system, we have shown the applicability of fuzzy logic technologies for a complex control problem found in the automotive industry. The design of the fuzzy logic system has been done straightforward and without a mathematical model of the process. Existing engineering heuristics were implemented in fuzzy logic rules and linguistic variables. During optimization, we found the control strategy easy to optimize due to the linguistic representation in the fuzzy logic system. Tests and verification were expedited due to the transparency of the controller. The poor computational performance of early fuzzy logic software solutions has been overcome with the new generation of software implementation tools.

EXERCISES

1. What is the various application of fuzzy logic?
2. Explain the use of the fuzzy logic in industrial automation?
3. Explain the concept of fuzzy logic supervisory control for coal power plant?
4. Explain the fuzzy logic control design for coal power plant?
5. How we can perform optimization of a water treatment system?
6. How fuzzy logic replaces manual control in water treatment system?
7. What are the applications of fuzzy logic in chemical industry?
8. Explain the truck speed limiter control by fuzzy logic?
9. Explain the fuzzy logic controller for truck speed limiter control?
10. How we can use fuzzy logic and neuro-fuzzy in appliances?
11. Explain the use of fuzzy logic in adaptive heating system control?
12. Explain the neuro-fuzzy analysis in machines?
13. Explain the use of fuzzy logic in data analysis of environmental data for traffic control?
14. Explain the architecture of environmental data analysis?
15. Explain the use of fuzzy technology in sonar system?
16. Explain the use of fuzzy logic in automotive engineering?

CHAPTER 17

Neuro-fuzzy Systems

17.1 INTRODUCTION

Soft computing includes fuzzy logic, neural networks, probabilistic reasoning, and genetic algorithms. Today, techniques or a combination of techniques from all these areas are used to design an intelligence system. Neural networks provide algorithms for learning, classification, and optimization, whereas fuzzy logic deals with issues such as forming impressions and reasoning on a semantic or linguistic level. Probabilistic reasoning deals with uncertainty. Although there are substantial areas of overlap between neural networks, FL, and probabilistic reasoning, in general they are complementary rather than competitive. Recently, many intelligent systems called neuro fuzzy systems have been used. There are many ways to combine neural networks and FL techniques.

Neuro-fuzzy refers to combinations of artificial neural networks and fuzzy logic. Neuro-fuzzy hybridization results in a hybrid intelligent system that synergizes these two techniques by combining the human-like reasoning style of fuzzy systems with the learning and connectionist structure of neural networks. Neuro-fuzzy hybridization is widely termed as Fuzzy Neural Network (FNN) or Neuro-Fuzzy System (NFS) in the literature. Neuro-fuzzy system (the more popular term is used henceforth) incorporates the human-like reasoning style of fuzzy systems through the use of fuzzy sets and a linguistic model consisting of a set of IF-THEN fuzzy rules. The main strength of neuro-fuzzy systems is that they are universal approximators with the ability to solicit interpretable IF-THEN rules.

17.2 BASICS OF NEURAL NETWORKS

Neural networks are computing systems modeled after the brain's mesh-like network of interconnected processing elements, called *neurons*. Like the brain, the interconnected processors in a neural network operate in parallel and interact dynamically with each other. This enables the network to "learn" from the data it processes. That is, it learns to recognize patterns and relationships in the data it processes. The more data examples it receives as input, the better it can learn to duplicate the results of the examples it processes. Thus, the neural networks will change the strengths of the interconnections between the processing elements in response to changing patterns in the data it receives and the results that occur.

Thus, a neural network can be defined as a network of many simple processors (called units) each possibly having a small amount of local memory. The units are connected by communication channels (called connections), that usually carry numeric (as opposed to symbolic) data, encoded by any of various means. The units operate only on their local data and on the inputs they receive via the connections. The restriction to local operations is often relaxed during training. Most neural networks have training rules whereby the weights of connections are adjusted on the basis of data. In other words, neural networks learn from examples to recognize dogs and exhibit some capability for generalization beyond the training data.

In principle, neural networks can compute any computable function; i.e. they can do everything that a normal digital computer can do or even more. In practice, neural networks are especially useful for classification and function approximation or mapping problems that are tolerant of some imprecision and have a lot of training data available.

Neural networks can be implemented on microcomputers and other traditional computer systems by using software packages that simulate the activity of a neural network. In addition, special-purpose neural net microprocessor chips are being used in specific application areas such as military weapons systems, image processing, and voice recognition. Other areas of application include signature verification, investment forecasting, data mining, and manufacturing quality control.

17.3 ARTIFICIAL NEURAL NETWORK (ANN)

An artificial neural network is a system based on the operation of biological neural networks, in other words, is an emulation of biological neural system. Why would be necessary the implementation of artificial neural networks? Although computing these days is truly advanced, there are certain tasks that a program made for a common microprocessor is unable to perform; even so a software implementation of a neural network can be made with their advantages and disadvantages.

17.3.1 Advantages

Following are the advantages of ANN:

1. A neural network can perform tasks that a linear program can not.
2. When an element of the neural network fails, it can continue without any problem by their parallel nature.
3. A neural network learns and does not need to be reprogrammed.
4. It can be implemented in any application.
5. It can be implemented without any problem.

17.3.2 Disadvantages

Following are the disadvantages of ANN:

1. The neural network needs training to operate.
2. The architecture of a neural network is different from the architecture of microprocessors therefore needs to be emulated.
3. Requires high processing time for large neural networks.
4. Another aspect of the artificial neural networks is that there are different architectures, which consequently requires different types of algorithms, but despite to be an apparently complex system, a neural network is relatively simple.

Artificial neural networks (ANN) are among the newest signal-processing technologies in the engineer's toolbox. The field is highly interdisciplinary, but our approach will restrict the view to the engineering perspective. In engineering, neural networks serve two important functions: as pattern classifiers and as nonlinear adaptive filters. We will provide a brief overview of the theory, learning rules, and applications of the most important neural network models. Definitions and Style of Computation An Artificial Neural Network is an adaptive, most often nonlinear system that learns to perform a function (an input/output map) from data. Adaptive means that the system parameters are changed during operation, normally called the training phase. After the training phase the Artificial Neural Network parameters are fixed and the system is deployed to solve the problem at hand (the testing phase).

The Artificial Neural Network is built with a systematic step-by-step procedure to optimize a performance criterion or to follow some implicit internal constraint, which is commonly referred to as the learning rule. The input/output training data are fundamental in neural network technology, because they convey the necessary information to "discover" the optimal operating point. The nonlinear nature of the neural network processing elements (PEs) provides the system with lots of flexibility to achieve practically any desired input/output map, i.e., some Artificial Neural Networks are universal mappers . There is a style in neural computation that is worth describing.

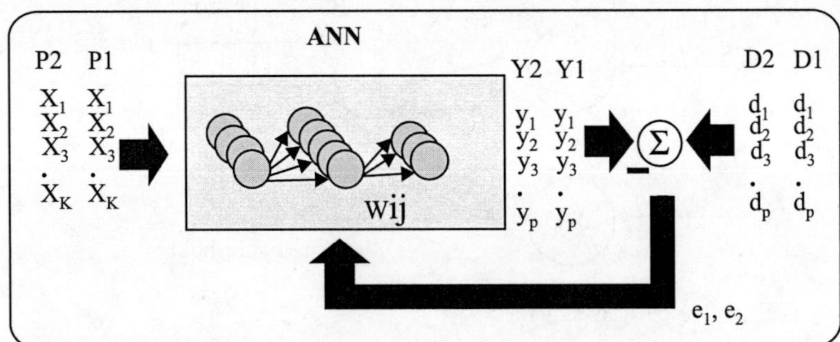

Figure 17.1: Working of artificial neuron

An input is presented to the neural network and a corresponding desired or target response set at the output (when this is the case the training is called supervised). An error is composed from the difference between the desired response and the system output. This error information is fed back to the system and adjusts the system parameters in a systematic fashion (the learning rule). The process is repeated until the performance is acceptable. It is clear from this description that the performance hinges heavily on the data. If one does not have data that cover a significant portion of the operating conditions or if they are noisy, then neural network technology is probably not the right solution. On the other hand, if there is plenty of data and the problem is poorly understood to derive an approximate model, then neural network technology is a good choice. This operating procedure should be contrasted with the traditional engineering design, made of exhaustive subsystem specifications and intercommunication protocols.

In artificial neural networks, the designer chooses the network topology, the performance function, the learning rule, and the criterion to stop the training phase, but the system automatically adjusts the parameters. So, it is difficult to bring a priori information into the design, and when the system does not work properly it is also hard to incrementally refine the solution. But ANN-based solutions are extremely efficient in terms of development time and resources, and in many difficult problems artificial neural networks provide performance that is difficult to match with other technologies. Denker 10 years ago said that "artificial neural networks are the second best way to implement a solution" motivated by the simplicity of their design and because of their universality, only shadowed by the traditional design obtained by studying the physics of the problem. At present, artificial neural networks are emerging as the technology of choice for many applications, such as pattern recognition, prediction, system identification, and control.

17.4 ELEMENTS OF ARTIFICIAL NEURAL NETWORKS

An artificial neuron as shown in Figure 17.2, is the basic element of a neural network. It consists of three basic components that include weights, thresholds, and a single activation function.

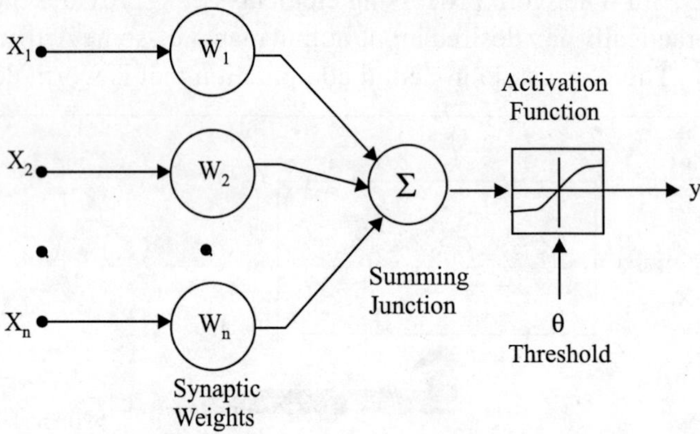

Figure 17.2: Basic elements of an artificial neuron

17.4.1 Weighting Factors

The values W_1, W_2, W_3,.....,W_n are weight factors associated with each node to determine the strength of input row vector $X = [x_1, x_2, x_3,...., x_n]^T$. Each input is multiplied by the associated weight of the neuron connection X^TW. Depending upon the activation function, if the weight is positive, X^TW commonly excites the node output; whereas, for negative weights, X^TW tends to inhibit the node output.

17.4.2 Threshold

The node's internal threshold è is the magnitude offset that affects the activation of the node output y as follows:

$$y = \sum_{i=1}^{n} (X_i W_i) \qquad (17.1)$$

17.4.3 Activation Function

In this subsection, five of the most common activation functions are presented. An activation function performs a mathematical operation on the signal output. More sophisticated activation functions can also be utilized depending upon the type of problem to be solved by the network.

17.5 NETWORK ARCHITECTURES

Two or more of the neurons shown earlier can be combined in a layer, and a particular network could contain one or more such layers. First consider a single layer of neurons.

17.5.1 A Layer of Neurons

A one-layer network with *R* input elements and S neuron follows. Inputs Layer of Neurons

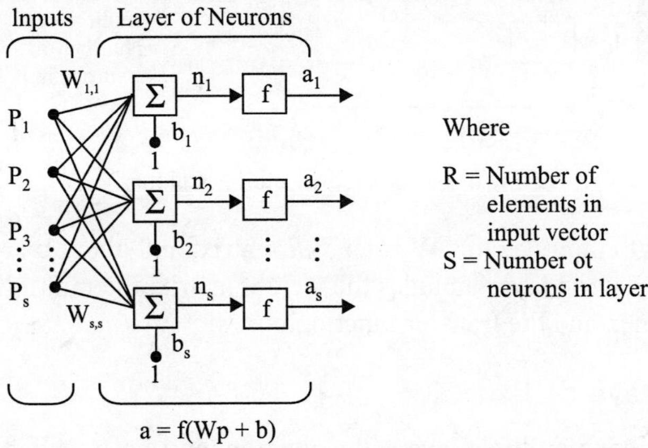

Figure 17.3: Input-layer neural network

In this network, each element of the input vector p is connected to each neuron input through the weight matrix W. The ith neuron has a summer that gathers its weighted inputs and bias to form its own scalar output n(i). The various n(i) taken together form an S-element net input vector n.

Finally, the neuron layer outputs form a column vector a. The expression for a is shown at the bottom of the figure.

Note that it is common for the number of inputs to a layer to be different from the number of neurons (i.e., R is not necessarily equal to S). A layer is not constrained to have the number of its inputs equal to the number of its neurons.

You can create a single (composite) layer of neurons having different transfer functions simply by putting two of the networks shown earlier in parallel. Both networks would have the same inputs, and each network would create some of the outputs.

The input vector elements enter the network through the weight matrix **W**.

$$w = \begin{matrix} W_{1,1} & W_{1,2} & \cdots\cdots & W_{1,R} \\ W_{2,1} & W_{2,2} & \cdots\cdots & W_{2,R} \\ \\ W_{S,1} & W_{S,2} & \cdots\cdots & W_{S,R} \end{matrix}$$

Note that the row indices on the elements of matrix **W** indicate the destination neuron of the weight, and the column indices indicate which source is the input for that weight. Thus, the indices in $w_{1,2}$ say that the strength of the signal from the second input element to the first (and only) neuron is w1, 2.

The S neuron R input one-layer network also can be drawn in abbreviated notation.

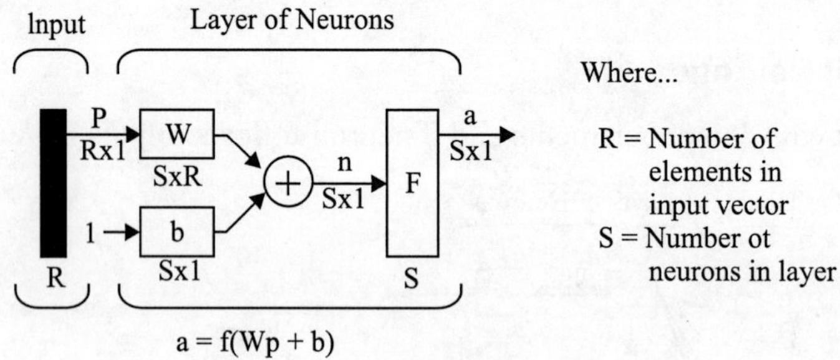

Figure 17.4: Abbreviated notation

Here **p** is an *R* length input vector, **W** is an *S*x*R* matrix, and **a** and **b** are *S* length vectors. As defined previously, the neuron layer includes the weight matrix, the multiplication operations, the bias vector **b**, the summer, and the transfer function boxes.

17.5.2 Inputsand Layers

To describe networks having multiple layers, the notation must be extended. Specifically, it needs to make a distinction between weight matrices that are connected to inputs and weight matrices that are connected between layers. It also needs to identify the source and destination for the weight matrices.

We will call weight matrices connected to inputs *input weights;* we will call weight matrices coming from layer outputs *layer weights.* Further, superscripts are used to identify the source (second index) and the destination (first index) for the various weights and other elements of the network. To illustrate, the one-layer multiple input network shown earlier is redrawn in abbreviated form below.

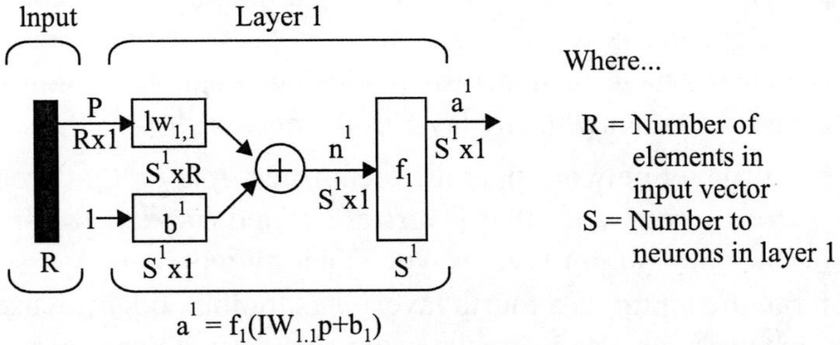

Figure 17.5: Inputs and layers

As you can see, the weight matrix connected to the input vector **p** is labeled as an input weight matrix (**IW**^{1,1}) having a source 1 (second index) and a destination 1 (first index). Elements of layer 1, such as its bias, net input, and output have a superscript 1 to say that they are associated with the first layer. "Multiple Layers of Neurons" uses layer weight (**LW**) matrices as well as input weight (**IW**) matrices.

17.5.3 Multiple Layers of Neurons

A network can have several layers. Each layer has a weight matrix W, a bias vector b, and an output vector a. To distinguish between the weight matrices, output vectors, etc., for each of these layers in the figures, the number of the layer is appended as a superscript to the variable of interest. You can see the use of this layer notation in the three-layer network shown below, and in the equations at the bottom of the figure.

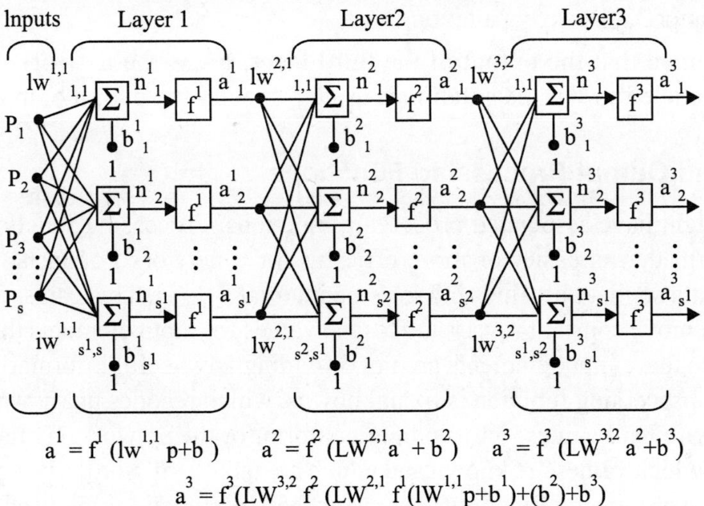

Figure 17.6: Multiple layers of neurons

The network shown above has R^1 inputs, S^1 neurons in the first layer, S^2 neurons in the second layer, etc. It is common for different layers to have different numbers of neurons. A constant input 1 is fed to the bias for each neuron. Note that the outputs of each intermediate layer are the inputs to the following layer. Thus layer 2 can be analyzed as a one-layer network with S^1 inputs, S^2 neurons, and an S^2xS^1 weight matrix W^2. The input to layer 2 is a^1; the output is a^2. Now that all the vectors and matrices of layer 2 have been identified, it can be treated as a single-layer network on its own. This approach can be taken with any layer of the network.

The layers of a multilayer network play different roles. A layer that produces the network output is called an *output layer*. All other layers are called *hidden layers*. The three-layer network shown earlier has one output layer (layer 3) and two hidden layers (layer 1 and layer 2). Some authors refer to the inputs as a fourth layer. This toolbox does not use that designation. The same three-layer network can also be drawn using abbreviated notation.

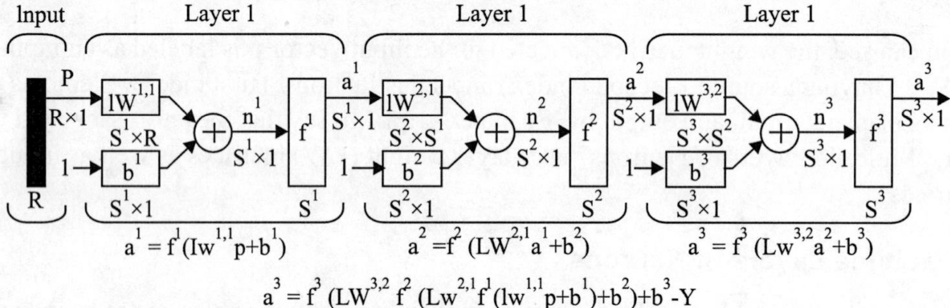

Figure 17.7: Abbreviated notation of multiple layers neural network

Multiple-layer networks are quite powerful. For instance, a network of two layers, where the first layer is sigmoid and the second layer is linear, can be trained to approximate any function (with a finite number of discontinuities) arbitrarily well. This kind of two-layer network is used extensively in Chapter 3, "Backpropagation."

Here it is assumed that the output of the third layer, $\mathbf{a}^3$, is the network output of interest, and this output is labeled as $\mathbf{y}$. This notation is used to specify the output of multilayer networks.

17.5.4 Input and Output Processing Functions

Network inputs might have associated processing functions. Processing functions transform user input data to a form that is easier or more efficient for a network.For instance, map min max transforms input data so that all values fall into the interval [–1, 1]. This can speed up learning for many networks. Remove constant rows removes the values for input elements that always have the same value because these input elements are not providing any useful information to the network. The third common processing function is fix unknowns, which recodes unknown data (represented in the user's data with Null values) into a numerical form for the network. fix unknowns preserves information about which values are known and which are unknown. Similarly, network outputs can also have associated processing functions. Output processing functions are used to transform user-provided target vectors for network use. Then, network outputs are reverse-processed using the same functions to produce output data with the same characteristics as the original user-provided targets.

17.6 NEURO FUZZY SYSTEM

Fuzzy neural network or **neuro-fuzzy system** is a learning machine that finds the parameters of a fuzzy system (i.e., fuzzy sets, fuzzy rules) by exploiting approximation techniques from neural networks.

17.7 COMBINING FUZZY SYSTEMS WITH NEURAL NETWORKS

Both neural networks and fuzzy systems have some things in common. They can be used for solving a problem (e.g. pattern recognition, regression or density estimation) if there does not exist any mathematical model of the given problem. They solely do have certain disadvantages and advantages which almost completely disappear by combining both concepts.

Neural networks can only come into play if the problem is expressed by a sufficient amount of observed examples. These observations are used to train the *black box*. On the one hand no prior knowledge about the problem needs to be given. On the other hand, however, it is not straightforward to extract comprehensible rules from the neural network's structure.

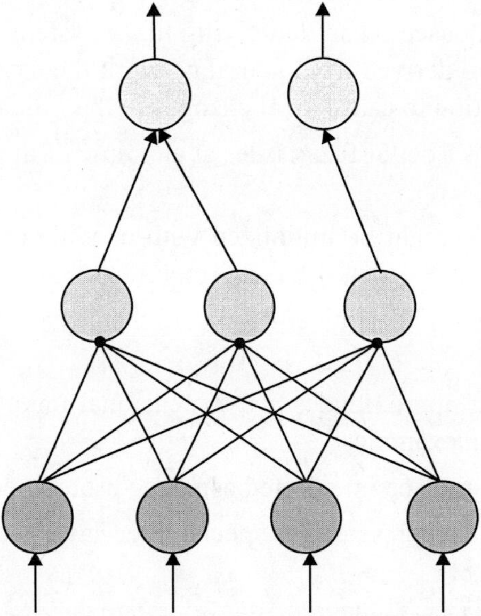

Figure 17.8: The architecture of a neuro-fuzzy system

On the contrary, a fuzzy system demands linguistic rules instead of learning examples as prior knowledge. Furthermore the input and output variables have to be described linguistically. If the knowledge is incomplete, wrong or contradictory, then the fuzzy system must be tuned. Since there is not any formal approach for it, the tuning is performed in a heuristic way. This is usually very time consuming and error-prone.

Table 17.1: Comparison of neural control and fuzzy control

Neural Networks	Fuzzy Systems
no mathematical model necessary	no mathematical model necessary
learning from scratch	apriori knowledge essential
several learning algorithms	not capable to learn
black-box behavior	simple interpretation and implementation

It is desirable for fuzzy systems to have an automatic adaption procedure which is comparable to neural networks. As it can be seen in Table 17.1, combining both approaches should unite advantages and exclude disadvantages.

17.7.1 Characteristics

Compared to a common neural network, connection weights and propagation and activation functions of fuzzy neural networks differ a lot. Although there are many different approaches to model a fuzzy neural network (Buckley and Hayashi, 1994, 1995; Nauck and Kruse, 1996), most of them agree on certain characteristics such as the following:

- A neuro-fuzzy system based on an underlying fuzzy system is trained by means of a data-driven learning method derived from neural network theory. This heuristic only takes into account local information to cause local changes in the fundamental fuzzy system.
- It can be represented as a set of fuzzy rules at any time of the learning process, i.e., before, during and after.
  - Thus the system might be initialized with or without prior knowledge in terms of fuzzy rules.
- The learning procedure is constrained to ensure the semantic properties of the underlying fuzzy system.
- A neuro-fuzzy system approximates a n-dimensional unknown function which is partly represented by training examples.
  - Fuzzy rules can thus be interpreted as vague prototypes of the training data.
- A neuro-fuzzy system is represented as special three-layer feedforward neural network as it is shown in Figure 17.8.
  - The first layer corresponds to the input variables.
  - The second layer symbolizes the fuzzy rules.
  - The third layer represents the output variables.
  - The fuzzy sets are converted as (fuzzy) connection weights.

– Some approaches also use five layers where the fuzzy sets are encoded in the units of the second and fourth layer, respectively. However, these models can be transformed into a three-layer architecture.

One can basically distinguish between three different kinds of fuzzy neural networks, i.e., cooperative, concurrent and hybrid FNNs.

17.8 COOPERATIVE FUZZY NEURAL NETWORK

In the case of cooperative neural fuzzy systems, both artificial neural network and fuzzy system work independently from each other. The ANN tries to learn the parameters from the fuzzy system. This can be either performed offline or online while the fuzzy system is applied. Figure 17.9 depicts four different kinds of cooperative fuzzy neural networks.

The upper left fuzzy neural network learns fuzzy set from given training data. This is usually performed by fitting membership functions with a neural network. The fuzzy sets are then determined offline. They are then utilized to form the fuzzy system by fuzzy rules that are given (not learned) as well.

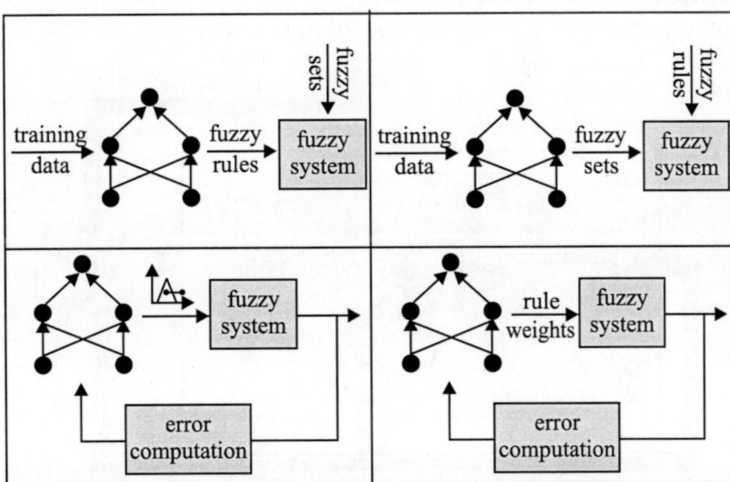

Figure 17.9: Different cooperative fuzzy neural networks

The upper right neuro-fuzzy system determines fuzzy rules from training data by a neural network. Here as well, the neural networks learns offline before the fuzzy system is initialized. The rule learning usually done by clustering on self-organizing feature maps (Bezdek et al., 1992; Vuorimaa, 1994). It is also possible to apply fuzzy clustering methods to obtain rules.

In the lower left neuro-fuzzy model, the system learns all membership function parameters online, i.e., while the fuzzy system is applied. Thus initially fuzzy rules and membership functions must be defined beforehand. Moreover, the error has to be measured in order to improve and guide the learning step.

The lower right one determines rule weights for all fuzzy rules by a neural network. This can be done online and offline. A rule weight is interpreted as the influence of a rule (Kosko, 1992). They are multiplied with the rule output. In (Nauck et al., 1997) the authors argue that the semantics of rule weights are not clearly defined. They could be replaced by modified membership functions. However, this could destroy the interpretation of fuzzy sets. Moreover, identical linguistic values might be represented differently in dissimilar rules.

17.9 HYBRID FUZZY NEURAL NETWORK

Hybrid neuro-fuzzy systems are homogeneous and usually resemble neural networks. Here, the fuzzy system is interpreted as special kind of neural network. The advantage of such hybrid NFS is its architecture since both fuzzy system and neural network do not have to communicate any more with each other. They are one fully fused entity. These systems can learn online and offline. Figure 17.10 shows such a hybrid FNN.

The rule base of a fuzzy system is interpreted as a neural network. Fuzzy sets can be regarded as weights whereas the input and output variables and the rules are modeled as neurons. Neurons can be included or deleted in the learning step. Finally, the neurons of the network represent the fuzzy knowledge base. Obviously, the major drawbacks of both underlying systems are thus overcome.

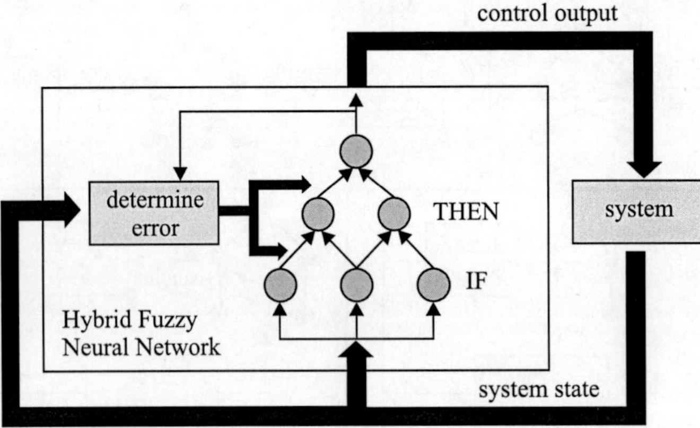

Figure 17.10: A hybrid fuzzy neural network

In order to build a fuzzy controller, membership functions which express the linguistic terms of the inference rules have to be defined. In fuzzy set theory, there does not exist any formal approach to define these functions. Any shape (e.g., triangular, Gaussian) can be considered as membership function with an arbitrary set of parameters. Thus the optimization of these functions in terms of generalizing the data is very important for fuzzy systems. Neural networks can be used to solve this problem.

By fixing a distinct shape of the membership functions, say triangular, the neural network must optimize their parameters by gradient descent (Nomura et al., 1992). Thus, aside information about the shape of the membership functions, training data must be available as well.

Another approach (Hayashi et al., 1992) is to group the training data $\{(x_i, y_i)| x_i \in X, y_i \in Y, i = 1, 2,...., l\}$ into M clusters. Every cluster represents a rule R_m where m= 1,2,..., M. Hence these rules are not defined linguistically but rather by crisp data points $x = (x_1, x_2,..., x_n)$. Thus a neural network with n input units, hidden layers and m output units might be applied to train on the pre-defined clusters. For testing, an arbitrary pattern x is presented to the trained neural network. Every output unit m will return a degree to which extend x may fit to the antecedent of rule R_m.

To guarantee the characteristics of a fuzzy system, the learning algorithm must enforce the following mandatory constraints:

- Fuzzy sets must stay normal and convex.
- Fuzzy sets must not exchange their relative positions (they must not *pass* each other).
- Fuzzy sets must always overlap.

Additionally there do exist some optional constraints like the following:

- Fuzzy sets must stay symmetric.
- The membership degrees must sum up to 1.

An important hybrid fuzzy neural network has been introduced in (Berenji, 1992). The ARIC (approximate reasoning-based intelligent control) is presented as a neural network where a prior defined rule base is tuned by updating the network's prediction. Thus the advantages of fuzzy systems and neural networks are easily combined as presented in Table 17.1.

17.10 PROPERTIES OF NEURO FUZZY SYSTEMS

Modern neuro-fuzzy systems are usually represented as special multilayer feedforward neural networks (see for example models like ANFIS, NEFCON). However, fuzzifications of other neural network architectures are also considered, for example self—organizing feature maps. In those neuro—fuzzy networks, connection weights and propagation and activation functions differ from common neural networks.

Although there are a lot of different approaches, we usually use the term *neuro—fuzzy system* for approaches which display the following properties:

1. A neuro-fuzzy system is based on a fuzzy system which is trained by a learning algorithm derived from neural network theory. The (heuristical) learning procedure operates on local information, and causes only local modifications in the underlying fuzzy system.
2. A neuro-fuzzy system can be viewed as a 3-layer feedforward neural network. The first layer represents input variables, the middle (hidden) layer represents fuzzy rules and the third layer represents output variables. Fuzzy sets are encoded as (fuzzy) connection weights. It is not necessary to represent a fuzzy system like this to apply a learning algorithm to it. However, it can be convenient, because it represents the data flow of input processing and learning within the model.

   Remark: Sometimes a 5-layer architecture is used, where the fuzzy sets are represented in the units of the second and fourth layer.

3. A neuro-fuzzy system can be always (i.e.\ before, during and after learning) interpreted as a system of fuzzy rules. It is also possible to create the system out of training data from scratch, as it is possible to initialize it by prior knowledge in form of fuzzy rules. ***Remark:*** Not all neuro-fuzzy models specifiy learning procedures for fuzzy rule creation.
4. The learning procedure of a neuro-fuzzy system takes the semantical properties of the underlying fuzzy system into account. This results in constraints on the possible modifications applicable to the system parameters.

   Remark: Not all neuro-fuzzy approaches have this property.
5. A neuro-fuzzy system approximates an n-dimensional (unknown) function that is partially defined by the training data. The fuzzy rules encoded within the system represent vague samples, and can be viewed as prototypes of the training data. A neuro-fuzzy system should not be seen as a kind of (fuzzy) expert system, and it has nothing to do with fuzzy logic in the narrow sense.

17.11 NEURAL NETWORKS AND FUZZY LOGIC

Neuro Fuzzy (NF) computing is a popular framework for solving complex problems. If we have knowledge expressed in linguistic rules, we can build a FIS (Fuzzy inference system), and if we have data, or can learn from a simulation (training) then we can use ANNs. For building a FIS, we have to specify the fuzzy sets, fuzzy operators and the knowledge base. Similarly for constructing an ANN for an application the user needs to specify the architecture and learning algorithm. An analysis reveals that the drawbacks pertaining to these approaches seem complementary and therefore it is natural to consider building an integrated system combining the concepts. While the learning capability is an advantage from the viewpoint of FIS, the formation of linguistic rule base will be advantage from the viewpoint of ANN.

Neural networks and fuzzy logic are two complimentary technologies. Neural networks can learn from data and feedback; however, understanding the knowledge or the pattern learned by the neural networks has been difficult. More specifically, it is difficult to develop an insight about the meaning associated with each neuron and each weight. Hence, neural networks are often viewed as a "black box" approach – we can understand what the box does, but not how it is done conceptually.

In contrast, fuzzy rule-based models are easy to comprehend because it used linguistic terms (linguistic expressions in general) and the structure of if-then rules. Unlike neural networks, however, fuzzy logic does not come with a learning algorithm. The learning and identification of fuzzy models need to adopt techniques from other areas (e.g. statistics, linear system identification, etc.) as we have seen in Chapter 14. Since neural networks can learn, it is natural to marry the two technologies. This marriage has created a new term – neuro-fuzzy system. A neuro-fuzzy system can be loosely defined as a system that uses a combination of fuzzy logic and neural networks.

Neuro-fuzzy systems can be classified into three categories:

1. A fuzzy rule-based model constructed using a supervised NN learning technique.

2. A fuzzy rule-based model constructed using reinforcement-based learning.
3. A fuzzy rule-based model using NN to construct its fuzzy partition of the input space.

17.12 NEURO-FUZZY ARCHITECTURES

A neuro-fuzzy system describes a fuzzy rule-based model using an NN-like structure (i.e., involving nodes and links). A neuro-fuzzy system differs from an NN in four major ways. First, the nodes and links in a neuro-fuzzy system usually are comprehensible because they each correspond to a specific component in a fuzzy system. For example, the first layer of a neuro-fuzzy architecture shown in Figure 17.11 describes the antecedent membership functions of input variables. Second, a node in a neuro-fuzzy system is usually not fully connected to nodes in an adjacent layer. In fact, the connections between nodes in a neuro-fuzzy system reflect the rule structure of the system.

For instance, the second-layer nodes in Figure 7.11 are connected to only two nodes from the first layer, each one of which describes a condition about an input variable. The nodes in the second layer thus perform the "AND" (conjunction) operator in fuzzy rules. Hence, the number of links connected to a node in the second layer equals the number of input variables. Third, the nodes in different layers of a neuro-fuzzy system typically perform different operations. We will elaborate on this point below. Finally, a neuro-fuzzy system typically has more layers than neural networks.

Typically, a neuro-fuzzy architecture has five to six layers of node. The functionalities associated with different layers usually include the following:

1. Compute the matching degree to a fuzzy condition involving one variable
2. Compute the matching degree of a conjunctive fuzzy condition involving multiple variables.
3. Compute the normalized matching degree.
4. Compute the conclusion inferred by a fuzzy rule.
5. Combine the conclusion of all fuzzy rules in a model.

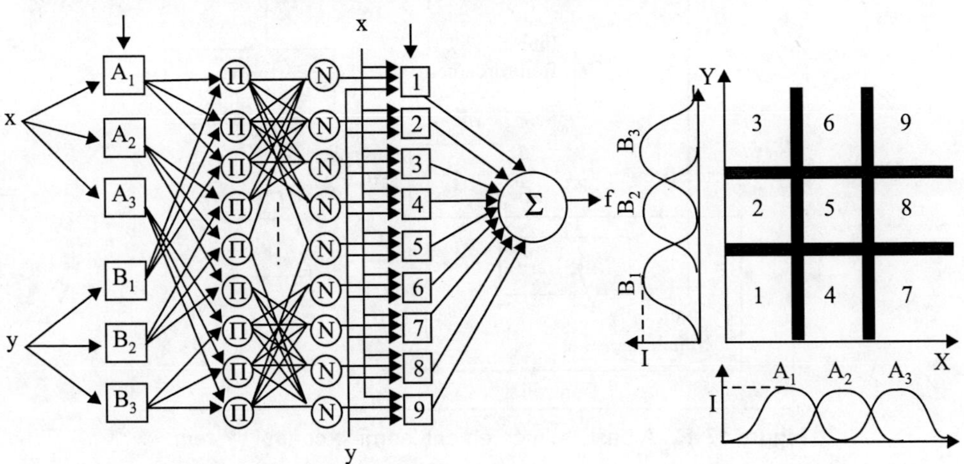

Figure 17.11: (a) ANFIS Architecture for a two-input sugeno fuzzy model with nine rules; (b) the input space that are partitioned into nine fuzzy regions.

17.13 REINFORCEMENT-BASED LEARNING OF FUZZY MODELS

Reinforcement learning used external reinforcement signals (rewards or punishments) to adjust parameters in a system (typically a rule-based system). Reinforcement learning was motivated by leaning theory in behavioral science that states people and animals can learn to change their behavior from positive reinforcements (rewards) and negative reinforcements (punishments).

The basic principles of reinforcement learning can be summarized as follows.

1. External reinforcement signals are generates based on the performance of the system being trained. For example, a system for balancing a pole will receive a negative reinforcement signal whenever the pole falls.
2. The external reinforcement signal is used to learn the desirability of recent states of the system being trained. A positive reinforcement will increase the desirability, while a negative reinforcement will decrease the desirability.
3. Because external reinforcements are generated infrequently and can be all negative or all positive, the learning algorithm generates a frequent internal reinforcement signal from both the external reinforcement and the change of state desirability. For example, changing from a less desirable state to a more desirable state without external reinforcement generates a positive internal reinforcement.

Reinforcement learning used two neuron-like units to carry out the ideas summarized above. It uses an Adaptive Critic Element (ACE) to generate internal reinforcement, and an Associative Search Element (ASE) to adjust the parameters of the system being trained. Figure 17.12 shows the basic architecture of a reinforcement learning system for training a rule-based controller.

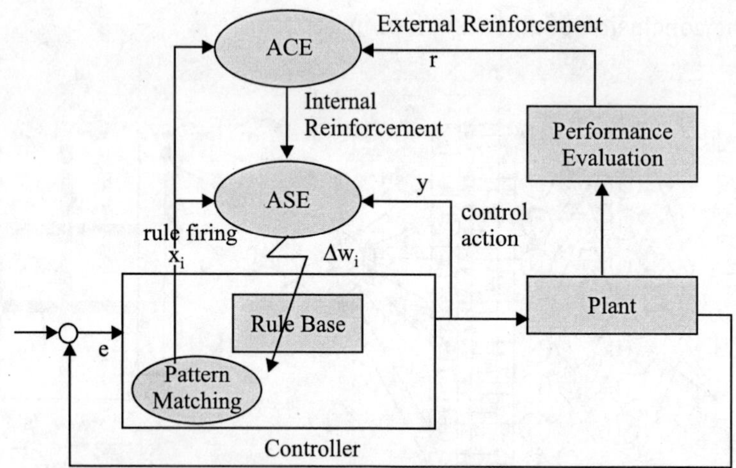

Figure 17.12: A basic reinforcement learning control system

17.14 USING NEURAL NETWORKS TO PARTITION THE INPUT SPACE

An important element of fuzzy rule-based modeling is the fuzzy partition of the input space. We have also discussed three major approaches to fuzzy partition: grid-based partition, tree-based partition, and scattered partition. However, the fuzzy subregions we have used to form these partition are all described in the form of "x_1 is A_{1i} and x_2 is A_{2i} ... and x_k is A_{ki-}" where x_1, x_2, ... x_k are linguistic variables and A_{1i}, A_{2i}, ...A_{ki} are linguistic labels of these variables. Such a fuzzy subregion forms a fuzzy hypercubes in the k-dimensional input space. Even though these fuzzy hypercubes are easy to comprehend, they do not offer the flexibility of partitioning using arbitrary nonlinear hypersurfaces. Since the latter can be achieved using NN, it offers an alternative way for constructing a fuzzy partition.

The basic idea of using a NN to construct a fuzzy partition is simple. We only need to construct a NN that takes input variables of a fuzzy model as input and generates the degrees the input data belong to a predetermined number of fuzzy regions. Figure 7.13 depicts a NN that partitions a two-dimensional input space into three fuzzy subregions. If the NN's output (i.e., A_1, A-$_{2-}$, A_3) were either 0 or 1, the NN performs a hard (nonfuzzy) partition. To perform a fuzzy partition, the NN's output needs to be a real number in the interval [0, 1]. Figure 17.13 (b) depicts the fuzzy partition generated by the NN. As shown in the figure, the boundary of each fuzzy region is a fuzzy hypersurface. Due to the flexibility of these fuzzy hypersurface, an NN can reduce the number of rules in a fuzzy model. We will leave this as an exercise.

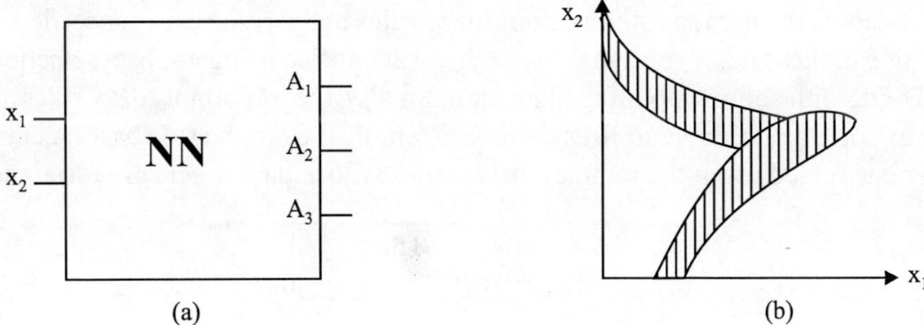

Figure 17.13: (a) An nn that partitions a two-dimensional input space (b) the corresponding fuzzy partition

In order to train the NN to partition the input space, we first need to have training data. The training data can be obtained in two ways: (1) by asking an expert of the problem domain to assign membership degrees to a sample set of input data, (2) by clustering a sample set of training data using a clustering algorithm (e.g., fuzzy e-means). The former approach is feasible only if such an expert is available.

Notice that the training data used in the latter approach contain desired input-output pairs for the fuzzy model being constructed. However, this training data cannot be used directly to train the NN for fuzzy partition because the target outputs of a fuzzy partition are the desired membership degrees in the partition's fuzzy subregions, which are different from the fuzzy model's outputs.

Hence, the data need to be first partitioned using a clustering algorithm. The classified dataset can then be used to train the NN for partitioning the input space.

17.15 NEURO-FUZZY MODELING EXAMPLES

In this section we provide two examples to show how the BP algorithm is used to estimate the parameters of a fuzzy model. For simplicity, we assume that the fuzzy model has a constant consequent constituents. That is,

R_i: If x_1 is A_{i1} and x_2 is A_{i2} and … and x_m is A_{im}

Then y is $\qquad C_i$, i = 1, 2, …, M. (17.2)

where c_i are the constant constituents. The antecedent membership functions are assumed to be Gaussian functions, as defined by

$$A_{ij} = \exp \frac{(x_i - m_{ij})^2}{2\sigma_{ij}^2} \qquad (17.3)$$

In order to determine the structure (mainly the number of fuzzy rules constituting the underlying model) and the parameters of the model in an integrated manner, the BP algorithm is combined with the SVD-QR with column pivoting algorithm. The main steps of the process are shown in Figure 17.14. First, a candidate fuzzy model is considered, which may exhaustive and oversized (i.e., have a large rule base) but not undersized. The parameters of the model are trained using the BP algorithm. Second, the number of important fuzzy rules in the rule base is specified using SVD. Third, the position of these fuzzy rules in the rule base is identified using a subset selection algorithm known as SVD-QR with column pivoting algorithm. Finally, the important fuzzy rules are retained, while the less important or redundant fuzzy rules are removed from the rule base. A compact fuzzy model is then constructed using the retained fuzzy rules whose parameters are retrained using BP.

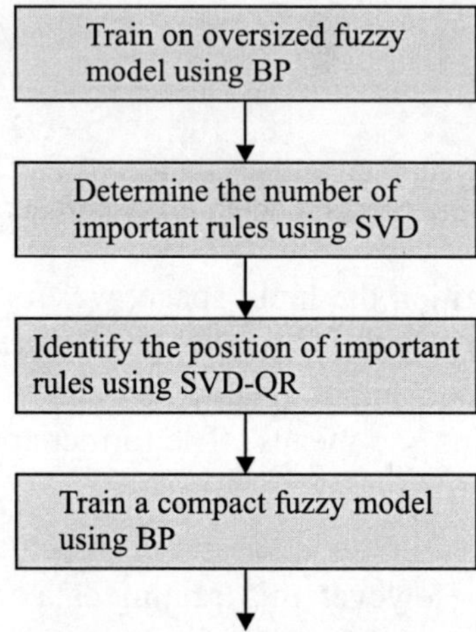

Figure 17.14: Fuzzy model identification using a BP-SVD combination.

Consider the nonlinear function

$$Y = \frac{\sin x}{x}$$

We want to approximate this function using the fuzzy model described in Equation 17.2 For this purpose, we generated 100 training data points using equally spaced x values in the interval [–10, 10].

We first built a fuzzy model with 30 rules whose antecedent and consequent parameters were trained using the BP algorithm with the initial parameter values $c_i(0)$ ε [–1, 1], $m_{ij}(0)$ ε[–10, 10] and $\sigma_{ij}(0)$ ε[1, 2]. These fuzzy rules were labeled as 1, 2, …, 30 to indicate their position in the rule base. For each of the 100 input data points x(k), k = 1, 2, …, 100 to the model, we computed the normalized firing strength of the 30 rules. A 100-by30 firing strength matrix P was then formed.

Applying SVD to P, the resulting singular values are shown in Figure 17.15. Based on the distribution of the singular values, we retained 12 rules that were used to construct a reduced fuzzy model. The position of these retained rules in the rule base was identified using the SVD-QR with column pivoting algorithm as 3, 5, 30, 16, 1, 13, 8, 24, 19, 29, 23, 14. The order of the position also indicated the importance of the associated fuzzy rules in the rule model.

The antecedent and consequent parameters of the reduced 12-rule fuzzy model were re-trained using the BP algorithm with the initial parameter values determined in the 30-rules fuzzy model.

Figure 17.16 shows the log-MSE (Mean Squared Error) curves of the 30-rule fuzzy model and the 12-rule fuzzy model over 1000 epochs of BP training. As a comparison, Figure 17.16 also shown a 12-rule fuzzy model trained using the BP algorithm with random initial parameter values $c_i(0)$ ε[–1, 2], $m_{ij}(0)$ ε[-10, 10], and $s_{ij}(0)$ ε[1, 2]. Table 17.2 gives the MSEs of the three fuzzy models after 1000 epochs. From Figure 17.15 and Table 17.2 we know that the reduced 12-rules model with predetermined initial parameter values has achieved its feasible parameter sets much faster than the one with random initial parameter values. This is because the BP algorithm is a nonlinear optimization algorithm and its convergence depends to a great extent on the choice of initial parameter values. The original 30-rule fuzzy model gives a small MSE compared with the two reduced 12-rule fuzzy models. This is not surprising because the former contains a larger number of fuzzy rules. However, good fit on training data points does not always assure good performance on untrained data points. A fuzzy model with a large number of rules may have a high risk of overfitting: capable of fitting training data points completely, but incapale of generalizing to untrained data points satisfactorily. We will see this point in the following example. Figure 17.17. shows the real output of the nonlinear function and the outputs of 30-rule fuzzy model and 12-rules fuzzy model with predetermined initial parameter values. Figure 17.18 shows the membership functions of the input variable x in the 30-rule fuzzy model and in the 12-rule fuzzy model with predetermined initial parameter values.

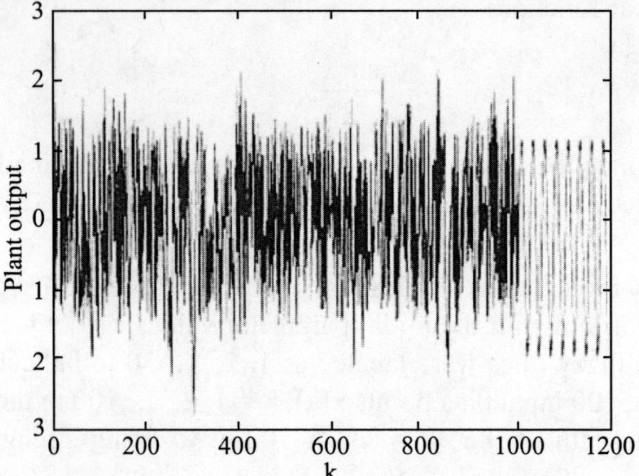

Figure 17.15: Distribution of singular values of the 100-by-30 firing strength matrix

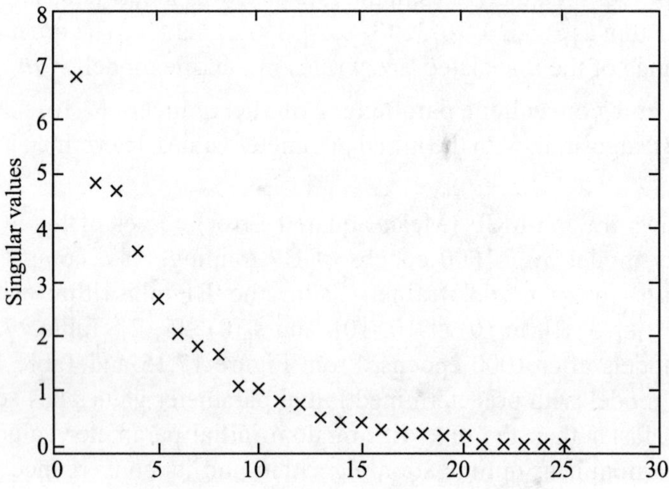

Figure 17.16 Log-MSE curves for three fuzzy models trained using the bp algorithm

Table 17.2: MSEs of three fuzzy models after 1000 epochs of BP training

Fuzzy Model	MSE
Original Model (30 rules)	2.7902e-6
Reduced model (12 rules, with predetermined intial values	2.8342e-6
Reduced model (12 rules, with random initial values)	6.8712e-6

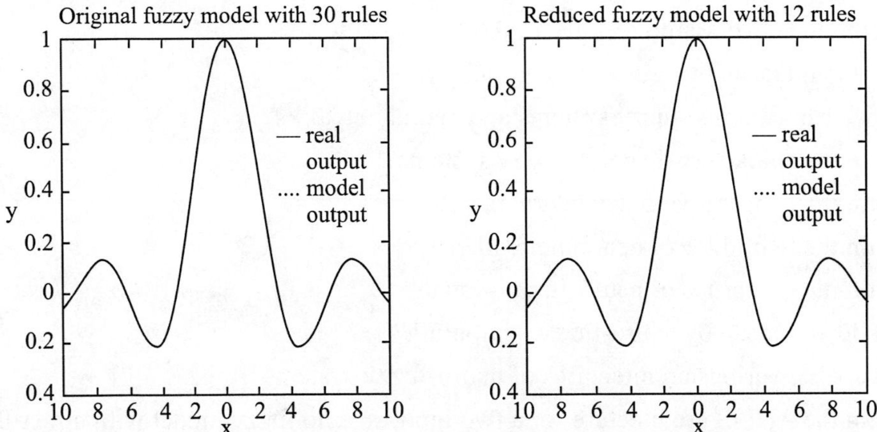

Figure 17.17: Comparison of outputs of real system and identified fuzzy models.

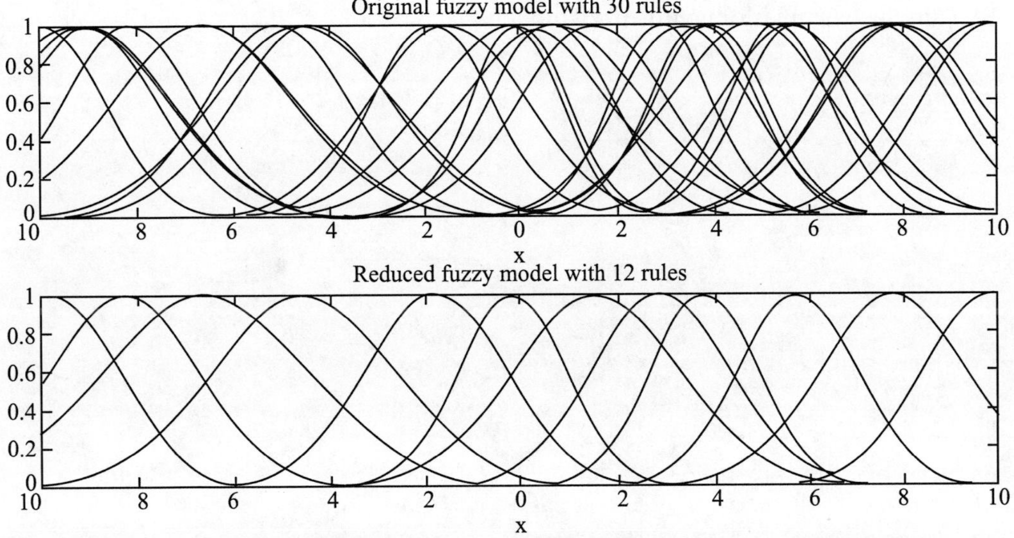

Figure 17.18: Membership functions of input x in the original and reduced models.

EXERCISES

1. What do you mean by neural networks?
2. What do you mean by artificial neural network?
3. What are the various advantages and disadvantages of neural network?
4. Explain the working of ANN?
5. What are the various element of ANN?

6. Explain the network architectures of ANN?
7. What do you mean by neuro-fuzzy systems?
8. How we can combine fuzzy systems and neural networks?
9. Explain the characteristic neuro-fuzzy systems?
10. Explain the cooperative fuzzy neural network?
11. Explain the hybrid fuzzy neural network?
12. Explain the properties of neuro-fuzzy system?
13. What do you mean by neuro-fuzzy computing?
14. What are the various architectures of neuro-fuzzy systems?
15. Explain the ANFIS architecture for a two input sugeno fuzzy model with nine rules?
16. Explain the reinforcement based learning of fuzzy models?
17. How we can use neural networks to partition the input space?
18. Explain the examples of neuro-fuzzy modeling?

CHAPTER 18

Genetic Algorithm

18.1 INTRODUCTION

Genetic Algorithms (GAs) are adaptive heuristic search algorithm premised on the evolutionary ideas of natural selection and genetic. The basic concept of GAs is designed to simulate processes in natural system necessary for evolution, specifically those that follow the principles first laid down by Charles Darwin of survival of the fittest. As such they represent an intelligent exploitation of a random search within a defined search space to solve a problem.

First pioneered by John Holland in the 60s, Genetic Algorithms has been widely studied, experimented and applied in many fields in engineering worlds. Not only does GAs provide an alternative method to solving problem, it consistently outperforms other traditional methods in most of the problems link. Many of the real world problems involved finding optimal parameters, which might prove difficult for traditional methods but ideal for GAs. However, because of its outstanding performance in optimisation, GAs have been wrongly regarded as a function optimiser. In fact, there are many ways to view genetic algorithms. Perhaps most users come to GAs looking for a problem solver, but this is a restrictive view [De Jong ,1993] .

Herein, we will examine GAs as a number of different things:

1. GAs as problem solvers
2. GAs as challenging technical puzzle
3. GAs as basis for competent machine learning
4. GAs as computational model of innovation and creativity
5. GAs as computational model of other innovating systems
6. GAs as guiding philosophy

However, due to various constraints, we would only be looking at GAs as problem solvers and competent machine learning here. We would also examine how GAs is applied to completely different fields.

Many scientists have tried to create living programs. These programs do not merely simulate life but try to exhibit the behaviours and characteristics of a real organism in an attempt to exist as a form of life. Suggestions have been made that a life would eventually evolve into real life. Such suggestion may sound absurd at the moment but certainly not implausible if technology continues to progress at present rates. Therefore it is worth, in our opinion, taking a paragraph out to discuss how a life is connected with GAs and see if such a prediction is far fetched and groundless.

18.2 GENETIC ALGORITHM

A **genetic algorithm (GA)** is a search technique used in computing to find exact or approximate solutions to optimization and search problems. Genetic algorithms are categorized as global search heuristics. Genetic algorithms are a particular class of evolutionary algorithms (EA) that use techniques inspired by evolutionary biology such as inheritance, mutation, selection, and crossover.

18.2.1 Methodology

Genetic algorithms are implemented in a computer simulation in which a population of abstract representations (called chromosomes or the genotype of the genome) of candidate solutions (called individuals, creatures, or phenotypes) to an optimization problem evolves toward better solutions. Traditionally, solutions are represented in binary as strings of 0s and 1s, but other encodings are also possible. The evolution usually starts from a population of randomly generated individuals and happens in generations.

In each generation, the fitness of every individual in the population is evaluated, multiple individuals are stochastically selected from the current population (based on their fitness), and modified (recombined and possibly randomly mutated) to form a new population. The new population is then used in the next iteration of the algorithm. Commonly, the algorithm terminates when either a maximum number of generations has been produced, or a satisfactory fitness level has been reached for the population. If the algorithm has terminated due to a maximum number of generations, a satisfactory solution may or may not have been reached.

Genetic algorithms find application in bioinformatics, phylogenetics, computational science, engineering, economics, chemistry, manufacturing, mathematics, physics and other fields.

A typical genetic algorithm requires:

1. a genetic representation of the solution domain,
2. a fitness function to evaluate the solution domain.

A standard representation of the solution is as an array of bits. Arrays of other types and structures can be used in essentially the same way. The main property that makes these genetic representations convenient is that their parts are easily aligned due to their fixed size, which facilitates simple crossover operations. Variable length representations may also be used, but crossover implementation is more complex in this case. Tree-like representations are explored in genetic programming and graph-form representations are explored in evolutionary programming. The fitness function is defined over the genetic representation and measures the *quality* of the represented solution. The fitness function is always problem dependent.

For instance, in the knapsack problem one wants to maximize the total value of objects that can be put in a knapsack of some fixed capacity. A representation of a solution might be an array of bits, where each bit represents a different object, and the value of the bit (0 or 1) represents whether or not the object is in the knapsack. Not every such representation is valid, as the size of objects may exceed the capacity of the knapsack. The *fitness* of the solution is the sum of values of all objects in the knapsack if the representation is valid, or 0 otherwise. In some problems, it is hard or even impossible to define the fitness expression; in these cases, interactive genetic algorithms are used.

Once we have the genetic representation and the fitness function defined, GA proceeds to initialize a population of solutions randomly, then improve it through repetitive application of mutation, crossover, inversion and selection operators.

18.2.2 Initialization

Initially many individual solutions are randomly generated to form an initial population. The population size depends on the nature of the problem, but typically contains several hundreds or thousands of possible solutions. Traditionally, the population is generated randomly, covering the entire range of possible solutions (the *search space*). Occasionally, the solutions may be "seeded" in areas where optimal solutions are likely to be found.

18.2.3 Encoding of a Chromosome

The chromosome should in some way contain information about solution which it represents. The most used way of encoding is a binary string. The chromosome then could look like this:

Chromosome 1	1101100100110110
Chromosome 2	1101111000011110

Each chromosome has one binary string. Each bit in this string can represent some characteristic of the solution. Or the whole string can represent a number.

Of course, there are many other ways of encoding. This depends mainly on the solved problem. For example, one can encode directly integer or real numbers, sometimes it is useful to encode some permutations and so on.

18.2.4 Selection

During each successive generation, a proportion of the existing population is selected to breed a new generation. Individual solutions are selected through a *fitness-based* process, where fitter solutions (as measured by a fitness function) are typically more likely to be selected. Certain selection methods rate the fitness of each solution and preferentially select the best solutions. Other methods rate only a random sample of the population, as this process may be very time-consuming.

Most functions are stochastic and designed so that a small proportion of less fit solutions are selected. This helps keep the diversity of the population large, preventing premature convergence on poor solutions. Popular and well-studied selection methods include roulette wheel selection and tournament selection.

18.2.5 Reproduction

The next step is to generate a second generation population of solutions from those selected through genetic operators: crossover (also called recombination), and/or mutation.

For each new solution to be produced, a pair of "parent" solutions is selected for breeding from the pool selected previously. By producing a "child" solution using the above methods of crossover and mutation, a new solution is created which typically shares many of the characteristics of its "parents". New parents are selected for each new child, and the process continues until a new population of solutions of appropriate size is generated. Although reproduction methods that are based on the use of two parents are more "biology inspired", some research suggests more than two "parents" are better to be used to reproduce a good quality chromosome.

These processes ultimately result in the next generation population of chromosomes that is different from the initial generation. Generally the average fitness will have increased by this procedure for the population, since only the best organisms from the first generation are selected for breeding, along with a small proportion of less fit solutions, for reasons already mentioned above.

1. Crossover

After we have decided what encoding we will use, we can make a step to crossover. Crossover selects genes from parent chromosomes and creates a new offspring. The simplest way how to do this is to choose randomly some crossover point and everything before this point copy from a first parent and then everything after a crossover point copy from the second parent.

Crossover can then look like this (| is the crossover point):

Chromosome 1	11011 | 00100110110
Chromosome 2	11011 | 11000011110
Offspring 1	11011 | 11000011110
Offspring 2	11011 | 00100110110

There are other ways how to make crossover, for example we can choose more crossover points. Crossover can be rather complicated and very depends on encoding of the encoding of chromosome. Specific crossover made for a specific problem can improve performance of the genetic algorithm.

2. Mutation

After a crossover is performed, mutation takes place. This is to prevent falling all solutions in population into a local optimum of solved problem. Mutation changes randomly the new offspring. For binary encoding we can switch a few randomly chosen bits from 1 to 0 or from 0 to 1.

Mutation can then be following:

Original offspring 1	1101111000011110
Original offspring 2	1101100100110110
Mutated offspring 1	1100111000011110
Mutated offspring 2	1101101100110110

The mutation depends on the encoding as well as the crossover. For example when we are encoding permutations, mutation could be exchanging two genes.

18.2.6 Crossover and Mutation Probability

There are two basic parameters of GA - crossover probability and mutation probability.

1. **Crossover probability** says how often will be crossover performed. If there is no crossover, offspring is exact copy of parents. If there is a crossover, offspring is made from parts of parents' chromosome. If crossover probability is **100%**, then all offspring is made by crossover. If it is **0%**, whole new generation is made from exact copies of chromosomes from old population (but this does not mean that the new generation is the same!). Crossover is made in hope that new chromosomes will have good parts of old chromosomes and maybe the new chromosomes will be better. However it is good to leave some part of population survive to next generation.
2. **Mutation probability** says how often will be parts of chromosome mutated. If there is no mutation, offspring is taken after crossover (or copy) without any change. If mutation is performed, part of chromosome is changed. If mutation probability is **100%**, whole chromosome is changed, if it is **0%**, nothing is changed. Mutation is made to prevent falling GA into local extreme, but it should not occur very often, because then GA will in fact change to **random search**.

18.2.7 Termination

This generational process is repeated until a termination condition has been reached. Common terminating conditions are:

- A solution is found that satisfies minimum criteria
- Fixed number of generations reached
- Allocated budget (computation time/money) reached
- The highest ranking solution's fitness is reaching or has reached a plateau such that successive iterations no longer produce better results
- Manual inspection
- Combinations of the above

Simple generational genetic algorithm pseudocode:

1. Choose the initial population of individuals
2. Evaluate the fitness of each individual in that population
3. Repeat on this generation until termination: (time limit, sufficient fitness achieved, etc.)
   (a) Select the best-fit individuals for reproduction
   (b) Breed new individuals through crossover and mutation operations to give birth to offspring
   (c) Evaluate the individual fitness of new individuals
   (d) Replace least-fit population with new individuals

18.3 BASIC GENETIC ALGORITHM

Following are the steps of the genetic algorithm:

1. **[Start]** Generate random population of *n* chromosomes (suitable solutions for the problem)
2. **[Fitness]** Evaluate the fitness f(x) of each chromosome x in the population
3. **[New population]** Create a new population by repeating following steps until the new population is complete
   (a) [Selection] Select two parent chromosomes from a population according to their fitness (the better fitness, the bigger chance to be selected)
   (b) [Crossover] With a crossover probability cross over the parents to form a new offspring (children). If no crossover was performed, offspring is an exact copy of parents.
   (c) [Mutation] With a mutation probability mutate new offspring at each locus (position in chromosome).
   (d) [Accepting] Place new offspring in a new population
4. **[Replace]** Use new generated population for a further run of algorithm
5. **[Test]** If the end condition is satisfied, **stop**, and return the best solution in current population
6. **[Loop]** Go to step **2**

18.4 WORKING OF GENETIC ALGORITHMS

Genetic Algorithms (GA) are global search and optimization techniques modeled from natural genetics, exploring search space by incorporating a set of candidate solutions in parallel. A Genetic Algorithm (GA) maintains a population of candidate solutions where each candidate solution is usually coded as a binary string called a chromosome. A chromosome, also referred to as a genotype, encodes a parameter set (i.e. a candidate solution) for a set of variables being optimized. Each encoded parameter in a chromosome is called a gene. A decoded parameter set is called a phenotype. A set of chromosomes forms a population, which is evaluated and ranked by a fitness evaluation function. The fitness evaluation function plays a critical role in GA because it provides information about how good each candidate solution is. This information guides the search of a genetic algorithm. More accurately, the fitness evaluation results determine the likelihood that a candidate solution is selected to produce candidate solutions in the next generation. The initial population is usually generated at random.

The evolution from one generation to the next one involves mainly three steps: (1) fitness evaluation (2) selection, and (3) reproduction as shown in **Figure 18.1.** First, the current population is evaluated using the fitness evaluation function and then ranked based on their fitness values. Second GA stochastically select "parents" from the current population with a bias that better chromosomes are more likely to be selected. This is accomplished using a selection probability that is determined by the fitness value or the ranking of a chromosome, as shown in Figure 18.2. Third, the GA reproduces "children" from selected "parents" using two genetic operations: crossover and mutation. This cycle of evaluation, selection and reproduction terminates when an acceptable solution is found, when a convergence criterion is met, or when a predetermined limit on the number of iterations is reached.

The crossover operation produces offspring by exchanging information between two parent chromosomes. An example of crossover operation for binary GA is shown in Figure 18.3. The mutation operation produces an offspring from a parent through a random modification of the parent. The chances that these two operations apply to a chromosome are controlled by two probabilities: the crossover probability and the mutation probability. Typically, the mutation operation has a low probability of reducing its potential interference with a legitimately progressing search.

The genetic algorithm differs from the conventional optimization techniques in that it is inherently parallel. All individuals in a population evolve simultaneously without central coordination. They operate on a set of solutions rather than on one solution, hence multiple frontiers are searched simultaneously. The only feedback used by the genetic algorithm is the fitness evaluation. The GA has been shown to be an effective search technique on a wide range of difficult optimization problems.

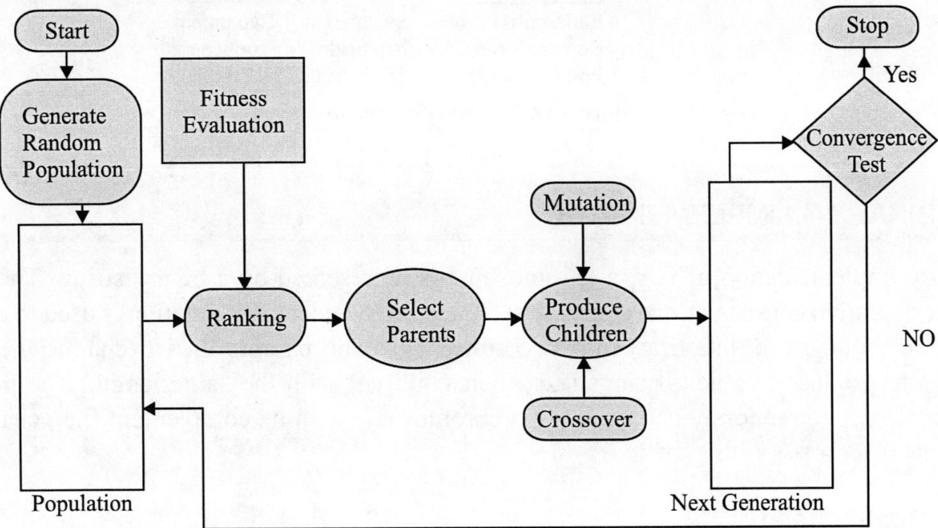

Figure 18.1: Architecture of the genetic algorithm

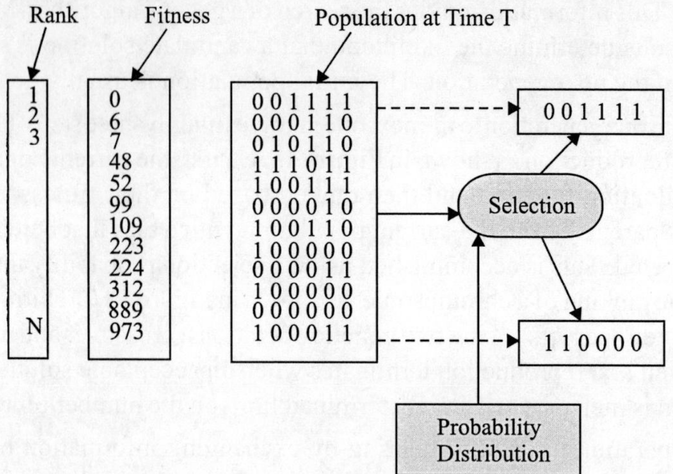

Figure 18.2 : Selection of parents

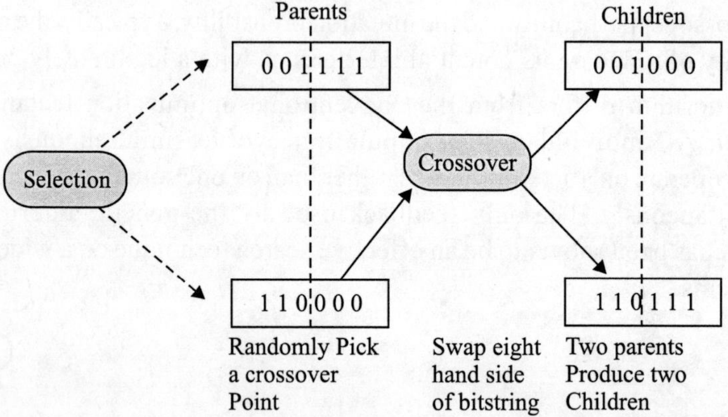

Figure 18.3: Binary crossover

18.5 BINARY GA IMPLEMENTATION

In a binary implementation of GA, a chromosome is represented by a binary string. The binary crossover operation consists of two steps. First, a randomly selected bit position is used to cut each parent chromosome (i.e. bitstring) into two substrings. The parents then exchange their right substrings to produce two new strings (i.e., their children) with the same length. The mutation operation replaces a randomly chosen bit of a chromosome with its complement (i.e., changing a "1" with a "0" or a "0" with a "1").

18.5.1 Real-coded GA

A real-coded GA is a genetic algorithm representation that uses a floating point. A chromosome in real-coded GA becomes a vector of floating-point numbers. With some modifications of genetic operators, real-coded GAs have resulted in better performance than binary-coded GA for certain problem. We briefly describe below some modified genetic operators recommended for real-coded GA.

The crossover operator of a real-coded GA is analogous to that of binary-coded GA except that its crossover points fall between genes (i.e., encoded parameters). Two mutation operators have been proposed for real-coded GA. A random mutation changes a gene with a random number in the feature's domain. A dynamic mutation stochastically changes a gene within an interval that narrows over time.

18.5.2 Dynamic Mutation of Real GA

The basic idea is to gradually reduce the range of the mutation operator over time such that the GA gradually changes from "explorative" search to focused search. The dynamic mutation operator is defined as

$$v_k = \begin{matrix} v_k & (t,\ UB \quad v_k) \text{ if a Random digit is 0} \\ v_k & (t,\ v_k \quad LB) \text{ if a Random digit is 1} \end{matrix} \tag{18.1}$$

$$(t, y) = y \cdot 1 - r^{\,1 \; \frac{1}{t}^{\,b}} \tag{18.2}$$

where r is a uniform random number from [0, 1], T is the maximal generation number, a and b are system parameters determining the degree of dependency on an iteration number (a typical choice is b = 5).

18.6 DESIGN ISSUES IN GA

18.6.1 Choice of Encoding

For binary GA, the choice of an encoding scheme is one of the important design decisions. Because binary GA encodes each parameter value using a binary string (i.e., a fixed length of binary numbers), we need to find a scaling function that maps the real parameter alue into an integer in the interval $[0, 2^n - 1]$ where n is the length of the binary string. Such a scaling function can be easily constructed from (1) the range of the parameter values we wish GA to search, and (2) the length of the binary string. The role of the scaling function and its inverse in encoding and decoding a parameter set is shown in Figure 18.4.

In designing GA, we usually first decide the range of each parameter value based on background knowledge of the problem being optimized. Based on the range and the desired precision of the optimal value for each parameter, we can then calculate the length of the binary string required.

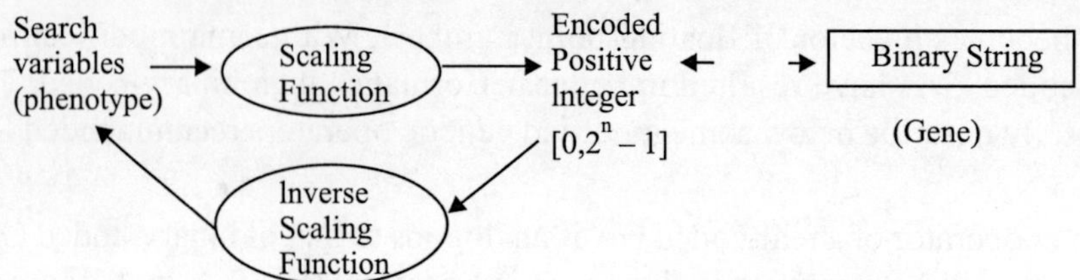

Figure 18.4: Encoding and decoding of search variables

18.6.2 Selection Probability

The probability that a chromosome is selected is selected to be a parent for reproduction can be based on (1) its fitness value or (2) its ranking. Most GA experiments reported in the literature recommend ranking-based selection probability, because using fitness-based selection probability often results in premature convergence. This is because the fitness of chromosomes in generation often varies widely, especially during the early stage of the search. Hence, a fitness-based selection probability may biase the selection process to such an extent that medium-ranked chromosomes are rarely selected if their fitness values are rarely selected if their fitness value are much lower then the fitness of those ranked on the top.

18.6.3 Mutation and Crossover Probability

The design of mutation and crossover probability differs significantly for binary GA and real – coded GA. This is because their roles are different in the two GA schemes. A binary GA mainly relies on the crossover operation to produce new point in the search space. The mutation operations plays a secondary role in binary GA by introducing "Stochastis randomness" into the reproduction process. In contrast, a real coded GA primarily uses its mutation operator to generate new point in search space. The crossover operation plays a secondary role of "Exchanging parameters". Because of these differences, the crossover probability of a binary GA is usually much higher then the mutation probability. IN contrast, the mutation probability of a real coded GA is usually much larger then the crossover probability.

18.6.4 Fitness Evaluation Function

A good design of fitness evaluation function is probably the most important factor in a successful application of GA. However, its importance can be easily overlooked. When a GA does perform well in solving an optimization problem, a natural temptation is to change a GA design parameter (e.g. population size, the crossover probability, or the mutation probability). Even though changing these parameter does effect the performance of GA, Tuning GA parameter will be in vain if the fitness evaluation function does not correctly reflected the desired optimization criteria.

There are atleast two type of fitness evaluation function: fitness-based and performance-based. A fitness-based function calculate how well a model using a parameter set in a chromosome fit a set of input output training data. In other words, the function computes the error between the target's output and the module's output. A performance-based evaluation function determines how well a system using the parameter set in a chromosome achieves a set of performance objectives.

EXERCISES

1. What do you mean by genetic algorithms?
2. Explain the methodology of genetic algorithms?
3. How we can encode a chromosome?
4. Explain the various genetic operators?
5. What do you mean by crossover reproduction?
6. What do you mean by mutation reproduction?
7. What are the two basic parameters of GA?
8. Explain the termination process of GA?
9. Write down the basic steps of the genetic algorithm?
10. Explain the working of genetic algorithm?
11. Explain the binary GA implementation?
12. What are the various design issues in GA?

PART - III
Probabilistic Reasoning

19. Probability Theory
20. Random Variable and Mathematical Expectation
21. Theoretical Distributions
22. Fuzzy Logic and Probability Theory

CHAPTER 19

Probability Theory

19.1 INTRODUCTION

Probability theory is the branch of mathematics concerned with analysis of random phenomena. The central objects of probability theory are random variables, stochastic processes, and events: mathematical abstractions of non-deterministic events or measured quantities that may either be single occurrences or evolve over time in an apparently random fashion. Although an individual coin toss or the roll of a die is a random event, if repeated many times the sequence of random events will exhibit certain statistical patterns, which can be studied and predicted. probability theory is essential to many human activities that involve quantitative analysis of large sets of data. Methods of probability theory also apply to descriptions of complex systems given only partial knowledge of their state, as in statistical mechanics.

Probability, or chance, is a way of expressing knowledge or belief that an event will occur or has occurred. In mathematics the concept has been given an exact meaning in probability theory, which is used extensively in such areas of study as mathematics, statistics, finance, gambling, science, and philosophy to draw conclusions about the likelihood of potential events and the underlying mechanics of complex systems.

19.2 BASIC CONCEPTS

1. **Random Experiment:** An experiment is said to be a random experiment, if it's out-come can't be predicted with certainty.

   Problem: If a coin is tossed, we can't say, whether head or tail will appear. So it is a random experiment.

2. **Sample Space:** The sent of all possible out-comes of an experiment is called the sample space. It is denoted by 'S' and its number of elements are n(s).

   Problem: In throwing a dice, the number that appears at top is any one of 1, 2, 3, 4, 5, 6. So here:

   S ={1, 2, 3, 4, 5, 6} and n(s) = 6

Similarly in the case of a coin, S = {Head, Tail} or {H,T} and n(s) = 2.

The elements of the sample space are called sample point or event point.

3. **Event** Every subset of a sample space is an event. It is denoted by 'E'.

   Problem: In throwing a dice S={1, 2, 3, 4, 5, 6}, the appearance of an event number will be the event E={2, 4, 6}.

   Clearly E is a sub set of S.

4. **Simple event** An event, consisting of a single sample point is called a simple event.

   Problem: In throwing a dice, S={1, 2, 3, 4, 5, 6}, so each of {1},{2},{3},{4},{5} and {6} are simple events.

5. **Compound event** A subset of the sample space, which has more than on element is called a mixed event.

   Problem: In throwing a dice, the event of appearing of odd numbers is a compound event, because E={1,3,5} which has '3' elements.

6. **Equally likely events** Events are said to be equally likely, if we have no reason to believe that one is more likely to occur than the other.

   Problem When a dice is thrown, all the six faces {1, 2, 3, 4, 5, 6} are equally likely to come up.

7. **Exhaustive events** When every possible out come of an experiment is considered.

   Problem: A dice is thrown, cases 1, 2, 3, 4, 5, 6 forms an exhaustive set of events.

19.3 CLASSICAL DEFINITION OF PROBABILITY

If 'S' be the sample space, then the probability of occurrence of an event 'E' is defined as:

$$P(E) = n(E)/N(S) = \frac{\text{Number of elements in 'E'}}{\text{Number of elements in sample space 'S'}}$$

Problem 1: Find the probability of getting a tail in tossing of a coin.

Solution: Sample space S = {H, T} and n(s) = 2

Event 'E' = {T} and n(E) = 1

therefore P(E) = n(E)/n(S) = ½

Note: This definition is not true, ifteb

(a) The events are not equally likely.

(b) The possible outcomes are infinite.

Sure event: Let 'S' be a sample space. If E is a subset of or equal to S then E is called a sure event.

Problem 2: In a throw of a dice, S = {1, 2, 3, 4, 5, 6}

Let E_1 = Event of getting a number less than '7'.

So 'E_1' is a sure event.

So, we can say, in a sure event n(E) = n(S)

Mutually exclusive or disjoint event: If two or more events can't occur simultaneously, that is no two of them can occur together.

Problem 3: When a coin is tossed, the event of occurrence of a head and the event of occurrence of a tail are mutually exclusive events.

Independent or mutually independent events: Two or more events are said to be independent if occurrence or non-occurrence of any of them does not affect the probability of occurrence or non-occurrence of the other event.

Problem 4: When a coin is tossed twice, the event of occurrence of head in the first throw and the event of occurrence of head in the second throw are independent events.

Difference between mutually exclusive an mutually independent events: Mutually exclusiveness id used when the events are taken from the same experiment, where as independence is used when the events are taken from different experiments.

Complement of an event: Let 'S' be the sample for random experiment, and 'E' be an event, then complement of 'E' is denoted by 'E' is denoted by E'. Here E' occurs, if and only if E' doesn't occur.

19.4 THEOREMS RELATED TO PROBABILITY

Theorem 1: The probability of an event lies between 'O' and '1'.

i.e. O <= P(E) <= 1.

Proof: Let 'S' be the sample space and 'E' be the event.

Then

$$O <= n(E) <= n(S)$$

$$O/n(S) <= n(E)/n(S) <= n(S)/n(S)$$

or

$$O <= P(E) <= 1$$

The number of elements in 'E' can't be less than 'O' i.e. negative and greater than the number of elements in S.

Theorem 2: The probability of an impossible event is 'O' i.e. P () = O

Proof: Since has no element, n() = O

From definition of Probability:

$$P() = n()/n(S) = O/n(S)$$

$$P() = O$$

Theorem 3: The probability of a sure event is 1. i.e. P(S) = 1. where 'S' is the sure event.

Proof: In sure event n(E) = n(S)

[Since Number of elements in Event 'E' will be equal to the number of element in sample-space.]

By definition of Probability:

$$P(S) = n(S)/n(S) = 1$$

$$P(S) = 1$$

Theorem 4: If two events 'A' and 'B' are such that $A \subseteq B$, then $P(A) <= P(B)$.

Proof: $A \subset B$

$$n(A) <= n(B)$$

or

$$n(A)/N(S) <= n(B)/n(S)$$

$$P(A) <= P(B)$$

Since 'A' is the sub-set of 'B", so from set theory number of elements in 'A' can't be more than number of element in 'B'.

Theorem 5: If 'E' is any event and E^1 be the complement of event 'E', then $P(E) + P(E^1) = 1$.

Proof:

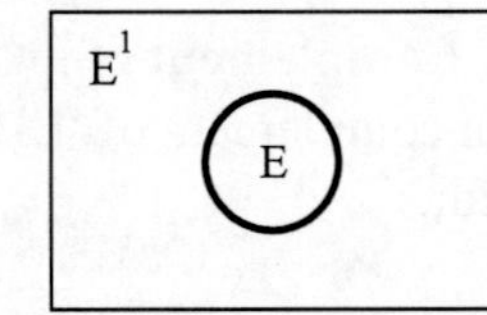

Let 'S' be the sample – space, then

$$n(E) + n(E1) = n(S)$$

or

$$n(E)/n(S) + n(E1)/n(S) = 1$$

or

$$P(E) + P(E1) = 1$$

Algebra of Events: In a random experiment, let 'S' be the sample – space.

Let $A \subset S$ and $B \subset S$, where 'A' and 'B' are events.

Thus we say that :

(i) $(A \cup B)$, is an event occurs only when at least of 'A' and 'B' occurs.$(A \cup B)$ means (A or B).

Problem 5: Suppose we conduct a simple statistical experiment. We flip a coin one time. The coin flip can have one of two outcomes-heads or tails. Together, these outcomes represent the sample space of our experiment. Individually, each outcome represents a sample point in the sample space. What is the probability of each sample point?

Solution: The sum of probabilities of all the sample points must equal 1. And the probability of getting a head is equal to the probability of getting a tail. Therefore, the probability of each sample point (heads or tails) must be equal to 1/2.

Problem 6: Let's repeat the experiment of Example 1, with a die instead of a coin. If we toss a fair die, what is the probability of each sample point?

Solution: For this experiment, the sample space consists of six sample points: {1, 2, 3, 4, 5, 6}. Each sample point has equal probability. And the sum of probabilities of all the sample points must equal 1. Therefore, the probability of each sample point must be equal to 1/6.

19.5 PROBABILITY OF AN EVENT

The probability of an event is a measure of the likelihood that the event will occur. By convention, statisticians have agreed on the following rules.

- The probability of any event can range from 0 to 1.
- The probability of event A is the sum of the probabilities of all the sample points in event A.
- The probability of event A is denoted by P(A).

Thus, if event A were very unlikely to occur, then P(A) would be close to 0. And if event A were very likely to occur, then P(A) would be close to 1.

Problem 7: Suppose we draw a card from a deck of playing cards. What is the probability that we draw a spade?

Solution: The sample space of this experiment consists of 52 cards, and the probability of each sample point is 1/52. Since there are 13 spades in the deck, the probability of drawing a spade is

$$P(\text{Spade}) = (13)(1/52) = 1/4$$

Problem 8: Suppose a coin is flipped 3 times. What is the probability of getting two tails and one head?

Solution: For this experiment, the sample space consists of 8 sample points.

$$S = \{TTT, TTH, THT, THH, HTT, HTH, HHT, HHH\}$$

Each sample point is equally likely to occur, so the probability of getting any particular sample point is 1/8. The event "getting two tails and one head" consists of the following subset of the sample space.

$$A = \{TTH, THT, HTT\}$$

The probability of Event A is the sum of the probabilities of the sample points in A. Therefore,

$$P(A) = 1/8 + 1/8 + 1/8 = 3/8$$

Problem 9: An urn contains 6 red marbles and 4 black marbles. Two marbles are drawn *with replacement* from the urn. What is the probability that both of the marbles are black?

(A) 0.16
(B) 0.32
(C) 0.36
(D) 0.40
(E) 0.60

Solution: The correct answer is A. Let A = the event that the first marble is black; and let B = the event that the second marble is black. We know the following:

- In the beginning, there are 10 marbles in the urn, 4 of which are black. Therefore, P(A) = 4/10.
- After the first selection, we replace the selected marble; so there are still 10 marbles in the urn, 4 of which are black. Therefore, P(B|A) = 4/10.

Therefore, based on the rule of multiplication:

$$P(A \cap B) = P(A)\, P(B|A)$$

$$P(A) \cap B) = (4/10)*(4/10) = 16/100 = 0.16$$

Problem 10: A card is drawn randomly from a deck of ordinary playing cards. You win $10 if the card is a spade or an ace. What is the probability that you will win the game?

(A) 1/13
(B) 13/52
(C) 4/13
(D) 17/52
(E) None of the above.

Solution: The correct answer is C. Let S = the event that the card is a spade; and let A = the event that the card is an ace. We know the following:

- There are 52 cards in the deck.
- There are 13 spades, so P(S) = 13/52.
- There are 4 aces, so P(A) = 4/52.
- There is 1 ace that is also a spade, so $P(S \cap A) = 1/52$.

Therefore, based on the rule of addition:

$P(S \cup A) = P(S) + P(A) - P(S \cap A)$

$P(S \cup A) = 13/52 + 4/52 - 1/52 = 16/52 = 4/13$

Problem 11: A coin is tossed successively three times. Find the probability of getting exactly one head or two heads.

Solution: Let 'S' be the sample – space. Then,

S = {HHH, HHT, HTH, THH, TTH, THT, HTT, TTT}

n(S) = 8

Let 'E' be the event of getting exactly one head or two heads.

Then:

E = {HHT, HTH, THH, TTH, THT, HTT}

n (E) = 6

Therefore:

P(E) = n (E)/ n (S) = 6/8 = 3/4

Problem 12: Three coins are tossed. What is the probability of getting (i) all heads, (ii) two heads, (iii) at least one head, (iv) at least two heads?

Solution: Let 'S' be the sample – space. Then

S = { HHH, HHT, HTH, THH, HTT, THT, TTH, TTT }

(i) Let 'E_1' = Event of getting all heads.

Then E_1 = { HHH }

$n(E_1) = 1$

$P(E_1) = n(E_1)/n(S) = 1/8$

(ii) Let E_2 = Event of getting '2' heads.

Then:

E_2 = {HHT, HTH, THH}

$n(E_2) = 3$

$P(E_2) = 3/8$

(iii) Let E_3 = Event of getting at least one head.

Then:

E_3 = {HHH, HHT, HTH, THH, HTT, THT, TTH }

$n(E_3) = 7$

$P(E_3) = 7/8$

(iv) Let E_4 = Event of getting at least one head.

Then:

E_4 = {HHH, HHT, HTH, THH}

$n(E_4) = 4$

$P(E_4) = 4/8 = ½$

Problem 13: What is the probability, that a number selected from 1, 2, 3, ... 2, 5, is a prime number, when each of the numbers is equally likely to be selected.

Solution: S = {1, 2, 3, ..., 2, 5} n(S) = 25

And E = {2, 3, 5, 7, 11, 13, 17, 19, 23} n(E) = 9

Hence P (E) = n(E)/n(S) = 9/25

Problem 14: Two dice are thrown simultaneously. Find the probability of getting :

(i) The same number on both dice,

(ii) An even number as the sum,

(iii) A prime number as the sum,

(iv) A multiple of '3' as the sum,

(v) A total of at least 0,

(vi) A doublet of even numbers,

(vii) A multiple of '2' on one dice and a multiple of '3' on the other dice.

Solution: Here:

S = {(1, 1), (1, 2) ....., (1, 6), (2, 1), (2, 2), ... (2,6), (3,1), (3,2), ... , (3,6), (4,1), (4,2), ... (4,6), (5,1), (5,2), ... (5,6), (6,1,), (6,2), ... (6,6) }

n(S) = 6 ′ 6 = 36

(i) Let E_1 = Event of getting same number on both side:

E_1 = { (1,1), (2,2), (3,3), (4,4), (5,5), (6,6) }

$n(E_1) = 6$

$P(E_1) = n(E_1)/n(S) = 6/36 = 1/6$

(ii) Let E_2 = Event of getting an even number as the sum.

E_2 = { (1,1), (1,3), (1,5), (2,2), (2,4), (2,6), (3,1), (3,3), (3,5), (4,2), (4,4), (4,6), (5,1), (5,5), (6,2), (6,4), (6,6)}

$n(E_2)$ = 18 hence $P(E_2) = n(E_2)/n(S) = 18/36 = 1/2$

(iii) Let E_3 = Event of getting a prime number as the sum.

E_3 = { (1,1), (1,2), (1,4), (1,6), (2,1), (2,3), (2,5), (3,2), (3,4), (4,1), (4,3), (5,2), (5,6), (6,1), (6,5),}

$n(E_3) = 15$

$P(E_2) = n(E_3)/n(S) = 15/36 = 5/12$

(iv) Let E_4 = Event of getting a multiple of '3' as the sum.

E_4 = { (1,2), (1,5), (2,1), (2,4), (3,3), (3,6), (4,2), (4,5), (5,1), (5,4), (6,3), (6,6),}

$n(E_4) = 12$

$P(E_4) = n(E_4)/n(S) = 12/36 = 1/3$

(v) Let E_5 = Event of getting a total of at least 10.

E_5 = { (4,6), (5,5), (5,6), (6,4), (6,5), (6,6), }

$n(E_5) = 6$

$P(E_5) = n(E_5)/n(S) = 6/36 = 1/6$

(vi) Let E_6 = Event of getting a doublet of even numbers.

E_6 = { (2,2), (4,4), (6,6),}

$n(E_6) = 3$

$P(E_6) = n(E_6)/ n(S) = 3/36 = 1/12$

(vii) Let E_7 = Even of getting a multiple of '2" on one dice and a multiple of

'3' on the other dice.

$E_7 = \{ (2,3), (2,6), (4,3), (4,6), (6,3), (3,2), (3,4), (3,6), (6,2), (6,4) \}$

$n(E_7) = 11$

$P(E_7) = n(E_7)/n(S) = 11/36$

Problem 15: What is the probability, that a leap year selected at random will contain 53 Sundays?

Solution: A leap year has 366 days, therefore 52 weeks i.e. 52 Sunday and 2 days.

The remaining 2 days may be any of the following:

(i) Sunday and Monday

(ii) Monday and Tuesday

(iii) Tuesday and Wednesday

(iv) Wednesday and Thursday

(v) Thursday and Friday

(vi) Friday and Saturday

(vii) Saturday and Sunday

For having 53 Sundays in a year, one of the remaining 2 days must be a Sunday.

$n(S) = 7$

$n(E) = 2$

$P(E) = n(E)/n(S) = 2/7$

Problems based on finding $P(E^1)$, by the use of $P(E^1) - 1 - P(E)$:

Note: When an event has a lot of out comes, and then we use this concept.

Problem 16: What is the probability of getting a total of less than '12' in the throw of two dice?

Solution: Here $n(S) = 6 \times 6 = 36$

It is very difficult to find out all the cares, in which we can find the total less then '12'.

So let E = The event, that the sum of numbers is '12'.

Then $E = \{ 6, 6\}$

$n(E) = 1$

$= P(E) = n(E)/n(S) = 1/36$

Required probability, $P(E^1) = 1–P(E)$

$= 1 - 1/36$

$P(E1) = 35/36$

Problem 17: There are '4' envelopes corresponding to '4' letters. If the letters are placed in the envelopes at random, what is the probability that all the letters are not placed in the right envelopes?

Solution: We have to place '4' letters in 4 envelopes.

$$n(S) = 4!$$

Now:

Let E = The event, that all the 4 letters are placed in the corresponding envelopes.

So E^1 = The event that all the '4' letters are not placed in the right envelope.

Here $n(E) = 1$

$$P(E) = n(E)/n(S) = 1/4! = 1/24$$

Required probability, $P(E^1) = 1 - P(E) = 1 - (1/24)$

$$P(E^1) = 23/24$$

19.6 MATHEMATICAL OR CLASSICAL OR 'A PRIORI' PROBABILITY

Definition: If a random experiment results in N exhaustive, mutually exclusive and equally likely outcomes (cases) out of which m are favourable to the happening of an event A, then the probability of occurrence of A, usually denoted by P(A) is given by:

$$P(A) = \frac{\text{Favourable number of cases to A}}{\text{Exhaustive number of cases}} \quad \frac{m}{N} \qquad \text{...(19.1)}$$

This definition was given by James Bernoulli who was the first man to obtain a quantitative measure or uncertainly.

Remarks

1. Obviously, the number of cases favourable to the complementry event $\bar{A}$ i.e. non-happening of event A are (N – m) and hence by definition, the probability of non-occurrence of A is given by:

$$P(\bar{A}) = \frac{\text{Favourable No. of cases to } \bar{A}}{\text{Exhaustive number of cases}} \quad \frac{N \quad m}{N} \quad 1\frac{m}{N}$$

$$\rightarrow P(\bar{A}) = 1 - P(A) \qquad \text{...(19.2)}$$

$$\rightarrow P(A) + P(\bar{A}) = 1 \qquad \text{....(19.3)}$$

2. Since m and N are non-negative integers, $P(A) \geq 0$. Further since the favourable number of cases to A are always less than or equal to the total number of cases N, i.e. $m \leq 1$. Hence probability of any event is a number lying between 0 and 1, i.e..

$$0 \leq P(A) \leq 1, \qquad (19.4)$$

for any event A. If P(A) = 0, then A is called an impossible or null event. If P(A) = 1, then A is called a certain event.

3. The probability of happening of the event A, i.e., P(A) is also known as the probability of success and is usually written as p and the probability of the non-happening of A, i.e., $P(\bar{A})$ is known as the probability of failure, which is usually denoted by q. Thus from (19.2) and

(19.3), we get

$$q = 1 - p \rightarrow p + q = 1 \tag{19.5}$$

4. According to the above definition, the probability of getting a head in a toss of an unbiased coin is 1/2, since the two exhaustive cases H and T (assuming the coin does not stand on its edge), are mutually exclusive and equally likely and one is favourable to getting a head. Similarly, in drawing a card from a well shuffled pack of cards, the probability of getting an ace is 4/52 = 1/13. Thus, the classical definition of probability does not require the actual experimentation, i.e., no experimental data are needed for its computation, nor it is based on previous experience. It enables us to obtain probability by logical reasoning prior to making any actual trails and hence it is also known as 'a priori' or theoretical or mathematical probability.

19.6.1 Limitations of Classical Probability

The classical probability has its short-comings and fails in the following situations:

(i) If N, the exhaustive number of outcomes of the random experiment is infinite.

(ii) If the various outcomes of the random experiment are not equally likely. For example, if a person jumps from the top of Qutab Minar, then the probability of his survival will not be 50%, since in this case the two mutually exclusive and exhaustive, viz, survival and death are not equally likely.

(iii) If the actual value of N is not known. Suppose an urn contains some balls of two colours, say red and white, their number being unknown. If we actually draw the balls from the urn, then we may from some idea about the ratio of red to the white balls in the urn. In the absence of any such experimentation (which is the case in classical probability) we cannot draw any conclusion in such a situation regarding the probability of drawing a white or a red ball from the urn. This drawback is overcome, in the statistical or empirical probability which we discuss below:

19.7 STATISTICAL OR EMPIRICAL PROBABILITY

Definition: (Von Mises). If an experiment is performed repeatedly under essentially homogeneous and identical conditions, then the limiting value of the ratio of the number of times the event occurs to the number of trials, as the number of trials becomes indefinitely large, is called the probability of happening of the event, it being assumed that the limit is finite and unique.

Suppose that an event A occurs m times in N repetitions of a random experiment. Then the ratio m/N gives the relative frequency of the event A and it will not vary appreciably from one trail to another. In the limiting case when N becomes sufficiently large, it more or less settles to a number which is called the probability of A. Symbolically,

$$P(A) = \lim_{N} \frac{m}{N} \tag{19.6}$$

Remarks

1. Since in the relative frequency approach, the probability is obtained objectively by repetitive empirical observations, it is known as Empirical Probability.
2. The empirical probability provides validity to the classical theory of probability. If an unbiased coin is tossed at random, then the classical probability gives the probability of the head as 1/2. Thus, if we toss an unbiased coin 20 times, then classical probability suggests we should have 10 heads. However, in practice, this will not generally be true. In fact in 20 throws of a coin, we may get no head at all or 1 or 2 heads. However, the empirical probability suggests that if a coin is tossed a large number of times; say 500 times, we should on the average expect 50% heads and 50% tails. Thus, the empirical probability approaches the classical probability as the number of trials becomes indefinite large.

19.7.1 Limitations of Statistical Probability

It may be remarked that the empirical probability P(A) defined in (19.6) can never be obtained in practice and we can only attempt at a close estimate of P(A) by making N sufficiently large. The following are limitations of the experiment.

(i) The experimental conditions may remain essentially homogeneous and identical in a large number of repetitions of the experiment.

(ii) The relative frequency m/N may not attain a unique value, no matter however large N may be.

Problem 18: A uniform die is thrown at random. Find the probability that the number on it is:

(i) 5, (ii) greater than 4 (iii) even.

Solution: Since the dice can fails with any one of the faces 1, 2, 3, 4, 5 and 6, the exhaustive number of cases is 6.

(i) The number of cases favourable to the event of getting ‘5’ is only 1.

∴ Required probability = 1/6

(ii) The number of cases favourable to the event of getting a number greater than 4 is 2, viz, 5 and 6.

$$\therefore \quad \text{Required probability} = \frac{2}{6} \quad \frac{1}{3}$$

Problem 19: In a single throw with two uniform dice find the probability of throwing

(i) Five (ii) Eight

Solution: Exhaustive number of cases in a single throw with dice is $6^2 = 36$.

(i) Sum of ‘5’ can be obtained on the two dice in the following mutually exclusive ways:

(1, 4), (4, 1) (2, 3) (3, 2) i.e., 4 cases in all where the first and second number in the bracket ( ) refer to the numbers on the 1st and 2nd dice respectively.

$$\therefore \qquad \text{Required probability} = \frac{4}{36} \quad \frac{1}{9}$$

(ii) The cases favourable to the event to getting sum of 8 on two dice are:

(2, 6) (6, 2) (3, 5) (5, 3), (4, 4) i.e., 5 distinct cases in all.

$$\therefore \qquad \text{Required probability} = \frac{5}{36}$$

Problem 20: Four cards are drawn at random from a pack of 52 cards. Find the probability that

(i) They are a king, a queen, a jack and an ace

(ii) Two are kings and two are aces.

(iii) All are diamonds

(iv) Two are red and two are black

(v) There is one card of each suit

(vi) There are two cards of clubs and two cards of diamonds

Solution: Four cards can be drawn from a well shuffled pack of 52 cards in ${}^{52}C_4$ ways, which given the exhaustive number of cases.

(i) 1 kings can be drawn out of the 4 kings is ${}^{4}C_1 = 4$ ways. Similarly, 1 queen, 1 jack and ace can each be drawn in ${}^{4}C_1 = 4$ ways. Since any one of the ways of drawing a king can be associated with any one of the ways of drawing a queen, a jack and an ace, the favourable number of causes are ${}^{4}C_1 \times {}^{4}C_1 \times {}^{4}C_1 \times {}^{4}C_1$.

$$\text{Hence} \qquad \text{required probability} = \frac{{}^{4}C_1 \quad {}^{4}C_1 \quad {}^{4}C_1 \quad {}^{4}C_1}{{}^{52}C_4} \quad \frac{256}{{}^{52}C_4}$$

$$\text{(ii)} \qquad \text{Required probability} = \frac{{}^{4}C_2 \quad {}^{4}C_2}{{}^{52}C_4}$$

(iii) Since 4 cards can be drawn out of 13 cards (since there are 13 cards of diamond in a pack of cards) in ${}^{13}C_4$ ways.

$$\text{Required probability} = \frac{{}^{13}C_4}{{}^{52}C_4}$$

(iv) Since there are 26 reds cards (of diamonds and hearts) and 26 black cards (of spades and clubs) in a pack of cards.

$$\text{Required probability} = \frac{{}^{26}C_2 \quad {}^{26}C_2}{{}^{52}C_4}$$

(v) Since, in a pack of cards there are 13 cards of each suit.

$$\text{Required probability} = \frac{{}^{13}C_1 \quad {}^{13}C_1 \quad {}^{13}C_1 \quad {}^{13}C_1}{{}^{52}C_4}.$$

(vi) $$\text{Required probability} = \frac{{}^{13}C_2 \quad {}^{13}C_2}{{}^{52}C_4}$$

Problem 21: What is the chance that a non-leap year should have fifty-three Sundays?

Solution: A non-leap year consists of 365 days i.e., 52 full weeks and one over-day. A non-leap year will consist of 53 Sundays if this over-day can be anyone of the possible outcomes:

(i) Sunday (ii) Monday (iii) Tuesday (iv) Wednesday (v) Thursday (vi) Friday (vii) Saturday i.e. 7 outcomes in all. Of these, the number ways favourable to the required event viz., the over-day being Sunday is 1.

Problem 22: A bag contains 20 tickets marked with numbers 1 to 20. One ticket is drawn at random. Find the probability that it will be a multiple of (i) 2 or 5, (ii) 3 or 5

Solution: One ticket can be drawn out of 20 tickets in ${}^{20}C_1 = 20$ ways, which determine the exhaustive number of cases.

(i) The number of cases favourable to getting the ticket number which is:

(a) a multiple of 2 are 2, 4, 6, 8, 10, 12, 14, 16, 18, 20 i.e., 10 cases.

(b) a multiple of 5 are 5, 10, 15, 20 i.e., 4 cases.

Of these, two cases viz., 10 and 20 are duplicated. Hence the number of distinct cases favourable to getting a number which is a multiple of 2 or 5 are $10 + 4 - 2 = 12$.

$$\text{Required probability} = \frac{12}{20} \quad \frac{3}{5} \quad 0.6$$

(ii) The cases favourable to getting a multiple of 3 are 3, 6, 9, 12, 15, 18 i.e., 6 cases in all and getting a multiple of 5 are 5, 10, 15, 20 i.e., 4 cases in all. Of these, one case viz., 15 is duplicated.

Hence, the number of distinct cases favourable to getting a multiple of 3 or 5 is $6 + 4 - 1 = 9$

$\therefore$ $$\text{Required Probability} = \frac{9}{20} \quad 0.45$$

Problem 23: An urn contains 8 while and 3 red bails. If two balls are drawn at random, find the probability that

(i) both are white (ii) both are red (iii) one is of each colour

Solution: Total number of balls in the urn is $8 + 3 = 11$. Since 2 balls can be drawn out of 11 balls in ${}^{11}C_2$ ways.

$$\text{Exhaustive number of cases} = {}^{11}C_2 = \frac{11 \quad 10}{2} \quad 55$$

(i) If both the drawn balls are whit, they must be selected out of the 8 white balls and this can be done in ${}^{8}C_2 = \frac{8 \quad 7}{2} \quad 28$ ways.

$\therefore$ Probability that both the balls are white $= \frac{28}{55}$

(ii) If both the drawn are red, they must be drawn out of the 3 red balls and this can be done in ${}^{3}C_2 = 3$ ways. Hence, the probability that both the drawn balls are red $= \frac{3}{55}$.

(iii) The number of favourable cases for drawing one white ball and one red ball is

$$`{}^{8}C_1 \times {}^{3}C_1 = 8 \times 3 = 24$$

$\therefore$ Probability that one ball is white and other is red $= \frac{24}{35}$

Problem 24: The letters of the word 'article' are arranged at random. Find the probability that the vowels may occupy the even-places.

Solution: The word 'article' contains 7 distinct letters which can be arranged among themselves in 7 ! ways. Hence, exhaustive number of cases is 7!.

In the word 'article' there are 3 vowels viz., a, i and e and these are to be placed in, three even places viz., 2nd, 4th and 6th place. This can be done in 3!, ways. For each arrangement, the remaining 4 consonants can be arranged in 4 ! ways. Hence, associating these two operations, the number of favourable cases for the vowels to occupy even places is $3! \times 4!$.

$$\therefore \qquad \text{Required Probability} = \frac{3!4!}{7!} \quad \frac{3!}{7 \quad 6 \quad 5} \quad \frac{1}{35}.$$

Problem 25: The letters of the word 'failure' are arranged at random. Find the probability consonants may occupy only odd positions.

Solution: There are 7 distinct letters in the word 'failure' and they can be arranged among themselves in 7! ways, which gives the exhaustive number of cases.

In the word 'failure' there are 4 vowels viz., a i, u and e, and 3 consonants viz., f, l, r. These 3 constants are to be placed in the 4 old places viz., 1st, 3rd, 5th and 7th and this can be done in ${}^{4}C_3$ ways. Further these 3 consonants can be arranged among themselves in 3 ! ways and the remaining 4 vowels can be arranged among themselves in 4! ways. Associating all these operations, total number of favourable cases for the consonants to occupy only odd position is ${}^{4}C_3 \times 3! \times 4!$.

$$\therefore \qquad \text{Required probability} = \frac{{}^{4}C_3 \quad 3! \quad 4!}{7!} \quad \frac{4 \quad 3!}{7 \quad 6 \quad 5} \quad \frac{4}{35}$$

19.8 PERMUTATION AND COMBINATION

The word permutation in simple language means "arrangement" and word combination means "group" or "selection". Let us consider three letters A, B and C. The permutations of these three letters taken two at a time will be AB, BC, CA, BA, CB and AC, i.e.,6 in all whereas the combinations of these three letters taken two at a time will be AB, BC and CA that is 3 in all.

Permutation (Def): "A permutation of n different objects taken r at a time, denoted by ^nP_r is an ordered arrangement of only r objects of the n objects."

Combination (Def): "A combination of n different objects taken r at a time, denoted by ^nC_r or (n/r) is a selection of only r objects out of the n objects, without any regard to the order of arrangement."

Principal of Counting (Def): "If one operation can be performed in p different ways and another operation can be performed in q different ways. Then the two operations when associated together can be performed in p × q ways."

Problem 26: A bag contains '6' red, 4 white and 8 blue balls. If three balls are drawn at random, find the probability, that

(i) '1' is red and '2' are white, (ii) '2' are blue and 1 is red, (iii) none is red.

Solution: We have to select '3' balls, from 18 balls (6+4+8)

$$n(S) = {}^{18}C_3 = 18!/(3! \times 15!) = (18 \times 17 \times 16)/(3 \times 2 \times 1) = 816$$

(i) Let E_1 = Event of getting '1' ball is red and '2' are white

Total number of ways = $n(E_1) = {}^6C_1 \times {}^4C_2$

$= 6!/(1! \times 5!) \times 4!/(2! \times 2!)$

$= 6 \times 4/2$

$= 36$

$$P(E_1) = n(E_1)/n(S) = 36/816 = 3/68$$

(ii) Let E_2 = Event of getting '2' balls are blue and '1' is red.

= Total no. of ways $n(E_2) = {}^8C_2 \times {}^6C_1$

$= 8!/(2! \times 6!) \times 6!/(1! \times 5!)$

$= (8 \times 7)/2 \times 6/1 = 168$

$$P(E_2) = 168/816 = 7/34$$

(iii) Let E_3 = Event of getting '3' non – red balls. So now we have to choose all the three balls from 4 white and 8 blue balls.

Total number of ways :

$n(E_3) = {}^{12}C_3 = 12!/(3! \times 9!) = (12 \times 11 \times 10)/(3 \times 2 \times 1) = 220$

$P(E_3) = n(E_3)/n(S) = 220/816 = 55/204$

Problem 27: A box contains 12 bulbs of which '4' are defective. All bulbs took alike. Three bulbs are drawn randomly.

What is the probability that:

(i) all the '3' bulbs are defective?

(ii) At least '2' of the bulbs chosen are defective?

(iii) At most '2' of the bulbs chosen are defective?

Solution: We have to select '3' bulbs from 12 bulbs.

$n(S) = {}^{12}C_3 = 12!/(3! \times 9!) = (12 \times 11 \times 10)/(3 \times 2 \times 1) = 220$

(i) Let E_1 = All the '3' bulbs are defective.

All bulbs have been chosen, from '4' defective bulbs.

$n(E_1) = {}^{4}C_3 = 4!/(3! \times 1!) = 4$

$P(E_1) = n(E_1)/n(S) = 4/220 = 1/55$

(ii) Let E_2 = Event drawing at least 2 defective bulbs. So here, we can get '2' defective and 1 non-defective bulbs or 3 defective bulbs.

$n(E_2) = {}^{4}C_2 \times {}^{8}C_1 + {}^{4}C_3$ [Non-defective bulbs = 8]

$= 4!/(2! \times 2!) \times 8!/(1! \times 7!) + 4!/(3! \times 1!)$

$= 4 \times 3/2 \times 8/1 + 4/1 = 48 + 4$

$n(E_2) = 52$

$P(E_2) = n(E_2)/n(S) = 52/220 = 13/55$

(iii) Let E3 = Event of drawing at most '2' defective bulbs. So here, we can get no defective bulbs or 1 is defective and '2' is non-defective or '2' defective bulbs.

$n(E_3) = {}^{8}C_3 + {}^{4}C_1 \times {}^{8}C_2 + {}^{4}C_2 \times {}^{8}C_1$

$= 8!/(3! \times 5!) + 4!/(1! \times 3!) \times 8!/(2! \times 6!) + 4!/(2! \times 2!) \times 8!/(1! \times 7!)$

$= (8 \times 7 \times 6)/(3 \times 2 \times 1) + 4 \times (8 \times 7)/2 + (4 \times 3)/2 + 8/1$

$= 216$

$P(E_3) = n(E_3)/n(S) = 216/220 = 54/55$

Problem 28: 6 boys and 6 girls sit in a row randomly, find the probability that all the '6' girls sit together.

Solution: We have to arrange '6' boys and '6' girls in a row.

$n(S) = 12!$

Now, we have to arrange '6' girls in a way, such that all of them should sit together.

Regarding all the 6 girls as one person, we have to arrange 7 person in a row.

Total no. of ways = 7!

But 6 girls can be arranged among themselves in 6? ways.

$$n(E) = 7! \times 6!$$

$$(E) = n(E)/n(S) = (7! \times 6!)/12! = (6\times5 \times 4 \times 3 \times 2 \times 1)/(12 \times 11 \times 10 \times 9 \times 8)$$

$$P(E) = 1/132$$

Problem 29: If from a pack of '52' playing cards one card is drawn at random, what is the probability that it is either a kind or a queen?

Solution: n(S) = Total number of ways of selecting 1 card out of 52 cards.

$= {}^{52}C_1 = 52$

n(E) = Total number of selections of a card, which is either a kind or a queen.

$= {}^4C_1 + {}^4C_1 = 4 + 4 = 8$

$P(E) = n(E)/n(S) = 8/52 = 2/3$

Problem 30: From a pack of 52 playing cards, three cards are drawn at random. Find the probability of drawing a king, a queen and a jack.

Solution: Here

$$n(S) = {}^{52}C_3 = 52!/(3!\ '\ 49!)$$
$$= (52 \times 51 \times 50)/(3 \times 2 \times 1)$$
$$= 52 \times 17 \times 25$$
$$n(E) = {}^4C_1 \cdot {}^4C_1 \cdot {}^4C_1$$
$$= 4!/(1! \times 3!) \times 4!/(1! \times 3!) = 4!/(1! \times 3!)$$
$$n(E) = 4 \times 4 \times 4$$
$$P(E) = n(E)/n(S) = (4 \times 4 \times 4)/(52 \times 17 \times 25) = 16/5525$$

Problems Based on Finding $P(E^1)$, by the use of $P(E^1) - 1 - P(E)$

Note: When an event has a lot of out comes, then we use this concept.

Problem 31: What is the probability of getting a total of less than '12' in the throw of two dice?

Solution: Here $n(S) = 6 \times 6 = 36$

It is very difficult to find out all the cares, in which we can find the total less then '12'.

So let E = The event, that the sum of numbers is '12'.

Then E = { 6, 6}

$$n(E) = 1$$

$$P(E) = n(E)/n(S) = 1/36$$

Required probability, $P(E^1) = 1\text{-}P(E) = 1 - 1/36$

$P(E^1) = 35/36$

Problem 32: There are '4' envelopes corresponding to '4' letters. If the letters are placed in the envelopes at random, what is the probability that all the letters are not placed in the right envelopes?

Solution: We have to place '4' letters in 4 envelopes.

$$n(S) = 4!$$

Now:

Let E = The event, that all the 4 letters are placed in the corresponding envelopes.

So E1 = The event that all the '4' letters are not placed in the right envelope.

Here $n(E) = 1$

$$P(E) = n(E)/n(S) = 1/4! = 1/24$$

Required probability, $P(E^1) = 1 - P(E) = 1 - (1/24)$

$$P(E^1) = 23/24$$

19.9 ADDITION THEOREM OF PROBABILITY

If 'A' and 'B' by any two events, then the probability of occurrence of at least one of the events 'A' and 'B' is given by:

$$P(A \text{ or } B) = P(A) + P(B) - P(A \text{ and } B)$$

$$P(A \cup B) = P(A) + P(B) - P(A \cup B)$$

From set theory, we have :

$$n(A \cup B) = n(A) + n(B) - n(A \cap B)$$

Dividing both sides by n(S) :

$$n(A \cup B)/n(S) = n(A)/n(S) + n(B)/n(S) - n(A \cap B)/n(S)$$

or $P(A \cup B) = p(A) + P(B) - P(A \cap B)$

Corollary: If 'A' and 'B' are mutually exclusive events,

Then $P(A \cap B) = 0.$ [As we have proved]

In this case:

$$P(A \cup B) = p(A) + P(B)$$

Addition theorem for '3' events 'A', 'B' and 'C' :

$$P(A \cup B \cup C) = P(A) + P(B) - P(A \cap B) - P(B \cap C) - P(A \cap C) + P(A \cap B \cap C)$$

Proof: $P(A \cup B \cup C) = P[(A \cup B) \cup C]$

$= P(A \cup B) + P(C) - P[(A \cup B) \cap C]$ [By addition theorem for two events]

$= P(A \cup B) - P(C) - [P(A \cap C) + P(B \cap C) - P(A \cap C \cap B \cap C)]$

$= P(A) + P(B) - P(A \cap B) + P(C) - P(A \cap C) - P(B \cap C) + P(A \cap B \cap C)$

$P(A \cup B \cup C) = P(A) + P(B) + P(C) - P(A \cap B) - P(B \cap C) - P(A \cap C) + P(A \cap B \cap C)$

Corollary : If 'A', 'B' and 'C' are mutually exclusive events, then $P(A \cap B) = 0$, $P(B \cap C) = 0$, $P(A \cap C) = 0$ and $P(A \cap B \cap C) = 0$.

In this case:

$$P(A \cup B \cup C) = P(A) + P(B) + P(C)$$

19.10 CONDITIONAL PROBABILITY

Conditional probability is the probability of sombe event A, given the occurrence of some other event B. Conditional probability is written P(A|B), and is read "the probability of A, given B".

Conditional probability provides us with a way to reason about the outcome of an experiment, based on **partial information**. Here are some examples of situations we have in mind:

(a) In an experiment involving two successive rolls of a die, you are told that the sum of the two rolls is 9. How likely is it that the first roll was a 6?

(b) In a word guessing game, the first letter of the word is a "t". What is the likelihood that the second letter is an "h"?

(c) How likely is it that a person has a disease given that a medical test was negative?

(d) A spot shows up on a radar screen. How likely is it that it corresponds to an aircraft?

In more precise terms, given an experiment, a corresponding sample space, and a probability law, suppose that we know that the outcome is within some given event B. We wish to quantify the likelihood that the outcome also belongs to some other given event A. We thus seek to construct a new probability law, which takes into account the available knowledge and which, for any event A, gives us the **conditional probability of** A **given** B, denoted by **P**(A|B). We would like the conditional probabilities **P**(A|B) of different events A to constitute a legitimate probability law, that satisfies the probability axioms. The conditional probabilities should also be consistent with our intuition in important special cases, e.g., when all possible outcomes of the experiment are equally likely. For example, suppose that all six possible outcomes of a fair die roll are equally likely. If we are told that the outcome is even, we are left with only three possible outcomes, namely, 2, 4, and 6. These three outcomes were equally likely to start with, and so they should remain equally likely given the additional knowledge that the outcome was even. Thus, it is reasonable to let **P**(the outcome is 6 | the outcome is even) = 1/3.

This argument suggests that an appropriate definition of conditional probability when all outcomes are equally likely, is given by

$$\mathbf{P}(A|B) = \frac{\text{number of elements of A} \quad \text{B}}{\text{number of elements of B}}$$

Generalizing the argument, we introduce the following definition of conditional probability:

$$\mathbf{P}(A|B) = \frac{P(A \quad B)}{P(B)}$$

where we assume that **P**(B) > 0; the conditional probability is undefined if the conditioning event has zero probability. In words, out of the total probability of the elements of B, **P**(A|B) is the fraction that is assigned to possible outcomes that also belong to A.

Problem 33: We toss a fair coin three suoccessive times. We wish to find the conditional probability P(A|B) when A and B are the events

A = {more heads than tails come up}, B = {1st toss is a head}.

Solution: The sample space consists of eight sequences,

Ù = {HHH, HHT, HTH, HTT, THH, THT, TTH, TTT},

which we assume to be equally likely. The event B consists of the four elements HHH, HHT, HTH, HTT, so its probability is

$$P(B) = 4/8$$

The event $A \cap B$ consists of the three elements HHH, HHT, HTH, so its probability is

$$P(A \cap B) = 3/8$$

Thus, the conditional probability **P**(A|B) is

$$\mathbf{P}(A|B) = \frac{P(A \quad B)}{P(B)} \quad \frac{3/8}{3/4} \quad \frac{3}{4}.$$

Because all possible outcomes are equally likely here, we can also compute **P**(A|B) using a shortcut. We can bypass the calculation of **P**(B) and **P**(A∩B), and simply divide the number of elements shared by A and B (which is 3) with the number of elements of B (which is 4), to obtain the same result 3/4.

Problem 34: Let's try working through an example. "Given that you have been dealt an Ace as your first card, what is the probability of being dealt a blackjack?"

Solution: By using conditional probability formula, we get:

P[Blackjack|Ace has been dealt] = P[Blackjack and Ace has been dealt]/P[Ace has been dealt]

For independent events, P[A and B] = P[A] * P[B]. The probability of receiving a blackjack is (4/52)*(16/51) + (16/52)(4/51). But because we are specifying that the Ace must come first for our Blackjack, we must not include any blackjacks where the 10-valued card comes first. Therefore, the blackjack is made up of an Ace first and only then a 10-value card, so we can say that P[Blackjack and Ace has been dealt first] = (4/52 * 16/51). Therefore, P[Blackjack|Ace has been dealt first] = P[Blackjack and Ace has been dealt first]/P[Ace has been dealt first] = (4/52 * 16/51)/(4/52) = 16/51.

Problem 35: A math teacher gave her class two tests. 25% of the class passed both tests and 42% of the class passed the first test. What percent of those who passed the first test also passed the second test?

Solution:

$$P(\text{Second}|\text{First}) = \frac{P(\text{First and Second})}{P(\text{First})}$$

$$= 0.25/0.42 = 0.60 = 60\%$$

Problem 36: A jar contains black and white marbles. Two marbles are chosen without replacement. The probability of selecting a black marble and then a white marble is 0.34, and the probability of selecting a black marble on the first draw is 0.47. What is the probability of selecting a white marble on the second draw, given that the first marble drawn was black?

Solution:

$$P(\text{White}|\text{Black}) = \frac{P(\text{Black and White})}{P(\text{Black})}$$

$$= 0.34/0.47 = 0.72 = 72\%$$

Problem 37: The probability that it is Friday and that a student is absent is 0.03. Since there are 5 school days in a week, the probability that it is Friday is 0.2. What is the probability that a student is absent given that today is Friday?

Solution:

$$P(\text{Absent}|\text{Friday}) = \frac{P(\text{Friday and Absent})}{P(\text{Friday})}$$

$$= 0.03/0.2 = 0.15 = 15\%$$

Problem 38: At Kennedy Middle School, the probability that a student takes Technology and Spanish is 0.087. The probability that a student takes Technology is 0.68. What is the probability that a student takes Spanish given that the student is taking Technology?

Solution:

$$P(\text{Spanish}|\text{Technology}) = \frac{P(\text{Technology and Spanish})}{P(\text{Technology})}$$

$$= 0.087/0.68 = 0.13 = 13\%$$

19.11 INVERSE PROBABILITY

One of the important applications of the conditional probability is in the computation of unknown probabilities, on the basis of the information supplied by the experiment or past records. For example, suppose an event has occurred through one of the various mutually disjoint events. Then the conditional probability that it has occurred due to particular event is called inverse probability

.these can be computed by Baye's Rule, named so after the British mathematician Thomas Bayes who founded it in 1763.

Baye's Theorem

If an event A can occur in conjunction with one of the n mutually exclusive and exhaustive events $E_1, E_2 .... E_n$ and if A actually happens, then the probability that it was preceded by the particular event $E_i(i = 1, 2, ... n)$ is given by:

$$P(E_i|A = P(A \cap E_i)/\sum_{i=1}^{n} P(E_i)\cdot P(A|E_i) = P(E_i)\cdot P(A|E_i)/\sum_{i=1}^{n} P(E_i)\cdot P(A|E_i)$$

Proof: Since the event A can occur in combination with any of mutually exclusive and exhaustive events $E_1, E_2, ...E_n$, we have

$$A = (A \cap E_1) \cup (A \cap E_2) \cup ...... \cup (A \cap E_n)$$

where $A \cap E_1, A \cap E_2,.... A \cap E_n$, being the subsets of mutually exclusive events $E_1, E_2,... E_n$ are all disjoint events. Hence,by the addition theorem of probability, we have

$$\begin{aligned} P(A) &= P(A \cap E_1) + P(A \cap E_2) + ... + P(A \cap E_2) \\ &= P(E_1) \cdot P(A|E_1) + P(E_2) \cdot P(A|E_2) + ... + P(E_n).P(A|E_n) \\ &= \sum_{i=1}^{n} P(E_i)\cdot P(A|E_i) \end{aligned}$$

For any particular event E_i, the conditional probability, $P(E_i|A)$ is given by:

$$\begin{aligned} P(E_i \cap A) &= P(A)\, P(E_i|A) \\ P(E_i|A) &= P(E_i \cap A)/P(A) \\ &= P(E_i)\cdot P(A|E_i) \Big/ \sum_{i=1}^{n} P(E_i)\cdot P(A|E_i) \end{aligned}$$

which is the Baye's rule for obtaining the conditional probabilities.

Problem 39: You enter a chess tournament where your probability of winning a game is 0.3 against half the players (call them type 1), 0.4 against a quarter of the players (call them type 2), and 0.5 against the remaining quarter of the players (call them type 3). You play a game against a randomly chosen opponent. What is the probability of winning?

Solution: Let Ai be the event of playing with an opponent of type i. We have

$$P(A1) = 0.5, P(A2) = 0.25, P(A3) = 0.25.$$

Let also B be the event of winning. We have

$$P(B|A1) = 0.3, P(B|A2) = 0.4, P(B|A3) = 0.5.$$

Thus, by the total probability theorem, the probability of winning is

$$P(B) = P(A1)P(B|A1) + P(A2)P(B|A2) + P(A3)P(B|A3)$$

$$= 0.5 \cdot 0.3 + 0.25 \cdot 0.4 + 0.25 \cdot 0.5$$

$$= 0.375.$$

Problem 40: A Gambler has two coins in his pocket, a fair coin and a two-headed coin. He picks one at random from his pocket, flips it and gets heads. (a) What is the probability that he flipped the fair coin? (b) If he flips the same coin a second time and again gets heads, what is the probability that he flipped the fair coin?

Solution: Let F be the event he picked the fair coin and B the event he picked the biased coin. There are two coins in his pocket so the probability of picking the either coin is 0.50. Let H_1 be the event "the first flip is heads" and H_2 be the event "the second flip is heads".

For (a)

$$P(F|H_1) = P(H_1|F) * \frac{P(F)}{P(H_1)} \quad \frac{P(H_1|F)\,P(F)}{P(H_1|F)\,P(F) \quad P(H_1|B)\,P(B)}$$

where

$$P(H_1|F) = 1/2$$

and

$$P(H_1|B) = 1$$

$$P(F|H_1) = \frac{1/2 * 1/2}{1/2 * 1/2 \quad * 1/2} \quad \frac{1}{3}$$

For (b)

This question is solved in the same way as (a)

$$P(F|H_1 \text{ Ç } H_2) = \frac{P(H_1 \quad H_2|F)\,P(F)}{P((H_1 \quad H_2|F)\,P(F) \quad P((H_1 \quad H_2|B)\,P(B)}$$

$$= \frac{1/8}{1/8 \quad 1/2} \quad \frac{1}{5}$$

Problem 41: In a class of 75 students, 15 were considered to be very intelligent 45 as medium and the rest below average. The probability that a very intelligent student fails in a viva-voce examination is 0.005; the medium student failing has a probability 0.05; and the corresponding probability for a below average student is 0.15. If a student is known to have passed the viva-voce examination, what is the probability that he is below average?

Solution: Let us define the following events:

E_1: The student of the class is very intelligent

E_2: The student is medium

E_3: The student is below average

E : The student passed in the viva-voce examination

Then we are given:

$$P(E_1) = \frac{15}{75} \quad 0.2; \quad P(E_2) = \frac{45}{72} \quad 0.6; \quad P(E_2) = \frac{15}{75} \quad 0.2$$

$P(A \mid E_1) = 1 - 0.005 = 0.995$; $P(A \} E_2) = 1 - 0.05 = 0.95$; $P(A \mid E_3) = 1\text{-}0.15\text{=}0.85$

We want $P(E_3 \mid A)$.

If a student is known to have passed the viva-examination, the probability that he is below average, is given by Bayes' rule as follows:

$$P(E_3 \mid A) = \frac{P(E_3)P(A \mid E_3)}{P(E_1)P(A \mid E_1) \quad P(E_2)P(A \mid E_2) \quad P(E_3)P(A \mid E_3)}$$

$$= \frac{0.2 \quad 0.850}{0.2 \quad 0.995 \quad 0.6 \quad 0.950 \quad 0.2 \quad 0.850}$$

$$= \frac{0.170}{0.199 \quad 0.570 \quad 0.170} \quad \frac{0.170}{0.939} \quad 0.181$$

Problem 42: In a railway reservation office, two clerks are engaged in checking reservation forms. On an average, the first clerk checks 55% of the forms, while the second does the remaining. The first clerk has an error rate of .03 and second has an error rate of .02 A reservation form is selected at random from the total number of forms checked during a day, and is found to have an error. Find the probability that is was checked (i) by the first, (ii) by the second clerk.

Solution: Let us define the following events:

E_1: The selected form is checked by clerk 1.

E_2: The selected form is checked by clerk 2.

E_3: The selected form has an error.

Then we are given:

$P(E_1) = 55\% = 0.55$; $P(E_2) = 45\% = 0.45$; $P(E \mid E_1) = 0.03$; $P(E \mid E_2) = 0.02$ ..(*)

We want $P(E_1 \mid E)$ and $P(E_2 \mid E)$. By Bayes' Rule, the probability that the form containing the error was checked by clerk 1, is given by:

$$P(E_1 \mid E) = \frac{P(E_1)P(E \mid E_1)}{P(E_1) \quad P(E \mid E_1) \quad P(E_2)P(E \mid E_2)}$$

$$= \frac{0.55 \quad 0.03}{0.55 \quad 0.03 \quad 0.45 \quad 0.02}$$

$$= \frac{0.0165}{0.0165 \quad 0.090} \quad \frac{0.0165}{0.0255} 0.647$$

Similarly, the probability that the form containing the error was checked by clerk 2, is given by

$$P(E_2 \mid E) = \frac{P(E_2)P(E \mid E_2)}{P(E_1) \; P(E \mid E_1) \quad P(E_2)P(E \mid E_2)}$$

$$= \frac{0.45 \quad 0.02}{0.55 \quad 0.03 \quad 0.45 \quad 0.02} \quad \frac{0.0090}{0.0255} \quad 0.353$$

or $\qquad P(E_2 \mid E) = 1 - P(E_1 \mid E) = 1 - 0.647 = 0.353$

Problem 43: An urn contains four balls. Two balls are drawn at random and are found to be white. What is the probability that all the balls are white?

Solution: Since two balls are drawn and they are found to be find, the urn must contain at least two white balls. Let us defined the following events?

E: (i = 2, 3, 4): The event that the urn contains i white balls.

E: The event that two white balls are drawn.

Since the events E_2, E_3 and E_4 are equally likely, we have:

$$P(E_2) = P\,(E_3) = P(E_4) = \frac{1}{3} \qquad \text{(i)}$$

$P(E \mid E_2)$ = Probability of drawing two white balls, given that the urn contains 2 white balls.

$$= \frac{{}^2C_2}{{}^4C_2} \quad \frac{1}{6} \qquad \text{(ii)}$$

Similarly, we have:

$$P(E \mid E_3) = \frac{{}^3C_2}{{}^4C_2} \quad \frac{3}{6} \quad \frac{1}{2} \quad \text{and} \quad P(E \mid E_4) \frac{{}^4C_2}{{}^4C_2} \quad 1 \qquad \text{(iii)}$$

We want the conditional probability P (E_4/E).

By Bayes' rule, we get:

$$P(E_4 \mid E) = \frac{P(E_4)P(E \mid E_4)}{P(E_2) \; P(E \mid E_2) \quad P(E_3)P(E \mid E_3) \quad P(E_4)P(E \mid E_4)}$$

$$= \frac{\frac{1}{3} \quad 1}{\frac{1}{3} \quad \frac{1}{6} \quad \frac{1}{3} \quad \frac{1}{2} \quad \frac{1}{3} \quad 1} \quad \frac{\frac{1}{3}}{\frac{1}{18} \quad \frac{1}{6} \quad \frac{1}{3}} \quad \frac{\frac{1}{3}}{\frac{10}{18}} \quad \frac{3}{5} \quad 0.6$$

(From (i), (ii) and (iii))

Problem 44: Marie is getting married tomorrow, at an outdoor ceremony in the desert. In recent years, it has rained only 5 days each year. Unfortunately, the weatherman has predicted rain for tomorrow. When it actually rains, the weatherman correctly forecasts rain 90% of the time. When it doesn't rain, he incorrectly forecasts rain 10% of the time. What is the probability that it will rain on the day of Marie's wedding?

Solution: The sample space is defined by two mutually-exclusive events - it rains or it does not rain. Additionally, a third event occurs when the weatherman predicts rain. Notation for these events appears below.

- Event A_1. It rains on Marie's wedding.
- Event A_2. It does not rain on Marie's wedding
- Event B. The weatherman predicts rain.

In terms of probabilities, we know the following:

- $P(A_1) = 5/365 = 0.0136985$ [It rains 5 days out of the year.]
- $P(A_2) = 360/365 = 0.9863014$ [It does not rain 360 days out of the year.]
- $P(B|A_1) = 0.9$ [When it rains, the weatherman predicts rain 90% of the time.]
- $P(B|A_2) = 0.1$ [When it does not rain, the weatherman predicts rain 10% of the time.]

We want to know $P(A_1 \mid B)$, the probability it will rain on the day of Marie's wedding, given a forecast for rain by the weatherman. The answer can be determined from Bayes' theorem, as shown below.

$$P(A_1 | B) = \frac{P(A_1)\, P(B \mid A_1)}{P(A_1)\, P(B \mid A_1) + P(A_2)\, P(B \mid A_2)}$$

$$P(A_1 | B) = (0.014)(0.9)/[(0.014)(0.9) + (0.986)(0.1)]$$

$$P(A_1 \mid B) = 0.111$$

Note the somewhat unintuitive result. Even when the weatherman predicts rain, it only rains only about 11% of the time. Despite the weatherman's gloomy prediction, there is a good chance that Marie will not get rained on at her wedding.

Problem 45: A die is rolled, find the probability that an even number is obtained.

Solution: Let us first write the sample space S of the experiment.

$$S = \{1, 2, 3, 4, 5, 6\}$$

Let E be the event "an even number is obtained" and write it down.

$$E = \{2, 4, 6\}$$

We now use the formula of the classical probability.

$$P(E) = n(E)/n(S) = 3/6 = 1/2$$

Problem 46: Two coins are tossed, find the probability that two heads are obtained.
Note: Each coin has two possible outcomes H (heads) and T (Tails).

Solution: The sample space S is given by.

$$S = \{(H, T), (H, H), (T, H), (T, T)\}$$

Let E be the event "two heads are obtained".

$$E = \{(H, H)\}$$

We use the formula of the classical probability.

$$P(E) = n(E)/n(S) = 1/4$$

Problem 47: Which of these numbers cannot be a probability?

(a) –0.00001 (b) 0.5

(c) 1.001 (d) 0

(e) 1 (f) 20%

Solution: A probability is always greater than or equal to 0 and less than or equal to 1, hence only **a)** and **c)** above cannot represent probabilities: –0.00010 is less than 0 and 1.001 is greater than 1.

Problem 48: Two dice are rolled, find the probability that the sum is

(a) equal to 1

(b) equal to 4

(c) less than 13

Solution:

(a) The sample space S of two dice is shown below.

$$\begin{aligned} S = \{&(1, 1), (1, 2), (1, 3), (1, 4), (1, 5), (1, 6)\\ &(2, 1), (2, 2), (2, 3), (2, 4), (2, 5), (2, 6)\\ &(3, 1), (3, 2), (3, 3), (3, 4), (3, 5), (3, 6)\\ &(4, 1), (4, 2), (4, 3), (4, 4), (4, 5), (4, 6)\\ &(5, 1), (5, 2), (5, 3), (5, 4), (5, 5), (5, 6)\\ &(6, 1), (6, 2), (6, 3), (6, 4), (6, 5), (6, 6)\} \end{aligned}$$

Let E be the event "sum equal to 1". There are no outcomes which correspond to a sum equal to 1, hence

$$P(E) = n(E)/n(S) = 0/36 = 0$$

(b) Three possible ouctcomes give a sum equal to 4: $E = \{(1,3),(2,2),(3,1)\}$, hence.

$$P(E) = n(E)/n(S) = 3/36 = 1/12$$

(c) All possible ouctcomes, E = S, give a sum less than 13, hence.

$$P(E) = n(E)/n(S) = 36/36 = 1$$

Problem 49: A die is rolled and a coin is tossed, find the probability that the die shows an odd number and the coin shows a head.

Solution: The sample space S of the experiment described in question 5 is as follows

S = {(1, H), (2, H), (3, H),(4, H), (5, H), (6, H)
(1, T), (2, T), (3, T), (4, T), (5, T), (6, T)}

Let E be the event "the die shows an odd number and the coin shows a head". Event E may be described as follows

E = {(1,H),(3,H),(5,H)}

The probability P(E) is given by

P(E) = n(E)/n(S) = 3/12 = 1/4

Problem 50: A card is drawn at random from a deck of cards. Find the probability of getting the 3 of diamond.

Solution: The sample space S of the experiment in question 6 is shown below

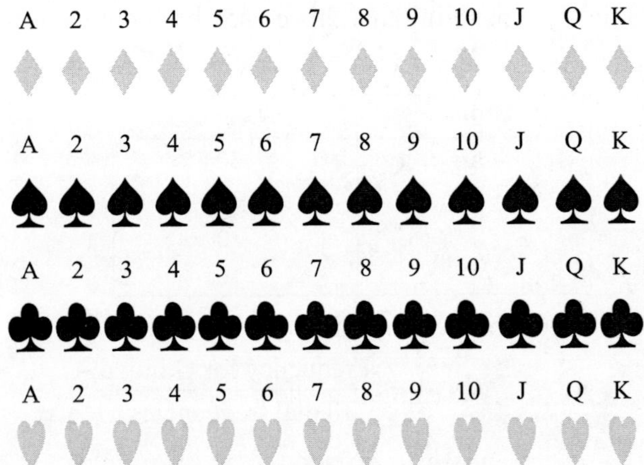

Let E be the event "getting the 3 of diamond". An examination of the sample space shows that there is one "3 of diamond" so that n(E) = 1 and n(S) = 52. Hence the probability of event E occuring is given by

P(E) = 1/52

Problem 51: A card is drawn at random from a deck of cards. Find the probability of getting a queen.

Solution: The sample space S of the experiment in question 7 is shwon above (see question 6)

Let E be the event "getting a Queen". An examination of the sample space shows that there are 4 "Queens" so that n(E) = 4 and n(S) = 52. Hence the probability of event E occuring is given by P(E) = 4/52 = 1/13

Problem 52: A jar contains 3 red marbles, 7 green marbles and 10 white marbles. If a marble is drawn from the jar at random, what is the probability that this marble is white?

Solution: We first construct a table of frequencies that gives the marbles color distributions as follows

Color	Frequency
red	3
green	7
white	10

We now use the empirical formula of the probability

$$P(E) = \frac{\text{Frequency for white color}}{\text{Total frequencies in the above table}}$$

$$= 10/20 = 1/2$$

Problem 53: The blood groups of 200 people is distributed as follows: 50 have type A blood, 65 have B blood type, 70 have O blood type and 15 have type AB blood. If a person from this group is selected at random, what is the probability that this person has O blood type?

Solution: We construct a table of frequencies for the the blood groups as follows

Group	Frequency
a	50
B	65
O	70
AB	15

We use the empirical formula of the probability

$$P(E) = \frac{\text{Frequency for O blood}}{\text{Total frequencies}}$$

$$= 70/200 = 0.35$$

More Problems on Probability

Problem 1: How many 3 digit numbers can you make using the digits 1, 2 and 3 without repetitions?

Solution: method (1) listing all possible numbers using a tree diagram.

First digit	Second digit	Third digit
1	2	3
	3	2
2	1	3
	3	1
3	1	2
	2	1

We can make 6 numbers using 3 digits and without repetitions of the digits.

method (2) counting:

Look at the Tree Diagram Above.

We have 3 choices for the first digit, 2 choices for the second digit and 1 choice for the third digit.

Using the counting principle, we can say:

The total number of 3-digit numbers is given by

$$3 * 2 * 1 = 6$$

There is a special notation for the product 3 * 2 * 1 = 3! and it is read 3 factorial.

In general n! is read n factorial and is given by

$$n! = n*(n-1)*(n-2)* \ldots *2 *1$$

We also define 0! = 1.

Problem 2: How many different words can we make using the letters A, B, E and L ?

Solution: We have 4 choices for the first letter, 3 choices for the second letter, 2 choices for the third letter and 1 choice for the fourth letter. Hence the number of words is given by

$$4 * 3 * 2 * 1 = 4! = 24$$

Permutations

Problem 3: How many 2 digit numbers can you make using the digits 1, 2, 3 and 4 without repeating the digits?

Solution: This time we want to use 2 digits at the time to make 2 digit numbers. For the first digit we have 4 choices and for the second digit we have 3 choices (4 – 1 used already). Using the counting principle, the number of 2 digit numbers that we can make using 4 digits is given by

$$4 * 3 = 12$$

The above problem is that of arranging 2 digits out of 4 in a specific order. This is also called permutating.

The most important idea in permutations is that order is important. When you use the digits 3 and 4 to make a number, the number 34 and 43 are different hence the order of the digits 3 and 4 is important.

In general permutating r (2 digit in the above example) items out of a set of n (4 digits in the above example) items is written as ${}_nP_r$ and the formula is given by

$${}_nP_r = n!/(n-r)!$$

Problem 4: Calculate

${}_4P_2$

${}_6P_5$

${}_4P_4$

Solution:

$$_4P_2 = 4!/(4-2)! = 24/2 = 12$$

$$_6P_5 = 6!/(6-5)! = 6*5*4*3*2*1/1! = 720$$

$$_4P_4 = 4!/(4-4)! = 4!/0! = 4! = 4*3*2*1 = 24$$

(We now understand the need to define 0! = 1)

Problem 5: How many 3 letter words can we make with the letters in the word LOVE?

Solution: There are 4 letters in the word love and making making 3 letter words is similar to arranging these 3 letters and order is important since LOV and VOL are different words because of the order of the same letters L, O and V. Hence it is a permutation problem. The number of words is given by

$$_4P_3 = 4!/(4-3)! = 24$$

Combinations

Problem 6: How many lines can you draw using 3 non collinear (not in a single line) points A, B and C on a plane?

Solution: You need two points to draw a line. The order is not important. Line AB is the same as line BA. The problem is to select 2 points out of 3 to draw different lines. If we proceed as we did with permutations, we get the following pairs of points to draw lines.

AB , AC

BA , BC

CA , CB

There is a problem: line AB is the same as line BA, same for lines AC and CA and BC and CB.

The lines are: AB, BC and AC ; 3 lines only.

So in fact we can draw 3 lines and not 6 and that's because in this problem the order of the points A, B and C is not important.

This is a combination problem: combining 2 items out of 3 and is written as follows:

$$_nC_r = n!/[\,(n-r)!\ r!\,]$$

The number of combinations is equal to the number of permutations divided by r! to eliminate those counted more than once because the order is not important.

Problem 7: Calculate

$_3C_2$

$_5C_5$

Solution:

$$_3C_2 = 3!/[\,(3-2)!2!\,] = 6/[1 * 2] = 3$$

(problem of points and lines solved above in example 6)

$$_5C_5 = 5!/[(5-5)!5!\,] = 5!/[0!5!] = 5!/[1 * 5!] = 1$$

(there is only one way to select (without order) 5 items from 5 items and to select all of them once!)

Problem 8: We need to form a 5 a side team in a class of 12 students. How many different teams can be formed?

Solution: There is nothing that indicates that the order in which the team members are selected is important and therefore it is a combination problem. Hence the number of teams is given by

$$_{12}C_5 = 12!/[\ (12 - 5)!5!\ ] = 792$$

Sample Space and Events

The **sample space** is the set of all possible outcomes in an experiment.

Problem 9: If a die is rolled, the sample space S is given by

Solution: $S = \{1, 2, 3, 4, 5, 6\}$

Problem 10: If two coins are tossed, the sample space S is given by

Solution: S = {HH, HT, TH, TT} , where H = head and T = tail.

Problem 11: If two dice are rolled, the sample space S is given by

Solution:

$$\begin{aligned} S = \{&(1, 1), (1, 2), (1, 3), (1, 4), (1, 5), (1, 6) \\ &(2, 1), (2, 2), (2, 3), (2, 4), (2, 5), (2, 6) \\ &(3, 1), (3, 2), (3, 3), (3, 4), (3, 5), (3, 6) \\ &(4, 1), (4, 2), (4, 3), (4, 4), (4, 5), (4, 6) \\ &(5, 1), (5, 2), (5, 3), (5, 4), (5, 5), (5, 6) \\ &(6, 1), (6, 2), (6, 3), (6, 4), (6, 5), (6, 6)\} \end{aligned}$$

We define an **event** as some specific outcome of an experiment. An event is a subset of the sample space.

Problem 12: A die is rolled (see example 1 above for the sample space). Let us define event E as the set of possible outcomes where the number on the face of the die is even. Event E is given by

Solution: $E = \{2,4,6\}$

Problem 13: Two coins are tossed (see example 2 above for the sample space). Let us define event E as the set of possible outcomes where the number of head obtained is equal to two. Event E is given by

Solution: E = {(HT), (TH)}

Problem 14: Two dice are rolled (see example 3 above for the sample space). Let us define event E as the set of possible outcomes where the sum of the numbers on the faces of the two dice is equal to four. Event E is given by

Solution: $E = \{(1, 3), (2, 2), (3, 1)\}$

How to Calculate Probabilities?

1. Classical Probability Formula: It is based on the fact that all outcomes are equally likely.

$$P(E) = \frac{\text{Total number of outcomes in E}}{\text{Total number of outcomes in the sample space}}$$

Problem 15: A die is rolled, find the probability of getting a 3.

Solution: The event of interest is "getting a 3". so E = {3}.

The sample space S is given by S = {1, 2, 3, 4, 5, 6}.

The number of possible outcomes in E is 1 and the number of possible outcomes in S is 6. Hence the probability of getting a 3 is P("3") = 1/6.

Problem 16: A die is rolled, find the probability of getting an even number.

Solution: The event of interest is "getting an even number". so E = {2,4,6}, the even numbers on a die.

The sample space S is given by S = {1, 2, 3, 4, 5, 6}.

The number of possible outcomes in E is 3 and the number of possible outcomes in S is 6. Hence the probability of getting a 3 is P("3") = 3/6 = 1/2.

Empirical Probability Formula: It uses real data on present situations to determine how likely outcomes will occur in the future. Let us clarify this using an example 30 people were asked about the colors they like and here are the results:

Color	Frequency
red	10
blue	15
green	5

If a person is selected at random from the above group of 30, what is the probability that this person likes the red color?

Let event E be "likes the red color". Hence

$$P(E) = \frac{\text{Frequency for red color}}{\text{Total frequencies in the above table}} = 10/30 = 1/3$$

Problem 17: The table below shows students distribution per grade in a school.

Grade	Frequency
1	50
2	30
3	40
4	42
5	38
6	50

If a student is selected at random from this school, what is the probability that this student is in grade 3?

Solution: Let event E be "student from grade 3". Hence

$$P(E) = \frac{\text{Frequency for grade 3}}{\text{Total frequencies}} = 40/250 = 0.16$$

mutually exclusive may be represented as follows:

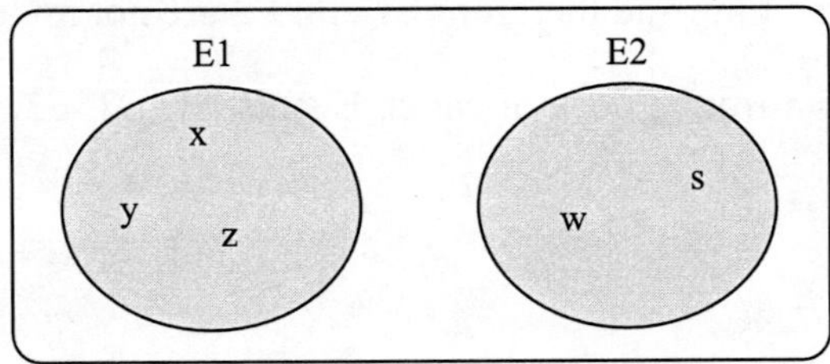

The two events are such that

$$\mathbf{E1 \cap E2 = \Phi}$$

The two sets E1 and E2 have no elements in common and their intersection is an empty set since they cannot occur at the same time.

Using Venn diagram, two events that **are not mutually exclusive** may be represented as follows:

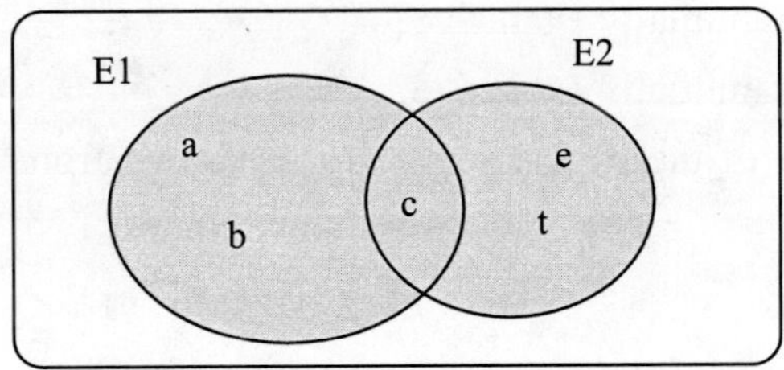

E1 ∩ E2 = {c} , the intersection of the two events E1 and E2 is not an empty set

Problem 18: A die is rolled. Let us define event E1 as the set of possible outcomes where the number on the face of the die is even and event E2 as the set of possible outcomes where the number on the face of the die is odd. Are event1 E1 and E2 mutually exclusive?

Solution: We first list the elements of E1 and E2.

$$E1 = \{2, 4, 6\}$$
$$E2 = \{1, 3, 5\}$$

E1 and E2 have no elements in common and therefore are mutually exclusive.

Another way to answer the above question is to note is that if you roll a die, it shows a number that is either even or odd but no number will be even and odd at the same time. Hence E1 and E2 cannot occur at the same time and are therefore mutually exclusive.

Problem 19: A die is rolled. Event E1 is the set of possible outcomes where the number on the face of the die is even and event E2 as the set of possible outcomes where the number on the face of the die is greater than 3. Are event E1 and E2 mutually exclusive?

Solution: The subsets E1 and E2 are given by.

$$E1 = \{2, 4, 6\}$$

$$E2 = \{4, 5, 6\}$$

Subsets E1 and E2 have 2 elements in common. If the die shows 4 or 6, both events E1 and E2 will have occured at the same time and therefore E1 and E2 are not mutually exclusive.

Problem 20: A card is drawn from a deck of cards. Events E1, E2, E3, E4 and E5 are defined as follows:

E1: Getting an 8

E2: Getting a king

E3: Getting a face card

E4: Getting an ace

E5: Getting a heart

(a) Are events E1 and E2 mutually exclusive?

(b) Are events E2 and E3 mutually exclusive?

(c) Are events E3 and E4 mutually exclusive?

(d) Are events E4 and E5 mutually exclusive?

(e) Are events E5 and E1 mutually exclusive?

Solution: The sample space of the experiment "card is drawn from a deck of cards" is shown below.

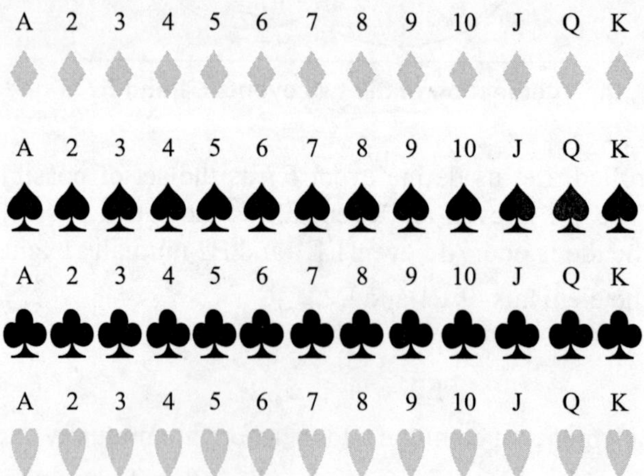

(a) E1 and E2 are **mutually exclusive** because there are no cards with an 8 and a king together.

(b) E2 and E3 are **not mutually exclusive** because a king is a face card.

(c) E3 and E4 are **mutually exclusive** because an ace is not a face card.

(d) E4 and E5 are **not mutually exclusive** because there is one card that has an ace and a heart.

(e) E5 and E1 are **not mutually exclusive** because there is one card that is an 8 of heart.

Problem 21: Two dice are rolled. We define events E1, E2, E3 and E4 as follows

E1: Getting a sum equal to 10

E2: Getting a double

E3: Getting a sum less than 4

E4: Getting a sum less to 7

(a) Are events E1 and E2 mutually exclusive?

(b) Are events E2 and E3 mutually exclusive?

(c) Are events E3 and E4 mutually exclusive?

(d) Are events E4 and E1 mutually exclusive?

Solution: The sample space of the experiment "2 dice" is shown below.

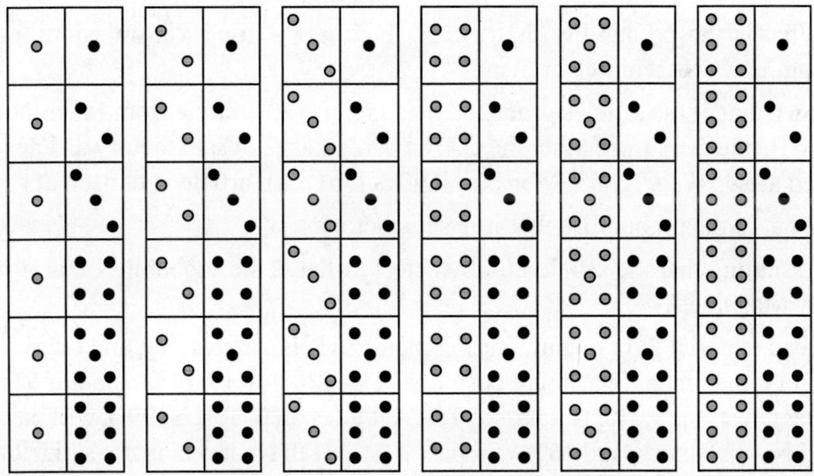

(a) E1 and E2 are **not mutually exclusive** because outcome (5, 5) is a double and also gives a sum of 10. The two events may occur at the same time.

(b) E2 and E3 are **not mutually exclusive** because outcome (1, 1) is a double and gives a sum of 2 and is less than 4. The two events E2 and E3 may occur at the same time.

(c) E3 and E4 are **not mutually exclusive** a sum can be less than 7 and less than 4 the same time. Example outcome (1, 2).

(d) E4 and E1 are **mutually exclusive** because a sum less than 7 cannot be equal to 10 at the same time. The two events cannot occur at the same time.

EXERCISES

1. A flood forecaster issues a flood warning under two conditions only: (i) if fall rainfall exceeds 10 cm and winter snowfall is between 15 and 20 cm, or (ii) if winter snowfall exceeds 20 cm regardless of fall rainfall. The probability of fall rainfall exceeding 10 cm is 0.10, while the probabilities of winter snowfall exceeding 15 and 20 cm are 0.15 and 0.05 respectively.
   (a) What is the probability that he will issue a warning any given spring?
   (b) Given that he issues a warning, what is the probability that fall rainfall was greater than 10 cm?
2. A certain company has two car assembly plants, A and B. Plant A produces twiceas many cars as plant B. Plant A uses engines and transmissions from a subsidiary plant which produces 10% defective engines and 2% defective transmissions. Plant B uses engines and transmissions from another source where 8% of the engines and 4% of the transmissions are defective. Car transmissions and engines at each plant are installed independently.
   (a) What is the probability that a car chosen at random will have a good engine?
   (b) What is the probability that a car from plant A has a defective engine, or a defective transmission, or both?
   (c) What is the probability that a car which has a good transmission and a defective engine was assembled at plant B?
3. It is known that of the articles produced by a factory, 20% come from Machine A, 30% from Machine B, and 50% from Machine C. The percentages of satisfactory articles among those produced are 95% for A, 85% for B and 90% for C. An article is chosen at random.
   (a) What is the probability that it is satisfactory?
   (b) Assuming that the article is satisfactory, what is the probability that it was produced by Machine A?
4. Of the feed material for a manufacturing plant, 85% is satisfactory, and the rest is not. If it is satisfactory, the probability it will pass Test A is 92%. If it is not satisfactory, the probability it will pass Test A is 9.5%. If it passes Test A it goes on to Test B; 99% will pass Test B if the material is satisfactory, and 16% will pass Test B if the material is not satisfactory. If it fails Test A it goes on to Test C; 82% will pass Test C if the material is satisfactory, but only 3% will pass Test C if the material is not satisfactory. Material is accepted if it passes both Test A and Test B. Material is rejected if it fails both Test A and Test C. Material is reprocessed if it fails Test B or passes Test C.
   (a) What percentage of the feed material is accepted?
   (b) What percentage of the feed material is reprocessed?
   (c) What percentage of the material which is reprocessed was satisfactory?
5. In a small isolated town in Northern Saskatchewan, 90% of the Cola consumed by the townspeople is purchased from the General Store, while the rest is purchased from other

vendors. Records show 60% of all the bottles sold are returned. According to a special study, a bottle purchased at the General Store is four times as likely to be returned as a bottle purchased elsewhere.

(a) Calculate the probability that a person buying a bottle of Cola from the General Store will return the empty bottle.

(b) If a Cola bottle is found lying in the street, what is the probability that it was not purchased at the General Store?

6. Three road construction firms, X, Y and Z, bid for a certain contract. From past experience, it is estimated that the probability that X will be awarded the contract is 0.40, while for Y and Z the probabilities are 0.35 and 0.25. If X does receive the contract, the probability that the work will be satisfactorily completed on time is 0.75. For Y and Z these probabilities are 0.80 and 0.70.

   (a) What is the probability that Y will be awarded the contract and complete the work satisfactorily?

   (b) What is the probability that the work will be completed satisfactorily?

   (c) It turns out that the work was done satisfactorily. What is the probability that Y was awarded the contract?

7. Two service stations compete with one another. The odds are 3 to 1 that a motorist will go to station A rather than station B. Given that a motorist goes to station B, the probability that he will be asked whether he wants his oil checked is 0.76. A survey indicates that of the motorists who are asked whether they want the oil checked, 79% went to station A. Given that a motorist goes to station A, what is the probability that he will be asked whether he wants his oil checked?

8. A class consists of 60% men and 40% women. Of the men, 25% are blond, while 45% of the women are blond. If a student is chosen at random and is found to be blond, what is the probability that student is a man?

9. It is known in a certain country that 20% of mothers use spanking as a method of disciplining their children. 85% of the mothers that spank their children use valium, while 25% of mothers that don't use spanking use valium. Does this data suggest that valium causes mothers to spank their children? Explain.

10. A jar contains black and white marbles. Two marbles are chosen without replacement. The probability of selecting a black marble and then a white marble is 0.34, and the probability of selecting a black marble on the first draw is 0.47. What is the probability of selecting a white marble on the second draw, given that the first marble drawn was black?

11. At Kennedy Middle School, the probability that a student takes Technology and Spanish is 0.087. The probability that a student takes Technology is 0.68. What is the probability that a student takes Spanish given that the student is taking Technology?

CHAPTER 20

Random Variable and Mathematical Expectation

20.1 INTRODUCTION

Corresponding to every outcome of a random experiment, we can associate a real number. This correspondence between the elements of the sample space associated to a random experiment and the set of real numbers is defined as a random variable. If a random variable assumes countable number of values, it is called discrete random variable. Otherwise, it is known as continuous random variable. We shall study these two types of random variables in the following sections.

20.2 RANDOM VARIABLE

In mathematics a **random variable** (or **stochastic variable**) is a variable whose value is a function of the outcome of a statistical experiment. Random variables are used in the study of probability. They were developed to assist in the analysis of games of chance, stochastic events, and the results of scientific experiments by capturing only the mathematical properties necessary to answer probabilistic questions. Further formalizations have firmly grounded the entity in the theoretical domains of mathematics by making use of measure theory.

The language and structure of random variables can be grasped at various levels of mathematical fluency. Beyond an introductory level, set theory and calculus are fundamental. The concept of a random variable is closely linked to the term "random variate": a random variate is a particular outcome of a random variable.

There are two types of random variables: discrete and continuous. A discrete random variable maps events to values of a countable set (e.g., the integers), with each value in the range having probability greater than or equal to zero. A continuous random variable maps events to values of an uncountable set (e.g., the real numbers). In a continuous random variable, the probability of any specific value is zero, although the probability of an infinite set of values (such as an interval of non-zero length) may be positive. However, a random variable can be "mixed", having part of its probability spread out over an interval like a typical continuous variable, and part of it concentrated on particular values, like a discrete variable. This categorization into types is directly equivalent to the categorization of probability distributions.

A random variable has an associated probability distribution and frequently also a probability density function. Probability density functions are commonly used for continuous variables.

20.3 INTUITIVE DESCRIPTION

Very commonly a random variable takes values which are numbers. This is by no means always so: for example there are random variables which as values have vectors, complex numbers, sequences, or functions. If the variables are real-valued then a random variable can be thought of as an unknown number that may change every time it is inspected. Thus, a random variable can be thought of as a function mapping the sample space of a random process to a set of numbers. A few examples will highlight this.

Examples

For a coin toss, the possible events are heads or tails. The number of heads appearing in one fair coin toss can be described using the following random variable:

$$X = \begin{cases} \text{head,} \\ \text{tail.} \end{cases}$$

and if the coin is equally likely to land on either side then it has a probability mass function given by:

$$\rho x(x) = \begin{cases} \frac{1}{2}, \text{if } x \quad \text{head,} \\ \frac{1}{2}, \text{if } x \quad \text{tail.} \end{cases}$$

It is sometimes convenient to model this situation using a random variable which takes numbers as its values, rather than the values *head* and *tail*. This can be done by using the real random variable *Y* defined as follows:

$$Y = \begin{cases} 1, \text{ if heads,} \\ 0, \text{ if } \quad \text{tails.} \end{cases}$$

and if the coin is equally likely to land on either side then it has a probability mass function given by:

$$\rho Y(y) = \begin{cases} \frac{1}{2}, \text{ if } y \quad 0, \\ \frac{1}{2}, \text{ if } y \quad 1. \\ 0, \text{ otherwise} \end{cases}$$

A random variable can also be used to describe the process of rolling a fair die and the possible outcomes. The most obvious representation is to take the set {1, 2, 3, 4, 5, 6} as the sample space, defining the random variable X as the number rolled. In this case,

$$X = \begin{cases} 1, & \text{if a 1 is rolled,} \\ 2, & \text{if a 2 is rolled,} \\ 3, & \text{if a 3 is rolled,} \\ 4, & \text{if a 4 is rolled,} \\ 5, & \text{if a 5 is rolled,} \\ 6, & \text{if a 6 is rolled.} \end{cases}$$

$$\rho X(x) = \begin{cases} \frac{1}{6}, & \text{if } 1, 2, 3, 4, 5, 6, \\ 0, & \text{otherwise} \end{cases}$$

An example of a continuous random variable would be one based on a spinner that can choose a horizontal direction. Then the values taken by the random variable are directions. We could represent these directions by North West, East South East, etc. However, it is commonly more convenient to map the sample space to a random variable which takes values which are real numbers. This can be done, for example, by mapping a direction to a bearing in degrees clockwise from North. The random variable then takes values which are real numbers from the interval [0, 360), with all parts of the range being "equally likely". In this case, X = the angle spun. Any real number has probability zero of being selected, but a positive probability can be assigned to any range of values. For example, the probability of choosing a number in [0, 180] is ½. Instead of speaking of a probability mass function, we say that the probability density of X is 1/360. The probability of a subset of [0, 360) can be calculated by multiplying the measure of the set by 1/360. In general, the probability of a set for a given continuous random variable can be calculated by integrating the density over the given set.

An example of a random variable of mixed type would be based on an experiment where a coin is flipped and the spinner is spun only if the result of the coin toss is heads. If the result is tails, X = "1; otherwise X = the value of the spinner as in the preceding example. There is a probability of ½ that this random variable will have the value "1. Other ranges of values would have half the probability of the last example.

20.4 FORMAL DEFINITION

Intuitively, by a random variable (r.v.) we men a real number X associated with the outcomes of a random experiment. It can take any one of the various possible values each with a definite probability. For example, in a throw of a die, it X denoted the number obtained, then X is a random variable which can take any one of the value 1, 2, 3, 4, 5 or 6, each with equal probability 1/6. Similarly in toss of a coin if X denotes the number of heads, then X is a random variable which can take any one of the two values: 0 (No head, i.e., head) each with equal probability ½.

Let us now consider a random experiment of three tosses of a coin (or three coins toward simultaneously). Then the sample space S consists of $2^3 = 8$ points as given below:

$$S = \{(H, T) \times (H, T) \times (H, T)\}$$
$$= \{(HH, HT, TH, TT) \times (H, T)\}$$
$$= \{HHH, HTH, THH, TTH, HHT, HTT, THT, TTT\}$$

Let us consider the variable X, which is the number of heads obtained. Then, X is a random variable which can take any one of the values 0, 1 or 2.

Outcome:	HHH	HTH	THH	TTH	HHT	HTT	THT	TTT
Values of X:	3	2	2	1	2	1	1	0

If the sample points in the above order be denoted by $w_1, w_2, w_3, \ldots, w_8$ then to each outcome w of the random experiment, we can assign a real number X = X(w). For example,

$X(w_1) = 3, \quad X(w_2) = 2, \quad X(w_3) = 2, \quad \ldots.. \quad X(w_8) = 0$

Thus rigorously speaking random variable may be defined as a real valued function on the sample space taking values on the real line $R(-\infty, \infty)$. In other words, random variable is a function which takes real values which are determined by the outcomes of the random experiment.

Remarks

1. A random variable is denoted by the capital letters X, Y, Z,... etc., of the English alphabet and particular values which the random variable takes are denoted by the corresponding small letters of the English alphabet.
2. It should be clearly understood that the actual values which the event assumes is not a random variable. For example, in three tosses of a coin, the number of heads obtained is a random variable which can take any one of the three values 0, 1, 2 or 3 as long as the coin is not tossed. But, after it is tossed and we get two heads, then 2 is not a random variable.
3. Discrete and Continuous Random Variables. If the random variable X assumes only a finite or countably infinite set of values it is known as discrete random variable X assumes only a finite or countably infinite set of values it is known as discrete random variable. For example, marks obtained by students in a test, the number of students in a college the number of defective mangoes in a basket of mangoes, number of accidents taking place on a busy road, etc., are all discrete random variables.

On the other hand, if the r.v. X can assume infinite and uncountable set of values, it is said to be a continuous r.v., e.g. the age, height or weight of students in a class are all continuous random variables. In case of a continuous random variable we usually talk of the value in a particular interval and not at a point. Generally discrete r.v.'s, represent counted data while continuous r.v.'s represent measured data.

20.5 PROBABILITY DISTRIBUTION OF A DISCRETE RANDOM VARIABLE

Discrete random variables take on integer values, usually the result of counting. Suppose, for example, that we flip a coin and count the number of heads. The number of heads results from a random process - flipping a coin. And the number of heads is represented by an *integer* value - a number between 0 and plus infinity. Therefore, the number of heads is a discrete random variable.

Let us consider a discrete r.v. X which can take the possible values $x_1, x_2, x_3, \ldots, x_n$. With each value of the variable X, we association a number.

$$P_i = P(X = X_i);\ i = 1, 2, \ldots, n$$

Which is known as the probability of X_i and satisfies the following conditions:

(i) $$P_i = P(X = X_i) \geq 0,\ (i = 1, 2, \ldots, n) \quad (20.1)$$

i.e. p_i's are all non-negative and

(ii) $$\Sigma p_i = p_1 + p_2 + \ldots + p_n = 1. \quad (20.2)$$

i.e., the total probability is one.

More specifically, let X be a discrete random variable and define:

$$p(x) = P(X = x)$$

such that $p(x) \geq 0$ and $\Sigma p(x) = 1$, summation being taken over various values of the variable.

The function $p_i = P(X = X_i)$or p(x) is called the probability function or more precisely probability mass function (p.m.f) of the random variable X and the set of all possible ordered pairs {x, p(x)}, is called the probability distribution of the random variable X.

Remark. The concept of probability distribution is analogous to that frequency distribution. Just as frequency distribution tells us how the total frequency is distributed among different values (or classes) of the variable, similarly a probability distribution tells us how total probability of 1 is distributed among the various values which the random variable can take. It is usually represented in a form given below:

Table 20.1: Probability distribution of r.v. X

X	X_1	X_2	X_3	....	X_n
p(x)	P_1	P_2	P_3	......	P_n

20.6 PROBABILITY DISTRIBUTION OF A CONTINUOUS RANDOM VARIABLE

Continuous random variables, in contrast, can take on any value within a range of values. For example, suppose we flip a coin many times and compute the *average* number of heads per flip. The average number of heads per flip results from a random process - flipping a coin. And the average number of heads per flip can take on any value between 0 and 1, even a non-integer value. Therefore, the average number of heads per flip is a continuous random variable.

Unlike a discrete probability distribution, a continuous probability can not be presented in a tabular form. It has either a formula form or a graphical form.A frequency polygon gets smoother and smoother as the samples size gets larger, and the class intervals become more numerous and narrower. Ultimately the density polygon becomes a smooth curve called the density curve. The function that defines the curve is called the probability density function.

20.6.1 Probability Density Function of Continuous Random Variable

Let X be a continuous random variable taking values on the interval [a, b].

A function p(x) is said to be the probability density function of the continuous random variable X if it satisfies the following properties:

(i) $p(x) \geq 0$ for all x in the interval [a, b].

(ii) For two distinct numbers c and d in the interval [a, b]

$$P(c \leq X \leq d) = \text{[Area under the probability curve between the ordinates (vertical lines) at } x = c \text{ and } x = d] \qquad (20.3)$$

(iii) Total area under the probability curve is 1, i.e.,

$$P(a \leq X \leq b) = 1 \qquad (20.4)$$

20.7 DISTRIBUTION FUNCTION OR CUMULATIVE PROBABILITY FUNCTION

If X is a discrete r.v. with probability function p(x) then, the distribution function, usually denoted by F(x) is defined as:

$$F(x) = P(X \leq x) \qquad (20.5)$$

If X takes integral values, viz., 1, 2, 3,.... then

$$F(x) = P(X = 1) + P(X = 2) + \ldots + P(X = x)$$

$$\rightarrow F(x) = p(1) + p(2) + p(3) + \ldots + p(x) \qquad (20.5a)$$

Remarks 1. In the above case,

$$F(x - 1) = p(1) + p(2) + \ldots. + p(x - 1)$$

$$\therefore \quad F(x) - F(x - 1) = p(x) \rightarrow p(x) = F(x) - F(x - 1) \qquad (20.5b)$$

Hence, if X is a random variable which can take only positive integral values, then probability function can be obtained from distribution function by using (20.5).

2. If X is a continuous r.v. with probability density function p(x), then the distribution function is given by the integral

$$F(x) = P(X \leq x) = \overset{x}{\ } p(x)dx \qquad (20.5c)$$

Problem 1: A die is tossed twice. Getting 'an odd number' is termed as a success. Find the probability distribution of the number of successes.

Solution: Since the cases favourable to getting an odd number in a throw of a die are (1, 3, 5) i.e., 3 in all,

$$\text{Probability of success(S)} = \frac{3}{6} \;\; \frac{1}{2}; \text{ Probability of value (F)} = 1 \;\; \frac{1}{2} \;\; \frac{1}{2}.$$

If X denotes the number of successes in two throws of a die, then X is a random variable which takes the values 0, 1, 2.

$P(X = 0)\ P[F \text{ in } 1^{st} \text{ throw and } F \text{ in } 2^{nd} \text{ throw}]\ P(FF) = P(F) \times P(F) = \frac{1}{2}\ \frac{1}{2}$

$P(X = 1) = P(S \text{ and } F) + P(F \text{ and } S) = P(S)\,P(F) + P(F)\,P(S) = \frac{1}{2}\ \frac{1}{2}\ \frac{1}{2}\ \frac{1}{2}\ \frac{1}{2}$

Hence the probability distribution of X is given by:

x:	0	1	2
p(x):	$\frac{1}{4}$	$\frac{1}{2}$	$\frac{1}{4}$

Problem 2: Obtain the probability of X, the number of heads in three tosses of a coin (0) a simultaneous toss of three coins).

Solution: Obviously, X is a random variable which can take the values 0, 1, 2 or 3. The simple space S consists of $2^3 = 8$ sample points, as given below:

$$S = \{(H, T) \times (H, T) \times (H, T)\}$$
$$= \{(HH, TH, TH, TT) \times (H, T)\}$$
$$= \{HHH, HTH, THH, TTH, HHT, HTT, THT, TTT\}$$

The probability distribution of X is given in Table 20.2.

Table 20.2: Probability distribution of number of heads in 3 tosses of a coin

No. of heads (x)	Favourable events	No. of favourable cases	Probability p(x)
0	{TTT}	1	$\frac{1}{8}$
1	{TTH, HTT, THT}	3	$\frac{3}{8}$
2	{HTH, THH, HHT}	3	$\frac{3}{8}$
3	{HHH}	1	$\frac{1}{8}$

Problem 3: Two Cards are drawn

(a) successively with replacement

(b) simultaneously (successively without replacement).

From a well shuffled deck of 52 cards. Find the probability distribution of the number of aces.

Solution: Let X denote the number of aces obtained in a draw of two cards. Obviously X is a random variable which can take the values 0, 1, 2.

(a) Probability of drawing an ace = $\frac{4}{52} \quad \frac{1}{13}$ → Probability of drawing a non-ace = 1 $\frac{1}{13} \quad \frac{12}{13}$.

Since the cards are drawn with replacement all the draws are independent.

$$P(X = 2) = P(\text{Ace and Ace}) = P(\text{Ace}) \text{ x } P(\text{Ace}) = \frac{1}{13} \quad \frac{12}{13} \quad \frac{1}{169}.$$

$$P(X = 1) = P(\text{Ace and Non-ace}) + P(\text{non-Ace and Ace})$$

$$= P(\text{Ace}) \text{ x } P(\text{Non-ace}) + P(\text{Non-ace}) \text{ x } P(\text{Ace})$$

$$= \frac{1}{13} \quad \frac{12}{13} \quad \frac{12}{13} \quad \frac{1}{13} \quad \frac{24}{169}$$

$$P(X = 0) = P(\text{Non-ace and Non-ace}) = P(\text{Non-ace}) \text{ x } P(\text{Non-ace}) = \frac{12}{13} \quad \frac{12}{13} \quad \frac{144}{169}$$

Hence, the probability distribution of X is :

x:	0	1	2
p(x):	$\frac{144}{169}$	$\frac{24}{169}$	$\frac{1}{169}$

(b) If cards are drawn without replacement, then exhaustive number of cases of drawing 2 cards out of 52 cards is ${}^{52}C_2$.

$$\therefore \quad P(X = 0) = P(\text{No ace}) = P(\text{Both cards are non-aces} = \frac{{}^{48}C_2}{{}^{52}C_2 51} \quad \frac{48 \quad 47}{52} \quad \frac{188}{221}$$

$$P(X = 1) = P(\text{one ace}) = P(\text{one ace and one non-ace} = \frac{{}^{4}C_1 {}^{48}C_1}{{}^{52}C_2} \quad \frac{4 \quad 47}{52 \text{x} 51} \quad \frac{32}{221}$$

$$P(X = 2) = P(\text{both aces}) = \frac{{}^{4}C_2}{{}^{52}C_2} \quad \frac{4 \quad 3}{51 \quad 52} \quad \frac{1}{221}$$

Hence, the probability distribution of X becomes:

x:	0	1	2
p(x):	$\frac{188}{221}$	$\frac{32}{221}$	$\frac{1}{221}$

20.8 MEAN AND VARIANCE OF A DISCRETE RANDOM VARIABLE

Let X be a discrete random variable which can assume values $x_1, x_2, x_3, \ldots x_n$ with probabilities p_1, $p_2, p_3 \ldots.. p_n$ respectively then

(a) Mean of X or expectation of X denoted by E(X) or m is given by

$$E(x) = \mathop{}\limits_{i\ 1}^{n} x_i p_i$$

(b) Variance of X denoted by s^2 is given by

$$\sigma 2 = \mathop{}\limits_{i\ 1}^{n} (x_i \quad)^2 p_i$$

$$= \mathop{}\limits_{i\ 1}^{n} x_i^2 \quad ^2 \quad 2x_i \quad)p_i$$

$$= \mathop{}\limits_{i\ 1}^{n} x_i^2 p_i \quad ^2 \mathop{}\limits_{i\ 1}^{n} p_i \quad 2 \quad \mathop{}\limits_{i\ 1}^{n} x_i p_i$$

$$= \mathop{}\limits_{i\ 1}^{n} x_i^2 p_i \quad ^2 \quad 2 \quad ^2$$

$$= \mathop{}\limits_{i\ 1}^{n} x_i^2 p_i \quad ^2$$

$$\sigma^2 = \mathop{}\limits_{i\ 1}^{n} x_i^2 p_i \quad \mathop{}\limits_{i\ 1}^{n} p_i x_i \quad ^2 \quad E(x)^2 \quad [E(x)]^2$$

Note: σ^2 is called the standard deviation and equal to $\sqrt{\text{variance}}$.

Example:

Two cards are drawn successively without replacement, from a well shuffled deck of cards. Find the mean and standard deviation of the random variable X, where X is the number of aces.

Suggested answer:

X is the number of aces drawn while drawing two cards from a pack of cards.

The total ways of drawing two cards $^{52}C_2$. Out of 52 cards these are 4 aces. The numbers of ways of not drawing an Ace = $^{48}C_2$. The number of ways of drawing an ace is $^4C_1 \times {}^{48}C_1$ and two aces $^4C_2$.

Therefore the r.v. X can take the values 0, 1, 2.

x:	x = 0	x = 1	x = 2
p(x = x):	$\frac{48_{C_2}}{52_{C_2}}$	$\frac{4_{C_1} \quad 48_{C_1}}{52_{C_2}}$	$\frac{4_{C_2}}{52_{C_2}}$

$$\text{Mean} = E(x) \quad \overset{2}{\underset{x_i \;\; 1}{}} \; x_i P(x \quad x_i)$$

$$= 0 \; \frac{48_{C_2}}{52_{C_2}} \quad (1) \; \frac{4_{C_1} \quad 48_{C_1}}{52_{C_2}} \quad (2) \; \frac{4_{C_2}}{52_{C_2}}$$

$$= \frac{4_{C_1} \quad 48_{C_1} (2) 4_{C_2}}{52_{C_2}}$$

$$= \frac{(4 \quad 48) \quad 2(6)}{\frac{52 \quad 51}{2}}$$

$$= \frac{204}{26 \quad 51}$$

$$= \frac{2}{13} = 0.1538$$

$$E(x)^2 = \quad \overset{2}{\underset{x_i \;\; 1}{}} \; (x_i^2) P(X \quad x_i)$$

$$= 0 \; \frac{48_{C_2}}{52_{C_2}} \quad 1 \; \frac{4_{C_1} \quad 48_{C_1}}{52_{C_2}} \quad 2^2 \; \frac{4_{C_2}}{52_{C_2}}$$

$$= \frac{192 \quad 24}{52_{C_2}}$$

$$= \frac{216}{26 \quad 51}$$

$$= 0.1629$$

$$\text{Variance} = E(x^2) - [E(x)]^2$$

$$= 0.1629 - 0.0236 = 0.13925$$

$$\text{S.D} = \sqrt{\text{Variance}} \quad 0.373$$

Let X be a continuous random variable which can assume values in (a, b) and f(x) be the probability density of x then

(a) Mean of X or Expectation of X is given by

$$\mu = \overset{b}{\underset{a}{}} \; x\, f(x) dx$$

(b) Variance of x is given by

$$\sigma^2 = \int_a^b (x - \ )^2 f(x)dx$$

$$= \int_a^b x^2 f(x)dx \quad \int_a^b x f(x)dx$$

20.9 MATHEMATICAL EXPECTATION

If X is a random variable which can assume any one of the values $x_1, x_2..., x_n$ with respective probabilities $p_1, p_2,....p_n$ then the mathematical expectation of X, usually called the expected value of X and denoted by E(X), is defined as:

$$E(X) = p_1x_1 + p_2x_2 + \dots + p_nx_n = \Sigma p \text{ x } x \quad (20.6)$$

where $$\Sigma p_{i-} = p_1 + p_2 + \dots + p_n = 1 \quad (20.7)$$

More precisely, if X is random variable with probability distribution {x, p(x)}, then

$$E(X) = \Sigma x \text{ x } p(x) \quad (20.8)$$

summation being taken over different values of X.

Physical Interpretation of E(X). Let us consider the following frequency distribution of the random variable X:

x	x_1	x_2	x_3	...	x_i	...	x_n
f	f_{1-}	f_2	f_3	...	f_i	...	f_n

Then the mean of the distribution is given by:

$$\overline{x} = \frac{f_1x_1 \quad f_2x_2 \quad ... \quad f_nx_n}{N} \quad \frac{f_1}{N}x_1 \quad \frac{f_2}{N}x_2 \quad ... \frac{f_n}{N} \quad p_n \quad (i)$$

We observe that, out of total of N cases, f_i cases are favourable to x_i.

$$\therefore \quad P(X = x_i) = \frac{f_i}{N} \quad pi(say,)(i \quad 1,2,..., n), \quad \frac{f_1}{N} \quad p_1, \frac{f_2}{N} \quad p_2,..., \frac{f_n}{N} \quad p_n$$

Substituting in (*) we get:

$$\overline{x} = p_1x_1 + p_2x_2 + \dots + p_nx_n \rightarrow \overline{x} = E(X) \text{ [By def. of E(X)]} \quad (20.9)$$

Hence, mathematical expectation of a random variable is nothing but its arithmetic mean.

Remarks

1. The term 'expected value' is unfortunate in that, it is not in any sense a value which one expects to occur in a particular experiment. But if an experiment is conducted repeatedly a large number of times under essentially homogeneous conditions, then the average of the actual outcomes is the expected value. Sometimes, expected value may given results which

are impossible or absurd. For example, the expected value of the number of heads in three tosses of a coin is 1.5 [c.f. problem 4]; the expected number of white balls drawn in a draw of 2 balls from an urn containing 7 white and 3 red balls is 1.4 [c.f. problem 8]; the results are unrealistic and absurd.

2. In a game of chance, suppose that a player grains a sum 'a' if he wins and loses a sum 'b' if he does not win i.e., if the fails. If p and q are probabilities of his success and failure respectively in a single trial, then regarding loss as negative gain, the mathematical expectation of his gain is

$$a \times p + (-b) \text{ x } q = ap - bq$$

If the mathematical expectation of the gain of the player is zero, the game is said to be 'fair'. If the mathematical expectation of the gain is greater than 1, then the game is said to be biased to the player and if the expectation is negative, the game is said to be biased against the player.

Problem 4: What is the expected number of heads appearing when a fair coin is tossed three times?

Solution: Let X denote the number of heads obtained in a random toss of 3 coins. Then the probability distribution of X is [c.f. Example 13.3]

x:	0	1	2	3
p(x):	1/8	3/8	3/8	1/8

$$\therefore \quad E(X) = \Sigma p(x)$$

$$= \frac{1}{8}(0 + 1 \text{ x } 3 + 2 \text{ x } 3 + 3 \text{ x } 1) = \frac{12}{8} \quad 1.5$$

Problem 5: A random variable X is defined as the sum of faces when a pair of dice is thrown. Find the expected value of X.

Solution: Let the random variable X denote the sum of points obtained on a pair of dice when thrown. Then the probability distribution of X is (c.f. Example 13.4):

x:	2	3	4	5	6	7	8	9	10	11	12
p(x):	$\frac{1}{36}$	$\frac{2}{36}$	$\frac{3}{36}$	$\frac{4}{36}$	$\frac{5}{36}$	$\frac{6}{36}$	$\frac{5}{36}$	$\frac{4}{36}$	$\frac{3}{36}$	$\frac{2}{36}$	$\frac{1}{36}$

$$\therefore \quad E(X) = \Sigma x \cdot p(x)$$

$$= 2 \quad \frac{1}{36} \quad 3 \quad \frac{2}{36} \quad 4 \quad \frac{3}{36} \quad 5 \quad \frac{4}{36} \quad 6 \quad \frac{5}{36} \quad 7 \quad \frac{6}{36}$$

$$8 \quad \frac{5}{36} \quad 9 \quad \frac{4}{36} \quad 10 \quad \frac{3}{36} \quad 11 \quad \frac{2}{36} \quad 12 \quad \frac{1}{36}$$

$$= \frac{1}{36}[2 \quad 6 \quad 12 \quad 20 \quad 30 \quad 42 \quad 40 \quad 36 \quad 30 \quad 22 \quad 12] \quad \frac{252}{36} \quad 7$$

Problem 6: A constructor spends Rs. 3,000 to prepare for a bid on a construction project which , after deducting manufacturing expenses and the cost of bidding, will yield a profit of Rs. 25,000 if the bid is won. If the chance of winning the bid is ten per cent, compute his expected profit and state the likely decision on whether to bid or not a bid.

Solution: Expenses incurred on preparing the bid = Rs. 3,000.

This will be his loss if the bid is not won by the contractor. Profit if bid is won = Rs. 25,000.
P(Winning the bid) = 10% = 0.10 (Given); P(losing the bid) = 1 – 0.10 = 0.90

∴ Contractor's expected profit

$$= \text{Rs. } [25,000 \times 0.10 + (-3,000) \times 0.90] = \text{Rs. } (2,500 - 2,700) = (\text{-})\text{ Rs. } 200$$

Since the contractor's expected profit is negative he should not bid.

Problem 7: A survey conducted over the last 25 years indicated that in 10 years the winter was mild, in 8 years it was cold and in the remaining 7 years it was very cold.

A company sells 1000 woolen coats in a mild year, 1300 in a cold year and 2000 in a very cold year.

You are required to find the yearly expected profit of the company if a woolen coat Rs. 1730 and it is sold to stores for Rs. 2480.

Solution: From the given data, we obtain the following probability distribution of the number of woolen coats sold in any winter (year).

Winter (p)	Probability	No. of woolen coats sold (x)	p.x.
Mild	$\frac{10}{25}$	1000	$\frac{10}{25} \times 1000 = 400$
Cold	$\frac{8}{25}$	1300	$\frac{8}{25} \times 1300 = 416$
Very cold	$\frac{7}{25}$	2000	$\frac{7}{25} \times 2000 = 560$

Hence, the expected number of woolen coats sold in any year is given by:

$$E(x) = \Sigma p.x = 400 + 416 + 560 = 1376$$

Since the cost of a woolen coat is Rs. 1730 and it is sold to the stores for Rs. 2480, the company makes a profit of Rs. (2480 – 1730) = Rs. 750 per coat.

Hence, the yearly expected profit of the company is Rs. 1376 × 750 = Rs. 10,32,000.

Problem 8: An urn contains 7 white and 3 red balls. Two balls are drawn together, at random, from this urn. Compute the probability that neither of them is white. Find also the probability of getting one white an done read balls. Hence compute the expected number of white balls drawn.

Solution: From an urn containing 7 white and 3 red balls, two balls cn be drawn in $^{10}C_2$ ways. Let X denote the number of white balls drawn. The probability distribution of X is obtained as follows:

$$p(0) = \text{Probability that neither of two balls is white}$$

$$= \text{Probability that both balls drawn are red}$$

$$= \frac{^{3}C_2}{^{10}C_2} \quad \frac{3 \quad 2}{10 \quad 9} \quad \frac{1}{15}$$

since 2 balls can be drawn out of 3 red balls in $^{3}C_2$ ways.

$$p(1) = \text{Probability of getting 1 white and 1 red ball}$$

$$= \frac{^{7}C_1 \quad ^{3}C_1}{^{10}C_2} \quad \frac{7 \quad 3 \quad 2}{10 \quad 9} \quad \frac{21}{45},$$

since 1 white ball can be drawn out of 7 white balls in $^{7}C_1$ ways and 1 red ball can be drawn out of 3 red balls in $^{3}C_1$ ways and all these ways can be associated with each other.

$$p(2) = \text{Probability of getting two white balls}$$

$$= \frac{^{7}C_2}{^{10}C_2} \quad \frac{7 \quad 6}{2} \quad \frac{2}{10 \quad 9} \quad \frac{21}{45}$$

Hence expected number of white balls drawn is:

$$E(X) = \Sigma x.p(x) = 0 \text{ x } \frac{1}{15} \quad 1 \quad \frac{21}{45} \quad 2 \quad \frac{21}{45} \quad \frac{21 \quad 42}{45} \quad \frac{63}{45} \quad 1.4$$

Problem 9: A die is tossed twice. Getting 'a number greater than 4' is considered a success. Find the mean and variance of the probability distribution of the number of successes.

Solution: Since the favourable cases for 'getting a number greater than 4' in a throw of a die are 5 and 6 i.e., 2 in all, we have:

$$\text{Probability of success (S)} = \frac{2}{6} \quad \frac{1}{3} \rightarrow \text{Probability of failure (F)} = 1 \quad \frac{1}{3} \quad \frac{2}{3}$$

Let X denote the number of successes. Then, X is a random variable taking the calues 0, 1 and 2.

$$P(X = 0) = P\text{ (F and F)} = P(F) \text{ x } P(F) = \frac{2}{3} \quad \frac{2}{3} \quad \frac{4}{9}$$

$$P(X = 1) = P(\text{F and S}) + P(\text{S and F}) = P(F) \cdot P(S) + P(S) \cdot P(F)$$

$$= \frac{2}{3} \quad \frac{1}{3} \quad \frac{1}{3} \quad \frac{2}{3} \quad \frac{4}{9}$$

$$P(X = 2) = P(\text{S and S}) = P(S)\ P(S) = \frac{1}{3} \quad \frac{1}{3} \quad \frac{1}{9}$$

Computation of Variance			
x	p(x)	x.p(x)	x^2.p(x)
0	4/9	0	0
1	4/9	4/9	4/9
2	4/9	2/9	4/9
Total		$\Sigma p(x) = \frac{6}{9}$	$\Sigma x^2 p(x) = \frac{8}{9}$

$\therefore$ Mean (m) $= \Sigma x.p(x) = \frac{6}{9} \quad \frac{2}{3}$

Variance $(s^2) = \Sigma x^2 p(x) - [\Sigma xp(x)]^2$

$$= \frac{8}{9} \quad \frac{2}{3}^2 \quad \frac{4}{9}$$

Problem 10: A random variable X has the following probability distribution:

x :	4	5	6	8
p :	0.1	0.3	0.4	0.2

Find $E[X - E(X)]^2$

Solution: $E[X - E(X)]^2 = \text{Var}(X) = E(X^2) - [E(X)]^2$

$$= \Sigma px^2 - (\Sigma px)^2$$

x	p	px	Px^2
4	0.1	0.4	1.6
5	0.3	1.5	7.5
6	0.4	2.4	14.4
8	0.2	1.6	12.8
Total	**1**	**$\Sigma px = 5.9$**	**$\Sigma px^2 = 36.3$**

$\therefore$ $E[X - E(X)]^2 = \Sigma px^2 - (\Sigma px)^2$

$$= 36.3 - (5 - 9)^2$$

$$= 36.30 - 34.81$$

$$= 1.49$$

Problem 11: A player tosses two fair coins. He wins Rs. 5 if 2 heads occur, Rs. 2 if 1 head occurs and Re. 1 if no head occurs

(i) Find his expected gain/

(ii) How much should he pay to play the game if it is to be fair?

Solution: In a random toss of two fair coins, n(S) = 2^2 = 4, and the probability distribution of the number heads (x) is as obtained below:

No. of heads (x)	Favourable events	No. of favourable cases	Probability (p)	Gain in Rs. (y)	p.y
0	TT	1	$\frac{1}{4}$ 0.25	1	0.25
1	HT, TH	2	$\frac{2}{4}$ 0.50	2	1
2	HH	1	$\frac{1}{4}$ 0.25	5	1.25

(i) The expected gain of the player is given by:

$$E(y) = \Sigma p \cdot y = 0.25 + 1 + 1.25 = \text{Rs. } 2.50$$

(ii) The game is said to be fair if the mathematical expectation of the gain of the player is zero. Hence, the player should pay Rs. 2.50 to play the game, if this is to be fair.

EXERCISES

1. In a business venture a man can make a profit of Rs. 2,000with probability of 0.4 or have a loss of Rs. 1,000 with a probability of 0.6. What is his expected profit?
2. If the probability that the value of a certain stock will remain the same is 0.46 the probability that its value will decrease by Re. 0.25 per share is 0.14, what is the expected gain per share?
3. You have been offered the chance to play a dice game in which you will receive Rs. 20 each time the point total of a toss of two dice is 6. If it costs you Rs. 2.50 per toss to participate, should you play or not? Will it make any difference in your decision if it costs Rs. 3.00 per toss instead of Rs. 2.50?
4. Define mathematical expectation.

   Three coins, whose faces are marked 1 and 2, are tossed. What is the expectation the total value of numbers on their faces?
5. A box contains 12 items of which 3 are defective. A sample of 3 items is selected at random from this box. If X represents the number of defective items in the 3 selected items, describe the random variable X completely and obtain its expectation.
6. Suppose an insurance company offers a 45 year-old man a Rs. 1,000 one year term policy for an annual premium of Rs. 12. Assuming that the number of deaths per one thousand is five for persons in this age group, what is the expected gain for the insurance company on a policy of this type.

7. The probability known is 0.99 that a 30-year old man will survive one year more. An insurance company offers to sell such a man a Rs. 10,000 one –year term life insurance policy at a premium of Rs. 110. What is the insurance company's expected gain?
8. A firm plans to bid Rs. 300 per tonne for a contract to supply 1,000 tonners of a metal. It has two competitors A and B and it assumes that the probability that A will bid less that Rs. 300 per tonne is 0.3 and that B will bid less than Rs. 300 per tonne is 0.7. If the lowest bidder gets all the business and the firms bid independently, what is the expected value of the contract to the firm?
9. A number is chosen at random from the set 10, 11, 12, …, 109; and another number is chosen at random from the set 12, 13, 14, …, 61. What are the expected values of their (i) sum and (ii) product?

CHAPTER 21

Theoretical Distributions

21.1 INTRODUCTION

In the previous section, we have already defined the random variable and mathematical expectation in terms of probability function. These provide us the necessary tools for the study of theoretical distributions. Now, we shall study the following univariate probability distributions:

(i) Binomial Distribution

(ii) Poisson Distribution

(iii) Normal Distribution

The first two distributions are discrete probability distributions and the third is a continuous probability distribution.

21.2 BINOMIAL DISTRIBUTION

In probability theory and statistics, the binomial distribution is the discrete probability distribution of the number of successes in a sequence of n independent yes/no experiments, each of which yields success with probability p. Such a success/failure experiment is also called a Bernoulli experiment or Bernoulli trial. In fact, when n = 1, the binomial distribution is a Bernoulli distribution. The binomial distribution is the basis for the popular binomial test of statistical significance.

It is frequently used to model number of successes in a sample of size n from a population of size N. Since the samples are not independent (this is sampling without replacement), the resulting distribution is a hypergeometric distribution, not a binomial one. However, for N much larger than n, the binomial distribution is a good approximation, and widely used.

A binomial random variable is the number of successes x in n repeated trials of a binomial experiment. The probability distribution of a binomial random variable is called a binomial distribution (also known as a Bernoulli distribution).

Suppose we flip a coin two times and count the number of heads (successes). The binomial random variable is the number of heads, which can take on values of 0, 1, or 2. The binomial distribution is presented below.

Number of heads	Probability
0	0.25
1	0.50
2	0.25

This important distribution applies in some cases to repeated trials where there are only two possible outcomes: heads or tails, success or failure, defective item or good item, or many other possible pairs. The probability of each outcome can be calculated using the multiplication rule, perhaps with a tree diagram, but it is usually much faster and more convenient to use a general formula.

The requirements for using the binomial distribution are as follows:

- The outcome is determined completely by chance.
- There are only two possible outcomes.
- All trials have the same probability for a particular outcome in a single trial.

  That is, the probability in a subsequent trial is independent of the outcome of a previous trial. Let this constant probability for a single trial be p.
- The number of trials, n, must be fixed, regardless of the outcome of each trial.

21.2.1 The Binomial Distribution Has the Following Properties

1. The mean of the distribution (μ_x) is equal to n * P.
2. The variance ($^{2}_{x}$) is n * P * (1 – P).
3. The standard deviation (σ_x) is sqrt [n * P * (1 – P)].

When a coin is flipped, the outcome is either a head or a tail; when a magician guesses the card selected from a deck, the magician can either be correct or incorrect; when a baby is born, the baby is either born in the month of March or is not. In each of these examples, an event has two mutually exclusive possible outcomes. For convenience, one of the outcomes can be labeled "success" and the other outcome "failure." If an event occurs N times (for example, a coin is flipped N times), then the binomial distribution can be used to determine the probability of obtaining exactly r successes in the N outcomes. The binomial probability for obtaining r successes in N trials is:

$$P(r) = \frac{N!}{r!(N \quad r)!} \quad ^{r} (1 \quad)^{N \quad r}$$

where P(r) is the probability of exactly r successes, N is the number of events, and ð is the probability of success on any one trial. This formula for the binomial distribution assumes that the events:

1. are dichotomous
2. are mutually exclusive
3. are independent and
4. are randomly selected

Consider this Simple Application of the Binomial Distribution:

Problem 1: What is the probability of obtaining exactly 3 heads if a fair coin is flipped 6 times?

Solution: For this problem, N = 6, r = 3, and π = 0.5. Therefore,

$$P(3) = \frac{6!}{3!(6 \quad 3)!}(0.5)^3\,(1 \quad 0.5)^{6 \quad 3}$$

$$= \frac{6 \quad 5 \quad 4 \quad 3 \quad 2}{(3 \quad 2)(3 \quad 2)}(0.125)(0.125) \quad 0.3125.$$

Two binomial distributions are shown below. Notice that for π = 0.5, the distribution is symmetric whereas for π = 0.3, the distribution has a positive skew.

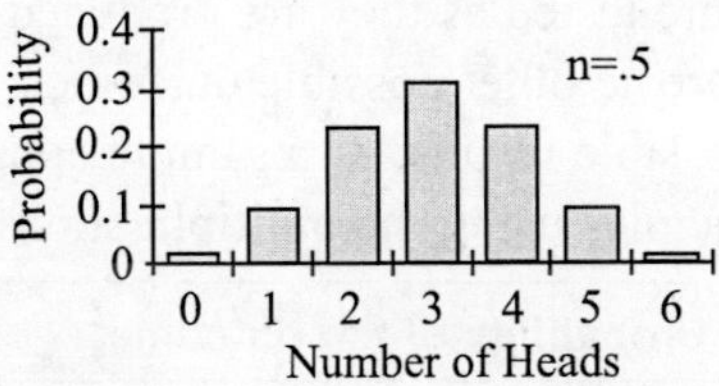

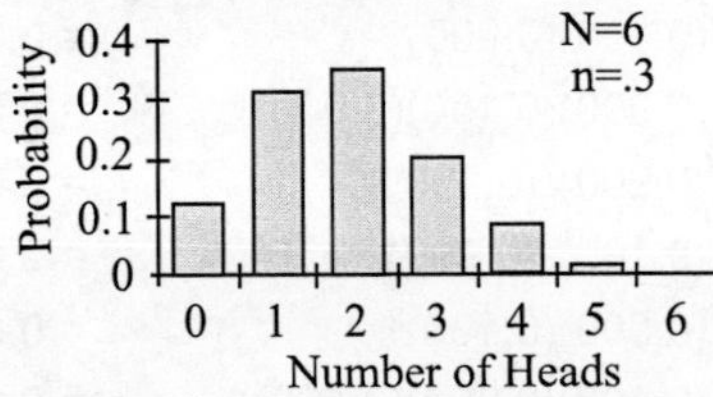

Often the cumulative form of the binomial distribution is used. To determine the probability of obtaining 3 or more successes with n = 6 and π = 0.3, you compute P(3) + P(4) + P(5) + P(6). This can also be written as:

$$\overset{6}{\underset{i \; 3}{}} P(r_i)$$

and is equal to 0.1852 + 0.0595 + 0.0102 + 0.0007 = 0.2556. The binomial distribution can be approximated by a normal distribution

21.2.2 Binomial Probability

The binomial probability refers to the probability that a binomial experiment results in exactly x successes. For example, in the above table, we see that the binomial probability of getting exactly one head in two coin flips is 0.50.

Given x, n, and P, we can compute the binomial probability based on the following formula:

Binomial Formula: Suppose a binomial experiment consists of n trials and results in x successes. If the probability of success on an individual trial is P, then the binomial probability is:

$$b(x; n, P) = {}_nC_x * P^x * (1 - P)^{n-x}$$

Problem 2: Suppose a die is tossed 5 times. What is the probability of getting exactly 2 fours?

Solution: This is a binomial experiment in which the number of trials is equal to 5, the number of successes is equal to 2, and the probability of success on a single trial is 1/6 or about 0.167. Therefore, the binomial probability is:

$$b(2; 5, 0.167) = {}^5C_2 * (0.167)^2 * (0.833)^3$$

$$b(2; 5, 0.167) = 0.161$$

Illustration of the binomial distribution

All items from a production line are tested as they are produced. Each item is classified as either defective (D) or good (G). There are no other possible outcomes. Pr[D] = 0.100, Pr[G] = 1 – Pr[D] = 0.900. Let us consider all the possible results for a sample consisting of three items, calculating their probabilities from basic principles using the multiplication rule:

Outcome	Probability of the outcome	
G G G	$(0.900)^3$	= 0.729
D G G	(0.100)(0.900)	= 0.081
G D G	(0.900)(0.100)(0.900)	= 0.081
G G D	$(0.900)^2$(0.1000	= 0.081
D D G	$(0.100)^2$(0.900)	= 0.009
G D D	(0.900)$(0.100)^2$	= 0.009
D G D	(0.100)(0.900)(0.100)	= 0.009
D D D	$(0.100)^3$	= 0.001
	Total	**= 1.000 (Check)**

Notice that the outcome containing three good items appeared once, and so did the outcome containing three defective items. The outcome containing two good items and one defective appeared three times, which is the number of permutations of two items of one class and one item of another class. The outcome containing one good item and two defectives also appears three times (as D D G, G D D, and D G D); again, this is the number of permutations of one item of one class and two items of another class.

Generalization of results

Now we'll develop more general results. Let the probability that an item is defective be p. Let the probability that an item is good be q, such that q = 1 – p. Notice that the definitions of p and q can be interchanged, and other terms such as "success" and "failure" can be used instead (and often are). Let the fixed number of trials be n. The probability that all n items are defective is p^n. The probability that exactly r items are defective and (n–r) items are good, in any one sequence, is p^r $q^{(n-r)}$. But r defective items and (n–r) good items can be arranged in various ways. How many different orders are possible? This is the number of permutations into two classes, consisting of r defective items and (n–r) good items, respectively. From previous section this number of permutations is given by n!/r!(n– r)! . But this is exactly the expression for the number of combinations of n items taken r at a time, ${}_nC_r$. Then the general expression for the probability of exactly r defective items (or successes, heads, etc.) in any order in n trials must be $p^r\ q^{(n-r)}$ multiplied by ${}_nC_r$, or

$$\Pr[R = r] = nC_r\, p^r\, q^{(n-r)} \qquad (21.1)$$

The lefthand side of this equation should be read as the probability that exactly r items are defective (or successes, heads, etc.). The name given to this discrete probability distribution is the binomial distribution. This name arises because the expression for probability in equation (21.1) is the same as the (n+1)th term in the binomial expansion of $(q+p)^n$.

Application of the binomial distribution

The binomial distribution is often used in quality control of items manufactured by a production line when each item is classified as either defective or nondefective. To meet the requirements of the binomial distribution the probability that an item is defective must be constant. The condition of constant probability is met to an acceptable approximation if the total number of trials is much less than the batch size, so for a sufficiently small sample from a large enough batch. Then the probability of a defect (or "success" etc.) on a single trial will be approximately constant.

The condition is met for sampling item by item from continuous production under constant conditions. It is also met for sampling from a small batch if each item which is removed as a specimen is returned to the batch and mixed thoroughly with the other items, once it has been examined and classified as defective or good. This, however, is not often a practical procedure: if we know that an item is defective, we should not mix it with other items of production. Indeed, sometimes we can't, because the test procedure may destroy the sample.

Problem 3: On the basis of past experience, the probability that a certain electrical component will be satisfactory is 0.98. The components are sampled item by item from continuous production. In a sample of five components, what are the probabilities of finding (a) zero, (b) exactly one, (c) exactly two, (d) two or more defectives?

Solution: The requirements of the binomial distribution are met. n = 5, p = 0.98, q = 0.02, where p is taken to be the probability that an item will be satisfactory, and so q is the probability that an item will be defective.

(a) Pr [0 defectives] = (0.98)5 = 0.9039 or 0.904.

(b) $\Pr[1 \text{ defective}] = {}_5C_1\,(0.98)^4(0.02)^1$

$= (5)\,(0.98)^4(0.02)^1 = 0.0922$ or 0.092.

(c) $\Pr[2 \text{ defectives}] = {}_5C_2\,(0.98)^3(0.02)^2$

$$= \frac{(5)(4)}{2}(0.98)^3(0.02)^2 = 0.038.$$

(d) $\Pr[2 \text{ or more defectives}] = 1 - \Pr[0 \text{ def.}] - \Pr[1 \text{ def.}]$

$= 1 - 0.9039 - 0.0922$

$= 0.0038$

Shape of the binomial distribution

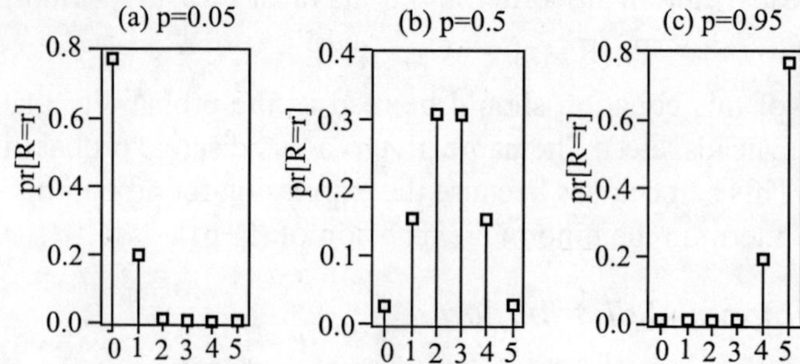

Figure 21.1: Effect of varying probability of success in a single trial when the number of trials is 5

Figure 21.1 compares the shapes of the distributions for p equal to 0.05, 0.50, and 0.95, all for n equal to 5. When p is close to zero or one, the distribution is very skewed, and the distribution for p equal to p_1 is the mirror image of the distribution for p equal to $(1-p_1)$. When p is equal to 0.500, the distribution is symmetrical.

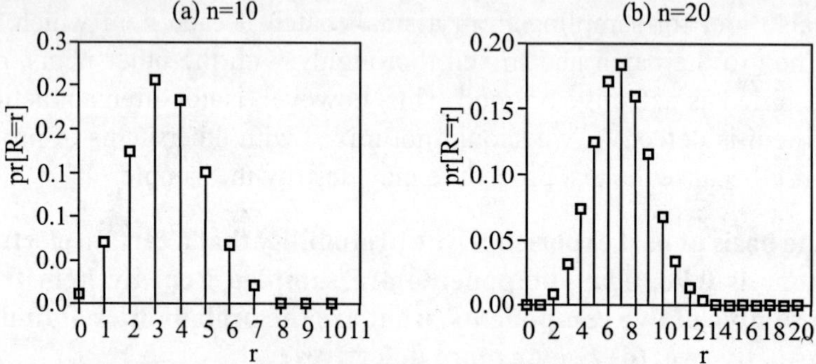

Figure 21.2: Effect of varying number of trials when the probability of success is 0.35

Figure 21.2 compares the shape of the distributions for n equal to 10 and 20, both for p equal to 0.35. At this intermediate value of p, the distribution is rather skewed for small numbers of trials, but it becomes more symmetrical and bell-shaped as n increases.

Expected mean and standard deviation

For any discrete random variable, gives that the expected mean is $E(R) = \mu(\text{or } \mu_R) = \Sigma$ (number of "successes")(probability of that number of "successes") for all possible results.

For the binomial distribution, from equation (21.1) the probability of r "successes" in n trials is given by

$$Pr[R \quad r] = \quad Cr(1 \quad p)^{n \quad r} p^r$$

Then

$$\mu = \sum_{r \quad 0}^{n} (r) Pr]R \quad r) \qquad \sum_{r \quad 0}^{n} (r)(\; C_r(1 \quad p)^{(n \quad r)} p^r$$

If the algebra is followed through, the result is

$$\mu = np \qquad (21.2)$$

Thus, the mean value of the binomial distribution is the product of the number of trials and the probability of "success" in a single trial. This seems to be intuitively correct.

For any discrete probability distribution,

$$\sigma^2 = E(r \qquad)^2 \quad \sum_{r \quad 0}^{n} (r \qquad)^2 Pr[R \quad r]$$

Substituting for the probability for the binomial distribution and following through the algebra gives

$$\sigma^2 = np(1 - p)$$

or

$$\sigma^2 = npq \qquad (21.3)$$

The standard deviation is always given by the square root of the corresponding variance, so the standard deviation for the binomial distribution is

$$\sigma^2 = \sqrt{npq} \qquad (21.4)$$

Problem 4: A merchant's file of 20 accounts contains 6 delinquent and 14 non-delinquent accounts. An auditor randomly selects 5 of these accounts for examination.

(i) What is the probability that the auditor finds exactly 2 delinquent accounts?

(ii) Find the expected number of delinquent dccounts in the sample selected?

Solution: We have:

$$p = \text{Probability of a delinquent account} = \frac{6}{20} = 0.3 \rightarrow q = 1 - p = 0.7$$

$\therefore$ p(r) = Probability that auditor finds r delinquent accounts in a random choice of n = 5 accounts

$$= {}^nC_r p^r q^{n-r} = {}^5C_r (0.3)^r (0.7)^{5-r} \qquad \text{(By Binomial Probability Law)} \qquad (21.5)$$

(i) The probability that the auditor finds exactly 2 delinquent accounts is given by:

$$p(2) = {}^5C_2\,(0.3)^2\,(0.7)^3 = \frac{5 \quad 4}{2} \quad 0.09 \quad 0.343 \quad 0.3087 \qquad \text{[From (21.5)]}$$

(ii) The expected number of delinquent accounts in the selected sample of n = 5 is : np = 5 × 0.3 = 1.5

Problem 5: The number of tosses of a coin that are needed so that the probability of getting at least one head being 0.875 is

(i) 2 **(ii) 3** **(iii) 4** **(iv) 5**

Solution: Let the required number of tosses of the coin be n. Then

$$\text{P[At least one head in n tosses of a coin]} = 1 - \text{P [No head in n tosses of a coin]} = 1 \quad \frac{1}{2}^{n}$$

We want n so that this probability is 0.875.

$$\therefore \qquad 1 = \frac{1}{2}^{n} = 0.875 \rightarrow \frac{1}{2}^{n} = 1 - 0.875 = 0.125 = (0.5)^3 = \frac{1}{2}^{3} \rightarrow n = 3$$

∴ (ii) is the correct answer.

21.3 POISSON DISTRIBUTION

In probability theory and statistics, the Poisson distribution is a discrete probability distribution that expresses the probability of a number of events occurring in a fixed period of time if these events occur with a known average rate and independently of the time since the last event. The Poisson distribution can also be used for the number of events in other specified intervals such as distance, area or volume.

The distribution was discovered by Siméon-Denis Poisson (1781–1840) and published, together with his probability theory, in 1838 in his work Recherches sur la probabilité des jugements en matières criminelles et matière civile ("Research on the Probability of Judgments in Criminal and Civil Matters"). The work focused on certain random variables N that count, among other things, the number of discrete occurrences (sometimes called "arrivals") that take place during a time-interval of given length. If the expected number of occurrences in this interval is λ, then the probability that there are exactly k occurrences (k being a non-negative integer, k = 0, 1, 2, ...) is equal to

$$f(k;\lambda) = \frac{e}{k!},$$

where

- e is the base of the natural logarithm (e = 2.71828...)
- k is the number of occurrences of an event - the probability of which is given by the function

- k! is the factorial of k
- λ is a positive real number, equal to the expected number of occurrences that occur during the given interval. For instance, if the events occur on average 4 times per minute, and you are interested in the number of events occurring in a 10 minute interval, you would use as your model a Poisson distribution with $\lambda = 10 \times 4 = 40$.

As a function of k, this is the probability mass function. The Poisson distribution can be derived as a limiting case of the binomial distribution. The Poisson distribution can be applied to systems with a large number of possible events, each of which is rare. A classic example is the nuclear decay of atoms. The Poisson distribution is sometimes called a Poissonian, analogous to the term Gaussian for a Gauss or normal distribution.

Definition

A Poisson random variable is the number of successes that result from a Poisson experiment. The probability distribution of a Poisson random variable is called a Poisson distribution.

Given the mean number of successes (μ) that occur in a specified region, we can compute the Poisson probability based on the following formula:

Poisson Formula: Suppose we conduct a Poisson experiment, in which the average number of successes within a given region is μ. Then, the Poisson probability is:

$$P(x; \mu) = (e^{-\mu}) (\mu^x) / x!$$

where x is the actual number of successes that result from the experiment and e is approximately equal to 2.71828.

The Poisson distribution has the following properties:

The mean of the distribution is equal to μ.

The variance is also equal to μ.

Problem 6: The average number of homes sold by the Acme Realty Company is 2 homes per day. What is the probability that exactly 3 homes will be sold tomorrow?

Solution: This is a Poisson experiment in which we know the following:

- $\mu = 2$; since 2 homes are sold per day, on average.
- $x = 3$; since we want to find the likelihood that 3 homes will be sold tomorrow.
- $e = 2.71828$; since e is a constant equal to approximately 2.71828.

We plug these values into the Poisson formula as follows:

$$P(x; \mu) = (e^{-\mu}) (\mu^x)/x!$$

$$P(3; 2) = (2.71828^{-2}) (2^3)/3!$$

$$P(3; 2) = (0.13534) (8)/6$$

$$P(3; 2) = 0.180$$

Thus, the probability of selling 3 homes tomorrow is 0.180

21.3.1 Cumulative Poisson Probability

A cumulative Poisson probability refers to the probability that the Poisson random variable is greater than some specified lower limit and less than some specified upper limit.

Problem 7: Suppose the average number of lions seen on a 1-day safari is 5. What is the probability that tourists will see fewer than four lions on the next 1-day safari?

Solution: This is a Poisson experiment in which we know the following:

$\mu = 5$; since 5 lions are seen per safari, on average.

$x = 0, 1, 2,$ or 3; since we want to find the likelihood that tourists will see fewer than 4 lions; that is, we want the probability that they will see 0, 1, 2, or 3 lions.

$e = 2.71828$; since e is a constant equal to approximately 2.71828.

To solve this problem, we need to find the probability that tourists will see 0, 1, 2, or 3 lions. Thus, we need to calculate the sum of four probabilities: P(0; 5) + P(1; 5) + P(2; 5) + P(3; 5). To compute this sum, we use the Poisson formula:

$$P(x < 3, 5) = P(0; 5) + P(1; 5) + P(2; 5) + P(3; 5)$$

$$P(x < 3, 5) = [(e^{-5})(5^0) / 0!] + [(e^{-5})(5^1) / 1!] + [(e^{-5})(5^2) / 2!] + [(e^{-5})(5^3) / 3!]$$

$$P(x < 3, 5) = [(0.006738)(1) / 1] + [(0.006738)(5)/1] + [(0.006738)(25) / 2] + [(0.006738)(125)/6]$$

$$P(x < 3, 5) = [0.0067] + [0.03369] + [0.084224] + [0.140375]$$

$$P(x < 3, 5) = 0.2650$$

Thus, the probability of seeing at no more than 3 lions is 0.2650.

Calculation of poisson probabilities

The probability of exactly r occurrences in a fixed interval of time or space under particular conditions is given by

$$\Pr[R = r] = \frac{(\ t)^r e^{\ t}}{r!}$$

where t (in units of time, length, area or volume) is an interval of time or space in which the events occur, and ë is the mean rate of occurrence per unit time or space (so that the product ët is dimensionless). As usual, e is the base of natural logarithms, approximately 2.71828. Then the probability of no occurrences, r = 0, is $e^{-ët}$, the probability of exactly one occurrence, r = 1, is ët $e^{-ët}$, the probability of exactly two occurrences, r = 2, is

$$\frac{(\ t)^2 e^{\ t}}{2!} \qquad (21.6)$$

and so on. Once one of these probabilities is calculated it is often more convenient to calculate other members of the sequence from the following recurrence formula:

$$\Pr[R = r + 1] = \frac{t}{r \quad 1} \Pr[R \quad r] \tag{21.7}$$

The basic relation for the Poisson distribution, equation (21.6), can be derived from a differential equation or as a limiting expression from the binomial distribution.

Problem 8: The number of meteors found by a radar system in any 30-second interval under specified conditions averages 1.81. Assume the meteors appear randomly and independently.

(a) What is the probability that no meteors are found in a one-minute interval?

(b) What is the probability of observing at least five but not more than eight meteors in two minutes of observation?

Solution: (a) $\lambda = (1.81) / (0.50 \text{ minute}) = 3.62 / \text{minute}$.

For a one-minute interval, $\mu = \lambda t = 3.62$.

Pr [none in one minute] $= e^{-\lambda t} = e–3.62 = 0.0268$.

(b) For two minutes, $\mu = \lambda t = (3.62)(2) = 7.24$.

$$\Pr[R = r] = \frac{(\ \ t)^r \, e^{\ \ t}}{r!}.$$

Then $$\Pr[R = 5] = \frac{(7.24)^5 \, e^{\ \ 7.24}}{5!} \quad 0.1189$$

From equation 5.14, $$\Pr[R = r + 1] = \frac{t}{r \quad 1} \Pr[R \quad r]$$

so $$\Pr[R = 6] = \frac{7.24}{6} (0.1189) \quad 0.1435,$$

$$\Pr[R = \Pr[R = 7] = \frac{7.24}{7} (0.1435) \quad 0.1484,$$

and $$\Pr[R = \Pr[R = 8] = \frac{7.24}{8} (0.1484) \quad 0.1343.$$

Then Pr [at least five but not more than eight meteors in two minutes]

= Pr [5 or 6 or 7 or 8 meteors in two minutes]

= 0.1189 + 0.1435 + 0.1484 + 0.1343

= 0.545

Problem 9: The average number of collisions occurring in a week during the summer months at a particular intersection is 2.00. Assume that the requirements of the Poisson distribution are satisfied.

(a) What is the probability of no collisions in any particular week?

(b) What is the probability that there will be exactly one collision in a week?

(c) What is the probability of exactly two collisions in a week?

(d) What is the probability of finding not more than two collisions in a week?

(e) What is the probability of finding more than two collisions in a week?

(f) What is the probability of exactly two collisions in a particular two-week interval?

Solution: $\lambda = 2.00$/week, $t = 1$ week, so $\lambda t = 2.00$.

(a) $Pr[R = 0] = e^{-\lambda t} = e^{-2.00} = 0.135$

(b) Pr [exactly one collision in a week]

$$= Pr[R = 1] = (\lambda t)e^{-\lambda t} = 2.00e^{-2.00}$$

$$= 0.271$$

(c) Pr [exactly two collisions in a week]

$$= Pr[R = 2] = \frac{(\ t)^2 e^{\ t}}{2!} = \frac{(2.00)^2 e^{200}}{2!}$$

(d) Pr [not more than two collisions in a week]

$$= Pr[R \le 2]$$

$$= Pr[R = 0] + Pr[R = 1] + Pr[R = 2]$$

$$= 0.135 + 0.271 + 0.271$$

$$= 0.677$$

(e) Pr [more than two collisions in a week]

$$= Pr[R > 2]$$

$$= 1 - Pr[R \le 2]$$

$$= 1 - 0.677$$

$$= 0.323$$

(f) Now we still have $\lambda = 2.00$/week, but $t = 2$ weeks, so $t = 4.00$ Then Pr [exactly two collisions in a two-week interval]

$$\frac{(\ t)^2 e^{\ t}}{2!} = \frac{(4.00)^2 e^{4.00}}{2!}$$

$$= 0.147$$

Mean and variance for the poisson distribution

Since the Poisson distribution is discrete, the mean and variance can be found from the previous general relations.

$$\mu = E(R) \qquad \underset{\text{all r}}{} (r)(Pr[R \quad r]$$

When the probability function is substituted in this expression and the algebra is worked through, the result is that the mean or expectation of the number of occurrences according to the Probability Distribution is

$$\mu = \lambda t \qquad (21.8)$$

Therefore an alternative form of the probability function for the Poisson distribution is

$$\Pr[R = r] = \frac{{}^{r}\ e}{r!}$$

Similarly, we can write

$$\sigma^2 = E(r \quad)^2 \quad \sum_{all}^{n} (r \quad)^2 \Pr[R \quad r]$$

Again, the probability function can be substituted. The result of this derivation for the Poisson Distribution is that

$$\sigma^2 = \lambda t$$

Thus, the variance of the number of occurrences for the Poisson distribution is equal to the mean number of occurrences, μ.

Problem 10: 5% of the tools produced by a certain process are defective. Find the probability that in a sample of 40 tools chosen at random, exactly three will be defective. Calculate a) using the binomial distribution, and b) using the Poisson distribution as an approximation.

Solution: (a) For the binomial distribution with n = 40, p = 0.05,

$$\Pr[R = 3] = {}_{40}C_3\,(0.05)^3(0.95)^{37}$$

$$= \frac{(40)(39)(38)}{(3)(2)(1)}(0.05)^3(0.95)^{37}$$

$$= 0.185$$

(b) For the Poisson distribution, ì = (n)(p) = (40)(0.05) = 2.00.

$$\Pr[R = 3] = \frac{(2.00)^3\ e^{\ 2.00}}{(3)(2)(1)} = 0.180$$

Problem 11: A manufacturer of blades knows that 5% of his product is defective. If he sells blades in boxes of 100, and guarantees that not more than 10 blades will be defective, what is the probability (approximately) that a box will fail to meet the guaranteed quality?

Solution. p = Probability of a defective blade = 5% = 0.05

Since the probability of a defective blade is small, we may use Poisson distribution. In the usual notations we are given n = 100.

Hence $\quad m = np = 100 \times 0.05 = 5$

If the random variable X denotes the number of defective blades in a box of 100, then (by Poisson probability law),

$$P(X = r) = \frac{e^{\ m} \cdot m^r}{r!} \quad \frac{e^{\ 5} \cdot 5^r}{r!}; r \quad 0, 1, 2, ...$$

A box will fail to meet the guaranteed quality if the number of defectives in it is more than 10. Hence the required probability is:

$$P(X > 10) = 1 - P(X \leq 10) = 1 - \overset{10}{\underset{r\ \ 0}{}} p(r)$$

$$= 1 - \overset{10}{\underset{r\ \ 0}{}} \frac{e^{\ 5}.5^4}{r!} \quad 1 \ e^{\ 5} \overset{10}{\underset{r\ \ 0}{}} \frac{5r}{r!}$$

Problem 12: In a certain factory turning out optical lenses, there is small chance 1/500 for any one lens to be defective. The lenses are supplied, in packets of 10. Use Poisson distribution to calculate the approximate number of packets containing no defective, one defective, two defective, three defective lenses respectively in a consignment of 20,000 packets. You are given that $e^{-0.02} = 0.9802$.

Solution: In the usual notation we are given: N = 20,000 ; n = 10 and

$$p = \text{Probability of a defective optical lense} = \frac{1}{500}$$

$$m = np = 10 \quad \frac{1}{500} \quad \frac{1}{50} \quad 0.02$$

Let the random variable X denote the number of defective optical lenses in a packet of 10. Then, by Poisson probability law, the probability of r defective lenses in a packet is given by:

$$P(X = r) = \frac{e^{\ 0.02}(0.02)^r}{r!} \quad \frac{0.9802 \quad (0.02)^r}{r!}$$

Hence in a consignment of 20,000 packets the frequency (number) of packets containing r defective lenses is

$$N.P. (X = r) = \frac{20000 \quad 0.9802 \quad (0.02)^r}{r!} \qquad (21.9)$$

Putting r = 0, 1, 2 and 3 in (21.9), we get respectively

No. of packets containing no defective lens = 20000 x 0.9802 = 19604

No. of packets containing 1 defective lens is

$$= \frac{20000 \quad 0.9802 \quad (0.02)}{1} \quad 19604 \quad 0.02 \quad 392.08 \quad 392$$

No. of packets containing 2 defective lenses is

$$= \frac{20000 \quad 0.9802 \quad (0.02)^2}{2!} \quad \frac{392.08x0.02}{2} \quad 3.9208 \quad 4$$

No. of packets containing 3 defective lenses is

$$= \frac{20000 \quad 0.9802 \quad (0.02)^3}{3!} \quad \frac{3.9208 \quad 0.02}{3} \quad 0.026138 \quad 0$$

Problem 13: The management of a photograph record company has discovered that the number of defects on records appears to follow a Poisson distribution with a mean equal to 0.4.

(i) What is the probability that a record selected at random will have three defects?

(ii) If management sets a policy that all photograph records sold to customers must not have any defects, what per cent of its records production will not be made available for sales because of defects?

Solution: Let the r.v. X denote the number of defects in a record. Then using Poisson probability model with mean m = 0.4, we have:

$$p(r) = P(X = r) = e^{-0.4}\,(0.4)^r/r\,!;\ r = 0, 1, 2, \ldots \qquad (21.10)$$

(i) Required probability = $p(3) = \frac{e^{\ 0.4}(0.4)^3}{3!} \quad \frac{0.6703 \quad 0.064}{6} \quad 0.00715$

(ii) The photographic records will not be made available for sales to the customers even if it contains at least one defect and the required probability is given by:

$$P(X\ {}^{3}\ 1) = 1 - P(X = 0) = 1 - p(0) = 1 - e^{-0.4} = 1 - 0.6703 = 0.3297.$$

Hence, 32.97% = 33% of its photographic record production will not be made available for sales because of defects.

21.4 NORMAL DISTRIBUTION

In probability theory and statistics, the normal distribution or Gaussian distribution is a continuous probability distribution that describes data that clusters around a mean or average. The normal distribution is the most important of all probability distributions. The normal distribution can be used to describe, at least approximately, any variable that tends to cluster around the mean. For example, the heights of adult males in the United States are roughly normally distributed, with a mean of about 70 inches. Most men have a height close to the mean, though a small number of outliers have a height significantly above or below the mean. A histogram of male heights will appear similar to a bell curve, with the correspondence becoming closer if more data is used.

By the central limit theorem, any variable that is the sum of a large number of independent factors is likely to be normally distributed. For this reason, the normal distribution is used throughout statistics, natural science, and social science as a simple model for complex phenomena. It is applied directly to many practical problems, and several very useful distributions are based on it. The normal distribution refers to a family of continuous probability distributions described by the normal equation.

21.4.1 The Normal Equation

The normal distribution is defined by the following equation:

Normal equation: The value of the random variable Y is:

$$Y = [1/\sigma * \text{sqrt}(2\pi)] * e^{-(x-\mu)2/2\sigma 2}$$

where X is a normal random variable, μ is the mean,σ is the standard deviation, π is approximately 21.14159, and e is approximately 2.71828.

The random variable X in the normal equation is called the normal random variable. The normal equation is the probability density function for the normal distribution.

21.4.2 The Normal Curve

The graph of the normal distribution depends on two factors - the mean and the standard deviation. The mean of the distribution determines the location of the center of the graph, and the standard deviation determines the height and width of the graph. When the standard deviation is large, the curve is short and wide; when the standard deviation is small, the curve is tall and narrow. All normal distributions look like a symmetric, bell-shaped curve, as shown below.

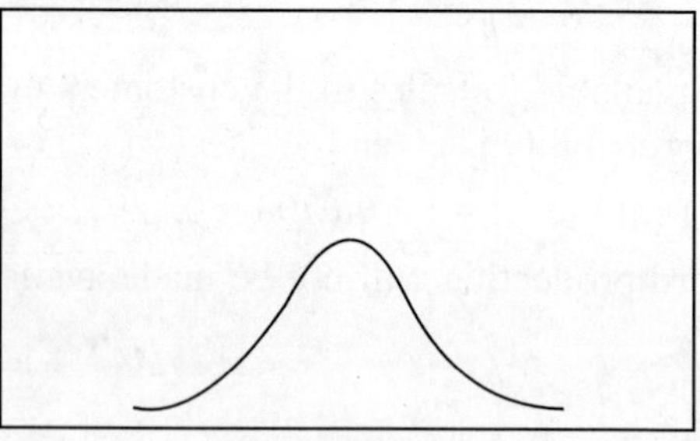

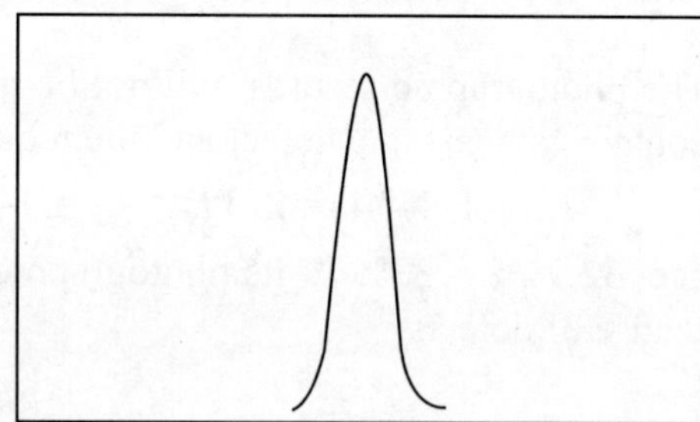

The curve on the left is shorter and wider than the curve on the right, because the curve on the left has a bigger standard deviation.

21.4.3 Probability and the Normal Curve

The normal distribution is a continuous probability distribution. This has several implications for probability.

- The total area under the normal curve is equal to 1.
- The probability that a normal random variable X equals any particular value is 0.
- The probability that X is greater than a equals the area under the normal curve bounded by a and plus infinity (as indicated by the non-shaded area in the figure below).

- The probability that X is less than a equals the area under the normal curve bounded by a and minus infinity (as indicated by the shaded area in the figure below).

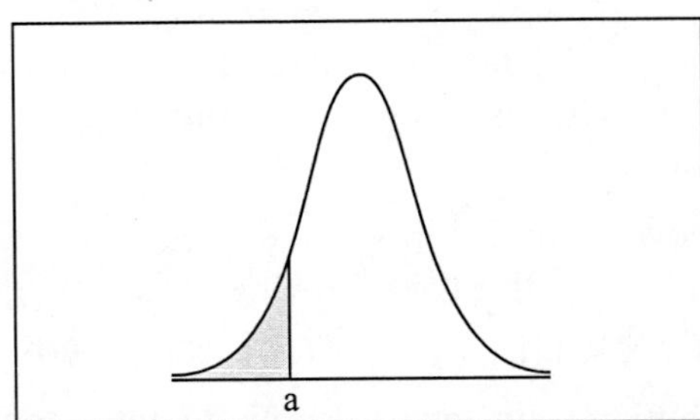

Additionally, every normal curve (regardless of its mean or standard deviation) conforms to the following "rule".

- About 68% of the area under the curve falls within 1 standard deviation of the mean.
- About 95% of the area under the curve falls within 2 standard deviations of the mean.
- About 99.7% of the area under the curve falls within 3 standard deviations of the mean.

Collectively, these points are known as the empirical rule or the 68-95-99.7 rule. Clearly, given a normal distribution, most outcomes will be within 3 standard deviations of the mean.

21.4.4 Characteristics

Many empirical frequency distributions have the following characteristics:

1. They are approximately symmetrical, and the mode is close to the centre of the distribution.
2. The mean, median, and mode are close together.
3. The shape of the distribution can be approximated by a bell: nearly flat on top, then decreasing more quickly, then decreasing more slowly toward the tails of the distribution. This implies that values close to the mean are relatively frequent, and values farther from the mean tend to occur less frequently. Remember that we are dealing with a random variable, so a frequency distribution will not fit this pattern exactly. There will be random variations from this general pattern.

Problem 14: An average light bulb manufactured by the Acme Corporation lasts 300 days with a standard deviation of 50 days. Assuming that bulb life is normally distributed, what is the probability that an Acme light bulb will last at most 365 days?

Solution: Given a mean score of 300 days and a standard deviation of 50 days, we want to find the cumulative probability that bulb life is less than or equal to 365 days. Thus, we know the following:

The value of the normal random variable is 365 days.

The mean is equal to 300 days.

The standard deviation is equal to 50 days.

We enter these values into the Normal Distribution Calculator and compute the cumulative probability. The answer is: $P(X < 365) = 0.90$. Hence, there is a 90% chance that a light bulb will burn out within 365 days.

Problem 15: Suppose scores on an IQ test are normally distributed. If the test has a mean of 100 and a standard deviation of 10, what is the probability that a person who takes the test will score between 90 and 110?

Solution: Here, we want to know the probability that the test score falls between 90 and 110. The "trick" to solving this problem is to realize the following:

$$P(90 < X < 110) = P(X < 110) - P(X < 90)\ 3$$

We use the Normal Distribution Calculator to compute both probabilities on the right side of the above equation.

To compute $P(X < 110)$, we enter the following inputs into the calculator: The value of the normal random variable is 110, the mean is 100, and the standard deviation is 10. We find that $P(X < 110)$ is 0.84.

To compute $P(X < 90)$, we enter the following inputs into the calculator: The value of the normal random variable is 90, the mean is 100, and the standard deviation is 10. We find that $P(X < 90)$ is 0.16.

We use these findings to compute our final answer as follows:

$$P(90 < X < 110) = P(X < 110) - P(X < 90)$$

$$P(90 < X < 110) = 0.84 - 0.16$$

$$P(90 < X < 110) = 0.68$$

Thus, about 68% of the test scores will fall between 90 and 110.

Problem 16: The income distribution of officers of a certain company was found to follow normal distribution. The average income of an office was Rs. 15,000.00. The standard deviation of the income of officers was Rs. 5,000.00. If there were 242 officers drawing salary above Rs. 18,500.00, how many officers were there in the company?

[The area under standard normal curve between 0 and 7 is 0.2580]

Solution: Let r.v. X denote the income (in Rs.) of the officers of the company. Then we are given salary above Rs. 18,500 is:

$$X \sim N(\mu, \sigma^2)$$

where μ = Rs. 15,000 and σ = Rs. 5,000

Let the number of officers in the company be N. Then the number of officers in the company drawing salary above Rs. 18,500 is:

$$N.P(X > 18{,}500) = 242 \text{ (Given).} \qquad \text{(i)}$$

When X = 18,500, $$Z = \frac{X}{} \quad \frac{18500 \quad 15000}{5000} \quad 0.7$$

$$\therefore \quad P(X\ ?\ 18500) = P(Z > 0.7)$$
$$= 0.5 - P(0 \le Z \le 0.7)$$
$$= 0.5 - 0.2580 = 0.242$$

Substituting in (i) we get: $N \times 0.242 = 242 \quad \rightarrow \quad N = \frac{242}{0.242} \quad 1{,}000$

Hence the number of officers in the company is 1,000.

Problem 17: Time taken by the crew, of a company to construct a small bridge is a normal variate with mean 400 labour hours and standard deviation of 100 labour hours.

(i) What is the probability that the bridge gets constructed between 350 to 450 labour hours?

(ii) If the company promises to construct the bridge in 450 labour hours or less and agrees to pay a penalty of Rs. 100 for each labour hour spent in excess of 450, what is the probability that the company pays a penalty of at least Rs. 2000?

Solution: Let X denote the time (in labour hours) to construct the bridge. Then in the usual notations, we are given: $X \sim N(m, \sigma^2)$ where $\mu = 400$ hrs. $\sigma = 100$ hrs.

(i) The probability (p_1) that the bridge gets constructed between 350 to 450 labour hours is given by:

$$p_1 = P(350 < X < 450)$$

X	$Z = \frac{X}{\quad} \quad \frac{X\ \ 400}{100}$
350	$\frac{350\ \ 400}{100} \quad 0.5$
450	$\frac{450\ \ 400}{100} \quad 0.5$

$$\therefore \quad p_1 = P(-0.5 < Z < 0.5), \text{ where } Z \sim N(0, 1)$$
$$= 2P(0 < Z < 0.5)$$
$$= 2 \times 0.1915 = 0.3830$$

(ii) The penalty for each labour hour delay (excess over 450 hours) is Rs. 100, (given) If the minimum penalty paid by the company is Rs. 2000 then the delay in completing the bridge is

$$\ge \frac{2000}{100} \quad 20\text{hours}$$

Hence, the company will take a minimum of $(450 + 20) = 470$ hours, to complete the bridge. Thus the required probability (p_2) is given by:

$$p_2 = P(X \ge 470) = P \quad Z \quad \frac{470 \quad 400}{100} \quad P(Z \quad 0.70)$$
$$= 0.5 - P(0 \le Z \le 0.70) = 0.5 - 0.2580 = 0.2420$$

EXERCISES

1. 12% of the items produced by a machine are defective. What is the probability that out of a random sample of 20 items produced by the machine, 5 are defective? (Simplification is not necessary)
2. The odds in favour of X winning a game against Y are 4 : 3. Find the probability of Y's winning 3 games out of played.
3. A salesman makes a sale on the average to 40 percent of the customers he contacts. If 4 customers are contacted today, what is the probability that he makes sales to exactly two? What assumption is required for your answer?
4. The average number of defective pieces, in the manufacturing of an article, is 1 in 10. Find the probability of getting exactly 3 defective articles in a packet of 10 articles selected at random.
5. If the chance that the vessel arrives safely at a port is (9/10), find the chance that out of 5 vessels expected, at least 4 will arrive safely.
6. Under normal operating conditions 1.5% of the transistors produced in a factory are defective. An inspector takes a random sample of forty transistors and finds that two are defective.
   (a) What is the probability that exactly two transistors will be defective from a random sample of forty under normal operating conditions?
   (b) What is the probability that more than two transistors will be defective from a random sample of forty if conditions are normal?
7. A control system is set up so that when production conditions are normal, only 6% of items from the production line gives readings beyond a particular limit. If more than two of six successive items are beyond the limit, production is stopped and all machine settings are examined. What is the probability that production will be stopped in this way when production conditions are normal?
8. A company supplying transistors claims that they produce no more than 2% defectives. A purchaser picks 50 at random from an order of 5000 and tests the 50. If he finds more than 1 defective, he rejects the order. If the supplier's claim is true and 2% of the transistors are defective, what is the probability that the order will be rejected?
9. An experiment was conducted wherein three balls were drawn at random from a barrel containing two blue balls, three red balls, and five green balls. We want to find the mean and variance of the probability distribution of the number of green balls chosen. Explain why this problem involving three colours can not be handled using a binomial distribution. Suppose we consider both the blue balls and the red balls together as not-green. Now find the required mean and variance.
10. Ten judges are asked to pick the best tasting orange juice from two samples labeled A and B. If, in fact, A and B are the same orange juice, what is the probability that eight or more of the judges will declare the same sample to be the best? Assume that no judge says that they are equal.

11. A sample of eleven electric bulbs is drawn every day from those manufactured at a plant. The eleven bulbs are tested before shipment to the customer. An analysis of the test data collected over a number of years reveals that the probability of finding no defective bulb in a sample of eleven bulbs is 0.5688. Probabilities of defective bulbs are random and independent of previous results.
    (a) What is the probability of finding exactly three defective bulbs in a sample?
    (b) What is the probability of finding three or more defective bulbs in a sample?
12. There are ten multiple choice questions on an examination. If there are five choices per question, what is the probability that a student will answer at least five questions correctly just by picking one answer at random from the possibilities for each question? State any assumptions.
13. The average number of customers, who appear at a counter of a certain bank per minute is two. Find the probability that during a given minute:
    (i) NO customer appears
    (ii) Three or more customers appear.

    ($e^{-2} = 0.1353$)
14. A guest house has two rooms which it hires out by the day. The number of demand for a room on any day follows Poisson distribution with mean 1.5. Calculate the probability that
    (i) all rooms are vacant on a particular day, and
    (ii) some demand is refused on that day.

    (Given $e^{-1.5} = 0.223$)
15. Suppose on an average 1 house in 1,000 in a certain district has a fire during a year. If there are 2,000 houses in that district, what is the probability that exactly 5 houses will have a fire during the year?
16. In a summer a truck driver gets on an average one puncture in 1000 km. Find the probability that he will have
    (i) no puncture,
    (ii) atmost one puncture, in a journey of 3000 km.
17. Assuming that on an average 1% of the output in a factory making certain part of an article are defective and that 200 units are in a package, find the probabilities that:
    (i) at most 2 defectives, and
    (ii) at least two defectives may be found in the package.
18. The number of cars entering a small parking lot is a random variable having a Poisson distribution with a mean of 1.5 per hour. The lot holds only 12 cars.
    (a) Find the probability that the lot fills up in the first hour (assuming that all cars stay in the lot longer than one hour).
    (b) Find the probability that more than 3 cars arrive between 9 am and 11 am.

19. Customers arrive at a checkout counter at an average rate of 1.5 per minute. What distribution will apply if reasonable assumptions are made? List those assumptions. Find the probabilities that
    (a) exactly two will arrive in any given minute;
    (b) at least three will arrive during an interval of two minutes;
    (c) at most 13 will arrive during an interval of six minutes.
20. Cumulative probability tables for the Poisson Distribution indicate that for $\mu = 2.5$, Pr $[R \leq 6] = 0.986$ and Pr $[R \leq 4] = 0.891$. Use these figures to calculate Pr [R = 5 or 6]. Check using basic relations.
21. Cumulative probability tables indicate that for a Poisson distribution with $\mu = 5.5$, Pr $[R \leq 6] = 0.686$ and Pr $[R \leq 7] = 0.810$. Use these figures to calculate Pr $[R = 7]$. Check using a basic relation.
22. Records of an electrical distribution system in a particular area indicate that over the past twenty years there have been just six years in which lightning has not hit a transformer. Assume that the factors affecting lightning hits on transformers have not changed over that time, and that hits occur at random and independently.
    (a) Then what would be the best estimate of the average number of hits on transformers per year?
    (b) In how many of the next ten years would we expect to have more than two hits on transformers in a year?
23. In 104 days, 170 oil tankers arrive at a port for unloading. The tankers arrive randomly and independently. Probabilities are the same for every day of the week. A maximum of two oil tankers can be unloaded each day.
    (a) What is the probability that no oil tankers will arrive on Tuesday?
    (b) What is the probability that more than two will arrive on Friday? This will mean that not all can be unloaded on Friday, even if no oil tankers were left over from Thursday.
    (c) Assuming that no oil tankers are left over from Tuesday, what is the probability that exactly one oil tanker will be left over from Wednesday and none will be left over from Thursday?
    (d) What is the probability that more than three oil tankers will arrive in an interval of two days?
24. Suppose the waists measurements W of 800 girls are normally distributed with mean 66 cms, and S.D 5cms. Find the number N of girls with waists-
    (i) Between 65 and 70 cms (ii) Greater than or equals to 72 cms
25. Assume the mean height of soldiers to be 68.22 inches with the variance of 10.8 inches^2. How many soldiers in regiment of 1,000 would you expect to be:
    (i) Over 6 feet tall.
    (ii) Below 5.5 feet? Assume heights to be normally distributed.

26. For a normal distribution with mean μ and standard deviation σ. Obtained the first and third quartiles and also the quartiles deviation.

27. For a normal distribution with mean 2 and variance 9, Find the value of x such that the probability of interval [2, x] is 0.4115.

28. In normal distribution, 31% of the items are under 45 and 8% are over 64. Find the mean and standard deviation of the distribution.

29. Let X be a continuous variable that follows a normal distribution with mean 12 and standard deviation 2. What is the probability that the value of X selected at random lie in the interval (11, 14)?

30. (a) If x follows normal distribution N (0, 1) and $P(x < 1) = 0.84$, then $P(|x| < 1)$ is

    (i) 0.68 (ii) 0.32 (iii) 0.16 (iv) None of these

    (b) Given that for standard normal variable Z, $P(0 < Z < 0.8) = 0.2882$. The value of $P(|Z| \geq 0.8)$ is:

    (i) 0.4238 (ii) 0.7119 (iii) 0.5762 (iv) none of these

    (c) If the distribution of the random variable X is normal with mean 0 and variance 1 with $P(0 \leq X \leq 1) = 0.3413$, $P(|X| > 1)$ is

    (i) 0.6578 (ii) 0.3413 (iii) 0.3174 (iv) none of these

    [Hint: $P(|X| > 1(= 1 - P(|X| \leq 1) = 1 - P(-1 \leq X d \leq 1)$; $X \sim N(0, 1)$]

31. The average daily sale of 500 branch offices was Rs. 150 thousand and the standard deviation Rs. 15 thousand. Assuming the distribution to be normal indicate how many branches have sales between?

    (i) Rs. 120 thousand and Rs. 145 thousand

    (ii) Rs. 140 thousand and Rs. 165 thousand?

32. The mean weight of 500 male students at certain college is 65.6 kg and the standard deviation is 10 kg. Assuming that the weights are normally distributed, find how many students weigh:

    (i) more than 75.5 kg;

    (ii) between 55.5 and 75.5 kg.

33. As a result of tests on 2,000 electric bulbs manufactured by a company, it was found that the lifetime of the bulb was normally distributed with an average life of 2,040 hours and standard deviation of 60 hours. On the basis of the information, estimate the number of the bulbs that is expected to burn for

    (a) more than 2,150 hours,

    (b) less than 1,960 hours

Proportions of Area under the Normal Curve from Z = 0 to Z = z;

z	Area	z	Area	z	Area
1.23	0.3907	1.33	0.4082	1.43	0.4236
1.63	0.4484	1.73	0.4582	1.83	0.4664

CHAPTER 22

Fuzzy Logic and Probability Theory

22.1 INTRODUCTION

Most of the applications chapters in this book deal with the quantification of various forms of uncertainty, both numeric and nonnurneric. Uncertainty in numerical quantities can be random in nature, where probability theory is very useful, or it earl be the result of bias or an unknown error, in which case fuzzy set theory, evidence theory, or possibility theory might prove useful. Probability theory also has been used almost exclusively to deal with the form of uncertainty due to chance (randomness), sometimes called variability, and with uncer-tainties arising from eliciting and analyzing expert information. Three other prevalent forms of uncertainty are those arising from ambiguity, vagueness, and imprecision. While vague-ness and ambiguity can arise from linguistic uncertainly, they also can be associated with some numerical quantities. Such as "approximately 5." Imprecision is generally associated with numerical quantities, although applications may exist where this type of uncertainty is nonnumeric (i.e., qualitative), for example, "the missile was close to the target." How do variability, ambiguity, vagueness, and imprecision differ as forms of uncertainty?

In the sections that follow, we detail the most popular methods used to address these various forms of uncertainly whether they arc quantitative or qualitative. While fuzzy set theory and probability theory have been used for all these forms of uncertainty, this chapter will extend this scope somewhat by commenting on the use of possibility theory in the characterization of ambiguity.

Fuzzy logic and probability theory are two different tools, lime screw drivers and hammers. They were designed for different tasks. One could conceivably use a hammer to hammer a screw, yet it is much more effective to use a screw driver for the job. Only after we fully understand the tasks these tools are designed for can we use them properly. Too often, unfortunately, we have a tendency to avoid learning how to use a new tool, simply because we are using to use an old tool that we are familiar with. Professor Zadeh once said, "if the only tool you know is a hammer, everything looks like a nail".

22.2 VAGUENESS, IMPRECISION, AND CHANCE: FUZZINESS VERSUS PROBABILITY

Often vagueness and imprecision arc used synonymously, but they can also differ in the following sense. Vagueness can be used to describe certain kinds of uncertainty associated with linguistic information or intuitive information. Examples of vague information are that the data quality is "good" or that the transparency of an optical element is "acceptable."

Moreover, in terms of semantics, even the terms vague and fuzzy cannot be generally con-sidered synonyms, as explained by Zadeh (1995). For example, "I shall return sornetime" is vague and "I shall return in a few minutes" is fuzzy, The former is not known to be associated with any unit of (seconds, hours, clays), whereas the latter is associated with an uncertainty that is at least known to be on the order of minutes. However, notwithstand-ing this distinction, the terms vague and fuzzy used herein will represent the same kind of uncertainly; i.e.. They will be used interchangeably in our discussions of this general form of uncertainty. As explained by Zadeh (1995), "Usually a vague proposition is fuzzy, but the converse is not generally true."

22.2.1 A Historical Perspective on Vagueness

Black (1935) defines a vague proposition as a proposition where the possible states (of the proposition) are not clearly defined with regard to inclusion. For example, consider the proposition that a person is young. Since the term "young" has different interpretations to different individuals, we cannot decisively determine the age(s) at which an individual is young versus the age(s) at which an individual is not considered to be young. Thus the propo-sition is vaguely defined. Classical (binary) logic does not hold under these circumstances; therefore, we must establish a different method of interpretation.

Black introduced a consistency profile as a graphical representation of the membership of a preposition in a set of states where 1 denotes absolute membership and 0 denotes absolute complementary membership. These profiles are established to represent a precise (crisp) or vague proposition: a precisely defined proposition has a consistency profile that is a step function (Figure 22.1), while a vague proposition has a consistency profile that gradually ranges between the two extremes (Figure 22.2).

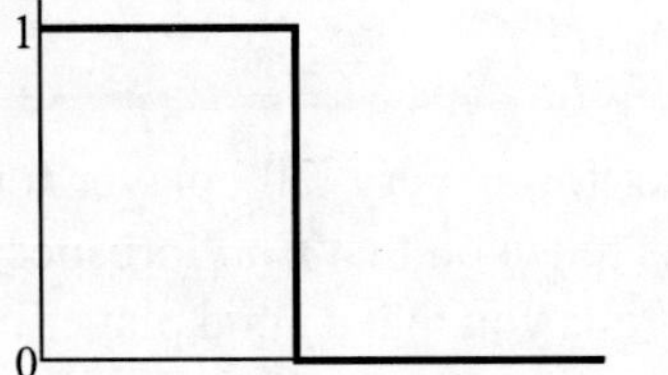

Figure 22.1: Precise consistency profile.

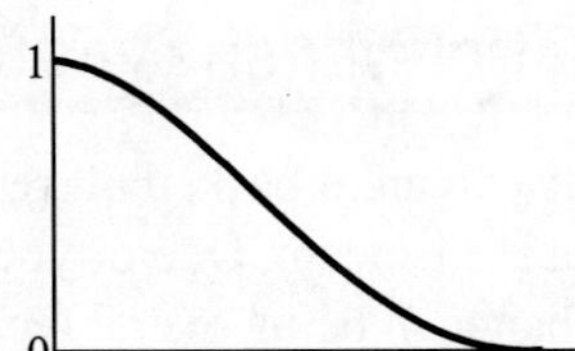

Figure 22.2: Vague consistency profile.

22.2.2 Imprecision

Imprecision can be associated with quantitative, or countable, data as well as noncountable data. An example of the latter might be, "the length of a flaw in an integrated circuit is long." An example of countable imprecision would be to report the length of such a flaw as 30 microns. If we use a microscope and measure the length of the flaw 100 times we will likely come up with 100 different values; the differences in the numbers will no doubt be on the order of the precision of the resolution limitations of the microscope and other measurement factors. Measurements using a light microscope (which has accuracy on the order of microns) will be less precise than those developed from an electron microscope (which has resolution on the order of nanometers). If we plot the flaw lengths on some sort of probit paper and develop a Gaussian distribution to describe the length of this flaw, we could state the imprecision in probabilistic terms. In this case, the length of the flaw is uncertain to some degree of precision that is quantified in the language of probability. Since we are not able to make this measurement an infinite number of times, there is also uncertainty in the statistics describing the flaw length. Hence, imprecision can be used to quantify random variability in the quantitative uncertainty, and it also can be used to describe a lack of knowledge for descriptive entities acceptable transparency, good data quality), Vagueness is usually related to non-measurable issues.

Many practitioners suggest that the uncertainty arising from vagueness makes use of fuzzy set theory, since this theory was developed to handle the vagueness inherent in natural language. Klir and Folger (1988) have shown that the relationships among Fuzzy set theory, probability theory, evidence theory, and possibility theory stem from a common framework of fuzzy measures in that they all have been used to characterize and model various forms of uncertainty. That they all are related mathematically (as fuzzy measures) is an especially crucial advantage in their use in quantifying the uncertainty spectrum. As more information about a problem becomes available, the mathematical description of uncertainty easily can transform from one theory to the next in the characterization of the uncertainty as the uncertainty diminishes or, alternatively, as the information granularity increases and becomes specific. There are various forms of fuzzy measures such as belief, plausibility, possibility, and probability, Yager (1993) has discussed the relationship between a possibility distribution and a fuzzy set. Ongoing research continues to provide theoretically based methods for translating uncertainties established in one of these measures into uncertainties in another without violating the fundamental axioms of either.

22.3 CHANCE VERSUS VAGUENESS

Suppose that you arc a basketball recruiter and are looking for a "very tall" player for the center position on a men's team. One of your information sources tells you that a hot prospect in Oregon has a 95% chance of being over 7 feet tall. Another source tells you that a good player in Louisiana has a high membership in the set "very tall" people. The problem with the information from the first source is that it is a quantity constrained by the law of the excluded-middle. There is a 5% chance that the Oregon player is not over 7 feet tall; this person could conceivably he of extremely short stature. The second source of information in this case, contain less uncertainty for the recruiter because if the player turned out to be less than 7 feet tail, then there is a high likelihood that this player would still he quite tall.

Suppose that we are allowed to measure the basketball players' heights. The prior probability of 0.95 becomes a posterior probability of 1.0 or 0.0; i.e., the player either is or is not over 7 feet tall. However, the membership value of 0.95 that measures the extent to which the player's height is over 7 feet remains 0.95 after measuring. This example illustrates very clearly the difference in the information content between chance and vague events.

This brings us to the clearest distinction between fuzziness and randomness: Fuzzi-ness describes the vagueness of an event, whereas chance describes the uncertainty in the occurrence of the event. The event will or will not occur; but is the description of the event clear and specific enough to measure its occurrence or nonoccurrence?

22.4 MANY-VALUED LOGIC

Binary logic pertains to propositions that are either true or false. However, Lukasiewicz (1930) recognized the existence of propositions that are simultaneously true and false at various levels. For example, a degraded yet functioning system cannot be classified as being in state 1(perfect Functioning), nor can it be classified as being in state 0 (total failure). For such propositions, their membership is neither 1 nor 0. Therefore, Lukasiewiez assigned a third number, $\frac{1}{2}$ as its associated truth value (ie., membership value) to account for any deviation from states 0 or 1. For example, a degraded component (system) would be considered in state $\frac{1}{2}$, This concept defines a three-valued logic.

Lukasicwicz (1930) defined the truth table corresponding to the implication X → Y for two propositions X and Y("if X, then Y") and negation X` (propositions complementary to X); see tables 22.1 and 22.2.

Table 22.1: Three-valued truth Table for X→ Y

X→ Y		**Values of proposition Y**		
		0	$\frac{1}{2}$	**1**
Values of proposition Y	0	1	1	1
	$\frac{1}{2}$	$\frac{1}{2}$	1	1
	1	0	$\frac{1}{2}$	1

Table 22.2: Three-valued truth table for X'.	
Values of proposition X	**Values of proposition X'**
0	1
$\frac{1}{2}$	$\frac{1}{2}$
1	0

From the logical equivalencies for conjunction ("AND," denoted $\wedge$) and disjunction ("OR," denoted), we have

$$X \wedge Y = (X \to Y) \to Y$$

and

$$X \vee Y = (X' \to Y')'$$

Truth tables can be found in Malinowski (1993); also see Tables 22.3 and 22.4. As a result,

Table 22.3: Three-valued truth Table for $X \wedge Y$

X ∧ Y		**Values of proposition Y**		
		0	$\mathbf{\frac{1}{2}}$	**1**
Values of proposition Y	0	0	0	0
	$\frac{1}{2}$	0	$\frac{1}{2}$	$\frac{1}{2}$
	1	0	$\frac{1}{2}$	1

Table 22.4: Three-valued truth Table for $X \vee Y$

X ∨ Y		**Values of proposition Y**		
		0	$\mathbf{\frac{1}{2}}$	**1**
Values of proposition Y	0	0	$\frac{1}{2}$	1
	$\frac{1}{2}$	$\frac{1}{2}$	$\frac{1}{2}$	1
	1	1	1	1

$$X \wedge Y = \min(X, Y)$$

and

$$X \vee Y = \max(X, Y).$$

These ideas can be generalized to define an n-valued logic in that propositions are true and false simultaneously but with varying degrees of truth (or falsity). Furthermore, extensions of the n-valued logic to the continuum lead to the notions of vagueness and fuzzy logic.

22.5 AXIOMATIC STRUCTURE OF PROBABILITY AND FUZZY LOGICS

To attempt to bring some relevance to the historical confusion between the logics associated with probability theory and fuzzy set theory, a paper by Gaines. (1978) does an eloquent job of addressing this issue. Historically, probability and fuzzy sets have been presented as distinct theoretical foundations for reasoning and decision-making in situations involving uncertainty. Yet when one examines the underlying axioms of both probability and fuzzy set theories, the two theories differ only by one axiom in a total of 16 axioms needed for a complete foundation! The material that follows is a brief summary of Gaines' paper which established a common basis for both forms of logic of uncertainty in which basic uncertainty logic is defined in terms of truth valuation on a lattice of propositions. Addition of the axiom of the excluded-middle to the basic logic defines standard probability logic. Alternatively, addition of a requirement for strong truth functionality yields a fuzzy logic.

In this discussion, fuzzy logic is taken to be a many-valued extension of Boolean logic based on fuzzy set theory in which truth values are a continuous function between the endpoints of the interval [0, 1]. This is seen to be an extension of the idea proposed by Lukasiewicz (1930) discussed in the previous section. The normal logical operations of both probability theory and fuzzy logic are defined in terms of arithmetic operations on values $x \in [0, 1]$: the vales are regarded as degrees of membership to truth. The logic operations and associated arithmetic operations arc those of conjunction, disjunction, and negation. Gaines (1978) points out that the use of the max and min operators in fuzzy logic is not sufficient to distinguish it from probability theory—both operators arise naturally in the calculation of the conjunction and disjunction of probabilistic events. Our association of addition and multiplication as natural operations upon probabilities comes from our frequent interest in statistically independent events, not from the logic of probability itself.

In developing a basic uncertainty logic (one that embraces both a fuzzy set theory and a probability theory), we begin first by defining a lattice consisting of a universe of discourse X, a maximal element T, a minimal element F, a conjunction $\wedge$, and a disjunction $\vee$. This lattice will he denoted L (X, T, F, $\wedge$, $\vee$), For the axioms (or postulates) to follow, the lower-case letters x, y, and z denote specific elements of the universe X within the lattice. The following 15 axioms completely specify a basic uncertainty logic. The basic uncertainty logic begins with the lattice L satisfying the following axioms:

1. Idempotency: for all $x \in L$, $x \vee x = x \wedge x = x$;
2. Commutativity: for all $x, y \in L$, $x \vee y = y \vee x$; $x \wedge y = y \wedge x$;
3. Associativity: for all $x, y, z \in L$, $x \vee (y \vee z) = (x \vee y) \vee z$;
4. Absorption: for all $x, y \in L$, $x \vee (x \wedge y) = x$ and $x \wedge (x \vee y) = x$;
5. Definition of maximal and minimal elements: $x \in L$, $x \vee T = T$, $x \wedge T = x$.

22.6 POSSIBILITY VERSUS PROBABILITY

Among all concepts and techniques in fuzzy logic, possibility theory is the one that is most often confused with probability theory. For this reason, we will first clarify the differences between them. Possibility and probability measure two different kinds of uncertainty. As we have mentioned in Chapter 2, the best way to introduce possibility theory is to start with the notion of interval values.

Imagine that you were a witness of a bank robbery. When the police asked you about the height of a male suspect, your answer may be one of the following:

- He is betweent 5 feet and 6 feet.
- He is somewhat tall.

Both of these answers impose a constraint (based on your impression) on the possible heights of the suspect. The first answer imposes a crisp constraint. That is, the suspect cant possibly be shorter than 5 feet, nor can he be taller than 6 feet. The second answer on the other hand, typically imposes an imprecise constraint on the suspect's height. Unlike the interval-value answer, the second response does not have a well-defined short boundary between the possible heights and the impossible ones. Rather, it suggests that a certain height is more possible than another one.

In general when we assign a fuzzy set, a variable whose value we don't know exactly, the assignment introduces an imprecise constraint on the variable's value. We call such a constraint a possibility distribution, because it specifies the degree of possibility for the variable to take a certain value. The constraint imposed by an internal-value assignment is a special kind of possibility distribution. In other words, the notion of possibility distribution generalizes the notion of intervalue to smooth the boundary between the possible values and the impossible values so that possibility becomes a matter of degree. We use $\Pi(x)$ to denote the possibility distribution of a variable x.

Possibility measures the degree of ease for a variable to take a value, while probability measures the likelihood for a variable to take a value. Therefore, they deal with two different types of uncertainty. Possibility theory handles imprecision, and probability theory matical properties of their distributions. Being a measure of occurrence, the probability distribution of a variable must add up to exactly 1. The possibility Distribution, however, is not subject to this restriction since a variable can have multiple possible values. Returning to our example about the robbery suspect, we may use the following normal distributions with $\mu = 5$ ft, $\sigma = 0.2$ ft to describe the probabilities of the suspect's height:

$$P(h) = \frac{1}{0.2\sqrt{2}} e^{\frac{1}{2}\frac{h\;\;5}{0.2}^{2}} \tag{22.1}$$

It is well known that the area under a normal distribution is 1.

22.7 PROBABILITY OF A FUZZY EVENT

An event is a subset of the sample space that shares a common characteristic that we are interested in. a day in Houston with a temperature between 70°F and 80°F is an event. The relevant sample space is all possible temperatures in Houston. Having more heads than tails in 20 tossing's of a coin, is a classical event in statistics textbooks.. the relevant sample space included all 21 possible outcomes (ranging from no head to 20 heads). There are situations when the event we are interested in does not have well-defined sharp boundaries. We call them fuzzy events. Formally, a fuzzy event is a fuzzy subset of the sampling space. For instance, "a day with a warm temperature" is a fuzzy event. Another example of a fuzzy event is "in 20 tosses of a coin, there are several more heads than tails."

The formula for calculating the probability of a fuzzy event A is generalization of the probability theory:

$$P(A) = \quad mA(x) \quad Px(x)\,dx \tag{22.2}$$

If X is continuous, or

$$P(A) = \underset{i}{\quad\quad} A(x_i) \quad P_X(x_i) \tag{22.3}$$

If X is discrete where P_X denotes the probability distribution function of X.

22.7.1 Properties About Probability of Fuzzy Events

For any two events A and B of a sample space, we know from probability theory that

$$P(A \cup B) = P(A) + P(B) - P(A \cap B) \tag{22.4}$$

Does this relationship hold for fuzzy events? The answer to this question depends on the choice of the fuzzy union (i.e., fuzzy disjunction) and fuzzy intersection (i.e., fuzzy conjunction) operators. In fact, it is straightforward to show that Equation 22.4 holds for the following two choices:

1. Union: max, intersection: min
2. Union: algebraic sum, intersection: algebraic product (i.e. multiplication).

22.7.2 Conditional Probability of Fuzzy Events

Suppose A and B are two events of a sample space the conditional probability of A given B is defined in probability theory as

$$P(A/B) = \frac{P(\qquad)}{P(\;)} \tag{22.5}$$

It is easy to show that the conditional probability of A given B and the conditional probability of A's complement given B adds to 1, i.e.,

$$P(A/B) + P(A^C/B) = 1 \tag{22.6}$$

The conditional probability of fuzzy events can be defined in a similar way using Equation 22.5 However, Equation 22.6 holds only if we choose multiplication as the fuzzy intersection operator.

22.7.3 Independent Fuzzy Events

In probability theory, two events A and B are independent if the occurrence or non-occurrence of either one does not affect the occurrence of the other one, i.e., P (A/B) = P(A) and P(B/A) = P(B).

If we substitute P(A) for P(A/B) into Equation $P(A \cap B) = P(A/B) \times P(B)$, we have $P(A \cap B) = P(A) \times P(B)$, which we will use to formally define the independence of fuzzy events.

Two fuzzy events A and B are independent if and only if $P(A \cap B) = P(A) \times P(B)$.

22.7.4 Bayes' Theorem for Fuzzy Events

Bayes' theorem is the basis for many probabilistic inferences schemes (e.g., Bayes' networks, influence diagrams, etc.) used in intelligent systems. If $A_1, A_2, \ldots, A_k$ forms a partition of the sample space S (i.e., they are mutually exclusive and exhaustive and $P(A_i) \neq 0$ for $i = 1, 2, \ldots, k$, then any event B is 5 such that $P(B) \neq 0$, Bayes' theorem enables us to infer $P(A_j/B)$ from and P(B/A):

$$P(A_j/B) = \frac{P(\ _j)\ P(\ /\ _j)}{\overset{k}{\underset{i\ 1}{}}\ P(\ _i)\ P(\ /\ _i)} \tag{22.7}$$

for $j = 1, 2, \ldots, k$.

If A_i and B are fuzzy events, we need to generalize the condition in Bayes' theorem to allow fuzzy events $A_1, \ldots A_k$ to form a fuzzy partition of S such that

$$\overset{k}{\underset{i\ 1}{}}\ _i(x) = 1 \text{ for x Î S}$$

We formally state the theorem below

If $A_1, A_2, \ldots, A_k$ are fuzzy events of S, such that

$$\overset{k}{\underset{i\ 1}{}}\ _i(x) = 1 \text{ for } x \quad S \tag{22.8}$$

$P(A_i) \neq 0$ for $i = 1, 2, \ldots, k$, and B is a fuzzy event of S such that $P(B) \neq 0$,

$$P(A_j/B) = \frac{P(\ /\ _j)\ P(\ _j)}{\overset{k}{\underset{i\ 1}{}}\ P(\ /\ _i)\ P(\ _i)} \tag{22.9}$$

for $j = 1, 2, \ldots, k$.

Proof: Form the definition of conditional probability for fuzzy events, we have

$$P(A_j/B) = \frac{P(\ _i\ \ )}{P(\ )} \tag{22.10}$$

In order to show that the right-hand side of Equation 22.9 equals the ratio above, we expand the denominator of Equation 22.9:

$$= \overset{k}{\underset{i\ 1}{}}\ P(\ /\ _i)\ \ P(\ _i)$$

$$= \overset{k}{\underset{i\ 1}{}}\ P\ \ _i$$

$$= \overset{k}{\underset{i\ 1\ x_k}{}}\ \ _i(x_k)\ \ \ (x_k)\ \ P(x_k)$$

$$= \underset{x_k}{}\ (x_k)\ \ P(x_k)\ \ \overset{k}{\underset{i\ 1}{}}\ \ _i(x_k)$$

$$= \underset{x_k}{}\ (x_k)\ \ P(x_k)$$

$$= P(B)$$

Since, $P(B/A_j) \times P(A_j) = P\ (A_j \cap B)$, we can substitute the numerator and denominator of Equation 22.9 to get Equation 22.10 The theorem is thus proved.

22.8 FUZZY PROBABILITY

In classical probability theory, a probability measure is a number between 0 and 1. There are cases, however, when such a precise probability measure is difficult to obtain. This motivated the development of interval probability theories, which can represent and reason about the lower bound and the upper bound of the probability measure. The interval formed by these two bounds contains the true probability value, which we do not know precisely. In other words, interval probabilities allow us to describe the imprecision of our probability estimates. The width of the interval reflects the degree of imprecision. The wider the interval, the less precise our probability estimates. In the literature of interval probability theory, this interval is sometimes referred to as the degree of ignorance.

22.9 FUZZY MEASURE

Finally, it may be worthwhile to point out that both possibility measure and probability measure belong to a more general class of measures called fuzzy measure.

A probability P over a set of events S is a function from 2^S to [0, 1] such that

1. $P(\phi) = 0$
2. $P(S) = 1$
3. If $A \cap B = 0$

then $P(A \cup B = P(A) + P(B)$

where A, B are subsets of S.

4. $P(B|A) = \frac{P(A \quad B)}{P(A)}$ if $P(A) \neq 0$

It is easy to show we get the following properties about probabilities from these axioms:

- $P(A) + P(A^c) = 1$
- If A Ì B, then P (B) ³ P(A)

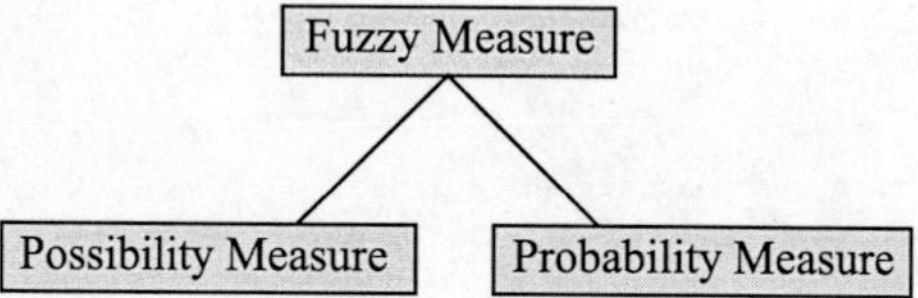

Figure 22.3: Relationships between fuzzy measure, probability, and possibility

A possibility measure $\prod$ over a set of events S is a function from 2^s to [0, 1] such that

1. $\prod(\phi) = 0$
2. $\pi(S) = 1$
3. If $A \subset B$ then, $\pi((A) \leq \pi(B))$
4. $\pi(A \cup B) = \max\{\pi(A), \pi(B)\}$

A fuzzy measure g over a set of events S is a function from s to [0, 1] such that

1. $g(\phi) = 0$
2. $g(S) = 1$
3. if $A \subset B$, then $P(B) \geq P(A)$

Since the set of axioms for fuzzy measure is a subset of the axioms of probability and possibility measure above, it is more general than both of them.

EXERCISES

1. What do you mean by vagueness?
2. What do you mean by imprecision?
3. What do you mean by chance?
4. Explain the difference between fuzziness and probability?
5. Explain the historical perspective of vagueness?
6. Difference between chance and vagueness.
7. What do you mean by many valued logic?
8. Explain the axiomatic structure of probability and fuzzy logic?

9. Difference between possibility and probability.
10. What do you mean by probability of a fuzzy event?
11. Explain the following:
    (i) Properties about probability of fuzzy events
    (ii) Conditional probability of fuzzy events
    (iii) Independence fuzzy events
    (iv) Baye's theorem for fuzzy events
12. What do you mean by fuzzy probability?
13. Explain the concept of fuzzy measure?

Index

F

G

H

T

U

V

W

X